MOUNTAINS
TOUCHED *with* FIRE

BOOKS BY WILEY SWORD

Shiloh: Bloody April (1974)

President Washington's Indian War: The Struggle for the Old Northwest, 1790–1795 (1985)

Firepower from Abroad: The Confederate Enfield and the LeMat Revolver (1986)

Sharpshooter: Hiram Berdan, His Famous Sharpshooters and Their Sharps Rifles (1988)

Embrace an Angry Wind: The Confederacy's Last Hurrah: Spring Hill, Franklin, and Nashville (1992; paperback, 1993)

MOUNTAINS TOUCHED *with* FIRE

CHATTANOOGA BESIEGED, 1863

WILEY SWORD

ST. MARTIN'S PRESS • NEW YORK

Design by Junie Lee
Maps by Irving Perkins

Library of Congress Cataloging-in-Publication Data

Sword, Wiley.
    Mountains touched with fire : Chattanooga besieged, 1863 / Wiley Sword : foreword by Albert E. Castel.
      p.   cm.
    ISBN 0-312-15593-X
    1. Chattanooga (Tenn.), Battle of, 1863.   I. Title.
E475.97.S92   1995
973.7'359—dc20   94-47255
                                           CIP

First St. Martin's Griffin Edition: May 1997

10 9 8 7 6 5 4 3 2 1

Who is the one who always cares;
 who is the one who's always there?

How can I ever repay
 the love and devotion every day?

Have I ever thought
 of the hopes and fears that she has not?

When will it be that I can see
 all that she has done for me?

What might an answer be
 to say with grace what it means to me?

Why does the starlight beam from above?
 It must be as a reminder of her love.

Dedicated to my mother,

Mrs. Genevieve Johnson Sword

CONTENTS

Foreword by Albert Castel   ix
Acknowledgments   xiii

PART I   THE GENERALS

1. To Serve One's Ambition   3
2. We Have Met With a Serious Disaster   10
3. "What Does He Fight Battles For?"   19
4. "Nothing but the Hand of God Can Save Us"   29
5. "Everything Will Come Out Right"   36
6. A "Dazed and Mazy Commander"   46
7. "What Does It Mean?"   55
8. Whom Should the Soldiers Trust?   63
9. Bragg's "Least Favorable Option"   70

PART II   THE MEN

10. "One of the Wildest Places You Ever Saw"   83
11. "Ain't That a Queer Kind of War?"   90
12. "This Is Starvation Camp"   99
13. "Oh, What Suffering This War Entails"   105
14. Brown's Ferry and Smith's Pontoons   112
15. "General Hooker's Balloon"   123
16. Jenkins's Patrol to Pick Up Wagons and Stragglers   131
17. "What Were Your Orders, General Schurz?"   138
18. "We Have the River"   145
19. "I Don't Think There Will Be Much Left
    After My Army Passes"   153

20. "I Have Never Felt Such Restlessness Before"   158
21. "Can't You Spare Me Another Division?"   164

PART III   THE FIGHTING

22. "Kicking Up Such a Damned Fuss"   175
23. "The Ball Will Soon Open"   186
24. What Is "Wrongly Laid Down"   195
25. "A Sickle of Mars"   202
26. The Battle Within the Clouds   213
27. Fireflies in the Night   222
28. "I Mean to Get Even With Them"   231
29. Hell Turned Loose on Tunnel Hill   240
30. An Ascent into Hell   248
31. Time for a Demonstration   259
32. One of the Greatest Blunders   266
33. A Matter of Survival   275
34. "Who in Hell Is Going to Stop Them?"   282
35. "You Kills Me mit Joy!"   290
36. "Give 'em Hell, Boys!"   296
37. "Here's Your Mule!"   306
38. The Night of the Long Shadows   313
39. "The Unaccountable Spirit of the Troops"   319
40. In the Wake of the Stampede   326
41. "Have You Any Troops That Won't Run Away?"   334
42. "Such Is Civilized War"   347
43. "Let the Past Take Care of Itself"   352

Order of Battle   360
Chattanooga Campaign Chronology   370
Reference Notes   377
Bibliography   407
Index   421

FOREWORD

For the North, the summer of 1863 marked the end of the beginning of the Civil War; for the South, the beginning of the end. On July 3, at Gettysburg, Pennsylvania, the Union Army of the Potomac won, insofar as actual fighting was concerned, its first major victory, in the process turning back Robert E. Lee's second attempt to carry the war into the North and inflicting on his forces casualties from which they never recovered, with the result that henceforth the Confederacy would be on the strategic defensive, seeking to hold the Yankees at bay in Virginia. A day later, July 4, Ulysses S. Grant captured Vicksburg, the South's last great stronghold on the Mississippi River: Not only was the Confederacy now cut in twain physically and psychologically, but more importantly the North had achieved an unchallengeable dominance of the Mississippi Valley and thus was in a position to penetrate the lower South on either side of the mighty Father of Waters as it, in Abraham Lincoln's words, flowed "unvexed to the sea."

Finally, in middle Tennessee, the third main theater of military operations, Northern power likewise asserted itself against Southern weakness. Starting out from Murfreesboro in late June, Maj. Gen. William S. Rosecrans's Army of the Cumberland, in a series of brilliant maneuvers, compelled General Braxton Bragg's Army of Tennessee to evacuate Chattanooga early in September and retreat into Georgia, closely pursued. For the Confederacy, this was a disaster both actually and potentially worse than those it had suffered at Gettysburg and Vicksburg. The former, after all, merely represented a failure to carry out a successful invasion of the North and the Yankees had made no serious effort to exploit their hard-won victory in Pennsylvania by launching another "On to Richmond" offensive in Virginia. When they did, Lee could be counted on to deal with them as he had in the past. Similarly, Grant had made no attempt to follow up his capture of Vicksburg and showed no sign of so doing in the near future. Besides, since the Confederates utterly lacked the means to recapture Vicksburg, it was pointless for them even to think about it—and they did not.

The loss of Chattanooga was different. It meant the loss of Tennessee and threatened the loss of Georgia. Together these states constituted the heartland of the Confederacy. Without them, victory would be impossible and defeat certain. Something, therefore, had to be done to retrieve Chattanooga. Moreover, thanks to the enemy's inactivity in Virginia, something could be done.

And it was. The Confederate government sent by railroad Lt. Gen. James Longstreet and two divisions of Lee's army from Virginia to Georgia. There, on September 19–20, along the banks of Chickamauga Creek, they joined Bragg's troops in assailing Rosecrans's Army of the Cumberland. Through a combination of good luck, a bad Yankee blunder, and, above all, hard and bloody fighting, the Confederates drove the Federals from the field, inflicting on them heavy casualties.

That, though, is all they did. The Army of the Cumberland, with Maj. Gen. George H. Thomas replacing Rosecrans as commander, still held Chattanooga, the gateway to Georgia, and was determined to keep holding it despite an increasingly precarious supply situation. On the other hand, the Confederates had suffered such heavy losses in winning—nearly one third of their total combat strength—that they dared not attack the strongly fortified enemy and so besieged Chattanooga in hope of starving the Yankees into retreating or surrendering. In sum, while tactically the Battle of Chickamauga had been a Southern victory, strategically it settled nothing. Only by taking Chattanooga and either destroying the Army of the Cumberland or forcing it to seek survival in flight could the Confederates assure the safety of Georgia and redeem Tennessee. By the same token, only by breaking out of Chattanooga and defeating Bragg's army could the Federals secure their control of Tennessee and resume their march into Georgia.

The story of how and why the Federals succeeded and the Confederates failed to do what each respectively had to do is a dramatic one, dramatically told in the pages of this book. It also is a story filled with paradoxes, ironies, and strange, even bizarre happenings. Thus, to give just a few examples, the reader will read about the following:

A commander who is more interested in battling with his own generals than he is the enemy's army, with the result that although he defeats his generals, he in turn is defeated by the enemy.

Another commander whose plan for winning the battle fails in all key respects, yet who wins the battle and claims that it was won exactly as he planned.

A general famous for his speed and aggressiveness who is so slow and cautious that he is defeated by a far smaller force headed by a former private. Adding paradox to paradox and irony to irony, had this general been slower and more cautious, he would have gained an easy victory.

Troops who, after being ordered by their commander not to attack because he deems them unfit for offensive operations, disregard that order and execute the most successful frontal assault of the Civil War.

Other troops, veterans who always have fought with almost incredible bravery, who flee in panic from a position that should have been impregnable—which is one of the reasons they flee, for neither they nor their generals thought that the enemy would be so foolhardy as to attack that position.

Now, reader, having done my best to encourage you to do what presumably you intend to do anyway—read this book—I turn you over to the author, Mr. Wiley Sword. That, incidentally, is his actual name, notwithstanding it being so singularly and suspiciously apt for a writer of military history. Moreover, as you will soon discover, he is a sword who wields a wily pen. So enjoy, and as you enjoy, learn about one of the truly decisive events of the Civil War: the Siege and Battle of Chattanooga.

Albert Castel,

author of *Decision in the West:
The Atlanta Campaign of 1864*

ACKNOWLEDGMENTS

For the generous cooperation of the following individuals and institutions, I am particularly grateful.

Dr. Albert Castel, Hillsdale, Michigan, read the manuscript and provided valuable suggestions and materials. His keen insight and vast knowledge is reflected in the foreword.

Zack Waters, Rome, Georgia, was especially helpful with the procurement of rare and hard-to-locate Confederate accounts, even copying by hand a lengthy personalized description.

Greg Beck, Livonia, Michigan, made available dozens of regimental histories from the extensive collection of the late Mil Lent.

Bill Mason, Morehead City, North Carolina, provided many books and several indexes.

James Ogden III, Historian at the Chickamauga-Chattanooga National Military Park, Ft. Oglethorpe, Georgia, helped with technical details and provided a variety of information pertaining to Confederate artillery units.

Dave Roth, Columbus, Ohio, made available many valuable photographs from his collection and the files of *Blue & Gray Magazine*.

For their assistance with various important aspects, I'm much indebted to the following individuals (listed in alphabetical order):

Harry H. Anderson, Milwaukee, Wisconsin; Susan Boardman, Sunbury, Pennsylvania; David Coles, Tallahassee, Florida; John E. Haas, Columbus, Ohio; Larry Hauptman, New Paltz, New York; John Huelskamp, Barrington, Illinois; Chris Jordan, Harpers Ferry, West Virginia;

Lewis L. Poates, Knoxville, Tennessee; Fred Prouty, Nashville, Tennessee; Dr. Richard Sommers, Carlisle Barracks, Pennsylvania

The following institutions contributed significant research materials, and I gratefully acknowledge their help:

The American Philosophical Society, Philadelphia, Pennsylvania
Duke University Library, Durham, North Carolina
Florida State Archives Library, Tallahassee, Florida
Milwaukee County Historical Society, Milwaukee, Wisconsin
Missouri Historical Society, St. Louis, Missouri
Ohio Historical Society, Columbus, Ohio
University of Michigan, William L. Clements Library, Ann Arbor, Michigan
University of North Carolina Library, Southern Historical Collection, Chapel Hill, North Carolina
U.S. Army Military History Institute, Carlisle Barracks, Pennsylvania
Western Reserve Historical Society, Cleveland, Ohio

Both Jeff Herman, my agent, and George Witte, my editor, have my sincere thanks for their efforts and encouragement. Carol Edwards's copyediting of the manuscript was superb.

Last but not least, my wife, Marianne, spent many evenings alone, curled up with a book or watching TV, in order that I might complete this project in a timely fashion. For her love and understanding, I'm particularly grateful.

Wiley Sword

Bloomfield Hills, Michigan
May 1994

MOUNTAINS
TOUCHED *with* FIRE

PART ONE

The GENERALS

CHAPTER I

TO SERVE ONE'S AMBITION

It was the damnedest mess Assistant Secretary of War Charles A. Dana had ever seen. "It was wholesale panic. Our soldiers turned and fled. . . . Vain were all attempts to rally them. The road [to Chattanooga] is full of a disordered throng of fugitives," he announced. "The total of our killed, wounded, and prisoners can hardly be less than 20,000, and may be much more." Dana's telegram to Secretary of War Edwin Stanton at 4:00 P.M. on September 20, 1863, precipitated one of the greatest crises ever to face the war-weary Lincoln administration.[1]

The critical two-day Battle of Chickamauga had been decisively lost. The federal government's great army of the then mid-American heartland, the Army of the Cumberland, was in disarray, with many of its officers and soldiers demoralized and discouraged.

The scene along the roads leading north to Chattanooga was unforgettable to an eyewitness. "The woods were full of the fleeing fugitives, running in every direction. Ambulances filled with wounded [clogged the roads], the drivers frantically urging the horses on, to they knew not whither. Artillerymen were trying to get their guns away, in many cases with but a single span of horses. Caissons, limber chests, guns, ambulances, and men were wandering in confusion over the hills and knobs like sheep without a shepherd. . . . we fully realized that two-thirds of the army was whipped and scattered to the winds." Another soldier considered that the entire army had degenerated into a mob. Most of the wounded had been abandoned and left to fend for themselves. "Were a division of the enemy to pounce down upon us . . . I fear the Army of the Cumberland would be blotted out," he wrote.[2]

This incredible circumstance, involving a most improbable change of personal fortunes, rested squarely on the shoulders of a veteran soldier recently noted for several significant victories, Maj. Gen. William Starke Rosecrans. It was a bizarre twist of fate, for Rosecrans had been credited with a brilliant campaign that once more had thrust his name into national prominence.

In the fall of 1863, Rosecrans was the Union's man of the hour in mid-America. As commander of the mighty Army of the Cumberland, he already had reclaimed much of the middle-Tennessee heartland from the Rebels. An ambitious, smart general, "Old Rosy" was loved by his soldiers, feared by his enemies, and respected by his peers. He had bested some of the Confederacy's most prominent generals on the field of battle, including Earl Van Dorn, Sterling Price, Robert S. Garnett, and Braxton Bragg. Many considered him as having "the first order of military mind." Even his Confederate opponents lauded him as "a wily strategist" and "a brave and prudent leader."[3]

Yet there always had been something mysterious and different about Rosecrans. An aura of vanity and perhaps instability seemed to enshroud his outgoing, congenial personality. George B. McClellan had privately termed him in 1861 "a silly, fussy goose." In fact, though there was much to admire about the ex–West Point instructor and engineer-businessman, his shortcomings seemed equally as disturbing, even to those who were his close friends.[4]

A somewhat rumpled, stockily built man of forty-four, Rosecrans clearly was woven of a mixed fabric. Likable, loyal in his friendships, and a tireless worker, he was also moody, nervous, and impulsive. In times of stress, his keen intelligence and perceptive judgment seemed clouded by an excitable manner and garbled, stammering speech. To many, he was precisely the general to win the war. To others, he was wrathful, inconsistent, and temperamental. Those not in daily contact with Old Rosy seemed impressed mostly by his restless manner and tireless energy, which was frequently devoted to such minute details as seeing to the proper attire of his men or monitoring camp discipline. Thus, he had become a favorite among his soldiers, who appreciated his sincere concern about their well-being. Moreover, Rosecrans's almost-fanatic obsession for perfection in planning, arrangements, and execution was considered as evidence of his great capacity to manage and administrate.[5]

Unfortunately, it was also the mark of a self-consuming eccentric. Lurking behind those "kindly blue eyes" was a penetrating, probing glare, the kind of a look that bordered on the bizarre. Often an able, crafty strategist and a tough, tenacious fighter, Rosecrans, nonetheless, exhibited a peculiar vulnerability—that of the mind.[6]

His greatest gift, intellect, also seemed one of his most glaring weaknesses—an inability to reason well under extreme stress and during severe crises. Moreover, what McClellan observed in Rosecrans as the

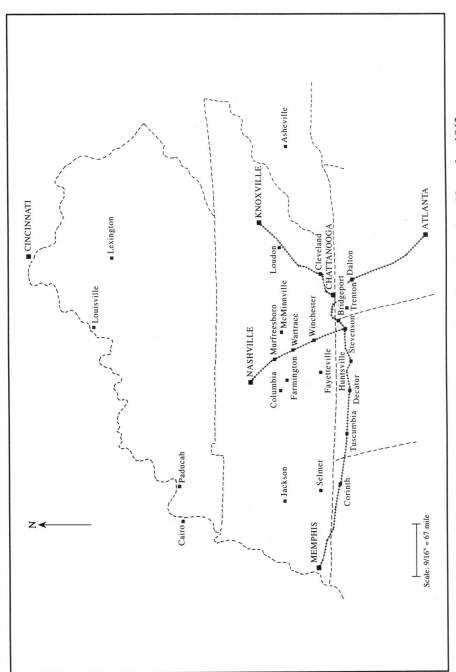

MAP 1   Theater of Operations, Chattanooga Campaign, September–November 1863
(*Source: O.R. Atlas, plates 149, 150*)

"silly, fussy goose" was perhaps a telltale manifestation of a manic disorder.[7]

Rosecrans's self-struggle was apparent in many ways. The eldest surviving son of a militia officer who was William Henry Harrison's adjutant during the War of 1812, Rosecrans had roots in America that went back seven generations, to Dutch immigrants who arrived in 1651. A youth whose motto, "lick and not get licked," made him somewhat of a ragtag leader among his Ohio schoolmates, Billy Rosecrans was always ambitious. When his family's modest means didn't allow for him to attend college, Rosecrans decided on West Point. A brilliant student, Old Rosy (as he came to be known to his fellow cadets) graduated fifth in his class of 1842, among such future luminaries as James Longstreet, and Earl Van Dorn. Ulysses Grant, a year behind, was not one of the more promising and elite young officers like Rosecrans, who received a choice engineering assignment upon graduation.[8]

Rosecrans's capacity for hard work and his engineering talent and practical success were not sufficient in themselves for this young lieutenant to remain in the army. The father of a rapidly growing family, he resigned in 1853, after ten years of service, for financial reasons. Annie, his young wife, and their four children required a greater income than the army provided. Yet Rosecrans's efforts in the coal-oil business not only met with varied fortune but also resulted in a harrowing brush with death. While experimenting with purifying coal oil, a "safety" lamp exploded in his face and Rosecrans was severely burned. After eighteen months' recovery, he still retained what some described as a permanent smirk due to this disfiguring injury.[9]

Of much importance from a psychological perspective was Rosecrans's conversion to Roman Catholicism. Although raised by a staunch Methodist family, young Rosecrans had converted while a cadet at West Point. His brother Sylvester had been similarly influenced, and even joined the priesthood, later becoming an auxiliary bishop. William Rosecrans had embraced his new faith with great enthusiasm, and he was fond of long discussions about religion. His espousal of the Catholic faith was an "intellectual decision," he conceded, based upon his experimental spirit and a need for "an authorized supernatural teacher." Not only did the devout Rosecrans carry a cross attached to his watch chain, but from his pocket he often withdrew "a dirty-looking string" of rosary beads—obviously well used, noted an observer. Later, of considerable import, Rosecrans literally adopted a displaced Catholic priest, Father Patrick Treacy, who became his close friend, confessor, and unofficial adviser.[10]

In 1861, Rosecrans, as a reflection of his faith in following his conscience, reluctantly determined to leave his increasingly successful civilian enterprise and reenter the army. By applying directly to the War Department for a commission as brigadier general, Rosecrans relied upon old Regular Army friends for endorsements and recommendations. In late May 1861,

Rosecrans received his prized appointment, and he soon earned considerable laurels in West Virginia.[11]

He was sent west in the spring of 1862 to the army besieging Corinth, Mississippi, and his star continued to rise rapidly. During the summer, he earned much recognition and command of a small army, the Army of the Mississippi, then led successful encounters at Iuka and Corinth before the year's end. Mindful of his burgeoning national stature, Rosecrans's vanity bubbled forth despite his having been elevated to major general prior to his Iuka victory. He fumed over his belated date of seniority, making it a major issue with the Washington authorities. "A feeling of shame and indignation came over me as I wrote the acceptance," he advised his friend Henry Halleck. "If fighting successful battles . . . deserved anything from the hands of government, it deserved my promotion from the date of those services crowned with success. . . . I find myself promoted junior to men who have not . . . had a tithe of the success. . . . I beg you to intercede for me, that some measure of justice may be done." This was characteristic of Rosecrans's self-image and temperament, even to the point where he allowed his emotions to outweigh discretion and better judgment. Finally, Lincoln interceded in the matter, and he backdated Rosecrans's commission to March 21, 1862.[12]

Old Rosy wasn't above using politics and all means at hand to gain an advantage, and the thought of being junior to the likes of Don Carlos Buell, Lew Wallace, Tom Crittenden, and "Bull" Nelson had made him furious. Also, there was new friction with Sam Grant, his emerging rival in the western theater. Although their initial relationship had been reasonably cordial, following the Iuka action Rosecrans became involved in an icy exchange with Grant, a onetime underclassman of his at West Point who was now senior in rank. Grant, after being thrust into national prominence following the capture of Fort Henry and Fort Donelson in February 1862, had rapidly risen to high command in the West. Despite a political setback as the victim of the devastating surprise attack at Shiloh, Grant had been named commander of the new consolidated force in the region, the Army of the Tennessee. Nonetheless, Ulysses S. Grant's career was marked with inconsistency and controversy. He inexplicably hadn't supported Rosecrans's attack at Iuka, as had been promised, resulting in the enemy's escape. The blame in the newspapers was cast largely upon Grant—due to "drunkenness in high places," said the *Cincinnati Commercial*. Even Rosecrans's brother Sylvester, the Roman Catholic auxiliary bishop of Cincinnati, condemned Grant's intemperance. "The awful charge made against Grant in today's *Commercial* is not so surprising as it is disgusting," wrote Bishop Rosecrans. "I am afraid it is true."[13]

Thereafter, the outspoken Rosecrans and the iron-willed Grant became bitter, internecine enemies—each conducting a backbiting behind-the-scenes campaign to discredit the other. Grant, in fact, became so embittered because of Rosecrans's innuendos that he said he was on the verge of removing him from command, on the very day Rosecrans's reassignment came.*

Although Rosecrans left behind him a formidable rival in Grant, he had yet to deal with another potential foe, Secretary of War Edwin Stanton. Having supplied and organized his new army in Nashville, Rosecrans repeatedly was prodded by the War Department into moving against Braxton Bragg's army at Murfreesboro. The ensuing Battle of Stones River, fought in miserable midwinter weather on December 31, 1862, and January 2, 1863, had resulted in Rosecrans's advance being counterassailed by Bragg's troops. The largely defensive battle Rosecrans won by tenaciously holding his positions was heralded in the North as a major victory. Coming close on the heels of Grant's failures to take Vicksburg, on the Mississippi River, and Burnside's bloody repulse at Fredericksburg, Virginia, Stones River was a major reason for Rosecrans's rising popularity.[14]

In early 1863, Old Rosy not only basked in widespread public acclaim; many considered him the nation's foremost military leader. He was the choice of several high-level administration officials to succeed Ambrose Burnside as commander of the Army of the Potomac. Yet a majority of Lincoln's cabinet preferred an eastern general, hence "Fighting Joe" Hooker was appointed.[15]

It was a strange phenomenon. Although Rosecrans's career was approaching its popular zenith, politically the Ohio general seemed already in decline. Pressured by Stanton and Halleck to move against Bragg's army once again, an almost haughty, reluctant Rosecrans feuded with Stanton over reinforcements and supplies. Old Rosy's curt language, indiscretions, and implied insults turned Edwin Stanton into an indignant foe. When Halleck demanded an advance in the West, saying a major general's commission in the Regular Army would be given to the general "who first wins an important and decisive victory," Rosecrans was livid. "As an officer and a citizen I feel degraded to see such an auctioneering of honor. Have we a general who would fight for his own personal benefit when he would not of honor and the country?" he angrily wrote. Rosecrans even privately criticized Halleck, his professed friend: "Does he seek to bribe me to do my duty? Does he suppose I will sacrifice the lives of my men to serve my ambition? The army is now to be administered on a plan of 'gift enterprise.' " As such, it was an "insult," raged Rosecrans.[16]

The feud with Washington continued to intensify. Noting the temperamental Ohio general's indignant attitude, Stanton, who increasingly served as the administration's spokesman, began pressing hard for Rosecrans's advance. At one point, Stanton even peremptorily ordered him to march at once. Yet by June 1863, Rosecrans had decided to ignore Stanton

---

*Rosecrans was relieved from duty on October 23, 1862, and was ordered a few days later to take command of the Army of the Cumberland, the successor to Buell's old Army of the Ohio.

and deal directly with President Lincoln. The result was a war within a war, and the political infighting divided many otherwise-neutral observers, including newspaper correspondents, into political camps opposed to or favoring Old Rosy.[17]

In the midst of this political imbroglio, Rosecrans was urged directly by Lincoln, who wanted to prevent Bragg from sending reinforcements to Mississippi for the defense of Vicksburg, to resume his offensive. "I will attend to it," responded Rosecrans unenthusiastically. At the time, Rosecrans was awaiting Ambrose Burnside's simultaneous advance in eastern Tennessee, in order to protect his vulnerable left flank. Although Burnside continued to procrastinate, Rosecrans began slowly moving south in early June 1863. But a three-week stall ensued, causing more controversy. Finally, Burnside's halting advance into east Tennessee enabled Rosecrans to push forward again toward Bragg's army, spread out along the line of the Duck River in Tennessee.[18]

In one of the most brilliant strategic maneuvers of the war, Rosecrans used deception—feinting in one direction while striking with his main force beyond the Confederate left flank—to threaten Bragg's vital line of communications. The Tullahoma campaign, lasting only eleven days, following a delay of six months, resulted in Bragg being outflanked around his strong, heavily fortified lines. Threatened with the loss of the railroad in his rear, Bragg had withdrawn from the main supply depot at Tullahoma on June 30, 1863, abandoning virtually all of Tennessee and retreating south of the Tennessee River to Chattanooga. Although a major victory, and an essentially bloodless one at that, Rosecrans's brilliant accomplishment was obscured by two other significant events that had occurred simultaneously— the fall of Vicksburg and the defeat of Robert E. Lee's army at Gettysburg.[19]

Despite Rosecrans's strategic victory, Grant had won the coveted prize—a major general's commission in the Regular Army—and, thanks to his Vicksburg victory, was clearly the dominant general in the West. Moreover, instead of being praised in the nation's press and receiving official commendation, Rosecrans was largely ignored, and he continued to be harassed by the Lincoln administration. Indeed, he was soon reminded that two primary objectives still remained on his front in Tennessee—the capture of the gateway city of Chattanooga and the destruction of Bragg's army.[20]

CHAPTER 2

WE HAVE MET WITH A
SERIOUS DISASTER

Secretary of War Edwin Stanton had become almost bellicose as week after week dragged on during the midsummer of 1863 without word of Rosecrans's further advance. Being plagued by a shortage of forage, supplies, and subsistence, Rosecrans continued to delay until he had twenty days' rations and the corn ripened for cavalry forage. Yet Stanton went so far as to demand, through Henry Halleck, Rosecrans's daily report of the movement of each corps until they crossed the Tennessee River. Rosecrans fumed about that "unprincipled Secretary of War['s]" meddling, and in a huff, he bluntly threatened to resign if not allowed his way. Sustained by Lincoln, who reassured this outspoken general that he was not watching him "with an evil eye," Rosecrans continued his deliberate preparations.[1]

In mid-August 1863, Old Rosy finally moved, again sending his army south in a familiar strategic movement intended to deceive Bragg. Basing his movements on the recently successful Tullahoma campaign maneuver, Rosecrans advanced in three separate columns and again swiftly duped Bragg. The bait was the northern column under the command of Thomas Crittenden, three divisions of the Twenty-first Corps. Their purpose was to deceive Bragg into thinking their presence north of Chattanooga represented Rosecrans's entire army. While mounted infantry, cavalry, and Crittenden's infantry maneuvered along the banks of the Tennessee River north of Chattanooga, Rosecrans, with two corps under George H. Thomas and Alexander McCook, had slipped across the Tennessee River near Bridgeport, Alabama, well downstream from Chattanooga. On August twenty-eighth, Rosecrans's advanced forces crossed the river, and by September fourth the movement was complete. When Burnside's occupation of Knoxville occurred on the same day, Bragg was strategically defeated, and on September sixth the Confederates abandoned Chattanooga.[2]

Having easily maneuvered Bragg out of a major objective, Rosecrans remained intent on marching eastward over the Lookout Mountain range, well south of Chattanooga, so as to reach the strategic railroads in Bragg's rear. Although this movement would effectively cut off the enemy's line of retreat and sever vital communications, the critical problem the Federal commander now faced was the dispersion of his three primary columns in mountainous terrain. Concentration of the army over the expanse of nearly sixty miles would be difficult in the event of a crisis. Thus, when McCook advanced far down Lookout Valley, his column remained nearly twenty miles south of and across Lookout Mountain from Thomas's corps, which had passed through Stevens Gap in the Lookout range. Thomas was posted in McLemore's Cove, a valley between the adjacent Lookout Mountain and Pigeon Mountain ridges.[3]

After occupying Chattanooga with Crittenden's troops on September tenth, Rosecrans had ridden south on the thirteenth to join Thomas in the vicinity of Stevens Gap. Riding with him was the acting second assistant secretary of war, Charles A. Dana, who had recently served as Stanton's observer at Grant's headquarters during the Vicksburg campaign. Dana had been sent by Stanton to scrutinize Rosecrans in a similar manner, and his instructions, according to Dana, were to "observe and report" on Rosecrans's conduct of the campaign. Although Dana's letter of introduction stated that he was there merely "for the purpose of conferring with you upon any subject you may desire," Rosecrans had greeted Dana as a pariah—a man intent on meddling with Rosecrans's career. Indeed, among many of the army's senior officers, he was regarded as "a bird of evil omen"—a spy intent on mischief and seeking gossip to funnel back to Stanton.[4]

Even worse, Dana's arrival had initiated a streak of ill tidings for Rosecrans. On September eleventh, some of Thomas's forward troops were severely attacked near Dug Gap in Pigeon Mountain, and Thomas had to pull back across McLemore's Cove towards Stevens Gap. After ordering McCook to join Thomas near Stevens Gap, Rosecrans had to wait five agonizing days for McCook's arrival—due to that general's confused meanderings over Lookout Mountain. In the interim, Rosecrans had learned with alarm of a formidable Confederate concentration east of Chickamauga Creek in McLemore's Cove. It became increasingly evident to Rosecrans that with a divided army, he was facing a rapid enemy buildup, including heavy reinforcements from the East. There was no time to lose, and even before McCook rejoined Thomas, he had Thomas begin shifting his troops northward up the cove, toward Lee and Gordon's Mill on the banks of Chickamauga Creek. Since Crittenden had been ordered south from Chattanooga over Missionary Ridge to the same site, the army would then be effectually concentrated.[5]

By the evening of September seventeenth, Rosecrans's three primary columns had moved within a mutually supporting distance and were positioned from Stevens Gap to Lee and Gordon's Mill. Even the reserve corps under Gordon Granger had been brought forward from the vicinity of Bridgeport to Rossville, south of Chattanooga. Here they were to protect against an enemy thrust northward toward Chattanooga.[6]

On the eighteenth, an anxious and apprehensive Rosecrans reported to Henry Halleck that Bragg's army had been greatly reinforced, particularly by troops from Virginia. He further warned that "everything indicates" that the enemy would swiftly attempt "to overthrow this army." Accordingly, Rosecrans stated his first priority was to protect the army's flanks, especially the Federal left, stretching northeastward in the direction of Chattanooga. By late afternoon on the eighteenth, this area appeared to be the point of the enemy's greatest concentration. Noting the rising dust clouds that swept to the northeast "three or four miles beyond" Chickamauga Creek, Rosecrans belatedly ordered George Thomas to shift farther to the north, bypassing Crittenden's troops, and to take a strong position forming the Federal army's extreme left. Intending to protect the vital main road through the valley to Chattanooga, Thomas's men marched throughout the night in order to reach their designated location in the vicinity of the Snodgrass farm by daylight.[7]

The bloody battle west of Chickamauga Creek, which began on the nineteenth in tangled thickets and rolling terrain, was somewhat of a surprise to both armies. Neither commander had foreseen the extent of their opponent's concentration along the extreme northern flank. Yet to Rosecrans, the result of the day's fighting was mostly favorable. Despite repeatedly having to send reinforcements to the critical left flank, so that virtually all of his army except for a few brigades and the reserves had been engaged, Rosecrans and his troops continued to hold the primary roads leading north. The Federal army's line of retreat was secure, and that night among a conference of his senior generals the renewal of the conflict was discussed. Thomas would continue in charge of the left flank and would command all troops now present there, amounting to the entire army except for ten brigades.[8]

Overstressed, nervous, and exhausted from a lack of sleep, William S. Rosecrans had heard Mass before daylight on Sunday, September twentieth. Perhaps as an omen, Rosecrans noted the sky was "red and sultry," with the thick woods enveloped in fog and a lingering battle haze. The day's action began relatively late, about 8:30 A.M., on the extreme Federal left. Although Thomas's stout defenders, aided by extensive breastworks thrown up during the night, quickly repulsed most of the Rebel attackers, the pressure became great as Bragg hurled more units into the action. When Thomas requested additional reinforcements, Rosecrans shifted even more frontline troops to the north. At one point that morning, responding to news of a pending gap in his line on the right, he ordered Brig. Gen. Thomas Wood's division to close up on Maj. Gen. Joseph J. Reynolds's division—presumed to be next in line. In fact, it was one division removed. A little more than an hour earlier, Wood had been berated by Rosecrans with great profanity in front of Wood's own staff for not promptly obeying orders. Now the resentful Kentuckian angrily reacted, with impulsive malice, said some. Although aware that Brig. Gen. John M. Brannan's division (between Wood's and Reynolds's divisions) had not withdrawn as earlier anticipated, Tom Wood peevishly determined to obey Rosecrans's orders immediately. Despite the admonition of the staff officer delivering the order—that considering Brannan's presence, Wood should at least wait until the matter could be clarified—Wood said no, he intended to move promptly as directed.[9]

In one of the more bizarre accidents in the history of the war, at the precise moment Wood directed his three brigades to leave their front line unoccupied and withdraw, Gen. James Longstreet, with about 11,000 Confederates, was poised to strike that very portion of the Union lines. At 11:10 A.M., just minutes after Wood's brigades withdrew and created more than a mile gap in the right center of Rosecrans's line, Longstreet's men, concentrated in five lines of eight brigades along a narrow front, struck Wood's abandoned breastworks. Only a single, understrength Union brigade from McCook's corps had time to begin moving into the vacated area. The immediate result was the systematic rout of the entire right wing of the Federal army.[10]

Stanton's man, Assistant Secretary of War Charles A. Dana, had been sleeping on the ground near Rosecrans's headquarters. "I was awakened by the most infernal noise I ever heard," wrote the stunned Dana. "I sat up on the grass, and the first thing I saw was General Rosecrans crossing himself. . . . Hello, I said to myself, if the general is crossing himself, we are in a desperate situation." Indeed, once in the saddle, Dana saw the troops on the right "break and melt away like leaves before the wind." Musket balls and cannon shells roared and zipped through the air. Everywhere Dana looked, there was confusion and tumult. Amid the deafening roar of battle, there was the frightening crash of treetops being torn from the trunks by whizzing cannon shells. As the limbs came cascading down upon the few men attempting to re-form, they invariably would break and run, he observed in horror. Dana dazedly wandered to the right, attempting to reach safety, but soon turned away and rode back to Chattanooga.[11]

William S. Rosecrans also had been caught up in the tumult and presented a pathetic sight along with his staff and escorts, noted an observer. Each with drawn saber was gesturing and flailing at the wildly running men. It was a frenzy of frustration. Following a futile attempt to rally the swarms of stragglers and bewildered, panic-stricken soldiers of his right flank, the distraught, exhausted Rosecrans had abandoned the battlefield about noon. Fearing the still-intact left wing of his army under Maj. Gen. George H. Thomas was about to crumble, and believing the enemy interposed between himself and Thomas's troops, Rosecrans disconsolately headed north for the crossroads village of Rossville. Amid the torrent of routed soldiers, he rode in stunned disbelief, an emotionally overwrought commander amid a frightened mob—the wreckage of the Army of the Cumberland. "[I] repeated to our Holy Lady the prayer of the Church very often," he later confided, "Monstra te esse Matra."[12]

Reaching the rear-echelon village of Rossville, Rosecrans continued to face a dire plight. No one seemed to know the fate of Thomas. It was suggested by Rosecrans's ubiquitous chief of staff, Brig. Gen. James A. Garfield, that he, Garfield, go to Thomas to learn of his situation. Further, Garfield would advise Thomas that protection of the army's commissary stores was vital until the officer in charge of the cumbersome wagon trains could withdraw with them to Chattanooga. The emotionally spent Rosecrans, meanwhile, would go back to Chattanooga to gather and reorganize the men.[13]

Rosecrans impulsively agreed, and about 2:00 P.M. the Federal commander, nearly in a stupor, turned and rode north along the road to Chattanooga. About 3:40 P.M., he arrived at the headquarters of Brig. Gen. George D. Wagner, the detached general earlier left in charge of that city. Rosecrans had to be helped from his horse into the house. He appeared completely broken in spirit, noted an observer, and yet the jaded Ohioan nervously began preparing dispatches.[14]

At the outset, the task of saving his army seemed overwhelming. Admittedly worn out, Rosecrans, just before 5:00 P.M., read Garfield's dispatch, relayed over the army field telegraph, which was still operating from Rossville. Written at 3:45 P.M., Garfield's telegram informed Rosecrans that Thomas, with a mixed command, still held his ground on the Snodgrass farm and ridges, as occupied that morning. Although "the hardest fighting I have seen today" was raging, said Garfield, Thomas had beaten off all attacks and appeared to be able to hold on until at least nightfall. Thomas "will not need to fall back farther than Rossville, perhaps not any," added Rosecrans's chief of staff, thus "we may in the main retrieve our morning disaster." All Rosecrans should do was order the army to halt and re-form at Rossville. Thomas's men were fighting superbly, and one general with Thomas was even speculating that the Rebels could be badly defeated the next day, "if all our forces come in." "I think you had better come to Rossville tonight and bring ammunition," urged Garfield.[15]

It was a ray of hope, an opportunity to act boldly and perhaps redeem the dire fortunes of the day. If Rosecrans seized the opportunity and returned with sufficient troops to Rossville, the Federal army might prevail after all.

Yet to William S. Rosecrans, Garfield's dispatch was couched in generalities and ambiguities—"I hope," "I think," and "if we can." To Rosecrans, on the edge of nervous collapse, it must have seemed a prescription for an even greater disaster. His response was revealing. He attempted merely to mollify Garfield, and he replied by telegraph: "What you propose is correct. . . . Ammunition will be sent up," he advised, also adding rather apprehensively, "I trust General Thomas has been able to hold his position."[16]

The truly decisive message of the day, however, which reflected Rose-crans's muddled state of mind, was his dispatch to Thomas, erroneously dated at 12:15 P.M. but actually sent from Chattanooga about 5:15 P.M.*

In substance, Rosecrans told Thomas to give up the battlefield despite his successful stand: "Assume control of all the forces [present] . . . and assume a threatening attitude at Rossville. Send all the unorganized force to this place for reorganization. I will examine the ground here and make such dispositions for defense as the case may require and join you. Have sent out ammunition and rations." That was it. Rosecrans was accepting battlefield defeat. In his mind, he was convinced the army except for Thomas's command was all but stampeded, a view accentuated by his own vivid eyewitness experiences.[17]

Minutes earlier, at 5:00 P.M., he had telegraphed to Washington the news of the humiliating defeat: "Have met with a serious disaster; extent not yet ascertained. Enemy overwhelmed us, drove our right, pierced our center, and scattered troops there. . . . Every available reserve was used when the men stampeded. . . . Troops from Charleston, Florida, Virginia, and all along the seaboard are found among the prisoners. It seems that every available man was thrown against us."[18]

Abraham Lincoln had spent September twentieth in his Washington, D.C., office, examining the hours-old dispatches providing news of the critical battle then raging along the Chickamauga Creek in Georgia. Aware of Rosecrans's telegram of the nineteenth, reporting ten pieces of Rebel artillery captured along with many prisoners, and considering his closing remark—"with the blessing of God will do more tomorrow"—Lincoln had been hopeful if apprehensive. Assistant Secretary Charles A. Dana, in the field with Rosecrans, had also dispatched various encouraging telegrams on the nineteenth, reporting "everything is going well" and "decisive victory seems assured to us." Although duly encouraged, Lincoln had remained ill at ease and pensive.[19]

That evening, Dana's fateful dispatch of 4:00 PM. was shown to Lincoln

---

*Rosecrans noted that the 12:15 P.M. time was incorrect in an addenda to Thomas's official report, suggesting that it must "have been written as late as 4:15 [P.M.]" (See O.R. 1-30-1-140, 256). Historians have accepted this 4:15 P.M. time as being accurate, which suggests it was sent *before* receipt of Garfield's 3:45 P.M. dispatch. From the content of this fateful message to Thomas, it is evident it was written *after* Rosecrans received Garfield's 3:45 P.M. dispatch. Far too many specific items cited by Garfield are addressed in Rosecrans's message to Thomas for it to have been coincidental. Specific among these are the need for ammunition at Rossville (cited by Garfield); Garfield's mention about the presence of mixed commands fighting with Thomas (Thomas was told to assume command of all); the order for Thomas to withdraw to Rossville (Garfield apparently planted this idea in Rosecrans's mind when he said in his dispatch there was no need "to fall back farther than Rossville"); and Rosecrans's statement to Thomas that "[I will] join you" at Rossville (Garfield requested Rosecrans come to Rossville that night).

by Edwin Stanton. Dana had hastened back to Chattanooga following the rout of the Federal right wing and arrived in that city before Rosecrans. "My report today is of deplorable importance," wired the exasperated Dana. "Chickamauga is as fatal a name in our history as Bull Run. . . . The lines of Sheridan and Davis broke in disorder, borne down by immense columns of the enemy. . . . Before them our soldiers turned and fled. It was wholesale panic. Vain were all attempts to rally them. . . . The road [to Chattanooga] is full of a disordered throng of fugitives. . . . Rosecrans escaped by Rossville road. Enemy not yet arrived before Chattanooga. Preparations making to resist his entrance for a time." Dana's preliminary wire clearly shocked Lincoln and Stanton, and they could but anxiously await further word. About an hour later, Rosecrans's own dispatch of 5:00 P.M. was received, and Lincoln began to comprehend the dire crisis suddenly thrust upon the nation. It would be a sleepless night.[20]

Abraham Lincoln characteristically kept his composure. To reassure Rosecrans, he wired a message just past midnight on the twenty-first, saying: "Be of good cheer. We have unabated confidence in you and in your soldiers and officers. In the main you must be the judge as to what is to be done. If I was to suggest, I would say save your army by taking strong positions until Burnside joins you, when I hope you can turn the tide. . . . We shall do our utmost to assist you." Minutes later, the President wired an imperative message to his independent commander in east Tennessee, Maj. Gen. Ambrose Burnside. Days earlier, Burnside had been ordered to reinforce Rosecrans and cooperate with him, and Lincoln now demanded: "Go to Rosecrans with your force without a moment's delay." Beyond that, there was little that could be done until Stanton organized a meeting with the cabinet and the general in chief, Henry Halleck.[21]

It was about dawn on the twenty-first when Lincoln wearily shuffled into the bedroom of his private secretary, John Hay. While sitting on the edge of Hay's bed, Lincoln agonized over the day's misfortunes: "Well, Rosecrans has been whipped, as I feared. I have feared it for several days. I believe I feel trouble in the air before it comes. Rosecrans says we have met with a serious disaster—extent not ascertained. Burnside, instead of obeying orders which were given him on the fourteenth, and going to Rosecrans, has gone up on a foolish affair to Jonesboro to capture a party of guerrillas."[22]

The President sadly gazed into space, as if in a trance. Hay may well have thought that it was the most depressed Lincoln had appeared since the early days of the war.

In Chattanooga, the night of September 20 had seemed without end. Reports began coming in about nightfall, but they were more optimistic in tone. Dana learned before 8:00 P.M. that the situation was not as bad as at first feared. News of Thomas's valiant and successful stand on Horseshoe

Ridge had arrived, and Dana wired Stanton that Thomas would belatedly fall back "to the strongest line of defense for the purpose of defeating enemy's design of regaining Chattanooga." Thomas was even reported driving back the Rebel hordes, said Dana, and so many Federal troops were intact and fighting that "it is not difficult to make good our lines until reinforcements can arrive."[23]

To substantiate Dana's optimism, Rosecrans's chief of staff, Garfield, wired from Rossville at 8:40 P.M. that the army's trains were safe, and "General Thomas has fought a most terrific battle and has damaged the enemy badly. . . . Our men not only held their ground, but at many points drove the enemy splendidly. Longstreet's Virginians have got their bellies full," offered the aroused Garfield, who added, "I believe we can whip them tomorrow. I believe we can now crown the whole battle with victory. [Maj. Gen. Gordon] Granger regards them as thoroughly whipped tonight, and thinks they would not renew the fight were we to remain on the field. . . . I hope you will not budge an inch from this place [Rossville], but come up early in the morning, and if the Rebs try it, accommodate them."[24]

As was fully apparent now, Rosecrans's 5:15 P.M. dispatch to Thomas to assume a defensive position at Rossville was a primary reason for Thomas ordering a withdrawal to Rossville after nightfall on the twentieth. With reports of Thomas being "in good shape," and that he "[will] be in a strong position before morning," Garfield had suggested another opportunity existed for Rosecrans to contest the final victory.[25]

Rosecrans hardly seemed to notice the supposedly altered situation. Instead of a Thermopylae, he envisioned only a pending Waterloo. Reports from commanders at Rossville, and even Garfield's message, were filled with pleas for food and munitions. "The troops here are utterly exhausted," wrote one general, adding that they were also "without rations." Garfield related how "nearly every division in the field exhausted its ammunition, got supplies, and exhausted it again." In his 8:40 P.M. report, Garfield also mentioned observing "clouds of dust to the eastward and northward, [which] seem[s] to indicate some movement on our left." Although Maj. Gen. Philip Sheridan thought it was the Rebels "projecting to come in directly on Chattanooga," Garfield said, "I do not think so."[26]

What went through Rosecrans's mind is not hard to envision. Added to the dire comments of various officers who had abandoned the battlefield and continued to tell stories of gloom and despair, there now seemed only the worst of circumstances to deal with—a major defeat, not a belated opportunity to reclaim victory.

Rosecrans's 9:30 P.M. telegram to Garfield expressed his concern with the "enemy drifting toward our left." Although again professing that "I like your suggestions [about making a stand at Rossville]," the Federal commander's mind was made up. His dispatch to President Lincoln the following morning reflected his lingering apprehension: "We have no certainty of holding our position here [Chattanooga]. If Burnside could come immediately it would be well; otherwise he may not be able to join us unless he comes on [the] west side of [the Tennessee] river."[27]

That night, a staff officer from Negley's division, Capt. Alfred L. Hough, found Rosecrans in the telegraph office at Chattanooga. Hough was seeking instructions; no one seemed to be able to dissipate the confusion and disorder then existing at Rossville. To Hough's surprise, he found Rosecrans out of sorts. "He looked worn and exhausted," reported Hough, "and was laboring under excitement. . . . [He] showed the want of one requisite of a great military commander, firmness and self-reliance under adverse circumstances. He was evidently crushed under the weight of his disaster." By Rosecrans's side was his friend and confessor, Father Patrick Treacy. Rosecrans was tearful, despairing, and seeking Treacy's spiritual dispensation. Amid all the remorse, Hough was dismissed and told to go back to Rossville. There he was to tell his general to preserve order until General Thomas might arrive to make a stand and save the army.[28]

Out on the front line at Rossville, the exhausted James A. Garfield was preparing his final dispatch of the night to Rosecrans. Pleadingly, Garfield wrote that the need for action was urgent. The report of the enemy attempting to get around the Federal left flank into Chattanooga (per the dust clouds earlier observed) had been disposed of as false, he said. Thus, Garfield urged with renewed energy: "I hope you will get here as soon as possible to organize the army and [win a] victory."[29]

CHAPTER 3

"WHAT DOES HE FIGHT
BATTLES FOR?"

Nathan Bedford Forrest, not yet known as the "Confederacy's Wizard of the Saddle"—but more as a bold and successful cavalry raider—had been in the saddle since before dawn on the crisp and clear morning of September 21, 1863. Forrest's adrenaline was flowing in the wake of the enormous victory along Chickamauga Creek on the twentieth. Although his men and horses were exhausted and suffering for want of water, Forrest had pushed his men hard that morning intent on pursuing the Yankees to Chattanooga. Along the LaFayette Road stretching north toward the village of Rossville, Forrest and his men had encountered vast numbers of Federal stragglers, wounded, and dead mingled among hundreds of arms littering the ground. While squads rounded up the prisoners and collected arms, using abandoned wagons and ambulances to send their booty to the rear, Forrest's main force proceeded to a spur of Missionary Ridge south of Rossville.[1]

Following a brief skirmish with Federal cavalry in which Forrest's horse was allegedy shot in the neck (Forrest is said to have plunged his finger into the hole to plug the artery until atop the ridge, when the horse fell dead as Forrest removed his finger to dismount), it was evident that a rare opportunity existed. Through a pair of field glasses captured from a Federal signal corps observer trapped in a nearby treetop, Forrest observed Chattanooga, about four miles distant. Forrest had climbed a tall oak, and upon coming down he sent an urgent dispatch to Lt. Gen. Leonidas Polk, to be forwarded to the Confederate commander Gen. Braxton Bragg. "We are within a mile of Rossville," wrote the aroused Forrest. "Can see Chattanooga and everything around. The enemy's trains are leaving, going around the point of Lookout Mountain. The prisoners captured report two pontoons thrown across for the purpose of retreating. I think they are evacuating as hard as they can go. They are cutting timber down to obstruct our passing. I think we ought to press forward as rapidly as possible."[2]

Due to the enemy's clearly visible efforts to defend Rossville Gap, Forrest knew it was unlikely he could force his way through without strong reinforcements. Nonetheless, the aggressive Forrest attempted the fight, dismounting a brigade and ordering them to attack. Although they were soon repulsed, when his artillery arrived he opened with a barrage and continued firing intermittently over the span of several hours. As the Yankees could not be moved, Forrest began to fret. No word had arrived from either Polk's or Bragg's headquarters.[3]

At 11:30 A.M., Forrest sent a second message. The enemy was "evidently fortifying, as I can distinctly hear the sound of axes in great numbers," he reported. In urging the army's prompt advance, the indignant Confederate cavalryman is said to have complained that "every hour was worth a thousand men," and asserted he could take Chattanooga if given a single brigade of infantry. Again the morning dragged on without a reply. Finally, nearly at the end of his wits, Forrest galloped back to army headquarters on the Chickamauga battlefield.[4]

Forrest found Braxton Bragg very reluctant to pursue en masse, seemingly unconvinced of the need for urgency. Busily engaged in administrative details and making arrangements for scouring the Chickamauga battlefield for small arms and equipment, Bragg allegedly told Forrest that exhaustion, disorganization, and a lack of supplies prohibited an immediate pursuit. "General Bragg, we can get all the supplies our army needs in Chattanooga," chided Forrest. Bragg glared in disapproval. Forrest eventually left in disgust. "What does he fight battles for?" announced the angry cavalry general.[5]

"[Braxton] Bragg is not fit for a general," observed a Confederate soldier in 1863. "If Jeff Davis will just let Bragg alone, I think he will do us more damage than the enemy." Perhaps the most despised commander on either side by mid-1863, Bragg, warned a Rebel physician, "is either stark mad or utterly incompetent. He is ignorant of both the fundamental principles and details of his noble profession. He has lost the confidence of both his men and officers." Even civilian observers in the South discredited him as a "worthless" general.[6]

It was quite a comedown from 1862, when Jefferson Davis had lauded Bragg as the only general who had accomplished all he had undertaken. Others had considered Bragg the greatest general in the Confederacy. A North Carolinian who graduated fifth in his class of 1837 at West Point, Bragg had gained notoriety and even celebrity status during the Mexican War. The apocryphal remark attributed to the *New Orleans Daily Delta,* March 31, 1847, "A little more grape, Captain Bragg," at the Battle of Buena Vista in 1847 had brought glory to Bragg as the hero of that battle.

After rising in the Regular Army to lieutenant colonel, he had retired in 1856, becoming a prosperous Louisiana planter. Yet the advent of the Civil War resulted in Bragg's receipt of a Confederate brigadier general's commission from his old Mexican War comrade in arms Jefferson Davis—"who hopes much, and expects much for you, and from you," wrote Davis in April 1861.[7]

Bragg's tenure in high command dated from his adept role in organizing the defenses of Mobile and Pensacola, which earned for him a major general's commission. Being stuck in a noncombatant role nearly a year after the beginning of hostilities, he chafed to enter active campaigning then under way in the early spring of 1862. In late February, Bragg had his chance. Following the loss of Fort Henry and Fort Donelson, he led a well-organized and disciplined force of about ten thousand men north to join Gen. Albert Sidney Johnston's army in defending the Mississippi Valley at Corinth, Mississippi. The subsequent Battle of Shiloh, which gave Bragg his first experience in managing large numbers of troops in combat, was a blunt hint of the methods he would embrace.[8]

Schooled in the theories of Mahan and Jomni at West Point, Bragg was convinced that the offensive dogma of "throwing masses upon decisive points" was the key to tactical success on the battlefield. At Shiloh, he had attempted to demonstrate the advantage of offensive over defensive warfare, per his admonition in January 1862: "I shall promptly assail him [enemy] in the open field with my whole available force, if he does not exceed me more than four to one." At Shiloh, Bragg had hurled his troops in repeated frontal attacks against the formidable Yankee line in the "Hornet's Nest," resulting in a series of disjoined piecemeal assaults. Nearly a dozen attacks were beaten off, with frightful slaughter of Bragg's men. It was only after the Hornet's Nest was flanked and surrounded that the defenders were routed and captured. Bragg, due to the resulting success, received scant criticism for his tactical mistakes. In fact, after the death of Sidney Johnston from a stray rifle ball, Bragg had assumed a new and dominant role in the army's hierarchy. Because of Pierre G. T. Beauregard's discomfiture in defending Corinth, and the Davis administration's feud with this temperamental Creole general, Bragg, who had been promoted to full general following Shiloh, was named commander of the Army of Tennessee in June 1862.[9]

Braxton Bragg, wrote the Confederate governor of Alabama, "is a master genius." The governor of Louisiana praised Bragg in the highest terms, saying he had more confidence in him than any other military man. Much was expected of the new commander, and in mid-1862 he had promptly set out to earn the Confederate army's respect. "What you can do . . . is the important question," observed his adoring wife, Elise.[10]

Bragg's reputation for achievement seemed quite appropriate. Following his early efforts as army commander, there was ample evidence to substantiate the high expectations of Jefferson Davis and others. Bragg had set about disciplining the army with a heavy hand, shooting deserters without mercy. A story even circulated that Bragg had a man shot for shooting a chicken. Actually, the man executed had violated a strict order prohibiting troops from firing guns when in camp. The guilty individual was shooting at a chicken, but instead, the bullet had struck and mortally wounded another soldier.[11]

Despite widespread grumbling, Bragg's strict discipline had molded the army into an effective fighting force, and a soldier noted: "There has been a marvelous change for the better in the condition, health, discipline and drill of the troops of this army since it left Corinth; it was a perfect rabble there." Another soldier reflected: "Bragg is beyond a doubt the best disciplinarian in the South. When he took command . . . the Army was little better than a mob. The din of firearms could be heard at all hours of the day. Now a gun is never fired without orders. . . . The discipline of the troops has improved very much. Men are not apt to disobey orders when they know death is the punishment."[12]

Yet the basis for this increased discipline, confided another observer, was outright fear of, rather than respect for, their commander. "So far as patriotism was concerned," wrote Pvt. Sam Watkins of the 1st Tennessee Infantry, "we had forgotten all about that. . . . [We] did not now so much love our country as we feared Bragg."[13]

Bragg's stern methods and attention to efficiency soon had everyone on their guard, even as Bragg seized the initiative and executed one of the war's more remarkable counteroffensives. Utilizing six separate railroads over a circuitous route of 776 miles through Mobile and Atlanta, during the span of a week in late July 1862 Bragg transported about thirty thousand troops from Tupelo, Mississippi, to Chattanooga, Tennessee. This bold, strategic use of the railroads set a new precedent in warfare. It initially gave Bragg an enormous advantage in recouping the disasters of early 1862, which had threatened the loss of the entire midwestern South. In fact, Bragg's move compelled the split-up and partial withdrawal of the major Federal concentration at Corinth, Mississippi. "Bragg had moved men farther faster than troops had ever been moved before," noted his contemporary biographer. Moreover, he had successfully united his troops with another smaller army (Maj. Gen. Edmund Kirby Smith's) beyond the enemy's flank. By advancing into Kentucky and Tennessee, Bragg and Smith soon attempted to take the war northward in a bold thrust that coincided with Robert E. Lee's offensive into Maryland. The intent of all this, wrote Bragg at the time, was "to gain the enemy's rear, cutting off his supplies and dividing his forces so as to encounter them in detail."[14]

Perhaps it was characteristic of Bragg that in the face of imminent success, he had found only failure. Once in Kentucky, a lack of supplies, the absence of expected recruits, and reckless action by subordinate and cooperating generals had so frustrated him that when active fighting occurred in October, Bragg badly bungled the Battle of Perryville. In the absence of adequate intelligence of enemy movements, Bragg hurled his troops at the enemy in a rash series of piecemeal assaults, much as he had at Shiloh. Instead of a significant victory, Bragg's soldiers suffered agonizing losses. Although his troops had fought well and had driven back the enemy, due to the separation of his forces, Bragg withdrew from the battlefield—and subsequently from Kentucky. The campaign had been a terrible failure, complained many of his despairing soldiers, and a Kentuckian wrote: "If Bragg is kept in command of the Western Army, the whole country of the Mississippi Valley will be lost."[15]

Jefferson Davis, who never liked to be proven wrong in the choice of his commanders, was prepared for that eventuality, and by year's end much of the Mississippi Valley was occupied by the enemy. Discounting reports that Bragg had lost the confidence of his army, the Confederate president sustained Bragg in command and sought to soothe his critics by claiming, "I have not seen how to make a change with advantage to the public service." The other generals "all have their defects," reasoned Davis, and Bragg's administrative abilities were such that "a new man would not probably for a time . . . be equally useful."[16]

Bragg's mandate was for victory, and with the Confederacy still reeling from Lee's retreat from Maryland, another offensive campaign was planned, as urged by Jefferson Davis.[17]

Middle Tennessee was the anticipated area of operations, and Nashville, defended by Bragg's old Perryville opponents, the Army of the Cumberland, was intended to be the focal point. Yet Bragg's planned offensive never got under way. Because Bragg's undersized Army of Tennessee was suffering from absenteeism and desertion, reorganization was necessary. In December 1862, when Jefferson Davis visited Bragg's headquarters at Murfreesboro, Tennessee, the Confederate president ordered nine thousand of Bragg's troops to Mississippi, where they might threaten Ulysses S. Grant's operations against Vicksburg.[18]

Like many of Davis's military schemes and campaign plans, the results failed to match expectations. On the day after Christmas, Rosecrans's army suddenly and boldly advanced through an icy rain toward Bragg's position at Murfreesboro. The resulting Battle of Stones River was an enormously bloody encounter, made more so by Bragg's offensive-based tactical concepts and foolish, isolated assaults against several nearly impregnable positions. Some of his units suffered nearly 50 percent casualties in charging massed Federal artillery across five hundred yards of open ground. Instead of entrenching and fighting Rosecrans's advancing army from prepared breastworks, Bragg had seized the tactical initiative and relied upon typical Mahan textbook attacks. Bragg scoffed at the idea of fighting defensively. "Heavy entrenchments demoralize our troops," a staff officer had earlier heard him say.[19]

Following Bragg's retreat from the Murfreesboro area on January 4, the clamor for his removal soon reached new and unprecedented heights. Several subordinate generals announced their intention never again to fight in battle under Bragg. "Bragg is cordially hated by a large number of his officers," conceded a government official. "No one man that ever lived . . .

ever had as much hatred expressed against him as Bragg," offered one of his soldiers. Even civilians seemed to despise him: "I wish you all could get rid of Bragg—everybody seems to hate him so," wrote the sister of a high-ranking general. All but crucified in the accounts of various regional newspapers, Bragg was so embittered and distraught after Stones River that he asked his staff for a vote of confidence, stating, "If he had lost the confidence of his army . . . he would retire." Shocked by their candid opinion that "under the existing circumstances the general interests required that Gen. Bragg should ask to be relieved," he shot back to a friend: "With so little support, my aching head rebels against the heart, and cries for relief—still I shall die in the traces."[20]

Thus proceeded the charade. Bragg was not truly considering resigning his command; he wanted only sympathy and understanding—a vindication of his methods and means. Once more, he polled the army's division and corps commanders, asking for their opinion of his military ability, so as "to save my fair name. . . . Be candid with me," he offered, "I shall retire without a regret if I find I have lost the good opinion of my generals."[21]

Again, Bragg was taken aback. The overwhelming opinion was decidedly against him. The most brilliant division commander in the army, Maj. Gen. Pat Cleburne, wrote: "I have consulted with my brigade commanders . . . and they unite with me in personal regard for yourself . . . and in a conviction of your great capacity for organization, but at the same time they see, with regret . . . that you do not possess the confidence of the army . . . in that degree necessary to secure success." Generals Breckinridge, Hardee, and various brigade commanders were even more candid. Hardee wrote: "Frankness compels me to say that the general officers whose judgment you have invoked are unanimous in the opinion that a change in the command of the army is necessary. In this opinion I concur."[22]

Bragg, although stunned and humiliated, began to fight back. To Jefferson Davis, he forwarded a rambling letter citing his reasons for retreating from Murfreesboro (due to alleged enemy reinforcements, and on the advice of his subordinate generals, said Bragg), and warning that various interests would attempt to influence Davis in the matter of his (Bragg's) removal from command. As for his army lacking confidence in him, this was limited to a few "new men under new officers," he scoffed. Although he included an offer to resign, considering the inherent political consequences, Bragg clearly was maneuvering for the only vote of confidence that now mattered, Jefferson Davis's.[23]

Davis was greatly disturbed by the events in Tennessee. With mixed emotions, he entrusted action to the overall theater commander in the West, General Joseph E. Johnston, who was directed to proceed to Bragg's headquarters at Tullahoma, Tennessee, and decide the issue.[24]

In one of the more unfortunate aspects of the Civil War from the Southern standpoint, Joe Johnston expressed little interest in replacing Bragg as the Army of Tennessee's commander. All but ignoring the whirlwind of discontent, Johnston soon reported to Davis: "[The army's] appearance is very encouraging, and gives positive evidence of General's Bragg's capacity to command. . . . the fact that some or all of the general officers of the army, and many of the subordinates, think that you might give them a commander with fewer defects cannot . . . greatly diminish his value. To me it seems that the operations of this army in Middle Tenn. have been conducted admirably. I believe . . . that the interests of the service require that General Bragg should not be removed."[25]

At the root of the matter was Johnston's reluctance to assume command himself. "I have been told by Lieutenant Generals Polk and Hardee that they have advised you to remove General Bragg and place me in command of this army. . . . The part that I have borne in this investigation would render it inconsistent with my personal honor to occupy that position."[26]

Thus was the matter settled. Despite repeated suggestions from the Davis adminstration, and at one point even an order to replace Bragg, Johnston refused to be party to it. His misplaced confidence in Bragg was matched only by his obstinacy in refusing on the basis of honor to be named as commander of the Tennessee army. Beyond "the great injustice" to Bragg that such an event would produce, wrote Johnston, "[it] would not look well, and would certainly expose me, [and] injure me." In essence, Johnston feared he would not have the confidence of the army if he was to relieve Bragg under the existing circumstances.[27]

Braxton Bragg, now growing more confident that he would be sustained, and yet bitter toward his detractors, who had caused him so much grief and misery, began to carry out a vendetta against his opponents in the army. Strong action was taken in the cases of Frank Cheatham, who was said to be drunk at Stones River; John McCowan, who was court-martialed following his alleged dilatory behavior during the battle and for slandering the commanding general; John C. Breckinridge, who was chastised for poor performance; and William J. Hardee, who was subsequently transferred to Mississippi due to his opposition to Bragg.[28]

The result was an internecine conflict within the Army of Tennessee's high command and officer corps, with factions split sharply on both sides of the Bragg issue. The net result proved to be a further disaster for the Confederacy.

Instead of a plan for decisive action against the enemy in the war to control much of Tennessee, the struggle within received precedence. While Bragg was busily conspiring against many of his generals, and they against him, the Federal army had suddenly lurched forth in a renewed offensive during midyear 1863.

The Federal army's Tullahoma campaign of June and July 1863 had proved to be one of the most devastating of the war. Over the span of eleven days, Bragg was forced to withdraw from the Duck River line to Tullahoma, then retreat to Chattanooga. Outflanked, outgeneraled, and forced to abandon middle Tennessee, he despaired to an army chaplain that "I am utterly broken down," and that "a great disaster" had occurred.[29]

Bragg's health was at a nadir. The stress and long ordeal had taken a heavy toll. Suffering from boils, migraine headaches, and weakness, he seemed to one officer "mentally and physically an old, worn-out man, unfit to actively manage an army in the field." His haggard appearance and sickly manner distressed his supporters, and his detractors, such as Hardee, considered him too feeble either to examine and determine a line of battle or to take command on the field.[30]

In mid-August 1863, Bragg had remained operationally inert while awaiting Rosecrans's next move—only to have Chattanooga suddenly shelled from Walden's Ridge on the twenty-first. Lacking intelligence of various Federal movements then under way to move around the Confederate army's left flank and sever communications in the vicinity of Rome, Georgia, Bragg still believed Rosecrans intended to outflank Chattanooga from the direction of Knoxville. The haggard forty-six-year-old Rebel commander thus vacillated over issuing orders for a countermovement. Not until September 5 did Bragg learn of the grave threat to his left flank, and not until the ninth did he abandon Chattanooga. After hastening to concentrate his army in the vicinity of LaFayette, Georgia, Bragg missed several excellent opportunities to fall on isolated units of Rosecrans's army as they came through several widely scattered mountain passes in the Lookout ridge. Largely due to ineffective planning and poor execution by incompetent subordinates, Bragg's major attacks planned on three successive days were aborted. By September 14 Bragg was thoroughly frustrated.[31]

Having allowed Rosecrans to concentrate his widely scattered army in the vicinity of Lee and Gordon's Mill, Bragg, on September 19, suddenly initiated the momentous Battle of Chickamauga. Learning of the imminent arrival of heavy reinforcements—two divisions of veteran troops coming from Robert E. Lee's Army of Northern Virginia, under the command of Lt. Gen. James Longstreet—Bragg once more began planning offensive operations on September 15. Yet he so frequently changed his plans that three additional days passed before major action occurred. Intending to shift beyond the Federal left flank to interpose his troops between Rosecrans and Chattanooga, Bragg instead learned on the nineteenth that major elements of Rosecrans's army were beyond his own right flank.[32]

The Battle of Chickamauga, fought on the nineteenth and twentieth in thick undergrowth and cedar forests along the western banks of Chickamauga Creek, involved desperate fighting, with a series of attacks and counterattacks primarily along the northern sector of the line. Bragg, utilizing units of John Bell Hood's division just then arriving from Virginia by railroad, was able to force Rosecrans's line back in several places on the nineteenth, but he suffered terrible losses in the process. Once again in anguish over the alleged failures of key subordinates during the campaign, Bragg decided to reorganize the army's high command before the morning's resumption of the battle. After ordering an attack at daylight on the twentieth against the enemy's far-northern flank, Bragg went to bed without discussing the change in commanders with key personnel or issuing detailed orders for carrying out the attack.[33]

Due to shoddy staff work, the attack order for the leading troops was mishandled in transmittal, and key units failed to get the order until after daylight. A heavy fog on the morning of the twentieth further delayed the anticipated attack. Bragg's temper was at the boiling point by the time the assault began at about 10:00 A.M.—more than four hours after daylight. Due to the enemy's fortified positions and unsupported piecemeal attacks, Bragg's primary assault on the far-northern end of Thomas's line had sputtered to a bloody halt by late morning. Consisting of log rails and large stones, the makeshift Federal breastworks loomed as defiant as ever. So many of Bragg's fallen soldiers now carpeted the ground that some unit casualties approached two-thirds of their overall strength.[34]

The furious fight on the Federal left, however, had led to a devastating error on the part of Rosecrans. The gap created in the main Federal battleline at precisely the time Longstreet initiated his attack in the central sector resulted in a rout that virtually destroyed the Army of the Cumberland's right wing, sending Rosecrans in stunned disbelief back to Chattanooga.

Bragg, however, knew little of what had happened.[35] Preoccupied with the repulse of his right wing, he refused permission to Longstreet to use idle troops in pursuing the routed Federals. Instead, Longstreet's subordinates were required to hurl their troops repeatedly at Thomas's line on Horseshoe Ridge, while Bragg prodded the right wing under Polk into advancing again. The fearful sledgehammer blows at Thomas's two positions resulted in horrendous casualties and repeated repulses, until Thomas withdrew after nightfall from both Kelly's Field and Horseshoe Ridge.[36]

Even on the morning of the twenty-first, Bragg was unaware that the Federals had abandoned the field, and he refused to order a pursuit, perhaps believing the noises the Yankees had made during the night indicated a disposition to fight again on the morrow. Forrest's pressing for an advance that day accentuated Bragg's anxiety and irascibility. His indecisiveness in pursuit merely intensified his befuddlement over the true status of the enemy's army. Finally, that afternoon Bragg issued orders for portions of the infantry to advance toward Chattanooga.[37]

On the morning of September 23, Bragg's troops had moved to the summit of Missionary Ridge, overlooking Chattanooga, to find Rosecrans's army not only still present in the valley below but fully entrenched about the city. Instead of retreating across the Tennessee River, as Bragg had anticipated, Rosecrans's army appeared to invite another contest for possession of the crucial Gateway City. As even the lowest private in the army understood, Bragg's victory at Chickamauga would not be significant unless the Yankees were compelled to evacuate Chattanooga.

Ironically, it was in June 1862, during the urgent, rapid transfer of his army from Mississippi to Tennessee by railroad, that Bragg had written that "no greater disaster" could befall the Confederacy than the loss of Chattanooga. Now the situation was strangely reversed. Bragg would attempt to regain Chattanooga, even while the enemy attempted a massive concentration of troops at that site by means of a full-scale, strategic use of the railroads.[38]

Matters had turned full circle. Yet Bragg's perspectives remained strangely focused—more on the internal situation within his army than on the military task at hand. Instead of a beneficial opportunity following the Confederacy's first major victory in the West, Chickamauga seemed to presage only another bizarre odyssey within the Army of Tennessee.

CHAPTER 4

"NOTHING BUT THE HAND
OF GOD CAN SAVE US"

It was the greatest victory of the Army of Tennessee, and one of the Confederacy's proudest moments. Newspapers heralded the success. Chickamauga was a renewal of Southern hope. In the aftermath of the disasters at Gettysburg and Vicksburg only a few months earlier, Chickamauga inspired widespread elation throughout the South. There was the real prospect of regaining Chattanooga and much of Tennessee. The initiative again had shifted to the Confederacy's western army. Even greater success was eagerly anticipated, not only by a hopeful populace but by the soldiers themselves. One of the Tennessee army's lieutenants eagerly wrote: "Having before been accustomed to defeat and retreat, no one can conceive what a change a victory so brilliant would make." Another soldier proclaimed in the aftermath of Chickamauga, "Our army never has been in better fighting trim and more anxious for a fight."[1]

Braxton Bragg was distant from it all. The battle hadn't so much defeated the Yankees as it had brought new prospects for personal vindication. "Every moment has been occupied, and my mind and body taxed to the utmost," he confided to his wife, Elise, two days after Chickamauga. "Thank God the latter has not failed me." For Bragg, the major task of the moment was not removing the enemy from Chattanooga; it was purging the Army of Tennessee of his detractors and personal enemies.[2]

Rather than trying to boost the morale of his officers and men following the only major Confederate victory of the war in the West, Braxton Bragg had already begun a vendetta against those senior generals whom he intended to discard.

This matter of personal priority, an outgrowth of hate and resentment, was fired by a deep, kinetic restlessness. Bragg intended to be the center of the Confederacy's military universe, at least in the West. Intolerant of others who differed with his views, Bragg was now in a position to repay the long-endured petty insults and snide remarks of many of his principal subordinates.

First to feel the North Carolinian's bitter wrath was an old and ardent detractor, Lt. Gen. Leonidas Polk. Although a former West Pointer and an ordained Episcopal bishop, Polk was formally accused of delay and incompetence during the Battle of Chickamauga. According to Bragg, hours after the attack on the twentieth was to have begun, Polk had been found "two miles from his troops, resting in a rocking chair at a house, waiting his breakfast." Although Polk's troops were to have led the attack, the fifty-seven-year-old general didn't know why the assault hadn't begun as ordered, fumed Bragg. A few days later, Bragg briefed Elise about his general campaign to rid the Army of Tennessee of Polk and other despised subordinates. "Again have I to complain of Genl. Polk for not obeying my orders, and I am resolved to bring the matter to an issue this time," he vowed. "One of us must stand or fall on the issue." Bragg said Polk had never given his subordinates orders for the attack, nor made proper dispositions. According to Bragg, Polk's delay cost the Army of Tennessee six hours, which the enemy utilized to advantage by fortifying their positions. As the enemy was routed "just at dark," complained Bragg, Polk's delay cost the Confederate army the ability to pursue quickly. "By this we have lost the opportunity of crushing Rosecrans and retaking Chattanooga." "I am not responsible for it and will not bear it," he raged. "I shall say candidly to the President [Davis] that he must relieve Genl. Polk or myself."[3]

Braxton Bragg had carefully calculated the situation. Bolstered by the Chickamauga victory, he had timed his campaign of purges mindful of the inherent political difficulty involved. Polk and Jefferson Davis had not only been classmates at West Point but were close friends. In fact, there was a risk of being deposed rather than sustained in a showdown involving Davis. Bragg's long-smoldering resentment of Polk dated from that general's repeated demands for Bragg's removal as commander following the Confederate failures at Perryville and Stones River. Now, after Chickamauga, old sores were festering anew.[4]

The open rift with Polk was heralded by a communiqué demanding a written explanation on September 22 for Polk's failure to attack as ordered on the morning of the twentieth. When Polk ignored the summons; three days later, Bragg again demanded a reply, even as he dispatched several letters to Richmond seeking Polk's replacement. The following day, Polk and several of the army's senior generals secretly met to confer on a course of action, both for recovering Chattanooga and for getting rid of Bragg. Present were Lt. Gen. James Longstreet, Lt. Gen. Daniel H. Hill, and Maj. Gen. Simon Buckner, all active Bragg detractors. Thereafter, letters openly seeking Bragg's removal were sent to Richmond by Longstreet and Polk, the two most politically influential among the generals. Meanwhile, as part of the ongoing charade, Polk belatedly replied to Bragg on the twenty-eighth, sending off an exculpatory letter shifting any blame for the delay on the twentieth to D. H. Hill, then his immediate subordinate.[5]

Bragg's reaction was probably premeditated. On the following day, he suspended Polk from command for "not obeying orders," along with Maj. Gen. Thomas C. Hindman, another anti-Bragg officer. Both were promptly sent to Atlanta, Georgia.[6]

The news of this dangerous and acknowledged rift in the high command traveled like wildfire. By the thirtieth, Jefferson Davis had been briefed about the major squabble within the "victorious" Army of Tennessee. Davis then endorsed the dispatch reporting Polk's removal: "General Bragg has power to arrest an officer of his command, but is bound in that case to show cause by preferring charges as prescribed." Accordingly, Adj. Gen. Samuel Cooper was instructed to tell Bragg on October 1 that "suspension from command" was considered "punishment without trial" and that Bragg would have to prefer charges if he chose to pursue the matter.[7]

Davis, clearly inveigling for his old friend Polk, had tried to sidestep the controversy, even suggesting that Bragg countermand the order. Braxton Bragg, determined to force the issue if need be, adamantly refused to do so. Bragg saw Polk as the ringleader of his opposition among the army. He told Davis he was acting equally on the basis of Polk's past sins and that he would accept only a replacement for Polk, not his restoration. To back up his demands, Bragg promptly prepared formal charges against both Polk and Hindman.[8]

By the end of the first week in October, an anguished Jefferson Davis was personally involved in what he regarded as a "public calamity." His aide-de-camp, Col. James C. Chesnut, was sent on about October 1 to investigate. After conferring with Polk in Atlanta on the third and Longstreet thereafter, Chesnut reported on the fifth that Davis's presence was urgently needed with the army to resolve the open hostility toward Bragg.[9]

The night before, at another secret meeting among the army's disaffected generals, a petition was initiated, eventually to be signed by twelve key commanders, asking for Bragg's removal. Moreover, having been banished to Atlanta, Polk had been busy soliciting statements from his key subordinates and others, attempting to whitewash his Chickamauga conduct. Even more pointedly, Polk railed against Bragg receiving undue credit for the Chickamauga victory, referring to Bragg's "incapacity" and damning his incompetence. Bragg had frittered away a great victory "by the most criminal negligence, or, rather incapacity," said Polk, "for there are positions in which weakness is wickedness." Furthermore, he asserted, "If there be a man in the public service who should be held to a more rigid accountability for failures, and upon the harshest scale . . . that man is General Bragg."[10]

In these heated tirades, Polk was supported by Longstreet, who condemned Bragg as having ordered "but one thing that he ought to have done" since Longstreet's arrival with the Army of Tennessee. "That was to order the attack upon the 20th," scoffed Longstreet. "All other things that he has done he ought not to have done. I am convinced that nothing but the hand of God can save us or help us as long as we have our present commander."[11]

Strong words, heated emotions, bitterness and personal animosity— they were as a fit of distemper rapidly permeating the Army of Tennessee's high command. Jefferson Davis's reaction was to visit the army immediately. Departing Richmond the day following receipt of Chesnut's dispatch, Davis was at Atlanta and conferring with Polk by October 8.[12]

Leonidas Polk's ire was intense. He virtually laid down an ultimatum, telling Davis he would resign before again serving under Bragg. Although Davis was anxious to dismiss the charges against his old friend, Polk wanted a court of inquiry, not only to clear his record but to pillory Bragg for his "incapacity." Davis now saw that he would have to give up as impractical any attempts at compromise. The next day he wearily traveled north to Bragg's headquarters.[13]

It was soon apparent that Davis, by contrived methods, would attempt to contain the wrath of the discontented generals. Various dissident officers, having learned of Davis's visit, accompanied him on the last leg of his journey to Marietta. They were insistent that Bragg must go. Yet Davis sat impassively, listening to their remarks without meaningful reply.[14]

Upon arrival at Bragg's headquarters, Davis met with his embittered North Carolina commander, and apparently the discussion centered around the blatant petition then circulating among the army's generals for Bragg's removal. Bragg was greatly distressed and mortified by the document, wrote his chief of staff. Yet "[he] is as blind as a bat to the circumstances around him," concluded the officer. Davis called for a meeting with the army's ranking generals. At this meeting on the night of October 10, Davis heard shockingly frank testimony about Bragg's incapacity. Maj. Gen. Pat Cleburne, among others, said a change in leadership was absolutely essential. Bragg, attested Cleburne, while being a good organizer and disciplinarian, had long been without the confidence of the army. The lack of positive results alone destroyed his usefulness as a commander, said the Irish-born general, and Bragg should be promptly removed.[15]

Bragg must have been embarrassed to the depths of his soul. He had just told a visiting staff officer how depressed he was over his troubles and had complained that the load was getting too heavy for his shoulders, especially since he was unassisted and unsupported. Thus, this curious, morbid meeting further cut to the quick. In humiliation, Bragg listened with intense resentment to the dire opinions of his subordinates about his woeful performance. Each of the petitioners for Bragg's removal was asked by Davis to explain his reasoning. Longstreet, followed by Simon Buckner,

Daniel Hill, and Frank Cheatham spoke frankly of their firm convictions. By the end of the discussions, there was an intensely charged atmosphere, alive with the current of disaffection with Braxton Bragg.[16]

The whole matter was a charade. Although Bragg had offered to resign during their meeting of the ninth, Davis had said no. In fact, Jefferson Davis's mind had long been made up, even before he departed from Richmond. At that time, he implied to Confederate Secretary of War James Seddon that he had no intention of removing Bragg. The practical and political alternatives just weren't acceptable.[17]

Davis abhorred the only ranking generals who might be persuaded to replace Bragg. Both P. G. T. Beauregard and Joe Johnston were severe critics of Davis, even regarded as personal enemies. To the prideful Davis, the thought of replacing Bragg with either was repugnant, and they were summarily dismissed from consideration. On October 10, Davis had ridden along the lines with another pretender, James Longstreet. Robert E. Lee wrote on October 26 to his "Old War Horse," telling him that "I think you can do better than I could. It was with that view I urged you going [west]."* If Lee expected Longstreet to replace Bragg, so did Longstreet. During his ride with Davis, Longstreet had indulged in heated conversation about Bragg. To the intelligent, perceptive Davis, it was all too obvious that Longstreet's burning ambition was to be named army commander. The former South Carolinian even had recently petitioned Seddon about Bragg's incompetence and professed that his views were "for the good of the country." "In an ordinary war I could serve without complaint under any one whom the Government might place in authority, but we have too much at stake in this to remain quiet," he declared. Davis, it appears, was clearly miffed about Longstreet and his obvious ambition. Longstreet would not do. The only other man capable of the task in Davis's eyes was the man he actually preferred. Although Davis had repeatedly sought to send him west, Robert E. Lee, just as adamantly, had refused to go. Beyond Lee, Beauregard, and Joe Johnston, there weren't any full generals worthy of consideration. To promote a junior general into Bragg's spot would create untold political friction.[18]

Jefferson Davis stood his ground. He admonished all, saying that Bragg would be retained as commander. The generals were enjoined to support rather than criticize their commander. "Shafts of malice" would be harmless against him, Davis later declared. Bragg was "worthy of all confidence," and "selfish aspiration" must not prevail over the public good.

---

*Lee's letter acknowledged Longstreet's letters of September 26, October 6, and October 11. In some of these, Longstreet had urged Lee to come west and take command. Lee's response, cited here, was negative. Obviously, Lee wanted no part of the notorious Western command imbroglio, but seemed to feel Longstreet would be a worthy successor to Bragg, considering the many rumors that Davis would replace the acerbic North Carolinian with a new commander. See OR 52-2-549, 550.

"He who sows the seeds of discontent and distrust prepares for the harvest of slaughter and defeat," warned Davis in a letter to the army a few days later.[19]

It was now clear that Jefferson Davis had visited the army for one basic purpose: to dispel the whirlwind of discontent. That he thought he could end the rampant discord merely by hearing complaints and speaking out on Bragg's behalf was characteristic of Davis's exaggerated self-image. In fact, despite all the strictures and posturing, Davis was already somewhat disillusioned by his visit to the Army of Tennessee.[20]

Davis had brought along from Richmond his friend, Lt. Gen. John C. Pemberton, who needed a job. Perhaps believing that Bragg would utilize Pemberton to replace one of the army's key subordinates, Davis had encouraged Bragg to consider his appointment, perhaps to command Polk's Corps. The furor within the army was intense and immediate. Pemberton was the immensely unpopular commander who had surrendered Vicksburg to Grant on July 4. A senator from Tennessee wrote a scathing letter to Secretary of War Seddon saying that the Tennessee troops would mutiny if this occurred. The governor of Mississippi warned that the paroled troops from Vicksburg and Port Hudson would refuse to serve under Pemberton ever again. Despite Bragg's evident willingness to accommodate Davis, the furor was too great within the army when presented to the senior generals. Pemberton was turned down. His presence thereafter was an embarrassment, and informed by Bragg's chief of staff that not even a division would have him as their commander, Pemberson dejectedly departed.[21]

Jefferson Davis's intuitive grasp of the politics involved in sustaining Bragg caused him, for once, to forgo his obstinacy in such matters. Forcing Pemberton on the Army of Tennessee would be too dangerous under the circumstances, and that general was allowed to leave without assignment. Eventually, the discredited Pemberton was compelled to resign as a lieutenant general, and he served the remainder of the war as an artillery colonel. To Davis, such setbacks reflected a more serious blow than was apparent on the surface.[22]

Jefferson Davis was proving to be the true sphinx of the Confederacy—a mystery to many due to his famed stubbornness and stoicism. An intelligent, deeply reasoning man, the Confederate president prided himself on his perceptive military judgments, gained from long experience in army matters. An 1828 graduate of West Point, a much publicized Mexican War hero, and the Pierce administration's secretary of war, Davis not only knew most of the principal generals of the North and South, but he harbored strong opinions of their worth.[23]

Despite his self-proclaimed expertise, Davis was noted for favoring personal friends from among his former colleagues and for arranging their appointment to high commands. In the case of a few competent commanders, such as Robert E. Lee and Albert Sidney Johnston, Davis's judgments were valid. Yet in very many cases, Davis's assessments of his generals were so poor as to be ultimately ruinous. As the war progressed unsatisfactorily, Davis's decisions about his generals, and stubborn pride in sustaining them, perhaps contributed the most to the ultimate defeat of the Confederacy. Worst of all, his unbending attitude was to risk widespread destruction rather than personal defeat. Thus, as in the case of Bragg, Davis ultimately sought to vindicate his position, often to the point of deceitful manipulation. "He retains his favorites long after they have blundered themselves out of the confidence of all their troops," wrote an angry observer, "and would rather lose a battle or give up a state than admit that Jeff Davis could have made an injudicious promotion."[24]

Although perhaps a distortion and an overstatement, such an assessment revealed Davis's flawed personality. His stubbornness, stoicism, and an inability to admit serious mistakes were proving to be some of his most glaring character traits. Although he often displayed a calm, reflective facade, there burned within his soul a flash fire of emotional turmoil that churned and twisted at his granite-firm sense of honor and pride. At the very heart of this intense pride was Davis's self-righteous attitude. Having risen to enormous power on the basis of mostly intuitive judgment, Davis was standoffish, uncompromising, and he simply would not allow himself to be proven wrong in his personal judgments. The consequences for the Confederacy were apparent in Davis's stubborn pride in sustaining Braxton Bragg.[25]

In striking contrast, on the very day Jefferson Davis departed from the Army of Tennessee near Chattanooga, leaving behind a circular encouraging the soldiers' "continuance in the patient endurance of toil and danger, and . . . self-denial," the man from Illinois, Abraham Lincoln, had acceded to a basic change in the hierarchy of the Federal army at Chattanooga.[26]

CHAPTER 5

"EVERYTHING WILL COME OUT RIGHT"

Matters at Rossville, Georgia, had been rather uncertain on the early morning of September 21, 1863. Rosecrans's chief of staff, James A. Garfield, wasn't sure what to expect. In his request of 1:30 A.M. for supplies and ammunition to be sent to Rossville, Garfield had observed: "We do not seem to be in the best trim for an early fight." Accordingly, he hoped Rosecrans would "get here as soon as possible to organize the army and victory before the storm sets in."[1]

For William Starke Rosecrans the storm had already begun. Before daylight, Rosecrans had learned of Lincoln's great concern, and that he should save the army "by taking strong positions until Burnside joins you, when I hope you can turn the tide." Then a further discomfiting report arrived from Garfield, sent via telegraph at 7:45 A.M. on the twenty-first. Therein, his chief of staff made a dire assessment that the Rossville position might not be a good one for a general battle, or that much reliance could be put on portions of the previously stampeded troops.[2]

By first light, however, Rosecrans had received George H. Thomas's report that all was quiet at the front. Less than an hour later, this was backed by an assessment from Maj. Gen. James S. Negley at Rossville that "everything is progressing most favorably." According to Negley, his men were well organized, armed, fed and posted for battle. "Affairs present a very satisfactory appearance," boasted Negley.[3]

What was Rosecrans to do? Should he withdraw everyone to Chattanooga, or allow Thomas to fight it out on the Rossville line? Nervous, apprehensive, and awkwardly unsure of the real situation, he sent for Garfield. Before noon, his jaded chief of staff arrived in the city, and

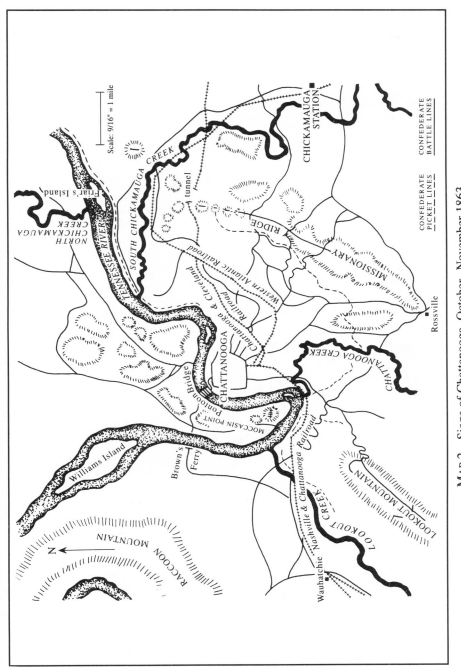

MAP 2   Siege of Chattanooga, October–November 1863
(*Source: O.R. Atlas, plate 49-2*)

Rosecrans sat down to confer with Garfield, while Stanton's man, Charles A. Dana, listened in.[4]

Garfield was graphic with details of Thomas's splendid fight and the utter devastation of Bragg's troops. Also, at midday Rosecrans received word from his cavalry chief that as late as 10:15 A.M. he had not heard a shot in front and several reconnaissance patrols had discovered nothing. Moreover, about midday Rosecrans learned the welcome news that William Tecumseh Sherman's troops had been ordered to Chattanooga from the vicinity of Vicksburg, Mississippi.[5]

It appeared that Rosecrans just might be able to hold on to the Rossville line. His courage bolstered, he had his aide draft a note to Thomas about Sherman's forthcoming reinforcements, giving "Three cheers!" and adding, "Tell the boys." Late that morning, George H. Thomas ordered several hundred axes for construction of breastworks at Rossville. Rosecrans then confided to Burnside in Knoxville: "We shall probably have to hold Chattanooga as a tete-de-point until reinforcements come up."[6]

Within minutes, everything changed. First alarming news arrived from the provost marshal at Rossville. A Kentucky prisoner had reported that Lt. Gen. Richard S. Ewell with twenty thousand troops from Stonewall Jackson's old corps was en route from Virginia to reinforce Bragg and was expected to arrive momentarily. The presence of additional enemy troops from Joe Johnston's command seemed to be corroborated by a few prisoners interrogated that morning. Suddenly, Rosecrans was convinced the Confederacy was again concentrating an overwhelming force in the Chattanooga region. Of further alarm, word arrived after 2:00 P.M. of heavy skirmishing near Rossville. "Two divisions of Longstreet's corps" were reported on the road to Chattanooga. Later it was stated that the enemy was advancing on both flanks. Although it proved to be only Forrest's cavalry, Rosecrans was so alarmed, he made another fateful decision.[7]

About 5:00 P.M., his orders went out to Thomas at Rossville: Maintain your present position, if possible, until nightfall, then quickly retire to Chattanooga. Rosecrans expected another severe battle within the next several days. As Dana tersely reported to Stanton by telegraph that afternoon, "If Ewell be really there [approaching Rossville], Rosecrans will have to retreat beyond the Tennessee." Otherwise, "R[osecrans] is determined not to abandon Chattanooga."[8]

By nightfall, there was additional confusing news. The firing had ceased at Rossville Gap. Thomas's assessment was that during the day the enemy had made only what amounted to a reconnaissance, and so far as was known, the enemy's infantry had not advanced in force. At 10:00 P.M., Rosecrans sent another message to Thomas: If this was true, he was to hold the ground at Rossville with the rear guard. Thomas replied only twenty minutes later that his troops were already en route back to Chattanooga.[9]

Rosecrans's impulsive decisions reflected his badly shaken confidence. Beyond overreacting, his planning was now defensive and based upon an assumed worst-scenario situation. Following merely the bold maneuvering of Forrest's cavalry that morning, and the unfounded rumor of the impending arrival of additional large Confederate reinforcements, Rosecrans had given up a key defensive perimeter and withdrawn his army into the immediate environs of Chattanooga. The consequences were enormous. Once confined to the valley and semi-peninsula formed by the loop in the Tennessee River, Rosecrans not only had a limited area for maneuver along the west bank but was confronted on all sides by the imposing peaks and ridges that ringed the Gateway City. Since the enemy was certain to occupy those heights east of the river, Rosecrans was gambling that "we can hold out for several days." "If reinforcements come up soon," he rather guardedly ventured to Halleck on the twenty-second, "everything will come out right."[10]

It was absurdity of the highest order. Rosecrans could not see what Thomas and a few others who had remained at the front seemed to realize. From a tactical perspective, the Confederate army was so disorganized and ravaged following their victory as to be about equally as discomfited as the Federal army. Moreover, instead of an overwhelming numerical superiority, Bragg on September 21 had approximately 10,000 more men than Rosecrans.[11]

Lincoln had been right. Chattanooga, the key point, was in danger, more so from within than without. Lincoln was worried by Rosecrans's obvious despair, and he instructed Henry Halleck how important it was to hold Chattanooga: "It keeps all Tennessee clear of the enemy," providing an opportunity to "bring [the enemy] to us, and saving us the labor, expense, and hazard of going farther to find him." Moreover, reasoned Lincoln, it would give "us the advantage of choosing our own ground and preparing it to fight him upon." "If he [Rosecrans] can only maintain this position without more, the rebellion can only eke out a short and feeble existence, as an animal sometimes may with a thorn in its vitals." Clearly, Lincoln wasn't expecting much from Rosecrans so soon after his crushing defeat; he merely wanted that commander to reorganize and prepare to fight again, on the defensive if need be, for control of a vital Chattanooga.[12]

Edwin Stanton was seething with rage. John Hay, Lincoln's personal secretary, recorded Stanton's reaction when presented with Rosecrans's initial account of the disaster at Chickamauga. The battle had been lost, Stanton asserted, because Rosecrans had run away from the battle and hadn't stopped for thirteen miles. Commenting on the alleged faults of two of Rosecrans's subordinates, McCook and Crittenden, who also had retreated to Chattanooga while the fighting raged, Stanton fumed, "[they] made pretty good time away from the fight to Chattanooga, but Rosecrans beat them both."[13]

Stanton was further angered by Dana's dispatch on the evening of the twenty-second that Rosecrans was considering a retreat from Chattanooga.

Although Dana telegraphed a few hours later that Rosecrans had decided to fight it out at Chattanooga if necessary, he reported only ten days' rations remained on hand and that the Confederates had closely invested the city's outer defenses that day. To Stanton, immediate action was required. Rosecrans's almost frantic dispatch to Lincoln of 5:40 P.M. on September 22, stating that the enemy was threatening his army's whole front and that it was certain Burnside would be too late in coming from east Tennessee, was a case in point. "Our fate is in the hands of God, in whom I hope," Rosecrans had irresolutely implored. To Stanton, this was further evidence of Old Rosy's weak inner fiber. The irate secretary anticipated the Ohio general's removal from command, preferring that the "noble" George H. Thomas be assigned in his place. Yet as James A. Garfield had learned upon visiting wartime Washington in 1861, Stanton was not all-powerful. Military decisions involving key personnel followed from the interaction of a mixed administrative and political circle. Lincoln, Halleck, Stanton, and other members of the President's cabinet were key players, but even senators and congressmen were often of influence. Stanton, until he had a strong consensus, would bide his time about removing Rosecrans. In Stanton's mind, the first urgency was for reinforcements—to get troops to Chattanooga with all haste.[14]

On the evening of the twenty-third, Secretary of War Stanton bolted into action. That day, another of Rosecrans's telegrams had arrived, saying, "I cannot be dislodged except by very superior numbers and after a great battle. . . . [Have] all reinforcements you can send hurried up." Following Garfield's telegram to Secretary of the Treasury Salmon P. Chase, which arrived at 10:00 P.M.—that the enemy outnumbered Rosecrans's army two to one, "but we can stand here ten days if help will then arrive"—Stanton felt compelled to act. Garfield suggested that "25,000 men should be sent to Bridgeport [Alabama] to secure Middle Tennessee in case of disaster to us." Since Garfield confirmed that a battle was "expected soon," Stanton considered the awful responsibility to "save the campaign" by holding Chattanooga, and he called for an immediate council of war that night.[15]

John Hay later reported how he rode by moonlight to summon the President at the Soldiers' Home, where he was lodged. Lincoln was in bed, and on being roused, he was much "disturbed," believing that perhaps a further disaster had occurred. Despite Hay's assurances that it meant "nothing serious," Lincoln continued to fret, "as it was the first time Stanton had ever sent for him." Also, Secretary of the Treasury Salmon Chase was awakened by a War Department messenger about midnight and told he was wanted immediately. "The summons really alarmed me," wrote Chase. "I felt sure that a disaster had befallen us." Others, including Henry Halleck and various cabinet members, were summoned under similar circumstances.[16]

It was Stanton's way of doing business in a crisis—address the issue posthaste. What the secretary of war had in mind was soon evident once the middle-of-the-night meeting began. Aware that great difficulties surrounded getting Sherman's troops rapidly from the Mississippi River to Chattanooga, the secretary of war had conceived a bold proposal. Said Stanton, "I propose to send 30,000 men from the Army of the Potomac. There is no reason to expect that General Meade will attack [Robert E.] Lee, although greatly superior in force, and his great numbers where they are, are useless. In five days 30,000 could be put with Rosecrans."[17]

Lincoln was incredulous: "I'll bet that if the order is given tonight the troops could not be got to Washington in five days." Others were shocked by the suggestion of removing troops from the primary army defending Washington, D.C.[18]

Stanton, however, was insistent: "On such a subject I don't feel inclined to bet, but the matter has been carefully investigated and it is certain that 30,000 bales of cotton could be sent in that time, and by taking possession of the railroad and excluding all other business I do not see why 30,000 men can't be sent as well. But if 30,000 can't be sent, let 20,000 go."[19]

A rather protracted debate followed, with Halleck and Lincoln against the proposal and Seward and Chase arguing for its implementation. During the discussion, various other telegrams from Chattanooga arrived, all pointing to the need for rapid relief. Waving the telegrams in his hand, Stanton pressed hard on the issue. The resigned look on the President's face foretold the final outcome. At 2:30 A.M. September 24, orders were issued for two Virginia-based army corps, the Eleventh and Twelfth Corps, to proceed to Chattanooga with five days' supply of cooked rations. Under the command of Maj. Gen. "Fighting Joe" Hooker, these two corps, 23,000 strong, would rush to reinforce Rosecrans. Yet the glaring question on everyone's mind, considering the obvious delay in moving Sherman's and Burnside's troops, was whether Hooker's troops would arrive in time to save Chattanooga, or the Army of the Cumberland.[20]

At that very hour on the night of the twenty-third, Rosecrans was in the process of making another momentous decision. Following the enemy's close approach to the Federal army's Chattanooga lines, Rosecrans ordered the withdrawal of the single brigade under Brig. Gen. James G. Spears, which had been posted at the head of Lookout Mountain in the aftermath of Chickamauga. According to Dana, both Garfield and Gordon Granger objected to this order. They claimed the precipitous mountain could be held by a minimal force so as to guard the army's vital line of transportation and communications along the south bank of the Tennessee River. Rosecrans, however, feared that Spears's isolated position would be difficult to supply and might lead to his brigade's capture. Following news of a skirmish on Spears's front, the withdrawal was completed on the twenty-fourth. Within a few days, Confederate control of Lookout Mountain was consolidated, inclusive of a signal station and emplaced artillery. The enemy's occupation of forbidding Lookout Mountain, Raccoon Mountain, and the Tennessee River's south bank would contribute significantly to Rosecrans's dilemma in the immediate future.[21]

* * *

Although the initial fear had been of a Confederate assault before the Chattanooga defenses were completed and the army reorganized, by September 24 it was clear that Bragg would not attack immediately. A different mind-set soon began to permeate the Army of the Cumberland's high command. Instead of fearing another military defeat, Rosecrans was growing uneasy about being unable to maintain the army. Not having taken the time to consolidate the territorial gain when Bragg was outflanked from Chattanooga, or to establish that city as a supply depot before resuming his late offensive, Rosecrans was now in a most difficult predicament. The railroads into Chattanooga from the north were inaccessible due to the enemy's occupation of the south bank. Indeed, perhaps the worst consequence of having lost the Battle of Chickamauga was the relative isolation of Chattanooga as the Federal army's place of refuge. It was a city surrounded by high and imposing mountain terrain on all sides. Due to prevailing low water in the Tennessee River, supply steamboats were unable to navigate the channel. All supplies had to be brought in by wagon train over difficult northern routes from the main depot at Bridgeport, Alabama, thirty miles distant by direct line, but about sixty by the tortuous route through the Sequatchie Valley and over rugged Walden's Ridge.[22]

Moreover, in anticipating an imminent fight at Chattanooga immediately after Chickamauga, Rosecrans was so preoccupied with details of fortification and reorganization that initially little was done to resupply the army. At first, it was believed that fifteen days' rations were on hand, but that estimate was soon reduced to a ten days' supply—which might be extended by reducing rations if necessary. Only enough ammunition was on hand for "two days' hard fighting." Since most of the cavalry was sent to guard the vital supply routes to Bridgeport, there was little means of gathering local forage. On September 23, Charles A. Dana estimated Chattanooga could be held under the current circumstances for from fifteen to twenty days. When a fifty-wagon ammunition train from Bridgeport came in that afternoon, everyone was greatly relieved, but within days new doubts began to arise.[23]

Rosecrans heralded the difficulty on the twenty-fourth when word was brought in by a "colored man" of a pending raid against Federal supply lines and communications by Nathan Bedford Forrest's cavalry. Rosecrans had dispersed his cavalry above and below Chattanooga, with instructions to watch the fords across the Tennessee River carefully.[24]

Unfortunately for Rosecrans, his cavalry commander, Brig. Gen. Robert B. Mitchell, had strung out his two divisions across a wide expanse of territory, primarily along the river north and south of Chattanooga. Being thus fragmented, Mitchell's troopers were unable to concentrate in effective force rapidly enough to contest a major Confederate cavalry raid. As such, they were preoccupied with watching for an enemy crossing rather than preparing to fight in concert. The price Rosecrans and the army would pay was fully evident on October 2.[25]

Heavy rains had begun falling on Thursday, October 1, and news that the Confederate cavalry raider Maj. Gen. Joseph Wheeler, was across the Tennessee River with an estimated ten thousand men and raiding westward toward McMinnville, Tennessee, added to the day's gloom. On the second, a portion of Wheeler's cavalry, striking south in the Sequatchie Valley, intercepted an immense Federal wagon train hauling supplies to Chattanooga. Most of the reported eight hundred wagons were captured, and the detonations of exploding ammunition were heard as far away as Chattanooga. When the damage was counted, an estimated four hundred wagons, hundreds of mules, and an enormous quantity of badly needed supplies, including forage, were tallied as lost.[26]

Rosecrans had miscalculated. Warned on the thirtieth that a large Rebel cavalry force was concentrating upriver, near Washington, Tennessee, he merely attempted to shuffle the responsibility to Burnside in east Tennessee: "I rely on you to protect my left flank," Rosecrans telegraphed that day. Hours later, when positive information arrived of the enemy's crossing, he could but plead with Burnside, "You will have to close up your force and cut them off." While organizing his own scattered cavalry to pursue Wheeler, Rosecrans began to fear an even greater danger—that Wheeler would tear up the vital north-south railroads in mid-Tennessee, even now being pressed to the limit to bring Hooker's soldiers from the east.[27]

Rosecrans had to order arriving infantry from the east dispersed along the rail lines to protect his main transportation routes. Only when it was learned Wheeler had turned south and west through middle Tennessee in a bid to escape the gathering concentration of Federal cavalry, did Rosecrans's fears begin to abate.[28]

The respite was brief. After taking stock of his supply situation at Chattanooga, the Federal army's commander found much cause for alarm in the wake of Wheeler's raid. The newly arrived quartermaster general, Brig. Gen. Montgomery C. Meigs, assessed the difficulties of transporting supplies as "immense." "I have never traveled on such roads before," wrote the exasperated Meigs of the main route across the mountains from Bridgeport. Indeed, Meigs said they were so "execrable" and difficult, the army's teams were rapidly "wearing out." During the drought, Rosecrans's assistant inspector general, Lt. Col. Arthur C. Ducat, had described the mountain roads as mere paths laden with rocks and treacherous gullies. Ominously, he had warned on September 25: "If we should have a rain it would bother us." Beginning with the deluge of October 1, the roads rapidly became quagmires of slippery mud, with vast washouts and water-choked gullies. Foundering teams and wagons could hardly make progress. Due to the heavy burden, many wagon masters had to throw portions of their cargoes away to lighten the loads. Narrow passageways prevented two-way travel, and many returning wagon trains were prevented from departing. By mid-October, an estimated five hundred teams were halted en route, immobilized by bad weather, impossible roads, and a lack of forage. Ducat had understated the obstacles. As Quartermaster Meigs later admitted following a personal inspection, the roads following a period of rain were "almost impassable."[29]

Following news of Wheeler's destruction of the wagon train, Rosecrans responded on the same day by placing the army on two-thirds rations. When necessary, there would be a reduction to one-half rations, he announced. Even before Wheeler's raid, the Army of the Cumberland was exceedingly short of "axes, spades, hatchets, picks, and clothing, especially shoes, canteens, and haversacks," the Federal commander had warned. Now he demanded that each corps keep their trains moving "as vigorously as possible" between Chattanooga and Bridgeport. So as to conserve on forage, all spare horses and mules were to be sent back to Stevenson, Alabama. "One-third of the artillery horses can safely be sent," estimated Rosecrans, who then discovered he was so short on pioneer details for construction, he had to "strongly urge" Halleck to send a portion of the Regular Army's engineers to Chattanooga.[30]

Chattanooga, instead of a place of refuge, seemed to become an insidious trap, threatening the army's very existence. Like a house of cards, ready to collapse at any moment, the army's morale now tottered at increasing risk.

In the midst of the many dire shortages, Assistant Secretary of War Charles A. Dana elaborated on the essence of the crisis as he saw it. "[General] Rosecrans . . . is sometimes as obstinate and inaccessible to reason as at others he is irresolute, vacillating and inconclusive," asserted Dana on October 12. Rosecrans's supply problems were interrelated: Many of the army's animals were gone, taken to Stevenson "to be fed as best they might." The remainder at Chattanooga were on one-quarter rations. Wheeler's destruction of the wagon train had depleted so much forage that for the past ten days there had been no regular supply. At least 250 animals had died of starvation. The surviving horses and mules were so infirm as to "render impracticable any efficient attack or pursuit of the enemy" if Bragg suddenly marched into Kentucky. Moreover, the movement of Hooker's troops from the east had burdened the railroad to the extent that spare forage couldn't be simultaneously brought from storage in Nashville to the head of the line at Bridgeport.[31]

Even worse, the men by now were reduced to two days' rations, and more rain seemed imminent. There was a steamboat at Chattanooga, which, considering the necessary twenty-seven inches of water over the shallowest shoals, was now able to run upriver to get supplies. Yet the boat couldn't move, fumed Dana. The problem was the "military error which gave the enemy control of the south shore between here and Bridgeport"— specifically the abandonment of Lookout Mountain. "Could the river be used, 400 tons freight might daily be delivered here," reasoned Dana. But Rosecrans had "pettishly rejected" Garfield's and Granger's insistence on keeping control of Lookout Mountain. "It is difficult to say which was the greater error, this order, or that [at Chickamauga] which . . . created the gap in our lines," complained Dana.[32]

The assistant secretary's fury was only building. "I have never seen a public man possessing talent with less administrative power, less clearness and steadiness in difficulty, and greater practical incapacity than General Rosecrans," Dana added. "He has inventive fertility and knowledge, but he has no strength of will and no concentration of purpose. His mind scatters; there is no system in the use of his busy days and restless nights, no courage against individuals in his composition, and [although] with great love of command, he is a feeble commander. . . . Under the present circumstances I consider this army to be very unsafe in his hands."[33]

Dana was adamant. The army was in a "helpless and dangerous" situation. "[With] our animals starved and the men with starvation before them," he could think of "no man except [George H.] Thomas who could now be safely put in his [Rosecrans's] place."[34]

Edwin Stanton was listening. It was obvious that another major crisis was at hand. Stanton was a man of action, and it seemed time to act. A few days later, he was on his way to Louisville, Kentucky. In his travel pouch, he carried an important document.[35]

CHAPTER 6

A "DAZED AND MAZY COMMANDER"

The genesis of the trouble with retaining Rosecrans followed the disaster at Chickamauga. Charles A. Dana, despite his reputation as a snoop, reckless informer, and distortionist, went to the heart of the matter when he first broached the subject on September 27 in a telegram to Edwin Stanton. As Stanton's confidential correspondent, Dana knew his mission well—to evaluate William S. Rosecrans's performance on the basis of subjective character assessments. Thus he brazenly suggested: "If it be decided to change the chief commander [Rosecrans] . . . I would take the liberty of suggesting that some Western general of high rank and great prestige, like [Ulysses S.] Grant, for instance, would be preferable as his successor."[1]

A former prominent newspaper journalist and editor who had worked for and been fired by Horace Greeley of the *New York Tribune,* Dana, while a civilian, was a self-styled military expert whose conceit was apparent in his prejudicial correspondence with Edwin Stanton. Dana owed his job to Stanton, who had hired him as his assistant after Greeley had terminated the outspoken managing editor of the *Tribune* for his zealous editorials defending Stanton. Dana not only knew the temper of his mentor; he catered to the secretary of war's larger-than-life self-image. Stanton was a man of deep emotional currents, passion, and consuming opinion. He was not a man to be trifled with, and Dana understood the implications. Stanton's wishes were Dana's command, and the select focus of these wishes in October 1863 was Rosecrans's position.

Stanton had decreed as much on September 30, ten days after the Chickamauga disaster. He then had wired to Dana: "If Hooker's command gets

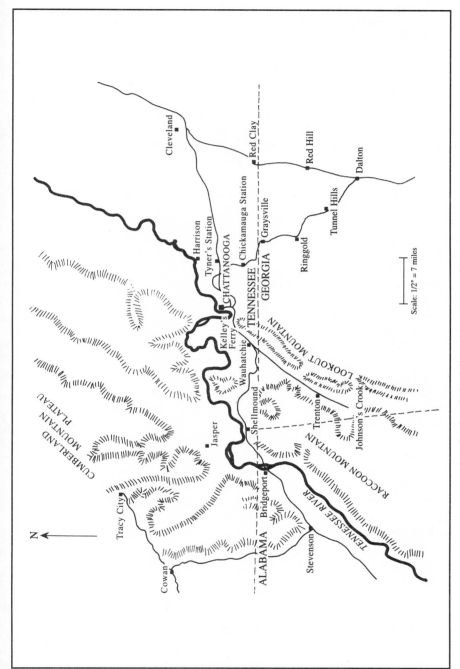

MAP 3   Logistical Situation–Siege of Chattanooga
(*Source: O.R. Atlas, plate 97-1*)

safely through, all that the Army of the Cumberland can need will be a competent commander. The merit of General Thomas and the debt of gratitude the nation owes to his valor and skill are fully appreciated here, and I wish you to tell him so. It was not my fault that he was not in chief command months ago." Taking a cue from Stanton, Dana almost immediately began a long series of criticisms of a highly derogatory nature against Rosecrans.[2]

Even while enjoying old Rosy's "personal hospitality, sitting at the same table, and sleeping in the same building," Dana displayed his duplicity in his secret correspondence with Stanton. One outraged correspondent later remembered how Dana "deliberately drew the general into confidential communications [discussions], the substance of which he used against him." Moreover, beyond eliciting from Rosecrans his plans and thinking, Dana conferred with various dissatisfied generals, gathering gossip and reporting their insinuations under the guise of fact.[3]

Stanton was equally outspoken about his low esteem for Rosecrans. When he had learned that Rosecrans had made a hasty retreat from the battlefield of Chickamauga while other generals remained to fight, Stanton scoffed: "I know the reasons [for the defeat] well enough. Rosecrans ran away from his fighting men and did not stop for thirteen miles."[4]

Despite their slander, the truth of the matter was that both Stanton and Dana were correct in their dire assessments of Rosecrans. After Chickamauga, the Federal commander was generally unbalanced and despairing, unable to put the pieces together to revitalize the army. If Dana was insidiously fashioning a portrait of ineptitude, Old Rosy was overtly writing to Washington in tones equally as damaging.

On October 3, Rosecrans sent a telegram to Lincoln suggesting that a general amnesty be offered to all Rebel officers and soldiers, probably in the belief that the Confederate army would thus be divided and weakened. Lincoln shrugged off the proposal, replying that he intended doing something of the sort when the time was right, but not "as a confession of weakness and fear." In the aftermath of a crippling defeat, Stanton evidently was particularly upset over the matter, considering it a political affront.[5]

Ironically, a few weeks after irresolutely giving up Lookout Mountain and the south riverbank, Rosecrans determined that a virtual "necessity" in maintaining his army at Chattanooga would be "to get possession of the line of the [Tennessee] river up to this place [Chattanooga]." Dana reported at the time how Rosecrans regarded this objective as "imperative," and he stated that Hooker would be ordered to concentrate his troops preparatory to seizing Raccoon Mountain—and, if possible, Lookout Valley. Two days later, however, Rosecrans wrote that he could not bring up Hooker's troops, since he could not feed them and Hooker had no transportation to move overland.*

*Hooker had been directed to leave his extensive transportation system behind in the East and to draw new horses, wagons, and quartermaster's supplies at Nashville. However, due to that depot's deficiencies, Hooker was without adequate transportation until late October.

For the first time, he talked of the possible loss of Chattanooga. Dana was so exasperated, he said Rosecrans believed that even with Hooker's reinforcements, the Army of the Cumberland would be too weak to take the offensive.[6]

Rosecrans seemed not only to be waffling on his decisions and plans but ineffective in utilizing his available resources. He was so short on engineers that he requested authority to enlist a regiment of veteran engineers from the present pioneer units for work on the roads and fortifications. Yet Dana acknowledged that the problem wasn't so much a lack of men as it was a lack of tools. Instead of working ten thousand men per day, "General [William F.] Smith is only able to work 1,000," complained Dana.[7]

Moreover, as October progressed, Rosecrans became convinced that the enemy was concentrating its troops and building pontoons to cross the Tennessee River north of Chattanooga. Bragg's men thus would "force us to quit this place and fight them, or lose our communications," warned Rosecrans. Despair seemed to be increasingly evident in each of Old Rosy's telegrams.[8]

Charles Dana reflected the tense mood at army headquarters on October 15 when he estimated that due to the rain and shortage of rations, "it will soon become necessary for all persons except soldiers to leave here." Rosecrans, he charged, besides being "obstinate and inaccessible to reason," was "irresolute, vacillating, and inconclusive." Instead of seeing to the needs of his men, Rosecrans was mostly "employed in pleasant gossip" with his friends and in composing "a long report to prove the fact that the Government is to blame for his failure." The basis for this claim, Dana asserted, would be that the secretary of war, and general in chief [Halleck], did not foresee that Bragg would be reinforced, and they had compelled an offensive campaign without adequate means. Meanwhile, at Chattanooga the army's animals were starving to death, and the men faced the same prospect. "In the midst of all these difficulties General Rosecrans seems to be insensible to the impending danger, and dawdles with trifles in a manner which can scarcely be imagined," wrote Dana on October 16. While there were "plenty of zealous and energetic officers ready to do whatever can be done, all this precious time is lost because our dazed and mazy commander cannot perceive the catastrophe that is close upon us, nor fix his mind upon the means of preventing it. I never saw anything which seemed so lamentable and hopeless," asserted Dana. "Nothing can prevent the retreat of the army from this place within a fortnight," he bluntly concluded.[9]

They were damning words from a man who in Washington, D.C., had become a highly respected source. Abraham Lincoln considered Dana "the eyes of the Government at the front." Already, Dana's condemnation of two of Rosecrans's subordinate generals had been instrumental in their having been removed from command. Not only were Maj. Gen. Thomas L. Crittenden and Maj. Gen. Alexander McCook relieved from command by Stanton's order following Dana's bitter personal tirades of September 23 through September 27 but their two corps, the Twentieth and Twenty-first, had been consolidated into a new corps, the Fourth, under Maj. Gen. Gordon Granger. Stanton, in particular, seemed alarmed by the increasingly frantic tone of Dana's dispatches.[10]

On October 16, the day following Dana's despairing telegram reporting that mud and rain had stopped all work and travel, troops were on half rations, and all but soldiers would soon have to leave Chattanooga, a decisive turn of events occurred. Not only had Dana denounced Rosecrans's leadership; he had also disparaged that general's own chief of staff. In a private letter evidently made available to key administration leaders at this time, Secretary of the Treasury Salmon P. Chase revealed to Lincoln highly damaging information about Old Rosy, written on July 27, 1863, by Brig. Gen. James A. Garfield, Rosecrans's supposed friend. Although not wanting to "do injustice to a good man," Garfield confided how he had "pleaded for an advance" in May 1863, but Rosecrans had "delayed through days which seemed months to me." Once the Tullahoma campaign proved successful, even "dissenting generals were compelled to confess that, if the movement had been made ten days earlier, while the weather was propitious, the army of Bragg would, in all human probability, no longer exist." Now, there had been further delay, to the point that Rosecrans was "singularly disinclined to grasp the situation with a strong hand and make the advantage his own." A "fatal delay" was the consequence, causing Garfield to assess: "If this inaction continues long, I shall ask to be relieved and sent somewhere where I can be part of a working army."[11]

Lincoln was allegedly shocked by Garfield's letter. It had, as an insider later noted, "the effect of a casting vote." Yet the President's well known magnanimity and a remembrance of what Rosecrans had accomplished at Stones River and elsewhere caused him to hesitate. At a cabinet meeting in which the Garfield letter was purportedly read, Stanton immediately suggested that Thomas replace Rosecrans. Yet Lincoln demurred, saying he did not wish to do Rosecrans an injustice. Lincoln was well aware of Stanton's ardent dislike of Rosecrans, and he believed Old Rosy "a true, and very able man." Nonetheless, in the back of his mind—considering the varied source of these severe allegations and Rosecrans's own despairing correspondence—was the lingering suspicion that Rosecrans might not be equal to the task at hand. Rosecrans had been acting "confused and stunned like a duck hit on the head," Lincoln later told his secretary. The President had long pondered the matter; of decisive importance in his decision was an indirect circumstance that became a major consideration.[12]

For nearly a month Lincoln, Stanton, Halleck, Rosecrans, and others had been urging, even demanding, that Maj. Gen. Ambrose Burnside reinforce the Army of the Cumberland by moving from the Knoxville region to Chattanooga. Burnside, although professing at first that he would immediately comply, had not done so. Instead, he had delayed and complained so loudly about abandoning east Tennessee while threatened by a professed enemy offensive, he had done nothing. Lincoln finally had been so exasperated that he allowed Burnside to remain in east Tennessee, fearing the enemy might make "a concentrated drive at Burnside."[13]

Yet as Burnside had so clearly demonstrated, a lack of coordination and practical authority in the western heartland was hamstringing the Federal effort. As officials of the War Department and others had suggested, the obvious solution was to establish a central department commander. If ever there was to be effective coordination of the three major armies then operating between the Mississippi River and the Allegheny Mountains, someone of great ability and established military reputation must manage their overall movements. As it stood, the independent commanders might profess to cooperate with one another, but in reality each had his own agenda and concerns. As was painfully evident during the recent campaign in Tennessee, little cooperation was evident during critical times, often resulting in disastrous results.

Realistically, there were only a few choices for a unified department commander among the then senior western generals. Ambrose Burnside had demonstrated his incapacity, both with the Army of the Potomac at Fredericksburg and in east Tennessee. Rosecrans's ability was severely in doubt following Chickamauga. George H. Thomas, although able, commanded merely a corps. Only the conqueror of Vicksburg, being as well the captor of Fort Henry and Fort Donelson, remained. As Halleck had promised, the victorious general in the west would be rewarded. There was only one viable choice: Ulysses S. Grant.[14]

Abraham Lincoln had long considered Charles A. Dana's suggestion of September 27 that Ulysses S. Grant, a man of "high rank and great prestige," be appointed to command at Chattanooga.[15]

Stanton had already made a preliminary decision on October 3, bringing Grant to Cairo, Illinois, to await orders. In light of the recent disaster at Chickamauga, there was obvious importance to this order. Grant's principal subordinate, Maj. Gen. William Tecumseh Sherman, wrote to Grant on October 10, telling him: "I feel sure you will be ordered to Nashville to assume a general command over all the forces operating to the southeast." Again, four days later, Sherman advised: "Accept command of the great army of the center: don't hesitate. . . . All success and honor to you."[16]

Grant, who had recently been injured in a fall from his horse, replied that his orders were to go to Cairo. Nonetheless, he had an inkling of what the administration was contemplating. On October 11, Henry Halleck advised: "You need not fear being left idle. The moment you are well enough to take the field you will have abundant occupation."[17]

It appears Lincoln was debating the overall consequences, and awaiting a major gubernatorial election before making a decision about changing commanders. A key political aspect was the Ohio elections, which were resolved favorably on October 9 when the pro-war Republican governor John Brough decisively defeated Clement L. Vallandigham, an antiwar

Democrat. Lincoln had feared that if removed, Rosecrans, a politically powerful Ohioan, might cost the Republicans Ohio by expressing a lack of support for Brough. All considerations of a major change thus had been deferred until after the election. Rosecrans's ardent support of the Lincoln administration was crucial, resulting in about 97 percent of the Army of the Cumberland's votes going to Brough. Lincoln was therefore grateful for Rosecrans's support and spoke of him as "a friend."[18]

Accordingly, despite Dana's increasingly damning assertions, including an outright remark that "I consider this army to be very unsafe in his [Rosecrans's] hands," Lincoln hesitated to consent to the outright removal of Rosecrans.[19]

On October 16, the matter abruptly came to a head. Probably based on Dana's despairing telegram of noon that day, asserting that "nothing [except the opening of the river] can prevent the retreat of the army from this place within a fortnight" and that Rosecrans, "dazed and mazy," could not perceive the approaching catastrophe, Stanton undoubtedly pressured the President to act before it was too late. Lincoln agreed, deciding that the time had come for a final decision.[20]

According to Lincoln, the consolidation idea was important to secure Chattanooga. Since Rosecrans seemed uncertain that he could hold that city, based upon the tone of his dispatches, Lincoln determined to place Grant in overall command.* Because he "knew and esteemed" Rosecrans as a general and patriot, Lincoln anticipated that Grant might retain Old Rosy in command. Yet, in deference to Grant's prerogative as overall commander, he would allow Grant to make that decision.[21]

By 9:00 P.M. that night, the crucial orders were prepared. An officer of the War Department would go to Louisville, Kentucky, to confer personally with Grant and deliver the order assigning Grant to command of the Military Division of the Mississippi. By express design, the War Department's messenger would carry two sets of orders pertaining to Rosecrans and the Army of the Cumberland. The first would retain Rosecrans as commander; the second would relieve Rosecrans and place George H. Thomas in command. As Halleck explained to Grant in the accompanying letter of conveyance taken to Louisville: "It is left optional with you to supersede General Rosecrans by General G. H. Thomas or not."[22]

From the moment of the President's decision, a glaring question was obvious. Whom would Ulysses S. Grant choose to work with, a man he seemed to abhor, Rosecrans, or a person he mistrusted and greatly resented, George H. Thomas? Since Edwin M. Stanton was particularly interested in this decision, he determined to deliver Grant's orders at Louis-

---

*This account was based upon a memo written December 16, 1863, by James A. Garfield, who interviewed Lincoln that month when he returned east to take his seat in the U.S. House of Representatives as a newly elected Ohio congressman.

ville personally, in place of the "officer of the War Department." Thus, there would be present at the time of decision a man who could hardly be considered an impartial participant. Stanton obviously was not taking any chances.[23]

Ulysses S. Grant knew nothing of the building pressures in Washington, D.C. Due to delays in telegraphic communications, it was 11:00 A.M. on October 17 before he received at Cairo, Illinois, Halleck's secretive telegram dated 9:00 P.M. October 16, instructing him to proceed to the Gault House in Louisville, "where you will meet an officer of the War Department with your orders and instructions." Only in the terse sentence "You will take with you your staff etc. for immediate operations in the field" was there a hint of the impending drama.[24]

Grant started by rail for Louisville via Indianapolis that morning. Amid ongoing speculation among his staff as to what Grant's orders would be, Grant was about to depart the Indianapolis depot on the morning of the eighteenth when a messenger came running up to stop his train. Secretary of War Stanton's special train was just then arriving at the station. Amid a flurry of activity, Stanton and Governor John Brough of Ohio boarded Grant's train. Stanton, eager and impulsive, mistook a staff surgeon for Grant and rushed up, vigorously shaking his hand as he blurted out, "How do you do General Grant? I recognize you from your pictures." Being much embarrassed, Stanton, amid the barely concealed smirks of various staff officers, was soon introduced to the chuckling Grant, and as they journeyed to Louisville, Stanton displayed Grant's optional orders.[25]

Although there probably never will be conclusive proof of the secretary of war's role in Grant's decision, Stanton's strong dislike of Rosecrans and his ardent support of Thomas may have surfaced in the conversation that followed. Grant had never met Stanton before but was well aware of Stanton's key role in the administration. According to one account, Stanton had already told Governor Oliver Morton of Indiana that he was removing Rosecrans based upon the general's dire communications after Chickamauga.[26]

Whatever their conversation, Grant quickly decided upon the removal of Rosecrans and his replacement with Thomas. The following day, Stanton said Grant's decision was based upon the prospect that Rosecrans "would not obey orders." Brig. Gen. John A. Rawlins, Grant's aide, wrote a month later that while Grant was "no enemy of General Rosecrans," the decision had been obvious because, following the campaign of 1862 around Corinth, Mississippi, he could never "think of again commanding" him. Rosecrans's disobedience of orders was one reason, but the "general spirit of insubordination toward General Grant" was the final straw, reasoned Rawlins. A few weeks before, when evidently asked by William T. Sherman how he would regard Rosecrans as an immediate subordinate should such occur in the imminent reorganization, Grant said he wondered whether he could be completedly objective in dealing with Rosecrans. "I may be wrong and judge Rosecrans from a rather prejudicial view instead of impartially as I would like, and try to do," he admitted to Sherman.[27]

Thomas, despite the clash of methods and personalities, was a true soldier and could be expected to do as ordered. That night, with a cold, drizzling rain falling on Louisville, Rawlins issued Grant's "General Order No. 1," removing Rosecrans and appointing Thomas to command of the Department of the Cumberland. Meanwhile, Grant, still lame from his fall and using a crutch but traveling with his wife, spent the evening of the nineteenth with some relatives in Louisville. During the general's absence from the hotel, Stanton received a copy of a rather frantic telegram from Charles A. Dana at Chattanooga, dated 11 A.M. October 18. Dana's assertions stood out in bold relief: ". . . our condition and prospects grow worse and worse." "The roads are in such a [bad] state that wagons are eight days making the journey from Stevenson to Chattanooga." Subsistence stores were "so nearly exhausted" that wagons were throwing overboard "precious cargo in order to get through at all." "A few days more and most of them [artillery horses] will be dead," Dana lamented. He then cut to the very quick: "If the effort which Rosecrans intends to make to open the river should be futile, the immediate retreat of this army will follow. It does not seem possible to hold out here another week without a new avenue of supplies. General [William F.] Smith says that as he passed among the men working on the fortifications yesterday several shouted 'crackers' at him. . . . If the army is finally obliged to retreat, the probability is that it will fall back like a rabble, leaving its artillery, and protected only by the river behind it."[28]

Dana's wire had Stanton pacing the floor in his nightshirt. The impression was that Rosecrans was on the verge of an imminent retreat. Stanton had messengers out looking for Grant in all directions. It was about 11:00 P.M. when Grant returned to the hotel, he remembered, and Stanton was in a frenzy. Immediately, Grant wrote an equally frantic telegram to Thomas telling him to hold Chattanooga "at all hazards" and report on the supplies on hand and how long they would last.[29]

Ulysses S. Grant had inherited a most difficult task, as he now well realized. On the morning of the twentieth he left for Nashville by train, having received Thomas's dispatch in reply to his of the night before: "204,462 rations in storehouses, 90,000 to arrive tomorrow. . . . I will hold the town till we starve." Soon Grant would witness the "condition of affairs that had prompted" Thomas's stout reply. "It looked, indeed," he later wrote, "as if but two courses were open [to the army]: one to starve, the other to surrender or be captured."[30]

CHAPTER 7

"WHAT DOES IT MEAN?"

For William S. Rosecrans, October 19 had dawned with renewed hopes of further progress in reopening the river supply route to Chattanooga. That morning, the rain of the preceding day had vanished, and splendid Indian summer weather warmed the air. James A. Garfield, Rosecrans's departing chief of staff, had left on the fifteenth for Washington, D.C., carrying Rosecrans's official report of Chickamauga, as well as instructions to see Stanton and Halleck in order to "explain to them in detail our condition here." While en route to Stevenson, Alabama, Garfield had reported on the sixteenth and seventeenth that the road was "pretty good," the creeks and rivers falling, and that many supply wagons loaded with forage and rations were on the road to Chattanooga. Upon reaching Stevenson on the seventeenth, Garfield's optimistic outlook seemed to be bolstered by the news that the steamboat under construction there would be ready in a week. Yet after arriving at Nashville on the evening of the eighteenth, Garfield heard rumors that the Secretary of War and Ulysses Grant were at Louisville and about to start for Nashville. "What does it mean?" Garfield wired to Rosecrans on the evening of the nineteenth.[1]

About the time Garfield made this query, Rosecrans was in the process of returning to army headquarters after being absent since early morning. He had started out that morning in the company of the army's new chief engineer, Brig. Gen. William F. "Baldy" Smith, who was going to make a reconnaissance in the vicinity of Williams Island "with a view to making the island a cover for a steamboat landing and storehouses." Yet when Rosecrans stopped to visit a hospital en route, Smith, after a lengthy wait, had grown impatient and departed without his commander. Despite this mishap, Rosecrans evidently remained in a good mood, and was seen joking with some of his troops about the favorable results from the recent Ohio election. Upon his arrival at headquarters shortly after 6:00 P.M., there was a telegram from Washington, D.C., waiting on the table. Due to Rosecrans's prolonged absence that day, some of his subordinates, Generals Gordon Granger, Daniel Butterfield, and even the new chief of staff, Maj. Gen. Joseph J. Reynolds, already knew of the directive. It was General Orders No. 337, relieving Rosecrans and assigning Thomas in his place. Later that evening, Rosecrans received Grant's telegram conveying the same orders and telling him to go to Cincinnati, Ohio, to await orders.[2]

William S. Rosecrans must have been stunned. To everyone at head-quarters, the order had been a complete surprise. Yet Old Rosy "took it coolly and composedly, exhibiting neither surprise nor chagrin," said an observer. Later he "laughed and talked with those who came in and had faces as if they were mourning the death of a near kin." George H. Thomas was sent for, and Rosecrans announced that he would depart the next morning at 5:00 A.M. Rosecrans's 6:20 P.M. dispatch to Washington, D.C., acknowledged receipt of the order, and thereafter, until past midnight, the stricken but remarkably composed Ohioan talked with Thomas about the army's circumstances and pending plans.[3]

Thomas was upset over the entire matter, Rosecrans later wrote. He felt that Rosecrans had been unjustly removed, and he was indignant at Old Rosy's callous treatment at the hands of the authorities in Washington. In fact, Rosecrans said he had to remonstrate with Thomas and urge him to take command for the country's sake—"You must do it," implored Old Rosy. Thomas finally yielded, and "in silence he accepted the situation." Later, when Grant's telegram to hold Chattanooga "at all hazards" arrived, both Rosecrans and Thomas were indignant at the implied concern that they might abandon Chattanooga. Already, Thomas was unfavorably impressed with Grant's attitude, believing that either malice or ignorance had inspired the wire to hold Chattanooga.[4]

Although Rosecrans said he couldn't bear the thought of meeting his troops, he prepared a farewell address, praising Thomas and asking God's blessing on the Army of the Cumberland. Then, early the following morning, a gloomy, gray day, William S. Rosecrans rode off in the company of a handful of officers. He kept a cheerful countenance despite the sorrow of aides and a few officers, some of whom wept openly. Rosecrans seemed to have a kind word for everyone present. It was not until after he was gone that most of the army knew what had happened. Old Rosy had vanished like a fire going out. He had "modestly left without fuss or dem-onstration," wrote one of his generals. Yet behind him there remained "deep and almost universal regret" among his stunned and disbelieving soldiers.[5]

Ulysses S. Grant had spent the afternoon of October 20 at Nashville. Word of his appointment to command of the military division had traveled fast, and a large crowd gathered at the St. Cloud Hotel. They wanted a speech, but Grant, haggard and stressed from the events in progress, said he had "never made a speech in his life, and was too old to learn now." Instead, Andrew Johnson, the military governor of Tennessee and his host, came to Grant's rescue with a long speech. Grant was content to shake everyone's hand until arm-weary. The following morning Grant and his staff resumed what they knew to be a rough three-day journey to Chattanooga. Traveling by rail to Stevenson, then by boat to Bridgeport, Grant planned to make the final leg of the journey on horseback, despite his crippled leg.[6]

Following his arrival on the evening of the twenty-first at Stevenson, Alabama, the southern end of the operating rail line, Grant learned that Rosecrans was present, being on his way to Cincinnati. Rosecrans went to Grant's railcar and briefly talked with the new commander. He seemed courteous, remembered a staff officer. Yet the meeting was short and strained. "They were far from sympathetic with each other," noted the staff officer. According to Rosecrans, Grant implied he had nothing to do with the removal decision. Rosecrans apparently pointed out that his plans were rapidly maturing when he was relieved. As was later confirmed by his correspondence, Rosecrans anticipated the crucial reopening of the Tennessee River supply route to Chattanooga. Only two days earlier, he had ordered Joe Hooker at Stevenson, Alabama, to be ready to march promptly to Chattanooga with his men. Yet Rosecrans had revealed to Halleck on the nineteenth that he had no intention of bringing Hooker up until Sherman arrived with his divisions—unless the enemy crossed the Tennessee River in force north of Chattanooga. Old Rosy reasoned that Hooker's men couldn't be fed at Chattanooga, and he knew they didn't have adequate transportation. In fact, the "preservation of our army" at Chattanooga had been so precarious, said Rosecrans, that he had told Hooker, "It will require almost superhuman efforts to sustain us here."[7]

To Grant, it seemed that Rosecrans was adrift. Although he had carefully calculated what needed to be done and how to do it, Rosecrans did not move. He appeared to be awaiting the prospect of certain success—specifically the arrival of Sherman's troops so as to secure the river—which probably translated in Grant's mind into a lack of nerve. Ulysses S. Grant, later remembering their interview, said Rosecrans's suggestions seemed excellent. "My only wonder was that he had not carried them out."[8]

It was apparent to many within the army's command structure that Rosecrans's successors were lacking neither in nerve nor determination. Both George H. Thomas and Ulysses S. Grant were men of strong will, with nerves of steel. The real problem to be confronted was the practical melding of their divergent personalities and perspectives.

Grant's fifty-five-mile journey on October 22 and 23 by horseback to Chattanooga over rugged, "nearly impassable" Walden's Ridge while still crippled from his September 4 fall was a testimony to his endurance and bulldog determination. The nature of the journey can well be imagined from the description of couriers who reported "from Bridgeport to the foot of the [Walden] mountain the mud is up to their horses' bellies." Once on the treacherous, rocky mountain roads, washouts, creeks swollen to six feet or more, and downed bridges made travel both hazardous for horsemen and extraordinarily difficult for wagons. Grant remembered he "had to be carried over places where it was not safe to cross on horseback." Traveling through torrents of rain over "the worst roads I ever saw," Grant became "very much fatigued." Moreover, he was shocked by the debris of broken wagons and the carcasses of thousands of mules and horses littering the roadway.[9]

After being compelled to halt on the night of the twenty-second near Anderson's Crossroads, Grant finally arrived the following evening at Chattanooga, only to have his horse fall "flat on his side." Luckily, Grant was unhurt, and he arrived at Thomas's headquarters "wet, dirty, and well." His reception, especially from George H. Thomas, however, was anything but cordial.[10]

Lt. Col. James H. Wilson of Grant's staff, who had ridden ahead and arrived the preceding night, walked into army headquarters and found Grant and Thomas seated in silence. It was a tense moment, noted Wilson. "Grant was sitting on one side of the fire over a puddle of water that had run out of his clothes. Thomas, glum and silent, was sitting on the other, while [Grant's chief of staff Brig. Gen. John A.] Rawlins and the rest were scattered about in disorder."[11]

Wilson perceived the situation at a glance. Neither general seemed conversant with the other. Wilson considered that it might relate to Thomas being upset about being placed under a man who had once been his junior as a general. Taking quick action, Wilson blurted out, "General Thomas, General Grant is wet and tired, and ought to have some dry clothes, particularly a pair of socks and a pair of slippers. He is hungry besides, and needs something to eat. Can't your officers attend to these matters for him?"[12]

It broke the awkward tension. At once, Thomas hurried about, doing everything to make Grant comfortable. As Wilson surmised, Thomas simply had not regarded Grant "as his guest," but more as a commanding general intent upon imposing his own ideas.[13]

Thereafter, Grant and his staff were treated with the utmost hospitality. Yet it had been an unsettling experience—and an inauspicious start for the two principal commanders who had to save Chattanooga for the Union.

George H. Thomas had his own concept for saving Chattanooga. When Rosecrans departed and Thomas took over, the change at headquarters was "strikingly perceptible," said Charles A. Dana. "Order prevails instead of universal chaos." Thomas's specific instructions prior to Grant's arrival were for Hooker to concentrate at Bridgeport or Stevenson, Alabama. He was instructed to be ready to make a forced march with the Eleventh and most of the Twelfth Corps to reach Rankin's Ferry along the south riverbank. This movement would occur within several days, Thomas wired to

Halleck on the twenty-second, the day prior to Grant's arrival. Its purpose would be to control Raccoon Mountain and occupy much of Lookout Valley, thereby reopening the wagon road and facilitating repair of the railroad line from Bridgeport to Chattanooga. Yet, as Dana perceived, Hooker had shown "no zeal in the enterprise." He was simply waiting for his wagons to arrive from Nashville before concentrating per Thomas's orders. This building impasse with Hooker, Dana concluded, would probably continue until after Grant's arrival.[14]

On the evening of October 23, Ulysses Grant had sat "as immovable as a rock and as silent as the sphinx," said one of Thomas's staff officers. Grant listened "attentively" to the various senior generals discuss the situation at Chattanooga. Then, suddenly straightening himself in his chair, Grant "began to fire whole volleys of questions at the officers present." There was the ring of authority in his voice and manner, noted an observer. Grant seemed to possess high mental capacity and reason and was keenly perceptive about crucial details. He soon made it clear that he not only expected a prompt opening of new supply lines but planned on seizing the initiative and taking the offensive.[15]

Thomas had a ready response, at least for the crucial supply difficulties. In addition to the proposed march from Rankin's Ferry, there were newly developed plans. Baldy Smith, during his return from the reconnaissance to Williams Island on the 19th, had chanced to stop at a small earthwork along the neck of land north of Moccasin Point. Here he found an artillery unit positioned so as to prevent an enemy crossing at Brown's Ferry, where a road from Lookout Valley led down to the river. Noting that the "sharp range of hills" on the opposite shore was broken at Brown's Ferry by a narrow gap, Smith was impressed with the potential importance of the position. By occupying that site, it would enable the Federal army to command the road through the valley to Kelley's Ferry, and might seriously disrupt enemy operations within and their control of Lookout Valley. It was Smith's idea, presented initially to Thomas following Rosecrans's departure, to seize the Brown's Ferry site in conjunction with the movement of troops from Bridgeport to open the river. Also, instead of laying another bridge across from Chattanooga to Moccasin Point as Thomas had sought, Smith proposed that the bridge materials then being fabricated by a detachment of the 1st Michigan Engineers and Mechanics be utilized for the Brown's Ferry site. Thomas had approved the plan, despite the grumbling of several of his generals, who, said Smith, had denounced it as "preposterous." It was this composite concept that Thomas presented to Grant on the night of the 23rd.[16]

Grant mused over the plan, but was unsure of its merit. Finally, he agreed to investigate the following morning by means of a personal reconnaissance. Thereafter, despite his fatigue, Grant remained at a table writing telegrams and directives, until nearly 11:00 P.M., when he limped off to bed in an adjoining room.[17]

About 10:00 A.M. the following day, October 24, the new military division commander rode to Brown's Ferry to see the riverbank site planned for the pontoon bridge being built near Chattanooga. Dismounting his horse, Grant went to the river's edge on foot—in full view of the Confederate skirmishers on the opposite shore. Thanks to an informal long-standing agreement among the opposing pickets not to fire on one another, not a shot was fired at him. After carefully examining the site, including the road leading through a break in the opposite hills, Grant returned to Thomas's headquarters on Walnut Street and confirmed the existing plans.[18]

Within a matter of hours after approving Thomas's operations, Grant began to have serious misgivings. An immediate crisis was thrust upon the Federal commander that evening when Henry Halleck wired news of the pending reinforcement of Bragg's army by more of Robert E. Lee's troops. According to Halleck: "It is pretty certain that Ewell's corps, from twenty to twenty-five thousand men, has left Lee's army, and gone to Tennessee. . . . You must guard against Bragg's entrance into east Tennessee above Chattanooga." That very day, deserters had reported Longstreet's Corps from Bragg's army moving north in the direction of east Tennessee.[19]

Grant, in rapid sequence, began making major operational changes. He dispatched a note to Sherman, en route to Chattanooga from the Mississippi Valley, telling him to "drop everything . . . and move with your entire force towards Stevenson [Ala.] until you receive further orders." Grant wanted Sherman's troops in position to block or attack Bragg should he "break through our lines and move on Nashville." Joe Hooker was instructed to leave a full division to guard the railroad from Murfreesboro to Stevenson. Realizing that the bulk of Hooker's troops was committed to opening the river supply route, Grant now lamented that "Sherman's forces are the only troops I could throw in to head [off] such a move [by Bragg]." The horrible condition of the roads, Grant foresaw, would make it difficult to follow Bragg with Thomas's army.[20]

Little did he then suspect the real difficulty at hand. Having just arrived, Grant had scant knowledge of the vastly depleted resources of the Army of the Cumberland. Its ability even to move from Chattanooga was in doubt. Within two days, however, Grant learned the truth. By the twenty-sixth, the new commander seemed convinced that Thomas's army was desperately compromised following its devastating defeat at Chickamauga.

The Army of the Cumberland just wasn't fit for battle. The chief ordnance officer reported only enough ammunition on hand to fight a single day's battle. So little forage remained at Chattanooga that all except one hundred artillery horses in each division were ordered on the twenty-fourth to be sent to Stevenson in order to keep them alive. Grant confided to his wife, Julia, on the twenty-seventh that "there are but very few people here and those few will have to leave soon." In fact, so devastated without the use of railroads was this remote, inaccessible spot that Grant termed it "one of the wildest places you ever saw." Comparing the hardships from the summer before, he wrote Julia: "People about Vicksburg have not seen war yet, or at least the suffering brought on by war [as have Chattanooga's citizens]."[21]

The army's rations, equipment, and even quartermaster's stores were so depleted that opening what the Union soldiers termed "the cracker line" remained a top priority despite the news of Bragg's reinforcement and possible movement northward.

Simply because Grant had little other option due to the critical time frame and Chattanooga's miserable supply situation, on October 25 Baldy Smith was put in command of the Brown's Ferry expedition and the go-ahead was given. Hooker was ordered to march from Bridgeport into Lookout Valley that same day. "I am making a desperate effort . . . to get possession of the river from here to Bridgeport," Grant admitted to his wife on the twenty-seventh. "If I do it will facilitate bringing [up] supplies very much."[22]

The terrible condition of the Army of the Cumberland's transportation and the meager logistics operations were already magnified in Grant's mind. More and more in the days ahead, Grant appeared to conclude that there was an inherent operational deficiency in Thomas's army. The whole spectacle of an army wasting away was simply disgusting. Thomas's soldiers didn't appear to measure up to the hardy, innovative campaigners of Vicksburg and the Mississippi Valley on whom Grant had always relied. From the military division commander's perspective, there was a growing and natural reluctance to utilize in large numbers troops so deficient.

Grant's telegram to Halleck the first night following Grant's arrival at Chattanooga was of ominous portent; it asked Halleck to approve his earlier order placing Sherman in command of the Army of the Tennessee. Clearly, a familiar star was rising in Grant's eyes, and it wasn't George H. Thomas. With the arrival of Sherman's columns, Grant would be able to rely on the man in whom he placed the utmost trust—his faithful campaigner since the days of Shiloh, William Tecumseh Sherman.[23]

Until then, Grant was entirely vulnerable. In fact, considering the Army of the Cumberland's confinement to the fortifications of Chattanooga, a great opportunity now existed for the enemy. Should Bragg strike northward, Grant admitted "a present inability to follow him [from here]." With little existing transportation, ammunition, or logistical support, not only was effective pursuit an impossibility but Grant lacked even the means to retreat from Chattanooga should such action become necessary.[24]

Of further dire consequence, Grant worried about the forthcoming winter climate. He told Halleck on October 26: "It is barely possible to supply this army from its present base. But when winter rains set in it will be impossible." Also, more bad news arrived in the lackluster performance of key personnel. From Bridgeport, Assistant Secretary of War Charles A. Dana sent word that Joe Hooker seemed to be dragging his feet at getting the movement under way for liberating Lookout Valley and the Tennessee River's south bank. Dana found Hooker on October 27 "in a unfortunate state of mind for one who has to cooperate [in such an important operation]. He is . . . fault finding, criticizing, dissatisfied . . . [and] is quite . . . truculent toward the plan he is now to execute."[25]

Grant's woes seemed to intensify rapidly. Writing to Halleck, he admitted: "If the enemy should break through our lines . . . and push north, it would greatly disturb us and lead to the abandonment of much territory, temporarily, and to great loss of public property."[26]

The only consolation Grant had at the time was in knowing the abilities of his opponent. From the days at Corinth, and earlier during the Mexican War, Grant had measured Braxton Bragg's capabilities. To Halleck, he confided: "I think the Rebel force making such a movement would be totally annihilated."[27]

CHAPTER 8

WHOM SHOULD THE
SOLDIERS TRUST?

During his October visit to the Army of Tennessee, Jefferson Davis had spoken of the crucial events then transpiring at Chattanooga. When serenaded on October 13 by the band of the 1st Tennessee Infantry, both Davis and Bragg had responded with brief speeches, "giving the privates their just praise" and citing the success of the present campaign as "proof of the soldiers' trust in their leaders."[1]

The following day, prior to his departure, Davis issued an emotional proclamation to the army: "Your movements have been the object of intensest anxiety. The hopes of our cause greatly depend upon you, and happy it is that all can securely rely upon your achieving whatever . . . human power can effect. Though you have done much, very much yet remains to be done." Our "holy cause," Davis asserted, required "patient endurance of toil and danger," from which would later come "the highest meed of praise . . . to him who has claimed least for himself in proportion to the service he has rendered."[2]

The real difficulty, Davis warned, was that there were those within the army who seemed to allow "selfish aspiration to prevail over a desire for the public good. . . . [Yet] he who sows the seeds of discontent and distrust prepares for the harvest of slaughter and defeat."[3]

Davis's proclamation was read on dress parade on October 17, and much of the reaction was skeptical. "He entreats us to be obedient and harmonious," wrote a diarist, who noted "it . . . [was] just what such a document might be expected to contain."[4]

Perhaps it was ironic that Jefferson Davis had focused on a key difficulty of the Army of Tennessee: widespread discontent due to factional strife.

Even more paradoxically, the very men the Confederate president intended to encourage, the soldiers, looked to their senior commanders for expert leadership. Yet, those Davis sought to admonish were in essence the command backbone of the army. It was a contradiction in cause, effect, and remedy. Specifically, the commanders most involved in a leadership role, and the vital basis for the troops' "trust in their leaders," were many of the generals Braxton Bragg now considered disgraced.

According to Bragg, Davis's proclamation was carte blanche to remove his most vocal and dangerous detractors. From Bragg's perspective, the "harvest of slaughter and defeat" Davis had alluded to in his proclamation was fair warning. It heralded the imminent resolution of the army's internal strife, with the victims, his own dissident generals, suffering their just fate.

Unfortunately for the South, the counterproductivity of a command shake-up at this critical time was apparent to neither Davis nor Bragg. Instead of focusing on the military task at hand—forcing the retreat of the Federal army from Chattanooga—Bragg and Davis had insisted on blind acquiescence to Bragg's controversial mandates. Politics and cronyism ever rife at Bragg's headquarters, now would have a larger consequence.

Bragg's bitter purge was evident almost from the moment of Davis's departure for Atlanta. Although urged by one general to heal the wounds among his chief subordinates now that he had prevailed, Bragg instead bristled with vindictiveness. Saying he wanted "to get rid" of them, Bragg angrily prepared to dismiss "any and every officer" who would not support him.[5]

First to feel Bragg's wrath was Daniel Harvey Hill, the abrasive Carolinian who had been transferred from Robert E. Lee's army following his ill-advised criticism of Lee. An outspoken maverick but a competent fighter, Hill had been accused by Bragg of delaying the attack at Chickamauga on the morning of September 20. This allegation followed in the wake of Hill's alleged active role in getting up the petition for Bragg's removal prior to Davis's arrival. To Bragg, such action was a form of mutiny. On October 15, Hill's removal was announced, and a few weeks later that embittered general was on his way to Richmond, chafing over his vindictive dismissal by Bragg.[6]

Simon Bolivar Buckner, the general who actually may have authored the Bragg removal petition, was removed from his independent department command and soon reassigned as a mere division commander. Even Buckner's close subordinate, William Preston, was reduced from a division to a brigade commander. Others were hobbled in their opposition or suitably chastened, including Thomas C. Hindman, who earlier had been suspended and banished from the army. Particularly satisfying to Bragg was the elimination of Leonidas Polk, Davis's special friend. Although Davis dismissed the charges against Polk, he was removed from Bragg's army and reassigned to duty in Joe Johnston's department of Mississippi and Alabama. In his place, Bragg had agreed to accept William J. Hardee, an old Bragg detractor who also happened to be one of Davis's longtime friends. Although a potential troublemaker, Hardee was certainly far preferable to Polk in Bragg's eyes.[7]

Of more significance to the army was Bragg's handling of Nathan Bedford Forrest. Outspoken in his frequent criticism and damnation of the North Carolinian's lack of leadership, Forrest had run afoul of one of Bragg's directives in late September. While conducting a reconnaissance to investigate reports of Burnside advancing from east Tennessee, Forrest was required to turn over nearly all of his corps to his rival and critic Maj. Gen. Joe Wheeler. Once before, during the 1862 Kentucky campaign, Bragg had similarly ordered Forrest to give up his command to Wheeler. The results had been disastrous. Thus, on October 5, Forrest was outraged when he learned that Bragg had placed him permanently under Wheeler's command. Seething with rage, Forrest arrived at Bragg's headquarters around October 7 and burst into Bragg's tent unannounced. Thrusting an index finger in Bragg's face for emphasis, the wrathful cavalry commander launched into a bitter tirade: "You commenced your cowardly and contemptible persecution of me soon after the battle of Shiloh, and you have kept it up ever since. . . . You robbed me of my command in Kentucky, and gave it to one of your favorites . . . in a spirit of revenge and spite, because I would not fawn upon you as others did. . . . Now this second brigade . . . in order to humiliate me, you have taken . . . from me. I have stood your meanness as long as I intend to. You have played the part of a damned scoundrel, and are a coward, and if you were any part of a man I would slap your jaws. . . . You may as well not issue any orders to me, for I will not obey them, and I will hold you personally responsible for any further indignities you endeavor to inflict upon me. You have threatened to arrest me for not obeying your orders promptly. I dare you to do it, and I say to you that if you ever again try to interfere with me or cross my path it will be at the peril of your life."[8]

Stunned, Bragg watched in silence as Forrest stormed from the tent. In an aside to a staff surgeon, who remarked that now he was "in for it," Forrest remarked, "No, he'll never say a word about it . . . and mark my word, he'll take no action in the matter. I will ask to be relieved and transferred to a different field, and he will not oppose it."[9]

Forrest was right. On October 13, Bragg wrote a letter to Davis citing Forrest's request to be transferred to another department. The Confederate president promptly approved, sending Forrest to west Tennessee and northern Mississippi.[10]

Bragg probably considered it another victory. Despite the verbal abuse from Forrest, that general, Polk, D. H. Hill, Hindman, Buckner, and Preston were gone or humbled. Other longtime critics such as John C. Breckinridge and Frank Cheatham were silent under the present circumstances, obviously fearful of losing their commands. Only one other major detractor remained to be dealt with in the ongoing purge.[11]

A key person in the army, long recognized as one of the most politically formidable of Confederate generals, was Robert E. Lee's "Old Warhorse," James Longstreet. Perhaps the most threatening of the opposition generals, he had come to Tennessee expecting to supersede Bragg. Although

Jefferson Davis had rejected Longstreet's overtures and plans during his recent visit, Longstreet remained a thorn in Bragg's side. His many high-placed friends in Virginia and his long-standing relationship with Robert E. Lee made Longstreet more than the ordinary troublemaker to be dealt with. Bragg had specific plans to rid himself of Longstreet, but in mid-October he seemed to be biding his time, seeking the proper opportunity to act.[12]

There was one other disaffected general who had signed his name to the removal petition and who, despite Bragg's earlier praise and request for his promotion, remained estranged from the Army of Tennessee's commander. A frustrating but special case, Maj. Gen. Patrick Ronayne Cleburne unquestionably was one of the army's most capable and brilliant fighters. Therein lay the difficulty for Bragg, who was well aware of Cleburne's outstanding ability. Despite Cleburne's prominently signed endorsement for Bragg's removal twice within a year, Bragg felt compelled to keep Cleburne in command of his division. In his mind, Bragg may have considered Pat Cleburne more of a misguided personality than a primary critic and part of the "mutinous" faction Bragg so intensely hated.[13]

In fact, Cleburne wasn't so much personally opposed to Bragg as he was alienated due to a professional estimate of his commander's lack of military competence.

To many who knew him well, Pat Cleburne was a walking contradiction: He had a mild-mannered personality and yet was a ferocious fighter, perhaps the very best infantry general of the Confederacy's western armies.[14]

Cleburne had once been a private, then a corporal in the British army before emigrating to the United States in 1849. A self-made man and a leading citizen of Helena, Arkansas, before the war, Cleburne was an overachiever with a driving zeal for success. The advent of the Civil War found Cleburne at age thirty-three quickly promoted from captain to colonel to brigadier general in the Confederate army. As a veteran of Shiloh, Richmond, Kentucky, Perryville, and Stones River, Cleburne was noted for his distinguished personal gallantry. By late 1862, he was a major general commanding a division in the Army of Tennessee.[15]

Despite his well-regarded reputation, perhaps the most frustrating aspect of Cleburne's life was his uncompromising integrity. Often he had resorted to rigid mental discipline to confront adversity in the wake of ignorance and the prejudices of others. Unwilling to compromise principle or personal dignity for political expediency, Cleburne had frequently run afoul of army politics. Pat Cleburne's actions were predicated on a commonsense estimate of what was right or wrong. In his mind's eye, he often saw only black or white, with very little gray area for compromising duty, honor, and judgment. Bragg, who had once praised Cleburne and recommended him for promotion, became alienated after hearing Cleburne's candid opinion of him following Stones River—that Bragg did not "possess the confidence of the Army." Instead of being promoted to lieutenant general and corps command, Cleburne had been relegated by Bragg to an uneasy "necessary" but unfavored status due to his support of the anti-

Bragg faction. Moreover, given his easygoing personality and his modesty in social situations, Cleburne had failed to attract widespread media attention. His refusal to become involved in political imbroglios while at the storm center of every heavy firefight ensured his continuing role as a remarkable fighting general, even while alienating him from the inner circle of command.[16]

Cleburne's response to adversity of this sort was characteristic of his attitude: "An honest heart and a strong arm should never succumb."[17]

Because Braxton Bragg's mind was preoccupied with subduing his dissident generals, the North Carolina commander's attention had been focused too long on the internal affairs of his army. Belatedly, at the end of October, in the wake of his enormous "showdown" victory over his many detractors, Bragg finally began to direct more attention to the enemy army occupying Chattanooga.

Bragg readily perceived that the strategic situation presented both opportunity and perturbation. For weeks, the Federal army had been penned up within Chattanooga. Word of their starving animals and short rations had encouraged Bragg to do little more than watch for the enemy's expected retreat into middle Tennessee. At first, once it had been understood the enemy would not immediately evacuate Chattanooga, Bragg had been wary of Rosecrans, believing he was concentrating all available troops for a renewed offensive. Bragg even sought reinforcements from Joe Johnston's command. Johnston had complied, sending Maj. Gen. Stephen D. Lee and about 2,500 cavalrymen to operate against the railroad "in [the] rear of Chattanooga." Johnston's communiqué of September 29 even urged Bragg on: "Might not a part of your own cavalry cross the river for the same object?"[18]

Bragg's woeful mismanagement of the available cavalry forces immediately following the Chickamauga battle had been a source of irritation to all. On September 22, relying on reports that Rosecrans was burning Chattanooga and recrossing the Tennessee River, Bragg had directed Wheeler's and Forrest's cavalry to cross the Tennessee River and intercept the fleeing enemy. Hours later, this order was countermanded when it was feared Rosecrans was preparing to advance again. Word that Burnside was coming to reinforce Rosecrans soon caused Bragg to send Forrest northward with his three brigades, only to order on September 28 that these cavalrymen merge with Wheeler's command.[19]

Wheeler, who had repeatedly received conflicting orders following Bragg's ever-changing estimate of what the enemy was doing, finally was instructed on the twenty-third to clear Missionary Ridge northward. Undoubtedly exasperated by the befuddlement at army headquarters, Wheeler probably conferred with Bragg prior to September 28 about the cavalry's proper role. At that time, he appeared to have persuaded the flustered Bragg to place Forrest's command permanently under his control. The basis for Wheeler's request apparently was the pending raid across the Tennessee River to destroy the enemy's railroad and supplies.[20]

Thus, when Joe Johnston's telegram arrived on the twenty-ninth, advising that S. D. Lee would independently raid the railroads behind Chattanooga from the south, Bragg was duly encouraged. Thereafter, a brigade of cavalry operating in northern Alabama under Brig. Gen. Phillip D. Roddey was ordered to join Wheeler's raiders by moving northward across the Tennessee River near Bridgeport, Alabama. Once across the river, they would move to link up with Wheeler near Jasper, in Tennessee.[21]

In view of Joe Wheeler's imminent raid against Federal supply lines across the Tennessee River, Bragg seemed to relish the prospect of seriously impairing the trickle of Yankee food stores reaching the besieged city. Yet, while promoting operations against the enemy's railroad communications as the means of forcing Rosecrans to retreat, Bragg had become exceedingly careless in implementing this potentially powerful blow.[22]

Wheeler's cavalrymen were allowed to proceed on September 30 via a northern route into the Sequatchie Valley behind Walden's Ridge without coordinating their efforts with either S. D. Lee or Roddey. Instead of concentrated and mutually supportive operations against the vital enemy supply lines, the raid became a disjointed and piecemeal effort that fell apart for want of proper planning and execution. Despite Wheeler's initial success at Anderson's Crossroads and on Walden's Ridge on October 2, by the fourth, Federal pursuers forced Wheeler into a hasty flight. Following spirited actions at McMinnville, Wartrace, and Farmington, Tennessee, Wheeler was fortunate to escape south across the Tennessee River at Muscle Shoals, Alabama, on October 9. Wheeler's command had been badly cut up in the action at Farmington, causing Wheeler to complain that a portion of his men had acted "shamefully."[23]

Just as the last of Wheeler's stragglers were recrossing the Tennessee River, Stephen D. Lee and his command arrived nearby, "much surprised" to learn of Wheeler's return south of the river. Lee had advanced with 2,500 cavalry from Mississippi on October 6, expecting to meet with Roddey and join forces for an advance northward into Tennessee. Instead, he met Wheeler's worn-out command, now "in no condition to return to Middle Tennessee." Moreover, since the large Federal cavalry force that had pursued Wheeler was known to be just across the river, S. D. Lee felt it imprudent to continue on alone.[24]

While Wheeler rested and refitted his men nearby, saying on October 13, "[I] would give anything if I could cross the river immediately," Lee waited for Bragg's reply to Wheeler's request for two fresh brigades, which had been left behind with the Army of Tennessee prior to the late raid.[25]

A week later, Wheeler and Lee were still awaiting word from Bragg. With the river rising due to heavy autumn rains, S. D. Lee grumbled that the chances of getting across the Tennessee River were slim. After complaining that such a large cavalry force should not be kept idle, Lee warned that he was planning a return to Mississippi due to the lack of a meaningful coordinated effort.[26]

Although Bragg ordered that he remain in northern Alabama, Lee soon learned that Bragg had instructed Wheeler to rejoin the Army of Tennessee for operations in east Tennessee. Moreover, with the approach of Sherman's columns en route to Chattanooga, S. D. Lee was prevented from doing anything more than harassing Sherman's troops as they passed through the vicinity of Tuscumbia. By October 31, Lee was fuming about the frustration of his every plan. Since Sherman was quickly gone, having crossed to the north bank of the Tennessee River, "there is little further use for cavalry in this valley," Lee scoffed. In early November, S. D. Lee returned to Mississippi, having accomplished virtually nothing of importance in the campaign.[27]

Even worse, Roddey had failed to cross the Tennessee River to cooperate with Wheeler until October 7. Once in Tennessee, Roddey became so confused about the existing circumstances that a week later, on October 14, he sent a courier to look for Wheeler, asking where he and S. D. Lee were. "I made this move under the impression that Generals Wheeler and [S.D.] Lee were both this side of the river," wrote the exasperated Alabama cavalryman. Once Roddey found out he was alone north of the river, he became intimidated and soon countermarched, recrossing the Tennessee River in late October.[28]

It was all terribly frustrating and embarrassing to those who knew the details. Directly implicated was Bragg, who, characteristically, was preoccupied with yet another festering internal crisis.

Bragg's concept for managing the siege of Chattanooga had evolved as early as October 3. Believing that to attack the enemy "in front, strongly intrenched as he is, would be suicidal," Bragg envisioned taking the offensive only after careful preparations were made. Specifically, Bragg told the Richmond authorities that to strike elsewhere involved crossing the Tennessee River. Yet, as his supplies were so short, the railroad from Atlanta had to be repaired before the army could become operationally mobile. Due to the want of adequate transportation, particularly a lack of artillery horses, Bragg would say only that "we hope soon to be ready."[29]

Within weeks, Bragg was again waffling about his course of action. At the time of Jefferson Davis's visit in October, Bragg was seeking reinforcements to counterbalance the enemy's heavy troop concentrations destined for Chattanooga. Following Davis's departure, Bragg was clearly in a defensive-reactive posture, seeking only to keep Burnside in east Tennessee from advancing toward Chattanooga. On October 17, he detached Maj. Gen. Carter L. Stevenson's Division in the direction of Knoxville "to threaten the enemy's rear" and thereby relieve pressure on Maj. Gen. Samuel Jones's Confederate force in the vicinity of Knoxville (which had reported Burnside advancing). This was one of the reasons for the sudden recall of Wheeler's cavalry from northern Alabama.[30]

In fact, the fast-developing situation in east Tennessee soon required so much of Bragg's attention as to provide an opportunity to eliminate the one remaining general he earnestly sought to rid himself of: James Longstreet.

CHAPTER 9

BRAGG'S "LEAST FAVORABLE OPTION"

James Longstreet's ego was at a nadir. The Virginia general's disenchantment with his assignment "on loan" to the western army, from which he had personally expected so much, was very apparent. Following the initial euphoria of the bloody Chickamauga victory, Longstreet had found the elements of time and circumstance much against him.

At first, he had been so convinced that Rosecrans's beaten army would promptly retreat from Chattanooga across the Tennessee River that he directed a subordinate to send forward a patrol "to listen for the rumbling of their vehicles [on the bridges]." Longstreet's September 24 orders were for his scouts to gather information "by putting their ears to the ground and listening," so as to discover the enemy's evacuation. This, he estimated, would allow the Confederates to attack and thus "prevent the escape of their whole army across the river, or at least to save the bridges."[1]

Two days later, it was apparent Rosecrans was entrenching, and would not evacuate Chattanooga. The frustration of a squandered opportunity caused James Longstreet to complain bitterly in a private letter to Secretary of War James A. Seddon that Bragg "cannot adopt and adhere to any plan or course, whether his own or someone else['s]. . . . [I] pray you help us, and speedily."[2]

Although Longstreet asked that Robert E. Lee be sent west to command, he was well aware of his old commander's great resistance to leaving the Army of Northern Virginia. Indeed, it appears that Longstreet never seriously considered that Lee would come west. Instead, the transplanted Longstreet appears to have anticipated only his own elevation to command of Bragg's army.[3]

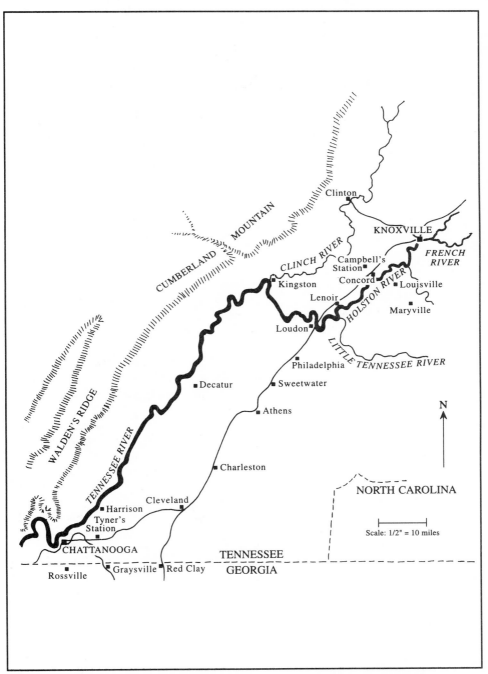

MAP 4 Chattanooga–East Tennessee Operations, October–November 1863
(*Source: O.R. Atlas, plates 149, 150*)

Specifically, Longstreet advocated offensive action. First, he proposed to advance northward and drive back Burnside's invading forces from east Tennessee. Should Burnside flee and escape, it was Longstreet's intention to swing westward against "Rosecrans's communications in the rear of Nashville." Although he had proposed this idea to Bragg as early as the morning of September 21, Bragg had vacillated in implementing Longstreet's plan, belatedly deciding instead to besiege Chattanooga.[4]

Although initially hopeful of shelling the enemy from their hastily prepared entrenchments after the heavy guns opened fire on September 25, Longstreet witnessed the impracticality of driving Rosecrans's troops from Chattanooga by artillery fire. These modified plans having thus fizzled, the irate eastern general again stewed with frustration.[5]

The following week, there was news of Jefferson Davis's pending visit, and with so many major subordinates conspiring to rid the army of Bragg, Longstreet anticipated a new opportunity to gain a personal victory based upon Bragg's discomfiture.

During Jefferson Davis's visit to the army, the prospects of Longstreet's taking command had been quickly dashed, causing Longstreet to bitterly reflect in his memoirs that discussions with Davis had been heated, and to little avail. Davis's stubborn reluctance to admit a mistake, and his rather callous personal treatment, thus rankled the increasingly despondent Longstreet.[6]

By this point, Bragg's resentment of Longstreet was fully evident. The North Carolinian's chief of staff reported the day before Jefferson Davis's departure, "Longstreet has done more injury to the general [Bragg] than all the others put together."[7]

Bragg's response was virtually to ignore Longstreet, who was assigned to the relatively remote Confederate left flank, on Lookout Mountain. Since the bitter feelings were mutual, a minimum of correspondence seems to have passed between the two headquarters during the critical mid-October period; it was carried on for the most part between Longstreet and Bragg's assistant adjutant general.[8]

During Davis's early October visit, Longstreet had revised his original plans to strike at east Tennessee, proposing instead specific plans to operate against the enemy's western flank in the vicinity of Bridgeport. Davis had not only endorsed this idea but anticipated its execution. Once Davis had departed, however, Bragg kept procrastinating, offering such excuses as "We cannot operate on our left for constant rains and bad roads." In fact, Bragg had no intention of adopting Longstreet's suggestion. In the face of mounting pressure from the administration, he had already made his decision to take action elsewhere.[9]

Longstreet's gloomy mood thus continued throughout the waning days of October. Writing to Bragg's headquarters about the detachment of a brigade that Beauregard wanted returned to the East Coast, Longstreet was obviously annoyed that an answer was not promptly forthcoming despite his expressed urgency. Then when Bragg removed Buckner's Division from its position adjacent to Longstreet's right flank on October 24, sending it to reinforce other troops without replacement, Longstreet protested, although to no avail. When the enemy seemed to threaten an attack beyond Longstreet's flank by sweeping south well below the north end of Lookout Mountain, Longstreet was at a loss to know what troops Bragg wished to utilize in countering this move. By early November, the absence of communications and the mutual mistrust permeating the relationship between the two ranking generals of the army only accentuated the disagreements in strategy and tactics that had long been evident.[10]

Despite his major personal victory in mid-October, Braxton Bragg found his days equally as vexing following Davis's visit. Having generally neglected many operational duties due to the political turmoil, Bragg finally had been compelled to cope with myriad problems, from directing the cavalry's operations to feeding and supplying his army. Even while accomplishing the purge of various subordinate generals, Bragg had begun seeking to replenish the depleted ranks of his infantry. Yet the burning issue occupying an increasing amount of the North Carolina commander's time was the growing Yankee threat from the northeast. The continuing occupation of east Tennessee by Ambrose Burnside's troops caused Bragg to complain and worry about a region beyond his immediate control and understanding.

For weeks, the Confederate commander in east Tennessee, Maj. Gen. Samuel Jones, had been dispatching reports of the enemy's activities in the region. Jones had been sent to the southwestern Virginia–east Tennessee border in early September to oversee the protection of the important saltworks and lead mines in that region. Instead of the expected cooperation from Maj. Gen. Simon B. Buckner's Division at Knoxville, Sam Jones was shocked to learn on September 6 that Buckner and his troops had departed from east Tennessee, having gone to Chattanooga to reinforce Bragg's army. Due to the advance of the enemy's columns under Burnside, Knoxville had fallen with but token resistance on September 2. Moreover, the sizable garrison at Cumberland Gap had been surrendered without a fight on September 9 by a frightened brigadier, John Wesley Frazer. Frazer had acted meekly, despite Jones's urgent orders to hold the position until reinforcements could go forward.[11]

Thereafter, Jones's woes had rapidly continued. With many of Burnside's 15,000 troops sweeping northward up the Holston River Valley toward Virginia, the beleaguered Jones, who had only about 2,800 men, had called repeatedly for help. Due to the threat to the salt and lead mines, the administration and Robert E. Lee responded quickly, sending several cavalry units and Brig. Gen. Montgomery D. Corse's Brigade from Pickett's Division of the Army of Northern Virginia. Before their arrival, however, Burnside had halted his northward advance in response to the disaster at Chickamauga. Sam Jones thus believed that Burnside was withdrawing to Knoxville, pending his expected march to relieve Rosecrans's besieged troops at Chattanooga.[12]

At this point, Jones had been so sanguine as to return Corse's Brigade to Lee, and he offered to send other troops to Virginia should they be needed. By pushing many of his main combat units forward into east Tennessee and garrisoning Greeneville in early October, Sam Jones anticipated the easy reoccupation of the northern end of the Holston River Valley.[13]

Within two weeks, Sam Jones had to swallow his pride and admit a serious mistake. The unpredictable Burnside had not marched to the relief of Chattanooga. Instead, the independent-minded Federal commander had decided to reconquer the northern Holston River Valley. Following the arrival about September 30 at Knoxville of six thousand men of his own Ninth Corps, previously sent on detached duty to Vicksburg, Mississippi, Burnside had resisted Lincoln's and Halleck's orders to go to the relief of Chattanooga. Instead, said Burnside, "I feel it my duty to first clear my left flank of the Rebel force there, and so destroy the railroad [East Tennessee and Virginia] and prevent the movement of any large force from Virginia." On October 9 Burnside had reinitiated an offensive in the direction of Greeneville.[14]

Little more than a week later, Burnside was back at Knoxville, proclaiming the defeat of Sam Jones's forces, which had been "driven . . . completely from the state [of Tennessee]."[15]

Sam Jones was so shocked by these events that he prepared to defend the saltworks at Saltville "to the last extremity," and he sought help from all directions, as "the emergency is great." Jones wrote to the Confederate secretary of war that "large reinforcements must be sent to this department, or much of this part of the state will be overrun by the enemy."[16]

Beyond the War Department's immediate return of Corse's Brigade to Jones, Braxton Bragg was provided with a copy of Sam Jones's telegram of October 15, in which he pleaded, "If you can send me any troops I beg you to do it." Bragg dutifully responded by sending a full division, Carter L. Stevenson's, up the valley railroad on October 17 "to threaten the enemy's rear . . . driving him back as far [as possible]."[17]

Sam Jones, who was puzzled to learn that very same day that Burnside had halted and many of his troops had withdrawn south in the valley, now began to consider that "it was not their purpose to attempt to hold any part of Southwestern Virginia." Accordingly, having initiated a beehive of activity, with Bragg's and other troops en route against Burnside in east Tennessee, Sam Jones contemplated a spur-of-the-moment offensive "to drive Burnside from East Tennessee." He told Bragg on October 22 that he would "move on the enemy as soon as practicable, which will be in two or three days."[18]

Braxton Bragg had been in a quandary ever since the departure of Jefferson Davis: What was his proper course of action, and how might he regain the lost Confederate initiative? With matters in a stalemate at Chattanooga, and considering the heavy pressure from the government to do something to regain Tennessee (so as to supply his army before the inclement weather intensified), Bragg was particularly receptive to alternative suggestions for active operations. On the preceding day, October 21, Bragg had learned of the success at Philadelphia, Tennessee, of cavalry cooperating with Carter Stevenson's troops, resulting in the capture of a reported seven hundred Federal cavalrymen and six field guns. Encouraged by the easy success of these troops and mindful of Jefferson Davis's instructions to act before myriad advancing Federal reinforcements arrived at Chattanooga, Bragg impulsively embraced Jones's pending plan for an east Tennessee offensive. On the night of October 22, he sent Brig. Gen. John K. Jackson's Division to reinforce Stevenson for operations against Burnside from the south. Bragg was so enthusiastic about this hastily conceived scheme, now termed an "expedition," on October 24 he ordered the main part of Wheeler's cavalry corps to the far right flank at Cleveland, Tennessee, to act in concert.[19]

Despite Jefferson Davis's mid-October endorsement of the Longstreet plan to operate in the Bridgeport region—which had been discussed in detail—Bragg, incredibly, opted for an impromptu scheme with little substantive planning or reasonable hopes of important success. Like many of Bragg's previous knee-jerk decisions, the Bragg-Jones east Tennessee operation fizzled out in less than a week. Stevenson's forces advanced to the Little Tennessee River at Loudon, Tennessee, but were blocked there by parts of the Federal Twenty-third and Ninth Corps, an estimated 10,000 infantry and 2,500 cavalry. To the north, Sam Jones failed to advance beyond Carter's Station and Kingsport, along the line of the Holston and Watauga rivers.[20]

As it turned out, Jones was relying on more troops being sent from the Army of Northern Virginia. Bragg's naïve concepts about the practicality of this impromptu joint offensive were thus exposed by Davis on October 29 when he warned the Army of Tennessee's commander, "My recollection of his [Jones's] condition does not permit me to hope that he will be able to effect much in East Tennessee. . . . General Lee cannot, I am sure, add materially to the force now serving under General Jones." Bragg, having lurched into a dubious undertaking, was faced with the prospect of another failure. By October 30, Jones informed Bragg: "I cannot move my infantry beyond the Holston [River—due to insufficient strength]." Instead, he would use his cavalry "to make raids" and, "if practicable, collect cattle and hogs." It was a major disappointment, and far from what Bragg had expected.[21]

Despite what was rapidly developing into another embarrassing Confederate campaign fiasco, Bragg at this point was the recipient of some unexpected and unsolicited help: the misguided efforts of Ambrose Burnside. As a result of Bragg having sent Stevenson up the railroad to Cleveland to relieve the pressure on Sam Jones, Burnside had reacted with great alarm. Following the loss of several outposts south of the Little Tennessee River, Burnside withdrew from Loudon across the river and fretted about "the very heavy force" threatening him.[22]

As a result of Henry Halleck's belief on October 24 that "Ewell's corps, from 20,000 to 25,000 men, has left [Robert E.] Lee's army and gone to [east] Tennessee," Burnside abandoned all thought of moving to Chattanooga. He did not want "to be caught on the south side of the Tennessee River" and said he was "not strong enough [with only about 30,000 troops present]" to attack Bragg in flank. Instead, he would withdraw all garrisons and outposts from the south side of the Tennessee River and attempt to hold only that portion of east Tennessee he now occupied. In essence, Burnside had opted for a strategic defensive as a result of two defensive moves by the Confederates: the sending of Corse's Brigade from Lee's army, which was mistakenly believed to be an entire corps, and Bragg's dispatch of Stevenson's Division to threaten Burnside's western flank and thereby halt his offensive up the Holston River Valley.[23]

To Bragg, however, Sam Jones's plea on October 30 for an additional force in east Tennessee was most opportune. Considering the rapidly deteriorating relationship with James Longstreet and in view of the nearly played-out offensive into east Tennessee, a timely opportunity existed to rid himself of the distasteful Longstreet and, as well, rescue the stalled Sam Jones–inspired offensive. To add to the intrigue, a complete fail-safe reason existed for the decision to continue the impulsive east Tennessee campaign: Bragg had Jefferson Davis's tacit approval.[24]

On October 29, after hearing of Hooker's movement from Bridgeport to reinforce Grant, Davis, then at Atlanta, Georgia, expressed his anticipation of Bragg striking this column before it approached Chattanooga. Yet due to Bragg's recent assertion that heavy rains had "interfered" with the Davis-proposed and -endorsed operation toward Bridgeport, the Confederate president, as an alternative, suggested the practicality of sending Longstreet with two divisions into east Tennessee "to expel Burnside." Although Davis continued to expect Bragg to attack the enemy column moving eastward from the vicinity of Bridgeport, Bragg was thwarted in making a major effort in this direction, especially following another Longstreet controversy, which occurred at Wauhatchie on the night of October 28 to 29.[25]

In fact, Bragg was already committed to a significant east Tennessee offensive. On October 24, he had transferred Wheeler's cavalry from the Alabama region to the opposite flank to aid in the east Tennessee expedition. With two divisions already present in the northern valley and Wheeler en route, Bragg was not anxious to reverse the plan. This was especially true given the fact that the Longstreet-devised Bridgeport plan had been personally presented by that despised general to Jefferson Davis.[26]

Due to the events of the past few days involving Longstreet's surrendering control of Lookout Valley and the south bank of the Tennessee River to the enemy, Bragg's options were greatly reduced. In fact, the movement of Hooker's troops into Lookout Valley on October 28 and the failure at Wauhatchie that night effectively eliminated the practicality of a Confederate movement in the direction of Bridgeport. As such, these events only greatly elevated Bragg's determination "to get rid of" the troublesome Longstreet.[27]

By November 3, rumors of Longstreet's pending detachment to east Tennessee were already circulating in camp. In fact, on October 31, Bragg had decided to utilize Jefferson Davis's remarkable suggestion as the basis for expanding the previously improvised expedition into east Tennessee.[28]

To justify his actions further, in several dispatches to Davis, Bragg chided Longstreet for "disobedience of orders and slowness of movements" plus "gross neglect resulting in a most serious disaster." On October 31, Bragg included in his indictment mention of receiving "disrespectful and insubordinate" correspondence from Longstreet. Sending Longstreet to east Tennessee would be a "great relief to me," admitted the calculating Bragg.[29]

Although James Longstreet apparently did not anticipate this development, he was called to Bragg's headquarters about November 3 and the plan was outlined for him. Despite much subsequent controversy over what was said in this council of war, it is quite apparent that the impulsive decision to send Longstreet into east Tennessee was an expediency—rooted in the emotionally charged hatred of Bragg and Longstreet for each other, as well as in the need to take offensive action. As Davis had outlined in his letter to Bragg of October 29, he would not consider the "further removal of general officers from their commands" but, instead, "must leave you to combat the difficulties arising from the disappointment or the discontent of officers by such . . . means as may turn them aside." In substance, Davis's edict meant Bragg was stuck with Longstreet unless he was detached from the army.[30]

Moreover, although a huge gamble and an unconventional decision, ostensibly the Longstreet east Tennessee movement allowed Bragg to satisfy the administration's demands that he promptly begin offensive operations. Furthermore, in case of a disaster, there was the added safeguard of placing ultimate responsibility for the specific plan on Davis. To Longstreet, who disagreed with its practicality at this late date, it was, nonetheless, a chance to escape the vengeful and incompetent Bragg and perhaps win new laurels.

That dividing his forces in the face of near-at-hand and overwhelming enemy reinforcements would be inviting disaster was evidently overlooked by Bragg at the time. Bragg's ad hoc plan was impelled by false premises, motivated as it was by the need to rid himself of lurking opponents. Ulysses S. Grant later observed that Bragg and Davis seemed to be collaborating on the basis of political expediency without due regard to the practical consequences: "[Jefferson] Davis had an exalted opinion of his own military genius. . . . On several occasions during the war he came to the relief of the Union army by means of his 'superior military genius.' "[31]

A facetious Grant notwithstanding, Bragg considered the east Tennessee offensive as an impending major blow against the Federal rear. What Bragg envisioned is alluded to in his letter of instructions to Longstreet of November 4: Wheeler's cavalry was "thoroughly acquainted" not only with east Tennessee but "Middle Tennessee, and many of the officers with him will know the route there." But first, Longstreet was to "drive Burnside out of east Tennessee, or better, to capture or destroy him" with the cooperation of Sam Jones.[32]

Clearly, Bragg was grasping at a viable plan. On November 5, Longstreet wrote to his friend Simon B. Buckner (who had been displaced from his former east Tennessee command), telling him that following Chickamauga he had considered it best to concentrate all forces in the local region, then send twenty thousand men to "move rapidly against Burnside and destroy him." "By continued rapid movements," the Confederates would thereafter threaten the enemy's rear so as "to draw him out" of Chattanooga. Yet, more than a month later, Bragg, after "wait[ing] till all good opportunities had passed," had "in desperation" seized upon "the least favorable" option. By sending Longstreet to east Tennessee with 12,000 men the army couldn't spare in its present circumstances, Bragg was risking failure on both fronts. There was "no chance to ourselves of great results [from this plan]," concluded the grim Longstreet.[33]

There was more. Bragg had scoffed at Longstreet's concern that the enemy could concentrate his masses "within twelve minutes march of any portion of our line" and successfully assault the too-long Confederate lines, which were to remain "as they now are." "I was assured that he [the enemy] would not disturb us," Longstreet later remembered. However, despite his many misgivings, as the east Tennessee movement would give the "promise of some result," it was "therefore better than lying here destroying ourselves [due to Bragg's incompetent leadership]," he concluded.[34]

On November 4, the day following the crucial Bragg-Longstreet council of war, James Longstreet's troops were ordered to prepare to embark on their east Tennessee offensive. "Every preparation is ordered to advance you as fast as possible," wrote Braxton Bragg, "and the success of the plan depends on rapid movements and sudden blows." Since James Longstreet was so rushed and ill-prepared, many details of the movement remained undefined. Indeed, Longstreet was first under the impression that Stevenson's Division, then at Loudon, would cooperate and form a part of the "expedition." Also, Longstreet had no specific knowledge of the size or locations of the enemy force he would face. By relying on the railroad for transportation, he hoped to avoid using his own ordnance and supply trains, which were drawn "by feeble animals" and lacked harnesses and equipment.[35]

On November 5, while embarking at Tyner's Station, Longstreet learned that Stevenson's Division would be immediately recalled to Bragg's army. Moreover, Bragg's instructions were to repair and rebuild the railroad to east Tennessee en route, which would considerably slow the anticipated rapid movement to "destroy" Burnside.[36]

Just how ill-prepared Longstreet was for a major offensive was revealed as early as November 8. Having reportedly been promised by Bragg that "preparations were already made, or would be made for all our wants," an alarmed Longstreet learned to his dismay that supply trains were not available, nor would they be soon forthcoming as his troops advanced northward. Moreover, on the ninth he learned that the enemy force opposed to him was 23,000, rather than the estimated 15,000 Bragg had suggested. Now outnumbered by the enemy he was supposed to drive away or destroy, Longstreet began a long series of daily dispatches to Bragg, complaining about everything from being delayed in moving north on the single-track railroad by Stevenson's troops moving south to a shortage of meat rations.[37]

Soon pressed by Bragg for a more rapid movement, Longstreet lashed out in anger. In reporting "the entire failure of the preparations ordered by you," he told Bragg on November 11, "My troops could have marched up in half the time that has been consumed in transporting them by rail. . . . Instead of being prepared to make a campaign, I find myself not more than half prepared to subsist." Longstreet acknowledged that his movement had been delayed, "but not by myself." Bragg's empty promises were to blame, he asserted, adding, "As soon as I find a probability of moving without almost certain starvation, I shall move, providing the troops are up." Give me another division, Longstreet urged, as "with the force that I now have I think it would be unreasonable to expect much."[38]

On the very same day, November 11, Braxton Bragg responded by reporting to Adj. Gen. Samuel Cooper in Richmond, Virginia, that Longstreet "ought to be over the Tennessee. But I hear nothing from him." That day, he had also written to Longstreet that he was unwilling to forward any additional reinforcements to east Tennessee, since "Sherman's force, fully 20,000, is now within six days' march" of Chattanooga, "[and] any further detachments from here [are] impracticable." Bragg's duplicity was thus fully evident. Within days, Jefferson Davis wrote to Bragg that "the failure of General Longstreet to keep you advised of his operations is unaccountable."[39]

Braxton Bragg was fully enjoying the discomfiture of his enemies. On the evening of November 14, he penned a brief note to his wife, stating that he had been vindicated by recent events. Reflecting his smug, ebullient mood, Bragg grandly described to his wife the lavish view from his headquarters on Missionary Ridge, saying, "No scene in the most splendid theatre ever approached it."[40]

James Longstreet, in contrast, assessed the bleak view from his headquarters at Sweet Water, Tennessee, on November 14. On the eve of active operations against Burnside, he wrote: "We know nothing of the enemy, as we have not been able to advance far enough today to see anything of him." Having just received the last of his troops and artillery on the night of the twelfth, Longstreet's mood was as somber as the blustery, cloudy skies overhead as he prepared to embark on this uncertain offensive. "There are many reasons for anticipating great results from the expedition against General Burnside's army with a proper force," he asserted, "but . . . [due to a lack of strength] it will, in all probability, be another fine opportunity lost." The "force now here is not strong enough to make any such effort . . . with any reasonable hope of success," Longstreet reflected. However, revealing his ulterior motive, he continued, "With the balance of my corps or any good marching division, I think that we may make a great campaign."[41]

Unfortunately for Longstreet, Braxton Bragg's idea of a great campaign had already been fulfilled. The likes of James Longstreet had been humiliated and banished to a lesser sphere. Bragg thus gloated to his wife on November 14: "My friends are aroused, and even the soldiers and inferior officers are coming out [for me]. . . . I am infinitely stronger than ever with my army."[42]

PART TWO

The MEN

CHAPTER 10

"ONE OF THE WILDEST
PLACES YOU EVER SAW"

The city of Chattanooga [is] a gay place with plenty of shoulder straps dashing around on hungry horses," wrote an Illinois soldier in parody of the dismal circumstances in which the Federal Army of the Cumberland had suddenly found itself. "Chattanooga . . . is a dirty, nasty, irregular town," mused a disgruntled Wisconsin volunteer wandering about in the aftermath of Chickamauga. Another scornful Federal agreed, saying he found the place to be "a shabby little town of few houses." "Any Indian house is better, more comfortable, and cleaner [than those here]," scoffed a full-blooded Seneca on Grant's staff. A disillusioned Minnesota sergeant noted that "Chattanooga is barren of anything worth having." Many of the inhabitants had previously fled, acknowledged a local minister, and only some women and children and a few families seemed to remain.[1]

Although in 1860, Chattanooga had been a bustling commercial village of 2,546 (including 451 blacks), Ulysses S. Grant discovered upon his arrival in late October 1863 that it was a town devoid of populace. "There are but very few people here and those few will have to leave soon," he told his wife. Noting the muddy, winter-barren mountain terrain and the isolated nature of this railroad village, now without running railroads, Grant cracked, "This is one of the wildest places you ever saw."[2]

A former Indian trading village once known as Ross's Landing, Chattanooga had fallen on evil days by 1863. The town of Chattanooga "must have been a nice place in times of peace," observed an Illinois officer, who was thoroughly amazed at the large network of railroad switches and side tracks at the southern end of town. Huge depots, warehouses, and two foundries dominated the scene, reflecting Chattanooga's status as a burgeoning railroad and industrial site before the Civil War.[3]

It was the railroads that had changed the town's destiny. Due to their influence, Chattanooga had become popularly known as "the gateway to the South." Located in the southeastern corner of Tennessee, and in close proximity to the borders of Georgia and Alabama, the village on the east side of the great horseshoe bend in the Tennessee River had been crisscrossed during the 1850s with a compass-circling grid of railroads. By 1861, connections to the great seaports of the East, the industrial cities of the North, and the flourishing commercial towns of the South were direct or easy. Another railroad line ran west to Memphis, while a popular valley route stretched toward Knoxville. At nearby Bridgeport, Alabama, the connecting railroad to Nashville joined the western route, completing the intrastate communications link with Tennessee's important cities.[4]

In prewar days, a visitor to Chattanooga had found the village bustling with commercial activity, amid swarms of people "with eager looks, as if lives [and] fortunes . . . hung upon the events of the next hour." Amid the dozens of trains constantly coming and going, investors and speculators in earnest conversation stood in corners of buildings, some handling bundles of paper, others examining maps. Rolls of banknotes were flashed and gold glistened from silk mesh purses. Everywhere there were animated conversations, with passersby hearing the words *stocks, quarter sections, dividends, railroads, ten thousands, hundred thousands, millions.*[5]

Wartime had brought a prolonged season of despair, noted the Reverend Dr. Thomas H. McCallie, the sole remaining local civilian minister following Chattanooga's September 9, 1863, occupation by the Federal army. "All without was winter. It was winter in the city and winter in the state. War had devastated everything," he sadly noted. His Presbyterian church on Market Street had been converted on September 21, 1863, into a hospital. Pews were torn out, cots installed, and hundreds of wounded Federals from the Chickamauga battlefield covered the floor. Confusion and chaos reigned in the city. Civil authority was suspended; stores and markets were closed. The town became white with a sea of tents, including a few sutler's shelters, which contained but little merchandise. There was barely enough food—no milk, no butter, no cheese, and hardly any fruit for the town's remaining populace. For sustenance, the citizens relied on bacon, bread, what salted meat and pickles they had preserved in barrels from earlier times, and a little coffee. Most families remained indoors. As the siege of Chattanooga progressed, an insidious despair had settled over the community.[6]

With the approach of the Confederate army on September 22, various outlying residences had been burned due to military expediency. The Federal commanders wanted no place of refuge for enemy sharpshooters between the lines, or a restricted view of Rebel positions. As a result, the blackened chimneys of once-prosperous residences stood stark against a sky hazy with smoke, noted a Federal lieutenant on the morning after the burning.[7]

Within the village, municipal buildings of every type had been appropriated for military use. Private dwellings became the personal residences of high-ranking officers, often being utilized as their headquarters. One church was soon converted into an arsenal. Only a single house of worship, the Catholic chapel, was not disturbed—by special order of General Rosecrans, who was a devout Catholic.[8]

Everywhere there was the relentless turmoil of war. Several hundred bales of confiscated cotton were fashioned into mattresses for the wounded. Old earthworks and fortifications were enlarged and new forts sprang up almost overnight. Shade trees, shrubbery, picket fences, and outbuildings were felled or torn down for kindling. So many stately trees were downed that by 1865 only fifty-one shade trees remained standing in the city. Then, with the advent of cold winter weather, so desperate for fuel became the multitude of soldiers that servants' quarters, smokehouses, doors from residences, and even household furniture were taken.[9]

Chattanooga's wretched facade had become all-pervasive. The town was only a dingy military camp, with the rights of citizens humbled, regardless of wealth or social standing. Many remaining townspeople were ordered to leave the city. Go north or go south, they were told, but leave Chattanooga.[10]

For good reason, many had already left in despair. A Yankee enlisted man was amazed to discover in one house the family's only calf and a disassembled board fence piled inside the parlor to protect them from pillage. "There is not a pig running loose inside our lines," he joked. Chattanooga was devoid of commercial activity, especially since most inhabitants were required to stay in their homes. A few managed to work for the Federal army, being paid in food, which was "the way the Rebels get their rights," decreed an unsympathetic soldier. Shrugging off all the manifest misery and squalor, Pvt. Bliss Morse of the 105th Ohio mused, "I suppose it [Chattanooga] looks no worse than many other Southern towns our army has been in."[11]

All of this agony and ordeal had been presaged, some said, by the meteor episode of 1860. Amid the presidential campaign of that summer and fall, various political speakers, including Stephen A. Douglas, had visited Chattanooga to address the citizens. During one of the frequent political speeches of that year, a meteor had streaked across the sky, breaking into two parts. Word soon spread that it was of ominous portent; the country would split into two halves. Chattanooga thereafter had suffered much. And now there was only more misery in the offing.[12]

Chattanooga's desolation was accentuated by its natural isolation. A large semicircle of mountain ridges and towering peaks overlooked the huge adjacent loop in the Tennessee River known as Moccasin Point (so named due to its shape, which resembled an Indian moccasin). Massive Raccoon Mountain guarded the approach to Chattanooga from the west, but it was Lookout Mountain, rising 2,146 feet above sea level, that was the dominant feature above the town. At its abrupt termination overlooking the southern bend of Moccasin Point, the face of Lookout Mountain loomed above Chattanooga, which was located about three miles from the summit. The strange Native American name Chattanooga was of ancient origin, said to be derived from an Indian name for Lookout Mountain—"Chatto-to-noo-gee" (a Creek term for "rock coming to a point" or "end of the mountain").[13]

Adjacent Lookout Valley on the west and Chattanooga Valley to the east were broad carpets of timber and farmland stretching as far as the eye could see northeast and southwest. East of Chattanooga, forming a barrier wall along the Chattanooga Valley at a distance of about three miles from the center of town, was imposing Missionary Ridge. Its heights rose irregularly about six hundred feet above the town, being broken only by the Rossville Gap south of Chattanooga and the terminus of Missionary Ridge northeast, where the Tennessee River flowed through. North of Chattanooga, beyond the twisting course of the mighty Tennessee River, which ran east and then northeast, stood Walden's Ridge, a rugged spur of the historic Cumberland Mountains.

Only twenty-five years after its founding, Chattanooga was surrounded on all sides by barren heights that served as a mute witness to the rapid despoliation brought by mankind. Although there once had been vast stands of tall trees, much of the region's centuries-old natural environment had been marred by the industrial, commercial, and finally military activities emanating from Chattanooga. The Civil War had only accentuated this effect; more timber had been felled, resulting in the land having been denuded across vast portions of the landscape. Hovering over the valley and blanketing the city, a haze of sooty smoke and dust often marked the town's site. One Tennessee soldier peering down from Missionary Ridge on September 27 found so much smoke obscuring his view that he couldn't even see Chattanooga. Another disgusted Confederate soldier noted on September 22 that a great dust cloud concealed much of both the town and the Tennessee River.[14]

Despite the anguish of the city, it wasn't the abandoned and rusting railroads or the stark blight of vacant commercial buildings and run-down warehouses that dominated every scene. Chattanooga, even in its darkest hour, was truly unique; the abundant quality of the setting offered a panorama of great beauty. From the lofty surrounding mountains, the scenery was so grand that many soldiers found it breathtaking.

The view of the Chattanooga Valley from the heights west of town was so impressive, a sergeant of the 34th Illinois Infantry wrote: "The valley [was] so far, far down that I could scarcely believe it was not a picture. I have often tried to imagine how the earth would appear to a person elevated thousands of feet. . . . As I stood on the mountain looking down into the valley I realized what imagination had failed to paint in true colors. A silver thread marked the course of the Tennessee [River] for miles until it was lost amid the dim blue mountain that bounded [one's] vision." Rugged mountains, so gigantic that the railroad tracks that ran below were minuscule lines across the valley, impressed even an engineer accustomed to scenic geography. Indeed, from various locations in the mountains, a sightseer could see forty or fifty miles, including three states, concluded another soldier.[15]

From a distance, the sights around Chattanooga were often magnificent, if not awesome. "At night," as a Confederate brigadier general, Arthur M. Manigault, observed, ". . . when all the campfires were lighted, the effect was grand and imposing." In the quiet of the evening, Manigault would sit on a prominent rock, admiring the impressive scene, "thinking of home [and] family," and pondering the future. To a young lieutenant of the 19th U.S. Infantry, the same sights from a knoll in the valley were equally compelling. The campfires appeared like "some great city illuminated" for the celebration of a holiday event, he wrote.[16]

The ground had been upheaved in long, irregular ridges, angled and serpentine in contour. Great earthen shapes disfigured the once-placid valley landscape. Nearly overnight, the scenery had vastly changed. Along the eastern and southern perimeter of Chattanooga, a network of forts and earthwork parapets jutted above the pick- and shovel-scarred terrain. "They fairly grow out of the earth," wrote an exhausted Federal private. Work details on the fortifications were long and arduous, continuing throughout the night during the period immediately following the Battle of Chickamauga. "Down go many fine houses this morning in order to make way for [earth]works," indifferently observed an Illinois artilleryman.[17]

At first, it had been feared the Confederates would make a frontal attack. At least some of Rosecrans's generals feared as much. This translated into dozens of false alarms and sleepless nights for many of the men, even for those behind the front lines. Nervous over the distant sound of train whistles coming from Chickamauga Station, many troops spread rumors that Bragg was being reinforced from Robert E. Lee's eastern army. "One has serious meditations laying in line of battle waiting momentarily for an attack," wrote an apprehensive Federal lieutenant on September 21. "Visions of home and friends come before [me] with the enemy in front and a thundering fight in hand." Although the preparations for battle were no longer intimidating to him, the "whistling of a bullet causes one to duck his head involuntarily," acknowledged the officer.[18]

Bragg's troops had moved up to invest the city on September 22, and beyond the sporadic roar of artillery fire that sent prolonged echoes along the sides of Lookout Mountain, the sharp crackle of skirmish and picket firing was commonplace. Yet once behind their hastily constructed earthworks, many of Rosecrans's men seemed sanguine and hopeful despite the recent debacle at Chickamauga. "Our army is all together again and in good order. Let them come on and God grant us the victory," wrote twenty-one-year-old Chesley Mosman, a lieutenant in the 59th Illinois Infantry Regiment. The random fighting along the front lines soon degenerated into scattered sniper firing, and aside from patrols or a few probing reconnaissances by small units, there were only occasional blasts of cannon fire to shatter the gathering quiet.[19]

On September 22, Rosecrans's outer lines were withdrawn to a semicircular three-mile-long perimeter about Chattanooga, extending a little more than two miles inland from the Tennessee River at its deepest point. This became the basic Union defensive line that was soon regarded by Charles A. Dana as impregnable to frontal attack. "When the inner fortifications are completed, 10,000 men could hold this place against the world," confided Dana in a message to the secretary of war. An observant Federal officer agreed, writing in his journal on September 23, "If the Johnnies are to attack us at all, they should do it at once, before the works are made too strong."[20]

Although several nervous-appearing generals were seen riding along the lines, peering through field glasses at the Rebel positions, only the low-lying haze and fog had advanced toward the Federal works that day. Sweating work details continued to labor on the breastworks, with twenty or thirty men often being required to lift and place a log in its proper position. "We have been fortifying here since last Tuesday morning [September 22]," wrote an increasingly confident soldier the following Monday. "We have worked hard at it . . . day and night, and it still goes on. . . . I am inclined to think that 'old Bragg' will not attempt to retake this place."[21]

Noting the various thirty-two-pounder siege cannon being mounted in Fort Wood and Fort Negley, an Ohio private informed his family at home that "our cannon peer out in all directions. . . . In front of Thomas's Corps it is an open field and should the Rebels make the atack they will get a raking fire on all sides. They never can come up in front of our breastwork[s] alive. We can sweep them off right and left."[22]

The soldiers' intuition—based upon the hard-earned wisdom of the front lines—soon proved to be correct. For days, the Confederate army languished behind their own improvised breastworks and made little sign of a general assault.

Once the initial concerns about a Rebel attack had abated, the men began to regard their circumstances and the results of the past few weeks in a different light. "We do not feel exactly whipped," announced a Federal soldier to his family on October 2, "neither do [we] feel we gained nothing. For we should have had a fight anyway to get this place. We have it to their sorrow. It is so much gained. I hope we can hold it. Let the reinforcements come." Another rejuvenated Federal noted the strong "works of every description" surrounding Chattanooga and wrote: "If they [Rebels] would only come in or try to drive us out we would be satisfied, for we could slaughter them by the wholesale." An Illinois enlisted man, impressed by the rows of imposing cannon guarding the Union perimeter, scoffed, "There is no danger of an attack [here], or rather no hope of one." "What few there are left of Longstreet's Corps are perfectly willing to go back to the Potomac, for Old Rosy's boys just whipped the conceit right out of them," reported a high-spirited Federal private on September 28.[23]

All of this was heavy irony. The attitude of well-being was soon revealed as so much false euphoria following a narrow escape from disaster. There were so many difficulties burdening the Federal army at Chattanooga that concern about a direct enemy attack was among the least worrisome. In fact, as the days and weeks progressed, it was the soul of the Federal army that was in doubt. The men and their leaders were to be tested psychologically to the fullest extreme. Instead of the prospect of facing an attack from behind well-prepared entrenchments, it was soon manifest that the bloodied and beaten Army of the Cumberland must attack the surrounding heights in order to survive.

Thus, in early October 1863, the crucial war for the minds and bodies of the soldiers on both sides had but fairly begun. The surrounding mountains were imposing an insidious fate. They were majestic barriers and yet a logistic curse. If they protected, they equally denied. If they provided a staging area for attack, they also impeded offensive operations. It was a great dilemma, but all very simple. The issue would turn on the practical coming or going. For the Union army in the fall of 1863, Chattanooga was not the gateway to the South; it was only a great wall.

CHAPTER 11

"AIN'T THAT A QUEER
KIND OF WAR?"

It may be chivalrous to stand up in an open field and be shot at," wrote Sgt. Ralsa C. Rice of the 125th Ohio Infantry, "but in our minds it was no indication of superior bravery. [Physical] protection, if no more than a pile of rails, was something to 'tie to.' " As Sergeant Rice later explained, "A breastwork, however slight, has a formidable look. All this came to our army intuitively and we were hardly encamped at Chattanooga before fortifying became a mania."[1]

Rice's comments were a revealing testimonial. The soldiers at Chattanooga in 1863 were no longer military innocents, inexperienced and unknowing. To stand up in line of battle and fight it out with an equally unprotected enemy was totally unrealistic, a bad idea, and against all common sense. The advent of superior defensive technology, including the rifle musket, canister, and effective explosive artillery shells had dictated the mode of warfare early in the Civil War. Frontal attacks against well-defended entrenched positions were seldom successful. The men on both sides knew it, many of their officers understood it, and some of the generals believed it. Yet mostly it was the soldiers who served in the front lines who lived and breathed this critical adage. They were the ones who paid the heavy toll in blood.

Following the Chickamauga defeat, the Federal army had reacted instinctively at Chattanooga. "This propensity to entrench became a part of our discipline," acknowledged a veteran infantryman. It was a simple matter of survival. With formidable fortifications such as Fort Wood and Fort Negley guarding the approaches to the town, even Braxton Bragg readily understood the impracticality of a direct assault. As the logical consequence of so much earlier bloodshed, the evolving battlefield was no longer assessed in simple topographical terms. By 1863, the extent and nature of the enemy's entrenchments or fortifications was the premise upon which key tactical decisions were made in both armies. Strategy had been duly effected. Maneuver, outflanking one's enemy, and the application of military pressure against an opponent's logistics were not only a primary reliance but the new way of thinking.[2]

Tactically, Rosecrans's troops were soon confident of Chattanooga's safety from direct attack due to their extensive fortifications. Likewise, Bragg and his officers regarded the full-scale occupation of the surrounding heights as a superior military position, precluding the prospect of a large Federal frontal assault. Thus, it seemed apparent to both armies that strategy rather than tactics would be the decisive factor in the loss or successful defense of Chattanooga.

The men responded accordingly.

The rather sharp fighting on the evening of September 24 and 25, involving units of Maj. Gen. James S. Negley's and Brig. Gen. Jefferson C. Davis's divisions, was part of several alarming post-Chickamauga flare-ups along the outer lines in front of Missionary Ridge. Several of Davis's regiments, the 22nd Indiana and 74th Illinois, probing beyond the banks of Chattanooga Creek on September 24, were suddenly ambushed and outflanked. Following a quick pullback, the affair degenerated into an artillery duel. The following evening, some of Davis's other troops were attacked from the cover of the opposite bank. Although a few Confederate troops pursued in the momentary confusion, they were soon driven back across the narrow creek. On the twenty-sixth, a dawn skirmish between picket lines in front of the Twenty-first Corps resulted in a flesh wound to Maj. Gen. John M. Palmer while he stood at an embrasure in Redan Palmer.[3]

Although only a few soldiers had been shot in these incidents, each day the general alarm had been sounded within the Federal lines. With units of both armies maneuvering in line of battle, artillery duels had been common. Rebel shells from Lookout Mountain fell in such profusion on September 25 that a soldier thought the ground had been sewn with them.

All of this fuss had amounted to little; it was soon recognized by many as so much random shooting. "All our men returned to the lines and things settled down to their old state," dryly noted an Illinois lieutenant. Finally, after eight straight days in line of battle with their equipment on, the men of the 5th Kentucky Infantry on the night of September 25 were able to pull off their accoutrements and rest.[4]

Two days later, the soldiers began to have it more their way.

It began on September 27, with a truce arranged following Rosecrans's request of the twenty-sixth for the recovery of Federal wounded from the Chickamauga battlefield. Braxton Bragg's reply on the twenty-seventh authorized the Federal commander to send a train of ambulances and hospital supplies to the relief of the thousands of Northern wounded overflowing the battlefield. The trains would be driven to the Confederate lines by Federal teamsters and turned over to their gray counterparts, who would then take the ambulances to the Chickamauga battlefield. There the Confederates would load the Federal wounded and return to the front lines, turning them over to the Federals as paroled prisoners of war. It was a calculating gesture on the part of Bragg, who sought the exchange of an equal number of uninjured Confederates, yet he knew at the very least it was a means of obtaining food and medical attention for the thousands of injured Yankees as well as removing the burden of their care. Bragg's logistic operations were hopelessly overwhelmed, and the few surgeons and medical attendants had insufficient medicines. By mutual agreement, during the several days' journey of the ambulance train, the pickets on both sides were ordered not to fire at one another.[5]

The importance of this truce as a subtle opportunity for the soldiers to chat and interact with their opponents was soon realized by troops in both armies. All along the lines, there were frank and practical discussions among both armies' rank and file. On the twenty-seventh, a Federal officer wrote how he was able to take a bath in Chattanooga Creek, within plain sight of a Rebel picket. "As he was so amiable, I went out to talk to him," wrote Lt. Chesley Mosman in his journal. "He didn't feel elated over the battle and says, 'we didn't whip you fellows much.' " One of Longstreet's men, the enemy picket acknowledged that they had found a big difference between eastern and western Yankees.[6]

Matters soon went beyond sociability. Some of the troops agreed that as an extension of the existing ambulance truce there would be no further shooting along the picket lines unless the other side made a general advance. This arrangement spread along the front lines until a general "understanding" prevailed. A Regular officer, a lieutenant in the 18th U.S. Infantry, described with amazement in a letter home the remarkable change that had occurred. "When we first took our position here after the battle [of Chickamauga] the pickets would have to lay down and keep under cover . . . for if he stuck his head up . . . a bullet would be sent after him." Since the lines were in places only about one hundred yards apart, under the new no-shooting arrangement, "They exchange papers, and even go down between the lines and have a social talk," he observed. To Lieutenant Mosman, the informal truce was appropriate. It "seems wrong to murder a fellow for not doing anything offensive," he acknowledged. "Instead of shooting at them we talk to them and ask them to come over to our side of the creek for a chat and a game of euchre."[7]

With the idle pickets in full view of one another on the evening of September 29, the returning ambulance train of about two hundred wagons loaded with 1,742 Federal wounded rumbled through the lines to the tune of bands playing at Fort Negley. Chesley Mosman found pickets from the 6th South Carolina Infantry in his front. To his surprise, they were "a fine, handsome, stout lot of fellows, better dressed than we are, their uniforms being apparently new." With soldiers from both armies filling their canteens from the same creek, a lively trade in tobacco for coffee and the exchange of newspapers was in progress. When Lieutenant Mosman found several privates from the 74th Illinois playing cards with the Johnnies, he recorded in his journal: "Ain't that a queer kind of war?"[8]

Another soldier, a member of the 85th Illinois, discussed the general situation with a nearby Confederate picket. "Say boys," said the Rebel, "this is all a damned piece of foolishness. Let's all quit and go home." The Yank benevolently agreed in principle, admitting that there was "some truth in that." As a Confederate captain noted, "If the terms of peace had been left to the men who faced each other in battle day after day, they would have stopped the war at once on terms acceptable to both sides."[9]

The common sense–inspired "no random small-arms firing" agreement soon became all-pervasive in front of Chattanooga and beyond, spreading to the fords up and down the Tennessee River. Friendly exchanges of goods, impromptu discussions, and innocuous fraternization, once begun, continued in no-man's-land throughout the siege, despite the uneasiness of many officers. It was perhaps a reflection of the veteran soldiers' practical attitude about what too often had become unnecessary fighting and killing. The men knew that the outcome of the campaign would not hinge on the death or maiming of a few front-line soldiers by snipers or in small-unit skirmishes.

This much-expressed "spirit of fairness and friendliness" extended to an enemy soldier who in battle would soon endeavor to kill his opponent may seem strange in the modern context. Yet as a practical arrangement, the lives of the men and the stress they endured was far less traumatic under the "no random firing" agreement. Also, there was the element of maturing perspectives. The all-consuming war fervor of 1861 had evolved; the fighting was now the physical means to a political end. In the prevailing Northern perspective, it was not an armed crusade against the Southern people. A particularly thoughtful Federal soldier acknowledged in a letter home: "One of the boys in my company was out and talked with them [Rebels], he traded his pipe and pocket knife to them for tobacco. It is strange that they will talk to one another one moment and maybe the next they may be in deadly conflict with each other. As for my part, I begin to think it is time for this thing [war] to stop. We have seen enough of men butchered."[10]

The sobering reality came in the form of a distant flash of fire and a dull puff of smoke, a count to five, then the resonating boom of a distant detonation. Prolonged reverberations momentarily echoed along the timbered mountain wall, terminating in the low-velocity whir of an incoming heavy projectile. Finally, there was a thunderclap burst and a dirty cloud of flame and smoke. The ground trembled, and the soldiers' senses were briefly jarred. Another thirty-two-pounder rifle shell from Confederate batteries atop Lookout Mountain had furrowed the earth amid the Federal lines.[11]

There was no truce among artillerists. The guns continued to roar during the ever-shortening autumn days, until an hour-long sporadic cannonading was considered commonplace. It was a constant reminder of the "realities of our circumstances," remembered a Federal soldier. Beginning on September 25, when heavy cannon began firing from Lookout Mountain, the long-range bombardment of Chattanooga had been a regular occurrence. Although at first a source of dread, the lumbering shells were randomly dispersed and inaccurate. For example, the October 5 bombardment had caused only a single injury, it was learned: that of a private in the Fourteenth Corps who was struck in the leg. After estimating that the Rebel guns were about two miles distant, one rather indifferent Ohio infantryman remarked in a letter home: "It would not seem very pleasant to any of you, I dare say, to have your sleep broken by cannonading [at] any hour during the night. Yet we have this music every night, and snooze away—perhaps asking the question: '[Do you] think that was our gun or the Rebs?' "[12]

To the battle-hardened Federal veterans who had faced many devastating close-range artillery blasts, the enemy's ineffective long-range practice, even if from commanding heights, was soon regarded as a minor annoyance.

"[The Rebels] have wasted a great deal of ammunition," wrote Capt. John S. H. Doty of the 104th Illinois Infantry, "for they have fired from the [Lookout] mountain every day, or almost every day, since we have been here, and I don't think they kill a man once in a month." Doty dismissed the danger, saying, "It seems that their shelling from that mountain does not amount to much, or has not so far." Another unimpressed officer agreed, scoffing that the "shells don't do [us] much harm." To a youthful Federal lieutenant, the Confederate cannon on Lookout Mountain were so notoriously inaccurate that he joked in a letter home about the scene witnessed on October 10. The men were all in line to answer roll call about noon when a shell from Lookout Mountain struck in the center of the 18th U.S. Infantry's camp. "It was a percussion shell, and struck on a rock and exploded beautifully" near Gen. Lovell H. Rousseau, noted the lieutenant. "The next shell passed . . . over General Rousseau's house and struck right in front of the door of General King's house, [only] about four feet behind a man who was carrying water. As the shell struck the ground he fell water and all, [then] kicked with his legs to see if he was still alive." The man hastily got up and walked away to the laughter of all.[13]

Firing at intervals of about ten minutes throughout the afternoon of the tenth, the Rebel artillery was so inaccurate as to be unable to hit the obvious target, General Rousseau's house, said Lt. Arthur B. Carpenter. The shells exploded on every side of the house and in the regular brigade's camp, yet didn't injure a man or the house during the entire day, he observed.[14]

When several shells fell in the camp of the 2nd Minnesota Infantry, a sergeant saw Gen. George H. Thomas standing on the wall of a nearby fort, looking nonchalantly at the scene. A few men were seen running as several shells passed overhead, causing the men of the 59th Illinois Infantry to have a good laugh. Instead of the supposed safety in scurrying away at the sound of an incoming shell, one soldier mused, "Motion is as likely to carry one into as [well] as out of its way." One wildly bounding solid shot, striking the ground in front of a campfire, knocked a frying pan out of a soldier's hand, then careened into a stump behind which another man was sitting. "The shell was hardly cool when the boys had it on exhibition, passing it from hand to hand," wrote an amazed onlooker.[15]

Although there was the ever-present element of danger, the impressive view of the enemy firing from the surrounding heights made the event somewhat fascinating and even entertaining. At night, the booming of the big guns seemed spectacular to an Ohio officer. "The roar of the artillery . . . and the beautiful moonlight, with the flash of the guns, was a magnificent sight," he wrote.[16]

With so little significant damage occurring, the occasional shell that found its mark was looked upon merely as ill fate. Yet while the Rebel "shelling machines" on Lookout Mountain were not particularly dangerous, when the enemy's batteries on Missionary Ridge and the adjacent high ground opened up at much shorter range, everyone had to "C sharp or b flat," cracked an officer.[17]

To counter the threat of the enemy guns firing from a commanding elevation, Federal batteries had been positioned opposite Lookout Mountain, on Moccasin Point. Here, from an abrupt ridge, a battery of twelve-pounder Parrott rifles fired with relative safety at the Confederate guns placed high above. The sides of the mountain were so steep and close that an Illinois sergeant found to his amazement that the Rebel guns were unable to fire at a sufficient deflection to strike their position. "The Rebel guns can throw shell[s] a mile beyond our camp," he reported. "[Yet] to shoot into our camp, which is in plain view [on Moccasin Point], their cannon would have to be lowered so much at the muzzle that the discharge would dismount them."[18]

Although some of the enemy shells with short fuzes occasionally burst overhead, nobody had been hurt. "Finding that nothing could be gained by shooting this way," they had directed their fire at other troops, reported the man. Meanwhile, the Moccasin Point Parrott rifles, which could throw a shell "clear over Lookout Mountain," were making life miserable for the Confederate cannoneers, he observed. "It is amusing to us to see the Rebs skedaddle when our shell[s] burst among them." The only problem, admitted the soldier, was when the twelve-pounder Parrott Rifles fired in unison from Moccasin Point. The noise was so loud "for about fifteen minutes I couldn't hear myself think."[19]

Fortunately for the soldiers' peace of mind, there were other, far more agreeable sounds emanating from around Chattanooga during the siege. One Federal private was almost homesick from listening to the sound of band music wafting across the valley on a balmy evening. Both armies contained various regimental bands, and the strains of favorite songs such as "Yankee Doodle," "The Battle Cry of Freedom," and "The Bonnie Blue Flag" entertained soldiers on both sides. Camp life seemed kind of easy, at first, noted various soldiers in their diaries and letters home. There was time to wash and boil clothes to kill the lice, watch wild ducks swimming on the Tennessee River—"they don't seem to care whether the world goes on or not" offered a soldier—and partake in a favorite pastime, gambling. Having just been paid for four months, some soldiers were promptly engaged in a game of Chuck-a-luck. This game would go on, despite interruptions, complained a Minnesota sergeant, until "a few get all the money there is, then it will stop until next payday." Noting there was nothing going on in their camp except gambling, an Ohio lieutenant reflected, "How strange it is that men are so thoughtless as to squander their hard earned money when so many of them have friends at home that need it, and are almost starving for want of it." It was a strange scene one Sunday, noted another soldier, with his regiment's brass band tooting away at the head of a funeral procession for a dead comrade while the big guns at Fort Wood were shelling the enemy's lines. The solemn procession passed by another part of camp almost unnoticed, where the soldiers were intently gathered together playing Chuck-a-luck.[20]

"You can't stop them from gambling," remarked an officer. Yet, as he witnessed, the good nature of most was reflected at night, when "the boys fell to singing, and it spread from company to company, and regiment to regiment. . . . The Johnnies must have thought we were holding a camp meeting," he joked.[21]

The rain began on the afternoon of September 30. At first it was very light, and barely noticeable. Most of morning had been dark, and to an Illinois soldier, the event represented much of "a miracle . . . a curious day, everything taken into consideration." This rain, the first in nearly two months of campaigning, had everyone abuzz. The drizzle that began about 3:00 P.M. was by evening a steady, pattering rain that continued into the night. On October 1, the men of both armies awoke to a downpour. "It was coming down in torrents," discovered a Federal officer who found himself "soaking wet from the hips down. . . . Strange how a fellow can sleep with the rain falling on him until he is wet through before he realizes his situation." To those who at first welcomed the end to the drought, there soon were unwelcome consequences. The trenches in the front lines became filled with water, and those without tents or adequate shelter were found to be "very mean and uncomfortable." Much of the day, wrote another soldier, was spent with extreme difficulty in attempting to "banish the water from our dog tents."[22]

This was only the beginning. Instead of the familiar rising cloud of choking dust at every step, within weeks both armies were foundering in a sea of mud. The rains of October and November 1863 proved to be some of the most relentless and devastating in recent memory. From October 1 to November 23, a period of fifty-three days, it rained during nineteen days, with many heavy thunderstorms and prolonged downpours, especially during a two-week period in October. For the men within the Chattanooga fortifications, it was the onset of misery beyond their wildest imaginings, for with the rain came cold weather.[23]

In late October, a Illinois infantry officer wrote in his journal how during a lull in a heavy storm he attempted to get some lumber to shore up his tent but instead got soaked to the skin. With the rain pelting down, he sat in his tent chattering. "It was very cold, and sitting in the tent I would shake so with the cold that I shook nearly all the mud off my feet. I was never tired of the service before, but I am pretty near it now. Will the rain ever cease?"[24]

One disgruntled Ohioan found that after a hard frost, the ground was so cold that he could not lie down to sleep. Instead, "I sit up by the fire," he wrote to his mother. "Better believe [me], they are long nights, and we look rather anxiously for old Sol [in the morning]."[25]

During the daylight hours, the ample mixture of water and mud had everyone foundering about in ankle-deep glop. To add to the difficulty, the constant tramping about of thousands of men so kneaded the camp-grounds and roads, it seemed impossible at times to move about in the heavy mire.[26]

With the coming of the hard frosts and wintry mountain blasts of frigid air, so many trees were being cut down for firewood, the supply was quickly exhausted. "We have to go quite a distance for wood [and now] cut the brush for fire[wood]," complained an Ohio soldier. "There were many hundred acres of timber inside our lines, but [they] are now cut away," he lamented. "Fuel is scarce," grumbled another besieged veteran on October 9. "Orders [are] received not to burn railroad ties."[27]

To Pvt. J. A. Reep of the 19th Ohio Infantry, the shortage of wood for fuel had a few positive aspects. With every man seeking to gather every available particle of wood, Reep saw "stumps cut off close to the ground and eventually dug out and cut into chips and small pieces. This was la-borious work." Yet there was a beneficial effect. "The exertion warmed the body . . . and [the resulting fire] warmed . . . food and fingers." Al-though there was an abundance of timber on the north bank across the Tennessee River, there were no spare wagons or animals to haul the wood. So desperate became many regiments that work parties were sent over the river to carry logs and large limbs by hand a distance of more than two miles.[28]

As the days of October 1863 waned, the soldiers grew more irritable and outspoken in their complaints. After trying to sleep on the bank of a trench to keep the water from "wetting me from below," Lt. Chesley Mosman gave it up as "no go" and sat up all night. The next day, it rained "so hard we could scarcely keep the fire going. We got wet clear through." He admitted, "it was the most disagreeable, discouraging rain I ever saw."

The following day when it rained "to make up time lost last summer through some error of the weather clerk," the only consolation to the angered Mosman was that "the Johnnies are out in it too."[29]

These are "gloomy times," mused a discouraged Illinois infantryman. The incessant rains had created shortages of everything, he complained, except a full ration of rheumatism from lying on the cold ground. "Rain, rain!! rain!!!" he scrawled in his diary. "This is . . . an awful time."[30]

Little did he know that the worst was yet to come.

CHAPTER 12

"THIS IS STARVATION CAMP"

The old Napoleonic maxim of an army traveling on its stomach might have seemed oddly appropriate to those in the Army of the Cumberland. The troops' stomachs were nearly empty, and the army wasn't about to do much traveling.

During the first few days following Chickamauga, the soldiers of the Army of the Cumberland had paid little attention to the imminent shortage of food. Anticipation of an enemy attack kept most focused on building fortifications and preparing for battle. An officer noted rather indifferently on September 24 that a work detail, sent out to construct breastworks, had labored "a day and a half, and all night, without rations."[1]

The true situation began to become evident once quartermaster's details were sent to Chattanooga to obtain supplies. By September 27, many of the men were on reduced rations. One Illinois lieutenant angrily recorded in his journal: "Our men are entirely out of rations and can't get anything to eat. Seventy thousand rations are said to have been issued from our [wagon] trains and we can't get any, while the center divisions have plenty." The following day, with the men "in very bad humor," the officers divided their rations with the "swearing mad" soldiers. Illinois artilleryman James E. Withrow wrote in his journal on September 27: "Great destitution of feed for our horses and half rations of everything but bread for man. Only a very few corn stalks, no corn, for our animals." The next day, Withrow noted: "we now draw only half rations of anything."[2]

Among the army's commanders, there seemed to be minimal concern about the dwindling supply of quartermaster stores until the first week of October. Although a food/forage shortage was evident, large supply trains were being gathered at and forwarded from Bridgeport, Alabama, all of which were routed along the Tennessee River's north bank to Chattanooga.[3]

Prior to early October, Rosecrans had routinely ordered a survey of the north-bank roads from Bridgeport and requisitioned more horses and wagons from St. Louis. Yet it was the evening of September 26 before an order to send rations to Chattanooga was received at the army's railhead supply depot at Stevenson, Alabama.[4]

With the destruction of an enormous quantity of supplies en route to Chattanooga in the Sequatchie Valley during Wheeler's early October raid, even Charles A. Dana suddenly became alarmed. Dana failed to mention the prospect of supply shortages in his dispatches to Washington, D.C., until October 9, when he abruptly reported twenty animals dying daily from starvation. Three days later, he fretted about losses of large numbers of animals, which now were on quarter rations of forage. Even worse, only a two days' ration supply was on hand for the troops. Bad mountain roads, "which a little rain will render impracticable," Dana warned, were a growing worry.[5]

The devastating, abrupt decline in available food was duly noted by Pvt. Bliss Moore of the 105th Ohio Infantry. Moore recorded the reduced bill of fare in his daily diary: "October 9th—We got some pork and [a] cracker for breakfast. For dinner beans and [a] cracker. Supper[;] crackers and coffee, no meat. October 10th—we drew five crackers for one day's rations, and a piece of meat. Our rations are scant. Boys grumble much." When general orders from Rosecrans put the army on two-thirds rations, an Illinois soldier sarcastically joked, "[I] wonder if he didn't know we have been on one-half rations for ten days."[6]

Hundreds of complaints filled the letters sent home by Rosecrans's suddenly famished soldiers. Despite the arrival of a supply train on October 8, two days later a soldier wrote in his diary: "Our rations are so short these days that for a few meals occasionally we have to go without." Whiskey rations provided little solace, and the overall situation continued to worsen. On October 20, a distraught Illinois soldier confided: "No hard bread for 12 hours, and scant prospects ahead." It was becoming "a life of suspense," he grumbled. The next day, he noted: "Our next five days' rations are: ⅔ hard bread, ¼ sow belly, ¼ beef, ¼ coffee, ¼ tea, ¼ sugar, no pepper, soap, or candles. Pretty rough times these."[7]

With morale plummeting and the weather continuing cold and stormy, many water-soaked soldiers resorted to ingenuity to fill their stomachs. Complaining that their rations had been cut so as to draw only "two spoonfuls of sugar, and ¾ rations of pork and beef for five days," an angry infantryman wrote home how he and another soldier had gone to the army's slaughter pen and stolen a beef heart, a liver, and an oxtail, from which "we made a good soup." "The continual gnawings of a growing appetite was a perpetual reminder of our condition," later remembered an Ohio private. "We have had four crackers three inches square issued to us as a day's rations of bread," an Illinois lieutenant grumbled on October 24. "That has been our bread ration for two weeks. . . . The men steal corn from the mules and roast and pulverize it and make a kind of mush. . . . I [just] saw two dead mules that are reported to have starved to death."[8]

By the middle of October, the few army animals remaining in Chattanooga were so famished that a soldier found horses and mules going without food for days on end and expressing their "hunger by gnawing at limbs and trees." Despite the fact that many of the animals around camp were barely able to stand, an Illinois soldier described how he offered a man in charge of the "mule commissary" seventy-five cents, "all the money I had," for one ear of corn. Being refused, the soldier admitted that before he returned to camp "one mule was minus three ears of corn—and I had the benefit of it at the mule's expense."[9]

"This is starvation camp," observed an Ohio sergeant who bribed a teamster, paying him ten cents to look the other way while he stole an ear of corn from his mules. "I ate it raw [but] I wasn't proud," he remembered. Col. John McClenahan of the 15th Ohio Infantry found he had to station a guard by his horse when fed in order to keep the "hungry soldiers from stealing the corn from him." "I would give $5.00 to have a good dinner," wrote one of the 96th Illinois Infantry's privates on October 20th. "I have not had all I could eat for over a month. I haven't had nothing but one ear of corn to eat today, and I gave a dime for that."[10]

Quartermaster General Montgomery C. Meigs's indictment was strong and direct. His curt communication on October 9 to Lt. Col. Henry C. Hodges, the Army of the Cumberland's chief quartermaster (who had gone to Nashville to oversee supply arrangements), expressed his displeasure; "Horses are dying for want of forage. Many are turned out on the north bottom to shift for themselves. It is more important to send forage than troops here now. This army, unless things improve, will be anchored for want of stout artillery and ammunition horses soon. A great oversight was not sending to Bridgeport grain in abundance as soon as the army retired to this place. Get it forward now."[11]

Only six days earlier, Meigs had written to Secretary of War Stanton about how everything seemed under control in "this guilty town [Chattanooga]." The men were working "cheerfully and with skill and ingenuity" on the fortifications, and "cavalry horses will be able to subsist for some time to come upon the country." Since "at this season of the year the corn is in the field and ripe," Meigs had quipped, "it furnishes food for man and beast."[12]

Meigs's transformation was typical of the sudden shift in perspectives and priorities among the Federal army's top command. Rosecrans and his staff were at first too preoccupied to see the practical consequences of the siege at Chattanooga, at least as keenly as did many of the troops. They were hungry. He and his staff were not. His joke to the troops about the

Irishman whose pocket was full and yet empty must have brought hollow laughter. "Do you understand how that was?" he remarked to some Illinois soldiers. "Why the pocket was *full* of holes."[13]

Rosecrans's larder was nearly empty. With the news of Wheeler's raid, resulting in the destruction of an estimated four hundred supply wagons, Rosecrans began increasingly to fear the loss of Chattanooga due to his dire logistic circumstances. Although he had begun the late offensive with twenty-five days' rations in wagons, the supply had rapidly dwindled in the face of his resupply difficulties. Moreover, there was little Rosecrans could do to hide his increasing plight from the men. The army's daily rations were cut to two-thirds on the very day news arrived of the destruction of the supply wagons in the Sequatchie Valley. Moreover, commanders were given discretion to reduce the allowance further—to one-half.[14]

On October 12, Rosecrans telegraphed Abraham Lincoln that the Rebels no longer were the chief worry at Chattanooga; "our danger is subsistence," he announced. Due to the lack of food and supplies, he couldn't bring up Hooker's troops, which would only increase the burden. Furthermore, Hooker's units were without most of their supply wagons and transportation, left behind in the East due to their urgent troop movement. To make matters psychologically worse, enemy-occupied Lookout Valley was said to be "full of corn," which Rosecrans couldn't reach, having evacuated Lookout Mountain. "We must put our trust in God, who never fails those who truly trust," he advised the President.[15]

By October 12, the Army of the Cumberland was so desperate for forage that Rosecrans told Hooker to "induce" the citizens along the railroads to bring in corn, which would be paid for at "liberal prices, and cash down." The insignificant result of these and other makeshift efforts caused Rosecrans to admit to the administration following the mid-October deluge of rain, "Our future is not bright." Although Quartermaster Meigs had left the Army of the Cumberland on October 13, saying his further presence at Chattanooga wouldn't be "of much service," Rosecrans continued to plead his sinking fortunes. On the eighteenth, he warned Meigs, "We must have some horses for our trains and cavalry. Relays will be necessary to maintain our position here. It will require a very great effort."[16]

The Army of the Cumberland was running out of time. Everyone knew the fate of the army hinged on getting adequate supplies forward. "Something has got to be done . . . in order to get command of the river from here to Bridgeport," complained a thoroughly perplexed infantryman. It was a universal plea among the rank and file. Finally, of necessity, it became a priority within the Federal high command. As was clearly defined by Meigs as early as October 9, the Army of the Cumberland was becoming increasingly immobile, unable to advance, retreat, or even follow in the wake of an invading enemy army. Forage was now more important than men. Meigs stated this very fact on the ninth in informing Stanton the army would be "unable to follow the enemy should he cross the river above in force. If the artillery and ammunition horses give out the army cannot move." Accordingly, said Meigs, it was vital to get control of the river, allowing supplies to flow freely by an easier, faster means.[17]

The critical tactical problem, most observers realized, was with the prolonged supply route to Chattanooga over nearly impassable roads from the army's Alabama supply bases. The round trip often took two weeks, and much of the load, of necessity, was hay and corn for the use of the teams in making the journey. Although Meigs's recommended using most of the army to repair and build the vital roads, foul weather was certain to hamper these efforts. "It will require much work, and more time than I fear can be spared," Meigs admitted on October 16.[18]

Rosecrans, driven to the point of near desperation, had begun to consider the only viable solution: the opening of the Tennessee River to Chattanooga. Despite the urgency, Rosecrans failed to commit to the immediate execution of this plan. On October 19, he had wired his explanation to Henry Halleck: "We expect to retake it [Lookout Mountain] as soon as we are prepared to hold it. That could be done only when the railroad [is] secured, the depots replenished, and Hooker's transportation provided. Without that he cannot subsist in a suitable position."[19]

It was vintage Rosecrans—unable to respond decisively or function effectively when under great stress. That evening, he learned the supply situation had contributed greatly to his undoing; Rosecrans was out, Thomas was in, and Grant was on his way to Chattanooga to rescue the army. George H. Thomas's famous telegram that night about "holding the town till we starve" tacitly acknowledged the army's critical circumstances.[20]

In practical terms, the change of command didn't make much difference to the men. Lt. Chesley Mosman seemed to sum up the perspective of the troops when he wrote in his journal shortly after Grant's arrival, "not knowing the situation, we assume that our commander does. . . . We have been here 31 days . . . and we surely can't be in a much worse situation, so go it 'Old Grant.' Make a spoon or spoil a horn, and whatever skies shine o'r us [t]here's a heart for any fate."[21]

Despite the natural rivalry of the Cumberland and Tennessee armies over the past year, it was evident Grant, the much acclaimed Vicksburg hero, would be given a reasonable opportunity by the soldiers. "Grant has immense responsibilities upon him—should he fail here, his past reputation will be dimmed, and he [will] be shelved again," wrote a pensive Ohio colonel, Emerson Opdycke. "But if he succeeds now, he will be in the flood tide of success at the death of the Rebellion, and will stand peerless in the annals of American Generals. His incentives to the greatest exertions are extraordinary, and with such power in his hands as the government has given him, and with such an able general as Thomas as his chief here, I think success can hardly be doubtful."[22]

The Army of the Cumberland sought relief from the daily plight of undue hardship. Yet the solution involved many complexities, and a critical point had more to do with Grant's common sense and intuition than his military abilities. At stake was the efficacy of the army, particularly the morale of the men, which was essential for victory. The critical point rested on Grant's ability to read the minds and hearts of his troops. The war at Chattanooga was not merely a matter of logistics; it also involved a question of resolve and execution—of taking swift, decisive action and, especially, not letting ennui and distress fester in the minds of the soldiers.

Sam Grant's attitude was evident even before his arrival. His three-sentence telegram to Thomas on October 19 reflected his priorities: "Hold Chattanooga at all hazards. I will be there as soon as possible. Please inform me how long your present supplies will last, and the prospect for keeping them up."[23]

Grant was very much the practical commander. He also knew that the essence of success was often as basic as a resolute point of view.

CHAPTER 13

"OH, WHAT SUFFERING
THIS WAR ENTAILS"

Our Virginia troops fight like tigers up here in the West," wrote an elated Georgia volunteer, one of Longstreet's men thrilled by the great victory at Chickamauga. "I think the western boys is all right. They are not as bad[ly] whipped as we heard they was. They all seem to be in good spirits." Another transplanted soldier from the East blurted out in a letter home, "Mother, I have not fared as well since I left Virginia. . . . The boys had a fine time plundering the Yankees' knapsacks. I got me a good knapsack and two pairs of socks . . . and the best blanket off of the battlefield that I ever saw, so I am fixed up for the winter." "The Yankees fought manfully," decreed an aroused Confederate captain from Alabama, but "when we raised a yell and went at them at a double quick . . . they went at a double quicker. I tell you they skedaddled in fine style."[1]

In the aftermath of the Battle of Chickamauga, there was a fiery Southern optimism—feelings of renewed purpose, a dismal fate redeemed, and a will to even greater success. The Confederacy's major western army seemed on the brink of long-overdue major achievement. The men in the late battle could hardly be restrained, wrote Capt. Joab Goodson of the 44th Alabama Infantry. "[My] men seemed to be almost carried away with the excitement. . . . I could scarcely keep some of my men back with the company." It was the thrill of winning, the euphoria of victory. Never had the men in the ranks of the Army of Tennessee experienced such joy and optimism.[2]

With Bragg's army in motion for the outskirts of Chattanooga on September 23, the men, "in fine spirits," said Capt. Thomas W. Davis of the 5th Tennessee Cavalry, had chased Old Rosy's boys to the limit. "The whole Yankee army presented one heterogeneous, jumbled, panic stricken . . . mass of men," noted Davis, who added, "The question on every lip is will Bragg attack Chattanooga?" "I am satisfied we will be in possession of the town in two hours," declared an excited Alabama private that same day, and he further boasted how "the Yanks are run out of Georgia."[3]

The subsequent days had proved anything but reassuring to the victorious Confederate ranks. After exchanging their obsolete smoothbore muskets for many Enfield rifles on the Chickamauga battlefield, the men of the 5th Tennessee Infantry had pursued the fleeing enemy toward Chattanooga, encouraged by local citizens along the way. While formed in line of battle before the Yankees' new position in Chattanooga Valley, the enemy began shelling the Rebel lines "so suddenly that it nearly scared us boys out of our wits," wrote a Tennessee rifleman. With pieces of shell whizzing about, "making a noise like a 'spinning wheel,' everyone began dodging. The Rebel line was soon withdrawn, and amid speculation about the prospect of charging "our old works," some of Bragg's men began swearing they would not do so, acknowledged a private. The next day, it was discovered the enemy was busily reconstructing and improving the old Confederate forts at Chattanooga, connecting them with long lines of formidable rifle pits and breastworks. "I see no hope of getting them out by fighting without great loss," wrote a battle-wise Tennessee soldier on September 25. Indeed, it was now apparent the Yankees would not retreat beyond Chattanooga; they were still full of fight. "Flanking seems impossible," commented a veteran Confederate infantryman, "to fall back would be to give up the fruits of victory. What will be done?" he asked.[4]

Bragg's answer was, essentially, to do little more than lay siege with his main army; he would partially fortify, then merely wait. The Confederate army having occupied Missionary Ridge, Chattanooga Valley, and Lookout Mountain, a wary observance of the enemy became the daily routine of the soldiers. Where there had been enthusiasm and optimism, with the inactivity there was soon only an anxious restlessness among the men. "No change in affairs" became the byword of the restive troops. "Every day we have a little artillery fighting, which amounts to just nothing," wrote an exasperated Confederate artillery officer. After firing forty-four rounds at a range of four thousand yards with several rifled guns, Lt. Andrew Jackson Neal decided that the enemy was "too well posted to be shelled out [of Chattanooga], and this business is all foolishness."[5]

Even worse for the morale of the men, with time to reflect on the staggering losses of Chickamauga, the reality of "this horrible war" was once more apparent.

"I rode over the [Chickamauga] battlefield," wrote Sgt. John Snow of Lumsden's Battery, "which can only be described as a world of bloody and mangled corpses. Some [had] the sweet smile of resignation to death . . . others [had] distorted features . . . produced by bodily pain or remorse of conscience. . . . I saw dead bodies . . . lying in the broiling sun, and their faces as black as ebony, and they were just beginning to bury the dead." Where there had been "one incessant, murderous roar of cannon and [small] arms," wrote Capt. Thomas W. Davis of Forrest's Cavalry, "now all is quiet as the midsummer's calm." Within a few days of the battle, the eerie quiet that prevailed along Chickamauga Creek's bullet-riddled Georgia pines reflected the now-somber mood of many Southern soldiers. Viewing the terrible carnage caused many to reflect upon the meaning of it all. One Confederate sergeant lamented: "We lost some of our best men killed and wounded. Men who are worthless both here and at home generally manage to keep out of danger, while good and true men are . . . at their post at all times. This I think is the cause of the best men being killed and wounded in battle." Others were too wrought up from the ordeal to comprehend. "Although this was the first time I ever saw such a sight, my feelings were scarcely moved at all," wrote one entirely numbed Tennessee soldier. "How unfeeling man becomes. . . . [That] none of them were suffering [now], was the reason in part, I suppose." The grisly battlefield was a sight that "I hope never to see again," wrote a despondent Sgt. John Snow, who "was glad to leave this scene."[6]

Like dark storm clouds gathering on the horizon, signs of serious disarray began to surface within Bragg's army. Many of the soldiers learned within days of their encampment on the heights surrounding Chattanooga that they were facing an insidious but excruciating, life-altering ordeal: crucial supply shortages. On October 3, a disillusioned soldier complained: "Our rations are pretty short, and men here are like children, they want to eat all the time. . . . It seems like they have a craving appetite, and can't be satisfied unless they are eating. Several [men have] deserted lately."[7]

As early as September 27, an envious Confederate private found some of his comrades in the 7th Florida Infantry resorting to theft in order to get enough to eat. "Some of the boys that were lucky enough to steal some ears of corn from the horses last night are busy grating it, and making mush . . . for we are almost starved to death. We draw enough in two days to make one good meal," complained Pvt. Robert Watson.[8]

Matters rapidly continued to worsen. On successive days, Robert Watson's journal provided a damning indictment of the Army of Tennessee's supply system: "September 28th: [I] drew one day's ration of corn bread and beef for tomorrow, but as everyone is very hungry they eat it all for supper. So we will have to fast tomorrow. September 29th: [I] drew one day's ration of corn bread and bacon; just enough for one meal, and we eat it up immediately, although it is for tomorrow. There is some rascality about [this] . . . for our full rations are drawn from the brigade commissary, and then cooked at the wagons [in the rear]. We think that our commissary sergeant sells it. September 30th: Nothing to eat but we are all well supplied with lice. Many of the regiment [are] sick from drinking bad water and [eating] poorly cooked food. I think we will all be sick soon if they don't give us more food. October 1st: All hands [are] as hungry as wolves and nothing to eat. October 2nd: [I] drew one day's ration of beef and cornbread, and one drink of whiskey. October 4th: I am very unwell having been up half the night with diarrhea. . . . October 8th: I am quite sick, and . . . all of the company are in the same fix from eating bad beef and drinking bad water. October 16th: I have a violent cold and pain in the breast. Nothing to eat, for the roads are so bad that the wagons can't get along. All hands as hungry as wolves. I went to bed but was so hungry that I couldn't sleep. When I would doze off, I would dream that I was at my mother's table, eating all sorts of nice things, then wake up and find it [was] all a dream. October 19th: [I] drew two day's rations of meal and beef, which was as lean as carrion. At 1 p.m. the regiment came back [to camp] as hungry as sharks."[9]

Robert Watson's ordeal mirrored the experiences of many of Bragg's troops. On October 24, Pvt. W. R. Montgomery of the 3rd Battalion Georgia Sharpshooters confided in a letter home: "I am almost crazy for something to eat." When provided with a stolen "old hen," Montgomery fairly jumped with joy: "You ought to have seen me eat chicken and dumplings. You may be sure they were good, though a little tough," he told his wife. A fare of half rations had an Alabama infantryman complaining about living "very hard," and he pleaded with his wife to send him some potatoes, dried fruit, and a few onions. To his wife's brother, who was considering joining the army, he had some tongue-in-cheek advice: Come here and join this company so he (the soldier) could get a furlough—promised for recruiting another man.[10]

Much of the trouble in getting adequate food into the hands of the troops originated with the makeshift arrangement of cooking in the rear, sometimes three or four miles distant from the front lines. A scarcity of utensils and inadequate transportation had resulted in makeshift consolidation. Yet transporting the prepared food to the front in a few rickety wagons was always uncertain, based upon the condition of the roads and the meager supply of horses. Moreover, the food was subject to prolonged delays en route, pillage, stormy weather, or even spoilage during periods of hot temperatures.[11]

At the root of the problem lay a nightmare of politics, inefficiency, and an overwhelming transportation burden. In the political spectrum, Bragg's logistical operations were complicated by a balky and peevish commissary general of subsistence, Col. Lucius B. Northrop, who ran matters from his headquarters in Richmond, Virginia. Northrop disliked Bragg, and he favored the eastern armies. Since the main commissary warehouses for both Robert E. Lee's and Braxton Bragg's armies were located at Atlanta, Georgia, Northrop ordered the chief commissary of subsistence at Atlanta, Maj. J. F. Cummings, to ship foodstuffs to Richmond as a first priority. Cummings was so exasperated by Northrop's restrictions and demands, he determined to tender his resignation when he could not "meet expectations." Bragg, who had complained even before Chickamauga that the army's morale was being "seriously injured," principally by the lack of rations, complained to Adjutant General Cooper in Richmond on September 29 that "our supplies are nearly exhausted at Atlanta."[12]

Northrop scoffed at Bragg's "superfluous" correspondence, saying his perspective involved a "delusion." Instead of grumbling about shortages, said Northrop, Bragg should have been attempting to drive the enemy from east Tennessee, where abundant food supplies could be obtained. The Army of Tennessee being inactive in a region of poor commissary supplies contributed to the difficulty, growled Northrop. As for the reserves of bacon and other supplies at Atlanta, which Bragg was now pillaging, they "were intended for the east," complained Northrop. "It being supposed that the armies of the west . . . could hold the country, which was amply sufficient to subsist them," Bragg was thus the one to blame. If he wants more food, decreed Northrop on October 7, "East Tennessee must be recovered and Rosecrans driven from the country."[13]

Bragg, additionally plagued with railroad problems in getting supplies forward from Georgia, already had begun improvising to reduce logistical demands. On October 16, he offered furloughs to soldiers who obtained a recruit. Stevenson's movement into east Tennessee at about the same time may have been at least partially motivated by subsistence shortages, and Bragg told that commander he would need to live off the countryside. Changes in the number of wagons assigned to headquarters units, artillery, and ordnance trains had already been made in the main army to bolster the quartermaster's supply. Foraging and commissary details were made up from various regiments to go into the distant countryside to obtain grain and food from the local residents.[14]

Still the problems continued to mount. On October 24, following heavy rains, a shivering Georgia soldier sat by a campfire and lamented about Chickamauga Creek bridge washing away, which prevented rations from reaching the army for two days. Blinded by the acrid log smoke, which "runs me almost crazy," he could do little but think about his hunger and the nearness of food, now inaccessible just beyond the swollen creek. "It [is] hard to be so near and have to suffer for something to eat," he grumbled. Another soldier complained the same day about having nine crackers for two days, "which will barely keep us alive." In the 5th Tennessee Infantry, officers had to post a strong guard to keep the men from ransacking their commissary's reserve stores. Angered and frustrated, some of the men had broken into a boxcar and "wantonly destroyed" some ordnance supplies, reported a private. Even the army's officers were reduced to hardship. Col. Robert Bullock of the 7th Florida Infantry admitted, "I suffer more from want of something to eat more than anything else. . . . We can get nothing now but bread and mush, and are only allowed to buy a soldier's ration, which is one pound each. I tell you, when it comes to eating boiled, poor beef and cornbread, it goes mightily against the grain."[15]

With the advent of cold, stormy weather, Bragg's bedraggled soldiers, caught on windswept high ground without adequate equipment, provisions, and shelter, suffered enormous misery. A barefoot Arkansas soldier, after hobbling about without shoes for two months, finally complained in early October about the heavy frosts hurting his feet. Another private who had "not been dry since the rain commenced," wrote on October 18 how "the whole face of the earth is about shoe-mouth deep in mud and water." There being only one tent for his company, he had given that up for use of the sick. The only shelter he now had was his blanket, "which I assure you is very poor," complained the private. In the 7th Florida, there were no tents, and on several autumn nights the men had to stand in ankle-deep mud during a pouring rain, without "a wink of sleep." Not having shelter, or even axes to cut wood for fires, they again had to "stand and take it" during a cold, driving rain on the night of October 6. "The mud is perfectly awful," wrote Col. Robert Bullock of the 7th Florida, and the "men are without tents, [have] thin clothing, and [are] scarce of blankets. Oh, what suffering this war entails."[16]

If the Union army was slowly starving at Chattanooga as the last week in October 1863 began, the Confederates seemed to be faring little better in the surrounding mountains and valleys. A scarcity of provisions and inadequate supplies and equipment had created a destitute, unhealthy existence. Sickness was rife; nearly everyone seemed to have respiratory ailments, fevers, and particularly diarrhea. "The regiment is suffering with dysentery; more than ever before. I have it pretty badly myself," wrote Colonel Bullock. Another Floridian described how he had been "never so near to death," after standing in a freezing rain for seven hours before he could change his wet clothes. Stricken by "diphtheria"—a high fever and a throat so sore, "the experience was about the same as if I had swallowed a pin cushion, and someone was trying to pull it backwards"—Sgt. Washington Ives of the 4th Florida Infantry wrote that he had been treated by several friends, including a black servant. After concoctions containing flour, sugar, and whiskey made into a "fly blister" were applied to his neck, Ives woke up to find his throat so swollen that it seemed he "would choke to death." A raw blister covered his throat from ear to ear, making it so painful, he could barely turn his neck. A "little [further] exposure would have killed me," Ives ruefully wrote following his recovery nearly two weeks later.[17]

The Confederate army was suffering, unlike many of the men had ever suffered before, and the attitude of the soldiers reflected their grueling ordeal. Remembering the relative innocence of a year earlier, Sergeant Ives reflected about how "war was then rather a romance, but alas, it has proved a reality [ever] since." There has been enough suffering here to end any war, he proclaimed, and he confided to his wife there weren't enough passions left in the soldiers on either side for "meddlers and politicians" to "stir up another war in my lifetime." On October 9, an Alabama infantryman wrote how "the men are getting so very badly worn out and tired of it [the war] I think it will most assuredly end before twelve months or sooner."[18]

Over the span of a month, the Confederate army that had won at Chickamauga had experienced a great metamorphosis. The men were sick, tired, hungry, and their morale was sagging. "I am very much afraid we will reap but little from the great battle [Chickamauga]," wrote a despairing colonel that month. It was perhaps fitting commentary for an army mired in its own inertia.[19]

CHAPTER 14

BROWN'S FERRY
AND SMITH'S PONTOONS

I do wish things would come to a crisis, this suspense is terribly wearing," wrote an anxious Capt. Alfred L. Hough of Maj. Gen. James S. Negley's staff. "To live, and go to sleep knowing that a hundred or so of cannon are looking one another in the face, and may at any moment open on each other, that is our daily life. But it must soon end, a fight or a fall back by one side or the other must take place before many days." Written in a letter to his wife in early October, this candid comment reflected the mood of many.[1]

Several weeks later, the day before Grant's arrival on October 23 at Chattanooga, Captain Hough commented: "I understand we have about 12 days rations ahead only . . . and if the roads do not get better by that time, we must starve or fall back. But we trust in Providence that we shall be preserved from so dire a calamity." Hough's thoughts mirrored those of Ulysses S. Grant, with one notable exception: Grant was determined not to fall back from Chattanooga under any circumstances.[2]

Grant was not only ready for a fight; the aggressive Vicksburg victor wanted to seize the initiative and take the offensive. In his mind, only the practical matters of supplying and reinforcing the army had to be addressed before executing his strategic plans. Grant's "inborn" dislike for being placed on the defensive was clearly apparent from the night of his arrival, said Capt. Horace Porter.[3]

"Opening up the cracker line" was what Grant had talked about the most that night, but it was his mental acuity, easy grasp of the situation, firm resolve, and administrative capacity that deeply impressed even Thomas's staff. Moreover, Grant's obvious mental toughness seemed to suggest

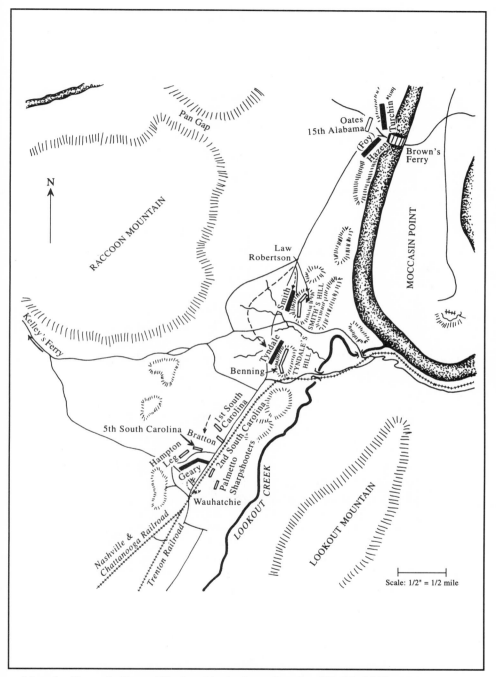

MAP 5   Brown's Ferry–Wauhatchie Actions, October 27–29, 1863

(Source: O.R. Atlas plate 47–8; O.R. 31-1-212; Edward E. Betts, 1896 Chattanooga Map)

that here was a commander to manage rather than be managed by future operations.[4]

On the following day, October 24, Grant, William F. Baldy Smith, Thomas, and various other generals had gone about five miles down the Tennessee River from Chattanooga, to Brown's Ferry, the key site that Smith hoped to seize in reopening an effective supply route. It was Baldy Smith's plan, presented to George H. Thomas on October 19 and approved before Grant's arrival, to seize the crossing here under the cover of darkness by floating a select detachment downriver from Chattanooga in pontoons. These boats then would enable the construction of a bridge, and supporting infantry would be brought over from the north bank to reinforce the beachhead. This assault would coincide with Hooker's march from Bridgeport south of Raccoon Mountain into Lookout Valley, providing a pincers movement against Brown's Ferry.[5]

Once Brown's Ferry, Raccoon Mountain, and much of Lookout Valley were controlled by Federal troops, the way would be open to utilize two small steamboats then being constructed upriver as a primary means of supplying Chattanooga. The road from Brown's Ferry led across the neck of Moccasin Point, providing an easy and direct route to Chattanooga, out of the range of Confederate guns on Lookout Mountain.[6]

It was a crucial plan. As one of Thomas's staff officers commented in a letter to his wife, the heavy rains had badly damaged the roads over Walden's Ridge, "so one of three things had to be done—open the river, retreat, or starve."[7]

Grant had already concluded that "this desperate effort" would be successful, and thus "the question of supplies will be fully settled." Because it was Baldy Smith's pet project, Grant placed Smith in direct tactical command of the operation, despite the fact that Smith was a staff officer, the chief engineer of the Department of the Cumberland. Smith, who received this assignment on Sunday, October 25, was given only two days to organize the operation. The assault at Brown's Ferry, in conjunction with Hooker's march into Lookout Valley, was planned for daybreak on October 27. Based upon his controversial past, Smith knew his reputation and perhaps the army's future depended upon the success of this significant expedition.[8]

Baldy Smith was an old army regular, a thirty-nine-year-old West Point-educated engineer whose outspoken comments had ruled out his further promotion in the Army of the Potomac. Sent west to help Rosecrans in the emergency following Chickamauga, the competent, but controversial Smith insisted on the practicality of the Brown's Ferry operation. He estimated that the enemy-held ridge line at the site was "thinly picketed," and "it seemed quite possible to take by surprise what could not have been carried by assault, if heavily occupied by an opposing force."[9]

While Smith's planning for the operation was detailed, it was predicated on many uncertainties. First and foremost, the pontoons, while nearing completion, were untried in the turbulent waters of the Tennessee River.

Built at Chattanooga by a three-company detachment of the 1st Michigan Engineers and Mechanics under the command of Capt. Perrin V. Fox, the pontoons were constructed from unseasoned and irregular lumber. After reassembling Chattanooga's dismantled sawmills from parts hidden by the Confederates but found by local slaves, Fox's men had cut the lumber and began assembling the boats despite a scarcity of nails. Lacking caulking, the Michigan Engineers were forced to use pressed cotton from stored bales. Fifty pontoons and two rafts were required to be assembled in less than twelve hours, some being loaded with additional construction materials to build a pontoon bridge at the Brown's Ferry site. At nightfall on the twenty-sixth, the Michigan engineers completed the pontoons but continued working feverishly to make 150 oars and oarlocks.[10]

For assault troops to man the boats, Smith had selected the best fighting men of Brig. Gen. William B. Hazen's and Brig. Gen. John B. Turchin's brigades, sixteen hundred men in total. All would depart in early-morning darkness on the twenty-seventh and glide nine miles down the Tennessee River, seven of which would be opposite enemy-controlled shoreline, to reach Brown's Ferry. Two nearby but separate landing locations were selected, and signal fires would be lighted on the Federally occupied opposite shore to mark the sites. Since the pontoon boats would use the swift current and stay close to the northern bank, Smith estimated that in the darkness the Confederates would not discover the assault force's presence until they were actually at Brown's Ferry. Should they accidentally do so while the boats were en route, reasoned Smith, they would not know the intended destination and thus would be unable to gather a strong force at the landing site. Beyond the pontoon-borne assault force, Smith had the remainder of Hazen's and Turchin's brigades march across Moccasin Point and camp out of sight in the woods.[11]

On Monday morning, October 26, William B. Hazen and Baldy Smith had visited Brown's Ferry, observing through field glasses the opposite shore, where Confederate pickets indifferently ambled about in full view. The informal "no firing" truce being in effect, Hazen had been able to bring many of his key commanders down to the shoreline, pointing out the exact locations for each landing and noting topographical features of the terrain.[12]

About noon that day in Hazen's camp, the grumblings of the men about scarce rations ("almost starved and there isn't a bit of bread in the house," a lieutenant of the 6th Ohio Infantry recorded at the time in his journal) were interrupted by special orders. Selections of officers and men distinguished for bravery on the battlefield were made from the various companies, and by 10:00 P.M. all were waiting with stacked arms "in readiness to march at a moment's notice." No one seemed to know what was planned, thus rumors abounded. "Something terrible [is in the offing] . . . I suppose," commented an officer, and a few hours later he learned his fears had been well founded.[13]

At 1:00 A.M. on the twenty-seventh, the various detachments of Hazen's brigade, about 1,150 men, were formed and marched to the river. The dozens of pontoon boats waiting there were "the first intimation" of what was planned, wrote Lt. William Glison of the 6th Ohio Infantry. Glison felt "the prospects were not very flattering," especially when old iron and standing water were found in some of the pontoons.[14]

Twenty-five men having embarked to the boat, about 2:00 A.M. the fleet began loading, when suddenly it was discovered that some of the boats would have to be dragged forward some three hundred yards so as to pass through a gap created in the main pontoon bridge at Chattanooga. By 3:00 A.M., all arrangements were completed and the first boat pulled steadily out into the river, gliding toward the right bank for maximum conceal-ment.[15]

The idea had been to constrict further the Federal army's basic line of communications along the tortuous fifty-five-mile wagon road over Wal-den's Ridge to Chattanooga. Aware that Wheeler's raid had torn at the vitals of Rosecrans's logistics operations, Bragg had continued to seek ways to cut off Rosecrans's supplies. During the first week in October, James Longstreet had been ordered to send a detachment of sharpshooters to prevent usage of the riverbank wagon road from Bridgeport—in the area along the "narrows" section of the river between Raccoon Mountain and Walden's Ridge. Due to the obvious vulnerability of these few sharpshoot-ers, the veteran all-Alabama brigade of Brig. Gen. Evander McIvor Law was ordered on October 8 to march from the vicinity of Lookout Mountain to support and augment the miniblockade of the Tennessee River opposite Raccoon Mountain. The specific tactical circumstances, observed Law, re-quired accurate firing against the enemy's wagon trains as they passed along the opposite riverbank road, some 300 to 350 yards distant.[16]

Law had thinly spread his riflemen along a five-mile front, utilizing only two regiments, the 4th and 15th Alabama, actually to picket the river. The remaining three units and a section of artillery remained in reserve, ready to rush to any point threatened by a sudden Federal attack across the Tennessee. The 4th Alabama's sharpshooters had gone to work with a will on October 8, promptly creating a significant disturbance.[17]

The first intimation of trouble became apparent to the Federal author-ities on October 7 when Rebel sharpshooters fired into the camp of the Pioneer Brigade, detailed to improve the road along the river. Rosecrans's chief telegrapher, Capt. John C. Van Duzer, in charge of repairing the line from Nashville, breathlessly reported the following day how a lone enemy sharpshooter had "killed everything he shot at, man, horse, or mule." The personal toll counted by the shaken Van Duzer was three men killed, two wounded, and "about a dozen mules" shot.[18]

It was but a prelude to the near debacle on October 8. About midday a virtual "turkey shoot' occurred near Little Suck Creek, which surprised both Federal and Confederate authorities due to the abrupt, serious devastation. A passing heavily laden wagon train of Maj. Gen. John M. Palmer's command, caught under only "a few" Confederate rifles, was severely bloodied and temporarily brought to a halt. The lieutenant in charge of the train was appalled to discover that in minutes two drivers had been killed, two or three others wounded, and twenty mules killed or disabled. While writing a hasty dispatch at 1:00 P.M., he found to his horror, "While I have been writing, three of my mules have been shot."[19]

Although the officer commanding the pioneers sent some of his men to the river to skirmish with the Rebel sharpshooters, these noncombatants were ineffective and suffered several losses. Rosecrans was so upset over the delay to the wagon trains, he became personally involved, ordering a battalion of Ohio sharpshooters attached to his headquarters to go to the site and stop these attacks. "They [Rebels] must be driven off, and that as quickly as possible," he demanded.[20]

A few days later, the local commander, Lt. Col. Hubbard K. Milward of the 18th Wisconsin Infantry, reported the enemy still present "in considerable force" along the opposite bank. By now, dead animals and the wreckage of army wagons so littered the narrow roadway that Milward had to send a work party to clear the road at night. When an infantry detachment and a single piece of artillery failed to dislodge the enemy riflemen, Milward complained that "work upon the road is suspended, as for nearly four miles the men are exposed to the fire of sharpshooters." The major commanding the infantry detachment reported his single Napoleon field gun was too limited in range to be effective, and his infantrymen had fired all day "without effect." With the Rebels securely posted behind rocks and in a thick woods along the mountain side, the major concluded, "It is impracticable to render it [road] safe for wagon trains unless we hold the opposite side of the river."[21]

Finally, the initial company of the 1st Battalion Ohio Sharpshooters, sent from Chattanooga, arrived about October 15. Despite their multishot Spencer repeating rifles, these fifty men were unable to make much difference. A perturbed Milward reported that day that work on the road was still suspended due to the enemy sharpshooters, and to make matters worse, the heavy rains had so inundated the river road that it was impassable. Rosecrans and other ranking officers had little choice. The river road was all but abandoned, and a new, more remote route through the mountainous terrain was utilized to avoid the deadly Rebel sharpshooters.[22]

It was an incredible circumstance. Responsible for much of this devastation were a mere six Confederate riflemen, the elite Whitworth sharpshooter contingent assigned to Hood's Division. As perhaps the deadliest killers in either army, these largely unheralded Whitworth sharpshooters were not only the selected best rifle shots in their division but had been armed with the most accurate military firearm available in the world. Firing an elongated .45-caliber hollow-based projectile, the technologically advanced Whitworth sharpshooter rifle was an English import, yet so costly at one thousand dollars each, that relatively few had been run through the blockade.* The rifle's secret lay in its polygonal bore, superior craftsmanship, and "fluid compressed cast steel barrel," which allowed use of enlarged high-pressure powder charges. So accurate as to repeatedly strike a man-sized target at four hundred yards, at longer ranges the elongated Whitworth bullet provided amazing accuracy, producing a mean deviation of 11.62 feet in tests at 1,800 yards (more than a mile). In the hands of an expert marksman, the single-shot muzzle-loading Whitworth was a consistent killer at ranges that far exceeded the width of the Tennessee River opposite Raccoon Mountain.† To add further to their effectiveness, many of the Whitworths were equipped with the side-mounted Davidson's telescopic sight.[23]

In a backhanded tribute to these deadly Whitworth riflemen, the still-exasperated Lieutenant Colonel Milward wrote on October 23 that there continued to be considerable firing by the enemy's sharpshooters against "the small extent of exposed road from the point where the new road begins." Their fire, said Milward, was so "well directed" that he would be forced to move his main camp if this deadly firing continued.[24]

When additional Ohio sharpshooters under Capt. Gershom M. Barber arrived at the river, bringing their total number to 125, an extraordinary confrontation occurred. Armed with one of the latest improvements in firearms—seven-shot Spencer Repeating Rifles using metallic cartridges—Barber's men engaged the few single-shot Whitworth sharpshooters and some of the 4th Alabama's mostly Enfield-armed riflemen. Due to the great disparity in numbers, the outcome was generally in favor of the Spencers' firepower. Barber claimed to have killed or wounded thirty enemy soldiers, while suffering only one casualty—a single Ohio Sharpshooter shot in the arm. Although his claim appears highly exaggerated, according to others the number of enemy troops visible along the river dramatically declined, causing Lieutenant Colonel Milward to believe the Ohio sharpshooters were "proving very effective."[25]

Despite the presence of these rapid-firing Spencer-armed Ohio sharpshooters, so dangerous were the few elusive Whitworth riflemen, it was conceded that until Federal troops occupied the opposite shore it would be impossible to protect the main river road fully. The Brown's Ferry expedition was intended in part to remedy this problem.[26]

Thereafter, the waning days of October had been mostly quiet along the river at Brown's Ferry and other major picket points. Due to the existing informal truce, honored by the pickets of both armies, little firing occurred unless wagon trains or significant military targets attempted to use the river

*In June 1864, a total of only twenty-six Whitworths were present in the Army of Tennessee, many being assigned to Cleburne's Division.
†A Whitworth-armed sharpshooter is credited with killing Maj. Gen. John Sedgwick at Spotsylvania in 1864, and possibly Maj. Gen. John F. Reynolds at Gettysburg in July 1863.

road. Since Rosecrans's engineers had hastily constructed new roads and directed supply traffic farther inland over Walden's Ridge, there generally was little military activity along the Tennessee River.[27]

Longstreet by now had learned that the enemy was using other roads, thus entirely avoiding his sharpshooters. Accordingly, on October 25, he ordered all but two of Law's regiments withdrawn to Lookout Mountain, leaving that commander without his reserves. The timing was most unfortunate. The men who remained posted on guard duty along the river had already begun to notice unusual activity within the Federal camps across the Tennessee River. Some began to fear their small numbers would allow the enemy to cross the river and "bag" both remaining regiments. Their concern about a pending Yankee raid was expressed to Col. William C. Oates, commanding the 15th Alabama Infantry; he said he promptly sent a report that day to Brig. Gen. Micah Jenkins at division headquarters on Lookout Mountain. Again on the twenty-sixth, Oates expressed concern about the enemy threat to "cross the river and clear the valley of Confederates." However, since Jenkins was expected to be absent for a few days, the local brigade commander, Evander Law, had departed for Lookout Mountain to take his place. Nothing was heard in reply.[28]

Later on the twenty-sixth, there were new signs of trouble. Oates said he received a message just after dark from a cavalry unit patrolling south of Raccoon Mountain that an enemy column of infantry, artillery, and cavalry was then attempting to cross the Tennessee River near Bridgeport. Oates, having had no luck with his messages to division headquarters, claimed he sent an urgent dispatch directly to Longstreet. Send reinforcements without delay—at least one more regiment that night—urged Oates. Later that night, Oates's courier returned, having delivered the message to Longstreet, but he had no specific orders. Oates, exhausted, then lay down "and tried to sleep."[29]

Early on the morning of October 27, most of Oates's men were asleep, "secure in our warm beds" fashioned of Yankee gum cloths and blankets captured on the Chickamauga battlefield, said a private, when the rapid crackle of gunfire sounded from the direction of the Tennessee River.[30]

On duty that morning at Brown's Ferry were Capt. N. B. Feagin and Company B of the 15th Alabama Infantry. Feagin's men were sleepily gazing at the several large signal fires burning across the river, speculating as to their significance, when their purpose became all too apparent. Out of the drifting fog and inky blackness abruptly appeared an eerie specter, a flatboat laden with soldiers. Feagin's men barely had time to raise their muskets; the boat was only about ten feet from shore when their first shots rang out. These bullets went right over the heads of the men in the boat, and a few men in the craft opened fire in reply. Suddenly, the bow touched shore, and fifty-two men led by Lt. Col. James C. Foy of the 23rd Kentucky Infantry scrambled up the steep bank. This was more than enough for Feagin and his few men. Behind the first flatboat, other boats, pontoons laden with soldiers, appeared through the fog. Feagin's pickets scrambled away in haste, even as their captain sent a messenger to Colonel Oates to alert the regiment.[31]

It was all too easy. Despite landing about 5:00 A.M. a few yards too far downriver past the road at the landing, where the steep sides of the riverbank caused momentary confusion, Foy and his infantrymen soon occupied the entire bluff and a nearby house. There was no opposition, and Foy pushed forward with other arriving troops into the predawn gloom. With clouds obscuring the bright moon, and amid an eerie stillness, Foy moved up the road some five hundred yards to the crest of a hill. Here he had his men build breastworks while skirmishers were sent forward. Foy than awaited the arrival of reinforcements—portions of Turchin's and Hazen's brigades—being ferried over from the north bank.

Elsewhere, above the Brown's Ferry landing, the other section of pontoon-borne troops had landed and occupied the adjacent hills. Only the dull chop of axes and the muffled crash of falling trees broke the early-morning stillness.[32]

William C. Oates had been one of the Confederates who had battled so arduously on Little Round Top at Gettysburg against Col. Joshua Chamberlain's 20th Maine. A veteran and skilled fighter, Oates was among the most respected commanders of Evander Law's Brigade. He was dozing fitfully on the early morning of October 27 when awakened by Feagin's messenger. Oates immediately had the long roll sounded in camp, and within minutes he started off with his men to begin a counterattack. Since five companies were absent on picket duty along the river, Oates had only the remaining portion of the 15th Alabama present with which to fight. Not knowing the strength of the enemy but hearing the sound of their axes, Oates deployed two companies in front, placing his men a single pace apart. They were told to "walk right up to the foe," with every man "plac[ing] the muzzle of his rifle against the body of a Yankee" before he fired.[33]

Foy's skirmishes heard Oates's men coming; their officers were audibly giving orders, and the crackle of brush alerted all of their progress. Foy barely had time to post his men farther to the right, before Oates's Alabamians loomed out of the darkness. The skirmishers opened fire and soon all began shooting and shouting, destroying Oates's plan to close before firing. Foy was still awaiting help from the landing area, and believing he was outnumbered four to one, he ordered a pullback when it appeared the enemy was outflanking him on the right.[34]

Oates plunged ahead on his mount, guiding his three companies on the left toward the Yankee flank so as to cut off their retreat. Boldly, the Alabamians swept forward over the crown of the ridge, only to come face-to-face with an advancing line of soldiers in dark uniforms. They were the 6th Indiana Infantry, some of Turchin's men, among the first reinforcements ferried over in the pontoons vacated by Hazen's assault force. Meeting Foy's men as they made their hasty retreat, the Indiana soldiers quickly formed a line across the road and opened with a crashing volley. With Foy's men soon reformed on their left, a withering fire swept through Oates's ranks. Many of Oates's riflemen were caught in an open field, with little protection, and many began to slump to the ground. Oates's horse was shot, and he already had a bullet through his coat sleeve, but he remained among his men, shouting encouragement. Daylight was beginning to brighten the sky, and Oates attempted to lead a rush toward the enemy line about thirty paces away when he was shot through the right hip and thigh. The blow came as if a "brick had struck me," he later remembered. It hurt so severely, he began to utter a curse as he fell to the ground. "God da—" he cried, cutting off the "damn" in midword, since the thought raced through his mind it was not well to die with an oath on one's lips. Seriously wounded, Oates was helped off the field by several privates just as his men fell back.[35]

That was the extent of fighting for Brown's Ferry. Within the span of about twenty minutes, the Confederate attempt to drive back the Yankee beachhead had fizzled miserably. Only six companies of a single Confederate regiment, about 250 men in all, had participated in the action. The vital terrain controlling the north bank of the Tennessee River had been meekly yielded for the want of sufficient troops, despite prior warnings of an imminent attack. Six dead and fourteen wounded was the toll among Oates's ranks.[36]

As the Confederates withdrew, posting several howitzers to cover their withdrawal into the valley, Foy's and Turchin's men initially followed behind, but they soon stopped at their abandoned breastworks to complete the defensive works earlier begun. The remainder of Turchin's and Hazen's men continued to move across the river in pontoons, so that five thousand men were transported to the south shore in about an hour. Meanwhile, construction of the pontoon bridge began under the direction of the Michigan Engineers and Mechanics. By 7:20 A.M., scouts reported the Confederates abandoning the valley entirely, moving off toward Lookout Mountain. Only the brief, distant shelling from several Rebel cannon against the construction engineers building the pontoon bridge marred the remainder of the morning. Lieutenant Colonel Foy reported accordingly: "After throwing a few shells towards us [the Rebels] were seen no more that day."[37]

By 4:30 P.M., the engineers had completed the bridge, and artillery, ammunition, and supplies were rumbling across it. Already, Federal reconnaissance patrols were probing deep into Lookout Valley. At the cost of twenty-one casualties, including only four killed, Brown's Ferry had been secured for the Union forces. To Capt. Alfred Hough, on duty at army headquarters, the news was splendid: "It was as fine a thing as was ever done," he proclaimed in a letter to his wife. Ulysses S. Grant that evening dispatched an uplifting telegram to Henry Halleck in Washington: "General Thomas's plan for securing the river and south side road . . . has proven eminently successful. The question of supplies may now be regarded as settled. If the Rebels give us one week more time I think all danger of losing territory now held by us will have passed away, and preparations may commence for offensive operations."[38]

"So far so good," concluded the ebullient Captain Hough. "We have a lodgment on the Rebel side."

The next day, however, there were second thoughts among the officers at headquarters. There was much uncertainty about the enemy's response, and the talk turned tentative among his fellow staff officers. "We wondered all day . . . what would be the next thing done," anxiously wrote Hough.[39]

CHAPTER 15

"GENERAL HOOKER'S BALLOON"

James Longstreet's mood was somber on the morning of October 27. High atop Lookout Mountain, he had looked down upon the scene and made his basic judgment. Braxton Bragg, having learned of the Brown's Ferry assault, had just sent word to make preparations "to retake the position." Yet Longstreet was wary. Any attacking force sent against the Brown's Ferry beachhead would have to cross Lookout Valley under fire of the enemy's guns on Moccasin Point, as well as from the just-captured ridges. This being impractical, "the only disposition" Longstreet had thus far ordered was to move a single brigade around from the other side of the mountain. "The enemy's designs," he informed Bragg by dispatch, "seem to be to occupy this bank of the river for the purpose of creating a diversion."[1]

This seemingly innocuous sentence was the key. Longstreet believed the enemy's true purpose was not yet evident; he expected they would try to capture Lookout Mountain by swinging south to its lower ridges, then march northward along the crest. Longstreet thus wanted to wait and see. Instead of counterattacking the Brown's Ferry beachhead, he would remain idle so as not to commit his troops prematurely.[2]

Longstreet's tepid reaction was not entirely unexpected, for he was a man caught in a thick web of political conspiracy and intrigue. Following Jefferson Davis's put-down during his mid-October visit, Longstreet had been increasingly frustrated and depressed. His poor relationship with Bragg's headquarters resulted in minimal communications and the personal distress of not knowing what was being planned or even having inside knowledge of important internal circumstances. In contrast to the favored and privileged relationship with Robert E. Lee in the East, Longstreet had found in the West only austere treatment, icy suspicion, and terse, formal communications from Bragg and his staff. Although mindful that he was very much a disliked outsider, Longstreet was particularly miffed when Bragg ignored Longstreet's revised plan to move against the Bridgeport region once Davis had departed from the army in mid-October. Instead, Bragg had endorsed operations in east Tennessee and began shifting troops away from Longstreet's flank. Bragg's demeaning innuendos and callous actions were regarded by James Longstreet as a personal affront. Yet at the time, there was little the aggrieved ex–eastern commander could do. Being trapped in a secondary role and subject to the whims of an obnoxious general, Longstreet had commanded the Confederate left wing on Lookout Mountain in a manner that had been uninspired and equivocating.[3]

Technically, Longstreet's assigned role to maintain the investment of Chattanooga from commanding Lookout Mountain was his essential task. Longstreet, however, had long fretted that "the enemy will cross below and move against our rear," which seemed "his easiest and safest move." In his mind, he was convinced that the enemy was on the verge of a major turning movement beyond the Confederate left flank. It was the basis for his concern on October 25 when his cavalry reported considerable enemy activity at Nickajack Cave, along the south side of the Tennessee River near Shellmound. Bragg, however, had again refused to listen, denying Longstreet's request to post significant troop concentrations along the southern regions of Lookout Mountain.[4]

To Longstreet, the surprise assault at Brown's Ferry on the morning of October 27 was further indication of just such an enemy movement—the initial deception Longstreet anticipated. Based upon messages recently received from Colonel Oates and the cavalry along the lower Tennessee River, Longstreet knew that other enemy movements were afoot. The major problem Longstreet faced was a shortage of sufficient troops to cover both his southern and western fronts. Since Bragg had pulled Buckner's Division from his right flank on October 24, Longstreet had recalled to Lookout Mountain most of Evander Law's Brigade from the Raccoon Mountain/ Tennessee River perimeter. This action was to help maintain the main line of investment and provide sufficient reserves on Lookout Mountain, which was especially important if the enemy approached from the south along the mountain's crest.[5]

Longstreet's obsession with protecting his rear thus was a major factor in that commander's determination not to counterattack at Brown's Ferry, as sought by Bragg on the morning of October 27. Believing Bragg's absence and lack of knowledge of the existing circumstances allowed him discretion in the matter, Longstreet made a decision that seemed fully justified late that afternoon when intelligence was received of an enemy crossing of the Tennessee River near Bridgeport. The enemy column "in force" was advancing toward Trenton, Georgia, along the southern approaches to Lookout Mountain, warned signal officers posted in the region.

Immediately, Longstreet sent a dispatch to Bragg's headquarters about the preparations he was making to defend mountain passes to the south "before the enemy reaches there." Nothing was mentioned about attacking the nearby Brown's Ferry lodgment. Longstreet's attention was focused and his priorities fixed. What the absent Bragg's intent might be seemed of minimal concern. Longstreet, Lee's "Old Warhorse," was present and knew what to do.[6]

In the Confederate lines now withdrawn to the base of Lookout Mountain, Brig. Gen. Evander Law had finally arrived from the mountain with the remainder of his and another brigade. Here he met the remnants of Oates's command. It was late in the afternoon and Law found Oates resting on the floor of a nearby house, his ugly wound having been dressed by a surgeon. Oates, who had sipped whiskey while his wound was bandaged, minced few words. Law was "too late," he gasped. The enemy had a heavy force across the river, and it would be futile to attack. Law then rode to a nearby hill and studied the Brown's Ferry region through field glasses. Soon returning to Oates's side, he agreed. "You're quite right," exclaimed Law. "The Yankees have laid a pontoon bridge, and have at least a corps in the valley."[7]

It was all very frustrating. In the absence of further instructions from Longstreet's headquarters, there was little else to be done. Law placed his men in a defensive line and began to wait. Even the handful of Whitworth sharpshooters seemed ill at ease; being posted further downriver, they hadn't so much as fired a shot at Baldy Smith's troops during the amphibious landing that morning. It was now 5:00 P.M. and Law's men were lolling about, discussing their narrow escape from the enemy's Brown's Ferry thrust when a courier dashed up. He had important news; scouts had detected a large force of Yankees on the march from Shellmound, moving in the direction of Chattanooga. They were then only about ten miles away, read the note. Moreover, Yankee cavalry were advancing from Kelley's Ferry, where another pontoon bridge had been placed across the Tennessee River.[8]

Evander Law knew immediately that the enemy was not looking to attack Lookout Mountain. They were seeking to hold Raccoon Mountain and portions of Lookout Valley so as to secure even further their lines of transportation and supply. Law sent a courier hastening to division headquarters with the latest news and his estimate of the enemy's objective. Again he sat down to wait.[9]

Joseph Hooker was a man who "seems to show no zeal in the enterprise," wrote a chagrined Assistant Secretary of War Charles A. Dana on October 23. Instead of rapidly concentrating his forces for the planned occupaton of Raccoon Mountain and Lookout Valley, Hooker offered excuses for not having done so; he said his wagons had not yet arrived from Nashville. Once Grant was present at Chattanooga and was informed of Hooker's "surprising unreadiness," Dana was sent on October 26 to Bridgeport to "observe" matters. Upon his arrival there the following afternoon, Dana found Hooker absent and the movement into Lookout Valley postponed for another day. When Hooker arrived at Bridgeport that night, he was, said Dana, "in an unfortunate state of mind . . . fault finding and . . . truculent toward the plan that he was now to execute." Although Hooker was administratively "behindhand" according to Dana, his three divisions from the Eleventh and Twelfth Corps, ten thousand men in all, were ready to march for the Brown's Ferry linkup early on the twenty-seventh. Since reconnaissance patrols into the valley had shown few Confederates present, and even a decreased number of pickets, "there was no evidence to show that the Rebels will oppose the undertaking," wrote Dana.[10]

Joseph Hooker may have felt like a pawn in a sideshow gambling pit. The chaos of the Rosecrans tenure had worn his patience thin. Rosecrans had issued various confusing orders, directing Hooker to spread out his troops from Murfreesboro, Tennessee, to Stevenson, Alabama, in order to protect the railroad from Rebel raiders. Then he had received Thomas's imperative orders to concentrate in northeastern Alabama so as to be able to move across the Tennessee River on short notice. The intent was rapidly to get possession of the Lookout Valley road and control the river all the way to Brown's Ferry, advised Thomas's chief of staff on October 24. Hooker, who was at Stevenson on the twenty-fourth and twenty-fifth, fumed that the plan was flawed; it allowed the enemy to gather two-thirds of his force on the southern portions of Lookout Mountain and, by swiftly descending, strike Hooker's column en route up the valley to Brown's Ferry. Rather unenthusiastically, Hooker sent orders for two divisions of Maj. Gen. Oliver O. Howard's Eleventh Corps and Brig. Gen. John W. Geary's division of the Twelfth Corps to concentrate at Bridgeport preparatory to the movement. Because several of Geary's units, including two artillery batteries, were still en route, Hooker had postponed the march until sunrise on October 27.[11]

The day had begun at 4:00 A.M. for the advance units of Hooker's Eleventh Corps. Following a breakfast of coffee, fried pork, and hardtack, the soldiers slung their knapsacks and began the day's long trek. The march was through rugged, scenic country along the Nashville and Chattanooga Railroad, across rocky hills, clear creeks, and along mountainous terrain with overhanging cliffs. Once beyond Shellmound, there was only a scattering of log huts, with ragged-looking women and children peering apprehensively out the door at the long blue column. "How do they live [in such desolate country]?" wondered a passing soldier. After a march of fifteen miles that day, the column halted near Whiteside, Tennessee.[12]

The following morning, October 28, the march continued over a rough road until about midmorning, when Hooker's column entered Lookout Valley. Eastward, the imposing barrier of Lookout Mountain loomed ominously, and Maj. Gen. Oliver O. Howard's Eleventh Corps, in the lead, halted so the entire command could be consolidated. By early afternoon, Howard's advance was at Wauhatchie, Tennessee, only about twelve miles from Chattanooga. Brushing aside brief resistance from Rebel cavalry along a high knoll, Howard's line of battle swept past the burning railroad bridge over Lookout Creek, then resumed its regular line of march. About 3:00 P.M., the boom of cannon from Lookout Mountain announced the enemy's full awareness of their passage. Although the loud whir of incoming shells caused many soldiers to duck, the bursting shells proved inaccurate at such long range. Despite prolonged artillery fire, only one man was killed and one wounded in Howard's entire corps as the long blue column marched along the base of Lookout Mountain.[13]

Late that afternoon, from the defensive breastworks along the Brown's Ferry perimeter, a heavy column was seen approaching. Their uncertain identity caused the defenders to gird for a coming struggle. It was widely feared "Bragg would not lose Brown's Ferry without some effort to get it back." The men stared intently into the gathering dusk, their rifles poised. "Suddenly, from the head of the column 'Old Glory' spread its folds to the breeze," wrote a tense artilleryman, and "there was a shout [of joy]" all along the Brown's Ferry line. "Oh, what a beautiful melodious sound those echoes [made]," remembered a soldier much relieved at the appearance of Howard's column. About 5:00 P.M., Howard's two divisions halted and went into camp near the outer perimeter. His tired soldiers, after preparing their coffee and hardtack, then flung themselves down for "a good night's rest."[14]

Distant about three miles up the valley, Brig. Gen. John W. Geary's division of the Twelfth Corps, the trailing segment of Hooker's command, went into camp about 4:30 P.M. at Wauhatchie. Having marched from Shellmound that morning after helping with construction of a pontoon bridge the previous afternoon, Geary's troops were much fatigued. Geary was only too happy to follow Hooker's revised instructions to guard the road intersecting from Kelley's Ferry rather than proceed to link up with Howard's corps, as originally intended. The basis for this change was Thomas's dispatch of October 27, received on the twenty-eighth, directing Hooker to take position so as "to command the road from Kelley's Ferry to Brown's Ferry." This seems to have originated from Grant's apprehensions: "There is every probability that the enemy will make every preparation possible" to reach the Tennessee River and interfere with the supply boat traffic intended to relieve Chattanooga, he informed Thomas.[15]

Since Hooker had been told that prisoners reported a mere two Confederate regiments present in the valley at the time of the Brown's Ferry attack, and only two brigades had been subsequently seen moving into the valley, it appeared that the essential object had been accomplished. Charles A. Dana, who had accompanied Hooker, had proceeded on to Chattanooga and telegraphed to Washington, D.C., that evening: "Everything perfectly successful." The river was now open, and Dana boasted about the success of Baldy Smith's Brown's Ferry assault. "Its brilliancy cannot be exaggerated," he bragged. Even the cautious Ulysses S. Grant's spirits were bouyed; he announced to Halleck and Burnside that night how Thomas had been "eminently successful" in getting possession of the river and roads along the south bank from Bridgeport to Brown's Ferry. The exciting news rapidly spread through the Federal army, and the soldiers began to rejoice. "Starvation camp," it seemed, was about to end. As a further uplifting sign, the cloudy skies and gloom of the past few days had given way that afternoon to bright sunshine.[16]

Everybody's spirits were soaring, except for Brig. Gen. William B. Hazen's. Hazen was still worried. From his perimeter at Brown's Ferry, he went to Hooker's headquarters and talked with Fighting Joe about consolidating the widely separated troop positions in the valley. Yet Hooker refused to change his encampments; not only was he following Grant's orders; he was also confident the enemy would not disturb him.[17]

That night, there was a full moon drifting in and out of scattered clouds. Yet as daylight neared, the dominant feature of the sky was a bright light, the morning star. "[It] was uncommonly brilliant," wrote an awed Union soldier camped along the river to the west. "[As] seen through the mists along the Tennessee River [it] appeared to be about one-third as large as the full moon. I could not believe the star was that large and could not understand what it was," he remarked. Being to the east, in the direction of where Hooker's forces lay, one wit cracked that it must be "General Hooker's balloon."[18]

Braxton Bragg was in a terrible mood. Having learned from a staff officer of Longstreet's apathy on October 27, Bragg, said Brig. Gen. St. John R. Liddell, "was very much incensed." On the twenty-seventh, Bragg and Longstreet had corresponded throughout the day, with Bragg impatiently waiting for Longstreet to carry out orders that would thwart the enemy's "designs." What was afoot on the part of the enemy was uncertain to Bragg, so he allowed Longstreet the discretion of planning accordingly, including use of his entire corps. Based upon Longstreet's fear about an enemy attempt along the southern crest of Lookout Mountain, Bragg that afternoon authorized "taking possession" of the entire mountain. That evening, Longstreet promptly ordered one of Micah Jenkins's brigades to march to Johnson's Crook, about sixteen miles southwest, to defend the southern flank of the mountain. Yet that night, at 11:00 P.M., after learning of additional details involving the Brown's Ferry lodgment, Bragg hastened to write a note to Longstreet indicating that an attack should be made on the enemy's main Brown's Ferry position if it was discovered the second enemy force was not moving northward from Trenton, as reported by Longstreet's signal officers. To carry out the attack, Longstreet should have his troops in motion before daylight, urged Bragg. In order to "witness" the attack, Bragg would go himself to Lookout Mountain the following morning and meet with Longstreet.[19]

When nothing further was heard from Longstreet, nor any report of pending action, Bragg, at first light on the morning of October 28, dispatched another more strident note, saying "the loss of our position on the left [Brown's Ferry] is vital, [since it] involves the very existence of the enemy at Chattanooga." Clearly, Bragg was expecting an offensive movement to be in progress when he met Longstreet on Lookout Mountain that morning.[20]

Upon Bragg's arrival, Longstreet was nowhere to be found. A staff officer subsequently found him at breakfast in camp several miles from his front lines. It was about 10:00 A.M. when Longstreet "came hastily up on foot," reported St. John Liddell. Although a long-range artillery duel was then in progress between Confederate guns on Lookout Mountain and the enemy's Moccasin Point batteries, Liddell wrote that the heated language exchanged between Bragg and Longstreet was more explosive. Bragg was annoyed at Longstreet's inaction at Brown's Ferry, based upon the eastern general's interpretation of sketchy reports from cavalry and his signal officers. Longstreet had no hard evidence of the enemy's supposed movement toward south Lookout Mountain. Bragg continued to pressure Longstreet on the Brown's Ferry matter, and both were examining the distant enemy lines through field glasses when one of Longstreet's excited signalmen suddenly appeared.[21]

The news was startling. A large enemy column had been observed proceeding north along the base of Lookout Mountain toward Brown's Ferry! According to Longstreet, Bragg at first scoffed at such "sensational alarms." When led to an overlook nearly a mile distant, however, Bragg discovered the column, Joe Hooker's, which he estimated at two brigades, marching north on the valley road from Bridgeport. Both generals were surprised, later remembered Longstreet, who thought the enemy troops numbered about five thousand. As he and Bragg watched closely, the column proceeded to a junction with the Brown's Ferry beachhead. Fully alarmed, Bragg now demanded that Longstreet attack. He would authorize the use of Longstreet's entire corps, said Bragg. Angry that Longstreet's cavalry had not given notice of this movement, Bragg then went off, stammering to Liddell about Longstreet's "inactivity and lack of ability." Longstreet was "greatly overrated," complained Bragg, who now appeared very restless.[22]

James Longstreet was in dire straits. Bragg's orders were imperative. He must do something. But to attack the Brown's Ferry concentration was not practical in his estimation.

The answer appeared almost miraculously. About an hour after watching Hooker's leading column join with Baldy Smith's troops along the river, another trailing column of enemy troops, "the rear guard," appeared along the valley road and went into camp near Wauhatchie, about three miles distant from the camps of Hooker's advanced units near Brown's Ferry.[23]

Although Longstreet later said in his report this enemy column numbered about fifteen hundred men, with a battery of artillery, to Micah Jenkins, the commander of the three brigades posted along Lookout Creek in the valley, it seemed to be only "a rear guard of a few hundred." Jenkins and Longstreet were together on the mountain late that afternoon when the situation was discussed in detail.[24]

Longstreet orchestrated an attack—but not against the formidable main enemy concentration near Brown's Ferry as Bragg expected. Instead, that night he planned to send three of Jenkins's brigades against the "rear guard" column under orders to move along the valley road and "pick up everything that was behind." Should "circumstances favor it," Jenkins might make a demonstration against the main force at Brown's Ferry and "endeavor to drive the enemy across the river."[25]

This appears to have been said tongue in cheek. In so many words, Longstreet would comply with Bragg's attack mandate, but it was essentially a ruse. Jenkins would advance Law's Brigade to occupy a hill in front, so as to command the road to Brown's Ferry and thereby prevent the enemy from joining forces. Jenkins might then sweep south along the valley road, gathering in a few stragglers, and probably chase away the "rear guards." It would surely satisfy Bragg's unreasoning mind, thought the calculating James Longstreet.[26]

CHAPTER 16

JENKINS'S PATROL TO PICK UP
WAGONS AND STRAGGLERS

Brig. Gen. Micah Jenkins's burning ambition was well known throughout the army. A South Carolinian whose wealthy background had allowed him high social status, Jenkins was much accomplished and polished, having graduated first in his class at the South Carolina Military Academy (now the Citadel). While being described as cheerful and popular with his men, Jenkins also was exceedingly proud, and his often-overbearing demeanor had resulted in many serious rivals in the army, including a key subordinate he commanded at Chattanooga on October 28, Brig. Gen. Evander McIvor Law.[1]

Although both were twenty-seven, Jenkins's commission as brigadier general, dated July 22, 1862, was about two months earlier than Law's, a critical aspect in the hierarchy of command. When division commander Maj. Gen. John Bell Hood had been badly wounded at Chickamauga, as earlier at Gettysburg, Evander Law had assumed command and capably led the division through the remainder of both battles. Only a few days following Chickamauga, however, Jenkins had arrived with Longstreet's rear echelon from detached duty in Virginia and assumed division command based upon his seniority in rank. Aside from their great rivalry for promotion to major general and permanent command of Hood's Division, the two South Carolina natives were opposites in personality and perspectives. Each disliked the other, but more importantly to Jenkins, he had gained the personal friendship of James Longstreet. Law, in turn, had earned the disapproval of his famous corps commander for his outspoken criticisms.[2]

On the afternoon of October 28, 1863, Micah Jenkins was looking to consolidate his position as division commander. Evander Law was looking for help.[3]

*   *   *

About noon on the twenty-eighth, Law's scouts had reported a heavy column of enemy approaching his mini-brigade's isolated position along Lookout Creek from the direction of Trenton, in the valley. Not having been earlier warned of this force, Law was perplexed; "I am fearful of my left up Lookout Creek. Will you protect it?" he anxiously asked Micah Jenkins, evidently by signal message. Jenkins, with Longstreet on Lookout Mountain, was almost disdainful. "Your left seems to be very well protected, [the enemy has] only a rear guard of a few hundred on your left," he tartly replied. Even Longstreet seemed unconcerned, and he signaled Law: "General Bragg, who is on the mountain, tells me that only two brigades have passed above you, and [I] will keep you advised." Since by this time his skirmishers were engaged with passing Federal infantry on the wagon road to Brown's Ferry, Law was not reassured; there were perhaps five or six thousand Yankees then passing to his right, and Law wanted to know the location of his supports. They were on south Lookout Mountain near Summertown, Longstreet curtly replied.[4]

This continued carelessness pointed to the still-lingering fear of James Longstreet that he would be attacked from the south along the Lookout Mountain crest. In spite of Hooker's column marching north to link up with the enemy's Brown's Ferry troops, Longstreet remained wary and was unwilling to commit to a major offensive movement involving the displacement of his corps from Lookout Mountain. He hadn't heard from cavalry units positioned near Trenton since the afternoon of the twenty-seventh. This seemed to be a major reason for the halfhearted effort planned for most of Jenkins's troops on the night of the twenty-eighth.[5]

Longstreet later cited the unexpected appearance of Joe Hooker's column marching north along the valley as the basis for criticizing his cavalry; they hadn't sent any warning beyond a preliminary 3:30 P.M. dispatch on October 27, he complained. For this failure, although never revealed, Longstreet himself was much to blame. After learning of the enemy's presence near Trenton from the cavalry and signal officers on the twenty-seventh, Longstreet had sent orders for Col. J. Warren Grigsby and his 6th Kentucky cavalrymen "to hold the mountain passes from Nickajack trail to Johnson's Crook." Since these vital passes to the southern Lookout Mountain region were *south* of Trenton, Grigsby and most of his men had gone in the opposite direction from Hooker's column, which on the twenty-eighth had turned north toward Brown's Ferry. Again, the root of the problem lay in Longstreet's conviction that the Federal column would sweep south to "gain possession of Lookout Mountain," then advance north along the crest.[6]

Evander Law was informed late on the afternoon of the twenty-eighth about Longstreet's pending plan to interdict the Brown's Ferry road that night. To do this, Law was to "cautiously advance" at dark about a mile and take position so as to "blockade the road and capture any trains that might attempt to pass." When Micah Jenkins arrived just before dark, Law learned of the basic plan. Jenkins would take the three other available brigades of his division and "cut off the enemy's trains and capture the rear guard and stragglers."[7]

Law was appalled. Being an eyewitness to what had just transpired in the valley, he "ventured to remark" to Jenkins that the enemy force was too large for even a division to attack. A bloody failure was in the offing, warned the aroused Law. Merely saying that he had "positive orders" to proceed, Jenkins brusquely ordered Law to advance with his brigade, then departed to bring up the other three brigades, which were still on Lookout Mountain.[8]

In the darkness and rugged mountain terrain, paths were indistinct and the progress of Jenkins's troops was slow. Since all of his units did not march until after dark on the twenty-eighth due to the need for concealment, Jenkins had much difficulty in getting his troops forward in a timely manner. It was about 9:00 P.M. before Brig. Gen. Henry L. Benning's Brigade, the last in Jenkins's column, arrived along the line of the railroad in the valley. Due to more delays, it was nearly midnight before the trailing two brigades, Brig. Gen. Jerome B. Robertson's and Benning's, reached the vicinity of the Brown's Ferry road.[9]

By now, both Jenkins and Longstreet had begun to fret. Upon their arrival at the valley road, no enemy traffic was found along the roadway; there was virtually "nothing there." Mindful of the delays and Law's explicit warning about the heavy force at nearby Brown's Ferry, Jenkins agreed to a major revision in plans. Instead of proceeding down the valley road with three brigades, he would post Benning's and Robertson's to support Law and send only what had been his own brigade, now commanded by Col. John Bratton, along the road to "see if he could find any wagons . . . and stragglers" before returning to camp.[10]

This being little more than an opportunistic patrol, Longstreet was convinced nothing of consequence would occur that night, and before 1:00 A.M. he went back to his Lookout Mountain headquarters. "There seemed to be no prospect of doing anything," he admitted the following day.[11]

Jenkins met with Law shortly after Longstreet's departure, and Law was told Bratton's Brigade would push south along the line of the railroad until they came in contact with the enemy. If he encountered only a small force, Bratton might "pick it up." Otherwise, should the enemy prove too strong, Bratton would retire across Lookout Creek under cover of Law's road-blockading force. Since Bratton planned to utilize only four of his regiments for the actual patrol, the tentative nature of the effort was evident from the start.[12]

Of lurking influence, however, especially in view of Longstreet having already given up on the project, were the unit commanders' personal ambitions. Clearly, Jenkins was hoping for some positive results so as to solidify his promotion to major general. Likewise, the new commander of his brigade, Col. John Bratton of the 6th South Carolina Infantry, was seeking his first star and permanent command of Jenkins's old brigade.

*　　*　　*

Union Brig. Gen. John W. Geary was a man of ambition, a fifty-three-year-old Pennsylvanian whose roustabout career had included terms as mayor of San Francisco, California, and territorial governor of Kansas. A large, hawk-eyed individual with a full beard and an outspoken manner, Geary was a soldier with a flair for self-serving publicity. Although a veteran of major eastern battles, including the furious night encounter on Culp's Hill at Gettysburg on July 2, Geary was controversial for his much-noticed minimal exposure in battle, even while in quest of his second star.[13]

On the afternoon of October 28, Geary had camped his bone-weary fifteen-hundred-man division at Wauhatchie, Tennessee, without fanfare. The trailing units hadn't reached camp until about 7:00 P.M., and Geary was in no mood to make his men entrench. Aware that Rebel signal posts had been active during the day on Lookout Mountain, Geary was additionally informed that evening of nearby enemy troops. A local resident, Judge Rowden, revealed that some of Longstreet's soldiers were camped at the foot of the mountain, on the other side of Lookout Creek, not more than a mile and a quarter distant. Although told there was a bridge at that site, Geary wasn't looking for trouble from the north; Howard's Eleventh Corps had just passed in that direction. "My anticipations were that we would be approached [by the enemy, if at all] from the southward," said Geary. Thus, most of his pickets were posted along the road leading south, toward Trenton. Geary did, however, order that his only artillery battery be unlimbered on a knoll near the Rowden house, sweeping both the road and railroad bed.[14]

Geary's men had been warned to be particularly watchful that night, and the division officer of the day, Col. William Rickards, Jr., of the 29th Pennsylvania, posted his few northern outposts nearly three-quarters of a mile from camp along the Brown's Ferry road. About 11:15 P.M., there had been an outburst of firing along this road. Rickards hastened to the outposts, only to find that the firing was beyond his main picket line and had already ceased.* Returning to camp, Rickards was surprised to find Geary's entire command formed in line and under arms. The men were jumpy, being in the enemy's territory, but after a half hour's uneventful wait, they were dismissed and sent back to their tents. Geary was not amused; it seemed to be another miserable, sleepless night, and he glanced at the "fitful moon" weaving in and out of the clouds, noticing that when the moon was hidden, a person couldn't see even one hundred yards.[15]

John Bratton was stalking the enemy. Utilizing the line of the valley railroad, Bratton's four South Carolina regiments had swept forward in the

---

*This firing was apparently the result of a 150-man patrol from the 141st New York, which proceeded toward the vicinity of the Ellis house on the road to Wauhatchie so as to "cut off" any enemy sharpshooters lurking in the area. Here they encountered Rebel skirmishers, opening a brief, scattering fire before withdrawing. See O.R. 31-1-98, 112.

darkness until reaching the Brown's Ferry road. Here they had captured several enemy stragglers before proceeding on toward Wauhatchie. A half mile down the road, Bratton's men had briefly skirmished with Yankee pickets along a rivulet before moving on. Now they were in view of the glowing campfires of the enemy's main camp. Bratton looked on with amazement. Firing had just broken out again in front, among his skirmishers, and within the camp, soldiers were dashing madly about, some attempting to extinguish the blazing campfires. Due to the great commotion, Bratton thought the enemy might be attempting to get away. He immediately put three of his regiments in line of battle and ordered them forward. They were not to fire, shouted Bratton, until past the picket line in front.[16]

All hell had broken loose in John Geary's encampment. It was discovered that the enemy was in close proximity and charging rapidly after the fleeing outposts and pickets. Geary's jolted troops rushed into line with arms already loaded from the previous alarm. Scattered flashes of rifle fire seemed to be fast approaching, marking the rapid progress of the enemy's line. Two sections of Knapp's Pennsylvania Battery (E) were hastily wheeled forward by hand to cover the open field west of the railroad. Yet the artillery brigade's commanding officer, Maj. John A. Reynolds, knew that close in front were a mixture of the outpost pickets and Geary's other troops rushing to form a line of battle. Canister would kill or maim his own infantry, but Reynolds was desperate. He ordered Knapp's gunners to fire shrapnel (spherical case shot) with short fuses, hoping the bursts would be just beyond the forming line.[17]

The gunners jerked their lanyards. There was a wall of flame, then a resounding crash. Bursting shells showered the sky with fire. A lieutenant of the 111th Pennsylvania, rushing into line, was flung to the ground, killed by a premature shell burst. Yet the tactic worked. The 2nd South Carolina Rifles, on Bratton's left flank, were caught in the open field and halted by the shell fire. Volleys of musketry, poured into the 2nd's ranks, soon caused their line to fall back. Bratton's other two forward regiments were unsupported, and they soon stalled in moving to the right. Although both continued to fire with deadly effect into Geary's line, distant about a hundred yards, Bratton hastily sought to bring up his reserves.[18]

The first volleys had been fired about an hour and fifteen minutes after the original alarm, at approximately 12:30 A.M., October 29, later wrote the exasperated John Geary. Due to the unexpected direction of attack and a lack of defensive breastworks, Geary had to improvise a line of battle. Placing three of his regiments facing north, along a rail fence in front of the open field, and two east, along the railroad embankment, Geary's battle line, in the shape of an inverted L—with the artillery firing across the shank segment, was constricted. There was much chaos, and a few men began running to the rear. Brig. Gen. George S. Greene, one of the heroes of the Culp's Hill fighting at Gettysburg, was riding along the line, rounding up stragglers, when he suddenly reeled in the saddle. A bullet had shattered his upper jaw. His mouth full of blood and unable to speak, Greene was helped to the rear. Nearby, a New York regiment, the 149th Infantry, was stampeded by mounted staff officers and orderlies scattering in haste amid the incoming fire. In the darkness, a "cavalcade" of horsemen mixed with ambulances and wagons trying to get to the rear so disrupted the regiment that it was "entirely broken to pieces and disorganized."[19]

Geary was in trouble. A few prisoners captured in the early confusion told Geary he was facing Hood's Division of Longstreet's Corps. Unaware that in reality it was a only few regiments of a single brigade commanded by Bratton, Geary began to fear the result, especially when an abrupt attack materialized beyond his western flank.[20]

Ironically, Col. John Bratton was equally ignorant about the extent of the enemy he now faced. Unaware that he had taken on two full brigades, Bratton continued to push for a quick victory over what Jenkins had suggested were only "a few hundred" enemy. Bratton had just managed to bring up the 6th South Carolina and Hampton's Legion regiments from the rear. Directing them to the right, he watched them swing beyond the line of flashing enemy muskets and dash forward into the Yankees' wagon camp. In minutes, this was easily captured, inclusive of Geary's reserve ammunition supply. Bratton seemed to be on the verge of an easy victory.[21]

The flank of the 137th New York Infantry, on Geary's far left, was now "in the air." Instinctively, the adjutant of the regiment pulled two companies out of line and formed them at right angles to the exposed flank. Their rifle fire, coming from another direction, was so effective that the Rebel attack was halted—probably because it was interpreted as the appearance of a new Federal battle line. Later, there was an amusing but false story of "a mule brigade" being stampeded by the intense firing and running roughshod through the Confederate lines, which disrupted their advance. Although the fighting soon tapered off along this western perimeter, the *zip* of incoming minié balls continued across the front of Geary's open field line.[22]

Meanwhile, heavy firing had broken out on the opposite Federal flank, along the railroad. Bratton had put in his last remaining regiments, the 6th South Carolina and Palmetto Sharpshooters, to outflank Geary's line from the east. Both units managed to get into the timber opposite Geary's flank, then forward to the railroad embankment, where they began firing at close range into the artillery and 111th Pennsylvania. Shouts of "pick off the Yankee artillerists" were repeatedly heard among the excited line of gray soldiers.[23]

Down went the artillery captain in charge of a section; he had suffered mortal wounds through the hip and spine. Exposed by the flash of the guns, gunners and animals became easy targets. One of Knapp's guns was hastily swung east behind the Rowden house to counter the terrific incoming fire. Lt. Edward R. Geary, the general's son, hurriedly aimed his piece and shouted, "Fire!" The order was barely out of his mouth when Geary sank to the ground, a bullet through his forehead. Around him lay dozens of dead horses and mules, shot in their harnesses. So many artillerymen had been hit that two guns had to be abandoned for want of men to serve them. Only two cannon remained firing, yet Knapp's gunners continued to use spherical case with effect, driving the Rebels from the woods beyond the railroad embankment despite many defective shells.[24]

The artillery seemed to be the key to the fighting. With so many men down, to Geary the issue tottered on either driving the enemy from their commanding flank positions or withdrawing from an untenable defensive perimeter. It was now nearing 3:00 A.M. The more than two-hour firefight had virtually exhausted the sixty rounds of ammunition carried by many of Geary's soldiers. Some units had to rummage through the cartridge boxes of the dead and wounded to find enough ammunition to sustain their fire. Worse yet, there was no ammunition available from the wagon train, which had been captured.[25]

Amid the terrifying, wild commotion, many men were showing signs of the strain. In the darkness, every sound or flicker of movement became a danger. Some soldiers were seen firing wildly and randomly into the night. Incoming minié balls filled the air from every direction as the enemy continued firing from three sides into Geary's constricted line. In replying to the crossfire, there was the danger of shooting one another.[26]

Responding to the crisis was the man who had commanded the outposts at the inception of the fighting, Col. William Rickards, Jr., Geary's division officer of the day. Rickards told Major Reynolds of the artillery to take one of his two remaining guns and wheel it outside the railroad embankment so as to fire down the line. "Oh, no," objected Reynolds. "The enemy would only capture the gun. Besides, there were no horses to pull it." Rickards glared at the major. "Do it," he ordered. "I'll take the responsibility and furnish the force." Two companies of the 29th Pennsylvania were sent for, and they quickly wheeled the gun under cover of a supporting fire over and outside the railroad embankment. Two other companies of the 29th ran forward to the woods on the right to cover the flank. With the Pennsylvania infantrymen maneuvering the gun and carrying ammunition forward, a few surviving artillerists loaded and served the cannon. Only two or three blazing shots were fired down the line of the railroad before the embankment was cleared. "This seemed to have a depressing effect upon the enemy," reported the jubilant Rickards. All across Geary's defensive perimeter, the firing suddenly began to abate, and many began to wonder whether the turning point had been reached.[27]

Col. John Bratton believed he finally had the Yankees at a serious disadvantage. His position seemed "entirely favorable to a grand charge." The Yankees were outflanked, their left driven back, and they were "crowded and huddled" together in a line barely 400 yards long and 150 yards deep. Then, just as he was about to give the order to charge, said Bratton, the turning point occurred—not Rickards's clearing of the railroad embankment, but an order to withdraw issued by division commander Micah Jenkins.[28]

CHAPTER 17

"WHAT WERE YOUR ORDERS, GENERAL SCHURZ?"

The men of the 33rd Massachusetts Infantry had been asleep on the night of October 28–29 near Brown's Ferry when the rumbling thunder of the guns at Wauhatchie brought forth the blare of bugles and the rattling "long roll." As the alarm spread rapidly through each of Hooker's encampments, the men formed in column, ready to march toward the sound of battle. Within half an hour of the first alarm, the troops were en route, guided by the booming of the guns at Wauhatchie, two and a half miles distant.[1]

Joseph Hooker had been abruptly roused by the distant firing and, being drowsy with sleep, was functioning haltingly. After discussing the situation with Maj. Gen. Oliver Howard, commanding the Eleventh Corps, it was at first feared their present position at Brown's Ferry might be in danger. Hooker told Howard to send a brigade to occupy the key hill, since known as Tyndale Hill, which controlled the Brown's Ferry–Wauhatchie road, where minor skirmishing on the twenty-eighth had occurred. Howard was also to push forward another brigade to Wauhatchie and reinforce Geary. These orders were then repeated to Hooker's aide-de-camp, Lt. Paul A. Oliver. Both Hooker and Howard talked thereafter with the commander of the division who was to execute these orders, Maj. Gen. Carl Schurz. Hooker's instructions to Schurz were to "push forward" rapidly, utilizing his troops nearest the line of march. Schurz, with Howard accompanying him, promptly stationed himself at the head of Brig. Gen. Hector Tyndale's brigade, and about 1:10 A.M. he started south along the road to Wauhatchie. The balance of his division and two additional brigades of Brig. Gen. Adolph von Steinwehr's division would march close behind, ready to deploy as needed.[2]

Moving at the double-quick through open fields, Schurz's advance approached a hill subsequently known as Smith's Hill, about a quarter of a mile north of the targeted Tyndale Hill. The sky was clear, with the moon full, and Schurz, Howard, and their staffs were riding close to the front, through a cornfield. Suddenly, a volley of shots rang out. Schurz's aide, Capt. Robert Lender, was struck in the leg, and the party halted. A scattering of shots was fired from some of Tyndale's troops before a staff officer shouted to cease firing—he thought they might be shooting into their own men. Veering westerly to avoid the rifle fire coming from Smith's Hill and the adjacent woods, Schurz's column soon continued ahead, sloshing into a marsh heavy with undergrowth. This brought the column to a halt, and Schurz's men were belatedly forced to move eastward, where they regained the roadway to Wauhatchie near Tyndale Hill. The enemy was found to be in possession of this hill, and Schurz was approached by Hooker's aide, Lieutenant Oliver.[3]

It was necessary to "take that hill," urged Oliver. Howard had already departed from the column, and Schurz, mindful of his instructions to post one brigade at Tyndale Hill, ordered three regiments deployed to attack and occupy the hill. As they advanced, there was scattered firing but very feeble resistance, and Tyndale's men soon took the crest and began entrenching there.[4]

Meanwhile, sharp firing had again broken out northward in the direction of Smith's Hill. A puzzled Carl Schurz soon learned that his next trailing brigade, that of Col. Wladimir Krzyzanowski, had been halted by General Hooker's order along the road to Wauhatchie. Schurz promptly went to the rear to find Hooker.[5]

On the Confederate side, Brig. Gen. Henry L. Benning was equally puzzled. Originally ordered by division commander Micah Jenkins to occupy Tyndale Hill so as to support Law's and Robertson's brigades in blockading the roadway from Brown's Ferry to Wauhatchie, Benning had been belatedly told by Jenkins to move again. Despite his troops' presence within thirty yards of the main roadway, Benning soon withdrew from Tyndale Hill to the line of the railroad in his rear. Benning thus left "a wide gap" between his new location and Law's and Robertson's positions near Smith's Hill. Although the firing was then abating in the direction of Wauhatchie, by the time Benning had taken position along the railroad, sharp firing was heard in the direction of Smith's Hill. This created more confusion.

Having already given the order for Bratton to disengage at Wauhatchie, Micah Jenkins had withdrawn Benning from Tyndale Hill so as to protect Bratton's withdrawal. Yet that order was given before the appearance of Hooker's main column along the road to Wauhatchie. As Benning's repositioned men began preparing breastworks to defend in two directions, south toward Wauhatchie and also westward, word came from skirmishers that the enemy had occupied the just-vacated Tyndale Hill and were close on the right. Benning worried that the advancing enemy would soon cut off his retreat over the Lookout Creek bridge. Anxiously, he looked for the appearance of Bratton's returning troops so all could withdraw.[6]

Col. John Bratton had expressed amazement when informed that Jenkins had ordered his withdrawal from Wauhatchie because "the enemy were pressing in the rear." After receiving a second notice that pickets in the rear were "about engaging the enemy," Bratton had ordered his men to disengage and withdraw. Before marching back to the bridge over Lookout Creek, however, Bratton delayed to gather up his wounded, even scouring the battlefield for "many of the guns left on the field." As his men wearily trudged across Lookout Creek bridge before dawn, John Bratton was unaware of the severe repercussions about to follow from his and Micah Jenkins's protracted attempt to turn a makeshift patrol into a little glory. Indeed, although the action at Wauhatchie had ended, the fighting that night would soon continue.[7]

Despite Bratton's withdrawal from Wauhatchie, and Benning's pullback from Tyndale Hill, Evander Law had remained unaware of these crucial events. Micah Jenkins's original instructions had been for Law to hold the designated position on Smith's Hill, both to prevent enemy reinforcements from passing along the road and to protect Bratton's eventual retreat. Therefore, Law's men had occupied an elevated position in thick timber about two hundred yards from the roadway. When first approached in the darkness by the vanguard of Schurz's troops (Tyndale's brigade), the Rebels had scattered the enemy's skirmishers with a sharp volley. Yet, as Law soon learned, other trailing Yankee troops were discovered approaching along the road from Brown's Ferry. Law knew from a captured prisoner that Howard's Eleventh Corps was in his front, and he had ordered the construction of log and rail breastworks. From these low defensive parapets, Law's soldiers peered into the moonlit darkness, their fingers poised on taut rifle triggers.[8]

Joe Hooker was "in a state of great anxiety." The earlier firing from Smith's Hill involving Tyndale's troops had given alarm, but it was an advance patrol of 150 men from Colonel Krzyzanowski's second brigade in line that had discovered Law's true position at Smith's Hill. Krzyzanowski's brigade had abruptly halted, and when Schurz's trailing brigade, that of Col. Frederick Hecker, attempted to pass Krzyzanowski's, it also was halted by a staff officer. Hecker, who talked with Hooker at the time, said Hooker was fearful of an attack. It was about 2:30 A.M., and several prisoners from two different brigades were being interrogated by Hooker's chief of staff. From them, Hooker learned Longstreet's men were present in force across Lookout Creek—at least two divisions, or possibly the entire corps, said the prisoners. Although the firing at Wauhatchie had already ended, Hooker feared "a renewal of the enemy's attack at daylight." At 3:00 A.M., he urgently called for reinforcements from Chattanooga. Since firing was still occurring on nearby Smith's Hill, there was little thought given at the time to getting the main column through to Geary. Hooker was preoccupied with defensive measures and efforts to take possession of Smith's Hill when Major General Schurz rode up.[9]

Hooker was obviously surprised at seeing Schurz. When told by Schurz that his men now occupied Tyndale Hill, Hooker learned that no troops had pushed ahead to reinforce Geary. Exploding angrily, he chastised Schurz: "What were your orders, General Schurz?" Being under the impression that Schurz had two brigades in front, rather than just Tyndale's, Hooker was unaware that Schurz had intended Krzyzanowski's brigade to be the one pushed forward to reinforce Geary. Since Krzyzanowski had halted due to the blockaded roadway to Wauhatchie, no units had gone forward to rescue Geary. The matter eventually led to a bitter court of inquiry, which exonerated Schurz and Col. Hecker, both of whom were accused by Hooker of having gotten lost and bogged down in a swamp. Hooker so misunderstood the tactical situation that night that he explained the difficulty as a "disobedience of orders." After ordering Schurz to take his division forthwith to Geary's rescue, Hooker again turned his attention to Smith's Hill.[10]

Col. Orland Smith's brigade of von Steinwehr's trailing division had been ordered to proceed to the Ellis house along a cutoff road adjacent to the Brown's Ferry–Wauhatchie road. When informed of the logjam ahead, occasioned by the firing at Smith's Hill, Smith's leading regiments were in a position to attack from a position presumed to be beyond the enemy flank. By sending two regiments, the 73rd Ohio and 33rd Massachusetts, forward to make a bayonet attack up the northern face of the hill, Smith hoped to advance his line close upon the enemy before they were discovered. Thus, his troops were instructed not to fire as they advanced up the nearly two-hundred-foot-high slopes.[11]

Ensnared by the thick underbrush and with their lines broken by a deep, winding ravine, the advancing 33rd Massachusetts soon became separated from the 73rd Ohio, on their left. As the 33rd neared the hill's crest, a few straggling shots were fired, then a dark line was visible against the moonlit sky. "Don't fire on your own troops," shouted a voice. "What regiment is that?" another yelled. "The 33rd Massachusetts," came the reply.[12]

Immediately, a volley of rifle fire exploded in the 33rd's faces. The adjutant and colonel of the 33rd were severely wounded, and the Federal line broke in confusion to the rear. Doggedly, the veteran Massachusetts officers began rounding up their men and quickly restored order. After re-forming on the roadway below, the 33rd Massachusetts again surged up the slopes, now more aware of the enemy's location.[13]

This time as they approached the enemy breastworks, by swinging suddenly to the right flank they broke through at the apex of an angle in the Rebel line. The 15th and 44th Alabama Infantry were seen streaming from

Law's breastworks, and Smith's Hill was soon occupied by Orland Smith's cheering troops.[14]

With word of other Yankee infantry advancing beyond his flank, north of the hill, Evander Law soon gave the order for his remaining men to fall back. At a cost of three killed, eighteen wounded and twenty-two missing (forty-three total casualties), Law had managed to delay Hooker's march to reinforce Geary for more than two hours. Their opponents, the 33rd Massachusetts had lost twenty-five killed and sixty-one wounded (total eighty-six), about one-third of their 230-man strength.[15]

While intending to defend their new position if need be, Law received belated information from one of Jenkins's aides that Bratton's South Carolinians, withdrawing from their Wauhatchie attack, had reached the bridge over Lookout Creek. Law thus gave orders for Robertson's and his own brigades to retreat. Before daylight, the last of Jenkins's troops were across the river without further incident.[16]

Among Joe Hooker's idle troops, the waiting had been irksome. Due to the apprehension that a large enemy force was in front in the valley, it was about 4:30 A.M. before Schurz's leading brigade, Hecker's, began to march to the aid of Geary. Schurz, alarmed by Hooker's "anticipation" of a pending enemy attack, had decided not to advance until reinforcements arrived and patrols were sent out to scout ahead. By the time Hecker's troops reached Geary, it was 7:00 A.M. At that hour, Schurz's second brigade, Krzyzanowski's, had only begun to march toward Geary. As Hecker's troops filed among Geary's weary soldiers, daylight was filtering through the trees on the eastern horizon. Revealed to all was an empty, desolate countryside. It was a fitting end to the sordid Wauhatchie affair, a night encounter notable for profound confusion and misperception.[17]

What had started out to be an opportunistic Confederate patrol had ended with little accomplished on either side. Yet the resulting reports and many claims initiated a whirlwind of paper, including boastful, inflated accounts and blatant cover-ups. Joseph Hooker claimed to have inflicted fifteen hundred enemy casualties, and he published orders announcing a glorious victory that would "rank among the most distinguished feats of arms of this war." His apprehension on the morning of October 29, however, were revealed by his correspondence in which he sought engineering help "at once" from Chattanooga to help him entrench. Later, Hooker was so stung by backbiting criticism about the delay in rushing reinforcements to the beleaguered Geary, he blamed Schurz for the failure to arrive "until long after the fight [at Wauhatchie] had ended."[18]

John W. Geary was equally outspoken in his interpretation of the events. Likening his predicament to that of a "Spartan band"—we were "considerably outnumbered," thought Geary of the Wauhatchie attack—he claimed he had defeated a veteran division sent to "surprise and capture or annihilate us." Concealed in the barely noticed after-action reports of some of his units was the fact that two thirds of his force had been unengaged. Moreover, Geary was so concerned about his tenuous predicament at 7:00 A.M. on the twenty-ninth that he pleaded with Hooker's chief of staff for seventy thousand rounds of ammunition. Immediately upon the 7:00 A.M. arrival of Hecker's brigade, which had marched to his relief, Geary had them dig entrenchments and take defensive positions along the railroad perimeter. It was hardly the behavior of a confident and aggressively victorious commander. Geary's personal gloom and depression at the tragic loss of his son was evident when Maj. Gen. Oliver Howard found him on the morning after the attack. "Geary's hand trembled, and . . . his tall, strong frame shook with emotion, as he held me by the hand and spoke of the death of his son," sadly noted Howard. Later, Geary wrote to his wife, "I feel this chastisement for the pride I took in him."[19]

Within the Confederate army the ruffled egos of Longstreet and Jenkins were equally apparent. Instead of carrying out a minor face-saving maneuver to appease Bragg, both Longstreet and Jenkins had become involved in a bitter controversy with Bragg over responsibility for an obvious failure and the inexpert nature of the operation. Longstreet blamed Law for withdrawing prematurely, his cavalry's lack of surveillance, and belatedly, "a feeling of jealousy among the brigadier generals [Law and Jenkins]." Jenkins cited Law's self-determined retreat from Smith's Hill as the basis for placing blame on Law for the overall failure. Law's withdrawal was the reason for pulling back Bratton, claimed Jenkins. On the contrary, it is certain Jenkins ordered Bratton's retreat prior to Law falling back, based upon the appearance of Tyndale's brigade and the almost unopposed occupation of Tyndale Hill, formerly held by Benning. The overwhelming numbers of enemy units moving forward from the Brown's Ferry perimeter and the ferocity of the attack on Law provided further impetus for the final retreat, although deemphasized by Longstreet. Jenkins's and Law's conflicting accounts of what had happened became the basis for open hostility between the two South Carolina generals. Law became so outspoken in his criticisms that Longstreet sought to press charges against him. In fully supporting his friend Jenkins, Longstreet wrote an endorsement to Jenkins's report, stating that Law had been much to blame: "Had Law pressed his advantage after the first or second repulse of the enemy [on Smith's Hill], we should have had a great success at a very light cost and trouble." The outraged Law would later offer his resignation when the allegations resulted in Longstreet's recommendation of Jenkins as permanent division commander.[20]

John Bratton's discomfiture at the lack of results and his heavy casualties suggests the structuring of his report to defray blame. In conjunction with Jenkins's effort to place responsibility on his rival, Evander Law, Bratton emphasized the Confederate withdrawal was mandated just as the "grand charge" at Wauhatchie was about to occur. Thus, Longstreet was given a basis for placing the blame on certain disfavored individuals. Bratton's losses had numbered 31 killed, 286 wounded, and 39 missing (356 total casualties). In comparison, Geary's were 34 killed, 174 wounded, 8 missing

(216 total casualties). It was further evidence of the failed Confederate effort at Wauhatchie.[21]

After the controversy abated, the night attack at Wauhatchie was relegated to a minor, confused, and badly interpreted status. Despite many wild claims on both sides of having faced overwhelming enemy numbers, with the exception of Geary's artillery being present, it was a fair fight. Five South Carolina regiments, in all not exceeding fifteen hundred men, had grappled with Geary's two veteran brigades—fifteen hundred Twelfth Corps soldiers who had fought so well on Culp's Hill at Gettysburg.*[22]

According to Longstreet, the outcome had been dictated by Micah Jenkins's pullback order to Bratton, based upon Law's "abandoning his position." Thus, the full truth was less than evident in Longstreet's official report. Bratton was making little progress with his assault; there were too many Yankees, and his several efforts had been beaten back. Jenkins's order to withdraw had provided merely a convenient excuse; Bratton's patrol to "pick up" stragglers and wagons had already gone awry. Jenkins simply hadn't committed enough troops for an effective night action. Law, burdened with the blame for his belated pullback, had been ill-served by both Longstreet's carelessness and Jenkins's animosity.[23]

At midmorning on October 29, a Federal soldier noticed that "General Hooker's Balloon," the morning star, was still bold in the light blue sky. It hung there like an apparition, a mysterious and ominous specter.[24]

In contrast, James Longstreet's dim, receding star was known to be falling within the Confederate hierarchy. Longstreet, who had come west with the bright prospect of assuming command of Bragg's Army, soon would be detached and sent forthwith to serve beneath the leaden skies of east Tennessee.

---

*The strength of Jenkins's entire four-brigade division was listed as 5,067 effectives on October 18.

CHAPTER 18

"WE HAVE THE RIVER"

Friday, October 30, 1863, was a day that would be long remembered. A light rain began before daylight, but by midday the rain was falling in torrents from hovering dark clouds. A soldier forced to march along a road that wagons had "ground up" found that the mud was knee-deep. "The boys were mad and yelled, jeered, hooted and swore defiance to the elements at every step," he noted. The air was cold, and despite orders not to burn rails, a lieutenant "stripped off naked" to dry his rain-soaked clothes by a roaring fire made of fence rails. Another thoroughly soaked victim of the weather wrote, "I felt it would be a great relief to die."[1]

Yet it was a remarkable day, one that had the entire Federal army elated.

The first indication came from towering signal rockets in the night sky, fired as notice of the pending arrival of desperately needed provisions. The pontoon bridge at Shellmound was soon opened to allow passage of the much heralded boat. She wasn't much to look at, a small two-hundred-ton-capacity river-draft steamboat that had been captured at Chattanooga and repaired. Yet the steamer *Paint Rock* represented the beginning of the end of the siege of Chattanooga. Ulysses S. Grant was so anxious to use the *Paint Rock* in bringing up provisions, he wrote on October 28 that it should "by all means be got down to Brown's Ferry . . . even if a house has to be torn down to provide the necessary fuel." As she sped downriver from Chattanooga to break the blockade on the night of October 29 to 30, the *Paint Rock* was discovered by Confederate pickets and fired into as she rounded Lookout Point. About fifty shots were aimed at her, but the only significant damage was a hole in a steam pipe, which was easily repaired. By late morning on the thirtieth, the *Paint Rock* was at Bridgeport and being loaded with supplies. Towing two scows loaded with provisions, the boat steamed upriver for Brown's Ferry that afternoon. It was the boat's premiere appearance as a vital element in the Union army's new logistical operations.[2]

Joined by the converted scow *Chattanooga,* built by Capt. Arthur Edwards at Bridgeport and just launched on the twenty-fourth, the two vessels soon became a familiar sight on the Tennessee River. Because the Federal army now controlled both riverbanks from Bridgeport to Brown's Ferry, the boats continued hauling supplies to that site around the clock. The road from Brown's Ferry across the neck of Moccasin Point provided direct access to Chattanooga, significantly shortening the route and expediting the delivery of the Army of the Cumberland's supplies.[3]

Although rations remained short for the next few weeks, Thomas's troops knew it was only a matter of time until full meals were restored. "Our cracker line was now open," wrote a much-relieved soldier of the 19th Ohio. The men, if continuing to grumble about wormy hardtack and "mouldy crackers," knew that they were no longer limited to supplies brought overland by a treacherous and exceedingly restrictive mountain route. "We have the river," jubilantly wrote Charles A. Dana on October 30. It was a psychological victory of major proportions.[4]

Thereafter, the mood of the Union soldiers was more tolerant and optimistic, and they began to anticipate the successful defense of Chattanooga. "This [Lookout Valley] movement brought us full rations," wrote a gleeful sergeant of the 40th Ohio Infantry. On November 10, an Illinois soldier was so excited to draw the first full rations of bread and meat "in a long time," he wrote that it was "a beautiful day" despite the heavy work details to unload boats and work on the roads.[5]

On the very same day, only a few miles distant within Bragg's lines, a distraught Confederate sergeant shivered in the cold and mused about not having "drawn a pound of meat in five days. . . . In cold weather like this a man wants beef if he has been raised to eat it," he grumbled. After dining on a skimpy meal of peas—"with three bugs to each pea"—the sergeant reflected, "I suppose our failure in the supply [system] . . . originated in the limited transportation." It was both an ironic and prophetic remark.[6]

Thomas's steamboats soon provided the means of improved subsistence, even to the point where there was a surplus in some quarters. A Federal lieutenant was able to buy from the commissary twenty pounds of bread, seventeen pounds of bacon, two pounds of sugar, two pounds of coffee, and one of salt for three dollars.[7]

Among Bragg's ranks, however, a soldier grumbled, "We would not have known how to have lived three or four years ago on what [little food] we draw now." Bragg hadn't adequately repaired the ramshackle railroad from Atlanta, supplies were short in the main supply depot, and Longstreet had lost control of a vital segment of the Tennessee River. With inclement weather imminent, Grant had acted to open the cracker line, but Bragg's logistics had only worsened due to his inaction. A hungry Confederate sergeant wrote on November 10: It was "so cold that no one wants to fight." In Thomas's army, a veteran wrote home at the time: "We have not hardly had a frost here yet . . . [and] we have a large force here and will clean them out [Rebels] in a few days." The difference in the Confederate and Union armies was manifest not only in terms of subsistence, but in attitudes.[8]

Braxton Bragg was in the foulest of moods, having to report the loss of Lookout Valley to Jefferson Davis on October 30. For this, James Longstreet was damningly blamed. Longstreet's excuse to Bragg, also written on the thirtieth, chided the cavalry for not notifying him of the enemy's movement through Lookout Valley. Bragg, who was not appeased, explained the situation to Davis in blunt terms: "We have thus lost our important position on the left, and the enemy holds the railroad within six miles of Chattanooga."[9]

On the thirty-first, with the arrival that morning of Lt. Gen. William J. Hardee, Polk's replacement, Bragg ordered Hardee, Breckinridge, and Longstreet to make an immediate evaluation of a full-scale attack on the enemy's main positions in Lookout Valley. Longstreet later spoke for the trio: An attack was "impracticable." Not only were too many enemy now in the valley but bringing Confederate troops forward across Lookout Mountain would necessitate their exposure to the Union batteries on Moccasin Point. Furthermore, Longstreet later wrote in his report, the idea of "trying to starve the enemy out by investing him on the only side from which he could not have gathered supplies" was the result of "faulty" positions, and thus "we could not accomplish that which was hoped for."[10]

Bragg fairly exploded with rage. In a letter to Jefferson Davis on October 31, Bragg cited Longstreet's further "disrespectful and insubordinate" correspondence. Longstreet, he determined, would be sent to campaign against Knoxville, in accordance with Davis's alternative suggestion of the twenty-ninth. More as an emotional reflex than a considered strategy, Bragg's action thus seemed to be motivated on ridding himself of the hateful Longstreet and his Virginians. That it nicely dovetailed into his previous plans to aid the Sam Jones–initiated offensive in east Tennessee was so much window dressing. Bragg could well afford a tongue-in-cheek comment when giving Longstreet his instructions on November 4: "I . . . sincerely wish you the same success which has ever marked your brilliant career." That Longstreet had had no success while besieging Chattanooga seemed to be a moot but pertinent point.[11]

Ulysses S. Grant's mood was decidedly upbeat. On the day following the Wauhatchie fight, Grant, Thomas, and their staffs had visited the Brown's Ferry positions. After riding his horse up the side of the steep banks while his staff followed on foot, Grant had studied the enemy's position on Lookout Mountain, and he seemed to believe the number of Rebel troops there was not as large as presumed. Accordingly, his plans remained unchanged. He would seek to resume offensive operations as soon as possible.[12]

Grant was much relieved at the course of recent events. After ordering several corrections in Hooker's defensive positions in Lookout Valley, Grant was convinced that his lodgment there was so strong that the Federal troops "could not be driven [out] except by vastly superior forces, and then only with great loss." The advantages thus secured were "of vast importance," concluded Grant. Noting that ten thousand animals had perished in "the vain attempt to supply half rations to the troops by the . . . Walden's Ridge [route]," Grant estimated that the men "could not have been supplied another week." The army at Chattanooga had been "practically invested," and due to the starved condition of the animals, "an attempt to retreat [from the city] must have been [made] with men alone . . . [leading] to almost certain annihilation." Now his army had "quiet possession of the short and comparatively good road on the south side of the river from the terminus of the railroad to Chattanooga." The importance of this move could not be overestimated, reflected Grant.[13]

"Gaining possession of the river below Lookout Mountain has remedied this [dire situation] so far as to enable [us] to hold on here," Grant told a friend. Once sufficient supplies were on hand, he would be able to "turn his attention to destroying all chance of the enemy's attacking Burnside from the southwest," Grant informed Henry Halleck on October 30.[14]

In ordering up extensive supplies, Grant was preparing to take the offensive. Matters were going well, and it was a confident, optimistic Grant who seemed to enjoy the moment to its fullest. Even his often-difficult subordinate George H. Thomas didn't seem to be much of a problem. Grant wrote to his wife that "The best of feeling seems to prevail with[in] the army here since the change [in commanders]. Thomas has the confidence of all the troops . . . [and] the consolidation of the three departments into one also seems to give general satisfaction."[15]

Grant's buoyant mood in early November was reflected by the atmosphere at headquarters. The humorous "mule charge" at Wauhatchie became a favorite joke, said a staff officer, who recited the story of Hooker's mules stampeding through Longstreet's ranks in the darkness and creating such a panic, it was thought to be a cavalry charge. According to the staff officer, a quartermaster sent in an official request that "the mules, for their gallantry in this action, may have conferred upon them the brevet rank of horses." For days, it was the subject of much fun-poking banter around army headquarters, and Grant had laughed "heartily."[16]

The news came like a thunderbolt: Lt. A. C. A. Huntington, Company E, 8th Georgia Infantry, wandered into the Federal lines on the night of November 6, a deserter from James Longstreet's Corps. Huntington said he was a northern man who had lived in Georgia before the war and was "forced" into the service. What made Huntington's case special, however, was his story of large-scale Confederate troop movements up the valley toward Burnside's position in east Tennessee. Cheatham's and Stevenson's Divisions had advanced in that direction some time ago, Huntington related. Two days before, Longstreet's entire command had withdrawn from Lookout Mountain, then moved by railroad on the fifth. It was understood among the officers that Longstreet's men would cooperate with a force sent from Robert E. Lee's army to drive Burnside out of east Tennessee.[17]

Huntington provided so many details that his "statements bear the stamp of truth," remarked Charles A. Dana. Grant agreed, and based upon scattered intelligence over the past few days, he said there was little doubt Longstreet was moving against Burnside in east Tennessee. This alarming news coincided with word just received from Burnside of the capture of a Federal battery and nearly half the garrison of Rogersville, Tennessee, in the eastern portion of the state. Together, they provided strong evidence of a major Confederate effort in that direction.[18]

Grant rushed into action. On the morning of November 7, he ordered George H. Thomas to attack the northern end of Missionary Ridge "not one moment later than tomorrow morning." "It was an imperative duty" for Thomas to draw the enemy's attention from Burnside to the Chattanooga front, said Grant. By threatening the Rebel line of communications, it was hoped Bragg would recall Longstreet, or at least many of his troops.[19]

Thomas and Grant had recently discussed projected operations against the enemy, and Grant intended as early as November 1 to make a "demonstration" to relieve the pressure on Burnside. On November 5, W. F. Smith had suggested a plan to advance the left-flank picket lines forward to Citico Creek near the northwestern extremity of Missionary Ridge. This would be intended as a threat, causing Bragg to retain his troops in front of Chattanooga. Yet Thomas had wanted to strike at Lookout Mountain with Hooker's troops and preferred to defer the Citico Creek movement until Sherman's column arrived from Memphis.[20]

On the seventh, before learning of Longstreet's departure, Grant had ordered Thomas to execute the Citico Creek movement evidently based upon Baldy Smith's recommendation. A major controversy had followed.[21]

According to Baldy Smith, Thomas was much upset, saying his army would be much incapacitated by this intended Citico Creek movement, and was seeking an excuse to call it off. That day, November 7, Thomas, Baldy Smith, and Brig. Gen. John M. Brannan, the Army of the Cumberland's chief of artillery, made a distant reconnaissance of Citico Creek and Missionary Ridge from the heights along the Tennessee River's opposite shore. Smith's plan of advancing the pickets was deemed "impracticable" and the attack on Missionary Ridge "out of the question." The maps utilized for this projected movement were discovered to be "wrongly laid down," and Thomas estimated he could commit only 18,000 troops to the operation. Most alarmingly, the artillery required for supporting this movement was unable to be moved due to the deficiency in animals, caused by the lack of forage.[22]

Thomas and the others reported back to Grant. Thomas said the move against Missionary Ridge was "utterly impracticable to make until Sherman could get up." Instead, Thomas proposed to attempt regaining the point of Lookout Mountain with Hooker's troops once more heavy cannon arrived from Nashville. Thomas's perspective was "to dislodge the enemy from the threatening position he had assumed in our front" by utilizing heavy-caliber siege guns. This would enable Thomas's troops to advance under the cover of counterbattery fire, or perhaps even drive the enemy off the point with heavy artillery shells. Although the anticipated thirty twenty- and thirty-pounder Parrott and four-and-a-half-inch Rodman guns were not yet available, eight siege guns were expected to reach Brown's Ferry momentarily. Thomas anticipated making within a few days a "demonstration with the view of completely opening our line of communications [by capturing the point of Lookout Mountain]." In effect, Thomas had disagreed with Grant about the urgency in keeping Bragg's troops at Chattanooga. His priority was to open the Tennessee River all the way to Chattanooga.[23]

Grant was stunned. Somewhat embarrassingly, he telegraphed to Halleck that it was "impossible" for Thomas to make the movement ordered. Being "forced to leave Burnside for the present to contend against superior forces of the enemy until the arrival of Sherman," Grant planned only to send a pontoon bridge upriver. He hoped that a crossing there might be made to enable a raiding party to cut the enemy railroad near Cleveland, Tennessee.[24]

Meanwhile, he unenthusiastically approved of Thomas's plan to establish heavy artillery along his western flank—to be used against the enemy at Lookout Mountain. "When Sherman crosses at Bridgeport, Alabama," offered the distressed Grant, "Howard will drive the enemy from the west side of Lookout and get possession of the road leading across the foot of the mountain; then join Sherman in his movement up the valley. Thomas will attack vigorously in this valley, and if the enemy give back, follow them up." This, then, was the master plan he explained to Halleck.[25]

Left unsaid in Grant's official correspondence was his bitter disappointment with Thomas's inability to conduct operations rapidly with his army. In Grant's mind, it seemed to imply an unreliability, or at least a want of opportunistic perspective. Thomas seemed partly accountable for the diminished operational capabilities and the less-than-brilliant combat record of the Army of the Cumberland. Accordingly, the cautious, methodical Thomas was not to be relied upon beyond a secondary role. It only confirmed their earlier strained relationship.[26]

In contrast, Sherman was the man Grant could count on no matter what the circumstances. The two thought alike—very aggressively. Thereafter, Grant would place increasing reliance on his trusted subordinate, Sherman, who would be called on to save the situation, where Thomas and the others had been found wanting. But first Sherman had to make his way to Chattanooga. Meanwhile, there was a glaring opportunity for Bragg to seize the initiative. Grant could only glumly predict on November 9, "Although a large force has gone up the Tennessee Valley that may annoy us, I feel that a decisive movement of the enemy in that direction must prove a disaster to him."[27]

Within days, Grant began to reconsider his prophecy. The news from various quarters was distressing. Food supplies were slow in reaching Chattanooga despite Grant's demands that forty carloads be loaded daily with rations and forwarded by rail for use at Chattanooga. At fault, Grant soon learned, were inefficiencies in the supply system. Adequate subsistence stores had not been warehoused at the current railroad terminus at Stevenson, Alabama, and Charles A. Dana complained, "Our steamboats actually have to come up the river with light loads." Difficulty with the pontoon bridges around Chattanooga was a further problem. These bridges were constantly breaking; if not from the rush of high water following heavy rains, it was due to the enemy drifting heavy log rafts downriver to crash into the lightweight pontoons. On November 2, sixteen pontoon boats were carried away, and the previous day four had been lost. Communication across the river was maintained by flatboat only until the breaks were repaired. Tool shortages were so acute that work on fortifications was suspended in Chattanooga until November 3, when the tools loaned out for the Brown's Ferry entrenchments were replaced by the quartermaster.[28]

When Thomas made an inspection trip to Hooker's positions in Lookout Valley on November 6, it was discovered the lines were "very negligently placed" and the rifle pits "badly done." Hooker "seems to pay little attention to his duties," chided Charles A. Dana, and Grant became so exasperated that, according to Dana, he wanted Hooker removed from his command and replaced with Howard. Adding to myriad minor difficulties were shortages that translated into decreased efficiency and reduced operations. The steamer *Dunbar,* another captured riverboat with a large freight capacity—350 tons—was still lying immobile at the wharf for want of machinery repairs "since Chattanooga was first occupied." To make matters worse, the telegraph lines were down at Knoxville for three days, and no word was received from Burnside as to his situation.[29]

Grant continued to fret. News arrived of Sherman's slow progress in crossing the Tennessee River at Eastport, Alabama, due to a lack of steamboats. Then it was feared Sherman would be "without anything to eat" en route. To add to these worries, enemy contingents were threatening Corinth, Mississippi, and Memphis, Tennessee, in the wake of Sherman's advance. The weight of a hundred worlds was building on Grant's shoulders, and still he was mired in inactivity at Chattanooga. It was "impossible to move a peg," as he put it.[30]

By mid-November, his inability either to reinforce Burnside, or move against Bragg's besieging army and force him to retain troops intended for east Tennessee had Grant at his wit's end. Instead of an easy victory and a successful campaign, Grant had thus far found only mounting frustration at Chattanooga.[31]

For much of his life, adversity had been a familiar companion to the former Illinois store clerk Sam Grant. Through the early war years, his attitude had remained resolute and his purpose fixed. Yet the burden and responsibility had become increasingly heavy. "Since Vicksburg fell this has become really the vital point of the rebellion, and requires all the care and watchfulness that can be bestowed upon it," Grant confided to his wife. "It has all [of] mine, and no fault shall rest upon me if we are not successful."[32]

Grant had long ago learned life's hard lesson about apprehension and despair: that it often was the consequence of fear and inertia. Initiative, he believed, was the engine of accomplishment. While perhaps not the Federal army's most brilliant strategist or outstanding tactician, Grant possessed an iron will and a courageous inner strength that enabled him to risk decisive action. There was no longer any worry about Grant's capacity to wage war. It was his patience that was in doubt. His bulldoglike tenacity to face a challenge and persevere until the task was accomplished would be fully tested at Chattanooga. A mistake might ruin everything that had been accomplished by the Federal armies in the West over the span of two years. At stake, he well knew, was his career and the fate of much of mid-America.[33]

Grant reflected upon his dilemma. The Rebels were not only marching into east Tennessee but were also threatening Memphis, Corinth, and Chattanooga. "The responsibility of guarding all, to a great extent, devolves upon me," he told his wife. "With all this I lose no sleep, except I do not get to bed before 12 or 1 o'clock at night, and find no occasion to swear or fret. I am [still] very hopeful."[34]

This optimism in the face of adversity was a measure of the man and the general.

CHAPTER 19

"I Don't Think There Will Be Much Left After My Army Passes"

He was coming much as a savior, and he knew it. William Tecumseh Sherman ("Cump" Sherman, to Grant) was "so fine an officer, and possessed of such fine judgement," Grant had placed unbounded trust in him. Grant's virtual insistence that Sherman be given his old commands—the Department of and the Army of the Tennessee—reflected their long association and friendship.[1]

Correspondingly, Sherman was one of Ulysses Grant's most ardent supporters. Sherman's early October prediction that Grant would become overall commander in the West had been proven correct. His close relationship with Grant led him to encourage and even insist that Grant accept the great responsibilities of overall command. Now Sherman was acting out the odyssey by bringing his—Grant's old—army to Chattanooga to conduct operations as Grant's right-hand man once more.[2]

Sherman's curious journey to Chattanooga had begun even before the Battle of Chickamauga. On September 13, Henry Halleck had ordered all of Grant's "available forces" sent to Tuscumbia, Alabama, to "co-operate" with Rosecrans in case Bragg and Joseph E. Johnston combined forces and advanced through northern Alabama. Due to the lack of telegraphic communications and a mix-up in delivery by steamboat, it was September 22 before Grant received an even later dispatch alluding to this movement. Although he immediately dispatched Sherman with one division to march to Alabama and assist Rosecrans, it became a protracted process just to get Sherman's troops to Memphis, Tennessee.[3]

Meanwhile, on September 15, Halleck had learned of Longstreet's movement to reinforce Bragg, and he wanted Grant to send to Rosecrans without delay "all the troops that can possibly be spared."[4]

Grant's absence in New Orleans until September 16 and the difficulty in communicating with Vicksburg due to the lack of telegraphic connections were in part responsible for the government's decision to send the Eleventh and Twelfth Corps to Rosecrans's relief following the Chickamauga disaster.[5]

Once Grant knew the true situation on the twenty-second, he ordered Sherman to march into Tennessee with two additional divisions, per Halleck's instructions. In addition to his own three divisions, Sherman would take one additional division, that of Maj. Gen. John E. Smith, on loan from the Seventeenth Corps.[6]

Yet the river movement of Sherman's troops was so slow due to low water in the Mississippi River and the scarcity of fuel for the gathering flotilla of steamboats that it was October 4 before all of his command reached Memphis.[7]

Once at Memphis, Sherman had received specific instructions from Halleck to advance and reinforce Rosecrans by following the Memphis and Charleston Railroad eastward, repairing it as he went. Halleck was concerned about the ability to transport food for so many troops at Chattanooga via the single route open from Nashville. Thus, Sherman's repair of the railroad en route would provide relief for Rosecrans's overtaxed logistical situation. Shortly thereafter, Sherman's various commands were strung out along the line of the Memphis and Charleston Railroad from Memphis to Corinth and beyond. Troop movements were delayed by the limited capacity of the ill-equipped railroad and the need to rebuild the badly damaged bridge at Bear Creek, Alabama. So many guerrillas and cavalry units were active along the railroad that Sherman was compelled to divert troops and fight several skirmishes. On October 11, while en route to Corinth, Sherman's special train was waylaid at Collierville, Mississippi, by some of Chalmers's cavalrymen, and he narrowly escaped capture.[8]

By the end of October, Sherman's column was laboring to cross the Tennessee River at Eastport, en route to Athens, Alabama. On the twenty-eighth, a special messenger, Corp. James Pike, 4th Ohio Cavalry, after a hair-raising canoe ride past Muscle Shoals, provided Sherman with an important dispatch. Grant, newly in midwestern command, had just reached Chattanooga when a warning from Halleck arrived that more reinforcements were reported en route to Bragg. Grant feared a Confederate crossing of the Tennessee and a strike toward Nashville—or else a major invasion of east Tennessee. Thus, his special dispatch of the twenty-fourth via Corporal Pike warned Sherman to "drop everything east of Bear Creek" and march to Stevenson, Alabama, as rapidly as possible. Sherman's were the only troops available to stop a Rebel breakthrough toward Nashville.[9]

The frenzied events of October were fresh in Sherman's mind. As the new commander of the Army of the Tennessee, he knew he was being relied upon to provide a primary means for Chattanooga's rescue. Even his troops understood their mission. A veteran Illinois infantryman, one of the "Vicksburg gophers," wrote on October 5 how they had learned through the newspapers that "Old Rosey got cleaned out" and they were to reinforce the Army of the Cumberland. "Our troops never have been whipped yet," he cracked, "and [when we get] there I'll bet the Rebs will get as big a chasing as they ever got."[10]

The mood of Sherman's men mirrored that of their ardent, confident commander. Sherman's "can do" attitude was evident from his first dispatch to Grant following receipt of the new "hasten forward" orders. After traveling to Eastport, Alabama, on the thirty-first, Sherman found that the progress of his men in crossing the river was slow. Only a single gunboat and a planked-over coal barge were available to ferry across the troops, but that afternoon a flotilla of three steamboats, a gunboat, and a small ferryboat arrived to aid in the work. Sherman wrote to Grant that he was working "day and night," saying he would have the entire Fifteenth Corps across by the next day.[11]

On November 1, Sherman passed to the head of his column, at Florence, Alabama, and began the march eastward. Yet his forced march came to an abrupt halt near Rogersville, Alabama, on November 5. Here Sherman found the rain-swollen Elk River two hundred yards wide and four and a half feet deep. Construction of a bridge would require an estimated five days, and the annoyed Sherman opted for a practical alternative—to detour northward about thirty miles so as to reach the stone bridge at Fayetteville, Tennessee.[12]

Although out of rapid communication with Grant at Chattanooga due to the remote route of travel, Sherman remained sanguine that "all is going on well." On November 8 from Fayetteville, Tennessee, Sherman wrote that his troops were "in fine condition, hardy and strong, most of them having marched the whole distance from Memphis." Noting the strung-out locations of his column, Sherman even suggested that if there was no "pressing haste" for his troops, he wished to assemble his entire army near Winchester, Tennessee, before marching to Chattanooga. Thus, for the next two days, Sherman "paused" at Fayetteville, "[waiting] for my column to close up."[13]

Ulysses S. Grant, unaware of this delay, continued to look with mounting anxiety for Sherman's arrival. Yet it wasn't until November 9 that Sherman received another of Grant's dispatches, that of the fifth, urging him to rapidly proceed to Stevenson, Alabama, after leaving a few troops behind to guard the middle Tennessee railroads and supplies.[14]

By the tenth, Sherman's column was again en route along the wagon road that led ever closer to the rugged mountains and water-drenched valleys just ahead. After reaching Winchester, Tennessee, the next day, Sherman was in telegraphic communication with Grant at Chattanooga and was quickly briefed on the situation. "I want your command to aid in a movement to force the enemy back from their present position, and to make Burnside secure in his," wired the eager Grant.[15]

Sherman's gritty reply must have struck a responsive chord with Grant. "I move tomorrow—brigades two hours apart—and expect to be in the mountains tomorrow night and the next day." Despite the lack of rations, Sherman boasted that his leading divisions were composed of "old soldiers [who] have plundered so much on the road that I have no doubt their wagons contain plenty to last them till they reach Bridgeport." Presaging the 1864 March through Georgia, Sherman had already jested about having fattened up his lean veterans. "I find plenty of corn, cattle, hogs, etc. on this route," he had remarked on November 6, "but I don't think there will be much left after my army passes. I never saw such greedy rascals after chickens and fresh meat. . . . [Maybe] it would be a good plan to march my army back and forth from Florence [to] Stevenson to make a belt of devastation."[16]

To Grant, whose discouraged soldiers scrimped on short rations in Chattanooga, such talk was a vivid reminder of the past successes of Sherman's jaunty, if often recklessly disposed, troops. Sherman's men not only won victories but displayed a bold, adventuresome spirit. Grant already had postponed all major operations pending Sherman's arrival.

By the evening of the thirteenth, Sherman was at Bridgeport, Alabama, in advance of his leading division and eager for orders. "Leave directions for your command and come up here yourself," replied Grant the same night. "Get ready for moving [your troops] as soon as possible," he urgently added.[17]

Late on the afternoon of the fourteenth, Sherman boarded a steamboat for Kelley's Ferry, then rode through Lookout Valley on horseback to reach Grant's headquarters in Chattanooga the next day. It was an important meeting, filled with emotion. Grant was bitter about the uncertain performance and immobile condition of Thomas's army, and thus "being forced to leave Burnside for the present to contend against superior forces of the enemy."[18]

Grant conferred at length with Sherman on the fifteenth. Then, on the sixteenth, Grant, Sherman, Thomas, W. F. Smith, David Hunter, and various staff officers rode upriver along the Tennessee River's northern bank for a reconnaissance opposite the mouth of South Chickamauga Creek.[19]

Pending Sherman's arrival, Grant had under consideration a plan to turn Bragg's right flank, proposed by Baldy Smith, who had made the exculpating reconnaissance opposite the north end of Missionary Ridge on November 7. Baldy Smith later claimed that as a result of his November 7 reconnaissance Grant had devised his specific plans to utilize Sherman. According to Smith, he pointed out the great probability of being able to capture the high ground beyond Bragg's right flank. Yet, said Smith, it was known that "no [final] plan of battle would be adopted until examined and approved by Sherman," hence the reconnaissance of the ranking generals on November 16. Smith said that Sherman rode with him to the same hill where Thomas and Smith had viewed the terrain on November 7. Sherman, mindful of the plan to seize the northern end of Missionary Ridge before Bragg could concentrate a large force there, carefully looked over the ground for a long time. Finally, snapping shut his long telescope, Sherman turned to Smith and remarked, "I can do it."[20]

By that afternoon, the plan was agreed upon. Sherman would proceed to bring his troops forward from Bridgeport through Lookout Valley, threatening the occupation of Lookout Mountain near Trenton, Georgia, to divert Bragg's attention. On the sixteenth, Sherman sent orders to one of his more reliable division commanders, Brig. Gen. Hugh Boyle Ewing (Sherman's brother-in-law), to be ready to march with light equipment and wagons. Then the next afternoon, Sherman returned downriver to Bridgeport via Kelley's Ferry to commence operations. To a newspaper reporter who questioned the wisdom of Sherman's movement to join Grant, he wrote in jaunty terms before leaving Chattanooga: "I have made the junction, and lived well on Confederate corn and pork. . . . I have been all day studying maps and positions and am ready for work."[21]

Grant was equally enthusiastic. "I am pushing everything," he wired Henry Halleck on the sixteenth. Sherman's troops were due to march on the seventeenth, and that day Grant confided to another officer, "I think our movements here must cause Longstreet's recall within a day or two. . . . There will be no halt until a severe battle is fought or the railroads cut supplying the enemy." By the eighteenth, Grant was predicting that "a falling back of the enemy is inevitable by Saturday [21] at the farthest."[22]

The mood at army headquarters now seemed much like that of an expectant father. Grant's staff officers talked among themselves about how strong and secure Chattanooga was, and Col. Ely S. Parker remarked on November 18, "To my mind the issue or result is not doubtful unless Bragg runs."[23]

The sound of band music wafting on the evening breeze that night drifted across to Grant's headquarters. The 79th Pennsylvania's band was serenading the general, who stood listening on the porch. When the band finished, Grant doffed his hat and returned to his room without saying a word. To Gen. David Hunter, who had derisively remarked about the great extent of card playing among the soldiers at Chattanooga, Grant said he thought it "the best possible amusement the troops can have."[24]

"Grant is in high spirits," noted a personal friend on November 16, and his joking and storytelling seemed to have put everyone at ease.[25]

Grant's confidence was brimming now that William Tecumseh Sherman was at hand. It was as if a great weight had been lifted from his shoulders. The army seemed to be on the verge of an important victory, and Grant wrote to his wife of his optimism about the decisive conflict that was imminent: "I am certainly happily constituted."[26]

CHAPTER 20

"I HAVE NEVER FELT SUCH RESTLESSNESS BEFORE"

William Tecumseh Sherman began to have an inkling that difficulty lay ahead when he returned to Kelley's Ferry on November 17 and found the steamboat gone despite his orders for it to wait. Instead of an uneventful cruise down the Tennessee River to Bridgeport, Sherman had to undergo a difficult night journey, being rowed by four soldiers in a small skiff. Occasionally, Sherman even manned an oar. The following morning, the eighteenth, he reached Bridgeport, only to find that his orders for two divisions to cross on the pontoon bridge and march for Shellmound were being implemented slowly.[1]

The problem, Sherman learned, was the narrow, frail pontoon bridge, which, added to the slippery riverbanks on each shore, made transit difficult with wheeled vehicles and field guns. Beyond the bridge lay Raccoon Mountain and the meager resources of Lookout Valley. Since Sherman had concluded "there is not a blade of grass or corn" between Bridgeport and Chattanooga, he "hated to put them [his troops and animals] up in that desolate gorge." In fact, due to the poor, mud-choked roads passing through Shellmound and Whiteside to Brown's Ferry, Sherman had requested that each wagon carry a maximum of only two thousand pounds of forage or provisions.[2]

Although Brig. Gen. Hugh Ewing had marched with Sherman's leading division on the seventeenth, advancing to the top of Raccoon Mountain and chasing off Confederate cavalry in the area, Ewing was uncertain of the intended result, which was to deceive Bragg into thinking an offensive was imminent against the far rebel left flank on southern Lookout Mountain. As such, Ewing's mission was to demonstrate against Lookout

Mountain in the vicinity of Trenton, then, when recalled, to turn and march promptly up the valley to Chattanooga in the wake of Sherman's other troops.[3]

Ewing was at Trenton by 10:00 A.M. on the eighteenth and proceeded to gather corn and flour from the countryside as well as act as if his troops "were the head of a strong column, waiting for the rear to close up." Ewing built numerous campfires at night and occupied the adjacent area, including the local crest of Lookout Mountain. After destroying several ironworks, Ewing wrote on the twentieth that the enemy was generally missing and that there were rumors from deserters and refugees of Bragg falling back from Chattanooga. On the twenty-first, Ewing began withdrawing his troops, and that afternoon he marched down the valley for Brown's Ferry, having made what he said was "a good demonstration."[4]

William Tecumseh Sherman seemed self-assured on November 18 when he wrote from Bridgeport that the entire Fifteenth Corps was en route for Chattanooga, twenty-eight miles distant. It would complete "one of the longest and best marches of the war," he boasted.[5]

The following day, he had to modify his optimism, notifying Grant that it was "rather slow work crossing the bridge [at Bridgeport]" and saying he would reach Chattanooga "as soon as possible." On the twentieth, Grant received a note from Sherman that due to delays it would be an impossibility to get his troops across at Brown's Ferry before the night of the twenty-first. Grant was still hopeful, and that day he notified Sherman, "Tomorrow morning I had first set for your attack. I see now it cannot possibly be made then, but can you get up for the following morning? . . . Time is of vast importance to us now. Every effort must be made to get up in time to attack on Sunday evening [November 22]."[6]

Sherman's subsequent reply was discouraging. On the twenty-first, Sherman told Grant that it would be impossible to get into position until the following day at best. The good weather of the past five days had given way to drenching rain on the afternoon of the twentieth, and travel along the rutted roads in Lookout Valley was slow and difficult. On the twenty-first, Grant glumly postponed offensive operations until Monday, November 23.[7]

On November 21, with heavy rain continuing throughout the day, Sherman's troops lagged even farther behind. Ewing's troops were still en route from Trenton, and Brig. Gen. Charles R. Woods's trailing division was virtually stuck in the mud, not having crossed at Bridgeport until the twentieth due to the congestion on the roads ahead.[8]

On the twenty-second, Grant was so angry as to dispatch a message directly to Charles R. Woods, demanding, "You must get up with your force tomorrow without fail. . . . I will expect the head of your column at Brown's Ferry by 10 a.m. tomorrow (23rd)."[9]

Sherman, who was in camp opposite Chattanooga prior to the arrival of his leading brigade on the night of the twentieth, was somehow not held accountable by Grant. Grant wrote on the night of the twenty-first that

"Sherman has used almost superhuman effort to get up . . . and his force is really the only one that I can move."[10]

As Charles A. Dana noted, Grant's favoritism was now suspect. The difficulty in getting Sherman's troops to Chattanooga involved a crucial mistake. Sherman had ordered his troops to march with wagons and artillery at the end of each division's column. This had so delayed travel for the troops immediately behind that the overall progress was exceedingly slow. Dana minced few words on the morning of the twenty-third when he informed Secretary of War Stanton about the "lamentable blunder." Sherman's enormous wagon trains had caused this congestion, and the rain greatly compounded the ordeal. Maddeningly, Grant had to issue orders to Sherman on the twenty-first for Sherman's troops to "pass your transportation and move up at once." Despite Sherman's insistence in sending forage and provision wagons within the troop column due to his "desolate gorge" perspective, "Grant says the blunder is his," wrote Dana. "[He said] that he should have given Sherman explicit orders to leave his wagons behind. But I know that no one was so much astonished as Grant on learning they had not been left, even without such orders."[11]

Instead of an attack being made on Saturday, November 20, as first planned, Grant's offensive was now "paralyzed," ranted Dana on November 23. Although Sherman sent an apology of sorts to Grant that day, Cump Sherman had no direct knowledge of his soldiers' circumstances. Being present at Chattanooga rather than with his troops en route, he could only comment sheepishly: "I know [Charles R.] Woods must have cause, else he would not delay."[12]

Sherman was off to a decidedly slow beginning as the savior of Chattanooga.

Those at headquarters perhaps sensed that Grant must have been deeply disappointed with Sherman's performance thus far. Yet instead of berating Sherman, Grant had turned his wrath on a favorite target, George H. Thomas and the Army of the Cumberland.[13]

The building pressure of imminent offensive operations and an inability to execute these plans due to various deficiencies had left Grant irritable and troubled. Particularly worrisome were the thousands of horses and mules belonging to Thomas's command that were literally starved to death due to the absence of forage. Dana complained that "nothing whatever is being done to repair the railroad between [Stevenson] and Nashville." Also, there was not enough rolling stock, and the track was so poor that derailments were frequent. As a result, an average of fewer than sixty rail cars were reaching Bridgeport per day, thirty-five of which were loaded with rations. "[The] other supplies [forage] fall short in proportion," admitted Dana. "Now that Sherman is here with 6,000 animals in addition to the thousands of dilapidated and dying beasts of Thomas's command, the matter is even more serious than it was before," he concluded.[14]

On November 20, Thomas had to borrow some of Sherman's horses in order to move a few pieces of artillery. In a frenzy, Grant lashed out at Thomas on the evening of the twenty-first, complaining to Halleck: "I ordered an attack here two weeks ago, but it was impossible to move artillery. Now Thomas's chief of artillery says he has to borrow teams from Sherman to move a portion of his artillery to where it is to be used." Grumbling that Thomas could move only about one gun per entire battery and that his infantry would go only as far as the rations they carried allowed [in contrast to Sherman's men, who could live off the country], Grant fairly exploded: "I have never felt such restlessness before as I have at the fixed and immovable condition of the Army of the Cumberland . . . the loss of animals here will exceed 10,000. Those left are scarcely able to carry themselves."[15]

This was only one of the many irritants. Thomas's rather placid attitude about getting Maj. Gen. Oliver Howard's troops into Chattanooga had Grant fuming. When it was suddenly decided to bring Howard's troops into Chattanooga on November 20 rather than have them move in the wake of Sherman's troops along the north bank, Thomas delayed. He told Grant, "I did not give the order . . . because by an arrangement with General [W. F.] Smith, chief engineer, he is to have exclusive use of the bridge all afternoon [to enable passage of equipment needed for Sherman's movements]."[16]

To Grant, it was just another example of the major differences in perspective and leadership that he had to cope with among his principal subordinates. Thomas wasn't up to the bold standard of Sherman's adaptable and aggressive style. Grant's estimation of Thomas continued to decline. Sherman was the only one Grant seemingly could rely upon. Meanwhile, in waiting for Sherman to get up, the difficulties continued to mount.

On November 15, Henry Halleck had wired a renewed warning that James Longstreet's invasion of east Tennessee was about to cause Burnside to abandon the state and retreat to Cumberland Gap. "Cannot Thomas move on Longstreet's rear and force him to fall back?" pleaded Halleck. Thereafter, Halleck had kept up a constant stream of messages, urging Grant at least to make a demonstration to avoid the "terrible misfortune" of Burnside's abandonment of east Tennessee.[17]

Grant was so worried about this new dilemma, he even sent Dana and Lt. Col. James H. Wilson of his staff to Knoxville to investigate "the real condition of Burnside." Due to the immobility of Thomas's army, Grant, meanwhile, could but plead with Burnside about "the necessity of holding on to east Tennessee." Were he there, he would withdraw only "after losing most of the army," Grant informed Burnside in urging him to stay put. Yet based on Halleck's wire of the sixteenth—"Unless you can give him [Burnside] immediate assistance he will surrender his position to the enemy"—and of the twenty-first—"The President feels very anxious that some immediate movement should be made for his relief," Grant was even more pressured to act. Burnside was allegedly surrounded in Knoxville, and the telegraph lines to east Tennessee suddenly went down for several days. There were also disturbing reports of cannon fire being heard at Knoxville by scouts from the garrison at Cumberland Gap.[18]

Grant thus far had only promised Halleck that he would give Burnside "early aid." Due to the difficulty in getting Sherman's men up, Grant was compelled to report delay after delay. On the twenty-first, he finally admitted: "Owing to heavy rain last night it will be impossible to attack Bragg before Monday [November 23]."[19]

It was all very embarrassing. Instead of a smooth, well-executed operation as had appeared imminent only a few days earlier, by November 21 the campaign to relieve Chattanooga was turning out to be a nightmare.

There was more: With Grant on the verge of ordering an attack as the last of Sherman's troops approached on November 22, another staggering blow occurred. Charles A. Dana had warned on the twenty-first that deserters were reporting the Confederates building heavy rafts in Chickamauga Creek, intended to be drifted downriver during high water to smash into and break the weak pontoon bridges at Chattanooga and Brown's Ferry. Due to the rain of the past two days, Dana fretted about the growing danger to the bridges.[20]

He was correct. On the twenty-second, the bridge at Brown's Ferry was ripped apart by Confederate rafts and the swift current. Grant had to delay for "yet another day." Most of Sherman's trailing two divisions, Ewing's and Wood's, were trapped on the south bank until six missing pontoons could be replaced. Although many of Ewing's troops crossed before the break on the twenty-second, Charles R. Woods's command was still strung out along the road to Bridgeport on the twenty-third. Grant was exasperated, yet there was little he could do. Until Sherman was ready, he could only anxiously wait.[21]

As if the stress of so many unforeseen difficulties wasn't enough, the strain of social and bureaucratic activities at headquarters further burdened Grant's mind. Maj. Gen. David Hunter, the inspector general, had arrived from Washington on November 15, eager to inspect the army. Grant, while admitting to a friend an inspection was impossible under the circumstances, was compelled to give Hunter much personal attention. Grant let him ride "his favorite warhorse," and even gave Hunter his own bed to sleep in when that general broke a cot put in Grant's bedroom for his use. Grant thereafter was reduced to sharing a bed with Dr. Edward D. Kittoe of his staff.[22]

On the night of November 14 to 15, there was a raucous party given by Col. Clark Lagow of Grant's staff at headquarters for his friends. Grant personally had to break up the party at 4:00 A.M., and Lagow was soon compelled to resign.[23]

If the long days of waiting involved bewildering frustration and intense stress, Grant seemed as yet unruffled. He is "modest, quiet, and never swears," noted a close observer. Although one staff officer intimated that Grant was prone to imbibe more than a convivial glass and required watching, there is no evidence he engaged in excessive drinking. David Hunter reported after the campaign that despite his almost constant presence with Grant for more than three weeks, he had seen him take only two drinks.[24]

Despite the toll on Grant's nerves as each time assigned for active operations passed and plans had once again to be revised, Grant seemed unruffled. Having just learned on the morning of November 23 of further trouble at Cumberland Gap, where Brig. Gen. Orlando B. Wilcox was "retreating too fast" even to get Grant's messages, much less help Burnside, Ulysses Grant found his patience tested yet again. Psychologically, however, he was unprepared for the shocking news he heard later that morning.[25]

Braxton Bragg was reported to be retreating.

CHAPTER 21

"CAN'T YOU SPARE ME
ANOTHER DIVISION?"

November 1863 was proving to be all that Braxton Bragg's rain-soaked and depleted army could endure. "Our army is lying idle in the ditches watching the enemy," gloomily complained Sgt. Lewis L. Poates of the 63rd Tennessee Infantry on November 15. "We have all been disappointed in not making a move during the fine dry weather we have had for the last twenty days," he added. With the advent of bad weather, the continued shortages of food, equipment, and even bare necessities had created an atmosphere of despair. Poates, an ordnance sergeant, had been able to find "plenty of bread and beef to eat" until early November. Now he was dismayed to discover in midmonth that his unit would receive only one day's rations of beef for six days. "I was hungrier day before yesterday than I ever have been in my life," Poates wrote to his wife, "and [I] paid four dollars for a little piece of bread which I divided with the boys of [our] mess. . . . Annis, you never was hungry with nothing to eat, and no where to get anything, so you don't know how it makes a person feel; but I know. . . . Great God! how earnestly I pray that this war may cease. I am tired of it tired, tired, tired! I want to be at home . . . with my family that I love."[1]

This sentiment was widespread within Bragg's bedraggled ranks. A sobered Florida sergeant reflected that "there is really a great deal of romance and affection yet in the South, which I wish would give way to something like the realities of life."[2]

The reality was, in fact, almost indescribable hardship. "We are in a bad fix, indeed," wrote a distraught Florida enlisted man in mid-November. "The weather is so cold and the wind blows so strong that I am nervous," complained Sgt. Washington Ives of the 4th Florida Infantry on November 8. Many men in the front lines had only one blanket apiece, and no tents, noted Ives on November 10. "Last night we had ice about an inch thick," and the men hadn't drawn "a pound of meat in five days." Food was so scarce that camp peddlers were selling oranges for $1.25 each, and apples at "$3.00 to $6.00 per dozen." Luxuries such as ginger cakes made of molasses and flour the size of "a card case" were going for a dollar apiece. On November 12, Ives reported: "Our brigade has not drawn but one day's ration of beef in eight days, so that there is not a particle of meat in any of the regiments—yet the brigade commanders, aides, etc. have as much bacon as they desire. . . . Still you hardly hear a murmur."[3]

This was an essential point. A crucial attitude among many of the long-suffering soldiers was their resilient, determined spirit. Despite their on-going ordeal, Sergeant Poates wrote on November 15: "I mean to stay at my post as long as I can get a pound of bread a week, and I mean to do all I can to get others to do the same." His perspective nearly mirrored that of Sgt. Washington Ives: "Our soldiers are willing to live as long as possible on bread and water rather than be conquered and our homes overrun by our enemies." Fighting for family, home, and their close-knit local ties—their comrades in arms—was what this translated to. It was the one sustaining force, the glue that had kept the Army of Tennessee in reasonable fighting trim despite all the shortages and suffering. Yet there was a reasonable limit; the prospect of ultimate success was the incentive upon which all personal effort was predicated. Within many soldiers' letters, there remained a measure of optimism at the final result. Hope was the basis of endeavor, but battlefield victory was the means of providing both.[4]

Braxton Bragg, now that he had prevailed over his many critics and antagonistic subordinate generals, had further considered the molding of his army into a properly compliant entity. This involved the complete restructuring—termed a reorganization—of the entire Army of Tennessee. On November 12 the final details of this major realignment were announced, effective immediately. Brig. Gen. George Maney's Brigade of Tennessee volunteers was transferred to the division of Maj. Gen. W. H. T. Walker. Also, John C. Brown's, William Bate's, Daniel W. Adams's, Marcelius A. Stovall's, and Edmund W. Pettus's brigades were moved to new divisions. Even certain Tennessee and Texas regiments were switched within brigades. This followed by three weeks a realignment announced shortly after Jefferson Davis's visit, whereby the troublesome Maj. Gen. Simon B. Buckner's Division had been reassigned to serve with what had become Hardee's Corps.[5]

The purpose of all this, according to Jefferson Davis, was to remove many troops enrolled in the same local or state region from a common-unit exposure in battle, thus preventing undue hardship in losses for a given community. Yet it seems certain that Bragg had self-serving and political purposes in mind. The powerful Tennessee and Kentucky factions in the army were now broken up and scattered among units commanded by Bragg supporters such as W. H. T. Walker. By dispersing the opposition generals, and, as in Frank Cheatham's case, removing all but six of twenty-two Tennessee regiments from the politically powerful Nashville native's command, Bragg was rigging the army to eliminate certain cliques and thus "keep down the anti-Bragg men."[6]

The consequences were soon felt in the ranks as units like the 7th Florida Infantry had to move their camp and equipment to a new camping ground— "a low, wet, nasty, muddy place." There was much grumbling as friendships, well-known commanders, and familiar circumstances were disrupted. Many units had to construct replacement log huts, "sheds, and shanties." The Floridians carried the needed wood three-quarters of a mile on their shoulders, even as work on improving or corduroying the roads continued, and without rations being issued.[7]

It was a heavy burden, and yet beyond the obvious mental and physical fatigue there remained the continued drudgery of army routine—drilling three hours per day and standing picket for hours on end. "A person at home has no idea of the suffering and hardships endured by the soldiers . . . It seems as if enough has been endured to end any war," wrote a discouraged enlisted man of Breckinridge's Division.[8]

The result of so much ordeal was a toll in effective fighting strength. Sickness was rife, especially "chills and diarrhea," noted an Alabamian on November 15. Such a continual stream of soldiers was observed coming and going to the hospital that in Breckinridge's command orders were issued that a man couldn't go to the hospital without the approval of his brigade commander. Much of the ill health was attributed to the absence of tents and vital clothing; "We have nothing here to protect us but the starry heavens," he grumbled. A Texas soldier, Pvt. Isaiah Harlan, wrote home in mid-November about how he had paid four dollars for a pair of cotton socks. "I was almost barefooted or I should not have done it," he admitted, adding, "We need blankets more than anything else—though clothing of every kind is in demand. . . . I could do well enough if [only] I could get a pair of pants, an overcoat, a blanket, and a few pairs of socks. . . . If I had money I would buy them at any cost." Having only one ragged blanket, Harlan now faced the prospect of freezing unless he slept side by side with his messmates. Already, his colleagues were so hungry, they had begun "pillaging the surrounding country," taking "everything they can get hold of—cows, hogs, sheep, poultry—nothing escapes them." Although he remained resolved "to live upon what ever I draw as long as I can do it," Harlan admitted, "when starvation stares me in the face . . . then I will take whatever I can find."[9]

It was perhaps ironic that on the very same day that Isaiah Harlan penned this letter, November 15, by Braxton Bragg's orders rations were further reduced to three-quarters of a pound of meat daily. In partial justification for this measure, Bragg published general orders blaming food shortages on the refusal of Federal authorities to exchange Yankee prisoners as agreed to by cartel. This "craft and cunning," said Bragg's orders, was an attempt to impose "upon us the maintenance of thousands of his prisoners that they may consume the subsistence which should go to the support of our gallant men and their families."[10]

Starved, ill-equipped, and without adequate clothing, much of the Army of Tennessee knew that the fault lay elsewhere. In fact, considering their misery, many soldiers felt they had endured enough. Desertions began increasing as the cold winds and raw, stormy weather pelted the soldiers in their makeshift camps.

One of Breckinridge's men from the 32nd Alabama Infantry deserted on November 7 and reported to his captors the men of his unit were very disheartened, they would make peace on "most any terms," he declared. "There is a great many men deserting and going to the Yankees," wrote Ambrose Doss of the 19th Alabama. "Thirty-two men went out of one brigade yesterday and last night to the Yankees. . . . They are deserting for want of something to eat." An Ohio private described how Rebel deserters came over despite knowing the Yanks were on half rations—the Yankee half was better than the Rebel full rations, they declared. To Pvt. Isaac Miller of the 93rd Ohio, the large number of enemy deserting was amazing: "If they [Rebel deserters] come in all around the whole line like they do in front of us they will soon lose their army. Three or four mornings ago it was awfully foggy and they say there was 500 came in all together. Their pickets could not see them." A New York soldier in the valley below Lookout Mountain wrote that it was an every-night experience to see enemy deserters come through the lines. "Some nights 150 come in," he asserted. "They say that they cannot stand the cold nights on the mountain without overcoats and not half enough to eat."[11]

Braxton Bragg's response was included in a dispatch to Joseph E. Johnston of November 19: "Deserters are an incumbrance to me and must be shot or they run off again."[12]

The Confederate army was an entity in disarray. Bragg's attempt to encourage his soldiers by offering forty-day furloughs to individuals who recruited another man paled in comparison to the prevailing ugliness. The entire matter was "a perfect humbug," wrote a disgusted soldier. Many of Bragg's men despised and distrusted him. Yet as a veteran Tennessee infantryman observed on November 15, "If he [Bragg] ever expects to be able to do anything with Grant and Thomas, now is the time." Indeed, the men in the ranks well knew the essential situation. The Confederate army was slowly growing weaker and their opponents stronger with each passing day.[13]

Braxton Bragg's thoughts were elsewhere, however, when on the night of November 14 he wrote to his wife, Elise. "Just under my headquarters [on Missionary Ridge] are the lines of the two armies, and beyond . . . are the Lookout, Raccoon and Waldren Mountains. At night all are brilliantly lit up in the most gorgeous manner by the myriads of camp fires. No scene in the most splendid theatre ever approached it. From my door we can see miles, right, left, front, and rear. Many persons . . . say it surpasses any sight they ever witnessed, and that it is worth a trip of a thousand miles to witness it."[14]

It was perhaps fitting that within the grand scene that Bragg so thoroughly enjoyed that night was another equally interested observer: William Tecumseh Sherman.

The news of his coming had arrived in bits and pieces. Gen. Joseph E. Johnston had warned Bragg on October 1 of Sherman moving with his entire force to Memphis. By late October, Bragg had reports that clarified the basic picture. A scout even provided a detailed sketch of the composition of Sherman's columns—six divisions, estimated at twenty-five thousand strong. With S. D. Lee's cavalry in northern Alabama reporting Sherman's progress, Bragg knew in early November that Sherman had abandoned repair of the Memphis and Charleston Railroad and, after crossing the Tennessee River, was moving his columns along the north bank to Stevenson, Alabama. Five of Sherman's divisions, twenty thousand men, were en route eastward, the last of his troops having left Florence, Alabama, on the sixth, Bragg advised headquarters in Richmond on November 11. On the nineteenth, his dispatch announced that Sherman had arrived.[15]

The troubling aspect to many observers was that Bragg had done virtually nothing to prevent the reinforcement of Chattanooga by Hooker's or Sherman's approaching columns or in preparing to counteract their arrival. In fact, Bragg seemed to ponder a sudden crisis when on November 18 he learned of Sherman's threat to his far-left flank near Trenton, Tennessee.[16]

Bragg's response was to alert his Chattanooga commanders to prepare to move or hold the present line, whichever was decided. To Joe Johnston, he wired an urgent request for additional troops.[17]

Bragg's thinking at the time is reflected by the note he sent to Jefferson Davis on November 20: "Sherman's force has arrived and a movement on our left is indicated. The same game may have to be played over [withdrawal to confront Federal troops moving through the lower mountain gaps, per Rosecrans's September offensive]. . . . Mobile could certainly spare some [troops]. Our fate may be decided here, and the enemy is at least double our strength."[18]

They were strange words for a general who two weeks earlier had sent nearly a third of his effective army to east Tennessee. On November 20, Bragg was "under the conviction that a serious movement is being made on our left," and he made arrangements to go in person and investigate. That night, Breckinridge's Division was alerted, and it was soon ready to go to Lookout Mountain based upon Bragg's order. Yet on the twenty-first, when the commander on the mountain, Maj. Gen. Carter L. Stevenson, reported Sherman's troops marching from Trenton up the valley to Chattanooga, Bragg began to consider that he had been duped. He immediately suspended the order for Breckinridge's movement, although he still remained wary. In fact, he directed that all approaches to Lookout Mountain as far down as Johnson's Creek be "protected by rifle pits and other defenses against the approach of the enemy." Even on the twenty-second, Bragg was not satisfied of the enemy's withdrawal from his far-western flank, and he ordered a strong cavalry reconnaissance to "ascertain whether there is any enemy at Trenton, or in that direction."[19]

Although Grant's brief ruse to deceive Bragg into thinking a movement was pending against the Confederate western flank had been exposed as such, Bragg's mind remained muddled. Amazingly, in the aftermath of Sherman's (Ewing's) march to Chattanooga on the twenty-first, Bragg was so naïve about an imminent enemy offensive as to prepare to send 11,000 more troops to east Tennessee.[20]

Bragg's growing preoccupation with east Tennessee reflected his tenuous position at Chattanooga. He was compelled to make something positive happen before it was too late.

As early as November 11, James Longstreet had sent a dispatch saying that "with the force that I now have I think it would be unreasonable to expect much." He needed another division at least, argued Longstreet; otherwise, it would be "another fine opportunity lost. . . . Burnside's force should not be allowed to escape without an effort to destroy it," Longstreet asserted.[21]

Little more than a week later, having pursued Burnside's troops into their Knoxville fortifications, Longstreet became even more insistent about the need for reinforcements. "His [enemy's] position is stronger here than at Chattanooga," declared Longstreet on November 20. "Hurry the Virginia troops up to help me shut up the place," he urged.[22]

For the next two days, Longstreet filled the wires with urgent requests for more troops. On the twenty-first, he complained that although close under the enemy's works, "my force is hardly strong enough to warrant my taking his works by assault." Again the same day, he telegraphed: "Can't you spare me another division? It will shorten the work here very much."[28]

Longstreet may well have been shocked to learn on November 22 that his persistence had paid off. Bragg's dispatch of that afternoon announced: "Nearly 11,000 reinforcements are now moving to your assistance . . . if practicable to end your work with Burnside promptly and effectively, it should be done now."[24]

Bragg's seeming benevolence was not in deference to Longstreet's wishes; it was couched in strictly practical terms. Bragg again had made a major revision in plans based upon a hasty interpretation of new evidence of enemy movements.

On November 21, Bragg advised Longstreet of hearing "rumors of some movement" from Chattanooga against Longstreet's left flank and rear. "Scout in that direction and keep me advised that I may counteract them," wrote the alarmed Bragg.[25]

The basis for Bragg's concern were Sherman's various columns, which on the twenty-third were reported moving into Chattanooga. From reports of deserters and civilians, Bragg had learned that Sherman's troops were on the north bank. Bragg now believed this column would march northward to "get in Longstreet's rear at Loudon and Charleston," thereby forcing him to raise the siege of Knoxville. This suggested that Grant was reacting to Longstreet's siege of Knoxville by sending Sherman to interpose between Bragg and Longstreet and thus cut off the later's communication and means of rejoining the Army of Tennessee. Accordingly, Hardee and others thought that Longstreet should "retire without delay."[26]

Bragg's decision was semiconservative: to have Longstreet hold Kingston "until reinforced" by the two divisions he ordered north via the railroad on the evening of the twenty-second. Bragg's basic concept was to counteract Grant's apparent move rather than to provide an offensive means for Longstreet to defeat Burnside. As such, it was a reaction rather than an initiative. The difference in reasoning was quite apparent. Bragg's mindset was to respond to what he thought was Grant's reaction to Longstreet's offensive. Grant's philosophy, however, wasn't that of reaction; he was a man of initiative. Had Bragg better judged his opponent, he wouldn't have been so surprised by the startling events that occurred on November 23.[27]

Patrick Cleburne had spent the night of November 22 moving his division from the rear of Missionary Ridge to the Chickamauga Station railroad depot for the trip up the valley and duty under Longstreet. Dutifully, the scattered troops remaining along that portion of the Missionary Ridge line had kept Cleburne's campfires burning so as to deceive the enemy as to Cleburne's departure. By the morning of November 23, Cleburne had his division at Chickamauga Station, on the Western and Atlantic Railroad, and was supervising the shipping of both his troops and those of Buckner's Division to their destination—Loudon, in east Tennessee. It was a cloudy yet pleasant day, and Cleburne's approximately seven thousand soldiers were awaiting the final pullout of Buckner's Division, about four thousand men commanded by Brig. Gen. Bushrod Johnson. All but A. W. Reynolds's Brigade of Buckner's Division had departed by midday, and these troops were on board the cars ready to start when a message arrived.[28]

It was from Bragg's headquarters. Cleburne was to halt all the troops not yet departed except for portions of brigades en route, and these were to halt at Charleston, Tennessee, about thirty miles northeast along the railroad. Cleburne was puzzled, but he pulled most of Reynolds's troops off the railcars and sent word for Bushrod Johnson to halt his entire division at Charleston.[29]

Immediately thereafter, another message arrived from headquarters:

"Order Johnson's troops at Charleston back here. Move up rapidly with your whole force."[30]

Cleburne barely had time to telegraph to Bushrod Johnson before another frantic message arrived from Bragg: "We are heavily engaged. Move up rapidly to these headquarters."[31]

It was Monday, November 23, 1863, and the sound of distant cannon fire wafted in on the breeze. Ulysses S. Grant had decided to wait no longer.

PART THREE

The FIGHTING

CHAPTER 22

"KICKING UP SUCH
A DAMNED FUSS"

November 23, 1863, was turning out to be a terrible day for Ulysses S. Grant. First there had been word of the difficulties at Cumberland Gap, where Brig. Gen. Orlando B. Wilcox was so intimidated as to be unable to help Burnside. Grant, reflecting his exasperation, wired Wilcox that morning: "You have got so far to the rear you can do nothing for him [Burnside]."[1]

Next, it was learned that repairs to the broken pontoon bridge at Brown's Ferry were running behind schedule, even as the steamer *Dunbar* was desperately attempting to catch more enemy rafts sent downriver to break the pontoons. Also, Charles R. Woods's division from Sherman's command was still strung out along the road from Bridgeport. The head of Woods's column had just arrived at Brown's Ferry at 10:55 A.M., and it was uncertain that this division would be able to get across before the next day. With more rain threatened, it seemed the difficulties of getting Sherman's troops into position would continue.[2]

Yet the crowning blow came on the morning of the twenty-third when an account was forwarded to Grant's headquarters that Bragg's army was then in the process of retreating. This important information was based on the interrogation of two Confederate deserters who had come in during the night; the message was then forwarded by Brig. Gen. Thomas J. Wood of the Fourth Corps at 3:30 A.M. Per Wood's report, the deserters had seen many troops moving over Missionary Ridge to the Chickamauga Station railroad depot on the twenty-second. Wagon trains had been ordered in, and the Rebel artillery had been wheeled to the rear. The deserters said that by that evening, there would be nothing but pickets left in front of the Yankees.[3]

This account corroborated reports from various sources that many of Bragg's troops were seen on the march throughout the day of the twenty-second, including specific evidence that they were retreating. On November 22, George H. Thomas's signal officers had reported "a heavy body of troops" passing over and moving down the east side of Missionary Ridge toward Rossville. One Union brigadier, Jefferson C. Davis, reported that afternoon: "All the enemy's camps upon his right look like they are deserted. The troops are evidently out of their camps for some purpose or other." Added to a statement from another Confederate deserter, Lt. David Gardiner of the 37th Tennessee Infantry, who reported on the twenty-second that several divisions were marching and "indications are that a general move is to be made," it was strong evidence that Bragg was shifting his army elsewhere.[4]

Grant now began to reassess recent events. Bragg had sent a flag of truce with a note to Grant on the afternoon of November 20. It read: "As there may still be some non-combatants in Chattanooga, I deem it proper to notify you that prudence would dictate their early withdrawal." This warning for noncombatants to leave the city had puzzled Grant at first.[5]

Obviously, it was intended for some purpose—to deceive the Federal commander, so it appeared. If Bragg was planning a retreat and wanted Grant to think that instead an attack was imminent, it was just the sort of device he might be expected to use.

In all, the evidence reflected terrible news. Grant and his staff had long worried that Bragg would move—escape—before Sherman's troops arrived to whip him decisively. Now it appeared that just such an unfortunate event was occurring. "The issue or result [of the pending battle] is not doubtful unless Bragg runs" was the way one of Grant's staff officers expressed his great confidence a few days earlier. Now it appeared all of Grant's offensive planning was in jeopardy.[6]

Unaware of Bragg's impulsive reaction to Sherman's threatening columns north of the Tennessee River and the Confederate commander's decision to send Cleburne with two divisions to protect his line of communications with Longstreet, Grant feared Bragg was intent on escaping.[7]

Although he had correctly read Bragg's intent in sending the warning for noncombatants to leave the city—to decoy Grant into thinking an attack was imminent on Chattanooga (and perhaps partially in retribution for the late unwillingness to exchange prisoners)—Grant was fooled about what was happening in his front.[8]

Late that morning, Grant sent an urgent dispatch to George H. Thomas that reflected his frustration. "The truth or falsity of the deserters who came in last night, stating that Bragg had fallen back, should be ascertained at once. If he is really falling back, Sherman can commence at once laying his pontoon trains, and we can save a day."[9]

That was as much as seemed possible. Grant simply wanted a probing

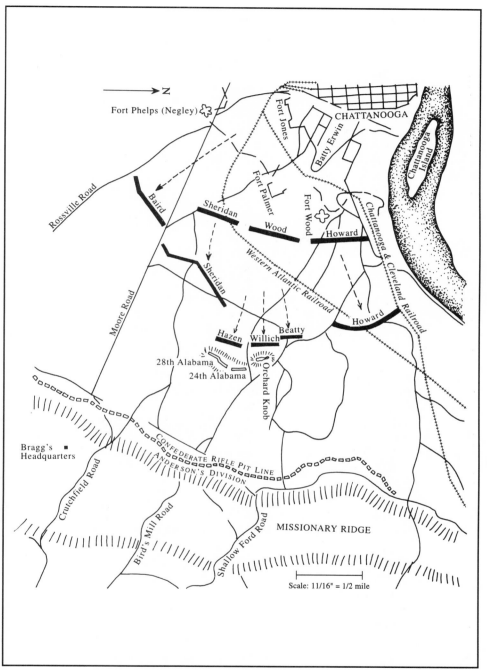

MAP 6   Assault on Orchard Knob, November 23, 1863
(*Source: Edward E. Betts, 1896 Chattanooga Map*)

reconnaissance made to see whether Bragg was still in front in large strength. Should Bragg be found departing, as it appeared, Sherman would be immediately ordered to recross the Tennessee River so as to save a day in the pursuit. Grant was not willing that Bragg "should get his army off in good order," if at all.[10]

George H. Thomas, careful, methodical, and conservative in his judgments, was not about to take lightly the matter of advancing against prepared enemy entrenchments, be it a reconnaissance or a major forward movement. Therefore, Thomas greatly overreacted. He ordered a reconnaissance "in force," committing four full divisions—about 20,000 men—to the operation, with two other divisions, another 6,600 men, formed in reserve.[11]

Thomas's primary commander, Maj. Gen. Gordon Granger of the Fourth Corps, was instructed at 11:00 A.M. by dispatch: "Throw one division of the IV Corps forward in the direction of Orchard Knob and hold a second division in supporting distance to disclose the position of the enemy, if he still remain[s] in the vicinity of his old camp. Howard's and Baird's commands will be ready to cooperate if needed."[12]

In turn, Granger had instructed his key commanders to carry out these orders, with Brig. Gen. Thomas J. Wood's division assigned as the primary offensive unit and Brig. Gen. Philip Sheridan's division in support. As Wood clearly understood, he was to "develop the position of the enemy" during the reconnaissance, but per his verbal instructions from Thomas and Granger, he was directed to return his division to its position within the Chattanooga fortifications after the reconnaissance was completed. Nothing more specific appears to have been discussed at the corps level, Granger evidently believing as the others did that Bragg was retreating. Accordingly, Wood's column would advance and drive the enemy's skirmish line in on their reserves, forcing the enemy to deploy what troops were available. Once the strength of the enemy was known, Wood would retire. No significant collision with the enemy was expected; "it was considered barely possible," said Wood. Thus the great display of reserves and supports was merely a precaution, "if needed" due to a Confederate counterattack.[13]

The morning of Monday, November 23, had been cloudy but pleasant. To the men of Brig. Gen. William B. Hazen's brigade, the day was much like the last few—with one exception: The men sensed that something was about to happen. A slow, desultory fire of heavy artillery against Missionary Ridge continued from Fort Wood, located along the northeastern outskirts of the Chattanooga defenses. On the twenty-second, there had been lively shelling of the ridge when heavy enemy troop movements were noted. This firing had only heightened the men's anticipation. That morning, one hundred rounds of cartridges per man had been issued, a heavier-than-normal allotment, causing much speculation and comment. One of Hazen's Ohio lieutenants wrote in his journal about how he felt "that this is the eve of battle with us." His thoughts wandered as he wrote about how the folks at home would be anxious if they knew their sons and fathers were preparing to face battle's iron hail and about "how many poor fellows are alive tonight that will sleep in death tomorrow night." How sad, he remarked, but, for one, he was glad the folks at home were ignorant of the pending fight. "Come what may we can only put our trust in God," he declared resignedly.[14]

The bugle's shrill notes broke the afternoon calm. Drums began beating, sounding assembly. The intense, labored commotion of an army scurrying into ranks caused dust to rise and hearts to beat faster.[15]

It was 1:00 P.M. and the troops began pouring out of their tents into the bright sunshine along their campgrounds. In long dusty blue columns, the men filed over the breastworks and marched onto the plain along the outer perimeter of Chattanooga's fortified lines. An observer watched eagerly from Fort Wood: "Flags were flying, the quick earnest steps of thousands beat equal time. The sharp commands of hundreds of company officers, the sound of the drums, the ringing notes of the bugle, companies wheeling and countermarching, and regiments getting into line, the bright sun lighting up ten thousand polished bayonets till they glistened and flashed like a . . . shower of electric spirits—all looked like preparations for a peaceful pageant, rather than for the bloody work of death."[16]

It was a martial spectacle at its finest. On the ramparts of Fort Wood at the time appeared a galaxy of high-ranking generals, including Grant, Thomas, Granger, T. J. Wood, Hunter, and even the civilian Dana. Arrayed in line of battle directly beneath the sloping walls of the fort, Granger's divisions stood in two lines, a nervous ripple of motion running along the serried ranks as soldiers adjusted their equipment. "It scarcely ever falls to the lot of man to witness so grand a military display," wrote the excited Thomas J. Wood. "My division seemed to drink in the inspiration of the scene," he continued. As far as the eye could see "troops in line and column checkered the broad plain of Chattanooga."[17]

Directly in front of the Union formations were open fields, through which the Atlantic and Western Railroad line passed. Beyond the line of the railroad lay a thick belt of timber, ranging from a quarter to three-quarters of a mile in width. East of the timber and 2,100 yards from Fort Wood loomed Orchard Knob, a rugged, craggy hill rising about 100 feet above Chattanooga Valley, and its adjacent spur ridge. This rock-strewn ridge, extending to the southwest, was not quite as high as Orchard Knob, but it was covered with timber and abrupt in its western slope. It was the target direction of the reconnaissance.[18]

In plain view in the open field within several hundred yards of the massed blue ranks were dozens of Confederate pickets. Like their Union counterparts, the gray pickets had dug individual rifle pits, with the earth thrown forward as a sort of rampart, and many were leisurely sitting on these little mounds. They looked like a colony of groundhogs in front of their burrows, and they were enjoying the scene immensely, noted a Federal officer.

Because of the long-standing truce between Confederate and Union pickets, there was no concern on the part of the Yankees about being fired upon. In fact, these Rebel pickets seemed to act like the Yankees were about to hold an inspection or a review, for which the Rebels would have grand seats.[19]

Of Thomas J. Wood's three brigades, two occupied the front line: Brig. Gen. August Willich's on the left and Brig. Gen. William B. Hazen's on the right. Brig. Gen. Samuel Beatty's Third Brigade would support Willich by marching in column on his left. Willich would proceed directly toward Orchard Knob, while Hazen would confront the line along the spur ridge southwest of the knob.[20]

The temperature was rather warm, remembered an Ohio soldier, and the men stood in ranks, wearing fatigue jackets, each man carrying sixty rounds of musket ammunition. There was a "nervous excitement" amid the ranks, and yet many felt uncertain. Some soldiers had formed ranks, believing that the day's events were just some "impromptu display or review" for the purpose of intimidating Bragg. For nearly three-quarters of an hour, many of Granger's men had been waiting. It was nearly 2:00 P.M., and behind the waiting blue lines their generals could be seen on the sandbag parapet of Fort Wood, smoking and chatting with one another.[21]

Gordon Granger was the man to direct the advance. The last of the troops were being aligned; all stood ready, awaiting the signal to start. Then there was a crucial last-minute modification in orders. While already formed in line of battle, August Willich was told to take Orchard Knob, a mile and a quarter distant, and hold it until further orders. Apparently, Wood had noted the absence of any significant Confederate troop strength along the high knob. Granger called for the bugler to signal Wood's division to advance. The bugle notes rang loud and clear. Officers began shouting commands. Hazen's and Willich's brigades surged forward with a sudden, prolonged motion.[22]

The day had been sort of a lazy one for Col. Newton N. Davis of the 24th Alabama Infantry. Davis's regiment was on picket duty in front of Orchard Knob, along with the 28th Alabama Infantry of Brig. Gen. Arthur M. Manigault's Brigade. As usual, everything was quiet along the line that morning except for an occasional shell fired from Fort Wood, and Colonel Davis was in his tent writing a letter home. Suddenly, a messenger arrived from the picket line; the Yankees were forming in strong force. Davis immediately pocketed his letter and ran to the top of a small knoll. To his astonishment, he saw the Union battle line only several hundred yards distant, formed in two ranks, with a third column behind, closed in mass. "My first impression," wrote the amazed Davis, "was that they were preparing for a review." When he heard the distant shouted order "Load at will!" he knew their intentions were far more serious. Davis hastily ordered his reserves to deploy along the line of small breastworks erected on the rocky ridge south of Orchard Knob, and he also sent an officer to warn his brigade commander, Manigault, on Missionary Ridge.[23]

Arthur Manigault was sitting in his tent, poring over the endless reams of paperwork for his brigade, when the officer sent from the picket line arrived "in a great hurry" with the startling news. In minutes, the shocked Manigault was standing along the edge of the ridge, peering through his field glasses at the gathering enemy masses. There must be at least fifty thousand men under arms, he thought.[24]

Immediately, Manigault ordered the entire brigade formed and his artillery brought into position. When acting division commander Brig. Gen. J. Patton Anderson appeared, a lively discussion began about the enemy's purpose. Although the Yankee line stretched imposingly across the plain, Manigault's pickets occupied a mere eight-hundred-yard front, with a total of 634 men combined in the two regiments. For protection, they had only a shallow ditch and improvised, low earthworks thrown up along the craggy ridge south of Orchard Knob. The embrasures for two field guns, constructed the previous week, were now empty. A section of two ten-pounder Parrott rifles had been withdrawn by corps commander Hardee's order several days earlier and relocated to Lookout Mountain, where their use was considered of more importance. Since it was uncertain what the Yankees would do, Manigault and Anderson decided to wait before altering any troop dispositions.[25]

Col. Newton Davis was not so uncertain. He saw the enemy deploy a second line of skirmishers to reinforce those already in front, then heard a bugle call and the shouted orders, "Forward!" The whole Federal center division lurched forward with flags flying and rifles poised. It was 1:50 P.M., and with a shudder, Davis realized the two isolated Alabama regiments would soon confront perhaps five thousand Yankees.[26]

The march forward over the open fields was fairly easy—too easy—thought an Ohio officer. Ahead, the skirmish line was pressing rapidly forward, so fast that some of the skirmishers dashed among a few of the startled Confederate pickets before they reacted.[27]

A spattering fire among skirmishers broke out before the advancing line had passed fifty paces, remembered one of Hazen's regimental commanders. Sweeping over the mounds of suddenly abandoned rifle pits in the open field, Willich's and Hazen's soldiers maintained an unbroken line. By the time the Federal skirmish line approached the belt of timber, the withdrawing Confederate pickets had disappeared into the underbrush.[28]

The Federal heavy artillery at Fort Wood had already opened with a ground-jarring roar against the enemy's camps along Missionary Ridge. The eerie shriek of shells passing overhead added to the bedlam and billowing smoke from the skirmish line.[29]

Within Col. Newton Davis's 24th Alabama regiment, there was a flurry of activity. In front of the rude breastworks along the craggy hill south of

Orchard Knob, the brush was so thick that it was impossible to see what was happening. Frustrated, Davis sprinted toward a nearby knoll to get a better view. He had gone but a few steps when he heard a shout and whirled around. The Yankee battle line had emerged from the brush and was but a few paces from his breastworks. His men were already scattering in flight.[30]

Davis thought fast. The 28th Alabama, on his left, was separated from his line by a few hundred yards, with two knolls in between. To try to hold the line against the overwhelming enemy numbers was useless. Davis joined his men and raced back toward the fortified line at the base of Missionary Ridge, twelve hundred yards distant.[31]

Lt. Col. William L. Butler, commanding Manigault's remaining skirmish-line regiment, the 28th Alabama Infantry, was also caught in a dilemma. Despite the great wall of blue uniforms surging toward his line, Butler had just received word to hold his position—he would be supported. Since Manigault later disclaimed knowledge of this order, it appears a staff officer may have issued these instructions as a temporary expediency, pending clarification about what to do.[32]

Butler was in a tight fix. Although the 24th Alabama had already disappeared from his right flank, Butler wasn't aware of it; the intervening knolls blocked his view. Butler had perhaps 300 men in line, facing Hazen's brigade of 2,256, which was seen double-quicking through the oak timber beneath the Confederate breastworks. Fortunately for Butler, there was about a one-hundred-yard open interval between his line and the timber.[33]

Hazen's brigade was deployed in two main lines, screened by a battalion of skirmishers in front. The first crashing volley from Butler's line abruptly halted Hazen's skirmishers. Yet the 41st and 93rd Ohio regiments of the brigade's first line were moving up close behind. Without waiting for instructions from Hazen, Col. Aquila Wiley of the 41st ordered a charge.[34]

Wiley and his men were out in the open, within fifty paces of the low breastworks, when the earth seemed to explode in their faces. A blazing volley from Butler's line felled nearly a fourth of the oncoming line in seconds. The major commanding the 93rd Ohio was mortally wounded, and Wiley's horse was shot. Although staggered, the Union ranks continued doggedly on—to within several dozen paces of Butler's line. Here an even deadlier fusillade ripped through their line, coming from the front and right flank. It was discovered, too late, that the enemy's breastworks ran in an irregular manner, creating a salient angle from which the enfilade fire occurred.[35]

It was military murder. Of 447 men in Wiley's line, 117 went down, and their charge was brought to a standstill. Wiley was on foot among his men, shouting encouragement and gesturing with his sword. They could not stay there; the line must go forward. Seconds became an eternity. Yet a rush began spontaneously along the left of Wiley's line, where two Kentucky regiments, the 5th and 6th, had joined from the skirmish line. Since on the north the 24th Alabama was gone, there was no protection for Butler's open flank.[36]

Through the drifting smoke sprinted Hazen's shouting soldiers, their leveled bayonets poised menacingly. Butler's Alabamians never had much chance. Some lay flat on their backs, shooting at the Yankees as they leapt over the breastworks behind them. Yet it was useless. Engulfed in a sea of blue uniforms, 146 of Butler's men surrendered, and the remaining survivors sprinted for the safety of Missionary Ridge.[37]

Within perhaps five minutes of the first firing along the craggy ridge, the action was over. Butler and Davis had suffered 186 casualties out of a force of 634, as well as losing the 28th Alabama's flag, presented by the ladies of Selma, which was captured by Corp. G. A. Kraemer of the 41st Ohio. Hazen, in turn, had suffered 167 casualties, 14 of whom were officers. It was a "brilliant" fight, "the work of a few short minutes," reflected one of Hazen's excited riflemen. Hazen later boasted that the enemy's works had been "carried at the point of the bayonet," and division commander Wood pridefully pointed out that the reconnaissance had resulted in "a substantial attack" and a "brilliant feat of arms."[38]

Of even greater importance, Willich's brigade, on Hazen's northern flank, had dashed up the steep slopes of Orchard Knob and chased off the few Rebel skirmishers found there, occupying the crest with little opposition. Instead of making a rather limited reconnaissance, Thomas J. Wood's troops had seized important terrain commanding the surrounding valley, to the extent of half its width. Yet these unexpected results posed a new problem: what to do next.[39]

It was about 2:20 P.M. While his winded troops rounded up prisoners and rested along the crest of the knob and ridge, Wood signaled Thomas at Fort Wood: "I have carried the first line of the enemy's intrenchments." Mindful of his instructions to retire once the reconnaissance was completed, Wood anxiously awaited his commander's reply.[40]

George H. Thomas was no fool. Signal flags wigwagged in reply: "Hold on, don't come back; you have got too much, intrench your position." To provide massive support, Sheridan's entire division, which had advanced only partially so as to cover Wood's flank, was ordered to move up and entrench adjacent to, and as an extension, of Wood's right flank. Also, Howard's corps was told to advance from their position in reserve and occupy the ground on Wood's left, along Citico Creek.[41]

Within an hour, the Chattanooga Valley landscape became a sea of marching Federal troops and hurrying wagons. Woodcutters swarmed into the newly captured woodlands, eager to get at the much-needed timber.[42]

As Wood's men dug in with tools hastened from Fort Wood by wagon following the division commander's urgent request, Grant and Thomas pondered the key question of the hour: What was the status of Bragg's army? The purpose of the reconnaissance had been to determine whether Bragg was withdrawing his army. The many prisoners taken said they knew nothing about a general retreat, yet the Rebels had fired only three small cannon at Wood's advancing troops, a sign of weakness. Although the evidence was inconclusive, the impression was that "they have withdrawn their main force," reported Charles A. Dana that afternoon.[43]

Although the Confederate artillery along Missionary Ridge finally opened with a sustained barrage about 4:00 P.M. against the Orchard Knob and craggy ridge Union entrenchments, perhaps only a dozen small-caliber cannon were involved. Dana said, "Nothing shows decisively whether the enemy will fight or fly. Grant thinks latter, other judicious officers think former."[44]

In order to have a better evaluation, Gordon Granger had been sent to Orchard Knob following the attack to assess the enemy's strength and the prospects for carrying the next line of works at the base of Missionary Ridge. At 3:00 P.M., Granger had signaled: "The enemy's rifle pits in front, 1,200 yards, very strong and filled with Rebels. They cannot be carried without heavy loss."[45]

Grant, Thomas, and Wood at that point had begun to prepare for the prospect of a counterattack against Orchard Knob. Late that afternoon, Grant and Thomas rode along the rear of the lines to view the distant Rebel camps. Since the artillery fire had died down and there was no sign of threatening enemy activity, the prospect of a counterattack was largely discounted. Grant, contrary to Granger's report, estimated that the enemy rifle pits below Missionary Ridge were assailable; they "seem to be but weakly lined with troops," he wrote on the morning of the twenty-fourth. Thomas seemed intent on telling the men of Hazen's brigade what a "gallant thing" they had done. Wood, however, remained apprehensive of a Rebel attack, and it was due to his concern that Sheridan was ordered about 10:30 P.M. on the twenty-third to advance further and bring up additional artillery. Bridges's battery—four three-inch Rodman guns and two Napoleon field guns—was ordered to Orchard Knob that night following the construction of embrasures by Wood's men. Before daylight on the twenty-fourth the construction of formidable entrenchments and the emplacement of several batteries had so fortified the captured ground that Grant considered the position secure. Again he turned his attention to further offensive operations.[46]

The terrible day Grant had anticipated on the morning of November 23 had given way during that afternoon to a satisfying maneuver and growing confidence. Great dividends seem to have been gained from Wood's expanded reconnaissance: Charles A. Dana boasted at the time that with the Orchard Knob heights in Grant's possession, any enemy attempt to counterattack through the valley toward the north end of Missionary Ridge could not now occur. Since Sherman's main thrust was pending in this area, it was a key point, estimated Dana.[47]

Grant, observed a visitor from Pennsylvania, seemed "well pleased with what had been accomplished." Moreover, "he seems perfectly cool, and one could be with him for hours and not know that any great movements were going on," wrote William Wrenshall Smith that night. "It is a mere matter of business with him."[48]

The fighting for the day had ended, and on the skirmish line some of Sheridan's soldiers heard a call from one of the Johnny Rebs across the way: "Hello, Yanks, what's got the matter with you all over there?" One of Sheridan's men yelled back, "We're out of wood." Another droll voice sounded from the Rebel position: "If you wanted wood why didn't you say so? We have more than we need out here, and if you had only asked us you might have sent out your teams and got all the wood you wanted without kicking up such a damned fuss about it."[49]

Up on Missionary Ridge, the conversation was not so pleasant. Brig. Gen. Arthur Manigault and others had remained silent spectators of the impressive and overwhelming Federal advance. "No effort to reinforce our advance posts was made," Manigault later wrote, "as our lines were very weak and we had not men enough to man them, and not knowing what was the ulterior intention of the enemy [nothing was done]." Manigault was thus shocked when about dusk an urgent message arrived from division commander Patton Anderson. Manigault was to retake Orchard Knob with his lone brigade. Immediately, Manigault rode to Anderson's headquarters and was told that he "must at once . . . attack and recover the hill which [his] picket force had lost."[50]

Manigault was mortified. It was pure folly; "madness and the most reckless stupidity," he thought to himself. The prospect of a single brigade recapturing Orchard Knob with at least six thousand enemy entrenched thereon and in close support would involve the sacrifice of his brigade. Yet orders must be obeyed. Manigault sadly returned to his brigade and gave the necessary instructions. Within minutes, his regimental commanders reported the men formed and ready to advance. It was now dark, and Manigault contemplated his own destiny—perhaps imminent death or a Yankee prison. Yet he steeled himself for the coming ordeal: "My orders, whatever I may have thought of them, were imperative."[51]

Manigault mounted his horse and galloped over to lead his command forward, never expecting to return.

CHAPTER 23

"The Ball Will Soon Open"

Braxton Bragg had been greatly upset and shaken by the sight of massed Federal ranks advancing in the direction of the ridge where his headquarters lay. Indeed, Bragg had nearly panicked. His repeated recall messages to Pat Cleburne, about to depart from the Chickamauga Station railroad depot for east Tennessee, reflected his utter dismay. It appeared to Bragg that he had been entirely wrong in estimating that the Yankee army would attack the Confederate left flank by enveloping Lookout Mountain with a turning movement. For this reason, William J. Hardee had been assigned as Longstreet's successor in guarding the Lookout Mountain flank with a heavy concentration of troops.[1]

Now, due to the enemy's massive deployment in line of battle in front of Missionary Ridge, there was a major revision in Bragg's thinking and dispositions. Reacting impulsively on the afternoon of the twenty-third, Bragg not only recalled Cleburne and a brigade of Kentuckians under Col. Joseph H. Lewis from Chickamauga Station but also directed Hardee to take his nearest division and "press forward" to the army's right flank. Hardee was personally to take command there. "Direct the balance of your command to hold itself in readiness to move at a moment's notice," ordered the alarmed Bragg. As for Lookout Mountain, it appeared that "a brigade is all that is necessary on the top of the mountain."[2]

Bragg's new priority was to confront the major Federal buildup in front of Missionary Ridge—especially following a Lookout Mountain signal officer's observation on the afternoon of the twenty-second that about six thousand Yankee troops were crossing into Chattanooga. These were presumed to be Sherman's men [they were actually Howard's, moved into

Chattanooga to avoid using the overcrowded pontoons at Sherman's intended point of crossing]. Other reports of lurking Federal troops in the vicinity of the mouth of North Chickamauga Creek added to the concern. During the afternoon and evening of November 23, Hardee, in obedience to Bragg's order, removed W. H. T. Walker's Division from the eastern base of Lookout Mountain and marched it across the valley to Missionary Ridge.[3]

It was cold and misting rain as Hardee's troops entered the zone of devastation on Missionary Ridge. The Federal artillery shelling of the ridge had ended as darkness fell, but the chaos remained. In the camp of a consolidated Alabama regiment, the men had crouched uncomfortably in their shallow ditches from late that afternoon until about 9:00 P.M. Their commander couldn't help but comment on the antics of about fifty new recruits who had experienced their first shell fire. When the firing first began, they were seen running wildly, hollering, praying, and hiding behind tents and virtually any cover they could find. It was all very amusing, if at the same time disturbing, wrote a knowing veteran.[4]

Arthur M. Manigault was "in a state of high indignation." He had just learned not only that his single brigade would attack Orchard Knob but that the units designated to support him had been recalled and only a skirmish line would go forward with his men. Manigault, having "fully made up his mind that that night would be his last," had once again protested to his unsympathetic division commander, Patton Anderson. The crusty Anderson told Manigault that the enemy's numbers were exaggerated, and he implied that Manigault was sulking. Furious, Manigault had bellowed out in full hearing of several staff officers about the rashness and recklessness of this foolish attack order. Galloping back to his brigade, Manigault called his brigade to attention and was about to issue last-minute instructions when one of Anderson's staff officers galloped up in great haste. Anderson had countermanded the order, said the staff officer. Manigault let out a sigh of relief; "Thank God!" he uttered. "There was scarcely an officer or man who did not regard himself as saved . . . from death, injury, or a Yankee prison," he later wrote.[5]

According to Manigault, Anderson had changed his mind only when the division officer of the day had protested that fully ten thousand Yankees were in line waiting to slaughter Manigault's brigade. Years later when writing his memoirs, Manigault remembered the incident and reflected on what had long become the bane of the Army of Tennessee: "[A] want of generalship, recklessness, and utter disregard for human life, did more on many occasions to weaken and impair the efficiency of our army than any losses inflicted by the enemy."[6]

Patrick Cleburne reported to Bragg's headquarters that night and was told by Bragg to rest his men immediately behind Missionary Ridge. His role would be to act as a reserve for the entire army, and he would report directly to Bragg's headquarters. It was now apparent that Bragg would fight the coming battle by responding to the enemy's initiatives. Since it was possible an attack on the center of the Confederate position was about to occur—something the Rebel commander had originally regarded as utterly impracticable due to Missionary Ridge's great natural strength— Bragg responded with revised tactical instructions. New orders went out that night for the soldiers to construct a line of defenses on the crest of Missionary Ridge. The artillery that was in position at the foot of the ridge would also be wheeled up the slopes to the crest.[7]

Under these new orders, the lower rifle pit line at the base of Missionary Ridge would be abandoned as the primary defensive position. This was a significant alteration in the basic conception of fighting the coming battle.

Since only a few reserves and various unit headquarters were then located along the crest of the ridge, the change required a major shift in troops. William J. Hardee, just arriving from the far Confederate left flank on Lookout Mountain, soon decided on an even more controversial disposition. He ordered Patton Anderson to divide his division, moving one half to the top of the ridge, while leaving the remainder at the bottom under command of Brig. Gen. Zachariah Deas.[8]

This attenuated line under Deas was intended much as a buffer force, and would retire to the crest if hard pressed by enemy troops. Hardee's engineer officer, Capt. John W. Green, was ordered to lay out a line of breastworks along the top of the ridge. This new line at the crest would serve as Hardee's main position for defense of Missionary Ridge.[9]

Braxton Bragg had occupied the heights overlooking Chattanooga for sixty-two days. Until now, many of the men had only randomly dug small trenches or ditches on Missionary Ridge for protection from the intermittent Yankee shell fire. Yet in the middle of the night, and on the eve of a pending battle, Bragg had finally ordered breastworks constructed along the crest of this crucial ridge. Arthur Manigault's premise was never more evident.[10]

Braxton Bragg, once again, had guessed wrong. Ulysses S. Grant had no intention of assaulting the formidable center of Bragg's Missionary Ridge lines. The long-standing master plan was to avoid the strength of Bragg's middle line and attack the exposed flank—the northern end of Missionary Ridge, where Sherman's poised veterans could envelop Bragg's right flank and cut off Longstreet from the Army of Tennessee.[11]

As early as November 15, Grant had explained this plan to Halleck, boldly asserting: "If Burnside can hold the line from Knoxville to Clinton, as I have asked him, for six days, I believe Bragg will be started back for [the] south side of Oostenaula [River] and Longstreet cut off."[12]

Grant's original concept, as explained in detail to all key commanders, had called for Sherman's four divisions to pass over the Brown's Ferry pontoon bridge onto the north bank. By utilizing the large hills of Moccasin Point to screen his troops from view, Sherman's units would pass along northern roads to a point west of the mouth of South Chickamauga Creek. Here they would remain hidden in heavy timber until all units were up and the attack coordinated. Using pontoon boats constructed by Baldy Smith's engineers at North Chickamauga Creek, Sherman's troops would then be ferried during predawn hours across the Tennessee River just south of the mouth of South Chickamauga Creek to establish a beachhead. Under the cover of artillery support from the north bank, a pontoon bridge would be quickly constructed across the Tennessee River in order to bring up all remaining troops. Meanwhile, Sherman's advanced units would launch an aggressive attack on the north end of Missionary Ridge before the enemy could concentrate against it. Thomas would contribute only one detached division to move northeast and support Sherman's right flank. Much of the remainder of Thomas's army would remain in a threatening but inactive posture, deployed along the center of Bragg's Missionary Ridge line. Cruft's division of the Twelfth Corps from the Army of the Potomac would hold Lookout Valley, while the other eastern unit, Howard's Eleventh Corps, would be held ready to support either Sherman or Thomas from its position on the north bank opposite Chattanooga.[13]

To complete the plan, following Sherman's lodgment on the south bank, a brigade of cavalry would be rushed across South Chickamauga Creek to raid and tear up the railroad between Chickamauga Station and east Tennessee, thus cutting off Longstreet's direct communications with Bragg.[14]

It was the blueprint for a Sherman victory. Thomas's Army of the Cumberland would play merely a supporting role due to Grant's reluctance to utilize an army severely immobilized and seemingly demoralized. Sherman remembered being told by Grant after reaching Chattanooga, "The men of Thomas's army had been so demoralized by the battle of Chickamauga that he feared they could not be got out of their trenches to assume the offensive." The Army of the Cumberland had so long been in the trenches, Grant related, that he wanted Sherman to hurry up and take the offensive, thereby setting an example so that the Cumberland men would fight well.[15]

A week later, Grant was aware some modifications would have to be made in his plan based upon the still-developing situation. On the afternoon of November 23, Sherman's four divisions were not yet up. Only three were in place opposite the mouth of South Chickamauga Creek. The fourth division, Brig. Gen. Peter J. Osterhaus's, was trapped on the south bank of the Tennessee River by the broken pontoon bridge at Brown's Ferry. Accordingly, Grant issued instructions for Osterhaus's men to report to and join Hooker on the twenty-fourth, if, as it appeared certain, they could not get over at Brown's Ferry by 8:00 A.M.[16]

Since Howard's Eleventh Corps had already crossed into Chattanooga on the twenty-second in order to better support Sherman by moving along the south bank "without trusting to the treacherous pontoons," Sherman was assured of strong support on his right flank. Together with Jefferson C. Davis's division of Thomas's Fourteenth Corps, assigned in compliance with Grant's original order, Sherman would have available for his attack on North Missionary Ridge on the morning of November 24 three divisions of his own command, two of Howard's ex–Army of the Potomac divisions, and one from Thomas's Cumberland army, a total of about 25,000 men.[17]

Being distressed and embarrassed that his troops had caused repeated delays, William Tecumseh Sherman had a point to prove on the night of November 23. According to Dana, Sherman's "erroneous calculations" caused him to blame himself for not getting all his troops forward; "it was his own duty to see that nothing hindered his arrival," explained Dana. Furthermore, Sherman knew Grant was relying on his men for the key role and an important victory. Sherman's apologetic but fiery letter on the evening of November 23 expressed his strong feelings: "We will move at midnight, and I will try the Missionary Ridge tomorrow morning, November 24, in the manner prescribed. . . . No cause on earth will induce me to ask for longer delay, and tonight at midnight we move. . . . Every military reason now sanctions a general attack. Longstreet is absent, and we expect no more reinforcements, therefore we should not delay another hour, and should put all our strength in the attack."[18]

These were reassuring words to Sam Grant. His old comrade and right-hand man obviously had his dander up. Sherman's ardent fighting qualities were much publicized. Grant could but well reflect on the events that tomorrow would bring.

They were dusty and dirty, ragged and often gaunt, hard-looking soldiers dressed in baggy uniforms and shapeless hats, and they fancied themselves Sherman's "boys." From stealing pigs on the march to fighting Rebels was what they knew best, and they had joked about Hooker's spick-and-span eastern troops as they passed their camps in Lookout Valley. They termed these easterners "brass mounted" troops—all decked out in cleanly brushed coats with polished brass buttons. Hooker's officers were seen wearing paper collars and fashionable kepis, and their men had neatly rolled blankets over their knapsacks. "We've come west to show you how to fight," boasted several broadly smiling Massachusetts soldiers.[19]

Sherman's men scoffed at these "paper collar" soldiers. Crude jibes and shouts of derision were commonplace as the dusty, winding columns passed Hooker's camps. "We expressed our earnest hope that they might not be compelled to eat their hardtack without butter," joked one of Sherman's veterans. Too bad these easterners "could no longer draw straw for their beds and Day & Martin's blacking for their brogans," sneered an Illinois soldier. Another quipped, "What elegant corpses they'll make in those fine clothes!" One ragtag western infantryman expressed his contempt: "There is some of the Eastern pimps here now, strutting around with their white collars. I think if they march up with our western grubs that their nice collars will get soiled before long."[20]

As for the Army of the Cumberland's soldiers, many of Sherman's men didn't much give a damn for them, either; they had been beaten too often and didn't seem to have the same grit as the victors of Vicksburg. Noting the corps badges displayed on many of Thomas's and Hooker's men, as well as their absence on Sherman's Fifteenth Corps veterans, an onlooker asked, "What's your badge?" Slapping his cartridge box, one of Sherman's riflemen smiled and replied, "Why, forty rounds here, and twenty in my pocket." Thereafter, the remark became so much of campfire lore that the cartridge box later became the official badge of the Fifteenth Corps.[21]

The point was well understood at the time. Hooker's easterners looked the part of "good society," but they were ridiculed as inferior soldiers. Thomas's men just didn't measure up, either, on the basis of past performance. The far-western boys knew it and acted accordingly. "In one respect our Western men are superior," wrote a veteran Indiana officer. "We are better fighters."[22]

Idly sitting around camp for several days had been taxing to many of William Tecumseh Sherman's men. The men knew something big was pending, but they weren't sure what. Even the officers were uncertain what was ahead: "There is evidently some strategic move on hand but of what character we are unable to conjecture," wrote a rather bored Iowa colonel on November 20. The following day, while still "hid away" in a mountain gorge, Sherman's troops were told to prepare three days' cooked rations and get ready for "an important movement." That this would involve hard fighting seemed evident to all: "We are to take 100 rounds of ammunition with us," wrote one of Sherman's suddenly pensive officers.[23]

On the evening of November 22, the plan had been outlined to all. The two Smith divisions, Morgan L.'s, and John E.'s, were to play the key roles. Morgan L. Smith's men would initiate the operation by crossing the Tennessee River before daylight in pontoons floated down from North Chickamauga Creek by his brother's (Brig. Gen. Giles A. Smith) brigade. They would entrench the beachhead and provide security while the remainder of Sherman's troops were crossed on a pontoon bridge fashioned from Giles A. Smith's pontoons. Once sufficient troops were present on the south bank, Sherman would promptly initiate his offensive against the north end of Missionary Ridge. It was regarded as a dangerous and decisive undertaking: Sherman's battle orders enjoined "the utmost silence, order, and patience." To prevent accidents due to the inherent commotion and excitement, the men's rifle muskets were to remain unloaded in crossing the river, unless ordered otherwise by on-site commanders.[24]

"Many of us may end our earthly career before tomorrow night," reflected the apprehensive Col. Jabez Banbury, one of John E. Smith's regimental commanders. "But our trust is in our commanders and our own brave hearts under Providence."[25]

The following day, November 23, there had been a brief reprieve.

Osterhaus's division being trapped at Brown's Ferry by the broken pontoons, Sherman postponed the crossing for twenty-four hours in hope that Osterhaus would get over to join in the assault. Sherman's terse communiqué on the morning of the twenty-third announced the postponement. Again his men had to wait in uncertainty. The suspense was building, causing one infantry officer to write apprehensively in his diary: "The ball will soon open, and we will dance to the [music of the] firing line." Another officer remarked: "We were at supper when the order came to . . . [begin the] assault at midnight. I laid down my knife and fork, and stopped eating. A strange sensation came over me. . . . Something told me that I was doomed—that some calamity was in store for me." His thoughts were shared by many; such thinking was inherent in facing up to the reality of personal experience in combat, made all the more excruciating during the hours of waiting.[26]

Col. Dan McCook, the former law partner of Thomas Ewing and William Tecumseh Sherman, had been given a most significant assignment. On November 17, McCook, commanding a brigade in Jefferson C. Davis's division of the Fourteenth Corps, had been informed by George H. Thomas of the pending plan for Sherman's troops to utilize pontoons and land below the mouth of South Chickamauga Creek prior to striking for the north end of Missionary Ridge. McCook would initiate the operation by providing much of the logistics. North Chickamauga Creek, where the pontoons were to be concentrated, lay about eight miles above Chattanooga. Although existing roads were available, McCook and his brigade would have to construct a new three-mile-long section along the north bank, upon which the pontoons might be brought in concealment from the city. Due to the Confederate occupation of Lookout Mountain and Missionary Ridge, it was necessary this road be constructed through low woodlands and valleys to prevent the enemy from viewing the large pontoon train. Since two sawmills at Chattanooga had been working day and night to provide the lumber for the 1st Michigan Engineers and Mechanics to construct these pontoons, Baldy Smith was confident the boats would be ready when needed.[27]

McCook had responded with great effort, even personally surveying the route. As his men set out to chop a new roadway through the timber on the eighteenth, McCook ordered the arrest of all local citizens on a pretext. By claiming his men had been "bushwhacked," McCook intended to keep the citizens' prying eyes from the roadwork and the pontoons. Many arrests were made despite angry protests, and on the eighteenth, pontoons began arriving by wagon at North Chickamauga Creek, about half a mile north of its mouth at the Tennessee River.[28]

By Friday night, November 20, 116 pontoon boats had been concealed in the creek, being guarded by McCook's men so as "to keep even our own soldiers away." Details were sent to clear the snags from the creek for easy passage of the pontoons, and by the evening of the twenty-third, wagonloads of oars were on hand and all necessary preparations made.[29]

Dan McCook was well pleased with the "secret accomplishment of the enterprise." Baldy Smith was so delighted with the effort and result, he said, "No trouble was anticipated in the mechanical part of the operation."[30]

Then what threatened to become a devastating nightmare suddenly occurred. On the twenty-third, a Rebel picket, on the opposite side of the Tennessee River, called across to one of McCook's pickets and "asked when we would be ready to move our pontoon boats out of the creek." "You Yankees think you will take us by surprise," scoffed the gray soldier. McCook was frustrated and alarmed. In passing along the information to George H. Thomas's chief of staff, he said the news was not unexpected, as about twenty citizens had escaped arrest and had seen the boats en route. To make matters even worse, McCook received a report that night that the Rebels were planting artillery along their side of the river. McCook immediately rushed a regiment, the 110th Illinois, to the shore opposite the intended landing site. Here they deployed under orders that if the enemy opened on the flotilla, they were "to silence their guns at all hazards."[31]

About midnight, the loading of the boats began. Two regiments, the 8th Missouri and the 55th Illinois, had been selected to lead the flotilla, and the designated loaders slid the bulky pontoons into the creek. Every boat was manned by four oarsmen selected for their experience with watercraft. Twenty-five men and officers were assigned to each boat. All guns were loaded but not capped; orders warned that no one was to fire unless by specific order. Every three minutes, a pontoon was loaded and launched, so that by 1:00 A.M. on the twenty-fourth a long line of pontoons floated silently down the narrow creek. "Not a loud word was spoken," later remembered a participant. "We hushed our very whispers, and the oars were carefully muffled." The weather was cool and the sky overcast, creating a darkness so intense that "we could hardly see the boat before or behind," noted an infantryman.[32]

There were 116 pontoons drifting southward, loaded with about three thousand infantrymen from Morgan L. Smith's division. The boats swirled out of the mouth of North Chickamauga Creek and into the rain-swollen Tennessee River. Hugging the forest-lined western riverbank for cover, the boats rapidly gained speed in the brisk current. Across the river, Rebel fires glimmered through the mist. Smith's men could see pickets throwing logs on the fires, and once there was an abrupt challenge from a sentry along the shore.[33]

Smith's pontoons swirled silently on. Then the leading boat suddenly veered across the channel toward the shoreline just north of the mouth of South Chickamauga Creek. The boats of two regiments followed, but the others continued on as planned—toward the designated bridgehead another quarter of a mile distant.[34]

With an abrupt jolt, the leading boat struck the eastern shore a little below the flickering fires of a Rebel picket post north of South Chickamauga Creek. Instantly, the twenty-five men jumped ashore. It was about 2:30 A.M. With hearts pounding, they plunged ahead into the misty darkness.[35]

CHAPTER 24

WHAT IS "WRONGLY LAID DOWN"

Out of the darkness came a shout: "Relief!" To the drowsy Confederate pickets and their reserves, eighteen men and a lieutenant, it seemed as if their replacements were at hand. The next thing they knew, they were staring into the leveled gun barrels of the 8th Missouri's surrounding landing party. Not a shot was fired. In an instant, the astonished gray soldiers were disarmed and herded into the waiting pontoon for a trip across the Tennessee River. Only one man, on the fringes of the campfire, had escaped in the darkness. Elsewhere along the shore north of South Chickamauga Creek, much of the same scene was repeated. Only a single shot was fired, by the last Rebel picket taken, and he merely discharged his rifle musket into the air.[1]

It was an important achievement. Just as planned, Giles A. Smith's main section of pontoons was able to land unopposed south of South Chickamauga Creek, guided to the proper location by a lantern on the opposite bank of the Tennessee River. Most of Smith's men had a spade, and in minutes the muffled sound of digging was heard all along the designated perimeter. "We digged like beavers," wrote an earnest Iowa captain. "What might happen any moment we knew not." "Every man worked with a will," observed an Illinois soldier, and "in an incredibly short time substantial earth works were thrown up." With a skirmish line thrown well in advance, Giles A. Smith's men continued improving their entrenchments, even as the first boatloads of pontoons filled with his brother's troops arrived from the western shore.[2]

Back and forth rowed the pontoons, discharging troops, then shuttling across the river for more soldiers. Some Ohio units swam their officers' horses across alongside, "holding their heads to the boats out of the water." "As [the river] was icy cold," wrote a lieutenant colonel, and the horses were forced to remain in the water for about thirty minutes, "they were so chilled and stiffened that they could scarcely ascend the bank to get out."[3]

By daylight, Morgan L. Smith's and most of John E. Smith's divisions were across the river, and construction of a permanent pontoon bridge had begun from both shores. Baldy Smith had earlier positioned twenty-four pontoons on wagons along the western shore, enabling engineers to begin construction almost immediately. As the construction party required a new pontoon, one of the in-service ferrying pontoons was appropriated, so that the bridge's completion proceeded rapidly.[4]

Everywhere there was the bustle of activity as blue-uniformed Federal troops swarmed over the low farmland perimeter, digging and fortifying, and yet there was not a sign of the enemy or any indication that Bragg's soldiers were even aware of the landing. Appearing through the mist and drizzle strode a lanky figure in a broad-brimmed hat—a Quaker farmer named Crutchfield. His farm was being ruined, he complained, and he demanded that the digging stop. Those within hearing began laughing at this ludicrous scene, and some of the soldiers gave a little derisive cheer for the old farmer. Suddenly, there was a swirling sound from afar, the rush of heavy air, and a close, jarring explosion. More incoming projectiles burst within seconds. A hole appeared in the ground "twice as broad" as the farmer's big-brimmed hat, only a few yards from where he stood. Two Iowa soldiers had been struck by the barrage, and the farmer disappeared in haste, all thought of contesting the occupation of his fields quickly forgotten.[5]

With desultory artillery firing continuing, it was decided about 8:00 A.M. to expand the beachhead perimeter to allow for more troops to occupy a broader front. Despite having just constructed substantial earthen parapets, most of John E. Smith's soldiers advanced about five hundred yards and the process of entrenching began anew. Although an occasional artillery shell burst within their perimeter, Sherman's troops were surprised at the lack of enemy activity. Where was the Rebel army? Why wasn't the whole enemy force coming down to attack? wondered many men.[6]

The steamer *Dunbar,* puffing clouds of black smoke into the leaden skies, arrived about 8:00 A.M. with a barge in tow, having been relieved from duty downriver transporting Sherman's horses to equip Thomas's artillery. It was a major addition and an important asset. Due to the pontoons' small carrying capacity, the *Dunbar* and the barge were a godsend. By noon, she had ferried across about five thousand troops, including horses of the generals and their staffs and a battery of artillery. Sherman was able to rush completion of the all-important pontoon bridge.[7]

The site Grant and W. F. Smith had selected for the crossing of Sherman's column was about six miles above Chattanooga, where Baldy Smith had calculated the Tennessee River to be 1,296 feet wide. The beachhead site was good, being opposite a knoll on the north riverbank, with positions for supporting artillery. Also, the river current was gentle here. Large quantities of balks (stringers) and chess (flooring) for the pontoon bridge had been transported by wagon to the opposite shore, and the engineers had been prepared to build two bridges to facilitate the rapid transit of Sherman's troops.[8]

Due to recent rains, however, the Tennessee River was now found to be about fourteen hundred feet wide, with only enough pontoons on hand for a single bridge. Construction had begun about 5:00 A.M., with the pioneer brigade clearing ground on the east shore and leveling it where necessary. William Tecumseh Sherman had personally supervised the work from the west shore; shortly after noon, he was found by Maj. Gen. Oliver Howard at the head of the pontoons being laid. Across the remaining gap, Howard reported his arrival with three regiments of Col. Adolphus Bushbeck's brigade, which had marched about 9:00 A.M. from the vicinity of Citico Creek. Ironically, as the gap was closed with the last pontoon at 12:20 P.M., Howard's presence all but completed the primary concentration of troops Sherman had sought. It was a major accomplishment for the now ebullient Cump Sherman.[9]

Although artillery units and Jefferson C. Davis's division of the Fourteenth Corps remained across the river, Davis's men were designated by Sherman as reserves; they were merely to occupy the beachhead while the striking column moved eastward against the north of Missionary Ridge.[10]

While Sherman made final preparations for his advance, Baldy Smith completed construction details. Due to the Confederate practice of sending heavy rafts down the creek to smash into the new pontoon bridge, Baldy Smith had a party rig ropes across South Chickamauga Creek to snare any drifting rafts. Five rafts were later caught and anchored to the shore.[11]

Earlier, at daylight, work had begun on a pontoon bridge across South Chickamauga Creek. By noon, the work was completed, providing support for the two regiments north of the creek and enabling Col. Eli Long's brigade of cavalry raiders to prepare to strike the enemy's railroad line near Tyner's Station.[12]

In all, the morning had proved to be a great success for Sherman and his troops. So little opposition had been encountered by the initial eight thousand men across that they now waited with arms stacked, idly chatting about the gathering sound of conflict far to the right on Lookout Mountain. When Grant's dispatch of 11:20 A.M. arrived, Sherman must have grinned broadly. "Until I do hear from you I am loath to give any orders for a general engagement," confided Grant. "Does there seem to be a force prepared to receive you east of the ridge? Send me word of what can be done to aid you." Sherman's reply was signaled by Dana—"four [three] divisions" were across the river, with Howard in close support. Rebels were visible in unknown strength behind the railroad at the foot of the ridge. Due to the deteriorating weather—low-hanging clouds and a light rain—Sherman foresaw his movements would be hidden from the enemy's observations. No additional help was needed.[13]

It was enough to make even Grant smile.

At about 1:00 P.M., orders went out from division headquarters to summon the men into line. Sherman's troops sprang to arms and were soon deployed in three primary columns. Morgan L. Smith's division was to follow the general course of South Chickamauga Creek on the left. John E. Smith's division would constitute the center column, marching en echelon on Morgan L.'s right flank. The end division, Brig. Gen. Hugh Ewing's, would maintain its distance to the right rear. The whole line thus was in stairstep formation from left to right.[14]

Since it was Sherman's intent to take the "Missionary Hills," or more specifically a high hill that was considered the head of the north end of Missionary Ridge, the line of advance would be directed accordingly.[15]

Of great importance, as confirmed by recent sighting reports, the north end of Missionary Ridge, from the railroad tunnel to South Chickamauga Creek, was not occupied by the Confederates. Although the existing maps in use by the Army of the Cumberland were discovered to be "wrongly laid down" as early as November 7, no particular importance was placed on this information. Clearly, the high promontory was the desired point from which Bragg's entire line might be easily enveloped.[16]

Sherman intended that it be an Army of the Tennessee affair. For this reason, Jefferson C. Davis's troops were to be left behind to guard the crossing site, and even Howard's easterners (Bushbeck's brigade) would merely skirmish on Ewing's flank. Howard was so unimpressed with this duty, he returned to his Chattanooga area headquarters, leaving a colonel in command of the detachment.[17]

The distance from Sherman's beachhead to the target hill was about a mile and a half, through low, undulating, and often swampy ground. It was a "splendid line of battle," noted an Illinois lieutenant colonel—and one of "the grandest sights" he had seen—when Sherman's columns poured forth across the open ground with flags flying. Under a drizzling rain and overcast skies, Sherman's columns moved onward at a steady pace, with strong lines of skirmishers well forward.[18]

Resistance was almost nonexistent from the beginning. Only the skirmish line was engaged with what seemed to be about two or three hundred rapidly retreating Confederates. After passing through swamps and thick underbrush, about 3:00 P.M. Morgan L. Smith's advanced skirmishers swept over the Western and Atlantic railroad bed and scrambled up the muddy slopes toward the top of the target hill. Despite the hill's stony and steep slopes, Smith's men reached the top with a trifling loss. The gray-clad soldiers who had been there were seen escaping through an adjacent valley. Immediately, the skirmish-line commanders ordered their men to halt and entrench, and within minutes strong supporting lines of blue-uniformed infantry occupied the summit.[19]

It was 3:30 P.M., and William Tecumseh Sherman could hardly believe his luck. Although he had remained behind at his headquarters near the river, Sherman was informed by signal relay of his columns' progress. Almost without firing a gun, his troops had taken possession of the designated hill. Sherman seemed to have secured the north end of Missionary Ridge, his primary objective—but not quite, as he soon learned.[20]

Brig. Gen. Joseph A. Lightburn, one of Morgan L. Smith's brigade commanders, noted that once on top of the hill, there was another larger knoll lying immediately in front of the one just occupied. Lightburn now considered that the height he had taken was "not the hill designated in the [Sherman's] order [of attack]." Quickly, he ordered a lone regiment, the 47th Ohio Infantry, to take the next hill. The colonel in command, Augustus C. Parry, scrambled forward with his men and reached the crest, only to find a line of gray infantry approaching through the valley from the south. Skirmish fire erupted along the knoll and spread into the valley. Parry sent for help. Within minutes, Lightburn had another regiment en route. Brig. Gen. Giles A. Smith, commanding Lightburn's sister brigade, was in the vicinity, and within minutes he appeared along the firing line to direct a portion of his brigade into position.[21]

In the confusion, Giles A. Smith was shot and soon carried to the rear. His older brother, Morgan L., was then too busy to stop. He began consolidating the lines on this key height, later popularly known as "Billy Goat Hill." Since the Confederates had already opened with two guns from yet another hill, Morgan L. Smith's priority was to bring up strong supports before his hastily entrenching advanced units were driven from the crest.[22]

Neighboring division commander John E. Smith managed to move two brigades quickly to the hill and even hastened forward a section of the 6th Wisconsin Battery. Yet the battery's horses were in such poor condition that they couldn't pull the guns up the muddy, sloping hillside. Two hundred men were detailed from Col. Jessie Alexander's brigade and put to work hauling the guns up the slopes by hand.[23]

Although the skirmish firing had already sputtered to a halt and the Confederates were seen retreating under cover of their artillery, the outbreak of firing had alarmed Sherman. Grant had already warned him that a "considerable movement [of Rebel troops] had taken place on top of the ridge toward you." This had been confirmed by observations made in the late morning from the artillery position at Sherman's crossing site. At the first report from his forward commanders of Confederates seen advancing, he made a major decision from his headquarters near the river. Instead of continuing his offensive movement, Sherman determined to assume the defensive immediately, apparently "in anticipation of an [enemy] attack through the valley at the base of the [Billy Goat] hill." It was about 5:00 P.M. and darkness was at hand. Sherman's reasoning was obvious. He had gained the key position desired and controlled the north end of Missionary Ridge. His orders were to take, hold, and fortify this crucial site.

As such, the enemy might be expected to counterattack to retake such a strategic position.[24]

By Sherman's orders, several brigades were relocated, being pulled from the high ground and sent into the nearby valley, only to be repositioned later that evening as part of a strong defensive line designated to thwart any Confederate attempt to outflank or isolate the crucial Billy Goat Hill. Suddenly going from the offensive to the defensive was confusing to many of Sherman's troops. Straining soldiers tugged at the wheels of additional artillery, four guns of Battery D, 1st Missouri Light Artillery, hauling the cannon up the steep slopes in the darkness. All across the heights and valleys, the chopping of axes and the crash of falling trees sounded through the night. Both sides continued busily to entrench. Whereas there seemed to be "no considerable force of the enemy north of the railroad tunnel" that afternoon, by darkness "the enemy appeared to be in considerable force" in front, noted a Minnesota officer.[25]

William Tecumseh Sherman had made a major mistake. His presence in the rear until after dark contributed to a misperception that remained uncorrected until daylight the following morning—when he saw the terrible truth. Sherman's men had not taken the head of the north end of Missionary Ridge. Billy Goat Hill was a separate height detached from the true ridge, being part of several clustered knolls and hills that overlooked South Chickamauga Creek but were separated from Missionary Ridge proper by an abrupt wooded ravine. From the distant western banks of the Tennessee River, the target Billy Goat Hill had appeared as a continuation of the ridge. Sherman's maps had been noted as incorrect on the date of the initial reconnaissance to the mouth of South Chickamauga Creek. Yet there is no indication any attempt was made to obtain corrected maps or determine the actual topography from local citizens. Sherman later acknowledged he had utilized the existing defective army maps; "from studying all the maps, I had inferred that Missionary Ridge was a continuous hill," he stated in his official report. To add to the confusion, Sherman remained out of communication with at least one of his key division commanders the entire night.[26]

As such, it was a rather sloppy and careless performance, the situation being accentuated by Sherman's absence from the front line. Instead of a dominating position and a lodgment on the northern terminus of Missionary Ridge, Sherman's troops had occupied a detached, adjoining height and were therefore unable to exert maximum offensive pressure on the exposed end of Bragg's line.

Even worse, Sherman, who was blithely ignorant of the true situation that night, forwarded inaccurate and misleading information to Grant via signal officers utilizing a high-intensity night-signal lantern. At 6:00 P.M., Grant telegraphed to Henry Halleck in Washington that Sherman had carried "the end of Missionary Ridge, and his right is now at the tunnel, and left at Chickamauga Creek." Grant also informed Thomas that Sherman had carried Missionary Ridge "as far as the tunnel." Sherman evidently had reported his troops extending as far along the ridge as the railroad tunnel through Missionary Ridge despite the fact that Ewing's division on his far right actually remained in the vicinity of Billy Goat Hill.*[27]

That evening, the skies cleared, revealing a cloudless and cold moonlit night. Yet at 12:24 A.M., a dark shadow crept across the face of the moon. It was a lunar eclipse, regarded by some as an evil omen. To Ulysses S. Grant, who sat on the porch at his headquarters, there was no presumption of ill tidings; rather, it seemed as if a terrible fate was imminent for the Confederates. Based upon the complete success of November 24, it now appeared that Braxton Bragg would be in full retreat before daylight.[28]

---

*This crucial message is missing from the reported official communications. Also, it appears further dispatches between Sherman and Grant similarly were not reported. A mysterious gap occurs in communications to and from these generals from November 24 to midday on November 25 (with two exceptions), despite the reference by signal officers to active communications during this critical period (OR 31-2-42,44,597).

CHAPTER 25

"A SICKLE OF MARS"

November 24, 1863, had dawned misty and with a drizzling, cold rain, which soon became a major element in the unfolding sequence of events. From Missionary Ridge, the valley below was shrouded by fog and low-hanging clouds. Thus, when Braxton Bragg had ridden north along the ridge that morning, there was little suggestion of an imminent Yankee attack.[1]

Bragg was worried about the Federal occupation of Orchard Knob and the threat to Missionary Ridge on that immediate front. For this reason, Bragg's troop deployment did not extend along the northern portion of Missionary Ridge; it reached only as far north as a point three-quarters of a mile south of the prominent railroad tunnel through the ridge. Here William H. T. Walker occupied the ridge and its western base with his division of mostly Tennessee and Georgia troops, recently transferred from Chattanooga Valley.[2]

Skirmish firing was lively in the valley below Missionary Ridge that morning, noted a much-harried division officer of the day, who had "quite a time of it" dodging enemy rifle fire. Those troops not directly exposed had begun working on fortifications, but due to a lack of tools, the rocky nature of the ground, and no logs, very slow progress was made.[3]

Posted along the extreme Confederate right flank near the mouth of Chickamauga Creek that morning was a cavalry brigade under the command of Col. J. Warren Grigsby. Grigsby knew the ground well and was among the first to report the Yankees threatening to cross the Tennessee River at that point. Yet due to the fog and lingering darkness, Grigsby's men couldn't tell whether the enemy was across in force or had merely

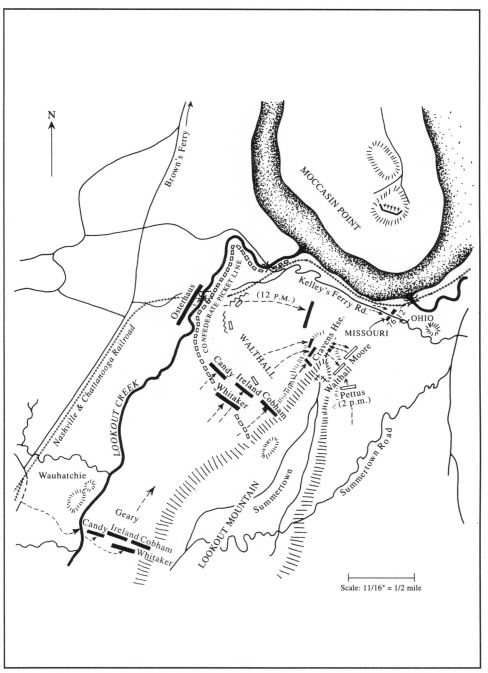

MAP 7   Assault on Lookout Mountain, November 24, 1863
(Source: Edward E. Betts, 1896 Chattanooga Map)

sent a reconnaissance patrol. By 8:30 A.M., Bragg's staff knew of this worrisome situation.[4]

Despite the potential threat to the north end of Missionary Ridge, Bragg was puzzled, being unsure of the Yankees' designs. Before returning to his headquarters, the only new disposition he made was to order Brig. Gen. Marcus J. Wright at Chickamauga Station, who had been recalled yesterday from duty at Charleston, Tennessee, to "proceed toward the mouth of the Chickamauga to develop the strength and designs of the enemy. Resist him every step. Should he not have crossed the Tennessee, resist his crossing," intoned Bragg. Unfortunately for Braxton Bragg, Wright's troops were still en route from Cleveland via the railroad, and by the time Wright arrived, obtained the message, and marched toward the mouth of Chickamauga Creek, it was early afternoon. Bragg's only other action was to alert several commanders of the possible threat and tell them to be ready to move at a moment's warning.[5]

Bragg's uncertainty as to what was occurring at the mouth of Chickamauga Creek was prolonged by ineffective communications. Significant information was already in the hands of commanders on the distant southern flank. The obscuring fog and mist had partially lifted shortly after dawn, permitting observers on Lookout Mountain to view Chattanooga and its environs. Accordingly, Brig. Gen. Edward Walthall had observed enemy troop movements prior to 7:30 A.M., and he reported at 8:00 A.M., "A steam boat is busy in the river beyond the town." Although thirty minutes later the fog was so thick that Walthall couldn't see anything below, his observations, including the certainty that Yankee troops were still deployed in their advanced positions of the previous day in front of Missionary Ridge, were of vital importance. It might have caused Bragg to look to his far-northern flank for a pending attack. Yet it appears this information failed to reach Bragg, who was riding along mid–Missionary Ridge, until after he returned to his headquarters about midday.[6]

While en route back to his headquarters late that morning, Bragg heard an unexpected sound—the heavy bombing of cannon being fired in the direction of Lookout Mountain. Bragg was greatly concerned. No significant attack was expected on Lookout Mountain. Earlier that morning, he had sent the commander there, Maj. Gen. Carter L. Stevenson, instructions to be prepared to move in any direction. In fact, Stevenson was told to send down his heavy artillery, preliminary to an anticipated movement to reinforce Missionary Ridge. Clearly, Bragg was most uncomfortable. It appeared he had been duped into carelessly overlooking the threat to his far-left flank.[7]

Carter L. Stevenson was not surprised by the morning's events. He had even sent a warning to corps headquarters on the evening of November 23. From his lofty perch near the Cravens house on Lookout Mountain, Stevenson that afternoon had seen what he believed was an enemy deception—to threaten the Confederate far-right flank and then attack the left. Stevenson's signaled message at 5:00 P.M. on the twenty-third reflected an anticipated crisis: "I observed closely the movements of the enemy until dark. [Their] object seemed to be to attract our attention. All of the troops in sight were formed from center to left. . . . If they intend to attack, my opinion is it will be upon our left." Stevenson's warning, however, had been ignored. Instead, he had been told to prepare to move.[8]

George H. Thomas had read Carter Stevenson's message almost as soon as its intended recipient, William J. Hardee. For weeks, Federal signal officers had attempted to intercept Confederate signal messages, and they had belatedly obtained the appropriate code. Truly, it was an important and timely interception.[9]

Ulysses S. Grant, as late as the afternoon of November 23, had expressed no specific intent to utilize Joe Hooker's troops in Lookout Valley during Sherman's pending offensive against the northern end of Missionary Ridge. Yet as a result of Carter Stevenson's intercepted message, Thomas immediately considered using Hooker's troops the following day. This might further deceive the Rebel generals in their apparent concern for the Lookout Mountain flank. At 10:00 P.M., Thomas telegraphed Hooker to "endeavor to take the point of Lookout Mountain" the following morning, and he authorized him to utilize some of Sherman's troops trapped by the broken pontoon bridge on the south riverbank. Yet after Thomas discussed the situation with Grant, this attack order was modified. Grant said that Hooker should make only a "demonstration" against Lookout Mountain on the morning of the twenty-fourth.[10]

Following the Grant-Thomas discussion, Hooker was informed at 12:30 A.M. November 24: "Intercepted Rebel dispatch is to the effect that Rebels expect us to attack them on their left in the morning. General commanding [Thomas] desires that you make demonstrations early as possible after daybreak on point of Lookout Mountain. General Grant still hopes [Brig. Gen. Charles R.] Woods's division [of Sherman's command] will get across to join Sherman, in which case your demonstration will aid Sherman's crossing. If Woods can't cross you can take the point of Lookout if your demonstration develops its practicality."[11]

That was it. Grant was leery of a full-scale attack without the aid of additional troops (Woods's). If Woods's men were used, Hooker might try to take the point of Lookout Mountain, but only if the preliminary demonstration suggested a favorable chance. In other words, Grant wanted no bloody failure from Hooker. He was skeptical, believing that this dominant mountain might be too difficult to assault and carry without a major sustained attack. Thomas, in essence, was to be held responsible for controlling Hooker's efforts.

Although an impromptu plan, within a few hours it was fully operational. At 2:00 A.M. and again at 3:15 A.M., Hooker announced that Woods's division would not be able to cross the river during the twenty-fourth and that he would make his dispositions accordingly. Hooker thus gave specific directions for an advance on "Lookout Nose," i.e. Point Lookout. His "demonstration" would begin "as soon after daylight as practicable." To Fighting Joe Hooker, these unexpected developments were a godsend. He was spoiling for a fight and an opportunity to win back his much-tarnished glory in the aftermath of his Chancellorsville defeat. Gloomily, he had anticipated being left entirely out of the major fighting. In fact, with his command divided due to the absence of Howard, Hooker had pleaded with Grant to allow him to accompany Howard's column so that he might "join that part of my command going into battle." Now, with a burst of renewed energy, Hooker announced to his leading division commander, "[I] am ordered to take Lookout Mountain." "Have your command in readiness to move at the earliest dawn of day," he alerted another key commander.[12]

The morning of the twenty-fourth had dawned appropriately foggy; "the elements seemed to frown on us as we lay in the valley [below Lookout Mountain]," wrote a glum Illinois soldier. Reveille had sounded at 4:00 A.M., ending a miserable night without blankets, overcoats, or shelter in the cold, sprinkling rain. That morning for many of Hooker's troops, there was no time for breakfast or even coffee before the men were called into line. "Each man seemed to [know] something unusually serious was before us," wrote an uneasy infantryman. While standing in line facing the foggy base of Lookout Mountain, the shivering men of the 96th Illinois were addressed by their grim colonel. "Boys, I have a few words to say to you," announced Col. Thomas E. Champion. "Before night I expect we will have to climb the side of yonder mountain. . . . I expect every man to do his duty; I shall try to do mine."[13]

The news fell on the men like a thunderbolt. "For a few moments not a word was spoken [along the line]," noted a private. "But we thought volumes." All eyes immediately peered at the hulk of the giant mountain. Through the drifting haze, an occasional break revealed Lookout Mountain in its imposing, massive height. From their camps on Moccasin Point, the men of Whitaker's brigade had long studied the craggy, forbidding slopes. They knew of the prominent nose, Point Lookout, with its crowning battery of Rebel cannon; of the glistening, sheer palisades above; and the steep, boulder-strewn slopes, broken by deep ravines with tangled vines and felled timber. They were willing to face the enemy, but to fight man and also contend with the overwhelming forces of nature seemed madness, considered a soldier. Another knew how in his regiment, the 60th New York Infantry, Lookout Mountain was regarded as "impregnable." It had become a joke among the men that Hooker was going to tell them to take the mountain—but this had been so ludicrous, it was dismissed. Now, as the men of Col. David Ireland's brigade formed at 6:45 A.M. and received their instructions to sweep the side of the mountain clear of the enemy, there was a noticeable change in attitude. "I am confident the brave men of my command can do it," division commander Brig. Gen. John W. Geary had cheerfully told his men. "What!" muttered the men of the 149th New York. "Does the general expect us to fly?" Their anguished comments were soon muted. In silence, the men stumbled off toward the looming, defiant slopes, many fully believing that they were being "asked to do an impossibility."[14]

Joseph Hooker had concocted an extraordinary plan. Aware of the many natural and Confederate-emplaced obstacles confronting any troops attempting to storm up Lookout Mountain's treacherous slopes, Hooker had decided on a practical expediency—attacking south to north along the side of the mountain rather than frontally up the slopes. By passing a large contingent of troops down Lookout Valley to a point two and a half miles below the prominent nose of the mountain, they might cross Lookout Creek and effect a lodgment on the side of the mountain without significant opposition. Then, by sweeping north along the slopes, stretched from Lookout Creek at the base of the mountain to the sheer face of the palisades midway up the slopes, this advancing line could take any enemy troops facing down the mountainside in flank. Meanwhile, the majority of Hooker's troops would remain poised at the base of the mountain, skirmishing with the Rebel troops below Lookout Point, so as to occupy the enemy's attention. When the flanking column appeared, led by Brigadier General Geary, Hooker's entire command would quickly advance, trapping the enemy in a deadly pincers.[15]

Actually, it was a scheme designed to capture the lower and middle slopes only, as Hooker had long regarded the crest of the mountain as unassailable. From detailed intelligence provided by deserters, Hooker knew the summit of Lookout Mountain was defended by three Rebel brigades. Since "the only means of access [to the crest] from the west for a distance of 20 miles up the valley was by two or three trails, admitting of the passage of but one man at a time . . . no direct attempt was [to be] made for the dislodgment of this force," confided Hooker.[16]

The fog, which at first seemed to be a curse, shrouding everything and resulting in confusion and uncertainty as to proper location, soon proved to be a blessing of major significance. Hooker's commanders were able to conceal their troop movements easily, which was especially important to Geary as he marched his combined command of 3,824 officers and men south in Lookout Valley to Wauhatchie. Yet at 7:30 A.M., Hooker reported his demonstration delayed. Swollen Lookout Creek was found too deep to ford, and Geary's pioneers were sent to bridge the stream near the site of an old dam. Hurriedly, while the pioneers began fashioning a bridge from logs floored with fence rails, two companies of the 29th Pennsylvania managed to get across Lookout Creek, deploying on the other side to establish a bridgehead. So unexpected was their appearance through the fog that the entire Confederate picket post of forty-two men was captured intact without firing a shot. By 8:30 A.M., the rude bridge was sufficiently completed. Geary's troops began clambering across even as the swift, swollen creek boiled under the logs and gurgled among the rails.[17]

Hastily, Geary's troops filed straight up the mountainside unopposed.

Within an hour, Geary's line stretched about a half a mile through the fog, from Lookout Creek to the steep rocky wall forming the palisades. Amazed, the men now realized it: The fog was their greatest ally, enabling them to reach without opposition the key position flanking the entire side of the mountain.[18]

About 9:00 A.M., Geary's men were joined by Whitaker's trailing six regiments. Extending across the side of the mountain was a long blue battle line of three parallel lines, 350 and 100 yards apart, preceded by a strong detachment of skirmishers. Shortly after 9:00 A.M., Geary's line briskly stepped off, led by the Pennsylvania brigade commanded by Col. George A. Cobham, Jr., on the far right near the palisades. The men were cautioned against making unnecessary noises, wrote a captain, but the suggestion was hardly necessary, he noted, "for the heart of every man was in his mouth." Cautiously, Geary's lines made their way forward along the rugged side of Lookout Mountain, climbing over or around boulders, loose stones, bushes, vines, and through thickets of dense timber. To veterans of nearly two years' warfare in the East, it seemed "undoubtedly the roughest battlefield of the war." Yet there were no shots being fired at them. "Our advance was unopposed and seemingly unnoticed," wrote a mystified soldier. In fact, he considered that the silence was "almost painful." "Every moment we expected to hear it broken by sharp shots from the rocks overhead, or by a rattling volley from the innumerable boulders in front. . . . But nothing was heard [except for] the trampling of many feet, and the hard breathing of men unused to mountain climbing." Only a few frightened jackrabbits and some scattering quail seemed to know of their approach. Indeed, where *were* Bragg's troops?[19]

Confederate Brig. Gen. Carter L. Stevenson hadn't slept at all that night. Suddenly called upon to command a nearly twenty-mile stretch of Lookout Mountain due to the transfer of William J. Hardee to Missionary Ridge the preceding evening, Stevenson had spent the night attempting to learn where all his troops were posted. At daylight, Stevenson become convinced that the northwest slopes, defended by a single brigade, Edward Walthall's, was no place to fight an approaching enemy. The trouble was obvious. The northern slopes were exposed to a raking artillery fire from the high hills across Lookout Creek and also from the devastating Federal heavy artillery batteries positioned across the Tennessee River on Moccasin Point. Moreover, Stevenson had only one other brigade midway along the mountainside, that of Brig. Gen. John C. Moore, which was positioned on the plateau at the Cravens house. At best, Stevenson considered he could delay a Yankee attack on the mountain only before they reached the Cravens house plateau, where a strong defensive position existed. Since Walthall's line of pickets and skirmishers along Lookout Creek, at the base of the mountain, were the first line of defense, Stevenson relied upon Walthall and his men to provide notice of any threatening enemy movement.[20]

Edward Walthall was a Mississippi lawyer and a recently promoted brigadier with two years' experience in the war, and he had a reputation for valor and hard fighting. On the morning of November 24, Walthall was puzzled. He had learned from his scouts before 8:00 A.M. that an unknown number of enemy troops were moving down the opposite side of Lookout Creek, toward Wauhatchie. Yet Walthall reported at 8:00 A.M. that the veil of fog had so thickened during the last half hour, he "could see nothing." Uneasily, Walthall strengthened his picket reserve near the mouth of Lookout Creek, then awaited developments.[21]

It was nearly 9:00 A.M. and, amazingly, the dense fog in Lookout Valley began to lift, although the mountain remained obscured in mist. It was an apparent break for Walthall and his troops. Visible in his immediate front near the mouth of Lookout Creek was a brigade of Federal troops that was maneuvering as if to force a crossing. With the outbreak of sudden skirmish firing, Walthall alerted his brigade, which was camped in a hollow along the middle slopes. They were soon formed behind a series of rude breastworks fronting Lookout Creek and ready for battle. Although an irregular barrage of Federal artillery fire began to burst on the adjacent slopes, Walthall remained calm. His dispatch to Brig. Gen. John C. Moore at the Cravens house plateau asked for artillery support. Upon receiving this, wrote Walthall, he believed he could hold the enemy in check.[22]

Walthall was still writing this dispatch when word arrived from several scouts sent to investigate the earlier movement of Yankee troops traveling along Lookout Creek, toward Wauhatchie. The enemy had crossed the creek in force, read the message, and they now occupied the slopes above the position of Walthail's picket line. Immediately, Walthall knew that a strong attack was in progress. On the bottom of Moore's dispatch, he scrawled a hasty note about the pending threat from the southern flank. Yet Walthall was uncertain where the enemy's main attack would be launched. Would it be from the front, or would it be along the distant mountainside? To add to the confusion, the Federal artillery bombardment from across Lookout Creek now intensified, being joined by the big guns on Moccasin Point. Walthall had nearly a third of his 1,489 troops extended in a picket line over a mile long. There were no reserves, and Walthall had only five regiments, four of which were so understrength as to be consolidated. Since three of these units were on the firing line along Lookout Creek, only two regiments remained to cover the slopes of the mountain. It was evident to Walthall that he must have reinforcements. Anxiously, he sent to the top of the mountain for help. With the enemy advancing from the lower valley and also at right angles along the middle slopes, it was now up to Stevenson and his immediate subordinate, Brig. Gen. John K. Jackson, to save Lookout Mountain.[23]

His line had advanced about a mile and a quarter, reported John W. Geary, angling higher and higher up the mountainside in the direction of the palisades, all without opposition. It was hard work, holding in one hand a rifle musket and grasping with the other a bush, tree limb, rock, or anything else that would assist in the steep ascent. The men were soon sweating despite the crisp November temperatures, and some began to flop on the ground to rest and catch their breath.[24]

Suddenly, shots rang out. From the skirmish line ahead, there was an answering volley. Bullets began to zip overhead, but it was soon discovered the opposition was only an enemy picket line. From out of the mist appeared a Confederate soldier, running, his hands uplifted in surrender. Badly frightened, he was shoved to the rear, and Geary's men began to sense victory. They scrambled ahead with gathering excitement. Through the drifting vapor, Geary's soldiers chased after the scattering line of Rebel pickets for nearly a mile. Progress was slow due to the rough terrain, but "we made up for lack of speed with yells," wrote an Ohio infantryman. The chase was on, yet the men of Ireland's brigade, in the center of Geary's line, suddenly found in their front formidable enemy breastworks.[25]

These breastworks were fashioned of boulders and rocks, filled in with earth, and barricaded with tangled timber slashings. Behind the breastworks were several of Walthall's Mississippi regiments, deployed for battle. Yet "to our joy," observed an Illinois soldier, the rebel fortifications were laid out to defend against an attack originating from the slopes below. Being uncompleted, they were not refused in flank, and as Geary's men approached along the mountainside, they could easily enfilade their entire length, as well as attack from the rear. "We found that the Rebels were but poorly prepared to defend themselves by the direction we were advancing," wrote an elated lieutenant.[26]

Geary's officers didn't hesitate. As their skirmish line opened a brisk fire, the cry "Fix bayonets" rang out along the approaching blue line. "Double quick!" "Forward march!" came the commands, but a rifleman who heard no orders in the tumult said it was really a matter of "soldier instinct." Geary's line surged ahead spontaneously, with bayonets glistening in the vapor and loud yells ringing in their ears. Despite the obstacles, Geary's assault was "like the rush of an avalanche," noted a participant. The wild hurrah of the oncoming line mixed with the rapid volleys of musket firing. It was a sight and sound never to be forgotten, reflected an eyewitness. This "wall of steel," with flags waving and men scrambling over the breastworks amid a mad swirl of hand-to-hand fighting, was like a whirlwind of death.[27]

Within the earthwork perimeter, Col. William F. Dowd of the 24th Mississippi knew in an instant his line was gone. His orders had been to "hold this post till hell froze over," said the colonel. Later he remarked that at this point the ice seemed about five feet thick; he ordered his handful of men to fall back. Desperately, his remaining men scrambled out of their trenches and hastened to climb the rocky slopes. A Mississippi color sergeant, struggling with his regiment's bulky flag, was seen attempting to get away. Ignoring shouted orders to halt and surrender, he kept going despite losing ground to several pursuers. Raising his Enfield rifle musket, a soldier of the 60th New York fired at close range, striking the sergeant in the leg.

Before they could pounce on him and wrest the flag from his grasp, however, the man was back on his feet, struggling to escape. With drawn sword, a captain of the 60th bounded after him. Soon surrounded, and with the captain's sword at his chest, the color sergeant finally yielded his flag and collapsed to the ground. It was one of four flags taken by Geary's men that morning. There were too many prisoners to count, but Walthall's Brigade later reported 845 missing for the entire day. In all, the brief encounter had lasted less than fifteen minutes.[28]

Before the fighting, a soldier had nervously considered the grim prospects they faced: "The mountain itself was terror enough without thinking of the graybacks and their leaden messengers," he admitted. Now this was replaced by exhilaration and excitement. "The whole brigade [camp] was ours," wrote the jubilant Geary, and everywhere were strewn Rebel dead, wounded, camp equipage, and abandoned small arms.[29]

As the last few fleeing enemy disappeared into the shrouding cloud banks, a renewed terror swept across the mid-mountain slopes. Having glimpsed the fight through the scattered, drifting clouds, Hooker's artillerists were eager to join in the fray. From across Lookout Creek, the bombardment of artillery shells now rose to a deafening crescendo. Twelve-pounder guns, twenty-pounder Parrott rifles, and batteries of howitzers and field guns rained shells as fast as the guns could be served from Bald Hill, and on Moccasin Point. The effect upon Lookout Mountain was devastating. Walthall's troops, escaping toward the plateau at the Cravens house about a half mile distant, had to run a gauntlet of hundreds of exploding shells. The terror of that experience was never forgotten. The ground literally quaked beneath their feet, said one of Whitaker's wide-eyed riflemen, who was watching from Geary's second line. The bursting shells seemed like thunderbolts. Their explosions amid the obscuring clouds high above ripped the misty cloud banks with spurts of fire. To an Illinois soldier familiar with the biblical story, "It seemed like a fire and cloud capped Sinai." So devastating was this rain of fire that prisoners by the score were gathered in after running down the hill to avoid the deadly barrage.[30]

It was about 11:30 A.M. From the ground below, Brig. Gen. Peter J. Osterhaus had been watching and waiting for the appearance of Geary's troops. That morning, before the firing began, Osterhaus had ridden up to the 13th Illinois and addressed the men. Sitting on his bobtail horse, with the cape of his overcoat thrown back over his shoulders, revealing a scarlet lining, Osterhaus presented a grand appearance. To an amused Confederate picket watching from across Lookout Creek, it seemed quite a spectacle. "Say, Yank," he hollered to a picket opposite, "is that old U.S. [Grant] sitting on that horse yonder?" Yes, it was, came the snickering reply. Minutes later, the informal frontline truce was broken as Osterhaus sent his skirmishers forward to the banks of the creek. Meanwhile, a brigade slipped across the creek on a bridge built during the initial cannonading. By midmorning, Osterhaus's troops were across Lookout Creek in force, and Walthall's Mississippians had been forced to retreat partway up the slopes. About 11:00 A.M., Osterhaus heard the sound of Geary's guns and ordered a general advance under the cover of the heavy artillery bombardment. With about 3,375 men, Osterhaus ascended the mountain directly up the slopes toward Lookout Point, anxious to trap Walthall's remaining infantrymen before they could escape from the closing pincers.[31]

From high above, it looked to John W. Geary as if a vast piece of machinery had been set loose on Lookout Mountain, advancing relentlessly toward their objective at Point Lookout. A nearby infantryman marveled at the grand spectacle: the long blue lines of infantry resolutely moving along the shoulder of Lookout Mountain from the palisades to the base. It was "a sickle of Mars whose blue blade and fire tipped edge" was poised to "reap a glorious harvest" of destruction beneath the crest, he thought.[32]

CHAPTER 26

THE BATTLE WITHIN
THE CLOUDS

Brig. Gen. Edward Walthall was exasperated. He had been fighting to hold back the enemy for two and a half hours. Yet despite having pleaded for help since about 9:30 A.M., no reinforcements had arrived, and no one had even bothered to inform him what to do, or what action would be taken. With Hooker's combined force under Osterhaus and Grose advancing from the lower slopes across Lookout Creek and Geary's flanking column sweeping the side of the mountain, Walthall was caught in an untenable tactical situation. Walthall, however, was by nature a stubborn fighter. "I endeavored in falling back . . . to yield the ground as slowly as possible with the hope that support might reach me," Walthall later tartly wrote in his after-action report. "Many officers and men were captured because they held their position so long as to render escape impossible."[1]

Walthall simply couldn't believe that the ranking generals would abandon Lookout Mountain without a hard fight. Now, with his camp captured and his brigade divided and fighting on two fronts, he knew it was only a matter of minutes before his scattered troops were driven back to the Cravens house plateau. Angrily, he looked in vain up the rocky slopes for the appearance of a messenger from acting division commander John K. Jackson.[2]

Daylight on Lookout Mountain that morning had found the Confederate commander, Carter L. Stevenson, much relieved from the anxiety and uncertainty of the previous evening. Having transferred his headquarters from Chattanooga Valley to the Cravens house before sunrise, the exhausted Stevenson had then ridden to the top of the mountain to check on two brigades posted along the crest. Here, after warning the local commanders to be ready to march to any threatened point, Stevenson finally began to relax, believing his dispositions were the best possible under the circumstances. Stevenson had arrayed his troops evenly; two brigades along the foot of the mountain at Chattanooga Creek, two brigades midway up the slopes along the northwestern face, and two brigades guarding the crest and southern ridges.[3]

At 10 A.M., Stevenson's rest came to an abrupt end. He was alerted by messenger from J. K. Jackson, near the Cravens house, that Walthall had seen Yankee troops moving along Lookout Creek in the direction of Wauhatchie. Immediately riding to the crest, Stevenson saw Hooker's troops bridging Lookout Creek near the mouth of that stream. Yet simultaneously with this observation came the fog—the damnable, obscuring vapor that quickly made visibility of the slopes below impossible. Was Hooker preparing to attack in front, or was the column that Walthall reported moving toward Wauhatchie about to attack in flank? Unable to see much, Stevenson merely sent a staff officer to Jackson to place his troops in line of battle along the Cravens house plateau. He would rely upon Jackson to defend the midslopes below Point Lookout. Stevenson remained on top of the mountain. Before noon, he wrote: "No demonstration anywhere upon the line so far heard. Signal corps thinks they [Hooker's column] have advanced nearly to the road leading down from Summertown. They have opened fire from their batteries upon our left center. Mist and fog so dense [we] cannot see anything at all. . . . Have sent about 50 men down a trail toward Cravens house to open a brisk fire upon the enemy's flank." Stevenson obviously was preparing for what he anticipated—a Federal thrust around the northern base of Lookout Mountain toward Chattanooga Creek. It seemed that Hooker's troops wouldn't be so foolish as to attack directly up the mountainside.[4]

John K. Jackson was a curious figure in the Confederate command structure. A former South Carolina lawyer whose troops had suffered frightful losses in previous battles, Jackson, nonetheless, had a reputation as being less than bold in battle. His nickname, "Mudwall," was a derisive parody of the late, more famous Jackson—Thomas J. "Stonewall" Jackson.* Mudwall Jackson had his headquarters on the morning of the twenty-fourth at the fork in the Summertown Road, where one path led to the crest of the mountain and the other to the Cravens house. When the distant firing began that morning, Jackson had walked to a small overlook to view the events below. "All was quiet, no massing, no movements of any kind," he wrote. After sending a staff officer to the Cravens house to "report anything of interest," Jackson returned to his fork-in-the-road headquar-

---

*There appear to have been at least two "Mudwall" Jacksons in the Confederate Army. William Lowther Jackson is usually referred to as *the* "Mudwall." Yet according to Gen. Edmund W. Pettus, the sobriquet was also applied to John K. Jackson based upon his timid behavior. See E. T. Sykes, *Walthall's Brigade*, pp. 539, 600.

ters. When a message from Stevenson arrived, asking if he needed rein-forcements, Jackson replied that until there were more developments, nothing was planned. Jackson continued to loll about his headquarters. The minutes passed and the dense clouds of fog rolled in. Soon the top of Lookout Mountain was enshrouded in an eerie mist.[5]

Brig. Gen. John C. Moore, at the Cravens house, couldn't understand why so little action was being taken to defend the northern slopes. Learning from personal observation and Walthall's urgent requests for help that the enemy was boldly advancing, Moore had formed his brigade in line of battle. Yet there were no specific instructions. After sending to Jackson for orders, Moore fretted about the absence of Jackson and Stevenson. Where were they? Why hadn't they bothered to investigate Walthall's re-peated alarming reports personally?[6]

It was nearly noon when one of Jackson's staff officers trotted up. Moore was told to place his brigade behind the prepared breastworks along the plateau, just to the north of the Cravens house. Walthall's troops would simultaneously form adjacent to Moore's along the breastworks south of the house, where two six-pounder Napoleon guns of Howell's Georgia Battery had been posted. This was all very confusing. Walthall was still fighting along the northern slopes below. If Moore took position where designated in the trenches, a gap would exist beyond the Cravens house. Moore looked to Jackson's staff officer for an answer. That officer nervously demurred. "[He] told me to wait until he could see the general [Jackson] and get more definite instructions," said the aroused Moore. The staff officer quickly departed, but Moore could now hear heavy firing just beyond the plateau, with the sound rapidly growing louder. Fearing that the enemy was close at hand, Moore ordered his brigade to advance to the Cravens house breastworks, only three to four hundred yards distant. His men had just started to rush forward, said Moore, when chaos suddenly erupted across the entire plateau.[7]

The advance was laborious, said an Ohio sergeant. The side of Lookout Mountain as Geary's troops approached the shoulder near the Cravens house plateau was so boulder-strewn and rough that the panting men were struggling to keep pace with the retreating fragments of Walthall's troops. Although some men continued to yell in the excitement of the pursuit, the deafening roar of artillery along the slopes had reached stunning propor-tions. The rocky ground was like "a sounding board," noted an Illinois soldier. Over the mountain's shoulder, the big Federal guns on Moccasin Point continued to fire ahead of the advancing blue line and at the "white-house farm" plateau. Above the heads of Geary's men, three Rebel cannon posted along the crest had begun firing canister down the slopes. Although the muzzles of these guns couldn't be sufficiently depressed to hit Geary's close-in troops, their blasts added to the terrible noise. Due to the re-bounding sound waves of exploding shells and crashing cannon, it seemed to an awed infantryman as if the sky had suddenly exploded. The artillery fire quickened our movements he said, and Geary's line suddenly clambered over the edge of the midmountain plateau, meeting only a scattered skirmish fire.[8]

Abruptly, the vapor obscuring the slopes began to lift as if by magic. To the disbelieving Geary, he saw a cloud bank "hovering above us," shrouding the mountain, and "fogs darkening the hills below." In between was open sky. It was as if "our path [was] a well defined stratum," wrote the amazed Geary. Even to the ranks of Thomas's soldiers in Chattanooga Valley far below the sight of a dark line of blue uniforms emerging from the vapor with the stars and stripes waving above was an incredible sight, one never to be forgotten. Amid the reverberations of cannon and small-arms fire rolling from the mountainside, the moment was such an imposing one, a sergeant of the 34th Illinois noted, "Our group of spectators, excited to the highest pitch of enthusiasm, [impulsively] burst forth . . . into three loud cheers."[9]

Up on Cravens house plateau, several of Ireland's regiments rushed toward the landmark white clapboard house long visible to the Federal campsites below. "We were yelling so loud the Rebels thought there were a million of us," an elated soldier later wrote.[10]

Although Confederate sharpshooters were firing repeatedly from the rocks above the palisades into the onward-moving crowd of blue uniforms, the two Rebel six-pounder brass guns positioned in the garden of the Cravens house remained silent. Walthall's scattered troops were falling back in disorder in front, and to shoot these guns would kill and maim dozens, the section's commander realized. Days earlier, he had sent his horses down the mountain for forage, and now there was no way to move the guns. Being without support, and since Walthall's broken ranks hadn't rallied, the lieutenant in command ordered his men to fall back. "There was no possibility of either moving my guns or repulsing the enemy," he said.[11]

Through the Cravens peach orchard sprinted several of David Ireland's regiments, the 60th New York and the 137th New York, racing for the stone wall along the edge of the house. Despite the deadly fire of sharp-shooters and the shrieking iron missiles overhead, "we took the works on the run," wrote an excited rifleman. The flag of the 137th New York was briefly draped over the brass guns as a sign of triumph, then the men sped on after the wildly running enemy. They ran head-on into a gathering smallarms fire. In the 60th New York, the major went down with a face wound, and the color sergeant was shot twice. The men began to hesitate. "The colors are down! Who will take them?" shouted an officer. A sergeant sprang forward and grasped the flag staff, carrying it onward. The 60th again lurched forward. Nearby, some of Whitaker's troops also had pressed ahead, past a few of Ireland's exhausted riflemen. "Go it boys, we have chased them up for you; pour it into them; give 'em hell," they cried.[12]

Ireland's impetuous advance was ill-advised. His other front-line regiment, the 149th New York, had passed through the yard north of the

Cravens house and was badly scattered in the drifting gunsmoke. Suddenly, about three hundred yards beyond the Cravens house, Ireland's advanced units encountered a deadly musketry fire from two directions. Too late, they realized their dire predicament. The 60th and 137th New York in their hasty pursuit had gotten beyond the Rebel rear north of the Cravens house perimeter and were suddenly isolated, in danger of being crushed by an attack from their left flank and front. The colonel of the 60th hastily ordered his men to halt and cease firing. The New Yorkers flung themselves to the ground and began to scurry for cover.[13]

On their right, one of Whitaker's regiments, the 40th Ohio, 333 men strong, had joined in the impetuous rush along the narrow plateau, working their way even farther forward than the New Yorkers during the hasty pursuit. Now the Ohio commander found his unit in great difficulty. A strong Rebel infantry force was in front, along the edge of timber near the Summertown Road. On his left flank, another enemy column was in position to overwhelm his small command. Desperately, he gave the order to fall back.[14]

Confederate Brig. Gen. John C. Moore had witnessed a near disaster. Unaware that Walthall's troops had been so scattered, broken, or captured as to be unable to form on his left to hold the Cravens house line of works, Moore had been shocked to find the enemy in possession of a portion of the stone wall when his brigade rushed forward to occupy the trenches below the Cravens house. Here the plateau, which is narrow along the upper bench where the white farmhouse stood, drops off in stair-step fashion to another flatland north of the Cravens house. This lower, mostly level terrain was greatly exposed from the upper bench. Yet here Moore attempted to form his men while under heavy fire from Geary's New Yorkers near the Cravens house.[15]

Moore's advance had chased a few of the 149th New York out of the trench line, but these parapets, he quickly saw, were untenable. With Ireland's other regiments already past his left flank and firing from above into his rear, Moore had no thoughts of staying there. He ordered his men to fall back to the line near the Summertown Road. Yet, before his men withdrew a hundred yards, they found the isolated 40th Ohio beyond their flank, attempting to get away. The colonel of the 40th Alabama, seeing an opportunity, ordered his men to charge. They managed to press forward after the retreating Ohioans until, abruptly, they encountered a hailstorm of rifle fire.[16]

It was from the 96th Illinois of Whitaker's second line. Although most of Whitaker's brigade had halted in reserve along the stone wall near the Cravens house, the 96th had passed to the right in the vacuum created by the scattering of Walthall's troops. Observing the situation in an instant, Col. Thomas E. Champion of the 96th ordered his men to left wheel and charge. Down the intervening declivity, "we slipped and rolled," wrote an Illinois rifleman. The effect was instantaneous. The 40th Alabama halted, then scattered to the rear. Yelling loudly, the Illinois soldiers rushed to a nearby rude rail fence and fired repeatedly into the enemy's vanishing ranks.[17]

As the 40th Ohio recovered and moved up to the line of the 96th Illinois, it was apparent that their excited major, Thomas Acton, wanted to charge after the retreating enemy. He was standing next to a kneeling soldier when the man, noting his light blue overcoat—a conspicuous target—grasped the major's coat and told him to get down. Bullets were zipping about, but Acton paid no attention. An instant later, with a loud *whack*, a minié ball struck him full in the chest. Acton threw up his hands and with a chilling cry of anguish sank to the ground, mortally wounded. It was but one of several telling casualties among the ranking commanders of Geary's units.[18]

In the lower line, Col. Charles Candy, in climbing over a boulder, slipped and dislocated his hip. The resulting delay due to confusion, intermixed commands, and the exhaustion of Geary's men lasted about an hour. During the interval, an "impenetrable fog" again settled over the Cravens house plateau, cloaking the region in an obscuring mist for the remainder of the day.[19]

At about 12:30 P.M., Brig. Gen. John W. Geary began to consolidate his position, ordering Cobham's brigade to work their way over the steep cliffs on the right so as to reach beyond Lookout Point and enfilade any attacking enemy line. Scaling the heights by means of a mere path, Cobham soon placed several regiments along a narrow ledge facing nearly eastward. With the arrival on the plateau of Hooker's initial units from the mouth of Lookout Creek after 1:15 P.M., Geary began to anticipate a further advance. Instead, he was ordered to halt and strengthen his position. According to Joseph Hooker, Geary had already gone too far—beyond the intended point.[20]

Fighting Joe Hooker's heart had beaten a little faster that morning when he learned of Geary's successful sweep of the midmountain slopes. At 1:25 P.M., he telegraphed to Thomas's headquarters of "our great success," which "has far exceeded my expectations." Reporting the capture of an estimated two thousand Rebels and stating that the bulk of his infantry was assembling on the nose of Lookout Mountain, Hooker proclaimed a significant victory. Yet his simultaneous orders to halt along the plateau recently captured were rooted in apprehension.[21]

Hooker's instructions had been to take the point of Lookout Mountain if practicable. He had already told Osterhaus's troops to proceed no farther than the crest of the plateau, based upon the technical definition of Thomas's original orders. "Not knowing to what extent the enemy might be reinforced, and fearing from the rough character of the [ground] that our lines might be disordered," Hooker later wrote, he had directed that all his troops halt along the Cravens house plateau.[22]

Essentially, Joe Hooker's apprehensive perspective didn't permit reorganizing for a final push to wrest total control of the northern face of the mountain from the enemy. "Make yourself strong in the [present] position you occupy [for] tonight," he told Geary at 2:00 P.M. Hooker feared the negative consequences of making an all-out attack—of perhaps losing what he had so easily gained. Fighting Joe wanted no disaster at this point, having already fashioned a notable victory from what army headquarters had intended only as a diversion, a mere demonstration.[23]

Although some of Geary's unit commanders were clamoring to attack and capture the vital Summertown Road, thus splitting apart the enemy's troops at the top and the bottom of Lookout Mountain, Hooker's abrupt order to halt changed everything. As Osterhaus's troops moved onto the plateau through the dense fog, firing along the front lines had sputtered to a near halt. This led to a virtual impasse. Even worse, the fog bank masked the arrival of Rebel reinforcements sent from the top of Lookout Mountain.[24]

About an hour after Geary's halt, at 2:45 P.M., that commander anxiously dispatched a message: "We are pressed heavily and need reinforcements. We must have ammunition." Geary's dire report reflected the dramatically changed circumstances on Lookout Mountain. Joe Hooker's imposed halt had yielded a key element for ultimate success, the initiative.[25]

At 1:30 P.M., disaster had seemed imminent for Carter L. Stevenson's Confederates on Lookout Mountain. Walthall's Brigade had been shattered and nearly destroyed; the remnants were barely able to hang on along the fringes of Moore's line. John C. Moore had re-formed his brigade along a boulder-strewn copse in front of the Summertown Road. Both Moore's and Walthall's troops were in such disarray that Walthall told a staff officer if the enemy attacked, they couldn't hold their position. Walthall's men were nearly out of ammunition, and Moore's troops had been largely supplied with improper ammunition for their old, defective arms. Moreover, there was no sign of the division commander, John K. Jackson. Mudwall Jackson said he had started out to join them but was delayed in attempting to rally some of Walthall's retreating men. After allegedly failing to stop them, he had returned to his headquarters.[26]

Due to the lengthy impasse after the loss of the Cravens house, a semblance of order was restored in the Confederate Summertown Road line. Most importantly, however, about 1:45 P.M. the all-Alabama brigade of Edmund W. Pettus moved into position behind Walthall's thin line. Responding to urgent requests from Moore and Walthall for reinforcements, about 12:30 P.M. Carter L. Stevenson, at the mountain crest, had sent Pettus and his troops rushing to the defense of the Cravens house plateau. Although it was Stevenson's intention to defend the nose of the mountain along the plateau, Pettus arrived too late—the Cravens house and its line of breastworks were already lost. After replacing Walthall's exhausted men, who quickly went to the rear, Pettus made a limited advance along the base of the palisades, displacing some of David Ireland's soldiers.[27]

This soon created an interesting situation. Ireland asked for support from Geary's other troops. Walter C. Whitaker was nearby, in charge of the reserve line. Although a veteran brigade commander, Whitaker had been drinking heavily, said one of David Ireland's aides. Most of Whitaker's men were resting with stacked arms near the Cravens house, and he refused to order his troops forward as requested by David Ireland. Already, said the tipsy Whitaker, he had asked some of Hooker's newly arriving troops to help take the Summertown Road. The colonel of one of Cruft's brigades, William Grose, had flatly refused to do so, displaying a copy of Hooker's order to halt at the plateau.[28]

Although Ireland pleaded with Whitaker to move forward, he was only offered a drink from Whitaker's large flask. Thereafter, since Pettus's troops had halted in the heavy timber adjacent to the bluff, Geary's mixed front-line troops became ensnarled in a desultory, ragged firefight through the thickening mist. Visibility was restricted to less than a hundred yards, yet the fighting was vicious and often deadly. The Confederates rolled giant boulders down from the heights, the huge rocks hurtling out of the mist and crashing randomly through the Federal lines. Mixed among the boulders were artillery shells hurled by hand, their fuses cut and ignited so as to explode among the Yankees below.[29]

For nearly two hours, the grueling in-place struggle continued, causing Geary nervously to request reinforcements and ammunition. Even Whitaker anxiously reported "the enemy massing rapidly on my right."[30]

Although it was apparent to Edmund Pettus that the Yankees were in force along his front, he was hopeful of receiving strong reinforcements. Meanwhile, noting Moore's weak line on his right and hearing reports of the enemy moving around the northern face of Lookout Mountain to cut off the Summertown Road below, Pettus sought instructions. Unfortunately, there were few to be had. Mudwall Jackson, it was discovered, had gone up the mountain to confer with Stevenson. "Hold your position as long as possible," offered a staff officer. Walthall, Moore, and now Pettus had been fighting an isolated, stopgap action for about five hours without command coordination. Outraged at the lack of communication and want of unified action, all were to write scathing after-action reports, condemning the poor performance and absence of Jackson.[31]

Mudwall Jackson was unsure how to proceed. Learning belatedly of Hooker's attempt to move troops across the northern face of the mountain while others attacked the Cravens house plateau, Jackson feared the loss of the Summertown Road along the lower slopes, or else at the plateau. Accordingly, he sought out Stevenson to learn where he should withdraw his troops.[32]

Carter L. Stevenson, however, was in no mood for a withdrawal just yet. That morning, in response to instructions from Bragg's headquarters to call on Breckinridge's adjacent corps for reinforcements as needed, Stevenson had already sent for help. Stevenson hoped to take the offensive once the fog lifted and Breckinridge's troops arrived. He intended to use his sharpshooters to keep the enemy pinned down, then, "descending

Smith's trail [a path over the palisades to the western slopes], take him in rear, and, I doubted not, drive him from the [mountain]." Repeatedly, Stevenson had sent the same message at intervals of a half hour by at least four different staff officers, to both Breckinridge and Bragg. Instead of the expected reinforcements, however, Carter Stevenson was stunned by the verbal message he finally received from Bragg about 4:00 P.M.[33]

Braxton Bragg was having a bad day. While returning from the far-right flank late that morning, he had been alerted of the serious fighting on Lookout Mountain by the distant thunder of Federal cannon. Belatedly, a message from Carter Stevenson provided news of the enemy's attack and estimates of their advance toward the Summertown Road. With fog shrouding much of the mountain by early afternoon, it was difficult to know of the current status there, and Bragg became increasingly alarmed—but not particularly for the safety of Lookout Mountain.[34]

That morning, Bragg's communiqué to Carter Stevenson had outlined his fears and also provided a few contingency plans. If attacked in overwhelming numbers, Stevenson was primarily to look to the defense of the Chattanooga Creek line in the valley. As such, Bragg's main concern was not so much for the retention of Lookout Mountain as for the protection of his vulnerable left flank along Missionary Ridge. Should the enemy penetrate along the valley in the direction of Rossville Gap, his entire Missionary Ridge line would soon be outflanked and become untenable. Thus, above all else, Stevenson was instructed to prevent his troops from being cut off from the main army on Missionary Ridge. Bragg's earlier decision to remove the artillery from Lookout Mountain confirmed the premise that the giant mountain was regarded as expendable. Bragg, accordingly, didn't equivocate when finally located by one of Carter Stevenson's staff officers about 2:30 P.M. Instead of sending the reinforcements Stevenson requested to drive back Hooker's troops and recapture Lookout's northern slopes, Bragg made a quick, fateful decision. He told the staff officer to return to Stevenson with the hard facts. No reinforcements could be sent, and Stevenson must withdraw from Lookout Mountain "as best he could." Later, Bragg's chief of staff wrote out a confirming dispatch for Stevenson. The message read: " . . . you will withdraw your command from the mountain to this side of Chattanooga Creek, destroying the bridges behind. Fight the enemy as you retire. The thickness of the fog will enable you to retire, it is hoped, without much difficulty."[35]

Abruptly, the battle for Lookout Mountain was over; it had been fought only in the minds of the generals. The gray soldiers, who never were involved in anything more than a ragged, sporadic skirmish, must have been as amazed as the red-faced Carter L. Stevenson when he received the unwelcome news; the lives and blood of Walthall's, Moore's, and Pettus's veteran troops had been as expendable as Lookout Mountain.

CHAPTER 27

FIREFLIES IN THE NIGHT

Retreating from Lookout Mountain in the midst of an overwhelming enemy force during the night of November 24 may well have been regarded by Carter L. Stevenson as a nightmare. His six brigades were strung out from across the top of Lookout Mountain at Nickajack Pass (ten miles distant) to the northern base near Chattanooga Creek. Due to the fog, Stevenson's artillery had been unable to accomplish much firing from the top of the mountain. Stevenson, therefore, could not rely on artillery support during the entire withdrawal phase. The captain commanding the Cherokee (Georgia) Artillery had been able to fire only thirty-three shells during the clear interval that morning. Later, following Geary's occupation of the Cravens house plateau, the situation had been considered so desperate that the gunners were ordered to fire into the mist in the supposed direction of the plateau. Nearly thirty shells were expended before the battery was ordered to retire about 3:45 P.M.[1]

The fog, if a damning curse in contesting the enemy's occupation of Lookout Mountain's northern face, now seemed to provide a welcome cloak for the escape of Stevenson's troops to the valley below. Due to the obscuring mist, the incoming Federal artillery fire was sporadic by midafternoon. Stevenson's wagons, artillery, and equipment were started down late that afternoon, even as a single brigade from Breckinridge's line, Clayton's, marched up the mountain to the relief of Moore's, Walthall's, and Pettus's troops along the Summertown Road.[2]

Clayton's all-Alabama brigade, currently commanded by Col. J. T. Holtzclaw, had double-quicked part of the way through the valley in a misting rain. The ground was "awfully slippery," discovered an officer, and a few enemy shells from batteries across Chattanooga Creek burst along the side of the mountain. After halting until dusk to conceal their movements, Clayton's men again resumed the march. About 8:30 P.M., his tense Alabamians relieved Pettus's troops. In the darkness, as they pressed forward to establish a connected line, some units mistakenly went too far, overrunning a portion of the enemy's picket line. A sharp firefight erupted in the night, but fortunately, noted a rifleman, most of the Yankee bullets were fired too high and passed harmlessly overhead.[3]

Stevenson, who was unaware of the presence of Clayton's Brigade until notified by Breckinridge after 8:30 P.M., had spent the evening arranging for the retreat and issuing orders. Much to Stevenson's surprise, he was visited about dark by Maj. Gen. Benjamin F. Cheatham, the division commander who was just now returning from a leave of absence following his attempted resignation over Bragg's fitness to command. Cheatham said he wouldn't take command, even though he was Stevenson's senior; he would act only as a consultant. Accordingly, Stevenson and Cheatham assessed the existing grave situation. Together, they concluded to go to the bottom of the mountain and confer with Breckinridge, who had accompanied Clayton's Brigade.[4]

By 10 P.M., Cheatham, Stevenson, Breckinridge, and J. K. Jackson were at the Gillespie house in Chattanooga Valley, where final plans were made to evacuate Lookout Mountain and withdraw to the east side of Chattanooga Creek, per Bragg's orders. It was decided to stagger the withdrawal, with Stevenson's mountaintop units moving first, followed by Clayton, and finally Cumming, who held the valley perimeter. About 11:00 P.M., the orders went out and the generals began to wait anxiously. An estimated three hours were needed to disengage and withdraw all the troops. To add to the obvious difficulty, the skies had abruptly cleared by 7:30 P.M. and a bright moon was now shining, casting a full eerie light through a canopy of twinkling stars.[5]

It was bitterly cold on Lookout Mountain that night, one of Holtzclaw's shivering Alabama officers recorded in his journal. Although the Yankee skirmishers continued to fire with intensity, "we had [shelter] from the rocks and trees, and [t]his fire was not destructive," he noted. In fact, it seemed to be equally dangerous just to walk about due to the rough terrain. Gray mountain rock, ranging in size from a "fist to a large house," covered the ground. The exertions of climbing the mountain had made Holtzclaw's men sweaty. Now they were chilled and many suffered painful cramps, being unable to move due to the enemy fire. Still, the boys had their fun, noted a soldier. "Our men would call out, 'Lookout Yanks,' then fire a volley, and crow [like a rooster]." The Federals would shout in return, "Lookout, Johnny Reb," and fire, then crow in reply. It was all very amusing, except for the toll in life; the consolidated 32nd and 58th Alabama of Clayton's Brigade suffered three killed and fifteen wounded. To add to their discomfort, a bitter wind began blowing, and both sides struggled to pile rocks and logs into makeshift breastworks along the timber-darkened slopes.[6]

On the outskirts of Chattanooga that night, Frank Wolfe of Quartermaster General Montgomery Meigs's staff was preparing to fall asleep after a tiring day riding along the lines below Lookout Mountain. There was a tap on the frame of his tent; it was Meigs's orderly. "He asked me to come out at once," wrote the surprised Wolfe. Wolfe soon emerged from the tent and stood in stunned silence. "There on the side of Lookout, like a thousand fireflies, the skirmishers were at it," observed Wolfe. Beneath a full moon, the "hunter's moon," said an engrossed officer, the muzzle flashes of musketry became "twinkling sparks upon the mountainside." It was such an awesome, beautiful sight that Wolfe roused even Meigs. All were amazed and only too glad to witness the dramatic scene. Amid a glowing belt of campfires skirting the mountain midway up the slopes, the rapid musket flashes, like "the gleaming of fireflies," shot streaks of fire across the slopes. "A stream of lightning seemed to run almost from the top to the bottom of the mountain," reflected an awed observer.[7]

It was one of the most imposing of sights, and from the porch of his headquarters, even Gen. Ulysses S. Grant admired the grand scene. "The full moon made the battlefield as plain to us in the valley as if it were day," wrote Charles A. Dana. To Grant, however, this beautiful sight was "not in the programme"—he expected the Rebels to evacuate Lookout Mountain that night. Until about 1:00 A.M., the firing and flashes continued, but by that time Grant and many of his headquarters staff had gone inside. "I fell asleep," wrote a guest at Grant's headquarters, only "to dream of the roar of cannon and the rattle of musketry."[8]

Joseph Hooker was both elated and awed by the events of November 24, 1863. Yet his performance reflected mostly the latter emotion. That morning, Hooker had been so conservative as to pass up an opportunity to attack Walthall's and Moore's thin line of pickets, and he had reported at 11:00 A.M., "I am in condition to cross the creek [with Osterhaus and Grose], but as it will be attended with some considerable loss, I have deemed it advisable to await the arrival of Geary's [flanking] command . . . before doing so." During the afternoon his caution had led to the order to halt along the Cravens house plateau.[9]

Even more significant was Hooker's handling of the column sent to march around the northern face of Lookout Mountain along the Kelley's Ford road. Under Hooker's personal direction, only two regiments were detached from Charles R. Woods's brigade and sent forward along the Kelley's Ferry road. These two units, the 12th Missouri and 76th Ohio Infantry, found their passage blocked by felled timber and a large rock slide. So little progress was made due to "expend[ing] a good deal of labor" in clearing these obstructions that at 6:40 P.M. Hooker didn't know what lay ahead of him in Chattanooga Valley.[10]

Several hours earlier, at 4:00 P.M., Hooker had complained, "It is so dark in Chattanooga Valley that it is impossible for me to see the position of the enemy or his numbers, and I deem it very imprudent to descend into it tonight." Since the enemy "continue[d] to hold the top of Lookout Mountain, and I cannot prevent it until I can move around and take possession of the Summertown road, which . . . requires me to descend into the valley," Hooker had decided not to advance.[11]

This cost him the chance to isolate Stevenson's troops atop Lookout Mountain, which is what Stevenson and J. K. Jackson had feared the most. In fact, Hooker's excessive caution after nightfall led to a remarkable request; due to a lack of knowledge of what was in front, Hooker suggested "that the operations of tomorrow be suspended until the fog lifts." Moreover, Hoooker was so uncertain of his position, he asked for a map from Baldy Smith, since he evidently did not have a very good one at hand.[12]

Hooker's conservative outlook was an incredible circumstance, much of which was rooted in the spur-of-the-moment "demonstration" planning. Yet Hooker simply lacked the aggressiveness and insight to capitalize on what had become a major Confederate command breakdown.

There soon were other embarrassments. At 5:15 P.M., Hooker had received a sizable reinforcement, Brig. Gen. William P. Carlin's brigade from Thomas's Fourteenth Corps, sent from Chattanooga Valley following Whitaker's seemingly urgent request of 2:00 P.M.* After rushing to ferry his troops across Chattanooga Creek in a large flatboat, Carlin was about to form his brigade to sweep forward into Chattanooga Valley and "attack the enemy in flank" when he was told to report in person to Hooker. By Hooker's direct order, Carlin was told to march instead to the Cravens house plateau and relieve the troops there. Hooker's concern was defensive, not offensive; "as the upper part of the line is most exposed it has been stiffened with reinforcements," he wrote late that afternoon. Carlin's men, thereafter, had taken the designated position, relieving some of Geary's troops. Soon they were "fiercely attacked" by the enemy. Yet it was only the tentative, mistaken advance of Clayton's Brigade, which had advanced too far in relieving Pettus's troops.[13]

Although this "attack" was repulsed most handsomely, said Carlin, and the firing sputtered to a halt after 1:00 A.M., this mistaken night encounter produced a strange sequence of events. Hooker was at once so alarmed, he feared that a major Confederate effort was taking place to break his line. Earlier, he had sent word to his chief of staff to have the bridges by which Geary had crossed Lookout Creek that morning destroyed, lest the Confederates use them to counterattack in Hooker's rear.[14]

Even more remarkable, as the desultory Clayton-Carlin night fighting

---

*Also a factor in Carlin being sent was Hooker's own dire midafternoon dispatch: "Can hold the line I am now on; can't advance. Some of my troops out of ammunition; can't replenish."

continued for more than two hours and provided the spectacular scene witnessed in Chattanooga Valley, this minor but highly visible midslope combat quickened the hearts of many at army headquarters.

Charles A. Dana, who observed this distant skirmish after 10:00 P.M., wrote in his dispatch to Washington, D.C., the following morning of "the sharp fight" on the eastern slopes the previous night. Grant, who had acknowledged that continued fighting on Lookout Mountain was not in the program, evidently implied to Dana that with all the troops Hooker had on hand, "the position can probably be held."[15]

It was a curious twist, involving the change from an opportunistic offensive to a cautious "wait and see" perspective. In contrast to Hooker's optimism at 4:00 P.M., when all seemed stable and the mountain was shrouded in fog, there was now much uncertainty. At the time, Hooker had told Geary what seemed obvious: "In all probability the enemy will evacuate tonight. His line of retreat is seriously threatened by my troops." Grant and nearly everyone at army headquarters seemed to agree. Yet following the outbreak of fighting during the 10:00 P.M. to 1:00 A.M. period, questions were raised about Bragg's willingness to yield Lookout Mountain.[16]

Due to the uncertainty and the difficult communications with Hooker's headquarters "in the field," nothing was specifically planned for Hooker on the following morning. Grant continued to rely on Sherman for the bulk of his offensive effort. Thus, Hooker was told by Thomas at 9:30 P.M. merely to "be in readiness to advance as soon as possible in the morning to seize and hold the Summertown road and cooperate with the XIV Corps by supporting its right."[17]

This was a very minimal and uninspiring role, and it was the extent of Hooker's instructions until late the following morning. Hooker, duly cautious from the previous evening's "attack," thus was in no hurry to push forward on the twenty-fifth. In fact, after sending scouts into the valley and idly peering through field glasses at enemy camps on distant Missionary Ridge while waiting for the valley fog to dissipate, Hooker became so bored and unoccupied on the morning of November 25 as to report at 9:20 A.M., "I await orders."[18]

The night of November 24 to 25 on Lookout Mountain had been a miserable one for most of the troops on both sides. One of David Ireland's men, Pvt. Peter Koppesser of the 149th New York Infantry, had captured a flag from one of Walthall's Mississippi regiments earlier that day. Being without adequate protection from the raw wind, Koppesser draped the flag shawl-like over his torso that night and slept soundly. To some of Grose's shivering troops, huddling around a small campfire with nothing to eat, the night was wretched and long.[19]

It had begun raining about 4:00 P.M., and after nightfall the rain had turned partially to sleet at higher elevations. "It felt sharp as needles to our faces," wrote a thoroughly soaked and miserable Ohio sergeant. After the rain ended and the skies cleared, the soldiers could see far below in the valley. The fires of both armies stretched for miles, and the waving and dipping of signal lights told of messages being transmitted for the morrow's fight, when nearly 120,000 men would grapple for possession of this rugged terrain. "It was a grand sight, and an awful thought," wrote an Illinois soldier.[20]

By 11:00 P.M., the moon was shining brightly, yet a shadow slowly crept across its face. With the moon in eclipse and the dead and scattered debris of battle lying about them, there was an eerie feeling among many of Hooker's soldiers—as if nature were grieving for the terrible drama being enacted. Above, on the crest of the mountain, some of Ireland's Pennsylvanians could hear the enemy noisily at work, "evidently strengthening their works." There was but little sleep that night.[21]

Among the equally cold and suffering Confederate soldiers of Clayton's command, there were whispered conversations shortly before 2:00 A.M. Commanders of the advanced pickets were ordered to pull back, leaving only three soldiers behind, who would withdraw after their regiments retired to the Summertown Road. Within a half hour, Clayton's men were on their way down the mountain, many limping due to cramps and stiff limbs.[22]

It was the final act of the sixty-three-day Confederate occupation of Lookout Mountain. John C. Brown's troops had begun the withdrawal about 7:00 P.M., followed by Walthall's at 11:00 P.M., and Pettus's and Moore's about 1:00 A.M. Campfires were left burning to deceive the enemy, and the noise the Yankee soldiers heard from the crest was probably the removal of camp equipage and supplies. By 10:00 P.M., many of Brown's men were across Chattanooga Creek, and the remainder of the Lookout Mountain troops proceeded to cross by two bridges. By 3:00 A.M., the Confederate evacuation of Lookout Mountain was accomplished. It seemed miraculous at the time. No enemy opposition had occurred.[23]

The morning of November 25 dawned misty and foggy along the lower slopes of Lookout Mountain. There was great uncertainty among Hooker's troops about the anticipated fight for the crest of the mountain. Many realized that the cloak of fog would soon be gone and they would be vulnerable to Rebel sharpshooters. As the fog began to dissipate, there was much trepidation. Yet "we look[ed] up at the summit, and to our surprise saw that some 'Yank' was waving," wrote an astounded lieutenant. Within minutes, cheering began, and "every man in the line from right to left was yelling with all his might." It was for the national flag of the 8th Kentucky Infantry, now waving prominently from the summit in the first brilliant rays of the sunrise.[24]

Before daylight, there had been indications of a Confederate evacuation of the mountain. In one of Osterhaus's units, the 13th Illinois Infantry, a captain told some of his men that he was sure the Rebels had evacuated. Although he volunteered to take a small detachment and climb the palisades to plant the 13th's flag there first, his colonel refused. Before sunrise, however, Brig. Gen. Walter Whitaker came to the 8th Kentucky and asked whether a small squad would again try to scale the heights to "take Lookout Rock." The previous day, when a small contingent of the 8th had attempted to reach the summit, they had been driven to cover by lighted shells thrown down by the enemy.[25]

Before daylight on the twenty-fifth, Capt. John Wilson of the 8th Kentucky Infantry, commanding the color company, volunteered to try this "bold undertaking." Taking five men, Wilson scaled the palisades beneath a glowing eastern horizon. Evidently, he utilized steps and a ladder made and formerly used by the Confederates to reach the top more easily.[26]

Wilson didn't know what to expect; the Rebels were still presumed to be on top of the mountain. Yet there was no one in sight. Jubilantly, the squad unfurled and planted the flag, originally presented by the ladies of Estill County, Kentucky. It was immediately illuminated in the first rays of sunlight striking the peak. At the time, soldiers of the 40th Ohio Infantry were dispersed along the plateau below, glumly eating their cold breakfast. Out of the corner of his eye, a sergeant caught a blur of motion from the mountaintop, where Rebel sharpshooters were expected to begin firing at sunrise. Incredibly, the national flag was flying there. "I . . . yelled, [and] at the same time the whole mountain side resounded with huzzahs," he later wrote.[27]

Below in the still-darkened valley, the sight of the Federal flag waving from the sun-gilded mountaintop was spectacular. Soon the air rang with mighty shouts and "immense cheering." "Our boys would take off their hats and wave them, and cheer at the top of their voice[s]," said an Indiana captain who was so excited, "I did not stop with waving my hat, but yelled and clapped my hands, jumped up and down, laughed and cried for joy. . . . In fact, the whole army in front of Chattanooga was simply wild with excitement."[28]

Later the "white star" flag of Geary's division and the flag of the 29th Pennsylvania, both from the Army of the Potomac, was added to the display at the summit. There was another round of cheers from the multitude below. "It was the happiest moment I ever experienced in the service," wrote a jubilant young Pennsylvania lieutenant to his family.[29]

By full daylight, Whitaker had sent the entire 8th Kentucky to the summit. Here they formed a line of battle and soon advanced to the Summertown Road. Everywhere, there were signs of a hasty Rebel retreat— abandoned camps with commissary stores, boxes of artillery ammunition, and even some ears of corn. Only six Rebel soldiers were encountered. It was now fully evident that Lookout Mountain was firmly in Federal hands.[30]

Joseph Hooker's confidence was suddenly renewed. From the Cravens house, he signaled in triumph to Chattanooga: "I have the honor to report that we have possession of the peak of Lookout Mountain. Present indications point to the enemy's having abandoned our front; prisoners think they have abandoned the valley entirely. Have ordered a reconnaissance."[31]

To some Ohio infantrymen, it was a godsend. In their assigned position of leading the advance up the Summertown Road that morning, the unit figured to suffer heavy casualties. The road was so narrow in spots that only four men could pass abreast. It was considered that the attack up that road would probably "use up the last man of our company [before it ended]," wrote a sergeant. It was a feeling of relief shared by many. Yet all but lost amid the joy and euphoria of having captured the neary impregnable "Gibralter" was the fact that, despite 1,251 overall casualties, Stevenson's Rebel troops had escaped intact.[32]

In fact, at that very moment, Carter Stevenson's troops were striding rapidly for the heights at Missionary Ridge. Behind them, a pall of smoke filled the once-placid Chattanooga Valley. Stevenson, ordered to destroy the crucial bridges over Chattanooga Creek, had done so before daylight, leaving a wide, deep watercourse separating Hooker's troops from their recent antagonists. Even more remarkable in the still-unfolding dramatic sequence of events, Stevenson's and the other troops had been summoned to Missionary Ridge as a part of Braxton Bragg's revised battle plan. Lookout Mountain had been abandoned, but its troops were the key element, not the heights, according to Bragg.[33]

Lookout Mountain had become dispensable in Bragg's eyes. Following the failures at Brown's Ferry, Wauhatchie, and the difficulties with Longstreet, Bragg simply didn't see the military usefulness of this giant mountain beyond that of an observation post. Its occupation had been marked with bad luck. Instead of what was first anticipated—a position from which the Yankees could be shelled from Chattanooga—the towering heights proved to be so remote that even Longstreet's skilled artillerists had been unable to effect more than minimal damage. Bragg's many disappointments with Lookout Mountain may have been reflected in his decision to evacuate it. Even in the final contest for its possession, in Bragg's view, Lookout Mountain's dominant topography had counted for little. Hooker's attack had been "met by one brigade only [Walthall's]," he complained. "Why this command was not sustained is yet unexplained," he fumed in his official report.[34]

If the Lookout Mountain encounter had proved to Bragg to be a forlorn hope, to the jubilant Federal army it had been a stunning, brilliant victory. It was soon known as the "Battle Above the Clouds," a phrase derived from the report of Brig. Gen. Montgomery Meigs that was written on November 26. "The day had been one of driving mists and rains and much of Hooker's battle was fought above the clouds," wrote the graphic but technically incorrect Meigs. Later amplified in press reports, Meigs's remark soon became the basis for enormous publicity and a variety of sensationalized accounts that settled into popular history as "one of the grandest military achievements of the age."[35]

Grant, who later termed all the hoopla over the fighting on Lookout Mountain "one of the romances of the war," eventually played down its interpretation as a battle. Considering the small number of Federal casualties attributed to the fighting—138 in Geary's units and perhaps 50 more in other commands—Grant implied that the Lookout Mountain fight was little more than a skirmish. "It is all poetry," he declared.[36]

His interpretation didn't set well with the men who had been there. The Battle Above the Clouds may have been controversial as to its severity, wrote a Lookout Mountain veteran after the war, but if the critics had experienced the action from the front ranks, they would have known that this "formidable undertaking" involved a hard climb and "a rough and tumble fight." Another veteran infantryman who had been present agreed, noting that only the part about "above the clouds" was inaccurate. This was pure fiction, he said; it was a battle "in the clouds."[37]

CHAPTER 28

"I MEAN TO GET
EVEN WITH THEM"

To the union high command in Chattanooga, the situation on the early morning of November 25 was uplifting. Charles A. Dana wrote at 7:30 A.M., "No firing at the front. This makes it pretty certain Bragg retreated." A major Union victory seemed all but proclaimed. "As soon as positively determined Bragg has gone, Granger, with 20,000 men, moves up south bank Tennessee . . . to cut off Longstreet's retreat and relieve Burnside," gloated Dana.[1]

Ulysses S. Grant had fallen asleep after midnight believing that Bragg's army would probably attempt to retreat during the night. Suggestions of this had been noted by Grant late on the afternoon of the twenty-fourth when "the enemy's wagon trains were seen passing . . . down the Summertown road from the top of the mountain to Chattanooga Valley." Accordingly, Grant's orders to his commanders on the night of the twenty-fourth were pursuit-oriented. Specifically, on the twenty-fifth Sherman would have the primary mission of moving along Missionary Ridge from north to south. Thomas's troops were to advance in front and carry the Confederate rifle pits at the foot of Missionary Ridge, or else "move to the left to [Sherman's] support," as the circumstances warranted. As such, Thomas's role was clearly ancillary; his main assignment was to cooperate with Sherman. In fact, Thomas's planned advance at dawn was intended primarily to compel the enemy "to show whether he occupies his rifle pits in our front [mid–Missionary Ridge]." This would provide specific evidence of a general Rebel retreat.[2]

Grant began to modify and revise his plans after daylight on the twenty-fifth when it was found that Bragg had evacuated the summit of Lookout

Mountain during the night but still held the rifle pits at the foot of Missionary Ridge, which appeared fully manned. Moreover, at daylight many Rebel troops were seen moving along the crest of Missionary Ridge toward the northern flank. Was it to oppose Sherman, or were they marching to the railroad depot and evacuating?[3]

As noted by Lt. Col. J. S. Fullerton at Fourth Corps headquarters, Grant now made a major change. For days, he had been fearful of Bragg escaping; "I was not willing that he should get his army off in good order," Grant confided a few weeks later. Believing the fighting on Lookout Mountain during the night was merely "a feint . . . to cover their retreat from the mountain top," Grant revised his plans. Instead of Thomas making a probing attack in front—for which there was no necessity, as Bragg's troops were clearly visible in their trenches—the Army of the Cumberland would merely pin the enemy down by occupying a threatening position in front of Bragg's center. Hooker, however, would now become a key player by turning the opposite (or southern) flank of Bragg's line on Missionary Ridge. Fighting Joe would advance from Lookout Mountain across the Chattanooga Valley to "carry the pass at Rossville, and operate against Bragg's left and rear." Bragg's army, perhaps trapped in the process of raising their siege, would be crushed between the two attacks and destroyed.[4]

Due to these revised plans, the order for Thomas to advance against the center was suspended. Sherman and Hooker would inflict the real damage; the flanks were to be the decisive points of attack.

Since these new orders didn't go out to Hooker until 10:10 A.M., Grant had a leisurely breakfast before riding to Fort Wood with several guests, including Inspector General David Hunter. Grant was so sanguine as to share a joke about John C. Fremont and how he had "used up" the Anderson troop of cavalry, later assigned to headquarters escort duty with the Army of the Cumberland. They had been so energetically run into the ground, joked Hunter, that had Fremont been given charge of the war, it surely would have ended six months later. Grant chuckled and agreed.[5]

There were few jokes being told at the Confederate army's headquarters on Missionary Ridge that morning. Beginning with the afternoon of November 24, a crisis-charged atmosphere had intensified at Bragg's command post. Beyond the unexpected engagement on Lookout Mountain, Warren Grigsby's cavalry along South Chickamauga Creek had warned of Federal cavalry crossing that creek about midmorning on the twenty-fourth. These Yankee horsemen were immediately recognized as a threat to the vunerable railroad line leading to east Tennessee. Bragg had promptly reacted, telling Maj. Gen. Patrick Cleburne, in reserve following his recall from the east Tennessee expedition the previous day, to send a brigade and a battery to guard the crucial East Tennessee and Georgia Railroad bridge over South Chickamauga Creek. Yet this was only the beginning of Bragg's many difficulties.[6]

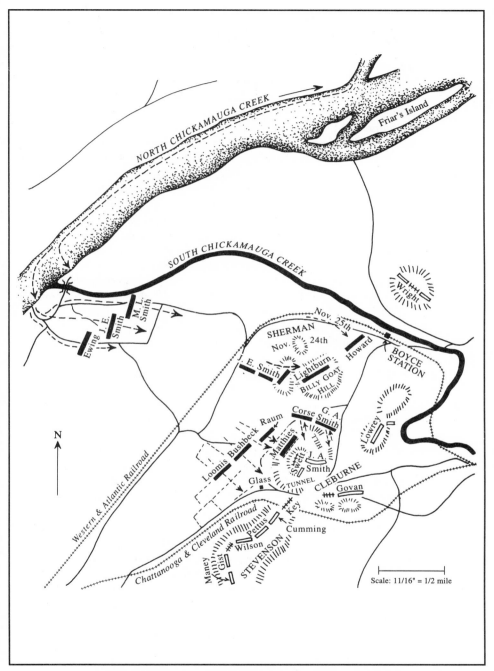

MAP 8   Sherman's Assault on North Missionary Ridge, November 24–25, 1863
(Source: Edward E. Betts, 1896 Chattanooga Map)

Early that afternoon, Grigsby's men had provided chilling intelligence of Sherman's heavy columns advancing along South Chickamauga Creek toward the northern terminus of Missionary Ridge. Considering that Stevenson was then heavily engaged on Lookout Mountain, it appeared to Bragg that a gigantic pincers movement was in progress. Stevenson was at least in place to fight for the eastern flank. Yet beyond W. H. T. Walker's troops south of the railroad tunnel, there were virtually no troops present on the north end of Missionary Ridge to stop Sherman. Delays in reaching the army's main Chickamauga Station railroad depot had hampered Marcus J. Wright's troops, en route from Charleston, Tennessee, that morning. It was early afternoon before Wright and his troops started for the mouth of South Chickamauga Creek, as directed by Bragg hours earlier.[7]

Due to Sherman's alarming advance, Bragg's only practical option was to send the remainder of Cleburne's reserve division, then building breastworks near Bragg's headquarters, to occupy the north of Missionary Ridge. Bragg explained the situation to Cleburne as he knew it about 2:00 P.M. on the twenty-fourth; Sherman already had a division in line opposite the railroad's Tunnel Hill, another was rapidly crossing the Tennessee River, and the enemy's pontoon bridge across that river was nearly complete. Bragg, at last, had begun to perceive the rapidly intensifying crisis on his right flank. You must preserve the vital railroad bridge in the rear "at all hazards," which would secure the army's line of retreat, Bragg instructed Cleburne.[8]

Pat Cleburne, fully aroused, issued immediate orders for his troops to march rapidly north along Missionary Ridge to the site above the railroad tunnel. Then, hurriedly, Cleburne galloped forward ahead of his command to find Gen. William Hardee, who would direct the overall defense of the northern flank.[9]

Cleburne discovered shortly after arriving on the ridge above the tunnel that he was in the midst of a burgeoning crisis. One of Hardee's staff officers pointed out the positions he was to defend—the detached Billy Goat Hill, Tunnel Hill (which was the highest point along North Missionary Ridge and about 250 yards north of the actual tunnel), and all of the intervening ridge extending to W. H. T. Walker's position about three-quarters of a mile south of the tunnel. Cleburne was aghast. He sent Hardee's staff officer to find that commander and tell him that with only three brigades it was impossible to cover so long a line.[10]

While Cleburne waited, several members of his signal corps staff went forward to scout the ground. Just as the head of Cleburne's leading brigade arrived, that of Brig. Gen. James A. Smith, a private from the signal corps rushed up to warn Cleburne that he had just come from Billy Goat Hill. The enemy was advancing against it in line of battle. Cleburne's orders to Smith were immediate: Get possession of that hill before the enemy. If he was too late, urged Cleburne, he would have to fall back to the main ridge. Smith dashed off with his men into the valley below Tunnel Hill and rushed toward the objective hill.[11]

Smith lost the race. The Yankees were found to be in possession of Billy Goat Hill, and Smith had to fall back while skirmishing to the northern terminus of the main ridge. When the enemy appeared to be working their way around Smith's right flank, Cleburne began to worry about the enemy turning his open flank and getting possession of the main ridge.[12]

At the time, Cleburne was in the process of placing his two trailing brigades, Govan's, and Lowrey's, south of the tunnel, so as to connect with W. H. T. Walker. Yet, recognizing the new danger, Pat Cleburne ordered Govan and his men to rush instead to the right, behind Smith. Here a spur of the main ridge jutted out just north of the tunnel and overlooked the gap between two detached hills north of Smith's position. It was a hasty, improvised move, and contrary to Hardee's original instructions. Yet Hardee, attracted to the north by the sound of skirmish firing, soon arrived and approved of Cleburne's dispositions. To both generals, it was apparent that defending the northern ridge terminus was the essential priority. The threat of Sherman's troops turning the right flank was obvious. Yet between Smith's position and W. H. T. Walker's troops south of the tunnel, a distance of nearly a mile, only two regiments of Lowrey's Brigade remained posted along Cleburne's opposite flank.[13]

It was such an impractical defensive situation that Cleburne anticipated a general retreat before Sherman's vast columns could attack this extended line in the morning. Accordingly, "hearing of the disaster at Lookout Mountain" and knowing of the weakened condition of Bragg's forces, Cleburne considered that the army would fall back beyond South Chickamauga Creek that night. Soon after dark on the twenty-fourth, he ordered his ordnance wagons and all but two pieces of artillery to cross over or remain on the east bank, so as to clear the roads for his withdrawing troops.[14]

About 9:00 P.M., Cleburne became increasingly anxious that no orders to withdraw had been received from Hardee's headquarters. He asked a staff officer, Capt. Irving Buck, to go to Hardee and find out when the expected orders would be issued. Buck went to find Hardee but learned that the general had been called by Bragg to an important conference at army headquarters. Riding there, Buck arrived just as the meeting was breaking up. Breckinridge emerged from the house, remarking, "I never felt more like fighting than when I saw those people shelling my troops off of Lookout [Mountain] today. [Now] I mean to get even with them."[15]

Breckinridge's comments startled Captain Buck. Finding Hardee nearby, Buck haltingly asked what he should tell Cleburne. "Tell Cleburne we are to fight," said Hardee. "His division will undoubtedly be heavily attacked, and they must do their very best."[16]

Buck could hardly believe what he was hearing, yet he managed a spirited reply: "The division has never yet failed to clear its front, and will do so again." Captain Buck hurriedly rode back to Cleburne's campsite with the grim news: The Confederate army would await the enemy's attack along Missionary Ridge. It was about midnight when Pat Cleburne learned of this shocking decision. With grim determination, he began to prepare for the next day and what was certain to be "a long day's fight."[17]

Braxton Bragg, when facing an unexpected crisis, generally became so flustered as to lean on the advice of even a drummer boy, his bitter enemy Simon B. Buckner once scoffed. On the night of November 24 to 25, Bragg disproved this adage; he was at this point so indecisive as to take the advice of one of his most notoriously inconsistent and rival subordinate generals.[18]

Bragg had called the evening conference at his headquarters to consider plans for the twenty-fifth based upon the inconclusive events of the twenty-fourth. Present were Breckinridge and Hardee, his senior commanders. That evening before the conference, Bragg had wired headquarters in Richmond news of the day's happenings: "We have had a prolonged struggle for Lookout Mountain today and sustained considerable loss in one division. Elsewhere the enemy has only maneuvered for position." Bragg's brief and misleading comments reflect a subtle misunderstanding that may well have permeated his thinking that night. Since Thomas's forces had remained virtually inactive in front of Bragg's center on Missionary Ridge that day—while Sherman's had "maneuvered" for position on the north and Hooker had attacked Lookout Mountain—was it not likely that Grant was merely attempting to outmaneuver Bragg from his strong position on Missionary Ridge?[19]

John C. Breckinridge, who disliked Bragg yet had been politically sensitive enough not to sign the petition circulating for his removal the preceding month, was vociferous in his ardent insistence that the Confederate army remain in its present position. Allegedly, Breckinridge stated that if the army "couldn't fight here with such advantage of position, they couldn't fight anywhere."[20]

Hardee, who knew of the serious threat to the far-right flank on the north end of Missionary Ridge, strongly disagreed. Noting the overwhelming concentration of enemy forces building on both flanks and mindful of the absence of Longstreet's troops, Hardee proposed an immediate withdrawal.[21]

Breckinridge promptly objected, saying that there was not enough time to withdraw the army that night without the loss of vast stores and equipment. Bragg agreed with this premise; it made sense that too few hours remained to effect an orderly retreat. Furthermore, Bragg considered his line on Missionary Ridge so strong that it could be held by "a line of skirmishers against any assaulting column." His decision, accordingly, was to remain in position and await the enemy's attack. Essentially, he would call Grant's bluff. The Federal commander would either have to attack Bragg's nearly "impregnable" positions along the heights or withdraw. Bragg, on the advice of Breckinridge, who was later accused (by Bragg) of being drunk at the time, intended to force a showdown on Missionary Ridge.[22]

Hardee, although his advice was disregarded, insisted that if he was to fight on the north end of Missionary Ridge, he must have reinforcements. Bragg, who shared Hardee's concern for the right flank, agreed to send Stevenson's Division from the far left, along with Frank Cheatham's Division. These units, although having participated in the Lookout Mountain fiasco, were still intact along the eastern banks of Chattanooga Creek. Verbal orders were given, and about midnight, said Carter Stevenson, he was alerted by two of Bragg's staff officers to send all troops that had been west of Chattanooga Creek to the army's extreme right. By daylight, most of Stevenson's troops were trudging along the crest of Missionary Ridge, en route to the far right. Their appearance surprised many of Bragg's midlevel commanders, who were still waiting for the expected orders to retreat across South Chickamauga Creek.[23]

William Tecumseh Sherman, contrary to the mood at Grant's headquarters, appears to have spent the night of November 24 to 25 in uneasy anticipation of an enemy attack on the following morning. Although about midnight he had received Grant's orders to "attack the enemy at the point most advantageous from your position at early dawn," Sherman was fearful of a counterattack by Bragg's troops. Soldiers along the picket line reported hearing the Rebels fortifying and emplacing artillery on Missionary Ridge during the night. Accordingly, at 5:00 A.M., Sherman had two brigades of Brig. Gen. John E. Smith's division moved to the right along the base of Billy Goat Hill, in "anticipation of [meeting] an attack through the valley at the base of the ridge." Smith soon put Alexander's and Matthies's brigades in line under cover of the woods, "ready to act in any emergency."[24]

Sherman, who was in the saddle before daylight, said he rode to the extreme left of his lines to attempt to gain an idea of the terrain and an approximation of the enemy's position "in the dim light of morning." What he found was shocking; instead of occupying the northern extremity of Missionary Ridge, his troops held only an isolated knoll, separated from the main ridge by a wooded ravine. Although Sherman later blamed imperfect maps for deceiving him as to what he had considered "a continuous hill," his absence from the forward positions before darkness fell on the twenty-fourth contributed significantly to the mistaken perspective.[25]

Due to the fog and lingering mist clinging to the valley, it was uncertain that the Confederate army was present in force. Sherman's initial order to Brig. Gen. Joseph A. J. Lightburn, then occupying Billy Goat Hill, was to send forward two hundred men "to occupy Tunnel Hill." Simultaneously, Brig. Gen. Hugh Ewing, one of Sherman's division commanders, ordered Col. John M. Loomis's brigade to "push the enemy's skirmishers, but under no circumstances to bring on a general engagement." Clearly, Sherman was in a cautious mood.[26]

This hesitancy was reinforced when Lightburn's reconnaissance discovered Tunnel Hill's northern terminus "occupied in force by the enemy." Although the patrol, reinforced by another regiment, soon occupied a portion of the breastworks abandoned by the enemy along the middle slopes, they could get no closer than within fifty to seventy-five yards of the main breastworks atop the hill. Loomis's brigade had even less success in "pushing the enemy's skirmishers." As they moved forward into open ground, Loomis's troops were fired upon by artillery positioned along the main ridge. When subjected to this "heavy cross-fire" of shells, Loomis moved his men to cover and halted.[27]

To Sherman, the crowning blow came soon thereafter when from a variety of locations strong enemy troop movements were reported along the crest of Missionary Ridge; they were moving in his direction. Sherman reacted impulsively. About 8:00 A.M., he sent an urgent message to Grant for additional help; he needed reinforcements, he said. Within forty-five minutes, Grant ordered Howard to march the Eleventh Corps to Sherman's relief, "looking well to your right flank and in readiness to form line on your right in case you should be attacked on the march." Howard received these orders about 9:45 A.M. and promptly started to move his nearly six thousand troops to join Sherman. Soon more than thirty thousand Federal troops would be concentrated on Sherman's front, representing more than a third of Grant's effective strength.[28]

By midmorning, Sherman had become so apprehensive of a gathering enemy force along the north end of Missionary Ridge as to be reduced to prolonged inactivity. Instead of attacking, as Grant had ordered, Sherman's soldiers spent much of the morning in anxious anticipation of a fight and awaiting orders.[29]

By midmorning, Ulysses Grant was lounging uneasily at Fort Wood. So quiet were events at his headquarters—even at the very hour Sherman's decisive action was to have occurred—that one of Grant's staff officers and a visitor rode back to Chattanooga for a drink. At the time, apparently, Grant was experiencing some misgivings. Despite his calculating plans and careful strategy, it appeared that Bragg hadn't been deceived after all; Bragg appeared to be concentrating his forces on the far-northern flank. Moreover, it was now evident Grant had been deceived by Stevenson's intercepted message into thinking Bragg expected an attack on the Lookout Mountain flank. With the strong columns of enemy troops seen moving along the crest of the ridge toward the far-right flank—the critical point of the Federal attack—Grant appeared to be checkmated.[30]

Grant's luck thus far had been excellent. Twice on successive days, he had advanced troops predicated on false information, both of which movements were intended as mere demonstrations. Yet an important victory or the occupation of significant enemy territory had been the result. Now, with the campaign outcome in doubt, where was Grant's fabled good luck? He had put his faith in William Tecumseh Sherman. Upon the success of that key commander, Grant expected to win the battle. Sherman had never before let him down. He was the man to be relied upon, Grant had written only a few weeks earlier in endorsing his promotion to command of the Army of the Tennessee.[31]

* * *

Instead of one of William Tecumseh Sherman's finest hours, the morning of November 25, 1863, found him wallowing in uncertainty and excessive caution. The net result had been added time for the hard-pressed Patrick Cleburne to prepare for the defense of the north end of Missionary Ridge. Yet about 11:00 A.M., when the head of Howard's Eleventh Corps column crossed a pontoon bridge over Citico Creek and reported their presence, it was apparent to Sherman that the initiative was again in his hands. Tentatively, he launched an attack spearheaded by a single brigade.[32]

CHAPTER 29

HELL TURNED LOOSE
ON TUNNEL HILL

Pat Cleburne had been born on St. Patrick's eve, 1828, an omen, some said, of forthcoming fame. Many of his staff officers fully agreed. At battles such as Richmond, Kentucky; Perryville, Stones River; and Chickamauga, Cleburne had been highly praised for his conduct and performance. Lt. Gen. E. Kirby Smith wrote that he was "one of the most zealous and intelligent officers in the army." Even Bragg had acknowledged Cleburne as "the admiration of his command as a soldier and a gentleman."[1]

Many of Cleburne's men had grown to idolize their Irish-born commander, and they reveled in their reputation as the elite troops of the Army of Tennessee. When regulations were issued May 1, 1863, requiring that all Confederate units utilize the so-called National Flag (the famous St. Andrew's Cross red flag), Cleburne's division had been allowed as a special honor to retain their distinctive blue flags with a white moon in the center. In the Army of Tennessee only Cleburne's Division was permitted to carry their old flags.[2]

Such honor accentuated the high opinion for and the enormous worth of the man whom Jefferson Davis later would ironically term the "Stonewall Jackson of the West." Accorded widespread recognition and the formal thanks of the Confederate Congress for Richmond, Kentucky, Pat Cleburne was one of the army's brightest stars, a man seemingly foreordained to greatness.[3]

Yet, for all of his dash and glory, there seemed to be a dark moon haunting Cleburne's career. Despite the many honors and his high reputation, Pat Cleburne continued to labor under a lingering sense of ill presentiment. If keenly intelligent and possessed of great common sense, he had been dogged by bad luck, army politics, and severe physical trauma. Gravely wounded by a pistol shot intended for his friend Thomas C. Hindman during a civil altercation at Helena in May 1856, Cleburne had hovered between life and death for days. Six years later, he had been severely wounded by a rifle ball in the lower left jaw at Richmond, Kentucky. The projectile had lodged in his mouth, knocking out two teeth and causing Cleburne thereafter to wear a short well-trimmed mustache and beard to mask the scar. Again at Perryville, only two months later, Pat Cleburne had been painfully struck near the ankle by a shell that killed his mount. Cleburne's grim humor reflected his attitude about the typical front-line exposure in battle, which often made him a conspicuous target: "I was trained in a school where running formed no part of the accomplishments."[4]

On November 25, 1863, Patrick Ronayne Cleburne's greatest military test was at hand. His many hard-fought campaigns had provided experience in confronting enormous battle odds, but on this occasion an extraordinary circumstance had occurred. By design, Bragg and Grant had committed their finest combat troops to what was understood to be the decisive action of the campaign—the defense or capture of the north end of Missionary Ridge. Since both zone commanders were operating on an isolated flank with full designated responsibility for that area, it loomed much as a personal confrontation between two separate combatants.[5]

Cleburne, perhaps the Army of Tennessee's best fighter, was defending a naturally strong position with about four thousand troops. Although aware he was outnumbered, he learned only later that he was facing a concentration of more than thirty thousand Yankee soldiers, a more than seven-to-one discrepancy. Moreover, Cleburne was up against a man considered by some to be the most ardent fighter in the Union army, Grant's favorite general, William Tecumseh Sherman. The odds seemed so overwhelming that the result appeared to be inevitable.[6]

Yet it was a contest of enormous fascination. Considering the various tactical options, replete with defensive strong points, narrow valleys of access, and hidden routes of maneuver, Cleburne's duel with Sherman loomed as a classic contest of generals, arguably the best against the best. The crucial question was that of applied combat leadership. The fight on the north end of Missionary Ridge thus was a momentous collision with immense stakes. For Cleburne, it was the test of a lifetime. For Sherman, it was the best chance of his career. No wonder that it would become one of the Civil War's most remarkable encounters.

Pat Cleburne's surprise at Bragg's decision to fight along Missionary Ridge was masked by an awareness of the heavy responsibility placed upon him and the enormous task ahead. After midnight, having immediately recalled his artillery and ordnance wagons from across the river, Cleburne was dogged by a bedeviling nuisance—the lunar eclipse. It was so dark, Cleburne said, that it was difficult to see during a "moonlight survey" of the ground he must defend. Moreover, the vital axes needed to cut trees for breastworks were with the division's train in the rear. The men would have to wait until they were brought up.[7]

Meanwhile, Cleburne assessed the coming day's battlefield. There were several primary defensive sites Cleburne relied upon to defend the north of Missionary Ridge. The northern apex and adjacent western perimeter of the main ridge's Tunnel Hill was defended by Brig. Gen. James A. Smith's Texas brigade, which would bear the brunt of any attack from enemy-occupied Billy Goat Hill. Four Napoleon guns of Swett's Battery (Lt. H. Shannon commanding) were ordered posted in Smith's support along the highest elevation of the crest (about 250 yards north of the railroad tunnel site). South of Swett's Battery, at a point directly over the tunnel, Calvert's Battery, commanded by Lt. Thomas J. Key, was unlimbered facing west. Key's infantry supports arrived about sunrise, being three regiments of John C. Brown's Brigade, Stevenson's Division, which had marched all night from Lookout Mountain. Cleburne placed them just north of Key's guns, to defend Tunnel Hill's western slopes.[8]

The other basic defensive positions Cleburne chose were actually separated from the main ridge. Cleburne's greatest fear was to be outflanked on his immediate north, enabling the enemy to cut off the line of retreat across South Chickamauga Creek and perhaps trap much of the Confederate army. Thus he retained Govan's Brigade in its position along a spur of the main ridge east of James A. Smith's line. Here they overlooked a small valley formed from the gap between Billy Goat Hill and the main ridge. A full battery, Douglas's, was posted in support along this line, in position to enfilade any enemy attack toward the right flank of Smith's position. Otherwise, two remaining regiments of Lowrey's Brigade were sent forward, across this valley to the next detached hill north of Govan's line, to join with the two previously sent to that location. Here Lowrey would be able to support Govan or Smith as needed and block any attempted Federal attack following the south bank of South Chickamauga Creek. Cleburne then completed his dispositions by moving Brig. Gen. Lucius E. Polk's small detached brigade to a prominent hill overlooking South Chickamauga Creek, on the opposite (northeastern) side of that stream. This effectively blocked an enemy passage along the north bank and also secured his line of retreat, estimated Cleburne.[9]

The net effect of Cleburne's planning was to throw a strong barrier to Sherman's progress to the north—Cleburne's right flank. Yet on the eastern perimeter of the ridge, where a gap existed between Cleburne's troops and Hardee's, the Tunnel Hill sector appeared vulnerable, being defended primarily by artillery. Clearly, Cleburne expected the primary fight to occur along the northern terminus.

Accordingly, he made one last significant change in his troops' positions. James A. Smith's men were ordered to fall back and to the right, higher up toward the crest of Tunnel Hill along its northern apex. Since Smith's men had previously prepared breastworks along the lower slopes, where they had defended against skirmishers from Billy Goat Hill on the evening of the twenty-fourth, these were abandoned. Smith's new line ran almost at right angles to the former perimeter. His single left-flank regiment remained about 150 yards north of the tunnel, stretching north along the western perimeter of Tunnel Hill. Beyond the gap left for Swett's artillery, Smith's remaining two regiments fronted northward. In all, Smith had fewer than fifteen hundred men to defend the most critical sector of Cleburne's line. When the few axes located from the division wagons arrived in the middle of the night, Smith's men went to work with befitting urgency.[10]

William Tecumseh Sherman's chat with his foster brother, Brig. Gen. Hugh Ewing, had set the tone for the morning's offensive: "I guess, Ewing, if you're ready you might as well go ahead." In discussing the method of attack, Sherman told Ewing to keep his lines intact, saying, "Don't call for help until you actually need it." Ewing, as division commander, had designated a single brigade, Brig. Gen. John M. Corse's, as the assaulting column. They were to advance from the base of Billy Goat Hill, pass through the intervening "gorge," and strike the northern face of Tunnel Hill. In support would be a polyglot aggregation of troops, selected for their ready accessibility that morning. Lightburn's brigade on Billy Goat Hill would provide a single regiment; Morgan L. Smith's remaining brigade, Giles A. Smith's, would move eastward in support around the base of Tunnel Hill. West of Corse's line, Loomis's brigade, another of Ewing's units, would be advanced simultaneously.[11]

Sherman's reasoning in utilizing a single brigade as the striking column seems have been based upon the narrow ridge of Tunnel Hill, which would limit the number of troops operating along the crest. Yet Sherman's caution was fully apparent, and the tentative nature of his advance was suggested by his statement that he retained three brigades on Billy Goat Hill to hold it as "a key point."[12]

As such, the tactical aspects of the attack appear to have followed from the events of the early morning, when Corse's men had crept forward to discover the enemy's strength and position.

Lt. Col. H. W. Hall of the 40th Illinois Infantry had been assigned to protect Battery D of the 1st Missouri Light Artillery, posted on Billy Goat Hill the evening before. Yet, before daylight, Corse had asked Hall to advance his regiment of 130 men at dawn and try to gain the hill in front. As it was then unknown whether the enemy was still posted in strength along the target hill (the northwestern face of Tunnel Hill), Hall's men had deployed in a skirmish line and pushed cautiously ahead into the semi-darkness. He would be supported, Corse encouragingly offered as Hall's line moved out.[13]

Confederate Capt. Samuel T. Foster's company of the 24th Texas (Dismounted) Cavalry, James A. Smith's Brigade, was on picket at the base of Tunnel Hill that morning. When one of his men saw movement in front and asked permission to fire, Foster told him to wait a few minutes and then shoot, since it was still too dark to see well. A few minutes later, with the sun glowing on the eastern horizon, Pvt. Theodore Cullen of Foster's company aimed his rifle at a shadowy figure and pulled the trigger. The sharp report signaled the morning's first shot in defense of Tunnel Hill. Other Confederate pickets then opened fire as Hall's men pressed forward. When Hall's men returned the fire, a rippled staccato of rifle fire erupted along the timbered slopes.[14]

Within minutes, Hall's extended line loomed beyond Foster's flanks, and Foster passed the word to "fall back slowly, but keep firing." Back past the line of Smith's abandoned works moved Foster's men, dodging from tree to tree. Perhaps a half hour after the first shot sounded, Foster's men tumbled over the brigade's new breastworks on Tunnel Hill and took their places next to Smith's riflemen. Only one of Foster's men had been shot, a private struck in the windpipe and mortally wounded.[15]

Lieutenant Colonel Hall watched his men of the 40th Illinois clamber over the makeshift log breastworks the Confederates had abandoned; he motioned them onward toward the crest. Suddenly, Hall saw a Rebel battery in the gathering light atop the hill. Hall looked around. Corse had promised him supports for his probing advance. Yet none were in sight. "We could easily have driven the enemy back and captured their battery," he later wrote. Yet as their own skirmishers were now out of the way, the Rebel cannon opened with a roar. Hall's skirmish line quickly beat a hasty retreat, falling back about eighty yards beyond the old enemy works, and took shelter under the lee of the hill. Here they were mistakenly fired into by the same battery they had been assigned to protect on Billy Goat Hill the night before. Some of our men were killed and wounded by this "friendly" fire before the error was discovered, Hall bitterly noted. It was an ominous beginning for Sherman's attempt to capture Tunnel Hill.[16]

As the 40th Illinois continued to cling to the slopes, sharpshooting at the Confederate line on the crest, Brig. Gen. John M. Corse suddenly appeared through the drifting smoke and found Hall. "What did you see?" he eagerly asked. Hall described the enemy's works and their cannon atop the hill. "Can we take them?" asked Corse. "With a strong force, yes, but not with my skirmish line," replied the exasperated Hall. Corse left in a hurry, telling Hall to get his men ready; he was going for the brigade, and then together they would charge and get those Rebel guns.[17]

Thereafter, about 11:00 A.M., the clarion sound of one of Corse's bugles signaled "forward," and Corse's assault began. It was an attack in four ranks, 920 men strong, against Smith's three regiments of slightly greater combined strength. Corse was in the front rank, leading three deployed lines of skirmishers straight for the blazing enemy battery atop the hill. In reserve, Corse had placed the remainder of his brigade under Col. Charles C. Walcutt of the 46th Ohio Infantry.[18]

Over and past the abandoned Rebel works swept Corse's front line, rushing toward the brow of the hill with gathering momentum. "Merciful Father," wrote an eyewitness, "what a dreadful roar . . . [now] shook the earth. I could almost see the [minié] balls fly through the air. Still not a shot came from our brave boys—only their bayonets glistened in the beautiful sunlight." It was the most terrific fire many of Corse's veterans had ever experienced. "General Corse shouted for 'all who are brave enough— follow me,' " said an officer. Smith's riflemen, on the top of the hill, had begun firing at a range of about four hundred yards. Yet it was the canister from Swett's Battery that made it seem "almost impossible for any troops to withstand it."[19]

It didn't matter. These were Sherman's men, the proud victors of Vicksburg. They kept going forward. Men began dropping by the dozens. Still they staggered onward. Their determination and fearlessness astounded even Colonel Walcutt in the rear line. Corse and his most advanced ranks pushed to within three hundred yards of the rim of fire on the hill's horizon. Here Corse was suddenly struck in the head and knocked senseless. Several men quickly carried the badly wounded general down the slopes to safety. His front line now began to waver and halt. Within seconds, the men began to fall back in fragments. Lieutenant Colonel Hall, who was in the front line, complained that once again the want of support had caused the attack to fail.[20]

On top of Tunnel Hill, Capt. Samuel Foster watched the Yankees run, "which I enjoy[ed] hugely." He and his men laughed and hollered, he wrote in his journal. Yet his celebration was premature, as Foster grimly noted. Within minutes, the Yankees were back again.

Corse's second and third skirmish line appeared through the drifting smoke, striking for the defiant line of breastworks along the crest. Again the ragged line of blue uniforms pressed onward into the hellfire of Smith's rifles and Swett's cannon. The whizzing canister and minié balls were too much. The line staggered to a halt, with most of Corse's men shooting blindly at the flashes of fire ahead. Caught in a static position, the Yankee line shuddered and wavered under the hail of missiles. "To see them blue coats fall is glorious," wrote Capt. Sam Foster. "We can see them dropping all along their lines. Sometimes great gaps are made—they can't stand it— and away they go to find shelter from our bullets."[21]

The hillside was in chaos. Corse's front ranks were riddled and in disarray. Even now, Sherman's veterans wouldn't give up the fight. Colonel Walcutt by this time had taken command of the brigade, and once more he pushed the lines forward, spearheaded by the main reserve line—portions of three regiments. Soon they emerged through the lingering smoke, climbing briskly toward those blazing Napoleons atop the hill.[22]

Here they come again, thought Capt. Samuel Foster. "They have a flag. I told my men to go [shoot] for [it]. . . . Down it came, [yet] another [man] picks it up, and down he went. Then another." Still Walcutt's ranks kept coming. They were Illinois, Ohio, and Iowa boys, yelling and shooting as they pressed onward to within one hundred yards of Smith's line. The roar of battle was deafening. Men along both lines were loading and firing as fast as they could. It was a frantic moment, where seconds seemed an eternity. There was no time to think, only to do. The two lines were within yards of one another. Foster said the enemy surged boldly forward "like they were going to walk right over us."[23]

Momentarily, it appeared as if they just might do so. Among the openly exposed Napoleons of Swett's Battery, both lieutenants and so many non-commissioned officers had fallen that a corporal now commanded. The brass gun tubes were almost too hot to touch, but the gunners kept firing canister into the oncoming blue ranks with such fury that an eyewitness watched Walcutt's men "fall like leaves in the fall of the year." "Still they advance, and still we shoot them down." wrote the amazed Sam Foster. "Oh, this is fun," he exclaimed. "[We] lie here and shoot them down and we don't get hurt—we are behind these logs. We give them fits."[24]

"[It was] a terrible storm of musket balls and canister, shot at short range," later said a veteran 6th Iowa infantryman. The men of the 6th Iowa, one of Walcutt's largest regiments, kept moving onward, bending low to the ground as if facing a driving sleet storm. When within fifty steps of Swett's blazing guns, their line staggered to an abrupt halt. Many considered it "impossible" to go farther, noted an Iowa man. Their line began to disintegrate. "Some keep coming, others hang back," noted Sam Foster. "Some are killed within 20 feet of our works." So many dead littered the smoldering slopes, with wounded men writhing in agony and others limping to the rear, that it seemed the very ground had become a maddened cauldron. To see the awful carnage, smell the pungent sulfurous odor of burned powder, and hear the shrieks and agonizing cries for help amid the roar of battle was the morbid experience of a lifetime. Yet it was but a blur— a frenzied, fear-filled glimpse of doom on earth.[25]

Suddenly, "without any command," noted the amazed Foster, "our men began jumping over the works like sheep, yelling like only Texans can, and charged into them." It was a countercharge of two regiments. Brig. Gen. James A. Smith led the rush with portions of Col. Roger Q. Mills's and Col. Hiram Granbury's regiments. They surged down the slopes with fixed bayonets, yelling the eerie Rebel yell and chasing the fleeing enemy over the brow of the hill. "I was standing on top of the logs yelling like an Indian," wrote the excited Sam Foster, when he was shot in the right leg. Instantly, Foster fell to the ground. "At first I couldn't realize that I was shot," he remarked with disbelief. "It felt like someone had struck me with the side of a ramrod . . . [but it was] benumbed somewhat." The rifle ball had crossed under Foster's knee, inflicting a severe wound and putting the captain out of the remainder of the fight.[26]

Foster's fate mirrored that of many who participated in Smith's ill-fated and impulsive countercharge. To Smith's dismay, Walcutt's scattering troops rallied upon the line of their brigade's previously fragmented skirmish line, still clinging to the slopes below the abandoned breastworks. While lying on the ground, Walcutt's infantrymen smothered Smith's attack with a severe rifle fire. Brigadier General Smith and Colonel Mills both were severely wounded while in the forefront, and the spirit of victory suddenly left the Texans. We severely "punished" the enemy, effecting a measure of revenge, noted the still-game Walcutt in his report. Thereafter, Smith's men took to their heels and hastily scrambled back into their breastworks, noted one of Walcutt's riflemen.[27]

The north face of Tunnel Hill presented a heartrending scene. A murky veil of smoke drifted over the embattled slopes, as if the ground was afire. Sharpshooting continued with ferocious intensity, and the cruel work of war endured. Two dazed Yankees were seen close in front of Smith's breastworks, one desperately attempting to help his wounded comrade escape. There was a burst of rifle fire, and both fell to the ground, riddled with bullets.[28]

Pat Cleburne was amazed. Sherman's main attack had been along a narrow front, at the apex of Tunnel Hill, where Swett's guns were posted. Instead of working their way around James A. Smith's right flank, the enemy's supporting troops had barely moved in that direction before halting and redeploying to the west. Rather than the anticipated major conflict along the far-right flank, it appeared to Cleburne that he had been wrong. The enemy was seen to be massing his troops on the opposite flank to attack the western perimeter of Tunnel Hill. This posed a new and even more difficult problem.[29]

Swett's Battery was shattered to such an extent that Hiram Granbury, now in brigade command following James A. Smith's wounding, had to detail infantrymen from the 7th Texas to man the battery and keep it firing. Moreover, this portion of Cleburne's line had many gaps, with missing infantry and too few guns.[30]

During the brief lull following Corse's attack, Cleburne rushed to make several important changes. Two of Swett's twelve-pounder Napoleons were pulled from the apex of Tunnel Hill and sent to Govan's position along the eastern spur. In their place, Cleburne ordered Key's four light field guns (Calvert's Battery) to move north from the tunnel site and take position on the apex with Swett's remaining cannon. Lieutenant Key, as senior officer, would command all the guns here. Cleburne then summoned a consolidated Arkansas regiment commanded by Lt. Col. E. Warfield from Govan's mostly unchallenged line and placed them in immediately in the rear of Key's cannon.[31]

By this time, it was nearly 1:00 P.M. and, said Cleburne, "it was evident that another grand attack was soon to be made on my division."[32]

CHAPTER 30

AN ASCENT INTO HELL

William Tecumseh Sherman faced a critical decision as the morning of November 25 progressed. His left flank supports, those of Morgan L. Smith's division, had run into considerable opposition, including "a massed force" of Rebels along the rugged hills and spurs of Missionary Ridge adjacent to South Chickamauga Creek. Giles A. Smith's brigade, now commanded by Col. Nathan W. Tupper, had encountered Govan's infantry and Douglass's Battery along the eastern spur beyond James A. Smith's Rebel line. Here they had taken a long-range volley of musketry from other Confederates (Lowrey's Brigade), posted on an adjoining hill to the northeast. Morgan L. Smith's front provided a limited capacity for maneuver due to the abrupt hills, narrow valleys, and the deep South Chickamauga Creek. Moreover, with strong enemy forces posted along the heights in this sector, Sherman saw that an attempt to force his way past the enemy's right flank would involve great difficulty and heavy losses. About noon, Sherman recalled Tupper's stalled brigade, ordering them to move to the right in close defensive support of Corse's men, who still occupied the lower northern face of Tunnel Hill at the abandoned old Confederate breastworks.[1]

Sherman's decision thus seemed the most practical option. He would strongly defend his left flank by moving most of Howard's arriving Eleventh Corps veterans to the extreme northern flank along South Chickamauga Creek. Meanwhile, his right-flank units, those of Ewing's and John E. Smith's divisions, would provide the main impetus of attack against the southwestern face of Tunnel Hill. Since Loomis's brigade, of Ewing's division, had already advanced in this direction to support Corse's morning attack, it was felt that a strong combined attacking force would carry the heights.[2]

Col. John M. Loomis had been given specific but cautious instructions early that morning: to probe the Rebel skirmishers but "under no circumstances . . . bring on a general engagement." Accordingly, Loomis had formed his approximately twelve hundred men and advanced to the right along the line of the Western and Atlantic Railroad to reach a point opposite the mouth of the prominent railroad tunnel through Missionary Ridge. This was the site Sherman reported he had reached the evening before and was now anxious to occupy. Here Loomis's troops had deployed in the valley along the edge of a woods, partially obscured by the rapidly dissipating lowland mist. In their front across a high rail fence was an old cornfield—almost perfectly level for the distance of about one-third of a mile to the base of the main ridge. At this point, there was a railroad embankment running along the line of the East Tennessee and Georgia Railroad (Chattanooga and Cleveland [Tennessee] Railroad), which entered the tunnel from the direction of Chattanooga.[3]

Loomis's two lines of skirmishers in attempting to cross the open field had drawn a heavy fire from two Confederate batteries along the heights—at the tunnel and on Tunnel Hill. Loomis then ordered his brigade to lie down and wait. For nearly two hours, his troops had waited for orders. Finally, about 11:00 A.M., when notified of Corse's pending assault, Loomis was ordered to advance simultaneously. Supporting Loomis on his left were three regiments of Col. Adolphus Bushbeck's brigade of Howard's Eleventh Corps, easterners from Pennsylvania and New Jersey. Also, two field guns from Battery D, 1st Missouri Light Artillery were moved over from Billy Goat Hill to support the effort.[4]

Loomis's soldiers had started across the level cornfield in their front when Confederate artillery shells from atop the ridge burst in their midst. Being in the open, Loomis's men knew they were inviting targets. "The order was 'double quick,' " wrote one of Loomis's sergeants, and "we were soon on a dead run toward the mountain." Loomis's brigade suffered intensely, drawing the fire of both Key's and Swett's batteries. Moreover, as they neared the base of the hill, two regiments of Confederate infantry occupying a cluster of buildings on the lower slopes near the mouth of the tunnel opened an accurate small-arms fire. Loomis hastily ordered his men to lie down. They had advanced only to within about one hundred yards of the railroad embankment that ran along the foot of the mountain. Although under a plunging fire from infantry and artillery, Loomis's men had remained stationary, hugging the ground even as Corse's brigade was repulsed along the northern face.[5]

Bushbeck's three regiments, however, had managed to penetrate farther, being sheltered by their trailing position on the left, and due to the fact that the enemy's attention was focused primarily on Loomis's brigade. The 73rd Pennsylvania of Bushbeck's line, advancing as skirmishers under the command of Lt. Col. Joseph B. Taft, reached the log barns and outhouses of the Glass house. With fixed bayonets, Taft's men chased the Confederate riflemen from the premises and took position behind a log barn. Yet their line wasn't strong enough to push on much farther. Bushbeck had halted his trailing two regiments in line with Loomis's brigade, but he soon sent the 27th Pennsylvania forward to support Taft's skirmish line. They moved up to occupy a ditch in the open field, about two hundred yards behind the 73rd. Here both units endured a terrible fire of musketry from Confederates still occupying the Glass house. By midday, it was evident to both Loomis and Bushbeck that due to Tunnel Hill's steep slopes in their front and the enemy's plunging fire, they were going nowhere without strong support.[6]

About 12:30 P.M., Sherman's orders for a new attack arrived. Loomis was to advance along the Tunnel Hill road "and hold the ground" while several brigades from Brig. Gen. John E. Smith's division moved up to assist.[7]

According to John E. Smith, he had been told about 11:00 A.M. that his initial detached brigade was merely going to the right to join Brigadier General Ewing and fill a gap in the valley as a defensive precaution. However, when the designated brigade commander, Brig. Gen. Charles L. Matthies, reported to Ewing, he was told to see Loomis. Colonel Loomis then went to Ewing for instructions; he soon returned with an order for Matthies to "move your brigade up and take that white house [Glass's]." Loomis, meanwhile, would advance along the line of the Tunnel Hill road. For added support, Loomis could call on the three regiments of Bushbeck's brigade.[8]

Loomis's effort to advance was decidedly a hesitant one. While his own regiments remained in place, about 1:00 P.M. Loomis ordered his skirmishers forward to carry the line of the railroad. Just as they reached this point, down the Tunnel Hill road from the ridge's summit streamed Confederate troops. "My entire front and left flank [were] threatened," said the anxious Loomis.[9]

It marked the onset of a terrible fiasco. The troops Loomis apparently saw were four companies of the 39th Georgia Infantry, commanded by Capt. W. P. Milton. Milton and his men were on a special mission—to burn the Glass house and outbuildings. Earlier that morning, Brig. Gen. Alfred Cumming had sent two Georgia regiments, the 39th and 56th, forward to occupy these buildings under the direct orders of General Hardee. By holding the Glass dwellings, the Yankees' approach would be made more difficult. If compelled to retire, the Georgians were told to burn the various buildings so as not to provide shelter to the enemy from the heights above.[10]

These two Georgia units had skirmished with Bushbeck's Pennsylvanians from about midmorning on. Yet when withdrawn by division commander Carter L. Stevenson's order (due to a threatened advance on their right flank—apparently the appearance of Matthies's troops), the Georgians had failed to set fire to the houses. Milton's four companies thus had returned to correct that mistake. Within minutes, they set fire to the Glass house, captured nine of Bushbeck's skirmishers, and retreated up the slopes.[11]

Lieutenant Colonel Taft, a veteran New Yorker temporarily commanding the 73rd Pennsylvania, had called for help in the face of Milton's oncoming riflemen. Taft was short on ammunition, and not having heard of any supports coming up, he started to the rear to get help. He was abruptly shot and mortally wounded. "Hold this position at all hazards," gasped Taft before he died. His supports were already en route, two companies of the 27th Pennsylvania, followed by the entire regiment. These soldiers, seeing Milton's Confederates retreating up the slopes and the Glass house on fire, were full of enthusiasm. Their commander, Maj. P. A. McAloon, made a spontaneous decision. He ordered an immediate pursuit by the 27th Pennsylvania Infantry.[12]

There was a gorge at this point, not very steep, but overgrown with brush and thickets as it ran upward to the ridge's crest about two hundred yards distant from the cluster of buildings. The Tunnel Hill road followed along the side of Tunnel Hill into this gorge and was exposed to fire from both the ridge above the tunnel and the highest elevation of the hill proper (to the north). The 27th's route was therefore not along the road into the gorge but, instead, up the partially cleared southwest slopes of Tunnel Hill, directly toward Key's guns at the summit. In all, McAloon and the 27th Pennsylvania faced climbing a height of about five hundred feet to reach Key's guns on the upper elevation. As such, it might as well have been an ascent into hell.[13]

Out of the valley surged the 27th Pennsylvania Infantry and left obliqued up the side of Tunnel Hill, being joined en route by Company B of the 73rd. Over the rough boulder-strewn ground struggled the thin blue line, straight into the fury of the enemy's fire. Many of McAloon's men were seen dropping from exhaustion and wounds, but the survivors continued onward. Their ragged line of blue spread over the southwestern side of Tunnel Hill and was visible miles distant in Chattanooga. Although McAloon had advanced without orders and his initiative had resulted in an unsupported, isolated attack, help was seen coming up from the valley, if in fragments. McAloon's assault, in fact, seemed to have ignited a whirlwind Federal effort against Tunnel Hill. The grim question to many observers in the valley was obvious: Would such a thin line be able to carry a rugged crest lined with blazing cannon and hundreds of enemy riflemen?[14]

Due to the steep slopes, much of the whizzing canister went over the 27th's heads as they approached the crest. Although McAloon was hit, eventually being struck three times and mortally wounded, he refused to leave the field. In fact, it was apparent the 27th was making good progress despite the intense fire. To many, it seemed they would gain the ridge in spite of the long odds.[15]

On the small, constricted knob of Tunnel Hill, both Key's gunners and

Cleburne's supporting infantry were hard-pressed to hit the Pennsylvanians from behind their log breastworks due to the contour of the slopes. Cleburne, who was personally directing the action, ordered Lieutenant Colonel Warfield, commanding the consolidated 2nd, 15th, and 24th Arkansas Infantry, to advance from behind their breastworks to the very edge of the hill. It was a crucial move. Here they began firing directly into the oncoming enemy ranks, their volleys stopping the Pennsylvanians just under the crest, "not 25 yards" from the muzzles of Key's guns. Yet, within minutes, the 27th Pennsylvania had opened a galling return fire from behind the shelter of trees, logs, and large rocks, driving Warfield's men back to cover.[16]

Added to the incoming crossfire from Corse's men occupying the abandoned Confederate breastworks along the northern face, the small battle zone was "one continuous sheet of hissing, flying lead," noted the awed Cleburne. The enemy's fire was concentrated on a front of not more than forty yards, which prevented Warfield's Arkansans from remaining sufficiently forward to fire with effectiveness down the hillside. Even as Warfield's men were being riddled by the oblique fire from Corse's riflemen, Cleburne noted the valor of these troops when they began rolling heavy boulders down from the crest into the line of blue uniforms just below.[17]

For more than a half hour, the fierce fight continued, with Key's gunners depressing the muzzles to the utmost and even elevating the trails for greater deflection. Blasts of canister tore into the ground, ricocheting from rocks, showering debris and gravel in all directions. It was an iron storm, where even a mouse couldn't survive in the open, thought a shaken veteran.[18]

Brig. Gen. Charles L. Matthies's brigade was known as "Old Ironsides," a veteran western unit of Illinois, Missouri, and Iowa troops whose experiences included Iuka and Vicksburg. Matthies, in carrying out Loomis's order to take the Glass house, had been able to double-quick his brigade forward to the foot of the ridge, suffering the loss of only two men to Rebel shells fired from three sites along the ridge. As his men sprinted forward along the road, Matthies ordered the 5th Iowa to take possession of the burning Glass house and grounds, then sent the Tenth Iowa farther to the right to secure that flank. Having now carried out his instructions, Matthies halted his two remaining regiments, the 26th Missouri and 93rd Illinois, in the road behind the Glass house to shelter them from the hot enemy fire.[19]

It was but a brief interlude. Within a few minutes, the commanding officer of the 93rd Illinois, Col. Holden Putnam, notified Matthies that the hard-pressed Pennsylvanians along the upper slopes of Tunnel Hill, having observed Matthies advance, "had sent down for reinforcements." With them "they could hold the hill," claimed the message from Major McAloon of the 27th Pennsylvania. Matthies told Putnam to go forward cautiously and sent word back to Loomis of their situation.[20]

It was about 1:30 P.M., and the 93rd Illinois struggled forward over cleared ground, attempting to reach the side of the 27th Pennsylvania. The climb was steep and the men became exhausted before they approached the 27th. "We lay down for a few minutes," wrote a private of the 93rd, but then the line surged upward again. The roar of the muskets was deafening. Men were falling on all sides of him, yet he could see no enemy to shoot at in the blinding smoke. Up by the side of the 27th scrambled the 93rd. The crest seemed only about twenty paces ahead. Here the whistling of the rifle balls intensified. The 93rd flopped to the ground beneath the brow of the hill and began firing frantically at the crest.[21]

Suddenly, there was trouble. "We hadn't been there 15 minutes," wrote a startled rifleman, "till the center gave way." Men were seen scattering down the hillside, with their officers shouting for them to halt and wildly gesturing with their swords. Col. Holden Putnam was there on horseback. Seizing the regiment's flag, he began waving it to rally his men. Now a conspicuous target, Putnam was struck in the head by a minié ball and instantly killed. His body was hastily carried off by four privates of Company D, but his rash effort paid off. The 93rd was rallied; they remained clinging to the ground below the brow of the hill, shooting at anything that moved along the crest.[22]

Again, another fragmented line appeared, moving up the side of the hill. It was Matthies, leading other regiments of his brigade into the "half circle" of death that poured from along the ridge's rim. Matthies had been ordered by Loomis to advance and "hold the hill, if possible." Accordingly, he pushed his men up Tunnel Hill to reach a line below the brow adjacent to the 27th Pennsylvania and 93rd Illinois. Matthies had just turned to direct the fire of his men when he was shot in the side of the head. Regaining consciousness a few minutes later, the dazed brigadier general propped himself up against a tree and gave instructions to his next-in-command about "the safest route to fall back on." As he finally departed the field, Matthies saw yet another line of blue-uniformed troops "advancing to our assistance."[23]

It was Col. Green B. Raum's brigade; John E. Smith's second brigade, which Smith had sent to the right about an hour after Matthies's departure. Ewing at that time had asked for additional reinforcements, and John E. Smith soon joined Raum's brigade in their new position in front of a portion of Ewing's entrenched line in the valley. Smith was angered, expecting his troops to be supports rather than formed in front as assault troops. After demanding an explanation from Ewing, Smith was so upset as to seek out Sherman, who merely approved of all Ewing had done. In fact, when John E. Smith returned, he discovered a line of troops ascending Tunnel Hill, which he presumed were Loomis's. Shocked to soon learn they were his own men—Matthies's brigade—he immediately ordered Raum forward to their support.[24]

Raum's advance began at about 2:30 P.M., noted one of his regimental commanders. After splitting his brigade into two lines of battle, Raum advanced the first line midway up Tunnel Hill to a rail fence and halted. Here he found the wounded Matthies and learned from him that his men were running low on ammunition—they had only another fifteen minutes worth remaining, gasped the blood-spattered Matthies. Raum ordered an immediate advance by his first line and moved into such a thunderous conflict that one of his officers said he couldn't hear himself holler in the deafening roar. Ahead, the line of the 93rd Illinois was outlined in flame and smoke. Their depleted ranks lay within sixty feet of the Rebel-held crest. What remained of their tattered flags was still flying, but the flagstaffs of both the national flag and the regimental colors were splintered and broken. Three color-bearers had been shot, and dozens of men lay groaning from gunshot wounds and severe injuries inflicted by large boulders rolled from the rim. Toward this cauldron on the "blood red heights" rushed Raum's men. They got no farther than halfway to the embattled regiments below the crest.[25]

The fighting had raged along the front of Key's Battery on Tunnel Hill for more than an hour and a half, later wrote the weary, exasperated Pat Cleburne. Reinforcements had been sent for, but one of Cumming's Georgia regiments, the 39th, in attempting to advance beyond the works to the rim where Warfield's men were still clinging, had fallen back in disarray. Their colonel, J. T. McConnell, had foolishly exposed himself by riding in front along the crest and had been shot in the head and killed.[26]

Next, Cleburne rode to the left to find Brig. Gen. John C. Brown, then defending the line near the tunnel. Cleburne wanted Brown to counterattack the enemy on his open flank, but Brown protested that he in turn would be exposed to "a terrible fire" on his left flank from "the enemy who was lying under the hill not more than 300 yards in my front." Cleburne allowed Brown to remain where he was, but he must have been very disappointed.[27]

The situation remained tense as Cleburne returned to the knob on Tunnel Hill. Key's cannoneers were so low on shells and canister that even they had begun rolling boulders down the slopes. Equally serious, Warfield's supporting riflemen were nearly out of ammunition. It was about 3:30 P.M. and the hour of crisis was at hand—it was that "critical period," said Cleburne, where victory or defeat tottered in the balance.[28]

Pat Cleburne, again up front in the breastworks with his men, decided to take a big risk. He would attack the enemy with virtually every soldier he could gather. It was certain to be either a forlorn hope resulting in a major defeat or the turning point in an enormous victory. The tactical concept was that of Lieutenant Colonel Warfield, his fellow Arkansan. Warfield came to Cleburne, pleading that his men were largely wasting their dwindling ammunition due to their inability to get farther forward and were becoming disheartened with the approach of each succeeding wave of enemy troops. Could he lead a bayonet charge down the hill to drive off the enemy?[29]

Cleburne never hesitated. "I immediately consented," he grimly wrote. Nearby stood Brig. Gen. Alfred Cumming, who had just arrived with the remainder of his brigade. Stevenson had hastened him to the right, to reinforce Cleburne in the heavy fighting for the Tunnel Hill knob. From Warfield and several other officers, Cumming had already heard of the dire situation along the crest. The anxious brigadier asked to lead the charge with two of his Georgia regiments. Cleburne agreed. More reinforcements had appeared, Maney's Brigade—from Hardee's line, with which Cleburne might provide additional support.[30]

While Warfield and Cumming made ready, Cleburne hastened to the left to alert Roger Q. Mills's consolidated Texas regiment, the 6th and 10th Infantry, and 15th (dismounted) Cavalry. Cleburne wanted Mills to participate in the attack "the moment that Cumming charged them in front." Within a few minutes, reported the eager Cumming, Cleburne sent word to begin the charge.[31]

Cumming's ranks were formed in two lines of battle, the 56th Georgia in front and the 36th ten paces behind. Both of these war-ravaged regiments were commanded by captains anxious to show their mettle. With a shout, the Georgians ran forward—straight into chaos.[32]

In Cumming's haste, he hadn't taken time to examine the exposed ground in front—adjacent to Key's artillery position. Cumming had been told there was an opening of about forty to fifty yards in the log breastworks immediately ahead, through which his men might charge unimpeded. Yet when his wildly yelling Georgians arrived at the site, they discovered the opening was much narrower—only wide enough to admit the passage of perhaps one-third of the 56th's regimental front. This nearly led to a disaster. With both regiments quickly piling up upon one another, confusion reigned. A firestorm of enemy bullets swept the opening. Cumming's Georgians reeled backward in disarray.[33]

Among the milling, bewildered throng ran their officers, shoving and prodding with their swords. "Re-form," they cried, and slowly the backward surge stopped. Within minutes, the captains had the line re-formed, and again Cumming urged them onward.[34]

This time, the Georgians knew what to expect. Scrambling past infantrymen in the ditches and climbing over the log breastworks, Cumming's men, shouting the high-pitched Rebel yell, dashed over the crest with bayonets leveled. On their left, Mills's Texans joined in the fray, jumping up from their position and running down the slopes with fixed bayonets on their empty rifles, noted the admiring Cleburne. Even one of George Maney's reserve regiments, the 1st and 27th (consolidated) Tennessee Infantry, moved forward in a spontaneous effort. Together with Warfield's Arkansans, the surging line of gray appeared simultaneously along a broad-enough front to outflank several of Sherman's now largely intermixed units below the brow of Tunnel Hill. This soon produced one of the wildest scenes of the entire battle.[35]

The plan presented by Cumming had been to attack on the double-quick with bayonet. "Don't open fire until the Yankees give way," was the way he put it. Instead, the assault had quickly become a vicious hand-to-hand brawl with point-blank gunshots, clubbed muskets, rocks, and even bare fists. Significantly, Cumming's attack fell on Major McAloon's much-depleted 27th Pennsylvania Infantry, which was out of ammunition. The sixty rounds carried by each man were exhausted, and they had been able to continue firing only by rummaging through the cartridge boxes of the slain and wounded, reported an officer.[36]

In an instant, the 27th Pennsylvania all but vanished in flight from the slopes. Next in line to the north, the 93rd Illinois suddenly found the enemy rushing in from the right flank. They, too, broke to the rear. Men were now seen streaming down the hill in the wildest disorder. Through the stunned ranks of Raum's advancing brigade ran the fugitives, momentarily throwing the right of their line into disorder. Yet Raum's two front-line regiments, the 80th Ohio and 17th Iowa, soon recovered, and their line continued on haltingly.[37]

Col. Clark R. Wever of the 17th Iowa in Raum's line looked to the right. Through the billowing white haze of battle, he saw a heavy Confederate force close on his flank, moving against his rear at the double-quick. Quickly, he shouted for his Iowans to fall back. They were swiftly joined by the 80th Ohio as Raum's entire front line gave way.[38]

On the far-right flank of what had been Matthies's line, the 5th Iowa had deployed as skirmishers farther down the slopes for added protection. Suddenly, an aide to General Matthies came running down the hill. "Retreat! Retreat!" he cried. The 5th Iowa's commander, Col. Jabez Banbury, ordered a retreat, yet he soon realized his men were trapped. Strung out in a dispersed line, they were at the mercy of the swarms of men in butternut uniforms rolling down the hillside to their left and rear. It was "madness," said Banbury, even to think of trying to resist such a heavy column. Through a shower of musketry and with yells of the enemy to halt ringing in their ears, Banbury and many of his men sped toward the valley below. Lt. Sam Byers, the 5th's adjutant, who had flopped to the ground, "hoping the storm would pass over and leave me," suddenly saw enemy troops running past, shooting at random. Byers jumped to his feet and surrendered. " 'Come out of that sword,' shrieked a big Georgian with a terrible oath. Another grabbed at my revolver and bellowed at me 'to get up the hill quicker than hell!' "[39]

Since Federal artillery across the valley had begun shelling the hillside, Byers hesitated only long enough to grab a blanket from a dead soldier before being hurried up the slopes at the point of a bayonet. His fate was shared by many. The 5th Iowa lost 106 of 227 men and 21 officers taken into the action, 82 of whom became prisoners. Most of the 5th's color company and also their flag was captured. The 93rd Illinois was similarly decimated, losing twenty-seven prisoners among their ninety-three casualties. The long list continued; the 27th Pennsylvania suffered eighty-four casualties; the 73rd Pennsylvania, which was surrounded near the Glass house, yielded ninety-nine prisoners.[40]

In the valley below, Maj. Thomas Taylor of the 47th Ohio Infantry looked up and saw the "stampede" coming at him. "I was mad and uttered a few expletives," he later wrote his wife. "I was sorry any division of our corps had disgraced itself by such conduct." The Rebels were "shrieking like fiends" in pursuit, and nearby he saw Sherman as he "chewed the stump of his cigar earnestly." Across the open field at the base of the hill ran the survivors. "I never saw such a sight before—it was like a flock of blackbirds [scattering]," wrote the amazed Taylor.[41]

Frantically, the 10th Missouri Infantry of Raum's reserve line scrambled across a fence and began firing into the pursuing enemy. Some of Raum's forward regiments rallied on their line, and although Raum himself was wounded, the thin line held.[42]

Cleburne's winded men, after being stopped at the base of the hill by the fire of Raum's reserves and a heavy Federal artillery barrage, returned to the crest with eight captured flags, four of which had been taken by Mills's Texans. Their total prisoners numbered an estimated five hundred. In fact, so many blue uniforms were seen pouring over the top of Tunnel Hill by one of Cleburne's staff officers, returning from duty elsewhere, that he feared the flank had been turned and the army was about to be attacked in the rear. Quickly locating Pat Cleburne, who had personally advanced with Mills's men during the charge, the aide gasped a warning. Cleburne only laughed. They were Yankee prisoners going to the rear, he hastily pointed out. The aide was astounded; it was true. So many Yankees were captured, including those taken in a belated advance ordered by Hardee from Pettus's Brigade in the direction of the Glass house, that more than the strength of an entire Yankee brigade—disarmed and distraught—was soon massed on Tunnel Hill.[43]

In all, it was a spectacular Federal disaster and the abrupt end of Sherman's attempts to capture Tunnel Hill. Already, many of Matthies's and Raum's survivors had fled across the cornfield in the valley to the next ridge under a heavy rain of Rebel shells. The intensity of the Confederate artillery fire from atop the ridge was now so great that it appeared to many of Loomis's and Bushbeck's mostly unengaged regiments along the base of the ridge that they were trapped beneath these deadly guns.[44]

By 4:00 P.M., there was little more Sherman planned to do. The order for the recall of Federal troops from the western base of the ridge went out, being issued by Ewing. An aide who dashed forward on horseback to carry the order to some of Loomis's troops had never been so scared, he later remembered. After dashing forward to an Illinois regiment across three ditches and four rail fences to deliver this message, he started back by the same route. Shells were bursting all across the field, and when he came to the last fence of seven rails, "I thought my horse couldn't jump it," said the nervous aide. Just then, a shell burst close by his horse's side, "frightening him so" that he jumped "clean over the fence," throwing the aide from the saddle. Grasping a blanket strapped to his saddle in midair, the aide awkwardly yanked himself back up. Minutes later, and white as a sheet, the aide galloped up to Ewing and reported. "My God," remarked the general, "I am glad to see you [safe], I never expected to see you come back alive."[45]

The aide's harrowing ride mirrored the experiences of many of Sherman's battle-weary veterans that evening as they discussed the day's events. "It is a gloomy sight, indeed, to look upon the small remnant of my brave little band," wrote the colonel of the 5th Iowa in his journal that night. Another soldier, a private in the decimated 93rd Illinois, wrote that this was his twenty-first birthday—one that he would never forget. Huddled miserably in the cold after the sun went down, and without blankets, it was too cold to sleep. In his diary, he confided, "I hope to be free [of the army] before I see another birthday."[46]

To another Illinois soldier, B. B. Tarman, the night shaped up to be one of arduous labor. His unit was ordered to throw up strong breastworks, as they "expected a harder day's fight [on] the 26th than on the 25th."[47]

Tarman and his comrades were in for a big surprise.

CHAPTER 31

TIME FOR A DEMONSTRATION

By the late afternoon of November 25, 1863, William Tecumseh Sherman was a man filled with anger and despair. Corse's attack on the north face of Tunnel Hill had failed; Ewing's and John E. Smith's primary assault on the western face had been severely defeated; and Morgan L. Smith's and Howard's soldiers were confronted along South Chickamauga Creek with unfavorable topography and "massed" enemy troops. Despite having more than thirty thousand available men, it was evident to Sherman that his offensive, Grant's main effort, was both stalled and defeated. Yet Sherman's ire wasn't the result of his isolated, piecemeal attacks, which had involved fewer than ten thousand men in the actual fighting. Rather, it was based on the alleged lack of support from Grant's other troops.[1]

At 12:45 P.M., when it was evident matters were going poorly on Corse's front and it appeared the Rebels were continuing to move troops to their right, Sherman had signaled a terse one-sentence message to Grant: "Where is Thomas?"[2]

Although Sherman hadn't met with Grant on the night of the twenty-fourth, he was referring to the dispatch received after midnight, stating that he was to attack at dawn in combination with an advance by George Thomas's Army of the Cumberland. Thomas, said Grant, would either carry the enemy rifle pits at the foot of Missionary Ridge "or move to the left to your support," whichever the circumstances required. Since these orders were issued before Grant's revised plans of daylight on the twenty-fifth, Sherman mistakenly had anticipated Thomas's active help along Missionary Ridge.[3]

Later, Sherman would use the lack of support by Thomas's troops as an excuse for the failed attack on the north end of Missionary Ridge. Sherman's postbattle perspective, in fact, was based not on the dire results of the fighting there, but on what hadn't been done in his support and on what others had accomplished as a result of his assault. Instead of acknowledging his role as the essence of Grant's offensive, Sherman was fond of portraying his attack as a diversion. Sherman was even so deceitful as to assert in his official report, "The real attacking columns of General Corse, Colonel Loomis, and General [J. E.] Smith were not repulsed."[4]

On the early evening of November 25, as his troops were preparing defensive works "to repel an anticipated attack from the enemy" and had already begun to bivouac, Sherman received an astounding signal message from Grant: "Thomas has carried the hill . . . in his immediate front. Now is your time to attack with vigor. Do so." It was a bizarre, bitter communiqué that cut to the quick. Sherman was out of the fight. There was no hope of mounting an attack; his failure was again magnified. Sherman's reply, which must have been despairing, was never reported in the official documents.[5]

Ulysses S. Grant's mood had been that of increasing frustration as the day progressed. The scene at army headquarters early that morning was dull, wrote a civilian observer. Grant had ridden forward from Fort Wood before noon to join with Thomas at Orchard Knob. Standing atop the rocky knoll with a cold wind blowing, it felt good to have an overcoat on, noted one of Grant's friends. Buffeted by the icy breeze and gazing at the top of Missionary Ridge, where the Rebels were seen looking down "as [if] from the third tier of a theater," Grant had awaited word of Sherman's progress on the far left. Although the booming of guns was heard at the north end of Missionary Ridge, visibility of the north face was restricted, and no report of any difficulty appears to have been received from Sherman until his 12:45 P.M. query about Thomas's location.[6]

Since Grant had seen enemy troop movements along the ridge and had reports of heavy Confederate columns marching toward Tunnel Hill, the Federal commander had already become concerned. About midmorning, Grant ordered Brig. Gen. Absalom Baird of Thomas's Fourteenth Corps to march with his division from Chattanooga Valley and reinforce Sherman, "then hotly engaged in the vicinity of Tunnel Hill." Thereafter, a dispatch from Sherman—apparently sent about 11 A.M., when Corse's attack was getting under way—had notified Grant that no more reinforcements were needed; Sherman "had all the force necessary." Accordingly, Grant sent word for Baird to take position on Thomas's left flank instead of supporting Sherman. Grant had even chided a concerned newspaper correspondent, saying Sherman would soon make things "all right."[7]

Grant's subsequent midday activities had been mostly those of idle routine while he awaited the planned pincer movements to develop on each end of Missionary Ridge. Grant was almost nitpicking; he sent a note to Sherman about properly using one of Howard's brigades. Thereafter, he

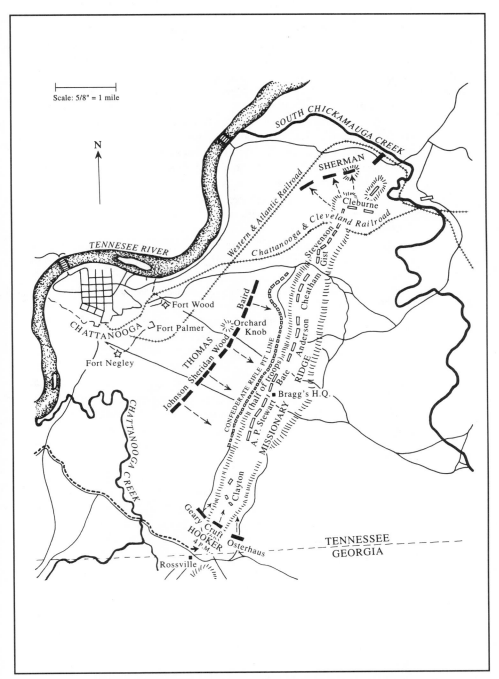

Scale: 5/8" = 1 mile

N

SOUTH CHICKAMAUGA CREEK

Western & Atlantic Railroad

Chattanooga & Cleveland Railroad

SHERMAN

Cleburne

TENNESEE RIVER

Stevenson

Gist

Cheatham

Anderson

CHATTANOOGA

Fort Wood

Fort Palmer

Orchard
Knob

Baird

THOMAS

Sheridan Wood

Fort Negley

Johnson

CONFEDERATE RIFLE PIT LINE
(half of troops)

Bate

Bragg's H.Q.

RIDGE

A. P. Stewart

MISSIONARY

CHATTANOOGA CREEK

Clayton

Geary Cruft

HOOKER
4 P.M.

Osterhaus

TENNESSEE
GEORGIA

Rossville

MAP 9   Situation at 4 p.m., November 25, 1863—Thomas's Assault
(Source: Edward E. Betts, 1896 Chattanooga Map)

joked with Thomas about the Rebels who were visible on the crest of Missionary Ridge, little more than a mile distant. When a civilian friend said he thought it a dangerous place to be so close to the Rebel lines and that it was astonishing the enemy wasn't shelling this exposed knob, Grant chuckled. Thomas remarked to Grant that if the Rebs knew who was then on the knob, they certainly would pay more attention. Thomas's humor wasn't very well received by the concerned visitor. Meanwhile, among Grant's staff officers there was an uneasy restlessness and a feeling of some embarrassment as matters continued to drag on and "nothing [was] done." John A. Rawlins, his chief of staff and Grant's closest confidant, was particularly "sullen" and finally became "indignant" to the point of urging Grant to take further action. Grant remained unruffled.[8]

About 2:00 P.M., Grant was hungry, so he walked down the reverse slope to have a lunch prepared by Bill Barnes, the general's servant. After eating and chatting idly with Gen. David Hunter and a visitor, Grant smoked a cigar, then walked back up Orchard Knob, having been gone about a half hour.[9]

What he saw on his return suddenly changed his mood. Visible on the west side of Tunnel Hill were Sherman's assaulting troops—those of Bushbeck, Matthies, and now Raum. Although Sherman's troops had been observed "across a large open field on the side of the ridge" before lunch, they were now seen falling back down the slopes in disarray. Grant was astounded. Was it possible Sherman would be defeated?[10]

Mindful of November's short daylight hours, Grant knew he was in serious trouble. Only a few hours remained to gain a victory. All morning, he had looked increasingly to the southeast for signs of Hooker's appearance along the south of Missionary Ridge. There were none. Hooker, in fact, had become bogged in what was much a self-inflicted inertia. This was a puzzling circumstance, since army headquarters had sent instructions the previous evening for Hooker to be ready to advance as early as possible into Chattanooga Valley. These orders had been updated at 7:00 A.M.— for Hooker to "immediately move forward." Thereafter, Thomas and his staff had anticipated little further delay, considering the anticipated Rebel evacuation of both Lookout Mountain and Chattanooga Valley.[11]

Hooker, who had remained unaware of Grant's new plans due to the morning's valley fog, which prevented signal messages, had merely awaited orders at his Cravens house headquarters on Lookout Mountain. From the plateau, Hooker could see the enemy's camps on distant Missionary Ridge as the fog lifted in the valley about 9:00 A.M. Smoke was then observed drifting up from the vicinity of Chattanooga Creek, where the enemy appeared to be burning camps. At 9:20 A.M., Hooker signaled Thomas he was awaiting orders.[12]

Nearly an hour later, a perturbed Thomas again issued imperative orders for Hooker to move immediately along the Rossville road toward Missionary Ridge. Finally, with the arrival of one of Thomas's staff officers about

9:30 A.M., Hooker learned of his specific role. Although his chief of staff issued immediate orders for a movement, by the time the troops were notified and began to move, it was nearly 10:00 A.M. Another hour was consumed marching down the mountain, and when Osterhaus's advanced units reached Chattanooga Creek, it was nearly noon. Here the smoldering ruins of several bridges lay amid the overflooded creek. Osterhaus had to call for pioneers, drive away Rebel skirmishers on the opposite shore, and establish a beachhead across the creek. Thereafter, nearly a three-hour delay resulted while a temporary bridge was constructed.[13]

Meanwhile, George H. Thomas had become increasingly angry. At noon, he again had urged Hooker "firmly and steadily" on. At 1:30 P.M., Hooker replied that construction of the bridge across Chattanooga Creek would require "perhaps" another hour. To both Grant and Thomas, it was increasingly apparent that relying on Hooker to roll up Bragg's southern flank was both unpromising and unlikely to occur soon.[14]

Accordingly, Grant was very much upset. Now, at about 3:00 P.M., with Sherman's troops obviously in difficulty along the slopes of Tunnel Hill, he had only one remaining option. Essentially, there was only Thomas. Several hours earlier, the situation had appeared so unpromising in front of central Missionary Ridge that Assistant Secretary of War Dana, who was with Grant on Orchard Knob, had telegraphed to Washington: "In our front here Rebel rifle pits are fully manned, preventing Thomas gaining ridge." According to a brigadier general present at headquarters, Grant had considered all along that a direct frontal attack on the ridge "could not be made with a reasonable prospect of success; or . . . if successful, it could only be at a great and unnecessary cost of life."[15]

But Grant was now increasingly desperate. Not knowing Sherman's true situation but presuming he was still fighting for the north end of Missionary Ridge, Grant approached Brig. Gen. Thomas J. Wood, who commanded a division in George H. Thomas's Fourth Corps. "General Sherman seems to be having a hard time," remarked the hard-bitten Grant. Wood agreed, and Grant spoke again: "I think we ought to try to do something to help him."

"I think so, too, General, and whatever you order we will try to do," replied Wood.[16]

Grant spoke deliberately: "I think that if you and Sheridan were to advance your divisions and carry the rifle pits at the base of the ridge, it would so threaten Bragg's center that he would draw enough troops from the right to secure his center, [and] insure the success of General Sherman's attack."[17]

Wood's reply was affirmative: "Perhaps it might work that way. If you order it we will try it, and I think we can carry the entrenchments at the base of the ridge."[18]

Moments later, Grant was seen talking to Thomas and Granger. "After perhaps a two minutes conversation," later wrote Wood, "[Granger] came to me and said: 'You and Sheridan are to advance your divisions. Carry the entrenchments at the base of the ridge if you can, and, if you succeed, halt there.' "[19]

It was that simple. Grant had made an impromptu decision to help Sherman. Another "demonstration" was contemplated, by which the day might perhaps be saved for Sherman. At the signal of six field guns fired from Orchard Knob, Thomas's troops would advance and attack the base of the ridge. Thomas's army would at last have an active role despite Grant's lingering concern about their efficacy. There really was little other choice. Grant's plans had once again been changed due to unforeseen circumstances.[20]

It was a blueprint for disaster. Grant had made a poor tactical decision, which was also impulsive and not very well thought out. As Col. Joseph S. Fullerton of Granger's staff later wrote: "This demonstration was to be made [only] to relieve the pressure on Sherman." What Grant had failed to consider was quickly perceived by many front-line commanders. By advancing to take the rifle pits at the foot of Missionary Ridge, Thomas's men would be caught in an untenable tactical situation. They would be trapped immediately under the frowning cannon atop the ridge and subject to such a severe bombardment that "it would be impossible to stay there." Already, Loomis's brigade in Sherman's column had endured such a devastating shelling during their more than four hours under the enemy's guns on the north of Missionary Ridge as to suffer 386 casualties from about 1,200 effectives.*[21]

Other mistakes in interpretation contributed to the Federal commander's faulty decision. The troops Grant and others had seen marching along Missionary Ridge that morning were mostly Stevenson's, en route from the Lookout Mountain sector. Bragg had not weakened his center to reinforce Cleburne, as was later asserted. All of the troops shifted during the fighting for the north end of Missionary Ridge had come from Hardee's Corps, which held ground near the tunnel. Moreover, there would be no drawing off of Rebel troops on Sherman's front until much later in the day. Even worse, Grant's primary reliance was placed on Sherman resuming his attack against the north of Missionary Ridge. Unaware that Sherman was soundly defeated and about to withdraw from the western face of the ridge, Grant was ordering an advance upon an entirely mistaken premise— that Sherman would again attack. His subsequent "now is your time to attack with vigor. Do so" order to Sherman reflected Grant's ignorance of the true situation.[22]

Grant's "diversionary" attack on the base of Missionary Ridge was so faulty in planning, concept, and out of touch with reality as to presage a

---

*Loomis's brigade had remained along the lower slopes, not participating in the actual assaults on Tunnel Hill. Their loss, the heaviest among Sherman's brigades, reflected their greater exposure due to the fact they were lying idle at the foot of the ridge rather than being partially sheltered by the slopes during an actual assault up Tunnel Hill.

total disaster. Essentially, the battle was already lost. With Sherman defeated on the north, Hooker floundering to the south, and Thomas about to take an exposed position directly under the enemy's guns, where his troops might be pounded into oblivion, Grant had already been soundly beaten—yet he didn't seem to know it.[23]

The only thing Grant had in his favor, and that even he then failed to consider, was that at Chattanooga every time he had ordered a "demonstration"—at Orchard Knob and at Lookout Mountain—an important victory had resulted.

CHAPTER 32

ONE OF THE GREATEST
BLUNDERS

In the stillness of the sunrise that Wednesday morning, November 25, an Ohio private, one of Phil Sheridan's men, had reflected upon the eerie quiet and the ominous prospect of battle. "[A] soldier intuitively knows that he will soon be called upon for bloody work," he wrote uneasily. With one's fate on the line, the only resolution, he considered, was to look to "the Almighty Hand which holds our lives." In his unit, many were seen thumbing through their pocket Testaments and silently offering a prayer for mercy in the coming fray.[1]

The irony was that despite the uneasy feeling among the men, there were no specific plans to use the Army of the Cumberland as the day wore on. For much of the day, George H. Thomas's men had listened to the booming of guns on the north of Missionary Ridge and watched the few thin clouds briskly drift across an azure sky. By midmorning, the sky was completely clear, noted a bored infantryman, and the tedious routine of watching and waiting continued.[2]

For Thomas's soldiers, it was a peculiar agony. Their pent-up emotions reflected both the anxiety of pending battle and the anguish of knowing they were not a part of the grand movements under way. The stigma of Chickamauga and the suspicion that they were being all but ignored in Grant's plans had the men on edge. "Standing [idle] for almost two days with the enemy maneuvering . . . in plain view, [we were] inactive, silent, [and felt] useless," wrote an Ohio private. "It is not to be wondered that there were signs of impatience."[3]

The war seemed to be passing the Cumberland soldiers by. In the 57th Indiana Infantry, the glint of gun barrels in the bright sunshine on

distant Missionary Ridge had many abuzz with talk of the enemy reinforcing his right flank. A nearby sergeant counted through field glasses
a total of thirty-two pieces of Rebel artillery arrayed along the distant
crest of the ridge. Yet there were no orders to move. "The day was passing; the sun had reached its zenith and was rapidly moving . . . toward
the west," wrote an Ohio officer. "Impatience was marked on every
face."[4]

It was about 3:00 P.M., and there was a sudden commotion along the
front of Sheridan's division line. A battery of artillery dashed forward and
unlimbered in the open, beyond the line of entrenchments. Troop movements were seen in the direction of Thomas J. Wood's division. A regimental chaplain speculated that an order might be pending to move to the
left and relieve some of Wood's troops, which perhaps were en route to
support Sherman on the north end of Missionary Ridge.[5]

Then, in whispered tones, some began to say that a general advance
was imminent. An aide dashed up to give instructions. Men began to move
about busily. In Wood's line, the 41st Ohio Infantry was seen unstacking
arms and forming in line. Color-bearers began unfurling the flags, shaking
the folds loose to catch in the brisk breeze. Surgeons were observed gathering squads of stretcher bearers behind the line. Thomas's sector had
suddenly become a beehive of activity.[6]

In the 6th Ohio, just returning from the skirmish line, the men were
joking and congratulating themselves about their good fortune in being
relieved without putting in a full day's duty. Then when they approached
Orchard Knob and saw the commotion along the fortifications, "we knew
something was up," wrote a suddenly grim officer. Minutes later, they were
standing in line of battle, awaiting orders to advance.[7]

In the 104th Illinois, one of Richard W. Johnson's units that had moved
over from the vicinity of Lookout Mountain that morning, the men were
making coffee when the order came to "fall in." It was shortly after 3:00
P.M. when the 64th Ohio of Sheridan's division crossed over the breastworks
and advanced several hundred yards down the valley into open timber. The
order "left-half wheel" was shouted, and suddenly the 64th came into line,
squarely confronting Missionary Ridge. Other regiments from Harker's
brigade filed out successively from left to right, and as soon as they were
in line, the men were ordered to lie down, leaving only the guides standing
to align the next approaching regiment.[8]

The Rebel artillery atop Missionary Ridge had begun to shoot, observed
one of the 64th's captains. Although their shells fell at a distance—"their
range was poor," he noted—lying there fully exposed was very stressful.
There was an unnerving "uncertainty as to where the next shell might
explode," he reported with grim candor.[9]

As Thomas's army moved into line of battle and lay anxiously waiting,
there was much uncertainty and nervous speculation among the men about
what the sudden commotion meant. Orders had come down through division headquarters, generally conveyed by staff officers, but they were

verbal due to the need for haste. As to be expected under these rushed, impromptu circumstances, there was much confusion and uncertainty about the specifics of the pending movement.[10]

Gordon Granger had personally told Brig. Gen. Thomas J. Wood, commanding his Third Division, to "advance your division and carry the entrenchments at the base of the ridge, if you can, and if you succeed, halt there." The signal to advance would be the rapid discharge of the six field guns on Orchard Knob, said Granger. Wood was to notify headquarters when ready to advance. As this directive was passed down the chain of command, Wood's brigades and regiments appear to have received generally uniform, if simple, instructions: to carry the line of enemy rifle pits at the base of the ridge.[11]

Yet the other key division commander, Brig. Gen. Phil Sheridan, who was general field officer of the day, apparently wasn't at Orchard Knob to talk with Granger. As a result, Sheridan received his orders indirectly, from a staff officer. In turn, Sheridan's orders were verbally conveyed to the brigade and finally to regimental commanders. As they were passed along, there was inevitably some confusion and garbled communications. Brig. Gen. George D. Wagner of Sheridan's line claimed he was told to carry the enemy's works at the foot of the ridge and "possibly storm the heights." Some of Wagner's regimental commanders understood their orders were to "take all before us." Col. Gustavus A. Wood of the 15th Indiana thought the order was to take the ridge.[12]

Sheridan's other brigades received instructions to carry the first line of Rebel works and conform to the movements of Wagner's brigade, on Sheridan's extreme left. The commander of the 42nd Illinois was told to capture the first of the enemy's rifle pits "and go only a few yards beyond." This confusion and lack of uniform orders resulted in further distortions. "Have your men fix bayonets and move slowly to the top of the ridge," were the instructions issued to the company commanders of the 15th Indiana. The major of the 15th next rode up and down the line, telling his men to stand firm, but if the first line gave way, to let them go but not to fall back. What Sheridan's soldiers understood from all this was that they were to attack. Some of the men were given no specific instructions, and in the 64th Ohio Infantry, "nothing was said as to what it was expected we were to accomplish."[13]

The situation was even worse in the two other divisions designated to participate in the demonstration. In Brig. Gen. Absalom Baird's division, on Thomas's extreme left, Baird received verbal notice about 3:30 P.M. from Baldy Smith, and then one of Thomas's staff officers, to move forward so as to be ready at a signal firing of six guns to dash forward and take the rifle pits in front. "And when I have captured the rifle pits, what then?" asked the incredulous Baird. Baldy Smith could but repeat the instructions Grant had personally given to him: to carry only the line at the base of the ridge. So little time remained that at least two of Baird's brigades had no idea that they were to advance, much less what the orders were, before troops were seen advancing on their right.[14]

On the opposite flank, the far right, Brig. Gen. Richard W. Johnson had so little notice of the pending operation that his troops were told merely to prepare to advance and conform to the movements of Sheridan's troops.[15]

In all, there was a sad lack of command coordination. Due to the rush to get the movement under way, few at the tactical level seemed to have a grasp of exactly what was intended or specifically how it was to be carried out. Along the skirmish line in Willich's brigade of Wood's division, the lieutenant colonel of the 15th Ohio Infantry asked Willich where they should stop. Willich, looking perplexed, replied, "I don't know, at Hell I expect."[16]

Farther down the more than two-mile-long line, Sheridan, astride a big black charger and in full dress uniform, galloped along the line of the 125th Ohio. Sheridan was animated and yet irritated; the more he thought about the existing circumstances, the more uneasy he became. The Rebel artillery was in full play along the line, and his men were obviously anxious and uncomfortable under the shelling. When a nearby exploding shell showered Sheridan with dirt, a private overheard him utter a profane oath and mutter, "That's damned unkind." Raising his silver whiskey flask toward Missionary Ridge, Sheridan then offered a mocking toast: "Here's to you, General Bragg." The nearby private remained unimpressed; "I only wished he would quit his foolishness, for it was drawing Rebel cannon shot down upon us," he grumbled.[17]

Sheridan's mood was sour. His men had gone forth over the entrenchments and formed in line of battle more than a half hour earlier. Yet still there were no orders to advance. Increasingly impatient, Sheridan sent an aide to Granger to clarify whether it was the first line of rifle pits that were to be taken or the ridge.

The staff officer hadn't returned when the thunderous boom of six field guns sounded in rapid sequence from Orchard Knob.[18]

Gordon Granger had remained on Orchard Knob, trusting to his staff and others to arrange the details of the movement, despite the fact that his troops numbered about two-thirds of Thomas's deployed force. Granger, an old army regular, had expressed his devil-may-care philosophy the day before when contemplating the anticipated fight for Missionary Ridge: "We'll all go to hell in twenty minutes after daylight, or make a name for life." On the afternoon of the twenty-fifth, Granger was intent on making proper arrangements for the firing of the six signal guns on Orchard Knob. According to *Chicago Times* reporter Sylvanus Cadwallader, who was present, Granger was seen sighting the guns "with all the enthusiasm of a boy," and had to be reprimanded by Grant. "If you will leave that battery to its captain, and take command of your corps, it will be better for all of us," Grant allegedly remarked. Assistant Secretary of War Dana later accused

Granger of devoting himself to firing a battery rather than commanding his corps. For this reason, said Dana, a delay occurred and orders had to be sent out a second time.*[19]

Actually, the delay seemed due to the wait for confirmation that Baird's division had moved into position adjacent to Wood and had been notified of the pending demonstration. While Granger waited on Orchard Knob, he sighted and arranged the cannon to be fired as the signal to begin. These guns were from Bridges's (Illinois) battery, four three-and-a-half-inch Rodman guns and two Napoleon smooth bores, brought to Orchard Knob on the night of the twenty-third. The gunners were old infantrymen, Company G of the 19th Illinois Infantry, detailed for artillery duty after the Battle of Stones River. Following word from the returning staff officers that all division commanders had been notified, Granger gave the order for the battery to fire. At exactly 3:40 P.M., the roar of Bridges's six cannon sounded in quick succession.[20]

Before the signal guns fired, his men had been quiet, noted an Ohio captain. Now there was a gathering commotion among the soldiers. Bugles sounded, and the men sprang to their feet amid the rustle of dried leaves and the snapping of twigs. In view as far as one could see through the open timber, Sheridan's division stood in two shimmering blue lines. Along their front waved clusters of bright red-white-and-blue flags, and the rippled gleam of polished gun barrels flashed in the afternoon sunlight.[21]

It was a scene that sent the blood rushing to his fingertips, an awed eyewitness later wrote. From along the rear heights, where hundreds of onlookers were clustered, the sight was impressive. There were four divisions of Thomas's troops facing Missionary Ridge, in all a total of about 24,500 infantry poised to advance against the base of the ridge.[22]

Although not all knew what to expect—"When the guns were fired on Orchard Knob we did not know what they meant," one of Baird's soldiers later wrote—the long infantry lines were swiftly ordered forward. Swinging their rifle muskets to right-shoulder shift, the troops lurched uncertainly toward the imposing heights before them.[23]

Thomas's lines were arrayed in a familiar assault formation. A double line of skirmishers covered each brigade front, with the main battle lines formed in two successive ranks, separated by about three hundred yards. Ahead of the 2nd Minnesota Infantry, deployed as skirmishers along Baird's front, were several dogs that had been adopted by the regiment during the siege. Racing ahead of the skirmish line, the dogs were busily chasing game as the 2nd's line emerged from the light timber and swept into the field beyond.[24]

Once in the open, one faced a vast panorama, enhanced by a broad, mostly level plain that jutted from beneath the rugged mountain ridge.

---

*Probably this "second" order was merely Granger's reply to Sheridan's query about the specific objective of the attack.

"For a few moments there was dead silence," said a soldier. Then all at once, the world seemed to explode in noise and flame.[25]

From along the crest of Missionary Ridge, an estimated fifty Confederate field guns began firing with shell and spherical case shot. "The tempest now broke upon us in all its fury," wrote a stunned Indiana infantryman. Suddenly, the air was ripped apart by the whir of plunging shells and sharp, thunderous detonations. Spurts of flame and wreaths of smoke spattered the sky. Men began to stumble and fall into the dried meadow grass. The 2nd Minnesota's dogs scattered in fright.[26]

From Forts Wood, Negley, and at Orchard Knob, answering artillery fire arched across the sky. The noise was deafening and the ground shook with jarring concussions. The experience was both frightening and fascinating. "Missionary Ridge appeared like a breathing, seething volcano, shooting out liquid fire and smoke," recorded an eyewitness.[27]

Within Sheridan's line, the men began instinctively to quicken their pace. His men were already moving at the double-quick past him, wrote the startled Capt. John Shellenberger of the 64th Ohio. Glancing up, Shellenberger saw jagged puffs of smoke "twenty or thirty feet in the air," where Rebel shells had burst. The enemy was firing too high, and most of the whizzing shell fragments were passing "harmlessly over our heads," he realized. Although a few men were hit, the fire represented more sound and fury than danger. Ahead, nearly a half mile distant, where the ground began to ascend toward the base of the ridge, "we could see the yellowish streak of dirt" that marked the line of the enemy's breastworks, Shellenberger said. His men began to break into a run.[28]

The sweep of Thomas's troops across that open valley, with shells bursting above the serried ranks, was the grandest sight he saw during the war, later reflected one of Wood's veteran officers. Their advance was like a raging prairie fire, thought another participant. Faster and faster, Thomas's soldiers dashed across the open ground. The advanced Confederate skirmishers, who had opened fire almost at the first barrage of cannon fire, were now seen retreating as fast as they could run. Yells and shouts rang out from the pursuing line of blue. The chase was on.[29]

Atop Missionary Ridge, the sight was like a scene from a grand theater. Brig. Gen. Arthur M. Manigault, commanding a brigade in Anderson's Division, thought it imposing in the extreme. "Such a sight I never saw either before or after, and I trust . . . never to see again," the amazed Manigault later wrote. The enemy seemed to have not fewer than fifty thousand men, he observed, and "I noticed some nervousness among my men as they beheld this grand military spectacle." "You'uns must have had more'n a million men," said a Confederate prisoner that night, declaring, "I seen 'em a marchin' an' counter marchin' fer three days, an' knowed thar warn't no use in fightin' that many." Another said it seemed like "all creation" was charging against only a few hundred soldiers in gray that he could see crouched about him.[30]

The sight of Thomas's army advancing was "like a huge serpent uncoiling his massive folds," remarked Brig. Gen. William Bate. Even Braxton Bragg had become impressed with the "heavy masses" and "immense force" formed in front of mid–Missionary Ridge. To Lt. Gen. William J. Hardee, the prospect of an attack along the center of the Missionary Ridge lines had been evident that morning when, in company with one of his division commanders, Patton Anderson, he rode along the line of trenches and rifle pits at the foot of the ridge. Hardee was recognized as one of the army's tactical experts, having written *Hardee's Tactics,* a widely acclaimed treatise on drill and soldiering, before the war. That morning, although preoccupied with the threat to Cleburne's northern flank, Hardee had taken the time to examine Anderson's trenches at the base of the ridge. During the ride, Anderson raised a serious question that already had many of his officers shaking their heads with disbelief. Were they to retreat up the slopes or fight along the lower trench line if the enemy attacked in force?[31]

By Hardee's instructions, issued on the evening of the twenty-third, following his transfer from Lookout Mountain, one half of Anderson's Division was to occupy the breastworks at the foot of the ridge while the other portion held the crest. Since there were then no breastworks along the crest, Hardee had assigned an engineer to lay out a proper line on the twenty-fourth. Despite a lack of tools, trees had been cut and the logs rolled to the edge of the crest to form a rude parapet that day. Furthermore, Hardee had directed the withdrawal of all artillery from the base of the ridge, then ordered it repositioned along the crest at multiple sites as selected by the division's chief of artillery.[32]

If necessary, Hardee clearly wanted to fight for the ridge from the high ground, given its impressive natural strength. Accordingly, Hardee was apparently shocked to learn on the twenty-fifth that Anderson had directed his men to defend to the last their position at the foot of the ridge. As he and Anderson rode along the lower line that morning, Hardee made a most significant tactical change. He specifically directed that the troops assigned to the breastworks at the foot of the ridge were *not* to resist strongly a full-scale enemy attack; instead, after the enemy approached to within two hundred yards, they were to retire while skirmishing to the top of the ridge. Here they would take position alongside the other troops for a decisive fight.[33]

Since these new instructions were received late on the morning of the twenty-fifth by the commander of the lower line, Brig. Gen. Zachariah C. Deas, there was much confusion about their intent and implementation. For two days, Deas had been angered that it was expected a fight would occur along the lower line at all. He had wanted to retire to the crest with all advanced troops. If his men made a stubborn resistance and were overpowered at the foot of the ridge, "capture or annihilation" were the alternatives, he believed. Common sense dictated the "impossibility" of making an orderly retreat up the slopes with the enemy close behind. Since

CONFEDERATES

Braxton Bragg. Intent on chastising or deposing many of his subordinate generals, he neglected the task at hand— winning a crucial victory at Chattanooga.

James Longstreet. Full of ambition and seeking to displace Bragg, Longstreet instead led the fruitless east Tennessee expedition.

William J. Hardee. Assigned to command of the Confederate right wing on Missionary Ridge, Hardee made unwise tactical dispositions at the base of the ridge, which led to disaster.

John C. Breckinridge. As commander of the Rebel left wing on Missionary Ridge, Breckinridge witnessed the breakthrough at Bragg's headquarters and a collapse on the Rossville flank.

COURTESY OF THE U.S. ARMY MILITARY HISTORY INSTITUTE

Patton Anderson. It was Anderson's lot to command the section of the line where the initial breakthrough on Missionary Ridge occurred. Of particular embarrassment, it was his old brigade that was the first to break.

COURTESY OF THE LIBRARY OF CONGRESS

Patrick Cleburne. Perhaps the best of the Confederate generals at Chattanooga, Cleburne soundly defeated William Tecumseh Sherman on North Missionary Ridge, then Joe Hooker at Ringgold Gap. Although awarded the formal thanks of the Confederate Congress, a year later he died unpromoted.

Top left: Alexander P. Stewart. His troops held the Missionary Ridge line on the left flank, but there was no stout defense here.

Top right: Carter Stevenson. Originally sent to east Tennessee, he returned with his division in time to suffer a stunning defeat at Lookout Mountain, but the following day helped defend the railroad tunnel on Missionary Ridge.

Bottom: John K. Jackson. Severely criticized for his absence on the front line during the Lookout Mountain fighting, "Mudwall" Jackson continued to suffer bitter accusations when his troops broke on Missionary Ridge the following day.

Top: Edward Walthall. His hard-fighting brigade alone was compelled to bear the brunt of Joe Hooker's assault on Lookout Mountain, after Walthall repeatedly called in vain for reinforcements.
Bottom left: William Bate. On November 25 his veteran division (Breckinridge's former command) was roughly handled along the region adjacent to Bragg's headquarters.
Bottom right: Evander Law. He was unfairly made the scapegoat of the Wauhatchie night action, based upon Longstreet's and Micah Jenkins's personal animosity.

Nathan Bedford Forrest. His disdain for and outspoken criticism of Braxton Bragg, in addition to his quarrels with Joe Wheeler, led to his transfer to western Tennessee after Chickamauga.

Joseph Wheeler. He commanded Bragg's cavalry and led a damaging raid on Union supply lines that was severely debilitating to Rosecrans's army, then wound up in east Tennessee and out of the major fighting.

FEDERALS

Ulysses S. Grant. The victor of Vicksburg was called upon to save the deteriorating situation at Chattanooga. Based upon a familiar credo—determination and action—he initiated the crucial offensive that broke the Rebel siege.

William S. Rosecrans. "Old Rosy's" antics in the days following Chickamauga seemed to President Lincoln like those of "a duck hit on the head." His removal from command was in marked contrast to Jefferson Davis's coddling of Bragg.

Top left: George H. Thomas. Perhaps the true hero of Chattanooga, Thomas was patient and reliable. His troops won the battle when Grant's plans were falling apart.
Top right: William Tecumseh Sherman. Always relied upon by Grant as his trusted chief subordinate, Sherman suffered a humiliating defeat on North Missionary Ridge, which was overlooked in the aftermath of Thomas's victory.
Bottom: Joseph Hooker. Once commander of the Army of the Potomac, "Fighting Joe" and his Eastern troops had their noses bloodied at Ringgold Gap, following their easy capture of undermanned Lookout Mountain.

Ambrose Burnside. Another less than successful Eastern commander, Burnside led the Union foray into east Tennessee, but balked at reinforcing Rosecrans, despite President Lincoln's direct orders.

William F. Smith. "Baldy" Smith was one of the Army of the Cumberland's behind-the-scenes leaders. As an old Regular, he knew the business of war well and organized the Brown's Ferry attack that opened the "cracker line."

William B. Hazen. A key
Federal brigade commander,
the aggressive Hazen led the
Brown's Ferry attack, then
later one of the crucial assaults
up Missionary Ridge.

Thomas J. Wood. It was
Wood's troops who first
broke the seemingly
"impregnable" line on
Missionary Ridge, which
helped salve the injury of
the infamous "gap" creat-
ed by Wood's withdrawal
at Chickamauga.

Philip H. Sheridan.
A division commander
whose troops shared in
the glory of the
Missionary Ridge
assault, "Little Phil"
was catapulted into
national prominence
when called upon to
reclaim the Shenandoah
Valley in 1864.

John W. Geary.
Having beaten off the
Wauhatchie night
attack, Geary and his
Eastern troops were
soon called upon to
spearhead the attack on
Lookout Mountain.

Morgan L. Smith. One of Sherman's key division commanders, Morgan Smith suffered personally when his brother Giles was wounded in the bloody debacle on North Missionary Ridge.

Emerson Opdycke. As commander of the 125th Ohio's "Tigers," the mercurial Opdycke led his regiment up Missionary Ridge, which later helped him earn brigade command.

Chattanooga Valley from Lookout Mountain.

Missionary Ridge battlefield, scene of Sherman's attack.

Captured Confederate guns in front of the Kindrick house, George H. Thomas's headquarters.

A Chattanooga street in 1864.

Grant's headquarters.

Sherman's headquarters.

Missionary Ridge.

The flanking gap. Rossville Gap in Missionary Ridge.

The skirmish line at Rossville Gap in Missionary Ridge.

half their unit strength already had been sent up the ridge and all field guns removed to the crest, Anderson's officers at the foot of the ridge considered their plight: to retreat while under attack meant climbing the steep slopes while their backs were exposed to the enemy's close-range fire. Chaos, confusion, exhaustion, and disarray were to be expected. Thus, Hardee's latest order was even more perplexing. If they weren't to fight along the lower line, why not withdraw before the enemy attacked?[34]

Now, about 4:00 P.M., as Thomas's vast lines of battle approached the rifle pits at the foot of Missionary Ridge, there was great consternation. "The plan of keeping [our men] down there was opposed by every officer with whom I conversed before the fight," later wrote an indignant Alabama colonel. Yet it was too late. A startled observer described the scene: "As soon as the Yankee lines commenced advancing [our batteries] opened on them with terrible effect. . . . Shells would plow through their lines, making great gaps, yet still they did not waver or falter, but kept steadily on. . . . Three lines of battle [extended] as far as you could see. [They advanced] with colors flying and keeping as accurately dressed as if on drill." Although "the grandest sight I had ever witnessed," said an officer, it was also one of the most frightening.[35]

"I watched with much anxiety the line below me," said Arthur M. Manigault. "They stood firm, and when the enemy arrived within about 200 yards, gave them their volley . . . but then followed a scene of confusion rarely witnessed. . . . The order had been issued to retire, but many did not hear it in the excitement of the fight, [the noise] of their own pieces, and the deafening roar of artillery." Some men were seen scrambling back up the steep ridge, although many continued to fight. Still others knelt dumbfounded in the rifle pits, not knowing what to do.[36]

Later, it was discovered that many of the men had not been informed of Hardee's new instructions. Not hearing the order to retreat and believing, as they earlier had been told, that they were to fight to the last, many continued to shoot from the rifle pits, even as others ran past them. Some men, seeing the gauntlet of fire facing them during a retreat, lay down in the trenches and waited for the inevitable.[37]

Soon the stampede from the lower breastworks was on. Deas's command, consisting of major portions from regiments belonging to four of Anderson's brigades, were forced to climb the steep ridge for three to four hundred yards under a devastating fire in order to reach the crest. As a result, said an eyewitness, "many threw away their guns, knapsacks, and in fact every [burdensome] thing." The men were soon "exhausted, demoralized, and unmanageable." "Each man, striving to save himself, took the shortest direction for the summit," noted an officer.[38]

"The consequence was," said the perplexed Manigault, "that many [troops] failed to reach the summit at all, but fell exhausted." Due to the heavy incoming fire, "which they could not return," many attempted to dash up the slopes too fast. Those that began reaching the crest were found "broken down, exhausted, and [in a] demoralized condition," wrote Manigault. "For many minutes . . . both officers and men were so jaded as to be utterly incapacitated." The moral effect was disastrous.[39]

The hell of retreating up those rugged slopes was remembered as an unforgettable ordeal and for its terrifying personal trauma. It was, decided a soldier, a by-product of one of the greatest blunders ever. Yet among the troops peering down from the crest, there was even greater trouble. Those at the top of the ridge couldn't fire accurately at the enemy because they feared hitting their own men, who were still retreating up the slopes. The cannon along the ridgeline were also compromised. In fact, when their muzzles were fully depressed, it was found the guns couldn't fire directly down the slopes so as to strike the breastworks below. The angle was too steep. An onlooking general saw that the effect of his artillery fire was not what he expected. "A plunging fire against infantry is far less effectual than over a level plain, or slightly undulating ground," he later commented. It was a painful lesson.[40]

Perhaps Hardee's orders to retire and fight at the top of the ridge had been conceptually sound. However, in the practical sense, they posed the prospect of an outright disaster.

CHAPTER 33

A MATTER OF SURVIVAL

The men of Thomas J. Wood's division were wild with energy, wrote an Indiana officer. "We had been held in restraint so long . . . that our enthusiasm knew no bounds." In fact, it was a chore, he said, to keep them in a reasonable semblance of a battle line. The thought crossed his mind that one might as well try to halt an avalanche as to try to stop the charge of the Fourth Army Corps.[1]

In the 41st Ohio Infantry of Brig. Gen. William B. Hazen's brigade, the soldiers sprinted toward the Confederate rifle pits at the base of the ridge with "new confidence." Despite the awful roar of artillery and the stunning air bursts, "it was plain that no harm was being done [by the shells]," wrote a veteran rifleman. "The much talked of moral effect of the big guns was missing; there was no wavering along the line." To further their excitement, as they approached the enemy breastworks at the foot of the ridge, there was a sudden commotion. The men could hardly believe their eyes.[2]

The enemy was running! Out from behind the log and earth parapets streamed hundreds of Rebel soldiers, dashing to the rear in irregular squads and clusters. Up the steep slopes scrambled the frantic gray troops, even as Bridges's cannon on Orchard Knob began shooting into them. The effect was electric. Wood's long blue line surged forward even faster.[3]

Unaware that the Confederate infantry had been ordered to withdraw upon their approach, the men of Brig. Gen. August Willich's brigade believed that the enemy was beaten. Most of the Rebel parapets were abandoned by the time Willich's skirmishers arrived in front. The commander of this skirmish line, Maj. John McClenahan of the 15th Ohio at first considered that he had gone too far, too fast. When one of his men looked around and saw there were no supports, the man blurted out to a comrade, "What are we going to do?" McClenahan's line abruptly slowed. Just then, the smoke cleared and the "grand, inspiring sight" of Willich's oncoming main lines, deployed in three ranks, sent their pulses racing. As the 35th Illinois, on Willich's left, sprinted ahead, McClenahan again urged his men forward. Together with a shout, McClenahan's soldiers and the 35th Illinois dashed among the abandoned rifle pits. They found only a handful of frightened enemy clustered behind the parapet walls. There was almost no resistance. The victory had been swift and easy.[4]

Their elation was but momentary. McClenahan and the others quickly saw the difficulty. Already, whizzing blasts of canister and a continuous angry zip of rifle balls foretold of the new danger. The men could not safely stay in the captured Rebel works due to the plunging fire from above. Exposed as they were to the direct fire from the ridgeline, there was virtually no protection among the breastworks. McClenahan and many of his men quickly sprinted onward toward some abandoned enemy huts along the lower slopes. A few panting soldiers from the 15th Ohio, on the brigade right, dashed to the same shelter and flopped down to rest.[5]

Although out of breath and taken aback by the intense incoming fire, Lt. Col. William P. Chandler of the 35th Illinois in Willich's main battle line also pondered his suddenly difficult situation. Having outdistanced the troops on his left, Chandler halted his men at the breastworks and fired a volley at the retreating enemy while waiting for the remainder of Willich's troops to arrive. Although the Rebel guns atop the ridge were annoying, their fire was not particularly destructive, noted Chandler. Soon he saw Willich dash forward through the smoke.[6]

August Willich was a fascinating soldier; a tall, liberal-thinking Prussian said to have royal blood lines. He had escaped from political intrigues in Europe to become editor of a German newspaper in prewar Cincinnati. Having led the 32nd Indiana Infantry at Shiloh and having been put in command of a brigade thereafter, Willich was a veteran fighter who was well liked by his men despite his thick accent and broken English. When first told he would be in the front rank in the assault on the rifle pits, Willich shrugged and said, "Vell, I makes my vill."[7]

Only minutes after arriving at the captured entrenchments, August Willich was both excited and astounded. Despite Thomas J. Wood's directive to attack only the rifle pits at the foot of the ridge, Willich somehow had misunderstood. He believed his specific orders were "to advance." As an old soldier, formally schooled in Prussian military science, Willich knew that despite the occupation of the rifle pits, he was in a terrible predicament. His troops, due to the delay of Baird's division on the left and the greater distance for Hazen's brigade to travel on his right, were in the very forefront of Thomas's assault.[8]

One of his regimental commanders, resting his men behind stumps, logs, and boulders, said the concentrated fire to which they were exposed had become "terrific beyond conception." Since by their return fire they were unable to diminish this incoming fire from the crest, "our only hope was to charge the hill," thought the officer. Willich agreed. "It was evident to everyone that to stay in this position would be certain destruction and final defeat," admitted the aroused Willich. "Every one saw instinctively that the only place of safety was in the enemy's works on the crest of the ridge."[9]

With the enemy peering down from above at their vulnerable ranks, and amid a shower of shell, canister, and minié balls, Willich sent his aide and another officer along the line to get the men moving forward. Ironically, it was unnecessary.[10]

The impetus seems to have come from Lieutenant Colonel Chandler of the 35th Illinois. Having rested his men for perhaps ten minutes while huddling miserably under the repeated blasts of canister from the ridge, Chandler was in no mood to remain where he was. "The slight resistance made by the retreating . . . enemy induced me to believe that a vigorous charge would succeed in silencing or capturing their battery," he later wrote. He hollered for his color sergeant to take the flag and advance with it directly toward the battery firing at them from the crest in front. Shouting "Forward," Chandler then sprang from the trenches and moved toward the flaming horseshoe-shaped ridgeline outlined above him.[11]

That was just enough of an impetus, for the feeling was mutual. Their common exposure to the enemy's scathing artillery fire and Chandler's example were contagious. Willich's men spilled out of the trenches with a shout and scrambled upward toward the crescent ridgeline distant about four hundred yards.[12]

Missionary Ridge's slopes along the lower levels were covered with downed timber felled for fuel and camp purposes. Among the topped branches and logs scattered over its face was heavy brush, all of which seemed to make scaling the ridge almost impossible, noted an Ohio soldier. The ridge, which appeared to be about a forty-five-degree angle of ascent, was steepest along the western slopes in front of several projections jutting out from the crest. Beyond the belt of timber, the open upper reaches were covered with loose rock and shale. Ravines, some deep and tangled with undergrowth, cut into the ridge at several points, presenting in all a rugged and difficult climb. Although various wagon roads were cut into the face of the ridge, they zigzagged across the slopes so as to make a practical grade for wagon travel. There simply was no easy way to reach the crest quickly, especially when ringed with opposing infantry and artillery.[13]

To an Indiana soldier, the distant crest looked like a solid mass of flame and smoke. Yet everybody was yelling and shouting, and the wild excitement of chasing after the fleeing enemy had made the men high from a surge of adrenaline. "We had no orders and no distinct purpose," wrote a flushed Ohio infantryman. "The enemy were fleeing up the slopes and we were bound to follow them. We didn't stop to think whether we could carry the crest or not—we didn't think at all! Each man just crowded on [after them]."[14]

On Willich's right flank, Brig. Gen. William B. Hazen's Ohio and Kentucky troops had reached the breastworks soon after Willich. Hazen knew his basic orders had been executed; they were in possession of the designated enemy line. Yet the Rebel musketry and cannon fire created a whirlwind. "We were completely enfiladed by artillery from both flanks [due to the concave shape of the ridge above us]," wrote Hazen. The particular problem no one had considered before the charge now was painfully evident. As Hazen's succeeding lines of infantry piled up behind the log parapets, which had been constructed at odd angles like a rail fence, the men discovered there was insufficient shelter for a single rank, much less three deployed lines of battle. The resulting chaos became an agony unto itself.[15]

With multiple units intermixed at the parapets, any semblance of discipline or order seemed impossible. Under the plunging fire from above there was a press of bodies forward to find shelter beneath the meager logs and rails. The roar of the guns was deafening on all sides, and no command could be heard beyond a few paces. Field officers dismounted and set their horses loose, most of which galloped in fright to the rear. Col. Aquila Wiley of the 41st Ohio Infantry was unable to control his bewildered mount. It stayed by Wiley, twisting and bucking nervously at each exploding shell. The horse's trampling hooves were a threat to the prone men lying there. Wiley jumped to his feet to shoo the horse away. He had grasped the animal's bridle to turn him away when a blast of canister felled the colonel, shattering his leg at the knee.[16]

Brigadier General Hazen lay on the ground and looked about. The chaos and confusion was spreading. To remain where they were "would be destruction," Hazen realized. "To fall back would not only be so, but would entail disgrace," he added. He had received no new orders, and ahead lay the comparative safety of shanties and log huts, which had been the enemy's camp. Hazen signaled an officer to go forward. Lt. Col. Robert L. Kimberly and a dozen men sprang to their feet. Shouting to the others, Kimberly plunged ahead over the works. Nearby, Lieutenant Colonel Langdon of the 1st Ohio also responded to Hazen's order, and soon his men began rushing forward.[17]

Not everyone heard these commands, however. In the 41st Ohio, the noise and confusion caused many soldiers to remain lying on the ground, even as the bulk of their regiment sprinted within the enemy's old camp. Kimberly briefly attempted to halt the line here to allow the regiment to close up. Yet the incoming artillery fire bowled over the log huts and the terrific musketry riddled the shanties with bullets. The men would not stay there. There was no safety in being shot at like rats running from pillar to post. Kimberly's men bolted forward up the slopes as fast as they could move. Here, they discovered, the steep angle of the slopes afforded both protection and a means to get at the enemy.[18]

To the north, beyond the sweeping concavity in Missionary Ridge, Brig. Gen. Samuel Beatty's brigade was similarly circumstanced. Two regiments, the 79th and 86th Indiana under the command of Col. Frederick Knefler, had pushed on ahead of their brigade line to reach the protection of the nearly vertical slopes. "Not having received any order to remain in the Rebel works, I ordered my command to advance," later wrote the fiery Knefler. However, his men, "protected by the steepness of the mountain," didn't stop along the lower ground. Like Hazen's men, they continued to move step by step up the ridge.[19]

Independently, by commonsense tactical decisions of front-line commanders, Thomas J. Wood's entire division had sprung forward within minutes of one another to attack Missionary Ridge. Despite the orders to take only the rifle pits at the base of the ridge, their bold initiative had set a remarkable precedent.

Phil Sheridan's three brigades had been slightly behind the progress of Wood's division in reaching the baseline enemy rifle pits due to a longer distance traveled. Reflecting the uncertainty about their specific tactical objective, there was much initial confusion among many of Sheridan's brigades once the soldiers reached the forward entrenchments. Most of the regiments were already badly intermixed, and there was much hesitation among the men. In the 74th Illinois of Col. Francis T. Sherman's brigade, their commander had great difficulty getting his troops to move from the safety of the parapets once it was determined to advance up the ridge. Another unit commander watched breathlessly as his men attempted to respond to the order to continue the attack. His men were exhausted from the long run under a heavy fire, and it seemed "that a farther advance was almost out of question." Slowly, however, the men began to go forward and follow their colors. A long, if scattered, line of blue uniforms inched up the slopes. "It was pretty much every man on his own hook," observed an officer.[20]

To Lt. Col. George W. Lennard, commanding the skirmish line in George D. Wagner's brigade, "the scene was truly sublime." Having given his panting men only a few minutes to rest following their sprint across the open plain, Lennard ordered his line onward from the captured rifle pits. The ground literally began to "reel and rock" under the intensive Rebel fire, but Lennard's men continued doggedly on. Behind them, Wagner's main line, understanding their orders were to "take all before us," followed their example. Col. Charles G. Harker's brigade, directed to follow the movements of Wagner's troops, also began to move beyond the entrenchments at the base of Missionary Ridge.[21]

Sheridan's entire division was thus slowly, inexorably going forward, just as Wood's troops simultaneously continued their advance on the adjacent parallel to the north. Although along much of Sheridan's front there were additional Confederate breastworks—a secondary line of log barricades about a third of the way up the ridge—Sheridan's men fixed their eyes on the enemy parapets and scrambled grimly onward.[22]

In Brig. Gen. Absalom Baird's division, on Thomas's extreme northern flank, the effort was almost the same. Baird's three brigades, Phelps's, Van Derveer's, and Turchin's, had swarmed over the abandoned Rebel entrenchments without great difficulty but were subjected to the same "heavy cross-fire [of artillery] from the crest." Their orders had been, as supports, to conform to the movements of Wood's troops on their right. Thus, when those troops began ascending the ridge, Baird's right-flank brigade, that of Brig. Gen. John B. Turchin, belatedly began to go forward also. Turchin's rationale was interesting. Seeing some of his men flopping down behind the captured parapets "to escape the murderous fire from the enemy's artillery and musketry," Turchin reacted impulsively. Believing that soldiers "dropping down under fire are very slow to get up and start again," he had hurriedly prodded his men onward. Soon the "bravest and strongest men [were] grouped around the regimental colors," noted Turchin. Within minutes, three of Turchin's regimental flags waved prominently along the rocky slopes, the soldiers behind forming an inverted V as they made their way slowly up the face of the ridge.[23]

It was quite a sight, an army rampant, feeding upon its old agony. Somehow, George H. Thomas's troops had found a way to fight the battle they weren't supposed to. What they were doing was against all odds. The men were veterans; they knew the hard-learned lessons of the battlefield— that frontal attacks against well-defended positions were seldom successful, much less against a dominant height crowned with enemy infantry and artillery. Yet the circumstances wouldn't allow careful logic or practicality. Their senior commanding general had placed them in a situation where they had no choice. They were an army being measured. It was no longer a matter of tactics; it was a matter of survival, and pride.

Ulysses S. Grant was aghast. From the high ground at Orchard Knob, Grant had watched George H. Thomas's "demonstration" slowly develop. Surrounded by Thomas, Gordon Granger, and their staffs, Grant had observed the rousing charge and victory at the rifle pits along the base of Missionary Ridge. Thomas's troops had fully carried out their instructions. Yet suddenly, in disobedience of Grant's specific orders, Thomas's troops were seen continuing forward—up the very slopes ringed with more than fifty cannon and thousands of Rebel infantry. Grant was both stunned and incensed. Only two hours earlier, he had watched Sherman's routed troops stream down the north end of Missionary Ridge's defiant slopes in complete disarray. The prospect of another bloody repulse at the crest loomed vivid in his mind.[24]

Angrily, he turned to Thomas and blurted out, "Who ordered those men up that ridge?" Emotionless, George H. Thomas stood transfixed. Slowly, he replied, "I don't know. I did not." Grant turned to Granger and demanded, "Did you order them up?" "No," he said quickly, nervously adding, "When those fellows get started all hell can't stop them." Grant wasn't amused. Menacingly, he grumbled that someone would pay dearly for it if the assault failed. Without another word, Grant grimly turned to look through his field glasses at the distant scene. He gave no further orders, said an uneasy staff officer.[25]

Gordon Granger was convinced the wrath of Job was about to settle upon him. In urgent tones, he turned to his chief of staff, Lt. Col. Joseph S. Fullerton, and told him to ride swiftly to the two division commanders, Wood and Sheridan, and find out who had ordered the troops up the ridge. The original order had been to carry only the first line of entrenchments, Granger reminded Fullerton. Yet perhaps as an afterthought, realizing that Wood's and Sheridan's troops were already partway up the ridge, Granger added that if in their judgment they could take the crest, they should do so. Before Fullerton dashed off, Granger said he would send another staff officer, Capt. William L. Avery, to give Sheridan the same instructions. Granger felt the intense enemy fire was so hot, Fullerton might not get through, hence the resort to Avery. Within minutes, both staff officers galloped off as fast as their horses could run.[26]

Granger's dispatch further intensified a remarkable situation. Only a half hour earlier, when found by the staff officer Sheridan had sent to learn what the specific objective was, Granger had told the officer it was only the first line that was to be carried. Thus, even before Fullerton's departure, this information was being conveyed to Sheridan and several of his brigade commanders. George D. Wagner, on Sheridan's left flank, was informed that it was Grant's orders that the troops not go beyond the first line of rifle pits. Wagner, shocked that he had exceeded orders, immediately sent his aides to recall the troops from the slopes. Wagner's movements were critical, since his was the guiding brigade from which Sheridan's other units would take their direction.[27]

The questions were thus grave. Would the orders to halt save a bloody repulse at the crest? Was it too late to stop the men? Would enough troops reach the ridge and capture it before ordered to retreat? It was an awkward race: Wagner's staff officers were scrambling after the men to stop them, even as the soldiers inched onward step by step up the fire-swept slopes.

In the offing was a decisive action: a terrible defeat, a stunning victory, or a practical stalemate. Grant, considering Sherman's fate on the north of Missionary Ridge, had already determined not to push his luck. He would settle for a drawn encounter. Thomas's men, however, were out of control. Their mistake was impelling events toward an unforeseen climax. Grant was merely a bystander. His reluctance to use Thomas's troops in a major fighting role had strangely backfired; now the final outcome would depend on them. Grant fretted. Was his legendary good luck about to desert him?

CHAPTER 34

"WHO IN HELL IS GOING TO STOP THEM?"

Lt. John Shellenberger of the 64th Ohio Volunteers prepared to cross the captured Confederate parapet at the base of the ridge. It was low on the outside, with a ditch inside, and as he jumped over the parapet, he could see that some of Wagner's troops on the left had already passed into the open, toward the belt of timber at the base of the ridge.[1]

Shellenberger promptly leapt out of the ditch, calling, "Forward!" to his company. The race across the open ground was terror-filled, remembered the captain. Canister felled men "like ten pens," and Shellenberger looked at the ridge ahead. "I seemed to be looking directly into the muzzle of one of those guns as it was discharged. . . . I saw the gunner pull the lanyard, stopped still, and with chin pressed to my breast, eyes closed, and teeth clenched, braced myself for the shock of an expected wound. I could feel the canister swish through the air close by me, but remained unharmed." By the time the 64th reached the cover of the timber, all were gasping for breath. Yet within minutes, some individuals began to work their way forward.[2]

While lying there recovering, Lieutenant Shellenberger noticed their colonel scurrying along the line and talking to the men. Abruptly, the soldiers jumped up in squads and went to the rear. When he reached Shellenberger, the colonel said, "Lieutenant, you must take your company and go back to the breastworks." Shellenberger was shocked. The order was such "a blunder" that he dared argue with the colonel. The Rebels were overshooting their line, said Shellenberger, and the heads of the enemy soldiers outlined against the sky made them a clear target. We should remain here, said the exasperated lieutenant. "I know," replied the colonel

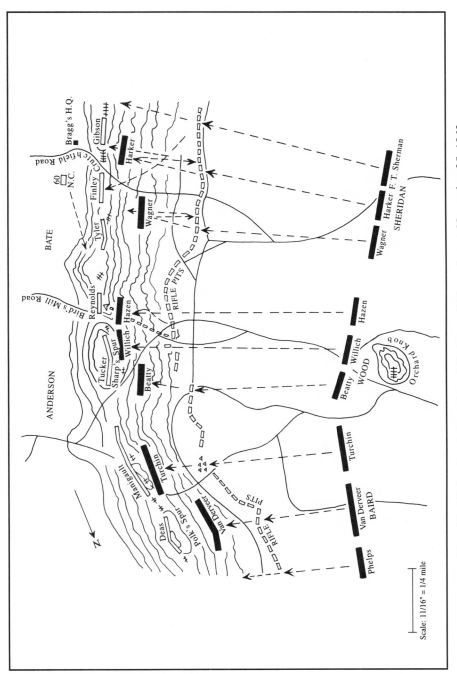

MAP 10   Union Breakthrough on Missionary Ridge—5 p.m., November 25, 1863
(*Source: O.R. 31-2-515; Baird's=Wood's Division Map–Turchin Mtls, Chick-Chatt*)

with some irritation, "but the orders are to go back, and we must obey orders."[3]

Wagner's aides had reached the line of advancing troops in quick time. "It was with the greatest reluctance, almost amounting to a refusal at first, that this order was obeyed," wrote an indignant lieutenant colonel. Wagner's brigade began withdrawing from the lower slopes, and the men were compelled to dash across the open ground back to the line of captured breastworks. Most of Harker's brigade, on Wagner's immediate right, also fell back to the baseline rifle pits after it was noticed that Wagner was retreating. Only Francis T. Sherman's troops, somewhat isolated on the extreme right of Sheridan's line, failed to get a direct order to withdraw.[4]

Within moments after returning to the crowded rifle pits, everyone lay hugging the ground under a devastating fire from the ridge above. An officer looked to the left, where the troops of Wood's division were still visible through the smoke. Their long lines "could be plainly seen, slowly but steadily pushing . . . up the hill[side]." What did it mean? By whose orders were they still advancing?[5]

Thomas J. Wood had his dander up. When approached by Lieutenant Colonel Fullerton, Wood was in no mood to apologize. Had he given the order to attack the ridge? asked Fullerton. "No," said Wood sharply. "The men had started of their own accord." Told by Fullerton that it was Grant's order that the line stop at the first line of entrenchments, Wood replied, "I would like to know who in Hell is going to stop them?" "If we are supported," continued the general, "we will take and hold that ridge!"[6]

The matter was thus practically decided. Fullerton went back to find Granger, and Wood's troops continued their onward movement unchecked.

August Willich's troops were by now well forward on the slopes, yet the going was slow due to the steep ascent. "We had to rest every few minutes," wrote an Ohio soldier. When a captain found that many of his men were getting ahead of him, he reached out and grabbed a private by the coattails, holding on until he passed him by. Yet it was only a momentary reprieve. Within moments, the man was ahead of him again.[7]

The fire along the mostly open slopes was murderous, wrote a soldier, and Willich's foremost men suffered the most. Especially dangerous was the apex of the many inverted V-shaped lines, where often a flag bearer led the attack. In the 35th Illinois, six color bearers were shot on the slopes. Each time, the flag was quickly raised again and the line crawled onward. It was purely an accident, but a fortuitous one, that Willich's brigade had formed directly in front of a prominent protrusion on Missionary Ridge later known as "Sharp's Spur." Here, due to the steepness of the slopes, Willich's men were greatly protected in front. Although a Rebel battery across the Bird's Mill Road swung about and began shooting into their ranks, there was an adjacent gully filled with underbrush that the men swarmed toward. "It was hard getting through the brush," wrote an Illinois soldier, but the depression afforded a large measure of protection.[8]

Beyond Willich's right flank, many in Hazen's brigade had also noticed the relative safety afforded by the convex slopes of the spur. Those units on Hazen's left now began moving in this direction, and many soon intermingled with Willich's lines, enlarging the multiple upside-down V-shaped formations.[9]

Although the lines were intermixed and the soldiers mostly going it alone, a growing, irregular mob of men in blue surged closer and closer toward the crest. Willich's and some of Hazen's men soon discovered they were within easy pistol range of the ridgetop. An officer shouted for his men to pick off the gunners at the enemy cannon. Shots rang out, and bodies collapsed about the smoking field guns. The cannon fired no more.[10]

Along the line below Sharp's Spur, the command "Fix bayonets!" sounded above the din of battle. The flash of polished blades and the metallic clank of metal was distinctly audible below the crest. "The Rebels heard [this], and it scared them mightily," wrote an excited officer.[11]

The Confederate colonel William F. Tucker knew he had a big responsibility. Now in command of division commander Patton Anderson's old brigade, Tucker anchored the line on the division's left flank. Although his position along the crest of Missionary Ridge now seemed to be the actual left of the entire main battle line, it was not intended to be such.

Tucker, a Mississippi lawyer who had fought at First Bull Run before being transferred west, had earned temporary brigade command only recently, following the absence of Col. Jacob H. Sharp. Like the other brigades in Anderson's Division, Tucker's had about half of its strength in the entrenchments at the foot of Missionary Ridge on November 25. Along the crest, Tucker's men occupied the prominent spur known within the army as "Sharp's Headquarters," located between two wagon roads leading over the ridge.* Most of the day had been spent in cutting and placing log breastworks along the spur's crest. Yet about 1:00 P.M., the brigade on Tucker's immediate left flank, that of Col. Randall Lee Gibson, had been ordered to rejoin its division, A. P. Stewart's, in its proper position south of Bragg's headquarters.[12]

The pullout of Gibson's troops left a void along the adjacent spur south of the Bird's Mill Road. To fill the gap, at about 2:00 P.M. Anderson ordered Brig. Gen. Alexander W. Reynolds's Virginia and North Carolina brigade to move from the rifle pits at the base of the ridge to the vacant position along the crest. In command of a small brigade of about 995 men, Reynolds inadvertently lost some of his strength when various companies of the 60th

---

*The site was named for the location of the brigade headquarters, as originally commanded by Jacob H. Sharp.

North Carolina Infantry were separated along the ridge during the pull-back. These troops later fell in with some of Bate's units in the vicinity of Bragg's headquarters farther south along the ridge. Meanwhile, Reynolds was in the process of moving up the ridge to join Tucker when some of Bate's troops appeared under orders to occupy the same site.[13]

Due to corps commander Breckinridge's assumption that the void would have to be filled with Bate's troops when Gibson was pulled from his position adjacent to Tucker, Bate had been ordered to move over and "touch Anderson's left." Bate was in the process of executing these orders when hastily notified to report to Bragg's headquarters. Here he was told Anderson wanted space for Reynolds's troops, and, accordingly, Bate was to shift back toward the Crutchfield Road, leaving room for Reynolds. Although his troops had nearly reached Tucker's flank, the order was countermanded, allowing Reynolds eventually to move into the gap.[14]

The net result was much confusion along Anderson's southern flank and a numbing feeling of semi-isolation among Tucker's men, who knew nothing of the reason for all the shifting and countermarching on their flank. In the face of the vast enemy columns forming for an attack on the plain immediately below, there was considerable anxiety and uneasiness.

An all-Mississippi brigade of combat-experienced units, Tucker's command numbered about fifteen hundred men and was supported by a Napoleon- and Parrott-armed battery of Alabama artillery just transferred from Lookout Mountain on the twenty-fourth, Capt. James Garrity's Battery. Although Tucker's men had belatedly attempted to construct breastworks along the prominent "Sharp's Spur," due to the topography the flimsy log barricades did not command the steep slopes directly in front. Tucker's difficulty was compounded when the enemy's columns advanced. His men at the bottom of the ridge had attempted to follow their instructions to fall back without fighting. Yet the result, said Tucker, was that these troops drifted back in fragments, much exhausted and unfit for duty. Some were so fatigued and ill as barely to be able to stand. Others were sent in ambulances to the hospital.[15]

Tucker's men, posted along the crest, seemed further confused and intimidated. Yet Tucker remained confident, appearing unconcerned about the threat in his front. Major General Anderson talked with Tucker when passing by Sharp's Spur shortly after the enemy had occupied the lower rifle pits. The Mississippians seemed to be fighting with a "coolness and composure," and there was little to be apprehensive about as to their role in the battle. Tucker said he could hold his position against all odds and he reassured Anderson that his old brigade was in safe hands.[16]

Thereafter, the fighting along Tucker's front had so stabilized that Anderson dashed off toward the next prominent spur to the north, "Polk's Headquarters," where it appeared the enemy's threat was more severe. In fact, so little firing was then occurring along Tucker's right flank and Manigault's left that Anderson detached the 34th Alabama Infantry from Manigault's extreme left and sent it to reinforce Deas's Brigade, then fighting along "Polk's Spur." The 34th was Manigault's largest regiment, and Tucker's men watched them go without knowing the reason for their departure. Suddenly, the Mississippians seemed to realize that they were once again unsupported on a crucial flank.[17]

The 32nd Indiana and 6th Ohio were the first to reach the crest, said August Willich. These regiments were intermixed, the Indianians being from Willich's brigade and the Ohioans from Hazen's. Here, on the right of Willich's line, they were slightly beyond the others as the men surged forward over the crest with a wild yell.[18]

"A volley was poured almost into our very faces," wrote an officer of the 6th Ohio. Some men were hit, but the fire went mostly over their heads. The Confederate breastworks were too far back from the crest for the Rebel soldiers to fire down the frontal slopes, yet they were close enough so that within seconds Willich's and Hazen's men "cleared the works and jumped right in among the Rebels." There was no time to reload, and Tucker's troops panicked.[19]

"Such a confused mass I never saw, nor expect to see again," wrote an amazed officer. As Willich's other units began swarming over the crest and were within a dozen yards of the entrenchments, the Rebel line suddenly broke "in wild confusion." The gray ranks then "fled in panic" toward the reverse slopes on the east, noted an amazed colonel.[20]

To Col. William F. Tucker, the enemy's sudden appearance over the crest at the center of his brigade was totally unexpected. The breastworks were back from the crest so that his men couldn't see well immediately below, and their line went to pieces before he could bring up two reserve regiments. Although Tucker attempted to get the reserves forward, they, too, "stampeded with the rest," he admitted.[21]

The chaos was never to be forgotten. Amid the smoke and terrible din, Confederate officers were seen trying to rally their men; Garrity's Battery had already limbered up, and everywhere clusters of gray soldiers were running in all directions. Willich's and Hazen's men were excited: "We started popping at them as if they were quail," wrote a jubilant Ohioan.[22]

Nearby, in the 15th Ohio Infantry of Willich's brigade, the regiment had arrived at the crest at a particularly steep point, and the men boosted Capt. J. C. Cummins over, the first man atop the ridge at that particular site. He was immediately shot and mortally wounded, yet past his sprawled form raced others; along with the other regiments, they spread rapidly out along the crest, yelling and shooting.[23]

The breakthrough was rapid, spontaneous, and like a wildfire fanned by the wind, raging out of control. Arthur M. Manigault was watching the approach of the Yankee line toward his right flank, in the direction of the Polk's Spur, when he learned from a staff officer that "the enemy had broken the Mississippi brigade on the left, and were in possession of a great part of their line." Manigault was incredulous when he heard the report. He couldn't see Tucker's position due to a rise in the ridge, but he rapidly rode in that direction. Manigault was shocked at what he soon found. Tucker's ground was entirely abandoned by Confederate troops. Two Yankee flags were flying amid troops forming in large numbers along the ridge. Confederate cannon were being swarmed over. It was a critical moment. Upon Manigault's reaction hinged the fate of the battle.[24]

The battery was the key. The 6th Ohio saw it in an instant and went for the guns. Garrity's cannon were rolling now, the lead horses struggling to jerk the heavy guns from their rocky placements. Hazen's and Willich's infantrymen began shooting at the front horses. Down in a tangle of harnesses and kicking hooves went several lead animals. A twelve-pounder Napoleon came to a stop. The 6th Ohio surged ahead, straight for the immobilized gun. A Rebel officer shot down two Ohioans with his revolver and refused to surrender even though surrounded. An instant later, he lay on the ground, a bloody victim.[25]

Around the captured gun perhaps a dozen Rebel cannoneers stood aghast. Quickly surrounded by excited, yelling men in blue uniforms, they were told to unlimber the cannon. At the point of leveled bayonets held by some of the 32nd Indiana Infantry, these captive gunners were made to swing the cannon about, load, and prepare to fire it into their own men. Within minutes, the twelve-pounder Napoleon was pointed in the direction of Manigault's line and the friction primer inserted. On the breech of the gun was an inscription: "Captured from Rosecrans' [army] on the 31st of December, 1862, Stones River."*[26]

Nearby, prisoners stood by the dozens behind the parapets, dazed and frightened. An Ohioan discovered a Rebel captain; he "made no attempt at resistance, but handed me his sword and asked what he should do." Willich's and Hazen's men began to exult. "Everybody seemed crazy with delight," said an Ohio officer.[27]

Arthur Manigault felt the pressure. With Tucker's line gone, his entire left flank was "now swinging in the air." He knew something must be done, yet he hesitated to act. "I regarded it for the moment as only a temporary [enemy] success, and [I] expected every moment to see the enemy driven back." His only reaction was to send a staff officer to find Patton Anderson and tell him of the crisis. Meanwhile, he rode toward the breakthrough, hoping to "observe the enemy's movements" more closely.[28]

The minutes ticked away. No word was received from Anderson. The enemy was seen forming at right angles across the ridge, "their numbers

---

*Garrity's Battery was charged with the loss of one twelve-pounder Napoleon in the Confederate Ordnance Report of Lt. Col. James H. Hallonquist, Chief of Artillery, dated December 3, 1863. Based upon listed Federal captures and the subsequent issuing of two three-inch rifles to Garrity's Battery, it appears this unit may have lost its two Napoleons at Missionary Ridge. Reportedly, the battery's two ten-pounder Parrott rifles were not engaged, perhaps due to a lack of suitable ammunition, which helps account for their escape.

increasing at every moment." Garrity's captured gun was being wheeled about. Where was Anderson? Where were the expected reinforcements to drive back the Yankees? Manigault "saw no such movement in progress." Although he knew that time was of the essence, Manigault took no initiative. He waited. The 34th Alabama had been removed from his left flank to reinforce Deas. Thus, he had no troops adjacent to Tucker's captured position.[29]

Manigault later said his own line was so weak, and having no reserves, he had awaited orders. It was the essence of defeat. Garrity's captured gun bellowed flame. Spraying canister shot whizzed through Manigault's ranks from the flank. Men began screaming with agony. Soldiers were seen leaving the line. The enemy was advancing.[30]

An aide dashed up with orders from Anderson. Manigault was to pull out a regiment from the front, form a line parallel to the enemy's along the ridge, and drive the Yankees off. Manigault turned to Captain Dent, whose six twelve-pounder Napoleons supported the brigade front. "Turn two of your guns on the enemy atop the ridge," he shouted. Staff officers scurried off to withdraw the troops and form a new line.[31]

Suddenly, there was undue commotion along the center of Manigault's line, at the point of the ridge's greatest elevation along the brigade front. Many of his men were running away. They were taking the brunt of the canister fire from the captured gun atop the ridge. Exposed and vulnerable, they had seen enough.[32]

Horrified, Manigault glanced to the right. Deas's Brigade seemed to be scattering in flight. Yankee infantry were pouring over the ridge here; the crest was swarming with blue uniforms. Even in the center of his own line, where the soldiers were seen running away, more enemy flags suddenly appeared below the crest. The crisis was simultaneous, instant, and expanding.[33]

Coming up from the right, Patton Anderson stood astonished. He saw his division line "slough[ing] off by fragments." Having only an orderly with him, Anderson was unable to send staff officers to rally the men. Desperately, he shouted for the soldiers to re-form, then rode among the fleeing men, gesturing wildly. Few paid any attention. Nearby, Manigault did the same, riding among his men to stop them in their "mad flight." "Threats and entreaties proved unavailing"; even the officers "generally seemed to lose their presence of mind," reported the wearied Manigault. "Panic seemed to seize upon all." It was shocking, sad, and maddening. A feeling of helplessness pervaded the minds of all.[34]

Manigault's and Anderson's reaction had been too little, too late. The Confederate army was on the brink of disaster.

CHAPTER 35

"You Kills Me mit Joy!"

Brig. Gen. Thomas J. Wood was like a man on the brink. "I expected the Rebels . . . would rise up, pour their fire into us, leap over their works, and charge us with their bayonets." If they did that, he grimly noted, it would surely "sweep us all back [down the ridge]."[1]

It was "a very great strain," and Wood breathlessly noted the events: "I expected every moment to hear the Rebel yell, and to see the Confederates pouring down on us like so many infuriated demons." Aware of Grant's chagrin over the assault up the ridge, he foresaw he would be severely dealt with and his career ruined if the attack failed. Yet riding immediately behind the second line of Willich's brigade, Wood was reduced to being merely an interested observer—"simply one of the boys," moving along with the crowd. Should the Confederates "bound over their works as they ought to," observed Wood, he would make sure he was shot down with his men. If he was killed, he reflected, "I would [be] beyond the reach of courts-martial, and the denunciations and curses of the public."[2]

"Fancy [my] relief," exclaimed the emotional Wood, when "I saw the Confederates begin to give way." It was "the proudest, most exultant moment of my life," he later claimed. As Wood saw the long blue lines break over the crest and their red-white-and-blue flags waving in triumph atop the ridge, he knew he had gambled his very reputation, career, and life, and won.[3]

Wood was most fortunate. He was not fighting the aggressive Pat Cleburne and his veteran soldiers, who had been positioned near this very area only a few days earlier. Instead, Wood was up against Patton Anderson's Division, which included troops that Bragg had shuffled about in the reorganization of mid-October. The difference was proving fatal to Bragg's army.

Like Wood, Arthur M. Manigault knew it was one of the greatest crises in his life. His brigade had been broken into several segments by Turchin's Yankee brigade sweeping over the ridge at various points. Although several regiments, the 10th South Carolina and the 28th Alabama, generally stood their ground, Manigault's artillery was in great difficulty. Two of Dent's Napoleons along the southern flank had already been overrun by some of Willich's troops sweeping north from the Sharp's Spur. Dent's remaining four guns had been limbered up so as to withdraw but were now in danger of capture as they ran a gauntlet of fire from Yankees attacking along the crest. In terror, the horses pulling one of Dent's retiring field guns ran between two trees and the cannon became jammed. Manigault dashed over to the gun and ordered the men to wheel it backward. Dent was there, looking at the oncoming enemy. "Leave the gun, General, and save yourself!" he shouted.[4]

Manigault glanced up. The Yankees were within fifty yards and closing fast. Manigault yelled to one of his staff officers that they must "ride for it." Ramming his spurs into his horse's flank, Manigault and the lieutenant bolted toward the rear. "Bullets whistled around me like a swarm of bees [and] my chances of escape seemed doubtful," noted Manigault. With a devil-may-care attitude, he urged his mount at top speed over the rough and rocky ground. "It was at imminent risk of [breaking] our necks," wrote Manigault, but they galloped four or five hundred yards before placing the intervening ridge between themselves and the foe. "We literally ran the gauntlet," he stated with amazement. "[Yet] only by God's mercy had we escaped."[5]

Behind him, the mixture of Dent's gunners and gray infantry hadn't been so fortunate. An isolated section of Dent's Battery had remained defiant to the last, firing double charges of canister at point-blank range into the faces of the oncoming enemy. Yet there was no time to reload. Many artillerists were shot or forced to surrender. On two opposite flanks, the 10th South Carolina and 28th Alabama—Manigault's only hope—had been successively attacked and routed by enemy troops rushing from the south along the length of the ridge. Manigault's efforts thus appear to have been misdirected. Instead of attempting to extricate an ensnared and about-to-be-captured cannon, a more judicious officer might have expended his efforts on rallying and uniting his troops for a concerted defense of the crest.[6]

Manigault was soon at his wit's end as he tried to re-form the panicked men along the lower reverse slopes. He said he had never before witnessed a routed army, "where panic seemed to seize upon all, and all order, obedience, and discipline were for the time forgotten and disregarded." The exasperated Manigault later wrote: "God grant that I may never again take part in another such affair." Although by the aid of subordinates he was able to rally a portion of his brigade on a rear ridge along the Shallow

Ford Road, the battle was beyond him now. Someone else would have to try to stop the exultant Yankees on Missionary Ridge.[7]

On the Confederate side, Brig. Gen. Zachariah C. Deas's Brigade had held the position that seemed to be the most threatened by the advancing ranks of Absalom Baird's division on Thomas's extreme left flank. Deas was still upset from the morning's events, when he had been denied permission to move his lower regiments to the crest of Missionary Ridge. As a result, when Thomas's columns attacked, his men from the base of the ridge were exhausted and demoralized as they reached the crest in broken fragments. Due to the ominous concentration of Turchin's and Van Derveer's brigades below the Deas-occupied Polk's Spur, all eyes had been on their progress.*[8]

At the time Tucker's line had broken well to the south, Deas was involved in a firefight with a heavy column of Van Derveer's infantry, spearheaded by three Yankee flags close by his right flank. Already a significant advantage had been created for Van Derveer, due to the massing of three regiments from Turchin's brigade on the ridge rim immediately to the south, formerly held by Manigault's right-flank regiments. Turchin's 11th and 31st Ohio were the first on the ridge in front of Manigault, and their abrupt swing to the north, together with the 36th Ohio, in the direction of Polk's Spur put enormous pressure on Deas.[9]

Turchin's three regiments had already chased Dent's retiring cannon along the slope toward the Blythe cabin and forge shop, overrunning one gun positioned near the shop. Meanwhile, the 17th Ohio Infantry, rushing forward over the crest and down the opposite slopes, captured two of Dent's other escaping guns after a fifteen-minute fight—including, apparently, the gun Manigault had attempted to save.[10]

Turchin's soldiers were on a rampage, overrunning the narrow ridge crest from south to north, even as his two separated units on the left flank joined with some of Van Derveer's regiments and pressured Deas's troops from the front. The 92nd Ohio and 82nd Indiana of Turchin's brigade had used a sheltering ravine to swing far to the left, then came rushing over the southern crest of Polk's Spur, to find two guns of Deas's artillery, Waters's Alabama Battery, immediately at hand.[11]

About the same time, some of Van Derveer's intermixed command, in the immediate front of the precipitous spur, were led by the 2nd Minnesota Infantry over the log barricade at the crest. Confronted by an enemy attack from two directions, the cannoneers serving Waters's section abandoned

---

*This is the point the Federals later termed "Signal Hill" and that the Confederates knew as "Polk's Headquarters." It was the apparent site of Col. Lucius E. Polk's command post. Polk commanded a brigade in Cleburne's Division and was located on Missionary Ridge prior to the division's movement under orders to go to Knoxville on November 22. The present area, encompassing a Federal National Military Park Reservation, is known as the De Long Reservation.

their guns while in the act of loading. There was a shout, a flurry of shots, and an instant later the 2nd Minnesota's exultant men were amid the guns. "Turn the cannon on 'em boys," shouted Sgt. Axel Reed, and one of Waters's twelve-pounder howitzers was wheeled about as others began rummaging through the debris for ammunition.[12]

For a moment, they stood dazed by the scene, a Minnesota infantryman later remembered. Then the rush forward began again. Van Derveer's men "were drunk with the frenzy of battle," remarked one of his Ohio officers, and a gathering mob of soldiers in blue streamed northward along the ridge. Elements of Beatty's, Turchin's, and Van Derveer's regiments were all mixed together in an enthusiastic crowd, said an officer. To add to the swelling mass, more of Van Derveer's troops began reaching the crest and joined with those already on the ridge. It was great fun to see the "gray-backs" run, noted an elated soldier.[13]

To Zachariah Deas, at this point "resistance now had ceased to be a virtue." He ordered his brigade back from the crown of the ridge and soon led the retreat, easterly over the opposite slopes. Three of Waters's guns were abandoned to the enemy. Although Deas said he hoped to organize a counterattack, his ammunition allegedly was found to be exhausted despite only a few minutes' intensive combat along the ridge. Deas later joined with fragments of other brigades from his division along the Shallow Ford Road and withdrew across Chickamauga Creek.[14]

Deas's pullout left only a single brigade along the line of Anderson's Division at the far right—the all-Tennessee brigade under the command of Brig. Gen. Alfred J. Vaughan, Jr. Vaughan had skirmished with the Yankees earlier while posted in the rifle pits below the ridge, and when he joined with the remainder of his troops along the crest north of Deas's position, Vaughan was fatigued and apprehensive.[15]

Although Col. Edward H. Phelps's Federal brigade was advancing in their front, Vaughan's Tennesseans had little trouble with these Yankees; Phelps's men had started late and then Phelps was killed while ascending the slopes. The major trouble for Vaughan was on his left flank, where Deas's, Manigault's, and Tucker's lines had given way. Vaughan sought to form a second line in that direction, pulling the 11th Tennessee Infantry out of line so as to "retake the [Deas] hill" on the left flank.[16]

It was a spectacular, if forlorn, effort. The Tennesseans came rushing forward along the crest, driving back some of Van Derveer's Indiana troops, and recaptured a section of Waters's Battery. Yet their onward impetus was brought to a halt due to the profusion of Yankee troops gathering for a renewed attack.[17]

When an Indiana color sergeant came rushing back through the ranks of the 11th Ohio, an Ohio private, Harvey M. Thompson, grasped the banner from his hands. Waving it beside the 11th's flag, Thompson sprinted toward the contested guns fifty yards distant. Within a few steps, he was knocked down by a blow on his right side. Looking down, he discovered the bullet had struck his cap box and deflected the ball. Jumping to his feet, Thompson again grasped the flag and ran forward. A bullet sliced through his side, inflicting a flesh wound. Thompson kept going. An instant later, the flagstaff was shattered and knocked from his hands; only about a two-foot section remained below the flag. Thompson looked back, to find there was no one advancing with him. After briefly ducking behind a stump, he attempted to sprint back to his own lines, which were thirty yards away. Thompson had nearly reached safety when he was shot in the ankle and fell to the ground. The Indiana flag was torn and muddied, but it was later restored to its original regiment.[18]

The brief impasse soon passed. The 2nd Minnesota was among the units in the forefront of a renewed Federal attack. It was "a charge en masse by the crowd," wrote a Minnesota officer. The 11th Tennessee reeled backward just as Vaughan was attempting to bring up two other regiments. Following a brief hand-to-hand struggle, Vaughan's line gave way and he ordered his entire brigade to pull back north along the ridge. Three guns of Scott's Tennessee Battery were lost to some of Van Derveer's troops. As the Confederates vanished into the drifting battle smoke, some of Phelps's soldiers crowned the ridge and fired a parting volley. There now was no organized Confederate battle line along Anderson's northern perimeter, and only Hardee's and Cleburne's previously victorious troops along the north of Missionary Ridge stood in the path of a complete Federal sweep of the northern ridge.[19]

At this point, only a single Confederate brigade attached to Anderson's division was still fighting—that of Brig. Gen. Alexander W. Reynolds, along the division's extreme southern position. Having just been repositioned along the crest following their former duty at the foot of the ridge, Reynolds's troops were both fatigued and shaken when Wood's and Sheridan's columns attacked Missionary Ridge. As Tucker's Brigade gave way, "this disgraceful and inexplicable panic" affected his men, Reynolds said. Hazen's Ohioans were in Reynolds's immediate sector, and although Reynolds partially changed front to meet the threat to his right, Hazen's southern-flank regiments were close under the crest.[20]

Within the ranks of the 41st Ohio Infantry of Hazen's brigade, there was a sudden shudder. The 1st Ohio, on their immediate left, was going over the ridge's crest with their lanky lieutenant colonel, Bassett Langdon, leading the rush. Langdon was shot in the face, the ball ranging through his cheeks side to side. The stricken officer staggered but recovered. Raising his revolver, he emptied its chambers before sagging to the ground. Clambering past him, his men poured over the crest and ran at Reynolds's troops, now attempting to defend the ridge in two separate directions. The 41st Ohio was right beside the 1st Ohio and soon overran the ridge along the Bird's Mill Road, shouting and yelling like "mad demons" in their excitement.[21]

Promptly, Reynolds's men all but disappeared in front, and Reynolds desperately attempted to retreat down the Bird's Mill Road to reach the pontoon bridge across Chickamauga Creek.[22]

They were the last of Patton Anderson's command to leave Missionary Ridge. For an expanse of a mile and a half, a huge gap existed where Anderson's Confederates had once been posted at the very center, the strongest portion of "impregnable" Missionary Ridge. This seemed incredible, beyond belief. It was "one of the greatest miracles in military history," some were already asserting. Charles A. Dana thought it "a visible interposition of God."[23]

Atop the still-smoldering ridge, August Willich was laughing now. With hat in hand, he was found among the captured cannon, broadly grinning and pointing to a broken spur. He had kicked a laggard on the way up the slopes, he said, and the man had seen his "point." Willich was still chuckling when several privates rode up on two captured battery horses and presented them as a gift. Willich was overjoyed. He blurted out in his best broken English, "My poys, you kills me mit joy, you kills me mit joy!"[24]

Thomas J. Wood was in the grandest of moods. Scattered enemy cannon, abandoned to or captured by his division, littered the ridge for as far as he could see. Galloping up to some of his soldiers, he began to shout. "Men, I'll have you all court martialled. You were ordered to take the rifle pits at the foot of the ridge, and here you've got the ridge itself, and all of Bragg's artillery." There was a great yell. Hats and kepis were flung into the air. The Army of the Cumberland was no longer an ugly orphan; the men were heroes. They had been redeemed.[25]

CHAPTER 36

"GIVE 'EM HELL, BOYS!"

Braxton Bragg seemed to be a man possessed by the fighting. Riding with his staff along the crest of Missionary Ridge, he was seen to dash past a cluster of infantrymen, with bullets whizzing past and shells exploding along the ridge. A rifleman heard one of his staff yell, "Give 'em hell, boys!" Just at that instant, a shower of Yankee rifle balls zipped through the air. An aide riding a cream-colored horse was shot and fell from the saddle, causing the animal to bolt in terror down the opposite side of the ridge. Bragg looked about. The flag of the 3rd Florida Infantry of Bate's Division lay on the ground; it had fallen for the third time that day. Bragg jumped down from his mount and grasped the banner. No sooner had he remounted than a lanky infantryman from that regiment ran forward and took it from his hands. Bragg, thought an observer, may be a tyrant to his men, yet he still is "a brave old soldier."[1]

Although Bragg appeared preoccupied with the fighting along the ridge adjacent to his headquarters, the men here were fighting well. Bate held the ground from Anderson's left flank along the Bird's Mill Road south to the Crutchfield Road, where Bragg's headquarters was established at the Thurman house. Beyond Bate, A. P. Stewart's Division of Breckinridge's Corps extended south along the ridge beyond the Crutchfield Road. In battery along Bate's and Stewart's front were various artillery units from the division and reserve battalions. Included among these was the famous 5th Company, Washington Artillery Battalion of New Orleans, popularly known as Slocomb's Battery. Commanded by Capt. Cuthbert H. Slocomb, the battery was positioned this afternoon along two prominent eminences

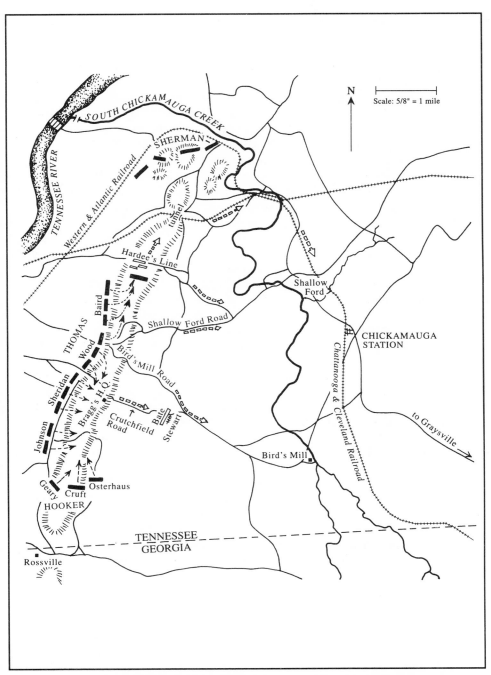

MAP 11 Confederate Retreat from Missionary Ridge, November 25, 1863
(*Source: Edward E. Betts, 1896 Chattanooga Map*)

on the far right of Bate's line, near where Reynolds's Brigade had filled the gap between Anderson's and Bate's flanks.[2]

Because the battery's two James rifles and four twelve-pounder Napoleons were in a key position to enfilade the Yankee lines attacking Sharp's Spur, Slocomb's guns had received much attention from some of Hazen's Federal troops on the far-right flank as they advanced up the ridge. Slocomb had three of his guns on the spur south of the Bird's Mill Road under the command of Lt. J. Ad. Chalaron and the remaining three under that of Lt. W. C. D. Vaught on a similar eminence farther to the south, near the Crutchfield Road. With Hazen's milling crowd re-forming along the ridge at Tucker's captured position, Slocomb had Chalaron swing his cannon to the right to fire at Hazen's attackers. Unfortunately, there were no infantry supports on the spur with Chalaron's guns, and only a few soldiers from Tyler's Brigade were scattered nearby.[3]

At this point occurred a random incident that helped change the complexion of the battle. Slocomb was running low on ammunition and had just sent for more. "I might have been warranted in withdrawing my battery [having little ammunition and no infantry support]," wrote the aroused Slocomb, "but firm in my reliance upon our infantry rallying and retaking [Tucker's captured] position on my right," he decided to stay and fight. With only a single caisson able to "run the gauntlet" of the enemy's fire and reach Chalaron, Slocomb watched as suddenly two of Chalaron's ammunition-filled caissons exploded in a towering ball of flame. A remarkably accurate shot from Bridges's guns on Orchard Knob, or, as William Bate thought, a shot fired by the captured artillery piece Hazen's and Willich's men were working on the adjacent spur, had struck one of Chalaron's Napoleon caissons, exploding both. When the smoke began to clear, Slocomb saw to his horror the wreckage: dead and wounded gunners, floundering horses, and the shattered debris of his half battery. What remained of Tyler's infantry fled in panic.[4]

Hazen's troops looked on in amazement. They had been exposed to a heavy fire from the adjacent ridge, especially when Slocomb's repositioned guns opened upon them. Now they saw only confusion and scattering enemy troops in the wake of the big explosion on the spur across the Bird's Mill Road. Although there was much disorder among their own ranks at the time and some of Hazen's troops had already gone to the north, most of the brigade had re-formed facing south.[5]

Hazen's soldiers were wild with excitement, and for the moment they had become careless, thought an officer. A flag bearer waving a large flag started with his banner toward the Rebel line, which was seen attempting to re-form at right angles across the crest. It generated an impetuous and spontaneous attack, due entirely to the reckless emotion of the moment, said an amazed lieutenant colonel. Despite their mad rush, he didn't dare attempt to stop them.[6]

Although of mixed regiments and only about thirty men in several clusters, when someone shouted, "Forward," others started at a run toward the frowning muzzles of Slocomb's Battery. Ahead, a few remaining gray gunners were seen desperately attempting to load the Napoleons with canister. Hastily, rounds of canister were rammed down the muzzles and the guns aimed at the charging blue line. Yet there were no friction primers. In the confusion, the primers required for detonation couldn't be found. Chalaron's gunners fled when Hazen's men were within thirty yards. Only a single gun was limbered up and pulled from the spur amid a volley of rifle fire.[7]

"It seemed incredible," reported an Ohio major, but before Hazen's onrushing line reached Slocomb's cannon, the Rebels broke and scattered in every direction. Yelling at the top of their lungs, Hazen's blue-clad soldiers quickly ran among Chalaron's half battery. Prisoners stood everywhere, their hands upraised in surrender. Behind the log barricades, a few lingering Confederate soldiers were found "rolled over on their backs," and they looked up with "pitiful" fright. "We didn't have a moment to lose on them," wrote a much-harried lieutenant colonel, and they ignored these men, leaving them for others to gather up.[8]

Looking to the right, down the western slopes, Hazen's men saw an inspiring sight: "Sheridan's left regiment [was advancing]; they being about one-half way up the ridge." It was all the incentive the handful of blue riflemen needed.[9]

One of Chalaron's abandoned guns was quickly swung about, in the direction of Rebel troops seen clustered about a small house known to be Bragg's headquarters. Although the gun was loaded, the absence of the friction primers posed a problem. Promptly, a quick-thinking soldier from the 41st Ohio Infantry emptied a musket cartridge into the vent, stepped back, and fired his Springfield rifle musket over the opening. The cannon roared and a blast of canister tore into the nearby ridge, showering projectiles and pulverized rock among the scattering gray ranks.[10]

William Bate was a man perplexed. The morning had been exasperating due to marches, countermarches, and an order for his troops at the foot of the ridge to return to the crest—only to have that order countermanded by Breckinridge. The Confederate command staff seemed in disarray, issuing confusing or conflicting orders following their frequently changed perspectives. Bate had told his men in the rifle pits below to fight to the last resort. Yet Reynolds's neighboring troops were ordered to retire to the crest upon the enemy's approach. Bate's greatest difficulty thus centered around the resulting confusion during the renewed Yankee assault.[11]

Bate had just seen "scattered troops a few hundred yards to my right making their way, apparently without resistance, to the top of the [ridge]. Believing them to be Confederates falling back from their trenches, I forbade my right [regiments] from firing on them," he wrote. It was a big mistake. Both Bate's and Tyler's brigades, on the division's right flank, had discovered too late the presence of Hazen's brigade along the adjacent crest—a flag flying where Anderson's Division was posted. Although Bate at first mistook it for a Southern flag, he saw on its "nearer approach" that it was a Yankee flag—the colors of the United States.[12]

Suddenly, the full impact of a disaster rapidly unfolding struck Bate's mind. Not only were Hazen's troops threatening his now-exposed right flank but a long line of blue infantry—Sheridan's division—was swarming up the ridge immediately in front. Ahead of their multiple ranks, scattered clusters of men in gray, Bate's Floridians, were arduously attempting to reach the safety of the crest. Both enemy threats seemed dangerous and perhaps might be fatal. What was Bate to do? He was without reserves. To withdraw troops from the front "would necessarily cause a gap in my line." To leave Hazen's infantry unopposed and in possession of Slocomb's artillery was unthinkable. His entire flank might be wiped out. Braxton Bragg was nearby, riding along the line, congratulating the soldiers for having repulsed the enemy along the slopes below. Bate turned to Bragg for orders.[13]

Lying along the line of captured Rebel rifle pits at the base of Missionary Ridge, a lieutenant of the 36th Illinois in Col. Francis T. Sherman's brigade looked up and saw several riders approaching. One man identified himself as being from Gordon Granger's staff and asked for brigade commander Sherman. "He's up the hill leading the attack," said the lieutenant, pointing. The attack was contrary to orders, announced the staff officer; he said the lieutenant must go up there and tell Colonel Sherman. The lieutenant declined, saying the staff officers would have to communicate with the colonel themselves. As the staff officers galloped off, the lieutenant looked up the slopes. Sherman's was the only brigade still moving forward, their ranks as yet in pyramid formation, with the colors of each regiment in the forefront. The lieutenant became alarmed. There didn't seem to be enough attackers to force their way over the crest. The lieutenant ran along the line, urging the soldiers to go forward and help in the assault. He nearly ran into Phil Sheridan, alighting with a jump from his large black charger. Sheridan was excited. He flung his cape to an aide and ran among the men at the breastworks. "Boys, we're going to take that ridge. Forward, and help your comrades!" he shouted.[14]

Sheridan had been lucky. After awaiting the return of his staff officer sent to Gordon Granger to determine the objective point of attack, Sheridan had joined his men, advancing behind the lines, being fully aware that it was Grant's order to go only as far as the lower rifle pits. Yet Capt. William L. Avery of Granger's staff managed to find Sheridan in the smoke and din and told him that the original orders had been modified to the extent that if in Sheridan's judgment his men could carry the ridge, he should do so. To Sheridan, it was a license for battle, and he acted immediately.[15]

Nearly all of Wagner's, many of Harker's, and some of F. T. Sherman's men were back at the rifle pits below the ridge. Under Sheridan's orders, the men were advanced again. "In going forward a second time," wrote

Lt. John Shellenberger, "the two lines were intermingled . . . [and] the color bearers strived with each other as to which should take the lead." It was a grand sight, never to be forgotten, wrote an observer. Before, as some of Wagner's men had withdrawn from the slopes, the Confederates atop the ridge had yelled out, "Chickamauga!" as a derisive reminder of the bitter defeat of more than two months ago. Now, with Hazen's men already on the crest and Wagner's and Harker's troops following in the wake of F. T. Sherman's, such cries were heard no more from the Rebels. They were too busy fighting in three directions.[16]

Braxton Bragg's reaction had been immediate. He told Bate to stop the flanking attack along the ridge. Although Bate hastily discussed the deteriorating situation in his front with the Confederate commander, Bragg remained insistent. He told Bate to withdraw those troops that could best be spared but to halt the enemy's progress southward along the ridge. Bate thought fast. A portion of the 60th North Carolina of Reynolds's Brigade had drifted back too far to the right during the pullback from the lower rifle pits and was now positioned behind Bate's center. Although only a handful, Bate sent them against Hazen's soldiers, leading them forward in person. For about five hundred yards, the North Carolinians rushed at a double-quick to reach the elevation just captured by the enemy. Suddenly, they stopped. The Yankees were discovered formed in heavy force immediately in front, with Slocomb's captured guns pointed in their direction. Neither Bate nor their regimental commander could induce them to go forward. The 60th North Carolina merely remained stretched across the crest at right angles to Bate's main line, shooting uncertainly at the enemy. Bate soon gave up the project as a forlorn effort, and believing the North Carolinians would at least keep the enemy in check, he returned to his main line, where Sheridan's advanced troops were now dangerously close to the crest.[17]

Most of Finley's Florida Brigade had been deployed that morning at the base of the ridge in a single skirmish line across Bate's division front. Their orders were to fight the Yankees to the last extremity if they attacked, said a Floridian, and they had fought accordingly. "We held our fire until they were about 300 yards of [sic] us . . . then made many of them bite the dust." Yet it was a profitless contest. There must have been 100,000 Yankees, thought a rifleman of the 7th Florida. "We mowed them down until they were within thirty yards of us," but a single rank of gray infantry proved to be no match for Sheridan's oncoming division. Finley's men scrambled back to the second line of breastworks, only about a hundred yards up the ridge, but that effort proved unavailing. The Yankees were too many. The colonel commanding the 1st Florida (dismounted) Cavalry was angered by "the inexplicable fact" that the troops on their right, some of Reynolds's men, had departed the rifle pits as soon as Sheridan's columns began advancing. Unaware that their withdrawal was by order, so as to plug the gap between Bate's and Tucker's lines, Col. Troup Maxwell considered his great dilemma. Bate had not only told Finley's men to hold the position at all hazards but had promised support if needed. Yet there were no troops seen coming down the slopes to reinforce Finley's line. Being outflanked on the right, where the enemy already had possession of the first line of rifle pits, Maxwell gave the order to fall back as F. T. Sherman's Yankees moved close in front. It led to a disastrous tactical circumstance.[18]

The ridge was "dreadful steep," considered a soldier, and the enemy kept up such a continual stream of fire that he felt it a wonder "that they didn't kill all of us." Having on a heavy knapsack, haversack, canteen, and blanket roll, the man didn't think he could make it to the top. Stopping several times to rest and try to remove his knapsack, he found to his chagrin he couldn't get it off. Instead, in frustration he "took a shot at the damned Yankees." As he finally crawled over the crest, there was a heavy blow on his back, and he lay so exhausted that for several moments he couldn't breathe or move. Finally recovering, the man discovered a bullet had struck his knapsack at the right shoulder and passed out diagonally on the left side, making twenty-three separate holes in his blanket roll. The private eventually scrambled behind a log and began shooting Yankees, but he found he was one of only a very few who managed to reach the top.[19]

Col. Robert Bullock, commanding the 7th Florida, was captured on the slopes; he was out of breath and unable to escape due to his beefy physique. In the 4th Florida, Sgt. Washington Ives found only 23 officers and men remaining of the 172 who had been present that morning. Even worse, the ranks of the Florida Brigade along the crest were so thin that an observer estimated there was only one man for every eight feet of breastwork.[20]

Francis T. Sherman's men were almost at the crest. It was steep here along the Crutchfield Road in front of the Thurman house. "The only shelter that we had was now and then a tree, a log, or a stump," wrote an Illinois captain. The flags had been moved up gradually, awaiting the approach of more soldiers, who kept firing at the ridgetop as they continued their climb. Here, just below the crest, the men of the 73rd Illinois, while waiting about twenty minutes to gather sufficient strength, endured rifle fire and an annoying rain of rocks and lighted artillery shells.[21]

In the 24th Wisconsin Infantry, on F. T. Sherman's left flank, eighteen-year-old Lt. Arthur MacArthur, Jr., adjutant of the regiment, looked up the rugged, forbidding ridge. "If you were only here to climb the elevation on a calm, clear day without any impediment it would be considered a big thing," he wrote to his father on the following day. About halfway up the ridge, the 24th's color-bearer became exhausted. "I immediately took [the colors]," wrote MacArthur, "and carried them the balance of the way." Now a conspicuous target, MacArthur, while struggling up the rocky slopes, saw a cannon fired in his direction. An instant later, "a whole dose of canister went through [my flag] tearing it in a frightful manner," wrote the amazed MacArthur. He was lucky. "I only received a scratch, and that through the rim of my hat."[22]

Behind F. T. Sherman's line, Phil Sheridan urged the 73rd Illinois on. "I know you, fix bayonets and go ahead," he had shouted at them. Incoming fire was heavy from the right flank. The lieutenant colonel commanding the 88th Illinois had halted his men, waiting for other troops to advance and draw some of the fire then enfilading his line. "This fire [was] not in any way diminishing," he noted, "[so] I ordered the colors forward."[23]

The rush to the top occurred almost simultaneously in several units. It was claimed the flag of the 74th Illinois was the first from the brigade on the crest. This was disputed by the 36th and 44th Illinois, who also claimed the honor. On F. T. Sherman's left flank, MacArthur dashed forward the last few yards and was among the first to plant a flag on the ridge in front of Bragg's headquarters.*[24]

It was a surprise to many that Confederate resistance was so minimal at the crest. The Floridians and Tyler's Tennesseeans and Georgians vacated the site without much of a fight, said the colonel of the 74th Illinois. For "some unaccountable reason they either fled or surrendered instantly upon the first few of our men reaching them," he added. Cobb's Kentucky Battery was captured almost intact, although the gunners attempted to defend their battery to the last, said Col. Charles G. Harker.[25]

The reason for the quick collapse was plainly evident in the after-action reports of commanders on both sides. Bragg's line was now being assailed from three separate directions. Hazen's advance along the crest from the north had put so much pressure on the 60th North Carolina that it "broke and retired in disorder," said Bate. Bate's own right flank, where Tyler's command of Tennesseeans and Georgians stood, was immediately thrown into disorder. Harker's brigade, on F. T. Sherman's left flank, and some of Wagner's much-delayed soldiers also began spilling over the crest. Amid all the turmoil, Slocomb had attempted to withdraw four of his remaining guns and had gotten off Vaught's and one of Chalaron's, but when they attempted to escape over the eastern ridge, they became mired "axle deep in mud." Scattered soldiers were running past, and Slocomb called for them to help save the guns. "My appeals to them were all in vain," the angry Slocomb later wrote. The enemy was advancing, and Slocomb gave the order to unlimber the guns and save the horses and limbers. Moments later, the guns were abandoned to the enemy, and Bragg's entire midridge line was in utter chaos.[26]

Yet the crowning blow, and what seemed to bother Braxton Bragg the most, was word that A. P. Stewart's Division was being rolled up on the far left flank by Hooker's troops, which had suddenly appeared from Chattanooga Valley. Fearing his position on the ridge was "almost surrounded," Bragg, clearly shaken, had given urgent orders to retreat.[27]

---

*For his action, MacArthur was awarded the Medal of Honor. Later commander of the 24th Wisconsin, MacArthur subsequently became a celebrated and important turn-of-the-century American general. His reputation was exceeded only by that of his son, General of the Army Douglas MacArthur of World War II fame.

Bate saw a Yankee flag waving to the left of Bragg's headquarters. Rifle fire was sweeping across the crest from that direction. His men were running away. Confusion was rampant everywhere he looked. Bate ordered his men to fall back, yet this was useless, said a Florida lieutenant. "The men [already] were retreating without orders." In Havis's Georgia Battery of the Reserve Artillery Battalion, a private looked to the right and left. The Yanks were coming from both directions. "We were ordered to retreat, and we got!" he exclaimed. With so many batteries attempting to limber up and withdraw, it added to the wild scene of confusion, despair, and frustration.[28]

Bate's and Stewart's men dashed for the safety of Missionary Ridge's eastern slopes. Amid "a shower of lead . . . we retreated in great confusion [with] men from different commands all mixed up together," admitted a terrified private. "When I saw a half dozen [enemy] flags across the breastworks," wrote a Florida private, "I tried to save myself." Yet, being loaded down with accoutrements and equipment, he couldn't move fast enough. A minié ball slammed into his leg. He tried to limp onward, yet was soon surrounded and forced to surrender. Minutes later, he was nearly shot again when, in the confusion, other advancing Yankees saw the milling gray soldiers and fired as they ran past. "The bullets whistled by me fast," he wrote, but he was not injured.[29]

"Missionary Ridge was ours!" wrote a jubilant Federal soldier. Such a scene could never be imagined, thought another. Amid deafening yells, the men "went wild with joy," wrote one of Harker's captains. "They shook hands, and hugged each other, tossed their hats in the air, danced, sung, cheered, and some of them whooped and yelled like a lot of drunken demons." Colonel Harker, overjoyed with the success, jumped from his horse and ran among the captured guns of Cobb's Battery. "One of the guns had the name 'Lady Buckner' and another 'Lady Breckinridge' painted on the trail." Harker jumped on the "Lady Breckinridge," seating himself astride the breech, and began yelling exultantly. An instant later, he bolted off the cannon and flung himself to the ground. His amazed men began laughing; the gunmetal was still so hot from repeated firing "that it would burn your fingers to touch it," joked a soldier.[30]

Phil Sheridan was soon among his soldiers, and the men gathered around him cheering. "How do you like this, General!" they joyously shouted. Arthur MacArthur, Jr., displayed his canister-ripped flag to Sheridan, and the general was impressed. Sheridan was still bantering with his men when an exploding shell threw mud "over horse and rider." Sheridan, shaken, yelled, "Form your lines, boys, and charge 'em." It was a sobering reminder of the work remaining. The enemy was attempting to escape, and, looking around, Sheridan's soldiers saw gray uniforms scattering into the nearby woods. Along the Crutchfield Road, there existed a scene of "wildest confusion." Wagons, caissons, and soldiers were jammed together in a crowded mass, all trying to get away.[31]

Dashing among the silent guns of Cobb's Kentucky Battery, some of F. T. Sherman's men wheeled the captured cannon about to fire into Bragg's fleeing ranks. They found rammers halfway down the muzzles in two of the guns—they were in the process of being loaded when abandoned. Within minutes, the roar of these big guns reverberated across the ridge and their projectiles tore into the crowd of fugitives escaping along the road. Beside the guns, a captured Confederate gunner sat crying. He had tried to defend the guns to the last, wielding a rammer menacingly when surrounded. An Irishman, he now kept moaning amid his tears, "This bathery was niver caphthured before."[32]

It was all over along the crest near Bragg's headquarters. The advance to, climbing of, and capture of mid–Missionary Ridge had taken about an hour and a half, observed an officer. It was now nearly sundown, and as various units re-formed to pursue the departed Rebels, souvenir hunters were seen picking over the scattered trophies. A lieutenant found a brass scabbard inscribed to one of Bragg's staff officers. Another soldier of the 73rd Illinois discovered a magnificent gray horse and presented it to his colonel, who had lost two horses at Chickamauga. Later given to Phil Sheridan, the horse was named Breckinridge because it allegedly came from one of Breckinridge's staff officers. In the last days of the war, Sheridan rode his captured gray "through the mud" at Petersburg and always remembered with pride that it came from the stunning victory at Chattanooga.[33]

On the captured ridge, the victors' emotions remained high as the sun began to sink low. "Was not Chickamauga avenged?" asked a veteran Ohio soldier. "The taking of Missionary Ridge was one of the marvelous feats of arms of all ages!" he proclaimed. At that time, not even a frazzled Braxton Bragg would argue the point.[34]

CHAPTER 37

"HERE'S YOUR MULE!"

Maj. Gen. Joe Hooker's progress from Chattanooga Creek on the afternoon of November 25 had been halting at best. Confronted about noon by the burned bridge along the Rossville Road at Chattanooga Creek, the pioneers had to work until about 3:00 P.M. to reconstruct enough of the bridge to get Osterhaus's leading troops across. Meanwhile, a single regiment, the 27th Missouri Infantry, was sent across on a makeshift bridge fashioned of stringers and driftwood in order to scout ahead. As the construction continued, they advanced and encountered Confederates posted in Rossville Gap, about a mile and a half southeast along the same road.[1]

The enemy had four field guns with infantry formed on both sides of the gap, so the Missourians opened a skirmish fire and waited for Hooker's column to arrive. It was nearly 4:00 P.M. when Osterhaus's leading brigade, that of Brig. Gen. Charles R. Woods, appeared along the Rossville Road. Osterhaus waited until portions of his second brigade appeared, then sent Woods to the right and Col. James A. Williamson with the trailing regiments to seize the ridge to the left. These units had hardly begun their advance when the Confederates in front, two regiments of Clayton's Brigade, abandoned their position and withdrew along the road south. The 27th Missouri promptly moved up to occupy the gap, discovering there much abandoned equipment, ammunition, wagons, ambulances, and even a house full of commissary stores. Yet it was a hollow victory.[2]

Thus far, the Federal occupation of Rossville Gap was as much a setback as a victory. Hooker had expended an enormous amount of time in reaching a point where Grant had expected him to be hours earlier. Hooker, who still remained cautious, having deployed several regiments in a defensive position to the north while Osterhaus advanced south, failed to realize that the Confederates were not in great strength on his front. When Osterhaus stopped after pursuing Clayton's fleeing men to a fork in the road about a quarter mile beyond Rossville Gap, there was no one present to give orders. An officer had to be sent back to find and obtain instructions from Hooker, who was still some distance in the rear. Although Dan Butterfield, Hooker's chief of staff, soon appeared with the specific orders, the sound of heavy fighting northward along Missionary Ridge warned all that a decisive fight was already in progress. This noise was so loud, "it seemed as though it would bring on an earthquake," thought an awed infantryman. The urgency of Hooker's rapid movement was now evident to all.[3]

Fighting Joe Hooker's spur-of-the-moment tactical plan conformed to what Grant had sought: to sweep northward along Missionary Ridge and roll up Bragg's left flank. Yet, so far as it now appeared, there were no Rebels present to drive northward along the ridge. Hooker made his dispositions accordingly. He ordered Osterhaus, in advance, to turn left and march northward along the eastern valley bordering Missionary Ridge. By merely following the Y in the road along the base of the ridge, Osterhaus would have a clear path to the enemy's rear, wherever that might be found. Meanwhile, Brig. Gen. Charles R. Cruft's demi-division of two brigades, which was marching in Osterhaus's rear, would climb to the crest of Missionary Ridge and follow it northward. Brig. Gen. John W. Geary's trailing division would march in tandem with Cruft in the valley along the western base of Missionary Ridge. In all, three main columns would advance northward, being mutually supportive and capable of sweeping any Rebels from their respective fronts.[4]

Before Hooker's troops advanced, there was a curious event that soon had many of the soldiers abuzz. Along the road south of Rossville appeared a Confederate lieutenant riding a small roan horse. The Rebel officer was completely oblivious that the gap was no longer occupied by his troops, and he rode among Osterhaus's men. Suddenly discovering he was among the enemy, he attempted to bluff his way out. After asking for an ambulance to remove a wounded officer on the ridge, he coyly turned his mount and attempted to ride away slowly. The lieutenant had reached the side of the ridge and "put spurs to his horse" when he abruptly ran into the skirmish line of the 9th Iowa. Brought to a halt by their leveled rifles, the lieutenant was made to dismount and surrender. It proved to be Lt. J. Cabell Breckinridge, the general's son. His horse was soon appropriated by Osterhaus for his personal use.[5]

Hooker's advance along the south ridge was under way shortly after 4:00 P.M. Cruft's was the biggest assignment, and he anxiously rode ahead with his staff and a small cavalry escort to scout the crest of the ridge. It nearly cost him his life. Riding up over the top, he came face-to-face with a skirmish line of Confederate infantry. A volley of shots rang out, and Cruft and his party scattered for their lives. Back through the advancing ranks of the 9th Indiana raced some of Cruft's cavalry escort.[6]

Immediately forming a line of battle, Col. Isaac C. B. Suman of the 9th Indiana Infantry ordered bayonets fixed and told his men to charge without firing a shot until they reached the enemy's first line. Suman's men never had a chance to close with the Rebel skirmishers. They fled before the 9th Indiana reached their breastworks. Suman's soldiers fired a sharp volley into the enemy's scattering ranks, then peered intently ahead.[7]

Three hundred yards distant, the main line of Confederate breastworks lay exposed, being the very works erected by Rosecrans's soldiers during their retreat from Chickamauga two months earlier. When Colonel Suman looked to his rear and saw Cruft's supporting infantry appear over the brow of the ridge, he ordered another charge. Again the 9th Indiana sprang forward; again the Confederates fled before their approach. Yelling at the top of their lungs, Suman's riflemen cleared the second line of breastworks and rounded up "some 200 prisoners." After pushing onward another two hundred yards, Suman halted to await the arrival of his supports. An amazed colonel of an Illinois regiment, just then puffing up to Suman's line, saw that there was nothing to do; "the gallant 9th [had] monopolized the entire affair," he later complained in jest.[8]

To the lieutenant colonel commanding the 58th Alabama Infantry of Clayton's battle line, John W. Inzer, the whole encounter had spelled disaster before it had fairly begun. Their all-Alabama brigade had retreated from Lookout Mountain early that morning, and after marching all night the men were exhausted and discouraged. To make matters worse, as the day wore on, Clayton's men were shifted from a position near Bragg's headquarters to the far-left flank, in the direction of the Rossville Gap, from which they had marched about daylight.[9]

Arriving near the gap, a single regiment, the 18th Alabama, took position as skirmishers in part of the old breastworks the Yankees had abandoned after Chickamauga. The balance of the brigade was then split into several segments for deployment along the ridge and at Rossville Gap. About forty minutes following their arrival here, the Yankees had appeared on the ridge. When the 18th Alabama gave way at the skirmish line, Clayton's men had attempted to form in line of battle. Yet two regiments, the 36th and 38th Alabama, broke and ran back through the brigade line, creating much confusion. Inzer, with the 58th Alabama, had attempted to defend the second line of breastworks, planting their battle flag and trying to rally his men when some of Cruft's Yankees were seen passing beyond the 58th's left flank. "I never worked so hard in my life," later wrote Inzer. Yet it was of little avail. Someone shouted, "Retreat," and the entire brigade scattered. "I stood there until every man left me," wrote the angered Inzer. He ordered them to stop. "Come back and fight," he yelled. They kept on running. A hundred yards in the rear, Inzer saw Col. J. T. Holtzclaw sitting on his horse. Running up to him, Inzer begged for help. Holtzclaw shook his head no. The order, said the colonel, was to fall back. Holtzclaw then put spurs to his horse, leaving Inzer to escape as best he could. Running to the right, down the face of the eastern slopes, Inzer plunged into some tall "hogweeds." They were so thick, he couldn't see anything. All the while, rifle fire from the hill on the left zipped through the weeds. Stumbling down to the bottom of the ridge, Inzer saw several men on an adjacent spur waving their hats. The noise and confusion was enormous. Inzer attempted to reach what he recognized as some of his officers. To his amazement, on his arrival he discovered they were prisoners. All around them stood Yankees with rifle muskets and gleaming bayonets. "I stuck my sword in the ground and became a prisoner," wrote the glum Inzer.[10]

Clayton's Brigade had broken apart in the face of Cruft's attack, only to run straight into Osterhaus's men along the eastern base of the ridge. "We've got 'em in a pen," the gleeful Osterhaus had yelled while watching nearby. About two thousand prisoners were claimed by Osterhaus, together with a single six-pounder brass field gun, captured during the earlier withdrawal from Rossville Gap. Cruft reported casualties numbering four men killed and thirty wounded. It was a disaster of the first magnitude for Bragg's army. Clayton's Brigade, all but obliterated, had been the only troops protecting the extreme Confederate left flank. Even more ominous, it represented the extent of fighting for Bragg's southern flank on Missionary Ridge.[11]

As Cruft's men re-formed and advanced along the crest, there was virtually no opposition. The Rebels seemed to have all but vanished. For more than a mile, Cruft's men streamed northward, with only a few enemy soldiers seen scattering from their front. "Old Gen. Hooker" was there, observed an eager officer, "riding along with his horse's nose just behind our file closers, as serene as if nothing of moment was going on." To a jubilant soldier of the 13th Illinois, reveling in the scene about him, it was a supreme moment. Their regiment had just captured the flag of the 18th Alabama, and "we were after them." Other troops "had shaken the tree, [and now] we were holding the bag to get the fruit."[12]

Those troops "shaking the tree" beyond Hooker's front were from the four-thousand-man division of Brig. Gen. Richard W. Johnson, posted on the extreme right flank of George H. Thomas's line. Johnson was up against A. P. Stewart's Division, extending southward from Bate's line along the Bragg's headquarters front and composed of three small brigades, Gibson's, Strahl's, and Stovall's, plus Clayton's detached brigade sent to guard the ridge along the far-southern flank.[13]

The Federal assault here, like those of T. J. Wood and Sheridan, was not without setbacks. Johnson's two brigades, those of Brig. Gen. William P. Carlin and Col. William L. Stoughton, had experienced difficulty after linking up on the southern flank with Sheridan's division. Carlin, who had cooperated with Hooker on the twenty-fourth, had been told by that general "to get out of the way" on the twenty-fifth, and he eventually rejoined the Fourteenth Corps, barely in time for the assault on Missionary Ridge. His brigade, on approaching the base of the ridge, discovered that they were overlapped on the right by the greater length of A. P. Stewart's line.[14]

Soon brought to a halt along the line of the lower rifle pits, Carlin's men had attempted to go forward to escape the heavy fire, only to be driven back. Here many of the 2nd Ohio's soldiers were thrown into confusion by a counterattack led by Georgians of Brig. Gen. Marcellus A. Stovall's Brigade. The ability to defend the imposing ridge successfully was thus well demonstrated by Stovall's men. They mirrored the successful tactics of Cleburne on the far-northern flank in seizing the initiative and counterattacking once the enemy's initial impetus had been stopped. Yet Johnson's two brigades were too many for the Georgians. The colonel of the 2nd Ohio was finally able to rally his men by having a bugler blow "halt," and "to the colors." In the 19th Illinois, someone shouted, "On, up the ridge!" Led by Stoughton's brigade on the left flank, which included many army regulars, Johnson's division scrambled toward the crest, pushing the detached infantry of Stovall's, Gibson's, and Strahl's brigades in front of them.[15]

The experience of one of Strahl's Tennessee riflemen was typical. With the enemy breaking over the lower rifle pits, Pvt. Joseph E. Riley of the 33rd Tennessee attempted to retreat from the second line of breastworks, halfway up the ridge. Bragg's artillery was firing rapidly at the attackers from atop the crest, and amid the incoming fire from Federal cannon along the Chattanooga perimeter, Riley didn't know whether it was a Confederate or an enemy shell that burst nearby. A heavy fragment struck Riley's left side, and he felt it pass through his body, just under his right shoulder. The thought raced through his mind that he was dying and had only moments to live. Catching his breath, he groped for the wound to stanch the flow. Instead of blood, he found a knot "the size of a goose egg." The projectile hadn't broken the skin, although he later discovered two broken ribs. Struggling to his feet, he saw some Yankees only about a hundred yards away. He attempted to run, but his legs wouldn't carry him. Riley collapsed to the ground, was captured, and later sent to Rock Island (Illinois) Prison.[16]

Like Riley, most of Strahl's, Gibson's, and Stovall's troops, detached by the order splitting their units in half (with part posted below and the other portion remaining on the crest), never made it to the top of the ridge. The thin Confederate line along the crest had very little chance. Johnson's two brigades spilled over the brow, with some of Stoughton's troops being among the first to plant their flags there.[17]

Like T. J. Wood's and Sheridan's troops elsewhere along the ridge, Stoughton's and then Carlin's men spread to the right and left, capturing many prisoners, including the colonel of the 7th Florida. When the 2nd Ohio finally reached the crest, Carlin sent them to the right. Here they ran head-on into the remnant of the 38th Alabama of Clayton's Brigade. The exhausted gray soldiers quickly surrendered, and the 2nd Ohio gathered up about 250 prisoners, including the 38th's lieutenant colonel and major.[18]

Following word of Clayton's rout and the advance of Cruft's troops along their southern flank, Bragg's line had all but disintegrated in panic when Johnson's division made their final push forward. "I can never forget the look of despair [etched on the face] of one poor wounded Rebel as he lay there begging us not to kill him," wrote a soldier of the 104th Illinois. "I stopped and gave him a drink of water from my canteen," he continued. The man later told him how their officers had warned them that if they fell into enemy hands, they would be killed.[19]

Nearby, through the drifting smoke, the Illinois soldiers saw a Confederate officer on a white horse, followed by his staff, galloping diagonally across their front. Shots were fired and many other soldiers raised their rifle muskets, but an officer cried out that it was General Hooker and not to fire. The men grumbled. It surely was Braxton Bragg, so the story later circulated. The men of the 33rd Ohio in Carlin's brigade were determined not to let another general, seen riding toward them in an overcoat with a fur collar, get away. Amid the leveled rifles of the Ohioans, the colonel of the 2nd Ohio rushed up to demand his sword. The general's face was creased with smiles. "Ah, colonel, this is glorious," he exclaimed. It was General Osterhaus, in the vanguard of Hooker's troops. The rifles were quickly lowered.[20]

It was near sundown, and as Cruft's men neared the vicinity of Breckinridge's headquarters at midridge, they saw the already-celebrating soldiers of Richard W. Johnson's brigade in their front. Hooker's men had at last joined Thomas's. "The cheering was tremendous," wrote an overjoyed lieutenant. Missionary Ridge was secured to the Federal army for more than four and one half miles. It was real evidence of an enormous Union victory, one that had seemed almost too easy at the critical moments. The soldiers' wild euphoria, involving the rounding up of the defeated enemy, presented "a fit scene for a painting," remarked an Ohio veteran. "It was a great sight," even surpassing the taking of Lookout Mountain, considered another. "I never before saw our men do so well, nor the Rebels so badly," gloated a jubilant major. The Federal army's great victory was soon formally proclaimed by Gordon Granger, who went forward to see for himself what had happened on the still-smoldering ridge. After rushing to Bragg's captured headquarters, Granger signaled at 6:00 P.M. a classic comment that seemed to sum up a remarkable day: "I think we have them."[21]

Granger's message was in marked contrast to the situation a mere two hours earlier. All but forgotten in the continuing celebration were the earlier events on the north end of Missionary Ridge, when it had appeared the battle was all but lost.

Braxton Bragg had suffered a crushing, almost incomprehensible defeat. His actions along the eastern ridge suggested as much as the last of his troops broke for the safety of the valley below. Chaos prevailed everywhere he looked. "[It was] a panic which I never before witnessed," admitted the shocked Bragg. He attempted to rally the men and got down off his horse. "I am here," he shouted. "Stop, don't disgrace yourselves, fight for your country!" The men around him kept on running. Bragg's cursing, yelling, and pleading had no effect. There was little respect for command authority among the bewildered, frightened throng, especially for Bragg. At one point, a burly private, irked by Bragg's continuing harangue, grabbed the Confederate commander around the waist. After carrying him backward for some distance, the man shouted, "And here's your mule," before dropping him unceremoniously on the ground.[22]

By the time he joined the crowd of fleeing soldiers, Bragg appeared to be scared. "He looked so hacked and whipped," noted a soldier. All along the road as the men noticed him, there were disparaging shouts. It was a special misery for the man who had created so much agony within his own army. With yells of "Bully for Bragg, he's hell on retreat" ringing in his ears, Braxton Bragg stumbled down the Crutchfield Road toward Chickamauga Station, a forlorn, beaten man.[23]

On Orchard Knob, a stunned but game Ulysses S. Grant was anxious to go and see the compelling sights atop the captured ridge. A civilian visitor, excited by the prospect of a victory ride with Grant, mounted his horse and galloped into town to fill his whiskey flask. He was gone only fifteen minutes, the man estimated, but when he returned, Grant, with Rowley and his staff, had already departed for Missionary Ridge. After the man caught up with the general atop the ridge, which was still hazy with battle smoke, Grant remarked to his friend that he was very lucky to be here. "It wasn't in half a dozen lifetimes one could see so much of a battle with comparatively so little danger," said the suddenly ebullient Grant. The Federal commander appeared truly amazed by the magnitude of this major victory, achieved with apparently minimal losses. "I can account for this only on the theory that the enemy's surprise at the audacity of such a charge caused confusion and purposeless aiming of their pieces," Grant later wrote in his official report. Grant rode along the lines of his celebrating men, taking off his hat and pausing to thank the soldiers as he passed some of Willich's troops. There were deafening yells and shouts.[24]

A few minutes later, a lieutenant attached to Grant's staff, dispatched for ammunition for the captured cannon, was suddenly shot from his horse while less than a hundred yards from the Federal commander. The Enfield rifle ball struck the aide between the shoulders, passed around his neck, and came out above the collarbone in front. Ulysses S. Grant's face never flinched. He knew now that it was all meant to be—his famous good luck was still intact.[25]

CHAPTER 38

THE NIGHT OF
THE LONG SHADOWS

Disaster was in the air along Missionary Ridge. In six locations along the crest, the breakthrough had occurred, resulting in the collapse of Confederate resistance a mile south of Tunnel Hill and beyond. Moreover, portions or all of the brigades of Hazen, Willich, Beatty, Turchin, Van Derveer, and Phelps had turned north along the crest, and an ever-expanding wave of blue began to engulf what had been intended as the objective point of Sherman's attack, but from the opposite direction.[1]

William J. Hardee was beside himself. Ironically, although on the previous evening he had urged a withdrawal, only to be ignored, Hardee was now being asked to save much of what remained of Bragg's army. As commander of Bragg's right wing, Hardee had no sooner begun to relax following Cleburne's repulse of Sherman than he learned of the collapse at midridge. Utilizing troops marched from the far left and Lookout Mountain during the night of the twenty-fourth, Hardee attempted to form a line at right angles across the ridge, about a quarter mile beyond the northernmost point of the Yankee breakthrough. Here, nearly a mile and a half south of the railroad tunnel, Hardee intended to make his stand.[2]

Frank Cheatham's Division clearly would bear the brunt of the initial onslaught, and already two of his brigades, John C. Moore's and John K. "Mudwall" Jackson's on the far left, had attempted to stem the tide of Yankees rolling northward along the ridge. The result was nearly another disaster. Jackson's line had hurriedly formed at right angles across the ridge and attempted to hold back the Yankees, mostly from Baird's division, just north of the ground where Phelps's brigade had crossed the ridge.[3]

Phelps's troops, now commanded by Col. William H. Hays, following

Phelps's death, had refreshed themselves from a mountain stream along the ridge's slopes and were mixed with Van Derveer's and Turchin's troops as they pressed forward along the narrow crest. Across a small gorge Jackson's men were seen formed in considerable force. Hays pushed his men onward, up to the edge of the gorge, and opened a brisk fire. Jackson's men began to waver. From the left, several regiments pushed ahead into the gorge and dashed toward Jackson's line. For a few minutes, the fighting raged "the hardest of the day," thought some Ohio soldiers, but soon "the enemy broke and fled precipitately." Pvt. James C. Walker of the 31st Ohio ran among the scattering gray ranks, shouting, "Surrender!" All around him were Rebels with their hands upraised. Suddenly, in the confusion, one defiant Confederate reached down and grabbed a rifle, shooting a passing Ohioan in the knee. Before Walker could strike the man down with his rifle butt, another private jammed the muzzle of his gun into the Rebel's chest and pulled the trigger. At the loud report, the man collapsed, dead. "Now, damn you, you have surrendered," shouted the angry Federal private.[4]

Behind Jackson's line, John C. Moore's troops were attempting, per Frank Cheatham's orders, to pass behind the line and form on the left flank. Yet, said Moore, Jackson's troops suddenly came "rushing back through the ranks of mine," creating chaos in both brigades. Moore attempted to rally his men, but Mudwall Jackson was nowhere to be found, said Moore.[5]

Fortunately for Hardee, John C. Brown's and Walthall's brigades were forming by Hardee's direction at right angles across the ridge less than a quarter of a mile away. The appearance of yet another seemingly strong Confederate line atop a large knoll was enough to dissuade Hays and the other mixed-command troops. The Yankees never approached closer than two hundred yards, noted Ed Walthall, who was painfully shot in the foot in the gathering darkness. Aided by Moore's and Jackson's rallying men, the grim but determined Walthall was prepared to sacrifice his command if necessary to save the Confederate right wing.[6]

Although division commander Absalom Baird was present, he ordered that the pursuit be halted. The enemy could be reached "only over a long, narrow neck of ground," wrote the battle-weary Baird, and the near darkness and disorganization among his troops made him apprehensive. At dusk on November 25, 1863, the north end of Missionary Ridge appeared more as a forbidding series of hills rather than an extended ridge. Abrupt knolls, tangled ravines, and a tortuous crest, sometimes less than a hundred feet wide, hindered easy communications and transit. Baird had gathered enough laurels for the day and was soon fretting about the Rebel artillery captured by his men being appropriated by troops of other commands.[7]

The major fighting of the day was over. With ammunition running low, the exhausted Federal field commanders were only too glad to halt, entrench, care for the wounded, and count the many captured cannon and prisoners. An Ohio infantryman watched as the sun sank low on the western horizon, gilding the crest of Missionary Ridge in golden rays. Then as darkness fell, the scattered firing sputtered to a halt and an eerie quiet prevailed on the tortured ridges overlooking Chattanooga.[8]

Hardee had been lucky. His message to Pat Cleburne following the rout of Jackson's and Moore's troops revealed his mounting desperation. Cleburne was given the "appalling news" that the enemy now controlled the center of Bragg's position along the ridge. The Confederate army was split into two isolated segments and was in jeopardy of being cut off and forced to surrender. Cleburne was told to prepare to meet an imminent attack; the safety of the right wing was in his hands, warned Hardee.[9]

Cleburne, moments before, could hardly conceive of a Southern defeat, yet he hastily acted to form a reserve line, and he personally went forward with two brigades dispatched to the aid of Cheatham's line. It was a race with nightfall, Cleburne seemed to realize. As his troops went forward to help Cheatham, he ordered a force to guard the vital Shallow Ford bridge across Chickamauga Creek so as to secure the right wing's line of retreat. When the enemy failed to advance, at 7:45 P.M. Hardee gave the order to retreat behind the covering banks of Chattanooga Creek. One by one, the Southern units withdrew, until by 9:00 P.M. everything was across, said Cleburne, except the dead and a few stragglers. The last to leave the north of Missionary Ridge was Smith's Texas Brigade, which had fought so well along the bloody Tunnel Hill perimeter. "Sadly, but not fearfully," wrote the prideful Cleburne, "this band of heroes left the hill they had held so well and followed the [retreating] army across the Chickamauga."[10]

On nearby mid–Missionary Ridge, an Illinois soldier sat down to record in his journal how the Rebels had been last seen fleeing in utter disarray. "We had more fun laughing over it than we have had since the Battle of Pea Ridge," he penned in gleeful spirits.[11]

Not far distant, a private in the 35th Ohio, an excellent soldier and a member of the color company, wearily sat down to eat. From the opposite side of the ridge, there was the angry zip of a rifle ball and a dull thud. The private collapsed to the ground, mortally wounded. A stray rifle ball had found its mark, claiming perhaps the last victim of the Battle of Chattanooga.[12]

For both Cleburne's men and the unlucky Federal soldier, it was but a sad misfortune, befitting the injustice and insanity of war.

Along the Crutchfield Road, some of the "debris" from Braxton Bragg's left-wing segment had been rallied with much difficulty before nightfall by Bragg and William Bate west of Chickamauga Creek. Here they hoped the men would stand long enough to hold back Sheridan's pursuit, enabling the army to cross on the pontoon bridge at Bird's Mill. It was a mixed Confederate command, mostly of Bate's and A. P. Stewart's men, formed along a ridge and high knoll about two-thirds of a mile beyond the captured main ridge. Bate had eight field guns, mostly from the reserve battalion, which he put in charge of Captain Slocomb. Bate's orders were to hold as long as possible, then retreat across Chickamauga Creek to Chickamauga Station, where Bragg hoped to reunite the army.[13]

Phil Sheridan's ardor was at fever pitch. From the top of Missionary Ridge looking eastward, he could see Bragg's routed troops fleeing in crowds through the valley below. Jammed along the Crutchfield Road within half a mile was a large Rebel wagon train, with artillery and ambulances snarling and delaying the traffic flow. For Sheridan, the tempting target was too much to overlook. Without orders, he sent portions of two brigades, Wagner's and Harker's, in pursuit, ordering them to take as much of the wagon train as possible.[14]

The 40th Indiana and 97th Ohio of Wagner's brigade were in advance, animated by the "rout of the enemy." Boxes of stores, about two hundred prisoners, and two wagons with their teams were soon captured at the foot of the eastern ridge. Wagner's two regiments eagerly hastened on, urged forward by Wagner in person. About a half mile farther down the road, Wagner's men encountered a crescent-shaped ridge, along which the enemy was posted. The Ohioans were particularly confident; the beaten enemy seemed only to be desperately attempting to get away. Undoubtedly, once these remnants were pushed, they, too, would flee.[15]

The 97th Ohio was on the 40th's left flank and took the lead in rushing forward in gathering darkness over level ground toward the steep ridge. They ran head on into a butcher's bill of casualties. Swept from the ridge by blasts of canister from Bate's guns, and with rifle balls passing "almost in every direction, front and flanks," the 97th and 40th suffered a quick and bloody repulse. The heavy swish of canister sounded to one rifleman "like flocks of wild geese sweeping past." Indeed, this "murderous" fire claimed more men in the 97th than had been lost in assaulting Missionary Ridge. The Ohio regiment reported a loss of 149 officers and men of the 434 present. Forty of the 40th Indiana were killed and wounded, and added to their previous loss of 118, nearly 45 percent of those engaged now numbered as casualties. Later, the colonel of the 40th wrote, "To storm the hill with the force we then had was clearly impossible." Wagner's two regiments thus took shelter in the dark valley and continued firing at Bate's troops. This disastrous incident was discussed among Sheridan's soldiers. An officer admitted, "The opinion prevailed among us that . . . the attack had been made too rashly." Bragg's men were still dangerous and would fight, they now understood, which "was surprising considering how anxious they seemed to be to get away."[16]

Sheridan soon heard of the bloody repulse and came forward with two of Wagner's other regiments, the 15th Indiana and 26th Ohio. The fighting continued for more than an hour, when Opdycke's demi-brigade from Harker's brigade came up, and about 9:00 P.M. Sheridan ordered an attack. The 26th Ohio and 15th Indiana swung wide to the left, gaining the top of the ridge unopposed, then came rushing along the crest to stampede Bate's soldiers. Two field guns were abandoned and Bate's infantry once more streamed to the rear. Sheridan watched from below as Wagner's men were outlined by the rising moon, which provided "a medallion view of the column . . . as they crossed the moon's disk."[17]

Despite Sheridan's claim that it had been "a gallant little fight," the whole affair had been unnecessary, according to one of Wagner's officers. A strong skirmish line might have done equally well in capturing stragglers, abandoned guns, and equipment. Moreover, outflanking any stand by the enemy's rear guard was the way the pursuit should have been conducted, he asserted.[18]

Harker was in the act of organizing a further pursuit when Sheridan called a halt—he noticed his troops were the only ones chasing after Bragg's army. For several hours, the men rested, then about 1:00 A.M. Harker's and Wagner's men were again aroused, issued ammunition, and ordered to pursue in the direction of Chickamauga Station. The weary men stumbled along the road for about three miles, but upon arrival about 3:00 A.M. at the Bird's Mill site, they found the bridge burned and no way to cross. Once again, Sheridan had been thwarted. Soon he was complaining his men had been sent in pursuit while T. J. Wood's division remained on Missionary Ridge, enabling Hazen's Brigade to gather up and claim the capture of artillery that Sheridan said his men had taken. Wood's subsequent report was "untruthful," growled Sheridan, and eleven of his captured guns were "gleaned from the battlefield and appropriated [by Hazen] while I was pushing the enemy on to Chickamauga Station."[19]

At 7:00 P.M., as Sheridan's men had begun their pursuit, Braxton Bragg was at Chickamauga Station, telegraphing a brief message to the Davis administration in Richmond: "After several unsuccessful assaults on our lines today, the enemy carried the left center about 4 o'clock. The whole left soon gave way in considerable disorder. The right maintained its ground, repelling every attack. I am withdrawing all to this point."[20]

Bragg's murky pretense was fully evident when within hours his circular orders went out to the troops. "Corps commanders will immediately put their commands in motion toward Ringgold, [Georgia] keeping their trains in front." When it was found the troops were too disorderly to march immediately, the orders were revised to start the troops at 2:00 A.M. Only the inky blackness of the night sky obscured the towering column of smoke as the bridges across Chickamauga Creek went up in flames. "Fortunately, it was . . . nightfall and the country and roads in our rear were fully known to us, but equally unknown to the enemy," Bragg reasoned. It was a remarkable admission. Bragg's planning had now been reduced to the bare essentials of survival.[21]

It was the night of the long shadows, remembered a haunted Federal enlisted man. About 10:00 P.M., the moon was shining peacefully across the landscape, revealing the awful carnage of war. "How ghastly the faces [of the dead and wounded] look in the moonlight," observed a soldier. To a Federal chaplain, the scene of suffering at the foot of the ridge, amid the old Rebel huts, was terrible. "In every direction could be seen fires which had been kindled, and about them lay the wounded, trying to keep warm." A wounded soldier of the 58th Indiana pleaded with the chaplain—if nothing was done for him, he would die, he gasped—yet, grieved the chaplain, "I could do nothing to afford the poor fellow relief, and he died the next day."[22]

All across the battlefield, about six miles in length along the rugged ridge, lay wounded men groaning and crying out for help. Scattered amid the debris of battle, they were suffering with intense cold. Yet the chaplain saw "parties of thieves" prowling among the dead and wounded, looking for valuables and trophies. "I am in favor of leaving a detail . . . to shoot down these cowardly scoundrels who remain behind to rob the dead," he soberly declared. "It must have been midnight when I reached my quarters," the chaplain wrote wearily. "My horse and myself were worn down. It seemed as if the experience of a month had been crowded into a [single] day."[23]

"It is awfully cold tonight," noted an Illinois officer in his journal, and he thought of the effect on the wounded men "who must lie on the field all night." Soldiers in the 59th Illinois carried canteens of water to some wounded Confederates lying nearby. A few men with stretchers were seen gathering up some of the wounded. There was a distant "ki yi ki yi." A small dog along the skirmish line had been hit by a minié ball. A thousand fires glimmered in the evening darkness; they were beacons of survival and a testament to the resilience of the soldiers. These were the impressions and sounds of the aftermath, vignettes of a war beyond measure in agony and ordeal.[24]

CHAPTER 39

"THE UNACCOUNTABLE
SPIRIT OF THE TROOPS"

The fighting on Missionary Ridge was a disgrace, reflected a still-appalled Confederate general many years later. "We were beaten . . . because of the great numerical disparity . . . and because the disposition of our forces was injudicious in the extreme." Bragg, said Arthur M. Manigault, was the main culprit. He had been "completely out generaled," was overconfident, and had badly underestimated his enemy. Manigault marveled that Hooker's force had been so dilatory in reaching the Confederate left flank. Had they appeared at an earlier time, said Manigault, the Confederate army "must have been forced to surrender or been destroyed on the following day."[1]

Bragg, writing shortly after the battle, termed the conduct of his troops on Missionary Ridge "shameful," this "bad conduct" being attributed to the intimidating sight of the enemy "marshaling his immense forces in plain view." The "great disaster and disgrace" would be investigated, promised Bragg, and "full justice shall be done to the good and bad." Three days after the fight, William Bate chastised many of his men for being so panic-stricken as to throw away their rifles during the fighting, calling each "a coward and a traitor to himself, his family, and his country." Even unit commanders such as Capt. Cuthbert H. Slocomb of the Washington Artillery were so incensed as to complain in after-action reports of the "unusual timidity of our infantry," who were found "abandoning their works without a struggle."[2]

Federal commanders, searching for a suitable explanation, chose phrases such as the enemy had been "dumbfounded by the audacity of the assault" and had become "sick of the war" and thus were "demoralized by the attack." To Charles A. Dana, the result had been "a visible interposition of God," as reflected by "the unaccountable spirit of the troops which bore them bodily up those impracticable slopes." Ulysses S. Grant attributed the victory on the ridge to confusion among Bragg's soldiers and the "purposeless aiming of their pieces." Years later, he would write in his memoirs that one of Bragg's gravest mistakes was "in placing so much of a force on the plain in front of his impregnable position."[3]

For years, the popular concept of the Confederate infantry inexplicably giving way from an "impregnable" location without reason or justification was to be nurtured and embellished until it became the fabric of history. The Confederate defeat at Missionary Ridge was unexplainable to so many Southerners that it became a psychological millstone around the neck of their soldiers. It was denounced and deplored at every opportunity, even while otherwise being analyzed and the question posed as to how such an "unthinkable" result might have occurred.

The attitude of "unthinkability" involved a cruel mystique. The dire military consequences for the Confederates at Missionary Ridge were not a random aberration or an enemy "miracle"; they were rooted in one very explainable circumstance: bad decisions. Strategically, Bragg had planned for a siege, not a frontal assault on his lines. He intended either to starve the enemy into surrender or to force a retreat. Bragg's concept didn't allow for much of a fight at Chattanooga. His strong natural positions precluded a direct attack, he reasoned. As a result, breastworks along the crest, cleared fields of fire, artillery emplacements, and strategic deposits of munitions were all lacking or neglected until the last moment. Worst of all, this perception of "natural strength," combined with political infighting among the army's senior commanders, resulted in Longstreet's Corps, nearly one-third of Bragg's effectives, being detached and therefore absent during the decisive action.[4]

Tactically, many of Bragg's subordinates contributed to the enormous disaster by issuing conflicting or confusing orders. Hardee's ill-fated decision to split brigade strengths between the top and bottom of the ridge was the decisive tactical mistake that directly led to the breakthrough and collapse on the crest. Some units had been told to fight to the last at the rifle pits below; others had followed Hardee's explicit orders to retreat to the crest. The confusion among the men, the physical exhaustion of climbing the ridge under heavy fire, and the dire effect on morale of seeing one's own fellow soldiers fleeing precipitously up the slopes was infectious and debilitating. Psychologically, Bragg's troops were probably beaten at that very moment.

Conversely, the unanticipated easy capture of the lower rifle pits, with a sizable enemy force fleeing up the ridge, only inspired Thomas's soldiers to continue the pursuit. An escaping enemy, seemingly routed and in terror, has been the incentive for immediate, spontaneous pursuit over the ages. This factor, when coupled with the heavy fire directed at the exposed breastworks below, was strong inducement for continuing on. The combination of these circumstances pushed Thomas's soldiers beyond the lower rifle pits, despite what Grant had intended.

Their progress was abetted by various other Confederate tactical mistakes. Hardee's engineer officer, Capt. John W. Green, had belatedly laid out a line of breastworks atop the ridge, based more on the topographical rather than the military crest. The proper military crest, below the actual crown of the ridge, would have given Bragg's soldiers a more direct and destructive line of fire. The resulting inability to see many of the enemy troops as they advanced up the slopes, as well as the overshooting caused by the breastwork placement, contributed to the defeat. Furthermore, the artillery was dispersed along prominent spurs, often without protective breastworks or modifications made in the ground to enable both a vertical and lateral field of fire. The guns' muzzles thus were unable to be depressed sufficiently to hit infantry crawling upward along the irregular slopes. In order to shoot at the enemy, the artillerists often had to fire at troops distant from their own sector, which generally meant aiming to one side and not head-on. The lack of a sufficient front-line supply and the inadequate protective shelter for artillery ammunition was well illustrated by the blowing up of Slocomb's caissons, which contributed to the crumbling of Bate's flank.[5]

Yet in the final analysis, the lost battle was merely a by-product of a lack of anticipation, of being at the last moment confronted by what was regarded as most unlikely: a massed frontal attack. Ironically, such perspective was based upon a valid premise. Had it not been for Grant's impulsive "mistake," observed an astute Federal officer, the storming of the ridge would not have occurred.[6]

Such was the essence of fate. At Missionary Ridge, human nature became the arbiter and common sense the decisive element. The military equation had been reduced to its basic common denominator.

Charles A. Dana fairly bubbled with excitement as he reported the results of the three days' fight. His telegram to Secretary of War Stanton at 10:00 A.M. November 26 proclaimed the captures: three thousand prisoners, fifty-two cannon, five thousand stand of small arms, and ten flags. Even Grant was carried away by the exaggerated early reports. Grant wired Halleck on November 27: "I think Bragg's loss will fully reach sixty pieces of artillery." The next day, Grant expanded his estimate to "near 7,000 prisoners, 42 cannon, and many colors." George H. Thomas, reflecting his more conservative nature, reported to Halleck on the twenty-fifth the capture of two thousand prisoners and about forty pieces of artillery, a remarkably accurate tabulation given the final figures.[7]

No matter what figures were given, by all accounts the profile was clearly that of an army bloodied and battered. Braxton Bragg acknowledged a "heavy loss" of artillery and small arms, which translated into thirty-eight pieces of field artillery captured by the enemy on November 24 and 25 and two twenty-four-pounder rifled siege guns abandoned at Chickamauga

Station after their carriages were burned. His losses in troops were set at 361 killed, 2,180 wounded, and 4,146 missing, a total of 6,687. Cheatham's and Anderson's divisions had suffered the most, each reporting more than 1,670 casualties. Based upon the estimated total of about 46,000 Confederates engaged at Chattanooga, Bragg had lost nearly 15 percent of his army, a devastating figure considering the large number of prisoners.*[8] Moreover, the loss in artillery and ordnance was particularly worrisome and embarrassing. Included among the forty captured Confederate guns were twenty-two smooth-bore twelve-pounder Napoleons or howitzers, six of which were of Leeds & Co., New Orleans, manufacture. Furthermore, the Rebels, noted the Federal chief of ordnance, had lost 6,175 small arms, "mostly Enfield [rifle muskets]," which were increasingly harder to replace, being first-class arms run through the blockade from England.[9]

Grant accurately assessed that Confederate losses in *killed and wounded* were "probably less than ours," since "he [Bragg] was protected by his entrenchments, while our men were without cover." Indeed, the Federal casualty reports reflected 753 killed, 4,722 wounded, and 349 missing, for a total of 5,824. This represented about 10 percent combat losses, based upon the reported 102,903 U.S. forces present for duty, of which only about 56,000 were actually engaged in the battles.[10]

The numbers didn't tell the full story. Among the ragged and dispirited gray ranks trudging south in the freezing night and early morning of November 26, there was talk only of survival. "I will never forget that night retreat," later wrote a glum Tennessee infantryman. "It was bitter cold. . . . As the enemy had cut us off from the rest of the army, we had to make a detour and cross Chickamauga Creek . . . at a ford unknown to the enemy. Just before day the head of the column reached the ford. [It was said] the enemy was passing parallel to our line of march on the main pike. General Cheatham stood on the bank and as each file passed going down the bank, he would say, 'Boys, keep quiet! If you make the least noise we are lost.' File after file plunged into that icy flood, four feet deep, struggling to reach the opposite shore. The men held their guns and accouterments on top of their heads. With bated breath and chattering teeth they waded waist deep in that ice cold water. Oh! how I dreaded my turn! As my file reached the edge of the water we plunged in with clinched teeth for fear our breath would come out in such force that it would end in a scream. It proved to be too severe for one of my file. As we stepped into the icy water . . . he hollered out to the top of his voice, 'Jesus Christ! God Almighty!' . . . [Finally] about sunrise we reached a safe place with our clothes frozen stiff upon us."[11]

The ordeal was ongoing. A Tennessee rifleman saw the looks on the

---

*Per the Federal army's final accounting for the campaign, 6,142 deserters and prisoners of war were listed as taken from October 20 to December 1, all but 573 of whom were captured.

faces of the retreating gray soldiers as they passed across the bridge to Chickamauga Station. "Some were mad, others cowed, and many were laughing. Some were cursing Bragg, some the Yankees, and some were [even] rejoicing at the defeat." When a weaponless and particularly bedraggled column of Alabamians passed, said to be from Deas's Brigade, the men standing by the side of the road began yelling in derision, "Yellow hammer, Alabama, flicker, flicker, flicker." "They all seemed to have the possum grins, like Bragg looked," noted a guffawing soldier.[12]

At Chickamauga Station, the extent of the tragedy was fully apparent to all. Immense stores of army quartermaster's goods and provisions were piled everywhere. To the weary, starving Confederate infantrymen, it was a particularly bitter sight. Great piles of sacked corn, bacon, crackers, molasses, sugar, coffee, rice, potatoes, onions, peas, and hundreds of barrels of flour were there but, in the confusion, the retreat toward Dalton, Georgia, began before rations were issued to many. Then the remaining regiments set the warehouses and piles of provisions afire to prevent them from falling into enemy hands. Before the flames consumed the enormous stockpile, the remaining soldiers randomly loaded their haversacks with rations. Two rear-guard brigades, Maney's and Lucius Polk's, were ordered to complete the destruction. "Every one of us had cut open the end of a corn sack, emptied out the corn, and filled it with hard tack," wrote a private. Others were seen with a side of bacon hung on their bayonets, or canteens "gummed up" with molasses. Then the flames devoured all, wrote an eyewitness.[13]

"Most of our army had already passed through hungry and disheartened, and here were all these stores that had to be destroyed . . . For months we had been starved for the want of these same provisions," a soldier reflected in outrage. It was enough to make "the . . . most patriotic soul . . . think of rebelling against the authorities."[14]

"Who do you think was to blame?" he mockingly asked.

It was a night of indescribable misery, wrote a Tennessee captain. He had been wounded and he painfully made his way to Chickamauga Station, hoping to get on board a railcar for the trip south. There were no cars, and none would come up, he was told. Together with "many other wounded," he limped down the railroad track toward Dalton, finally arriving at Ringgold Gap before daylight. The day's events whirled through the mind of an exhausted Alabama colonel who lay down by the roadside, hungry and cold. He soon became sick with "the thought of our defeat." "We had been whipped and driven from our strong position without making scarcely any resistance," and he was ashamed, he later wrote. Although the enemy outnumbered his men three to one, "still we had the advantage in position [and] ought to have whipped them . . . We will never have another such opportunity of completely destroying the Yankee army," grumbled the colonel.[15]

Word quickly spread among the men that it was a single brigade that had prematurely broken and "involved the whole army in defeat." "I regard the affair as shameful and disgraceful," wrote a Florida lieutenant. "I hope that out of this disaster some good may yet come . . . This thing never happened to Confederate soldiers before—God grant that it may never be again."[16]

The assessment of Chattanooga was far different for one of Cleburne's soldiers, a lowly rifleman. He plainly wrote: "[The Yankees] have driven us from the strongest position that we have got, just because some of our men are so tired of the war that they won't fight at all."[17]

On the retreat, a Tennessee sergeant noted in his journal how "several of our men were barefooted, yet they travelled without complaint through mud, over rocks, and sometimes on frozen ground. Our army is very much in need of clothing, blankets, and tents, but we will hardly get many tents this winter. Thus ends my second year of the war." A wounded Alabamian, wrapped in blankets and left on the cold ground, told his captors, "Well, we have received nothing, lived on nothing, been fighting for nothing, and could expect nothing from our enemies." Yet noting the kind treatment now given to him by the Yankees, he said from that night on things would be different—he would see things in another perspective.[18]

In the distant confines of the old Chattanooga railroad depot, Lt. Col. John W. Inzer of the 58th Alabama, a prisoner of war, reflected upon his fate. There were no blankets, it was freezing cold, and sleep was difficult. Before leaving his men, captured with him, he had told them some "encouraging things . . . [I] told them I hoped we would soon meet again in Dixie to fight the enemy."[19]

The Yankees just looked at him and said nothing. His men may well have done the same.

Ulysses S. Grant and his staff were celebrating. A few days earlier, Capt. Ely S. Parker of Grant's staff had observed that "a great battle" was pending "if our enemy does not run away from us. We intend to thrash them soundly and give the rebellion such a blow as to stagger its longer continuance in this region. General Grant feels confident of success, and so do we all."

Now Chattanooga was a prophecy fulfilled.[20] Parker excitedly wrote home following the fight how this "most terrific battle" had featured cannonading "like continuous thunder," and "deafening" crashes of musketry. Yet Grant had remained composed through it all. From Orchard Knob, Grant, Thomas, Granger, and their staffs had watched as "the music of the screaming shell" played about them. Charles A. Dana noted how an occasional bursting shell fired from Missionary Ridge would cause everybody to duck—except for Grant, Thomas, and Granger. "It was not according to their dignity," he observed.[21]

On the evening of November 25, Grant's eased mood was reflected in his 7:15 P.M. telegram to Henry Halleck. There had been "a complete victory over Bragg," announced Grant, and "I have no idea of finding Bragg here tomorrow." Fresh from his visit among the celebrating troops on Missionary Ridge, Grant considered that he had driven "a big nail in the coffin of rebellion." He had seen his troops tearing up captured Rebel battle flags for souvenirs and had listened to the humorous accounts of Bragg's narrow escape, the acerbic North Carolinian having fled "but a few minutes before" Sheridan's troops arrived.[22]

That night at headquarters, everyone talked in excited tones about the prospects for the morrow, and Grant ordered three days' provisions placed in an ambulance for him and his staff. The next day, they would follow after the great Chattanooga skedaddle, joked a mirthful staff officer.[23]

CHAPTER 40

In the Wake
of the Stampede

It was as pretty and white as a snow bank," observed a staff officer. "The ground was covered with corn meal about 2 feet deep" for more than one hundred yards. Chickamauga Station had been the principal supply depot for the Rebel army, noted Capt. Ely S. Parker, and it was amazing to see the extent of abandoned provisions. Sacks of cornmeal and shelled corn, storehouses filled with corn in the ear—taken all together, "it would make a heap as large and as high as a barn," observed Parker. Although the Rebels had set fire to some piles and several buildings, before they could destroy all, the Federal army had arrived and driven them off.[1]

To the cold and famished soldiers of the 86th Illinois Infantry, the sight of so many storehouses laden with provisions caused them to race into the burning buildings to salvage what they could. In one smoke-filled building, the men hurriedly filled their haversacks with "brown sugar" before being chased out by the flames. The men were celebrating their good fortune when someone decided to try out this new delicacy. He immediately spit it on the ground. Amid some loud swearing and hollering, the men began emptying their haversacks. Instead of brown sugar, they had found a cache of brown salt. Soon the orders came to fall in, and "we commenced a running race with the rear guard of the retreating army," wrote a disappointed soldier.[2]

The morning of November 26 was frosty, and hazy with the lingering smoke of burning campfires. Sherman had acted about midnight to organize a pursuit, following receipt of Grant's belated instructions. Ulysses S. Grant's reaction had been mostly cautious immediately following the victory on Missionary Ridge. While writing Sherman that evening about the

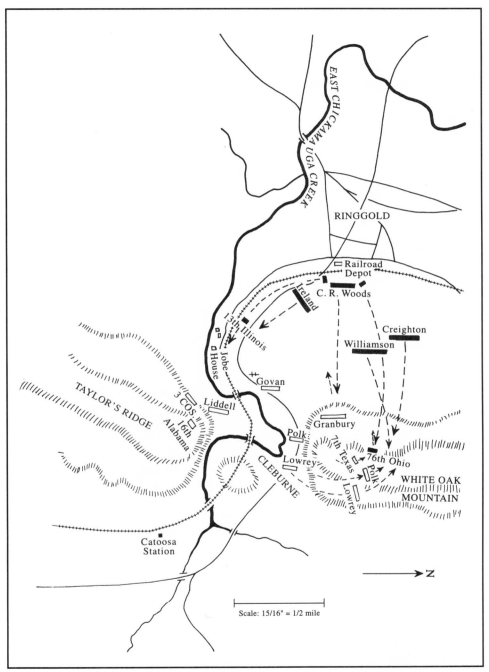

MAP 12   Action at Ringgold Gap, November 27, 1863
(*Source: Purdue, Pat Cleburne: Confederate General; O.R. Atlas, plate 101-2*)

day's events, he seemed to be organizing his thoughts. He thus confided to Sherman: "I take it for granted that Bragg's entire force has left. If not, of course, the first thing is to dispose of him. If he has gone the only thing necessary to do tomorrow will be to send out a reconnaissance to ascertain the whereabouts of the enemy.—P.S. On reflection, I think we will push Bragg with all our strength tomorrow, and try [to see] if we cannot cut off a good portion of his . . . troops and trains. His men have manifested a strong desire to desert for some time past, and we will now give them a chance."[3]

The plan was spontaneous. While writing out orders for the morning of the twenty-sixth, Grant had revised his thinking. Instead of merely probing Bragg's disorderly retreat, he would send in pursuit Sherman and all of Thomas's troops, except for Granger's Fourth Corps, which would march to the relief of Knoxville. Grant expected Bragg to be prepared to fight another battle rather than abandon Longstreet's line of retreat from Knoxville, and the object, said Grant's chief of staff, would be "to bring him to battle again, if possible."[4]

The building excitement was obvious on the morning of the twenty-sixth, noted a visitor at Grant's headquarters. Grant had ridden with William F. "Baldy" Smith and several staff officers to the front after a late breakfast. Meeting Thomas along Missionary Ridge, Grant gave him verbal orders not to order Granger to leave until the situation was clearer. Grant said he feared Bragg's troops "might be over their stampede" and would either fight to protect their Tennessee communications or move toward Knoxville with the intention of reuniting with Longstreet to attack Burnside. Then, riding past dead stretched in rows on Missionary Ridge, the Grant party passed down into the eastern valley until they reached Chickamauga Creek. The water was too high to ford, so Grant and Smith rode to the stone railroad bridge, where only a small trestle section had been destroyed. While Baldy Smith attended to the reconstruction, Grant and the other sat on the "soft grass," eating their lunch and drinking "the cold, crystal, delicious water" of Chickamauga Creek.[5]

About 12:30 P.M., Smith's construction detail of about fifty men had fashioned a flooring of railroad iron and cross ties, and Grant and the others were soon across and off "at a sharp gallop for the front." At Chickamauga Station, Grant found immense piles of corn burning, with sacked corn and meal heaped up along the railroad track. Pontoons, abandoned siege cannon, and much equipment were scattered about on the ground. Through the still-smoldering station trudged columns of Sherman's troops, many of them with sacks of corn or meal on their backs. Ambulances and wagons were filled with captured provisions. "The fat storehouses of the enemy were a perfect godsend to our half famished troops," noted an observer.[6]

Ahead sounded the roar of cannon and sharp musketry, and Grant and his party moved onward, taking to the fields to avoid the road, now completely jammed with advancing troops. Soon Grant came up with Sherman and his staff, sitting on horseback in the woods, about three miles south of Chickamauga Station. Although the firing here was loud and not far distant, a visitor noted that Grant's visage had begun to change. It was evident Bragg was in "full retreat" and only a rear guard action was being fought. The valley for a distance of ten miles was in flames, wrote Charles A. Dana, and there was no prospect of a major battle. Grant ordered Sherman to send Howard and the Eleventh Corps east to Red Clay, Georgia, on the twenty-seventh. Here, Howard would destroy the vital East Tennessee and Georgia Railroad line between Dalton, Georgia, and Cleveland, Tennessee, effectively cutting communications between Bragg and Longstreet. Meanwhile, Sherman would continue to pursue along the Graysville to Ringgold road, as the Rebels seemed to be protecting a large wagon train just ahead. Grant determined to return to Chattanooga as soon as the moon was up to light their way; then, the following morning, he would return to go with Howard's troops to Red Clay.[7]

Sherman's advance on the morning of the twenty-fifth had been delayed by fog and a decision to countermarch to the mouth of Chickamauga Creek, where the pontoon bridge had been constructed on the twenty-fourth, following Sherman's crossing of the Tennessee River. Since Cleburne and the Confederates had destroyed the bridges at the Shallow Ford crossing and elsewhere during the night of the twenty-fifth, there seemed to be no other quick, practical way to cross Chickamauga Creek. Sherman had thus been unable to push Bragg hard along the road to Graysville. The fight at Chickamauga Station, about 11:00 A.M., had been brief, only two regiments of Brig. Gen. James D. Morgan's brigade being needed to clear the site.[8]

In following the withdrawing enemy along the Graysville road, the delays had been frequent, due to brief stands made by the Rebel rear guard. There would be several shots fired from a few Confederate guns posted along the road, then, as Morgan's men formed in line of battle, the enemy cannon and their cavalry supports would withdraw. A short distance down the road, another similar stand would be made. In this manner, the Federal pursuit was much delayed, so that Sherman, present with division commander Jefferson C. Davis along the front line since about 2:00 P.M., had advanced only about three miles beyond Chickamauga Station by sundown.[9]

Here, near Mrs. Shepherd's log farm and in front of a densely wooded swamp, the Rebels suddenly seemed to be making a determined stand with infantry and artillery. By the time Jefferson C. Davis's three brigades deployed and advanced through the marsh, it was so dark that Davis felt "a night attack was not prudent." Although Brig. Gen. George Maney had been wounded on the Confederate side, the only Federal casualty seemed to be one man wounded by a shell fragment. In passing by Mrs. Shepherd's log cabin, Lt. Col. Allan Fahnestock "supposed there were Rebels in it," and he "leveled his revolver at the open door." There were an old man and woman peering out, and they quickly ducked their heads. Fahnestock ran on, but no sooner was he past the open door than two shots rang out from the doorway, narrowly missing him.[10]

Skirmish firing continued until well after dark, yet at that hour, as the shooting abated in front of Jefferson C. Davis's troops, about four miles to the south a heavy outbreak of firing told of a night encounter west of Graysville.[11]

George H. Thomas's pursuit from Missionary Ridge had gotten off to a slow start that morning following confusing orders and a delay in bridging Chickamauga Creek at Bird's Mill, beyond Rossville. Two brigades, Carlin's and Stoughton's of Richard W. Johnson's division, were in the advance, with corps commander Maj. Gen. John M. Palmer present. The men were restless and hungry, noted an army chaplain that morning. When a solitary rooster crowed at a neighboring farm early that morning, "it was his last crow," reported the chaplain. The soldiers "who had driven Bragg's army from Missionary Ridge were not in a humor to be crowed over." Soon the rooster was being cooked along with a frugal breakfast of johnnycakes made of coarse cornmeal.[12]

While the 33rd Ohio Infantry rebuilt the bridge at Bird's Mill, the distant echo of cannon fire from Chattanooga's Fort Wood sounded on the breeze. At 11:40 A.M., noted a soldier, thirty-six shots were fired from the fort as a salute to the great victory of the twenty-fifth. Later, the brigade bands played as the men cheered. To a restless infantryman, who watched as burial details gathered up dead Confederates and others scoured the battlefield for guns, it gave a sobering perspective, and he wrote in his journal, "Well, I'm glad I'm alive and well."[13]

The bridge at Bird's Mill was constructed in less than two hours, said a captain, and about 3:00 P.M. Carlin's troops took the lead on the road toward Graysville. It was a frustrating march.The column soon came to a halt at Pea Vine Creek, where another bridge was destroyed and had to be rebuilt. It was dusk when Carlin's men crossed the creek and came to a fork in the road. The left road led to Graysville and the other, to the right, toward Ringgold. John Palmer split his two brigades, sending Carlin toward Graysville, while the trailing brigade, under Col. William L. Stoughton, waited at the crossroads.[14]

Carlin hadn't gone very far before campfires were seen through the woods, and several stragglers confirmed that a large Rebel camp lay nearby. Carlin halted his men and reported to corps commander Palmer, who promptly planned a surprise attack. Stoughton would advance directly down the road toward Ringgold while Carlin watched the northern road. The enemy, which lay camped along a crossroad, seemed completely surprised. Their pickets were captured in the dark woods without alarm, and Stoughton's troops crept up on the unsuspecting Rebel camp.[15]

The first indication of the Yankees' presence was a volley from the darkness. Then, with fixed bayonets, Stoughton's men charged the camp, sending the enemy wildly scattering into the night. The fruits of the quick action were sixty prisoners, four brass Napoleon twelve-pounder guns taken from Capt. T. B. Ferguson's South Carolina Battery, two caissons, and one battle flag.[16]

After occupying Graysville before midnight, Carlin's men found another abandoned Napoleon field gun and took forty "Georgia militia," along with three commissioned officers from the 16th South Carolina Infantry of Brig. Gen. States Rights Gist's Brigade. In all, it was a productive evening, and Maj. Gen. Joseph Hooker, who had moved up with three divisions to Pea Vine Creek, eagerly reported at 10:00 P.M. that Palmer's troops had struck the rear of Hardee's column. "We have reached a ridge said to be 2½ miles from Ringgold," said Hooker. "If not otherwise directed, I shall move on Ringgold at daylight."[17]

Fighting Joe Hooker was quite a handsome man, observed a curious lieutenant on the march during the afternoon on the twenty-sixth. "He must be fully six feet tall, and . . . heavily built . . . [has a] very florid complexion and light hair, with a little patch of gray whiskers under each ears and extending down on his cheek." Beside him rode his chief of staff, Butterfield, a small, dumpy-looking man in a rumpled army blouse with two stars pinned on each shoulder but no shoulder straps.[18]

The predawn morning of November 27 found Hooker along the road leading to Ringgold, with his tired soldiers slowly marching along in the darkness, stopping and starting with maddening frequency. "Two hundred yards in half an hour," grumbled an officer, was no way to march an army. "Everybody was tired and sleepy," when suddenly down the road from the top of a hill came the sound of galloping horses. It was a runaway caisson, thought the men of the 59th Illinois Infantry, and they jumped to the side of the road. Everybody lay down, and the sound of cocking muskets filled the air. Not a shot was fired—the caisson apparently swerved away—and a few minutes later, no one knew what it was all about, said a lieutenant. Behind the 59th Illinois marched the 9th Indiana, which had also scattered. In their midst at the time, so it was said, was General Hooker, who had dismounted and was walking up the road with his staff. In the commotion, the scattering men had virtually run over Hooker, knocking him down. Thereafter, the march halted and the men camped until daylight. It was a rather inauspicious beginning for November 27, 1863, a day Joe Hooker would long remember.[19]

Hooker had asked George H. Thomas on the morning of the twenty-sixth for permission to march in pursuit of the enemy. The [battle-]field was as silent as the grave," said Hooker, and "knowing the desperate extremities to which [the enemy] must be reduced by our success," he felt confident Bragg "must be in full retreat."[20]

Hooker's attitude and burning quest for military glory was reflected in his eager anticipation on the morning of November 27. At daylight, as Peter J. Osterhaus's division led the march, followed by those of Geary and Cruft, Hooker knew of the rout of the Rebel camp near Graysville the previous evening. "I was now fairly up with the tail end of the enemy's column," Hooker realized, and anticipating further captures and a fleeing foe, he hastened onward to reach Ringgold, Georgia, less than five miles distant. Here, Hooker suspected the Rebels might attempt another stand. "The troops were wrought up to an intense degree of excitement," Hooker noted, and despite the lack of adequate provisions, the past few days seemed both the most eventful and "happiest of their lives." The chase was on, said Hooker, and "we lived on the excitement."[21]

Brig. Gen. Peter J. Osterhaus's Prussian military background and his aggressive manner seemed to make him an instant favorite with Hooker. On the twenty-seventh Osterhaus was on the road to Ringgold at 5:30 A.M., with a few mounted infantry leading the advance. The road was muddy and rutted, and along the way abandoned equipment was strewn, reflecting the urgency of the enemy's retreat. A few stragglers were captured, and as Osterhaus approached East Chickamauga Creek in front of the town, the mounted infantry chased a handful of Confederate cavalry pickets from the ford and secured a covered trestle bridge before it could be burned. Osterhaus's infantry supports arrived belatedly due to the meandering path of the road, but before 9:00 A.M. two Missouri regiments crossed the covered bridge and drove the Confederate skirmishers and cavalry through Ringgold, then into the gap in Taylor's Ridge behind the town. It was all very easy and almost bloodless.[22]

Joe Hooker had ridden to the front immediately upon hearing the firing. Arriving just as Osterhaus's skirmishers rushed through the town, Hooker reported at 9:00 A.M.: "The town is much cleaned out." Four pieces of Rebel artillery, weakly escorted, had been run into the nearby gorge. Had a small force of cavalry been present, said Osterhaus, he could have captured the battery. Hooker was duly encouraged. Among the citizens and "contrabands" venturing out of doors, it was soon learned that the Rebels had passed through Ringgold "sorely pressed." There were a number of Union citizens in the town, and Hooker eagerly listened as they told of a "disorganized and demoralized" Rebel throng, "about one-third of them without arms . . . and herded together like cattle." All the Rebel rank and file were heard "swearing they would not serve the damned Confederacy any longer." Hooker was almost jubilant. "I was convinced . . . with the force I then had it was in my power to follow [Bragg's] army until I had captured or destroyed it."[23]

Hooker looked to the east. "Only a feeble line of gray skirmishers appeared in sight." We had "fairly jammed [the Rebels] into the ravine in the mountain through which his [retreat] led." Hooker ordered Osterhaus to attack immediately through the gap. A single brigade, that of Brig. Gen. Charles R. Woods, was deployed to ascertain the enemy's "strength and position." "Our success, if prompt," envisioned Hooker, "would be crowned with a rich harvest of [captured] materiel."[24]

Without artillery support—Hooker's guns were still miles behind due to a delay in adequately bridging Chickamauga Creek—Charley Woods's infantrymen formed their lines, and about 10:00 A.M. swept forward across the open plain east of town.[25]

Joe Hooker watched them go. "Bragg's army," he scoffed, "have no heart in the[ir] cause. Their own officers appear to distrust the fidelity of the enlisted men, and they have no discipline like that of [Robert E.] Lee's army." Almost contemptuous of the Rebel "rabble," he was confident "they will retire as soon as a forward movement is made by our troops."[26]

CHAPTER 41

"Have You Any Troops
That Won't Run Away?"

Braxton Bragg had established his headquarters in a large freight room at Catoosa Station, about three miles south of Ringgold on the Western and Atlantic Railroad. On the night of November 26 to 27 he had learned with alarm of the rout of a portion of Hardee's column at Graysville, including the loss of Ferguson's Battery. Bragg, said a staff officer, evidently hadn't slept during the night, and he "exhibited more excitement than I supposed possible for him." The normally phlegmatic Bragg was upset and suffering from anxiety. His orders to the staff officer were: "Tell General Cleburne to hold his position at all hazards, and keep back the enemy, until the artillery and transportation of the army is secure, the salvation of which depends upon him." Grasping the staff officer's hand in both of his own, Bragg, by the light of a single candle, seemed unusually emotional and distraught. It was past midnight, and the staff officer, Capt. Irving A. Buck of Cleburne's staff, soon departed, more embarrassed than awed by the Confederate commander.[1]

Patrick Cleburne was again being asked to save the army. During the retreat of the twenty-sixth, Cleburne's command had wearily passed along the road from Graysville to reach the ford of East Chickamauga Creek at Ringgold about 10:00 P.M. Evidently unaware of the covered bridge farther south, Cleburne had refused to pass across the waist-deep creek in the freezing cold. Although in receipt of instructions to cross the creek, encamp, and then arise at 4:00 A.M. the following morning to serve as the army's rear guard, Cleburne had objected to what was an obvious mistake. If his men waded that ice-cold stream and slept in their wet clothing he would lose more men from pneumonia than he would if attacked, Cleburne told a staff officer.[2]

Pat Cleburne was thus upset when at 3:00 A.M. he received Bragg's order to take a strong position in the gorge behind Ringgold "to check pursuit of [the] enemy." "He must be punished until our trains and the rear of our troops get well advanced," continued Bragg's instructions. Cleburne considered that this would result in the loss of his command, especially if the enemy outflanked his position and cut off their retreat. Yet to Capt. Samuel A. Harris of Bragg's staff, Cleburne merely grinned and said, "I always obey orders."[3]

It was the beginning of yet another crisis, as well as a new odyssey for the man who had just beaten Sherman on the north end of Missionary Ridge. From Cleburne's perspective, the extreme peril was secondary to the great responsibility. With 4,157 men and two field guns, he must protect the retreat by holding off the enemy's overwhelming numbers. In this situation, although then unknown to Cleburne, he would initially confront three divisions under the command of Fighting Joe Hooker, numbering 8,868 effective troops.[4]

Pat Cleburne's mind began racing. While his troops were roused and waded across the creek, he rode ahead to examine the gap in Taylor's Ridge and form a plan for its defense. About twenty miles southeast of Chattanooga, Taylor's Ridge was abrupt and thinly wooded, running nearly north and south, and similar in height to Missionary Ridge. This ridge, on the north side of the gap, was locally known as White Oak Mountain. Only a single gap existed here, about a half mile east of Ringgold, and was perhaps one hundred yards wide at the western mouth, where Cleburne planned his major defensive line. Although the gap was about a half mile long and thick with pine undergrowth, the most difficult travel was beyond its eastern mouth, where meandering East Chickamauga Creek created multiple fording sites along the fifteen-mile road to Dalton. It was a nightmare for a retreating column. The roads were already axle-deep with mud, and in the first light of day, Bragg's large wagon train, mired and in difficulty, could be seen struggling to cross at the varous fords.[5]

Cleburne planned for a cushioned, multi-tiered defense, where successive layers of troops might absorb an enemy attack or be available to rush to any threatened point. Four lines of infantry were soon strung across the interior of the gap and concealed amid a woods and small ravine. Where a thick fringe of young timber ran north toward Ringgold for nearly four hundred yards along the foot of White Oak Mountain, Cleburne placed the Texas brigade under the command of Col. Hiram Granbury. A single regiment was sent atop this ridge to watch the flank and were told to "keep out of view."[6]

Cleburne's thinking was fully apparent when he concealed in front of the gap a section of Semple's Alabama Battery, commanded by Lt. Richard W. Goldthwaite. Two twelve-pounder Napoleon guns were placed behind a screen of withered pine branches, and since there was an open field south of the town and cleared ground where the railroad and roadway approached the gap, Goldthwaite had a favorable field of fire. Cleburne thus planned to defend the gap primarily along the base of the heights, rather than to embrace Bragg's, Hardee's, and Breckinridge's split-force tactics that had proved so disastrous at Missionary Ridge.[7]

Although his three other brigades were quickly posted in and about Ringgold Gap, Cleburne had "scarcely half an hour" before Hooker's skirmishers were seen crossing the creek in front of Ringgold. When the cavalry retreated through the gap at a trot soon thereafter, Cleburne knew his were the only Southern troops remaining. About 8:00 A.M., the enemy's skirmishers came into full view, advancing.[8]

The chaplain of the 13th Illinois had been riding with the regiment's Maj. Doug Bushnell and Capt. Walter Blanchard at sunset the previous evening. "Chaplain," said Blanchard, "I never look upon a setting sun of late but I am reminded that my life will soon be done. . . . I'm [convinced] that the next will be my last battle. I will never live to get out of the service." Beside him, Major Bushnell assented, saying, "I, too, feel . . . that the next battle is to be my last." The nervous chaplain said a silent prayer and offered some encouraging but frivolous remarks. On the morning of the twenty-seventh, the chaplain's special friend, Jimmy McCollum of Company C, confessed his premonition of coming death. Such fears were unusual; no battle was expected from a fleeing enemy. Yet the chaplain sensed a "ministration of the Divine Spirit." Was it the promptings of the spirit that these men might be better prepared? he wondered.[9]

The men of the 13th Illinois were animated by the prospect of chasing Rebels. As part of Brig. Gen. Charles R. Wood's brigade, Osterhaus's division, the regiment was in the vanguard of Hooker's column on that clear and pleasant morning of the twenty-seventh. "The boys were as chipper as could be," noted an officer as the 13th marched through Ringgold and filed past the old stone railroad depot at the end of town. Once on the open ground east of town, a battle line was formed. Quickly, at their officers' commands, the regiment strode forward, sweeping over the uneven ground toward some houses on the right of the gap, only a few hundred yards away. Their march was measured and precise. On their left, other regiments were moving in line directly toward the gap. Down the line of the railroad track swept the column of blue uniforms, with "the beautiful order and precision characteristic of well-drilled troops." Peter J. Osterhaus wanted the 13th Illinois to take these houses, including a brick farmhouse and outbuildings, Mr. Jobe's, only about one hundred yards from the gap. The 13th Illinois was aimed directly for these buildings.[10]

Pat Cleburne, intently peering through field glasses, stood beside Goldthwaite's two Napoleons. Closer and closer moved the line of blue soldiers, until their ranks were about 150 yards away. "Now, Lieutenant, give it to 'em," shouted Cleburne as he sprang into the air, clapping his knee. The first round, a solid shot from the left gun, tore through the center line, and the second, a blast of canister, ripped into the ranks of the 13th Illinois. Again, both guns fired canister in the direction of the 13th. Due to the high weeds, masking piles of branches, and the billowing smoke, nothing could be seen in front for anxious moments, said Goldthwaite. Yet a minute later, as the smoke lifted, the ground in front was empty.[11]

In the ranks of the 13th Illinois, the carnage was terrible. Dozens of men were down. The surprise had been devastating. A soldier wrote: "[We] were mowed down in swaths by the grape and canister that swept the field. It was simply murderous, and horrifying to look at." The ranks of the 13th went flat on the ground, but the lieutenant colonel tried to get two companies forward to shoot at Cleburne's artillerists. They were riddled with canister and musketry. Next, he ordered the whole regiment forward. The men jumped up and, bending low as though facing a hailstorm, ran forward. Just where they were to go, no one was quite sure, said a soldier, but the broken ranks ran ahead to a log house, barn, and pigpen, where many men took cover behind a pile of old railroad ties. In the rush forward, the regiment's color-bearer was shot and fell on the flag, soaking the Stars and Stripes in his blood. The incoming fire was too heavy to carry the flag aloft, so a soldier stuck the flagstaff through the fork of an old apple tree, then ducked behind the thick trunk.[12]

By now, the lieutenant colonel had been shot through the hand, and he ordered Major Bushnell to take command. The major was unable to respond. While he was lying behind the pile of rails, a bullet had grazed the end of a tie and struck him squarely in the forehead. He died instantly, his premonition fulfilled.[13]

Capt. Walter Blanchard was standing behind the corner of the log house when a whizzing canister ball shattered his knee. Some of the 13th's riflemen were inside the buildings, shooting out of the windows. One rifleman was taking aim when a minié ball struck him in the right arm. "He gave a little shriek as the bone snapped," said a grimacing onlooker, then sank to the floor.[14]

The 13th was being shot to pieces. Yet they continued to hold their ground for more than an hour. Their rifles were becoming fouled, and so much ammunition had been expended that many were out of cartridges despite having been issued one hundred rounds before the fighting. Most had to rummage through the cartridge boxes of the dead and wounded to keep fighting. Beside the pile of rails, Captain Blanchard leaned on his good leg and fired the guns of the dead soldiers about him. It was the fight of their lives, thought a soldier.[15]

Peter Osterhaus knew he was in trouble. Three Missouri regiments, the 17th, 29th, and the 31st had gone forward in a skirmish line with supports, but they had faced a whirlwind of fire. From the crest of White Oak Mountain and the timber along its edge, Granbury's Texans had fired repeated volleys at close range into their ranks, scattering the Missourians.

So confused and shaken were the survivors that they came running back in wild disorder and were not rallied until after the fighting was over. Two other Missouri units, the 3rd and 12th Infantry, were barely able to hang on behind the embankment, where the railroad curved before running directly toward the gap.[16]

On the far left, Osterhaus had sent a lone regiment, the 76th Ohio Infantry, straight up White Oak Mountain, intending for them to occupy the crest, then wheel to the right and come down above the gap. They were nearly annihilated for their effort, suffering 40 percent casualties in a stand-up twenty-minute firefight along the ridge. Both of the regiment's flanks were bent backward, and when the Confederate troops were reinforced along the crest, the major commanding gave the order to fall back. Although a nearby regiment, the 4th Iowa, belatedly rushed to their support and attempted to shore up the line, Osterhaus saw the 76th and 4th retreating and sent urgent orders for them to hold their positions until more help arrived.[17]

Fighting Joe Hooker was watching the fighting from the corner of the railroad depot, which was at the eastern edge of town. Obviously irritated at the sight of these "western" troops fleeing (Osterhaus's troops were from the Fifteenth Army Corps, William Tecumseh Sherman's men), Hooker turned to Brig. Gen. John W. Geary, who was standing beside him. "Have you any troops that won't run away?" asked Hooker sarcastically. Geary's reply was quick and assured: "I have no regiments that will run!" "Then, send some men into that gap," snapped Hooker, "and hold it until my artillery arrives." Geary immediately sprang into action and ordered his three brigades deployed. Hooker evidently began to feel better; his own eastern troops would soon be involved—Geary's Twelfth Corps veterans of Culp's Hill at Gettysburg. They were the ones to show Sherman's men how to fight.[18]

Pat Cleburne's Irish dander was up.The fighting was severe, as expected, and the enemy threatened to overwhelm his command. The most serious crisis, along the crest of White Oak Mountain, continued to be troublesome. Only the 7th Texas, Capt. C. E. Talley commanding, had been present there. Accordingly, Cleburne was wary. He had instructed Brig. Gen. Lucius E. Polk, commanding one of his reserve brigades, to move atop the ridge and support the 7th Texas if necessary. Polk was riding to the crest of White Oak Mountain to talk with Talley when "a breathless straggler" informed him he had just seen the enemy climbing the ridge beyond the right of the 7th Texas's line. Polk immediately sent for the 1st Arkansas Infantry, posted at the edge of the gap along the foot of the ridge.[19]

Riding at the head of this column, Polk, minutes later, trotted forward. He was just in time to see the 76th Ohio's skirmishers climb within twenty paces of the crest, beyond a knoll screened from Talley's Texans. The 1st

Arkansas ran ahead and began firing as they deployed into line of battle. Their timing was significant. For nearly a half hour, both the Arkansas and Ohio soldiers fought to hold their ground, yet the arrival of the 7th Texas on the 76th's flank, across the face of the ridge, finally sent the Ohioans streaming back halfway down the slopes.[20]

It was but a momentary victory. Polk's soldiers had no sooner begun to slacken their fire when other columns of blue infantrymen appeared from the lower timber and attempted to support the Ohioans at midridge. They were Iowans, four regiments of veteran troops from Osterhaus's Second Brigade, commanded by Col. James A. Williamson. Yet Williamson was leery of the concentrated fire coming from above. Two of his units moved up into line beside the 76th Ohio and 4th Iowa and lay down to fight at long range with Polk's and Talley's Confederates. On the far left, and screened by undulations in the slopes, Williamson's two left-flank regiments, the 25th and 30th Iowa, attempted to work their way up the steep face. At this point, no one anticipated the disaster that suddenly struck.[21]

John Geary had just ordered Col. William R. Creighton with two Pennsylvania and two Ohio regiments to "scale the mountain" to the left of Osterhaus's position and "attack the enemy in flank." Yet Creighton's men were under a false impression. Geary, evidently repeating what he had heard from Hooker, told his men that the Rebels were holding the ridge with only a small force. The implication was that another rout in the manner of Missionary Ridge was in the offing. Creighton, the former colonel of the 7th Ohio and a brave fighter but a hard drinker, promptly performed a ritual in front of his old command. Standing on a rock, he began flapping his arms and crowing like a rooster. The 7th Ohio, known as the "rooster regiment," was already wild with excitement and began crowing in reply. Their lieutenant colonel then jumped up on a rock and joined in the flapping and crowing. With brigade commander Creighton dressed in a newly purchased "elegant uniform" and carrying on in such a frenzied manner, it was quite a sight, noted a soldier.[22]

Minutes later, Creighton's battle line was formed near the stone depot, and at the command to move forward, they broke out with a yell, dashed over the open ground, and began climbing the steep slopes. As the fire intensified, the 7th Ohio in midline ducked into a ravine running up the side of the ridge. That was only their first mistake.[23]

Lucius E. Polk, on the crest, had seen Creighton's men coming and hastened up additional reinforcements. Meanwhile, acting by intuition, Cleburne had sent Brig. Gen. Mark Lowrey with his brigade to reinforce the critical right flank along the crest. Anxious about the sound of heavy firing ahead, Lowrey arrived on White Oak Mountain in advance of his brigade, just as Creighton's troops approached the line held by Williamson and the 76th Ohio at midslope. Lowrey saw that "nothing but the utmost prompt and rapid movement" would save the ridge, and he urged his brigade forward in column. They began sprinting forward, raising "a terrific Rebel Yell."[24]

Two of Creighton's regiments, the 28th Pennsylvania and 7th Ohio, had just reached the line held by the left-flank regiments of Williamson's line. As they attempted to pass through, there were angry words exchanged between the two Federal battle lines. The Iowans of Williamson's line wanted the Easterners to go around their flank. Some of Creighton's men only guffawed as they jammed past; they would teach "Western troops a lesson," they shouted. The colonel of the 25th Iowa again tried to stop them; the Rebels were rushing more troops along the crest to a point commanding both flanks. The advancing units would be caught in a cross fire, warned an officer.[25]

Too late, Creighton's line staggered to a halt not twenty yards in front of the Iowa line and attempted to fight standing up. Lowrey's regiments were on the right and Polk's on the left, facing up the hill. From three directions, bullets zipped through the exposed Federal ranks; it was "as terrific a musketry fire as I ever witnessed," wrote an amazed officer. The 7th Ohio, having been riddled by musketry while compacted in the ravine, was particularly exposed as they emerged in front. Immediately, its lieutenant colonel was killed near the top of the ridge. So many officers were being shot that only a single captain survived the fight unscathed. Nearly half the Ohioans were down, and the Iowa soldiers, immediately behind, were unable to shoot because of the looming line in front. Brigade commander Creighton ordered his men to fall back, but his line had already begun to break apart. They again ran over and through Williamson's Iowans like a "whirlwind," shouting, "The enemy have flanked us—they're coming." It soon became a stampede to the bottom of the hill, with Iowans, Pennsylvanians, and Ohioans all mixed together in a frenzied throng. It was "a perfect panic," admitted the colonel of the 25th Iowa. Down from the crest in pursuit poured Cleburne's Confederates, wildly yelling the high-pitched Rebel yell. It was all Creighton's and Williamson's officers could do to rally their men behind a fence at the base of the ridge.[26]

Almost frantic to stop his men, Col. William Creighton was struck in the chest by a rifle ball and suffered a mortal wound. Six hours later, he was dead. It was a butcher's bill of casualties, especially for Creighton's four regiments; when the 7th Ohio stacked arms in the streets of Ringgold that night, only thirty-three guns were counted. Twelve of thirteen officers who had been present were now missing. There was little crowing in the camp of the 7th Ohio that night. The "roosters" had been all but annihilated.[27]

These Easterners had attempted to fight the Rebels as if on dress parade, stand-up style, noted a saddened western officer. In the West, the troops knew better. A skirmish line and a cautious advance were the prudent, practical means. The eastern troops' "contempt for the Rebel soldiers," said an officer, had produced a disaster that left even Fighting Joe Hooker stunned and bewildered.[28]

*   *   *

Thanks to piecemeal, disjointed attacks and the enemy's inept battle plan, Pat Cleburne had thus far been able to hold off three divisions of Yankee troops. Yet Geary was still prepared to fight, and his two remaining brigades were intact. Observing Williamson's and Creighton's fleeing ranks streaming down the slopes, Geary told Col. George A. Cobham to advance and shore up the line beyond the railroad track. Cobham's Pennsylvanians promptly rushed to the site, faced the ridge, and lay down. Their presence checked the pursuit by Lowrey's and Polk's men, and soon the firing sputtered to a halt along White Oak Mountain's bloodied, smoke-obscured slopes.[29]

It was 10:40 A.M., and Geary no sooner had begun to look about when some Missourians from Charles R. Woods's brigade were seen streaming back along the railroad in disorder. It was a critical moment, thought Geary. The right flank seemed threatened, and Woods sent word that the Rebels appeared ready to attack. Hooker ordered Geary to put in his last brigade, the New Yorkers commanded by Col. David Ireland.[30]

Ireland's soldiers had to move from their shelter behind the stone railroad depot and sprint across the six-hundred-yard open field south of Ringgold to reach the houses and barn west of the gap. In the rush forward, Capt. Charles T. Greene, the son of General Greene, was struck by a shell that killed his horse and mangled his right leg. Once behind the buildings, Ireland's men began to improvise breastworks, having learned all too well on July 2 at Culp's Hill the value of frontal protection. Ireland's soldiers even utilized an old wagon bed, filling it with rails for shelter. Since Goldthwaite's Rebel guns were only a scant one hundred yards distant, the danger was fully evident. A soldier watched as the Rebels rolled one of their Napoleons forward and fired canister into the barn. Chips, splinters, and boards flew in every direction, he observed. Yet their fire was too high, and sharpshooters crept forward to shoot the cannoneers. Only four shots were fired at the barn before the sharpshooters made the gun's site too dangerous. The cannon was pulled away by prolonge.[31]

Thereafter, Ireland's troops lay behind the barn and natural cover for more than an hour, shooting only occasionally. By Ireland's orders, the men had been told "not to waste their ammunition, or [even] expose themselves." It was all according to Joe Hooker's latest orders. For the time being, Fighting Joe had given up on assaulting the gap or ridge. Hooker admitted he had been "disarmed" by the previous successes of his troops. Yet it was already apparent that fighting Pat Cleburne's command was unlike dealing with Bragg's other beaten and bedraggled troops.[32]

Joe Hooker was fretting, fuming, and waiting. The problem was his missing artillery. Hooker was now convinced he was facing "an overwhelming [enemy] force." He said, "I deemed it unwise to call up the commands of Palmer and Cruft [which were nearby] . . . to deliver a general attack without my artillery." Hooker thus ordered "no advance to be made" and "firing to be discontinued except in self defense." When scattered firing continued, Hooker became furious; despite his "emphatic and repeated instructions," some officers and men just didn't want to listen.[33]

Joe Hooker's artillery had been stacked up along the western bank of Chickamauga Creek since 4:30 P.M. on the twenty-sixth. The infantry had been able to cross on a temporary footbridge, but there was no way for the guns to get across; the creek was too deep to ford, and the bridge was inadequate. Butterfield, Hooker's chief of staff, had told an inquiring artillery officer to wait for the pontoons, due up momentarily. Yet by the morning of the twenty-seventh, they still hadn't arrived. Balks and chess planks had to be ordered up from Chattanooga and timber for the remaining portion had to be cut and hauled to the site. Due to the delay, construction of the replacement bridge had begun about 9:00 P.M. on the twenty-sixth and proceeded through the night with a work detail of about 450 men, mostly pioneers assigned to the Corps of Engineers. In the frigid five-foot-deep stream, the work was so difficult that three shifts had to be assigned. It was 6:30 A.M. on the twenty-seventh before the bridge was complete. By the time the leading battery was across, it was 8:00 AM., and soon thereafter the distant sound of cannon fire was heard in the distance.[34]

It was noon, and the men of the 149th New York Infantry were beginning to wonder whether they were ever going to escape their dire predicament. Enemy bullets kicked up the dirt about them and spattered mud in their faces. Yet the 149th could but lie quietly and endure it. Suddenly, they heard a rumbling on the macadamized pike in the rear. The noise grew louder, and the men, recognizing the telltale sound, began to cheer. Minutes later, from across the creek came the damnedest sight many of the men had ever seen.[35]

It was Capt. Clemens Landgraeber's Missouri horse artillery battery—four twelve-pounder howitzers. The "Flying Dutchman," as Landgraeber had been known since Vicksburg, was furious. The way along the road had been blocked with infantry columns, wagons, and the congestion incidental to an army on the move. Landgraeber, hearing the sound of the guns ahead, "was wild to go to the front," said a soldier. He dashed furiously about until he found a staff officer who would give him an order for the right-of-way. Then, lashing his horses into a gallop, he charged down the road, with cannons, limbers, and caissons wildly bounding, sending infantrymen scurrying for cover and clearing the road as if by magic.[36]

Landgraeber's appearance at Ringgold about noon was marked by prolonged cheering among Hooker's troops. The guns wheeled into battery at the end of the field fronting the gap, and minutes later they opened fire. The music of those guns was "sweeter to us than the notes of the dulcimer," wrote a much relieved soldier. Within a short time, Knapp's battery of ten-pounder Parrotts wheeled into town, and their fire soon added to the rain of projectiles arching toward Taylor's Ridge.[37]

Yet Joe Hooker continued to wait for the artillery fire to have an effect. He was contemplating sending some of Cruft's soldiers to the right to climb

Taylor's Ridge and approach the gap from the south when an unexpected visitor arrived. Minutes later, Hooker was standing in the street beside the depot, ardently talking about the enemy's stubborn stand and his own "great losses." It was all very embarrassing, as well as difficult to explain. The visitor peered at Hooker. The frown on his face clearly showed that Ulysses S. Grant was not pleased.[38]

It was one of Pat Cleburne's finest hours. For more than four hours, he had held off Hooker's vast columns. Generals Breckinridge and Joe Wheeler had been nearby, and hearing the heavy firing, they had come to the gap to see the fight. Cleburne was chatting with both when a dispatch from Hardee arrived at noon. The wagon trains were well advanced, said Hardee, and Cleburne might now safely withdraw. Cleburne talked over the matter with Wheeler and Breckinridge. Both urged him to pull back. Cleburne's men were still anxious to fight; some Arkansas officers wanted to charge and get that Yankee flag lodged in the crook of the apple tree. Cleburne wouldn't permit it; "it promised no . . . advantage to compensate for the loss of brave soldiers," he said. Cleburne's common sense was always prevalent; it was Cleburne's hallmark, which even the enemy be-grudgingly acknowledged. John W. Geary reported that at Ringgold Gap, he was up against the "best division in Bragg's army."[39]

Cleburne's decision was to withdraw. Some of the enemy's artillery was now present, and from the high ground more enemy troops were observed approaching Ringgold. Although some of Granbury's Texans were hidden along the fringe of timber, poised to make a countercharge across the plain if the Yankees attacked toward the gap, the enemy had not advanced, nor was there any indication they would soon do so. About 12:30 P.M., Cleburne had the brush screen masking Goldthwaite's artillery rebuilt, then withdrew the cannon. Cleburne's infantry pulled back simultaneously. Within an hour, the last of the skirmishers were withdrawn and the Ringgold Gap battlefield lay silent.[40]

At a cost of 20 killed, 190 wounded, and 11 missing, Cleburne had inflicted a heavy loss on Hooker's overconfident pursuers. Federal casualties for Ringgold Gap were listed at 507 by Hooker on the twenty-eighth. The price in depleted morale was even heavier.[41]

The scene at the railroad depot in Ringgold was both chaotic and astound-ing, wrote an amazed civilian observer, William W. Smith, one of Grant's party. A long procession of wounded were being carried past on litters and deposited in the brick tavern near the depot. Stragglers were roaming through town, "catching pigs and poking chickens from under sheds and houses with their ramrods." Peter Osterhaus, shaken by the heavy losses in his command, was disconsolate. His troops had been recklessly pushed ahead to certain destruction, he lamented. Osterhaus was particularly bitter over Fighting Joe's handling of the battle. One of Osterhaus's blood-smeared colonels wandered through the tavern, his hand partially shot off, moaning that every one of his officers had been slaughtered. It was a scene to tear at the very soul, noted Smith. Hooker was at the depot, sitting alone at a barrel and eating "a sandwich and . . . drinking tea from a tin cup." After reporting to Grant, Hooker wandered down the street to find better fare at a nearby house.[42]

Undaunted by the vast chaos and misery about him, Ulysses S. Grant, upon his arrival about 12:30 P.M., had taken prompt action to maneuver the enemy from their strong position. A dispatch to William Tecumseh Sherman, near Graysville, ordered Sherman to send a force down the valley east of Taylor's Ridge "to turn the enemy's position." The grim Grant wrote, "It looks as if it will be hard to dislodge them [from here]."[43]

A half hour later, Grant reported that the action at Ringgold was over. The Rebels had withdrawn just as some of Geary's men, noticing the lack of fire, pushed forward to check on the enemy's presence. They found an abandoned guidon and a Stars and Bars, the Confederate battle flag, which Hooker later claimed as captured in the fighting. Cleburne, the Confederacy's gray fox, was gone.[44]

Grant did not pursue. There had been enough futility that day. Although some troops advanced to a burning bridge beyond the gap and extinguished the flames, they were soon recalled. Finally, at 3:00 P.M., Grant authorized a reconnaissance by Grose's brigade in the direction of Tunnel Hill. By that time, Cleburne's Division was found strongly posted along "Dick's Ridge," about three miles from Ringgold, and Grose returned at dark with little more than gossip to report.[45]

November 27 had represented "the first great fault in this admirable campaign," wrote Charles A. Dana, who arrived after the fighting ended. He noted the grumbling about Hooker's lack of "common sense" in making a frontal attack. By outflanking the Rebels' position, wrote Dana, Hooker wouldn't have lost fifty men, much less the more than five hundred casualties he did suffer. Nonetheless, said Dana, the Federal army was now "perfectly concentrated." Indeed, despite Bragg's escape, the Rebels were "completely out of this portion of the country," and the campaign had ended, reflected Ulysses S. Grant.[46]

That night, the mood was relaxed at the gracious two-story brick homestead in Ringgold that had been chosen for Grant's headquarters. Following a meal of corn bread, pork, and coffee, a staff officer played the piano, and Grant "petted" the children's heads. The mother seemed to think General Grant was "not such a bad man after all," observed a guest. There were jokes aplenty among the staff officers, and when, due to the confined quarters at the homestead, Lt. Peter Hudson went next door to sleep, he soon returned. He had found a dead Rebel under a blanket, and it "smell[ed] too close." This had everyone shaking with laughter, said William Smith, Grant's guest. Capt. Ely Parker, a full-blooded Seneca, and Charles A. Dana then began "talking Indian" to the amusement of all. Later, when William Smith warned Dana that word of a pending Rebel night attack had just been received, Dana seemed scared. It was a good joke, thought Smith, and they all went to sleep chuckling.[47]

The chaplain of the 13th Illinois Infantry was roaming the battlefield that evening and came to the carnage at the cluster of buildings near the gap, where his regiment had fought. Behind an old corncrib lay a private of the 13th, shot six times and bloody from head to foot. He had been hit four times with rifle balls and twice with canister as he lay helpless on the ground, sadly noted the chaplain. Nearby was a horse lying in the wagon shed. The animal had been first hit in one leg, then a second. The third wound finally dropped the horse to the ground, where he died struggling to get up on his one remaining good leg.[48]

Among the wounded of his regiment, Chaplain Arnold T. Needham found Capt. Walter Blanchard, his leg horribly shattered at the knee. He was in the Jobe house, staining Mrs. Jobe's feather bed red as the blood trickled from his bandage. When he saw the chaplain, Blanchard stretched out his hands and uttered, "I told you it would be so, but I did my duty!"[49]

Remembering Blanchard's premonition, the chaplain offered spiritual comfort. Yet Blanchard wanted to confess. "I have been a terrible backslider," gasped the captain, "but God has been merciful to me; I would not give [up] . . . the peace I now have." Aided by another officer who was a lawyer, Chaplain Needham seated himself beside the dying captain and wrote out the man's will. When it was done, the will was read to him. "He nodded assent," wrote the chaplain, "for his tongue was already paralyzed. I gave him the pen with which to write his signature. [Yet] a circular mark was all he could make . . . He grasped my hand as best he could . . . [and] as I prayed he pressed my hand when I mentioned his family . . . When I rose to speak to him his hand was set in death, and he was gone."[50]

Jimmy McCollum, the chaplain's special friend, was found in town, on the floor of a vacant store. The surgeons had looked at him, but they had only shaken their heads. Nothing could be done for him; his wound was mortal. All around him, the wounded lay groaning, and the surgeons were busily amputating arms and legs. "I attempted to speak to Jimmy but broke down," gasped the chaplain. "I loved him as Jonathan loved David." They had shared a common experience as prisoners of war, and their bond was strong. "I attempted to sing Jimmy's favorite hymn, the one he had always sung at prayer meetings:

> 'Come sing to me of Heaven,
> When I'm about to die;
> Sing songs of holy ecstasy,
> To wait my soul on high . . .' "

The chaplain never finished the song. "We mingled our tears, and amid my sobs I asked Jimmy if [all] was well with his soul. 'Oh! God is so good,' he replied. 'He has received me in Christ.' " He wanted to see his mother once more, yet he was "resigned to God's will."[51]

The chaplain later learned Jimmy had died the next day while in a flatcar en route to Chattanooga. He was buried in his blanket on the banks of Chickamauga Creek, with the end of a hardtack box as his headboard.[52]

It was a painful reminder of the injustice of war. Jimmy McCollum was yet another of Joe Hooker's men who wouldn't run away.

CHAPTER 42

"Such Is Civilized War"

The high road to Georgia was now open," observed a Federal soldier, but Ulysses S. Grant had a difficult decision to make. He wanted to "pursue the broken and demoralized retreating enemy. . . . An army never was whipped as badly as Bragg['s] was," considered Grant. "So far as any opposition the enemy could make I could have marched to Atlanta or any other place in the Confederacy." Yet as Charles A. Dana observed, "The condition of the roads, and the impossibility of getting supplies even as far as Chattanooga . . . render a movement upon Rome, [Georgia] and Atlanta impracticable for the present. Such a movement cannot safely be undertaken until six months' supply for both troops and animals is accumulated here [Chattanooga], so that we shall no longer be under the necessity of employing a great part of our force to guard railroads in our rear." Grant admitted, "I had not rations to take nor the means of taking them, and this mountain country will not support an army."[1]

In a conference with William Tecumseh Sherman at Ringgold late on the afternoon of the twenty-seventh, Grant had discussed the various options. Yet Grant had already made up his mind. "I do not care about the pursuit being continued farther south," he wrote on the twenty-seventh, shortly after arriving at Ringgold. The only important aspect, said Grant, was to tear up the Cleveland to Dalton railroad, thus interrupting communications between Bragg and Longstreet. Sherman's assurance that Howard and his Eleventh Corps troops were already wreaking havoc on the railroad at Red Clay seemed to satisfy the Federal commander. As early as 1:00 P.M. on the twenty-seventh, Grant reported, "I do not intend to pursue [Bragg] farther," and he acknowledged to Halleck an hour later that he was "not prepared" at present to continue south.[2]

Grant's pursuit had been exclusively an infantry affair. The Federal cavalry was far distant, sent long ago from Chattanooga in order to provision the famished horses. For the same reason, a lack of horses, artillery support was limited, reduced as it was essentially to Sherman's and Hooker's light batteries. The Georgia country roads were so muddied and poor that their struggling animals couldn't make rapid progress during a pursuit. Both Sherman's and Hooker's columns thus had been spearheaded by infantry, without practical artillery or cavalry help. Continuing to pursue Bragg's army under these circumstances was an invitation to disaster, and after Ringgold Gap, Grant realized it.

On November 28, Grant departed for Chattanooga via Graysville, leaving instructions for Hooker to remain in the vicinity of Ringgold for a few days to protect the flank of Sherman's column as it advanced north up the railroad between Cleveland and Dalton. Sherman would tear up the track and prevent Longstreet from rapidly retreating south from Knoxville to join Bragg. It had begun raining during the night, and the twenty-eighth was "a miserable day," grumbled an officer, who added, "Our shebang mess club is played out and I am nearly starved."[3]

About 10:30 A.M., the rain ceased, and as Grant's party rode northward toward Graysville, they saw billowing smoke from "public buildings and factories ascending in fiery columns to [the] heavens." Along the line of the Western and Atlantic Railroad, groups of soldiers were working, piling ties along the track, ready to be burned, then stacking iron rails on top.[4]

At Graysville, William Tecumseh Sherman was found in the railroad depot, where a sumptuous lunch was prepared and Grant and the generals talked at length. Then, after about an hour's visit, Grant and his staff departed for Chattanooga, occasionally turning in their saddles to view the towering black cloud rising from Graysville. The railroad depot was now in flames, and one of Grant's party noted how it was a strange feeling to observe the flames shooting skyward from a venerable old building where "we had a few minutes before been refreshing ourselves." The man noted with resignation in his journal, "Such is civilized war."[5]

That night at Chattanooga, Ulysses Grant began attending to a festering difficulty that once again was greatly irritating him. Of immediate importance was the "rescue" of Burnside at Knoxville. Burdened by the intense pressure from Halleck and President Lincoln to advance rapidly and save east Tennessee from Longstreet's expedition, Grant began actively to regard the "imperative necessity of relieving Burnside."[6]

Owing to Grant's delay in issuing orders to start moving Granger's column, finally written at 1:00 P.M. on the twenty-seventh from Ringgold, George H. Thomas did not receive the dispatch until about 7:00 P.M. The head of Granger's column then marched from Chattanooga on the afternoon of the twenty-eighth, but Grant wasn't satisfied. Finding upon his return to Chattanooga that much of Granger's division "had not yet got off," Grant again lost patience with the Army of the Cumberland. He learned from Burnside that as late as the morning of the twenty-seventh, Longstreet was still besieging Knoxville. Since Burnside reported only enough rations on hand for another ten or twelve days, and thereafter he either "must surrender or retreat," Grant was greatly upset. Saying that any consideration of a retreat from Knoxville was "an impossibility," he noted that Granger was still bogged down in getting supplies, and he "didn't have the number of men I had directed." Fuming that Granger moved only "with reluctance and complaints" and claiming he had "lost all faith in his [Granger's] energy and capacity to manage an expedition of the importance of this one," Grant told William Tecumseh Sherman on the twenty-ninth, "I shall have to send you."[7]

"Notwithstanding the fact that two divisions of Sherman's forces had marched from Memphis, and had gone into battle immediately on their arrival at Chattanooga," Grant again chose to rely on his old favorite. Sherman would command his own and Granger's combined forces and move to relieve Knoxville with "all possible dispatch."* The entire situation was yet another example of how the Army of the Cumberland's generals just didn't measure up in Grant's eyes.[8]

The combat at Ringgold Gap was very rewarding, reflected an Alabama soldier after reaching camp at Dalton, Georgia. "We gave the [Yankees] a decent whippin' . . . killed a great many of them, and our company didn't get any man hurt." "I think that it was mis-management that caused us to have to retreat," he concluded in reflection. "The enemy was so elated with his victory [at Missionary Ridge] that he rushed blindly into the trap [Cleburne] had planned out for them," noted one of Manigault's colonels.[9]

In the aftermath of the wretched retreat to Dalton, the mood of much of the Confederate army was self-analytical. "Our army is in much better spirits than anyone would imagine," wrote a pensive Alabama colonel. Although "everybody, both officers and men, seem to be ashamed of our defeat [at Missionary Ridge], I honestly believe that it will have a good effect upon the troops. When they get a chance to meet the enemy again they will pay him back with interest." Missionary Ridge seemed but an aberration to some, an unfortunate, star-crossed encounter that due to bad luck had resulted in an unforeseen defeat.[10]

"The imbecility and cowardice of one brigade involved the whole army in defeat," considered a Georgia artillerist. Defiantly, he announced that he was "proud of the conduct of my men, and believe they would have stood with me to the guns until we were bayonetted. I left only when valor

---

*Sherman and Granger's combined forces approached Knoxvile in early December, causing Longstreet to break off his eighteen-day siege on the night of December 4 and withdraw eastward. Eventually, Longstreet was recalled (in the spring of 1864) to the Army of Northern Virginia. By December 9, 1863, Sherman's troops were en route "by slow marches" back to Chattanooga.

was in vain." To his father, he confided, "We have been overpowered in numbers and met with serious reverses, [yet] I hope, however, that out of the disaster some good may yet come . . . I never want to leave this army till we have punished the Yankees who drove us from Missionary Ridge."[11]

A veteran Alabama officer writing to his family found that raw emotions poured from his pen: "I fear that you all at home have become beclouded in doubts, fears, and despondency. Shake them off. This is doubtless our darkest hour. The sky of our political horizon is now dark and shadowed, but ere long the star of our independence will arise and shine forth, and gladden the hearts of our suffering people."[12]

A Florida soldier, numb with cold while at Dalton during the same week, had found temporary solace in a hospital building. Yet the man noted in his diary: "We moved into the woods in the afternoon, it being warmer there than at the hospital buildings." A sergeant of one of Breckinridge's units wrote home that having lost all of his spare clothing in the ditches at Chattanooga, he now suffered almost unbearably. "It is so cold that I can hardly write," he admitted. "The ground being frozen all day long, [is as it] had been for a week past." Another soldier recorded how "at 3 a.m. I was called to draw rations, and after standing in the rain for about three hours I got about enough half cooked corn bread and boiled beef for one day, but it is [to be] three days' rations."[13]

The men were willing; the spirit was still there. Yet the harsh reality was equally apparent. "We want now at the head of this army some general who will act with boldness and follow up every advantage he may gain," pleaded a Georgia officer. "This army will fight with all the desperation and valor displayed at Chickamauga, for they are heartily ashamed of their conduct at Missionary Ridge." "I have no heart to speak further of the matter," he concluded. "I regard the affair as disgraceful, and as shameful as it is humiliating and unfortunate."[14]

Cleburne's rear-guard action at Ringgold had changed everything and yet nothing. The Chattanooga campaign had ended as it had begun—with an impressive Confederate victory. Yet the consequences of the past two months for the Confederacy were self-evident.

The town of Ringgold, Georgia, was an impressive place, wrote a Federal soldier. "The houses are mostly of brick and are well built." "I never saw finer ones in a town of its size," agreed a Pennsylvania lieutenant. Beyond its macadamized road, large stone railroad depot, and impressive scenery, Ringgold also prided itself on cultural refinements that included a steepled church. Yet, noted a soldier, the town of perhaps two thousand citizens before the war was now reduced to about one hundred inhabitants. The ravages of war were particularly evident along the eastern side of town, where many houses were "shot full of holes" and dozens of shallow graves scarred the freshly shoveled ground.[15]

Amid this melancholy setting, Thomas's soldiers were seen busily playing chuck-a-luck. Others were pilfering "chickens, sheep, and bacon" from the local residents. The war at a private's level had progressed beyond an altruistic caring; life was from moment to moment in the army. Moreover, because Ringgold had been at the site near which the Andrews railroad raiders had been captured in 1862, and now was the scene of Hooker's bloody defeat on the twenty-seventh, there was a strong distaste in the mouths of many Yankees for this town. The house and barn of John Coombs, the local railroad agent, was burned on the twenty-ninth when some soldiers said they had seen "our men [being] shot from these buildings" during the battle. Another hapless civilian, an "able bodied man" who emerged from a cellar after the fighting ended, was eyed with suspicion by the authorities, and despite his claim of innocence, he "was counted among the prisoners given a free ride North."[16]

Yet Ringgold's hour of greatest agony was still ahead. It was endured only as the last of Hooker's soldiers prepared to evacuate the town early on the morning of November 30. Some of Geary's Easterners were the last to depart, and they witnessed the gloomy events.

During the previous afternoon, the remaining families in town had been herded into vacant buildings in the outskirts. Ringgold, they were told, was to be torched as "a military necessity." That night, the provost marshal and his men swiftly began their systematic work. As the lengthy columns of blue-clad soldiers marched across the creek and up a western hill, the midnight sky was aglow with flames. The depot, gristmills, hotels, commercial buildings, and private dwellings were all ablaze. Seen amid the conflagration were frantic figures running wildly about, striving in vain to put out the flames and save some of their belongings. In the center of town, a dense column of black smoke jetted skyward from the courthouse and jail. Minutes later, a deep explosion showered the scene with flaming debris and broken bricks. The main powder charge had detonated, completing the destruction of the village. To a lieutenant of Candy's brigade, the sight was but a fitting end: "I never witnessed a more sublime sight than the burning of that town." Particularly appropriate, thought the lieutenant, was the destruction of over $100,000 worth of property belonging to the man "who raised the first secession flag in that town."[17]

November 30, 1863, would be long remembered by the transplanted soldiers from the Army of the Potomac. "The officers of our brigade almost idolize old Joe Hooker," continued the lieutenant. "He handled us to perfection this time."[18]

CHAPTER 43

"LET THE PAST TAKE
CARE OF ITSELF"

November 30, 1863, was an equally remarkable day for the gray soldiers in and about Dalton, Georgia. The telegraph wires had been busy to and from Dalton since Bragg's arrival on the twenty-seventh. On that date, Bragg had telegraphed to Richmond that the army "could make no stand at Chickamauga [Station] against the enemy's superior forces" and, accordingly, had fallen back to Dalton. In a message to Joe Johnston at Meridian, Mississippi, Bragg acknowledged, "The disastrous panic [at Missionary Ridge] is unexplainable." A few days later, he published a circular ordering all corps commanders to forward the names of officers who abandoned the battlefield without authority, so their names could be sent to Richmond and "dropped from the rolls."[1]

Ironically, on November 30, it was Braxton Bragg who was dropped from the rolls of the Army of Tennessee. Bragg had become one of the South's greatest liabilities. Devastated by the events at Chattanooga, and now believing that the army might have to retreat farther south, to Resaca, Bragg was greatly depressed. The fractionalized command structure of his army and the deep-seated personal animosities and rival cliques were as a millstone that weighed heavily about his neck. Perhaps the most despised general associated with any Confederate army, Bragg became even more remorseful when he contemplated what had occurred. "My first estimate of our disaster was not too large, and time only can restore order and morale," he admitted in a communiqué to the Davis administration on November 29. In a fit of melancholia, Bragg then added, "I deem it due to the cause and to myself to ask for relief from command and an investigation into the causes of the defeat."[2]

Although in succeeding days Bragg sought to modify and even alter the prospects for his removal, on November 30, Jefferson Davis acceded to political pressure and notified Bragg he was "relieved from command." Two days later, Braxton Bragg bid farewell to the Army of Tennessee and departed for home. Bragg's attitude at the time was fully evident when he penned a fawning, plaintive letter to Davis. Despite his tacit admission that "the whole responsibility and disgrace rest on my humble head," Bragg's true purpose was self-evident: "Let us concentrate our available men, unite them with this gallant little army . . . and with our greatest and best leader at the head, yourself, if practicable, march the whole upon the enemy and crush him." Then, beyond his ill-disguised attempt at flattery, Bragg brazenly petitioned in the next sentence: "I . . . trust that I may be allowed to participate in the struggle which may restore to us the character, the prestige, and the country we have lost."[3]

Following three months' retirement, Bragg was called back to the side of his president as "special military adviser." Ultimately, he became in essence Davis's chief of staff, with responsibility for "the conduct of military operations in the Armies of the Confederacy." Jefferson Davis simply would not allow himself to be proven wrong in his personal judgments. Soon he was flaunting Bragg's prominence and allowing the acerbic North Carolinian to influence command decisions that would ultimately prove ruinous to the Confederacy.[4]

Lt. Gen. William J. Hardee, the man who six months earlier had supported, along with Leonidas Polk, Bragg's ouster, was temporarily assigned to replace Bragg on November 30. Hardee's initial proclamation to the soldiers of the Army of Tennessee asserted that "there is no cause for discouragement. . . . The overwhelming numbers of the enemy forced us back from Missionary Ridge, but the army is still intact and in good heart. Our losses were small and will be rapidly replaced. The country is looking to you with painful interest. I feel that it can rely on you. Only the weak and the timid need to be cheered by constant success. . . . Let the past take care of itself; we can and must secure the future."[5]

The future was uncertain for the Army of Tennessee. Hardee, who declined to accept permanent command of the army, perhaps in deference to protocol, pronounced the army "in fine condition" on December 24, 1863, three days before General Joe Johnston assumed command. The strength of the army was now greater than that engaged at Missionary Ridge, claimed Hardee, and the artillery losses had been replaced. New arms were issued, clothing, shoes, and blankets provided, and transportation improved. Even the commissary had been refurbished so that receipts were in excess of consumption.[6]

Four days later, following his inspection of the Army of Tennessee, and perhaps indicative of the man's cautious, apprehensive nature, Joe Johnston found that "this army is now far from being in condition to resume the offensive. It is deficient in numbers, arms, subsistence stores, and field transportation." Particularly worrisome, grumbled Johnston, was his inability to keep the army in condition to move and fight based upon an ineffective supply system that gave him "little if any power to procure supplies for the army." Complaint after complaint was to follow, so that little more than six months later Jefferson Davis and the authorities became totally fed up with Johnston's excuses and criticisms. This circumstance materially contributed to Johnston's removal from command following the retreat to Atlanta.[7]

To the hard-bitten veterans of the Army of Tennessee, Braxton Bragg's ouster on November 30 was looked upon with mixed emotions. Somewhat embarrassed by the newspaper criticism leveled at Bragg following Missionary Ridge, the men of Bate's and Finley's brigades later gave Bragg an elegant presentation sword inscribed: "[In] high appreciation of his military services and a compliment to his personal gallantry witnessed by them amid the misfortunes of the day at the Battle of Missionary Ridge." Some soldiers organized a serenade for Bragg on the night of December 1, but as one diarist recorded: "I did not go as it was too cold." To an Alabama private, the removal of Bragg was of uncertain effect: "[It] will make matter[s] better or worse, [but] I can't tell which it will be." William J. Hardee referred to Bragg as having "the steady purpose, the unflinching courage, and the unsullied patriotism of the distinguished leader." In his initial message to the soldiers, Hardee charitably stated, "[He] will be long remembered by this army and by the country he has served so well."[8]

Yet to many, Bragg's departure meant the prospect of a new beginning and an end to the prolonged agony of repeated defeat. "I am glad Bragg has been relieved," wrote a Georgia lieutenant on December 6, ". . . [because] it is necessary to have unity of action and unbounded confidence in our leader." Pat Cleburne had been disgusted with Bragg's mismanagement, and when he read a portion of his personal diary to several subordinates on December 9, his criticisms of Bragg, noted a captain, "were quite severe." Echoing the sentiments of a Richmond newspaper editor who declared it was better to have "an army of asses led by a lion" than "an army of lions led by an ass," a war-wise Tennessee private reflected upon Bragg's debacle at Chattanooga and wrote: "More depends on a good general than the lives of many privates. The private loses his life, the general his country."[9]

With ironic inequity, Patrick Cleburne, the Confederate general who had persevered through the disasters at Chattanooga, with credit due for some of the most brilliant tactical victories of the war, was soon all but ignored. Cleburne had succeeded where others had so miserably failed. His repulse of and victory over the celebrated warrior William Tecumseh Sherman on November 25 in the face of overwhelming odds was enhanced two days later when Cleburne's troops defeated Joe Hooker's vast ranks at Ringgold Gap. Cleburne's performance identified him as the outstanding combat commander in the Army of Tennessee, clearly a man to promote and rely upon. Yet Cleburne's star was dimmed by his former criticism of

Braxton Bragg. When his controversial proposal to enlist slaves for combat service with the army was forwarded to Richmond in January 1864, an outraged Jefferson Davis seems to have blacklisted Cleburne, denying him promotion to higher command.[10]

The best and the brightest had become manifest through trial and ordeal. The Confederate Congress clearly saw the evidence. On February 9, 1864, a joint resolution awarded the "thanks of Congress" to Pat Cleburne for his brilliant victory at Ringgold Gap. Unfortunately for the South, Jefferson Davis was blinded by an all too familiar weakness: his stoic pride and an inability to select and fully utilize competent military commanders. Ironically, Pat Cleburne would die at Franklin, Tennessee, on November 30, 1864, exactly one year after Bragg's removal from the army, a victim of misperception and incompetence characteristic of several of Davis's senior generals who commanded the valiant soldiers of the Army of Tennessee. Chattanooga, despite the overall defeat, had shown the promise of tactical victory under capable leaders. The Battle of Franklin exemplified the reality.[11]

It had been a remarkable campaign. Grant knew that his "magnificent victory" would count for much with the Lincoln administration, and the accolades were quick in coming. Halleck and Abraham Lincoln congratulated Grant heartily on his victories at Chattanooga. On December 8, Lincoln tendered Grant "more than thanks, my profoundest gratitude for the skill, courage, and perseverance with which you and [the army have], over so great difficulties . . . effected that important object. God bless you all." On December 17, the U.S. Congress passed a resolution of thanks and provided for the minting of a suitable gold medal to be presented to Grant in the name of the people of the United States for "gallantry and good conduct."[12]

Emerson Opdycke's earlier assessment had been correct. U. S. Grant, already a household word, was now the most famous soldier in the nation. Within a few months, Grant would be honored with promotion to lieutenant general, a rank specially authorized by Congress and previously held only by George Washington. Ulysses Grant's future was not only assured; he was destined to be regarded as one of the greatest of American heroes.[13]

There was an ironic twist to the popular conception of Grant's great victory. Among army insiders there was an awareness that Grant had been most fortunate. "The victory was quite as surprising to those who won it as to those who lost it," wrote James H. Wilson of Grant's staff. Even Charles A. Dana told Wilson: "The best brains supplied to Grant from any quarter [during the Chattanooga campaign] were [those of] . . . his own staff. Indeed, had the full story been known—that Grant's decisions at Chattanooga had been as often wrong as correct; that George H. Thomas and his soldiers had more to do with the actual victory than Grant, whose basic battle plan had failed; or that good luck, rather than William Tecumseh Sherman, had been the key element—the seeds of doubt would have once again been sown.[14]

Yet Grant was truly a man befitting the nation's hour of ordeal. His protégé, Sherman, said of him that he didn't scare worth a damn; "he is the great general, he makes his plans and goes ahead, cares nothing for what he cannot see, while some things I cannot see at times scare me like hell." Grant's tough inner fiber was never more evident than at Chattanooga, and above all else, the man was a tenacious fighter, a general who knew how to win. His remarkable composure under the stress that made others wilt in a crisis was well illustrated when on December 15 Grant rode from Chattanooga with Thomas and Baldy Smith to visit the Chickamauga battlefield.[15]

It was a grisly scene, with leering skulls stuck on poles and body parts laid on stumps and logs. Wild hogs had rooted up the shallowly buried carcasses and fed on the rotting remains. Due to heavy rains, the creeks had overflowed, washing out bodies and scattering debris. In one place, a skeleton was found lodged in a small tree. Grant, impressed by the ravaged wilderness, confided to an officer, "These trees would make a good lead mine."[16]

When crossing a creek, the horses stopped to drink and Grant pulled out his matchbox and a cigar. While he was lighting the cigar, his cream-colored horse "let fly with his hind hooves" at Baldy Smith's mount. Smith, perturbed, reached over and whacked the rump of Grant's horse with his riding stick, commenting at the same time that Grant had a "vicious horse." A major with the party had been watching Grant intently at the time. "He never for an instant changed the position of his hand or head in lighting his cigar, nor said a word, nor did he seem conscious of the episode, [despite the jerking of] his horse." The major was amazed at Grant's "stolid indifference." It was "very characteristic of his qualities as a soldier," he believed.[17]

Throughout the days and weeks following Chattanooga, Grant maintained a similar levelheaded indifference to all the political fuss and fawning over him. It simply was not his style. Allegedly, according to the sneering Joe Hooker, Grant said of the victory at Missionary Ridge: "Damn the battle, I had nothing to do with it." Yet beneath the rough-hewn facade, there was a lingering pride of accomplishment and a sense of greater destiny which even Grant was aware of. After announcing on December 7 that six thousand Rebel prisoners were on hand along with forty-two pieces of captured artillery, Grant could well boast to a friend, "Altogether I feel well satisfied and the army [soldiers] feel that they have accomplished great things. Well they may." To his wife, he acknowledged that "[it] is all over at Chattanooga," and he predicted. "I shall probably not remain in Chattanooga many weeks longer. Where I expect to go would not be proper for me to state, but I have no expectation of spending a winter in idleness."[18]

What Grant contemplated was a midwinter offensive to harass the enemy and prevent reorganization of their armies. As early as November 29, Grant had concocted a plan to sail with 35,000 men via the Mississippi River to invest Mobile and wreak havoc on the interior of Alabama. "It will go far towards breaking down the rebellion before spring," he advised Henry Halleck.[19]

Yet Lincoln and Halleck had more important campaigns in mind for the victor of Chattanooga. Twice within the past six months, Grant had earned national hero status for his crucial victories. By the spring of 1864, he was made commander in chief of the combined Union armies. Soon thereafter, Grant went to Virginia to direct operations against Richmond and Robert E. Lee's army.

Left behind as caretaker in the West was Grant's trusted favorite, William Tecumseh Sherman, who exercised command during the crucial campaign for Atlanta. Only by accident, during John Bell Hood's 1864 invasion of Tennessee, would George H. Thomas and units of the Army of the Cumberland again achieve a brief prominence and a measure of due recognition. Even today, many observers regard Thomas and his veteran army more with an austere indifference than with the recognition they deserve for their exceptional performance. It is but one of the many lingering inequities of popular history.

The die had been cast. Chattanooga had been a crucial and remarkable turning point in the war, a milestone on the path of doom for the Confederacy. The gateway to the Southern heartland was ajar. Thereafter, the wasting war of defense, of depleting resources in an ever-constricted territory, of irreplaceable manpower losses, and of personal despair for Southern citizens ravaged and economically ruined by invasion would be fully manifest. Lincoln had been right in his famous "thorn in its [Confederacy's] vitals" remark: the Federal army's holding of Chattanooga was crucial to the demise of the Confederacy. As Confederate War Department clerk John B. Jones confided in his diary, the loss of Chattanooga represented an "incalculable disaster" for the South. Mary Chestnut, the Richmond socialite, thus noted at the end of 1863, the "gloom and unspoken despondency hanging like a pall everywhere." In the North, the overall effect was the opposite. Celebrations, multigun salutes, and praise for the war effort by the media added to a growing popular expectation of victory and a quick end to a devastating war.[20]

Strategically, whereas the Confederacy had anticipated capitalizing on their great Chickamauga victory by reoccupying Chattanooga—this being the initial means of regaining Tennessee—that hope had been dashed. The ultimate military consequences after two months of siege had been nothing short of a humiliating defeat for the South. Ultimately, this was the final arbiter; upon battlefield victory or defeat hinged such vital elements as the popular will to continue the war, recruiting, and the total effort expended. Even more insidiously, the western theater loomed increasingly as the area of decision. The question of Southern independence was being inexorably shaped in the West, despite the political and practical attention given to the East. That the western regions continued to remain subordinate in the Richmond administration's perspectives was a major aspect of the Confederacy's ultimate defeat. Battles such as Stones River, Champion's Hill, and Chattanooga seem to have been regarded with a certain carelessness of interpretation. It was as if the consequences were momentary and isolated rather than directly contributory to a dire final result. Chattanooga, from Jefferson Davis's viewpoint, was but an aberration, blamable on the troops: "Our troops inexplicably abandoned a position of great strength, and by a disorderly retreat compelled the commander to withdraw," Davis informed the Confederate Congress on December 7, 1863. "It is believed that if the troops who yielded to the assault had fought with the valor which they had displayed on previous occasions . . . the enemy would have been repulsed with very great slaughter, and our country would have escaped [this] misfortune," he continued. Chattanooga, asserted the Confederate president, was the first defeat attributed to the misconduct of the troops. Despite this setback, and that success in driving the enemy from Southern soil had not equaled expectations, Davis concluded his message to Congress by saying the enemy's "progress [in winning the war] has been checked. . . . If we are forced to regret losses in Tennessee and Arkansas, we are not without ground for congratulation on successes in Louisiana and Texas," and there was never "any doubt of the [end] result"—Confederate independence. As many foresaw, Jefferson Davis's perspectives reflected a notable distortion, even at the end of 1863, with the fighting still to reach its grisly maximum in human carnage.[21]

The assessment of the Battles for Chattanooga, despite the fact that they were initially regarded as enormous Union victories, has evolved through the years to become today somewhat of a military paradox. The campaign had brought together perhaps the greatest galaxy of Union generals ever assembled on one battlefield of the war: Grant, Sherman, Thomas, Sheridan, Hooker, and Rosecrans were then, or soon would be, household words. Yet perhaps even more remarkable, these celebrity generals were tactically checkmated or beaten in major fighting by the largely unheralded Pat Cleburne, despite the incapacity of Bragg and the bungling of other senior Confederate commanders. Whereas Cleburne's brilliance was never more apparent, Longstreet, Hardee, John K. Jackson, and Breckinridge had contributed to the net disaster, notwithstanding their propensity to blame others. As subsequent events would demonstrate, the whole cloth of the Confederacy had long since been woven of a weakened fabric, despite the battlefield brilliance of commanders such as Forrest, Cleburne, and Walthall. Jefferson Davis's assessment about the fault resting on the performance of the men was reflective of the Confederacy's real weakness— a lack of proper perspective by key leaders.

*   *   *

In the span of a few minutes on Missionary Ridge the destiny of nations had been tested. Although there was a long and bloody path ahead, including an appalling butcher's bill of casualties at such once-obscure places as Cold Harbor and Kennesaw Mountain, the agonizing journey's end was fully in sight. After Chattanooga, the prospect of Southern independence flickered ever lower, like a solitary candle in the gathering breeze. The nation's most grueling ordeal was drawing to a close.

At Chattanooga, the careers of Ulysses Grant and Braxton Bragg had been influenced dramatically. Yet this change hadn't occurred because of the sublime wisdom or specific plans of either general. Both had often stood helpless and astounded by the events at hand. The final result was truly explained in the strong arms and resolute minds of George H. Thomas's soldiers. Their spontaneous and unauthorized charge up Misssionary Ridge became the application of ultimate courage as a decisive element.

If Chattanooga had reflected a unique crisis, the men had been equal to the task. Missionary Ridge was, in truth, a great revelation. The soldiers knew the end result had followed not so much from their leaders' prowess as from their own willpower. Their legacy endures today; it is written in the mettle of all who would strive to overcome in the face of severe adversity. Great events often are guided more by man's resilient spirit than by precise planning and reason. At Chattanooga, that dominant spirit made an indelible mark on history. Those in the ranks had witnessed an ultimate truth on Missionary Ridge: Despite the endless quest for worldly success, to conquer one's self is the greatest victory of all.

ORDER OF BATTLE
CHATTANOOGA CAMPAIGN

UNION MILITARY DIVISION OF THE MISSISSIPPI

Maj. Gen. Ulysses S. Grant

ARMY OF THE CUMBERLAND

Maj. Gen. William Starke Rosecrans,

superseded October 20, 1863 by

Maj. Gen. George H. Thomas

Headquarters

1st Ohio Sharpshooters; 10th Ohio

FOURTH CORPS

Maj. Gen. Gordon Granger

First Division—Brig. Gen. Charles Cruft
82nd Illinois, Company E, escort
1st Brigade—Col. D. A. Enyart (detached to Bridgeport, Alabama, with Battery M, 44th U.S. Artillery)
2nd Brigade—Brig. Gen. Walter C. Whitaker (assigned to duty with Gen. Joseph Hooker—Lookout Mountain assault)
96th Illinois; 35th Indiana; 8th Kentucky; 40th, 51st, and 99th Ohio
3rd Brigade—Col. William Grose (assigned to duty with Gen. Joseph Hooker—Lookout Mountain assault)
59th, 75th, and 84th Illinois; 9th and 36th Indiana; 24th Ohio

Second Division—Maj. Gen. Philip H. Sheridan (assault on mid–Missionary Ridge)
1st Brigade—Col. Francis T. Sherman
36th, 44th, 73rd, 74th, and 88th Illinois; 22nd Indiana; 2nd and 15th Missouri; 24th Wisconsin

2nd Brigade—Brig. Gen. George D. Wagner
    100th Illinois; 13th, 40th, 51st, 57th, 58th Indiana; 26th and 97th
    Ohio
3rd Brigade—Col. Charles G. Harker
    22nd, 27th, 42nd, 51st, 79th Illinois; 3rd Kentucky; 64th, 65th, and
    125th Ohio
Artillery—Capt. Warren P. Edgarton
    1st Illinois Light, Battery M; 10th Indiana Battery; 1st Missouri
    Light, Battery I; 1st Ohio Light, Battery G; 4th U.S., Battery G;
    5th U.S., Battery H

Third Division—Brig. Gen. Thomas J. Wood (assault on mid–Missionary
    Ridge)
1st Brigade—Brig. Gen. August Willich
    25th, 35th, and 89th Illinois; 32nd and 68th Indiana; 8th Kansas;
    15th and 49th Ohio; 15th Wisconsin
2nd Brigade—Brig. Gen. William B. Hazen
    6th Indiana; 5th, 6th, and 23rd Kentucky; 1st, 6th, 41st, 93rd, and
    124th Ohio
3rd Brigade—Brig. Gen. Samuel Beatty
    79th and 86th Indiana; 9th and 17th Kentucky; 13th, 19th, and 59th
    Ohio
Artillery—Capt. Cullen Bradley
    Bridges's Illinois Light Battery; 6th Ohio Battery; 20th Ohio Bat-
    tery; Pennsylvania Light, Battery B

COMBINED ELEVENTH AND TWELFTH CORPS FIELD COMMAND

Maj. Gen. Joseph Hooker

15th Illinois Cavalry, Company K, headquarters escort

ELEVENTH CORPS
(assigned to duty with Maj. Gen. William T. Sherman)

Maj. Gen. Oliver Howard

8th New York, Independent Company, headquarters escort

Second Division—Brig. Gen. Adolph von Steinwehr
    1st Brigade—Col. Adolphus Bushbeck
        33rd New Jersey; 134th and 154th New York; 27th and 73rd
        Pennsylvania
    2nd Brigade—Col. Orland Smith
        33rd Massachusetts; 186th New York; 55th and 73rd Ohio

Third Division—Maj. Gen. Carl Schurz
    1st Brigade—Brig. Gen. Hector Tyndale
        101st Illinois; 45th and 143rd New York; 61st and 82nd Ohio
    2nd Brigade—Col. Wladimir Krzyzanowski
        58th, 119th, and 141st New York; 26th Wisconsin

3rd Brigade—Col. Frederick Hecker
    80th and 82nd Illinois; 68th New York; 75th Pennsylvania
Artillery: Maj. Thomas W. Osborn
    1st New York Light, Battery I; 13th Battery New York Light; 1st
    Ohio Light, Batteries I, K; 4th U.S., Battery G

TWELFTH CORPS

Maj. Gen. Henry W. Slocum

First Division—Brig. Gen. Joseph F. Knipe (assigned to duty guarding the Nashville and Chattanooga Railroad from Wartrace Bridge, Tennessee, to Bridgeport, Alabama, with Slocum's headquarters at Tullahoma, Tennessee)

Second Division—Brig. Gen. John W. Geary (Lookout Mountain assault)
    1st Brigade—Col. Charles Candy; Col. William R. Creighton; Col.
        Thomas J. Ahl
        5th, 7th, 28th, and 66th Ohio; 28th and 147th Pennsylvania
    2nd Brigade—Col. George A. Cobham, Jr.
        29th, 109th, and 111th Pennsylvania
    3rd Brigade—Col. David Ireland
        60th, 78th, 102nd, 137th, and 149th New York
    Artillery—Maj. John A. Reynolds
        Pennsylvania Light, Battery E; 5th U.S., Battery K

FOURTEENTH CORPS

Maj. Gen. John M. Palmer

1st Ohio Cavalry, Company I, headquarters escort

First Division—Brig. Gen. Richard W. Johnson (assault on mid–Missionary
    Ridge)
    1st Brigade—Brig. Gen. William P. Carlin
        104th Illinois; 28th, 42nd, and 88th Indiana; 2nd and 94th Ohio;
        10th Wisconsin
    2nd Brigade—Col. Marshall F. Moore; Col. William L. Stoughton
        19th Illinois; 11th Michigan; 69th Ohio; 15th U.S., 1st Battalion;
        16th U.S., 1st Battalion; 18th U.S., 1st and 2nd Battalions; 19th
        U.S., 1st Battalion
    3rd Brigade—Brig. Gen. John C. Starkweather (held line of entrenchments and forts at Chattanooga)
        24th and 37th Indiana; 21st and 74th Ohio; 78th and 79th Pennsylvania; 1st and 21st Wisconsin
    Artillery—1st Illinois Light, Battery C; 1st Michigan Light, Battery A;
       5th U.S., Battery H

Second Division—Brig. Gen. Jefferson C. Davis (assigned to duty with Maj.
    Gen. William T. Sherman)
    1st Brigade—Brig. Gen. James D. Morgan
        10th, 16th, and 60th Illinois; 21st Kentucky; 10th and 14th Michigan

2nd Brigade—Brig. Gen. John Beatty
    34th and 78th Illinois; 3rd, 98th, 108th, 113th, and 121st Ohio
3rd Brigade—Col. Daniel McCook
    85th, 86th, 110th, and 125th Illinois; 52nd Ohio
Artillery—Capt. William A. Hotchkiss
    2nd Illinois Light, Battery I; 2nd Battery Minnesota Light; 5th
    Battery Wisconsin Light

Third Division—Brig. Gen. Absalom Baird (assault on mid–Missionary Ridge)
1st Brigade—Brig. Gen. John B. Turchin
    82nd Indiana; 11th, 17th, 31st, 36th, 89th, and 92nd Ohio
2nd Brigade—Col. Ferdinand Van Derveer
    75th, 87th, and 101st Indiana; 2nd Minnesota; 9th, 25th, and 165th
    Ohio
3rd Brigade—Col. Edward H. Phelps; Col. William H. Hays
    10th and 74th Indiana; 4th, 10th, and 18th Kentucky; 14th and 28th
    Ohio
Artillery—Capt. George A. Swallow
    7th and 19th Batteries Indiana Light; 4th U.S., Battery I
Engineers—Brig. Gen. William F. Smith
    1st Michigan Engineers & Mechanics (detachment); 13th, 21st, and
    22nd Michigan; 18th Ohio
Pioneer Brigade—Col. George P. Buell
    1st, 2nd, 3rd Battalions

ARTILLERY RESERVE

Brig. Gen. John M. Brannan

First Division—Col. James Barnett
1st Brigade—Maj. Charles S. Cotter
    1st Ohio Light, Batteries B, C, E, F
2nd Brigade—1st Ohio Light, Batteries G, M; 18th and 20th Batteries
    Ohio Light

Second Division—
1st Brigade—Capt. Josiah W. Church
    1st Michigan Light, Battery D; 1st Tennessee Light, Battery A;
    2nd, 8th, and 10th Wisconsin Batteries
2nd Brigade—Capt. Arnold Sutermeister
    4th, 8th, 11th, and 21st Indiana Light Batteries; 1st Wisconsin
    Heavy Artillery, Company C
Cavalry—2nd Brigade, 2nd Division—Col. Eli Long
    98th Illinois Mounted Infantry; 17th Indiana Mounted Infantry;
    2nd Kentucky Cavalry; 4th Michigan Cavalry; 1st, 3rd, 4th, and
    10th Ohio Cavalry
Post of Chattanooga—Col. John G. Parkhurst
    44th Indiana; 15th Kentucky; 9th Michigan

ARMY OF THE TENNESSEE
Maj. Gen. William T. Sherman

FIFTEENTH CORPS
Maj. Gen. Frank P. Blair, Jr.

First Division—Brig. Gen. Peter J. Osterhaus (assault on the north end of Missionary Ridge)
　1st Brigade—Brig. Gen. Charles R. Woods
　　13th Illinois; 3rd, 12th, 17th, 27th, 29th, 31st, and 32nd Missouri; 76th Ohio
　2nd Brigade—Col. James A. Williamson
　　4th, 9th, 25th, 26th, 30th, and 31st Iowa
　Artillery—Capt. Henry H. Griffiths
　　1st Iowa Light Battery; 2nd Missouri Light, Battery F; 4th Ohio Light Battery

Second Division—Brig. Gen. Morgan L. Smith (assault on the north end of Missionary Ridge)
　1st Brigade—Brig. Gen. Giles A. Smith; Col. Nathan W. Tupper
　　55th, 116th, and 127th Illinois; 6th and 8th Missouri; 57th Ohio; 18th U.S., 1st Battalion
　2nd Brigade—Brig. Gen. A. J. Lightburn
　　83rd Indiana; 30th, 37th, 47th, and 54th Ohio; 4th West Virginia
　Artillery—
　　1st Illinois Light, Batteries A, B, H

Third Division—Brig. Gen. James M. Tuttle (detached on duty in western Tennessee at Memphis, La Grange, and Pocahontas)

Fourth Division—Brig. Gen. Hugh Ewing (assault on the north end of Missionary Ridge)
　1st Brigade—Col. John M. Loomis
　　26th and 90th Illinois; 12th and 100th Indiana
　2nd Brigade—Brig. Gen. John M. Corse; Col. Charles C. Walcutt
　　40th and 103rd Illinois; 6th Iowa; 15th Michigan; 46th Ohio
　3rd Brigade—Col. Joseph R. Cockerill
　　48th Illinois; 97th and 99th Indiana; 53rd and 70th Ohio
　Artillery—Capt. Henry Richardson
　　1st Illinois Light, Batteries F, I; 1st Missouri Light, Battery D

SEVENTEENTH CORPS

Second Division—Brig. Gen. John E. Smith (assault on the north end of Missionary Ridge)
　1st Brigade—Col. Jesse I. Alexander
　　63rd Illinois; 48th and 59th Indiana; 4th Minnesota; 18th Wisconsin
　2nd Brigade—Col. Green B. Raum; Col. Francis C. Deimling; Col. Clark R. Wever
　　56th Illinois; 17th Iowa; 10th and 24th Missouri; 80th Ohio

3rd Brigade—Brig. Gen. Charles L. Matthies; Col. Benjamin D. Dean; Col. Jabez Banbury
    93rd Illinois; 5th and 10th Iowa; 26th Missouri
Artillery—Capt. Henry Dillon
    Cogswell's Illinois Battery; 6th Wisconsin Light Battery; 12th Wisconsin Light Battery

CONFEDERATE ARMY OF TENNESSEE

Gen. Braxton Bragg

Headquarters

1st Louisiana Infantry, 1st Louisana Cavalry

LONGSTREET'S CORPS

Lt. Gen. James Longstreet

(detached from the Army of Northern Virginia; present September 19 to November 5, 1863; detached November 4 to east Tennessee)

McLaws's Division—Maj. Gen. Lafayette McLaws
    Kershaw's Brigade—Brig. Gen. Joseph B. Kershaw
        2nd, 3rd, 7th, 8th, and 15th South Carolina; 3rd South Carolina Battalion
    Humphreys's Brigade—Brig. Gen. Benjamin C. Humphreys
        13th, 17th, 18th, and 21st Mississippi
    Wofford's Brigade—Col. S. Z. Ruff
        16th, 18th, and 24th Georgia; Cobb's Legion; 3rd Georgia Battalion Sharpshooters
    Bryan's Brigade—Brig. Gen. Goode Bryan
        10th, 50th, 51st, and 53rd Georgia
    Artillery Battalion—Maj. Austin Leyton
        Peoples's Georgia Battery; Wolihin's Georgia Battery; York's Georgia Battery

Hood's Division—Brig. Gen. Micah Jenkins
    Jenkins's Brigade—Col. John Bratton
        1st, 2nd, 5th, and 6th South Carolina; Hampton Legion; Palmetto Sharpshooters
    Law's Brigade—Brig. Gen. Evander McIvor Law
        4th, 15th, 44th, 47th, and 48th Alabama
    Robertson's Brigade—Brig. Gen. Jerome B. Robertson
        3rd Arkansas; 1st, 4th, and 5th Texas
    Anderson's Brigade—Brig. Gen. George T. Anderson
        7th, 8th, 9th, 11th, and 59th Georgia
    Benning's Brigade—Brig. Gen. Henry L. Benning
        2nd, 15th, 17th, and 20th Georgia
    Artillery Battalion—Col. E. Porter Alexander
        Fickling's South Carolina Battery; Jordan's Virginia Battery;

Moody's Louisiana Battery; Parker's Virginia Battery; Taylor's Virginia Battery; Woolfolk's Virginia Battery

HARDEE'S CORPS

Lt. Gen. William J. Hardee

(present to November 25; Assigned to Lookout Mountain November 12 to 24; redeployed to Missionary Ridge November 25)

Cheatham's Division—Maj. Gen. W. H. T. Walker; Brig. Gen. John K. Jackson; Maj. Gen. Benjamin F. Cheatham
    Jackson's Brigade—Brig. Gen. John K. Jackson
        1st, 5th, 47th, and 65th Georgia; 2nd Battalion Georgia Sharpshooters; 5th and 8th Mississippi
    Moore's Brigade—Brig. Gen. John C. Moore
        37th, 40th, and 42nd Alabama
    Walthall's Brigade—Brig. Gen. Edward C. Walthall
        24th/27th, 29th/30th, and 34th Mississippi
    Wright's Brigade—Col. John H. Anderson; Brig. Gen. Marcus J. Wright (detached to Charleston, Tennessee about November 6; recalled November 24; guarded north bank of South Chickamauga Creek, including Shallow Ford bridge, November 24–25)
        8th, 16th, 28th, 38th, and 51st/52nd Tennessee; Murray's Tennessee Battalion
    Artillery Battalion: Maj. Melancton Smith
        Fowler's Alabama Battery; McCants's Florida Battery; Scogin's Georgia Battery; Turner's (Smith's) Mississippi Battery

Hindman's Division—Brig. Gen. Patton Anderson (remained along Missionary Ridge front)
    Anderson's Brigade—Col. William F. Tucker
        7th, 9th, 10th, 41st, and 44th Mississippi; 9th Mississippi Battalion Sharpshooters
    Manigault's Brigade—Brig. Gen. Arthur M. Manigault
        24th, 28th, and 34th Alabama; 10th/19th South Carolina
    Deas's Brigade—Brig. Gen. Zachariah C. Deas
        19th, 22nd, 25th, 33rd, and 50th Alabama; 17th Alabama Battalion Sharpshooters
    Vaughan's Brigade—Brig. Gen. Alfred J. Vaughan, Jr.
        11th, 12th/47th, 13th/154th, and 29th Tennessee
    Artillery Battalion—Maj. Alfred R. Courtney
        Dent's Alabama Battery; Garrity's Alabama Battery; Doscher's (Scott's) Tennessee Battery; Hamilton's (Waters's) Alabama Battery

Buckner's Division—Brig. Gen. Bushrod R. Johnson (detached November 22 for operations in east Tennessee, but Reynolds's Brigade and the artillery were recalled the same day)
    Johnson's Brigade—Col. John S. Fulton
        17th/23rd, 25th/44th, and 63rd Tennessee

Gracie's Brigade—Brig. Gen. Archibald Gracie, Jr.
41st and 43rd Alabama; 1st, 2nd, 3rd, and 4th Battalions Alabama Legion
Reynolds's Brigade—Brig. Gen. A. W. Reynolds (served with Stevenson's Division November 24 and 25)
58th and 60th North Carolina; 54th and 63rd Virginia
Artillery Battalion—Maj. Samuel C. Williams
Bullen's (Darden's) Mississippi Battery; Jeffries's Virginia Battery; Kolb's Alabama Battery

Walker's Division—Brig. Gen. States Rights Gist (transferred from Longstreet's Corps November 12 in the general reorganization; assigned to the Chattanooga Valley front; moved November 23 to the Missionary Ridge line)
Maney's Brigade—Brig. Gen. George Maney
1st/27th, 4th, 6th/9th, 41st, and 56th Tennessee; 24th Tennessee Battalion Sharpshooters
Gist's Brigade—Col. James McCullough (senior officer listed)
46th Georgia; 8th Georgia Battalion; 16th and 24th South Carolina
Wilson's Brigade—Col. Claudius C. Wilson
25th, 29th, and 30th Georgia; 26th Georgia Battalion; 1st Georgia Battalion Sharpshooters
Artillery Battalion—Maj. Robert Martin
Bledsoe's Missouri Battery; Ferguson's South Carolina Battery; Howell's Georgia Battery

BRECKINRIDGE'S CORPS

Maj. Gen. John C. Breckinridge

Assumed command of corps Nov. 8 from Lt. Gen. Daniel H. Hill (corps present to November 25 along the Missionary Ridge front)

Cleburne's Division—Maj. Gen. Patrick R. Cleburne (assigned to the army's right wing [Hardee] on November 24, fought along the north end of Missionary Ridge)
Liddell's Brigade—Col. Daniel C. Govan
2nd/15th, 5th/13th, 6th/7th, 8th, and 19th/24th Arkansas
Smith's Brigade—Col. Hiram B. Granbury
6th/10th and 7th Texas; 15th/17th/18th/24th/25th Texas Cavalry (dismounted)
Polk's Brigade—Brig. Gen. Lucius E. Polk
1st Arkansas; 3rd/5th Confederate; 2nd and 35th/48th Tennessee
Lowrey's Brigade—Brig. Gen. Mark P. Lowrey
16th, 33rd, and 45th Alabama; 32nd/45th Mississippi; 15th Mississippi Battalion Sharpshooters
Artillery Battalion—Maj. T. R. Hotchkiss
Key's Arkansas Battery; Douglas's Texas Battery; Goldthwaite's (Semple's) Alabama Battery; Shannon's (Swett's) Mississippi Battery

Stewart's Division—Maj. Gen. Alexander P. Stewart (assigned to the left wing of Missionary Ridge)
Adams's Brigade—Col. Randall Lee Gibson
13th/20th, 16th/25th, and 19th Louisiana; 4th Louisiana Battalion; 14th Louisiana Battalion Sharpshooters
Strahl's Brigade—Brig. Gen. Otho F. Strahl
4th/5th, 18th, 24th, 31st, and 33rd Tennessee
Clayton's Brigade—Col. J. T. Holtzclaw
18th, 32nd, 36th, 38th, and 58th Alabama
Stovall's Brigade—Brig. Gen. Marcellus A. Stovall
40th, 41st, 42nd, 43rd, and 52nd Georgia
Artillery Battalion—Capt. Henry C. Stemple
Anderson's (Dawson's) Georgia Battery; Rivers's (Humphreys's) Arkansas Battery; Oliver's Alabama Battery; Stanford's Mississippi Battery

Breckinridge's Division—Maj. Gen. William B. Bate (assigned to mid–Missionary Ridge line near Bragg's headquarters)
Lewis's Brigade—Brig. Gen. Joseph H. Lewis (sent to the left wing on Missionary Ridge November 25)
2nd, 4th, 5th, 6th, and 8th Kentucky; John H. Morgan's dismounted cavalrymen
Bate's Brigade—Col. R. C. Tyler
37th Georgia; 4th Georgia Battalion Sharpshooters; 10th, 15th/37th, 20th, and 30th Tennessee; 1st Tennessee Battalion
Florida Brigade—Brig. Gen. Jesse J. Finley
1st/3rd, 4th, 6th, and 7th Florida; 1st Florida Cavalry (dismounted)
Artillery Battalion—Capt. C. H. Slocomb
Gracey's (Cobb's) Kentucky Battery; Mebane's Tennessee Battery; Vaught's (Slocomb's) Louisiana Battery

Stevenson's Division—Maj. Gen. Carter L. Stevenson; Brig. Gen. John C. Brown
(upon the division's return November 6 from east Tennessee, it was assigned to the tunnel region of Missionary Ridge to November 12, then transferred to Lookout Mountain until its evacuation November 24; reassigned to the Missionary Ridge tunnel region November 25)
Brown's Brigade—Brig. Gen. John C. Brown
3rd, 18th/20th, 32nd, and 45th Tennessee; 23rd Tennessee Battalion
Cumming's Brigade—Brig. Gen. Alfred Cumming
34th, 36th, 39th, and 56th Georgia
Pettus's Brigade—Brig. Gen. Edmund W. Pettus
20th, 23rd, 30th, 31st, and 46th Alabama
Vaughn's Brigade—Brig. Gen. John C. Vaughn
(paroled prisoners; few on duty)
3rd, 39th, 43rd, and 59th Tennessee
Artillery Battalion—Capt. Robert Cobb
Baxter's Tennessee Battery; Carnes's Tennessee Battery; Van Den Corput's Georgia Battery; Rowan's Georgia Battery

WHEELER'S CAVALRY CORPS

Maj. Gen. Joseph Wheeler

Wharton's Division—Maj. Gen. John A. Wharton
    1st Brigade—Col. Thomas Harrison
        3rd Arkansas Cavalry; 65th North Carolina (6th Cavalry); 8th and 11th Texas Cavalry
    2nd Brigade—Brig. Gen. Henry B. Davidson
        1st, 2nd, 4th, 6th, and 11th Tennessee Cavalry

Martin's Division—Maj. Gen. William T. Martin
    1st Brigade—Brig. Gen. John T. Morgan
        1st, 3rd, 4th, and 51st Alabama Cavalry; Malone's Alabama Regiment
    2nd Brigade—Col. J. J. Morrison
        1st, 2nd, 3rd, 4th, and 6th Georgia Cavalry

Armstrong's Division—Brig. Gen. Frank C. Armstrong
    1st Brigade—Brig. Gen. William Y. C. Humes
        4th, 5th, 8th, 9th, and 10th Tennessee Cavalry
    2nd Brigade—Col. C. H. Tyler
        Clay's Kentucky Battalion; Edmundson's Virginia Battalion; Jessee's Kentucky Battalion; Johnson's Kentucky Battalion

Kelly's Division—Brig. Gen. John H. Kelly
    1st Brigade—Col. William B. Wade
        1st, 3rd, 8th, and 10th Confederate Cavalry
    2nd Brigade—Col. J. Warren Grigsby
        2nd, 3rd, and 8th Kentucky Cavalry; Allison's Tennessee Squadron; Hamilton's Tennessee Battalion; Rucker's Legion
    Artillery—Huggins's Tennessee Battery; Huwald's Tennessee Battery; White's Tennessee Battery; Wiggin's Arkansas Battery
    Reserve Artillery—Barret's Missouri Battery; Duncan's Georgia Battery; Cribbs's Alabama Battery; Massenburg's Georgia Battery
    Detached—Roddey's Cavalry Brigade—Brig. Gen. Phillip D. Roddey
        4th, 5th, and 53rd Alabama Cavalry; Moreland's Alabama Battalion; Ferrell's Georgia Battery

CHATTANOOGA CAMPAIGN CHRONOLOGY

SEPTEMBER 1863 TO DECEMBER 1863

UNION	DATE	CONFEDERATE
Battle of Chickamauga, Georgia. Rosecrans reports a "serious disaster."	September 19–20	Longstreet's attack through gap in Union line routs center and right wing of Rosecrans's army on afternoon of twentieth.
Lincoln tells Burnside to reinforce Chattanooga. Rosecrans orders Thomas to retire to Chattanooga.	September 21	Forrest's reconnaissance reveals chaos, but Bragg ignores immediate pursuit.
Grant orders Sherman with two divisions to go to Rosecrans's relief.	September 22	Wheeler with cavalry ordered to cross Tennessee River and break up supposed Union retreat from Chattanooga. Bragg begins purge of subordinate generals.
Rosecrans seeks large reinforcements. Midnight conference results in Lincoln's order for Hooker, with two corps from Army of the Potomac, to reinforce Rosecrans.	September 23	Bragg suspends Wheeler's order; Confederate troops move up to invest Chattanooga.

UNION	DATE	CONFEDERATE
Rosecrans abandons Lookout Mountain.	September 24	Longstreet urges action to prevent Rosecrans's escape.
Sherman receives Grant's order to reinforce Rosecrans.	September 25	Signal officer reports large bodies of enemy troops crossing Tennessee River.
Hooker's Eleventh and Twelfth Corps en route to Chattanooga.	September 26	Longstreet complains of Bragg to Richmond headquarters. Lookout Mountain is occupied and artillery bombardment of Chattanooga begins in earnest.
Burnside balks at going to Chattanooga.	September 27	Armistice for removal of Federal dead leads to informal truce between pickets.
	September 29	Bragg continues purge of subordinate generals; suspends Polk, Hindman.
Stanton considers replacing Rosecrans.	September 30	Bragg seeks more troops. **Wheeler's Raid Begins.** (September 30 to October 9)
Sherman is delayed by low water. Burnside has 6,000 (Ninth Corps) at Knoxville.	October 1 (Heavy rain begins.)	Joe Johnson informs Bragg that Sherman is moving to Corinth, Mississippi and orders S. D. Lee to strike the railroad.
Rosecrans reports disaster to supply train in Sequatchie Valley; places army on two-thirds rations.	October 2	Wheeler attacks Rosecrans's supply train, destroying many badly needed supplies.
Sherman at Memphis. Eleventh Corps at Bridgeport. Grant is ordered to Cairo. Burnside and Rosecrans feud over reinforcing Chattanooga.	October 3	Bragg explains plans to Richmond headquarters— he will cross Tennessee River after gathering supplies. Chattanooga is now too strong to attack directly.
Halleck orders Sherman to repair railroad en route to Chattanooga.	October 4	Secret meeting between generals results in a petition for Bragg's removal.
	October 5	Heavy artillery bombardment of Chattanooga continues.

UNION	DATE	CONFEDERATE
Hooker is to repair mountain roads so as to get supplies into Chattanooga.	October 7	Six thousand men sick in army. S. D. Lee en route to join Wheeler in Northern Alabama.
Rosecrans has been out of touch with Burnside since October 1.	October 8	
Forage scarce, animals on one-quarter rations. Ohio gubernatorial elections.	October 9	Jefferson Davis arrives at Bragg's headquarters.
Quartermaster general reports horses starving.	October 10	Davis meets with generals and sustains Bragg.
Lincoln fears Confederate attack against east Tennessee.	October 12	S. D. Lee won't go into Tennessee due to Wheeler's return in poor condition.
Sherman at Corinth. Begins repairing railroad.	October 13	
Grant at Cairo, Illinois. Orders are drafted placing Grant in command of Military Division of Mississippi.	October 16	Bragg has copy of Sam Jones's telegram asking for reinforcements due to Burnside's advance up Holston River.
Grant en route to Louisville for orders. Rosecrans makes preparations for Hooker to march to Chattanooga.	October 17	Bragg sends Stevenson's Division to east Tennessee to help Sam Jones.
Conference at Louisville between Stanton and Grant.	October 18	
Grant chooses Thomas to command Army of the Cumberland. Baldy Smith makes reconnaissance to Brown's Ferry. Rosecrans is relieved at 6:20 P.M. Thomas says he will hold Chattanooga "until we starve."	October 19	
Grant en route to Chattanooga.	October 20	
Sherman delayed at Bear Creek. Thomas reports	October 22	Bragg sends J. K. Jackson and his brigade to east Ten-

UNION	DATE	CONFEDERATE
large Rebel force marched to east Tennessee about the twentieth.		nessee. S. Jones to begin offensive to drive off Burnside.
Grant arrives in evening at Chattanooga. Sherman learns he is to command Army of the Tennessee.	October 23	
Grant makes reconnaissance to Brown's Ferry. Grant orders Sherman to drop everything and march rapidly to Chattanooga.	October 24	Bragg sends Wheeler with most of his cavalry to east Tennessee.
Quartermaster Meigs reports 10,000 dead animals, troops on one-half rations.	October 25	
Assault at Brown's Ferry by Hazen in pontoons. Hooker marches into Lookout Valley.	October 28	Bragg orders a counterattack against Brown's Ferry, but Longstreet delays.
Steamboats begin moving downriver. Geary's rear guard division attacked after midnight, and Hooker marches to relieve him.	October 29	Bragg, present on Lookout Mountain, orders an attack against Federals in Lookout Valley. Longstreet's patrol results in the **Wauhatchie** night action.
"Cracker line" opened by *Paint Rock*. Rain delays Sherman at Eastport, Alabama.	October 30	Longstreet-Bragg conflict expands due to Wauhatchie action. Sam Jones won't go beyond Holston River.
Sherman receives Grant's instructions of twenty-fourth.	October 31	Reconnaissance by Longstreet, Hardee, and Breckinridge determines impracticality of attacking Brown's Ferry.
Grant tells Burnside to hold on to east Tennessee until reinforced.	November 1	Bragg has Jefferson Davis's permission to detach Longstreet to east Tennessee.
	November 3	Longstreet ordered to east Tennessee by Bragg.
Sherman in northern Alabama. Rain-swollen Elk River forces him to detour 30 miles to Fayetteville.	November 5	Longstreet departs for east Tennessee, and is to repair railroad en route. Stevenson's Division is recalled to Chattanooga.

UNION	DATE	CONFEDERATE
Confederate deserter reports in evening that Longstreet has gone to east Tennessee.	November 6	Attack in east Tennessee at Rogersville results in large capture of Federal cavalry.
Grant, per Rogersville and deserter's information, orders Thomas to prepare to attack on eighth.	November 7	
Thomas's attack called off, since he can't move artillery.	November 8	News of Sherman's presence in northern Alabama is sent to Bragg.
Sherman at Fayetteville, Tennessee, waits two days for column to close up. Grant sends orders for Sherman to cross at Bridgeport and march through valley to Chattanooga.	November 9	Longstreet at Cleveland, Tennessee, is short on supplies.
Artillery duel between Moccasin Point and Lookout Mountain.	November 10	S. D. Lee returns to Mississippi.
Telegraph to east Tennessee down for three days. Sherman passes through Winchester, Tennessee.	November 11	Sherman is reported advancing to Chattanooga with an estimated 20,000 troops.
Grant waits for Sherman before taking offensive to force Bragg to retreat.	November 12	Bragg reorganizes army with massive transfers.
Burnside reports Longstreet at Loudon. Sherman arrives at Bridgeport.	November 13	
Sherman en route to Chattanooga via valley; says he will need three more days to get all troops gathering at Bridgeport ready.	November 14	Hardee in command on far left flank; Stevenson in command on Lookout Mountain.
Sherman confers with Grant at Chattanooga.	November 15	Bragg reduces army's rations.
Grant and Sherman make reconnaissance along Tennessee River to mouth of South Chickamauga Creek.	November 16	Stevenson sends two brigades to Trenton, Tennessee, to guard lower Lookout Mountain.

UNION	DATE	CONFEDERATE
Sherman returns to Bridgeport; his advance begins by march into Lookout Valley.	November 17	Longstreet reports Burnside's retreat to Knoxville.
Ewing marches to Trenton, Tennessee, to deceive Bragg while Sherman's other columns march for Brown's Ferry.	November 18	Longstreet besieges Knoxville. Federals reported on march from Bridgeport. Bragg worries about an attack at Trenton.
Battle expected by November 21 at latest.	November 19	Bragg knows of Sherman's arrival at Chattanooga.
Rains interfere with Sherman's movement; wagons bog down in mud.	November 20	Longstreet asks for reinforcements. Bragg sends flag of truce to Grant; says evacuate civilians.
Bad roads delay attack, and all of Sherman's men are not across Tennessee River.	November 21	Bragg fears Sherman is about to march north of Chattanooga to cut off Longstreet.
Pontoon bridge at Brown's Ferry damaged by Confederate rafts; this delays Wood's division. In evening, deserter reports Bragg falling back from Chattanooga.	November 22	Bragg decides to send Cleburne with 11,000 men to reinforce east Tennessee, countering Sherman's move along river's north bank.
Grant, believing Bragg is withdrawing, orders Thomas to make reconnaissance in force to determine such, so as to save a day in pursuit. Thomas's advance results in the action at **Orchard Knob.** Federal troops occupy the knob and bring up artillery.	November 23	Bragg recalls Cleburne as he departs at Chickamauga Station. Manigault is ordered to make a counterattack with a single brigade after dark; this is rescinded at the last moment. Stevenson, at Lookout Mountain, believes an attack is pending against the Confederate left flank, but Bragg orders Hardee to the far right.
At 2:30 A.M., Sherman's pontoons land near South Chickamauga Creek; a bridge is constructed; Sherman advances in afternoon and occupies Billy Goat Hill without a fight. Hooker's troops are told to make a	November 24	Bragg, deceived by the crossing of Sherman's troops, ignores Lookout Mountain and orders an evacuation after poor command coordination results in only Walthall's Brigade fighting Hooker in the

UNION	DATE	CONFEDERATE
demonstration against **Lookout Mountain.** This results in the capture of Cravens house plateau due to weak opposition.		morning. Due to the fragmentary effort, Cravens house plateau is lost; Stevenson is told to march to the far-right flank during the night.
Sherman's piecemeal attacks against the **north of Missionary Ridge** fail by mid-afternoon. Hooker, after occupying top of Lookout Mountain, is delayed by burned bridges in Chattanooga Valley. Grant, desperate, orders Thomas to advance to relieve pressure on Sherman, not knowing Sherman, beaten, has given up the fight. Thomas's attack on the rifle pits carries them easily, but his troops can't stay under the plunging fire. Their spontaneous attack up mid–**Missionary Ridge** breaks the line in six sites and routs Bragg's army at dusk.	November 25	Cleburne's valiant fight against Sherman's overwhelming force results in a major victory. Yet on mid–Missionary Ridge, when units split between the bottom and top are attacked, confusion results, producing chaos in the main line atop the ridge. Tucker's Brigade gives way first, allowing Union units to spread both north and south along the ridge and overwhelm the demoralized defenders. Bragg's left and center break up, but Hardee with the right flank and Cleburne preserve order during the retreat to Chickamauga Station. Bragg, broken, acknowledges a disaster.
Pursuit of Bragg's columns begins. Sherman advances to Chickamauga Station and beyond. Thomas pursues to near Graysville and in a night action takes many prisoners.	November 26	Bragg's rear guard evacuates Chickamauga Station after burning many supplies. Scattered units retreat on various roads to reach the vicinity of Ringgold, Georgia.
Hooker's pursuit to Ringgold results in a bloody repulse at the gap beyond town. Grant arrives in the afternoon, but the artillery causes the Rebels to retreat. Grant calls off the pursuit of Bragg.	November 27	Cleburne's rear guard action at Ringgold Gap holds off Hooker's attack, allowing Bragg's wagon train to escape. Cleburne retreats in the afternoon after being notified the road is clear. Bragg's army withdraws to Dalton, Georgia.
Sherman and Granger are en route to east Tennessee.	November 30	Bragg resigns from army and is relieved by Hardee.

REFERENCE NOTES

ABBREVIATIONS

B&L: Johnson, Robert Underwood, and Clarence Clough Buel, eds. *Battles and Leaders of the Civil War,* 4 vols. New York, 1956

BHL: Bentley Historical Library, University of Michigan, Ann Arbor, Michigan

CHICK-CHATT: Chickamauga and Chattanooga National Military Park Library, Fort Oglethorpe, Georgia

CL: Clements Library, University of Michigan, Ann Arbor, Michigan

CV: *Confederate Veteran*

CWTI: *Civil War Times Illustrated*

MOLLUS: Military Order of the Loyal Legion of the United States

OR: *War of the Rebellion: Official Records of the Union and Confederate Armies,* series I, Government Printing Office, Washington, D.C. Cited with volume, part, and page numbers following (e.g., OR 31-2-235)

SHC: Southern Historical Collection, University of North Carolina Library, Chapel Hill, North Carolina

USAMHI: United States Army Military History Institute, Carlisle Barracks, Pennsylvania

WRHS: Western Reserve Historical Society Library, Cleveland, Ohio

CHAPTER 1: To Serve One's Ambition
1. OR 30-1-193.
2. B. F. McGee, *History of the 72d Indiana Volunteer Infantry of the Mounted Lightning Brigade,* p. 187; John Beatty, *The Citizen Soldier; or Memoirs of a Volunteer,* p. 345.
3. Peter Cozzens, *This Terrible Sound,*

The Battle of Chickamauga, pp. 6–9; Edward G. Longacre, "A General Vanquished in the West," CWTI, 24, no. 6 (October 1985): 16; William Lamers, *The Edge of Glory: A Biography of General William S. Rosecrans, U.S.A.,* general references.

4. Stephen W. Sears, *George B. McClellan, The Young Napoleon,* p. 86.
5. Cozzens, *This Terrible Sound,* pp. 6–9.
6. Ibid.
7. Ibid.
8. Lamers, *The Edge of Glory,* pp. 8–15.
9. Ibid., pp. 14–18.
10. Ibid., pp. 14,17; Cozzens, *This Terrible Sound,* p. 8; Theodore Clarke Smith, *The Life and Letters of James Abram Garfield,* vol. 1, pp. 272–273.
11. Lamers, *The Edge of Glory,* pp. 20–25.
12. Ibid., pp. 85–180.
13. Ibid., pp. 120–121, 175.
14. Ibid., pp. 177–183ff.
15. Ibid., pp. 245, 251.
16. Ibid., pp. 252–255.
17. Ibid., pp. 263, 265.
18. Ibid., pp. 269–277.
19. Ibid., p. 290; William B. Feis, "The Deception of Braxton Bragg, The Tullahoma Campaign, June 23–July 4, 1863," *Blue & Gray Magazine* 10, no. 1 (October 1992): 10ff.
20. Lamers, *The Edge of Glory,* p. 292.

CHAPTER 2: We Have Met with a Serious Disaster
1. Peter Cozzens, *This Terrible Sound, The Battle of Chickamauga,* pp. 23–36.
2. William Lamers, *The Edge of Glory: A Biography of General William S. Rosecrans, U.S.A.,* pp. 301–306.
3. Ibid., pp. 308–315.
4. Ibid., pp. 310–314; Charles A. Dana, *Recollections of the Civil War,* p. 104.
5. Lamers, *The Edge of Glory,* pp. 312–319.
6. Ibid., p. 321; OR 30-1-55.
7. OR 30-1-55,65,105–106.
8. Lamers, *The Edge of Glory,* pp. 325–329,333–335.
9. OR 30-1-57,58,59,635; Cozzens, *This Terrible Sound,* pp. 310–313, 363–367.
10. OR 30-1-635; Cozzens, *This Terrible Sound,* pp. 368–369ff.

11. Dana, *Recollections of the Civil War,* pp. 115–117.
12. OR 30-1-59,60; Cozzens, *This Terrible Sound,* pp. 403, 404.
13. Lamers, *The Edge of Glory,* pp. 325–329; Cozzens, *This Terrible Sound,* pp. 404–405.
14. OR 30-1-256; Cozzens, *This Terrible Sound,* pp. 405, 470.
15. OR 30-1-141,943.
16. OR 30-1-71,141.
17. OR 30-1-140.
18. OR 30-1-142,143.
19. OR 30-1-136,190–191; Carl Sandburg, *Abraham Lincoln, The War Years,* vol. 2, pp. 423–425.
20. OR 30-1-142,143,192,193.
21. OR 30-1-146.
22. Sandburg, *Abraham Lincoln,* p. 425; John Hay, *Letters of John Hay and Extracts from His Diary,* vol. 2, p. 92.
23. OR 30-1-193,194.
24. OR 30-1-144,145.
25. OR 30-1-145.
26. OR 30-1-143,145.
27. OR 30-1-145,150.
28. Alfred L. Hough, *Soldier in the West; The Civil War Letters of Alfred Lacey Hough,* pp. 150–151.
29. OR 30-1-146.

CHAPTER 3: "What Does He Fight Battles For"
1. OR 30-2-526; Peter Cozzens, *This Terrible Sound, The Battle of Chickamauga,* p. 519.
2. OR 30-4-675,681; Robert S. Henry, *First with the Most,* p. 191.
3. OR 30-2-525,526.
4. OR 30-4-675; B&L 3-662.
5. CV 4-10-358–359; Henry, *First with the Most,* p. 193.
6. Grady McWhiney, *Braxton Bragg and Confederate Defeat,* vol. 1, pp. vi–viii; Mary A. Chesnut, *A Diary from Dixie,* p. 316.
7. McWhiney, *Braxton Bragg,* pp. x,90–91,167.
8. Ibid., pp. 190,202.
9. Ibid., pp. 18–22,234–253; Wiley Sword, *Shiloh: Bloody April,* pp. 234ff, 277ff.
10. McWhiney, *Braxton Bragg,* pp. 225,252.
11. Ibid., p. 259.

12. Ibid., p. 265.
13. Ibid., p. 259.
14. Ibid., pp. 267–271.
15. Ibid., pp. 317–330.
16. Ibid., pp. 326,327.
17. Ibid., p. 337.
18. Ibid., pp. 337,345.
19. Ibid., pp. 346–357.
20. Ibid., pp. 374–376.
21. Ibid., pp. 376–377; OR 20-1-699.
22. OR 20-1-682–684.
23. Peter Cozzens, *No Better Place to Die: The Battle of Stones River*, p. 210.
24. OR 23-2-632,633.
25. Ibid.
26. OR 23-2-63.
27. OR 23-2-674; McWhiney, *Braxton Bragg*, p. 386.
28. Cozzens, *No Better Place to Die*, pp. 212–216.
29. Ibid., p. 201; William B. Feis, "The Deception of Braxton Bragg, The Tullahoma Campaign," *Blue & Gray Magazine* 10, no. 1 (October 1992): 10ff.
30. McWhiney, *Braxton Bragg*, p. 389.
31. Judith Lee Hallock, *Braxton Bragg and Confederate Defeat*, vol. 2, pp. 47–52; Cozzens, *This Terrible Sound*, pp. 36–55,85.
32. Cozzens, *This Terrible Sound*, pp. 39,89,115,120.
33. Ibid., pp. 91,299–304.
34. Ibid., pp. 305–320.
35. Ibid., pp. 357ff, 463ff.
36. Ibid., p. 456.
37. Ibid., p. 517; OR 30-2-34; OR 30-4-679.
38. McWhiney, *Braxton Bragg*, p. 267.

CHAPTER 4: "Nothing but the Hand of God Can Save Us"
1. Larry Daniel, *Soldiering in the Army of Tennessee, A Portrait of Life in a Confederate Army*, p. 136.
2. Braxton Bragg, letter to wife, September 22, 1863, Bragg Papers, Missouri Historical Society, St. Louis, Missouri.
3. Ibid., September 22, 27, 1863.
4. Thomas Lawrence Connelly, *Autumn of Glory: The Army of Tennessee, 1862–1865*, p. 235ff.
5. Ibid., pp. 237,254; OR 30-2-47,54.
6. OR 30-2-55,56.
7. OR 30-2-55,56; Connelly, *Autumn of Glory*, p. 236.

8. Connelly, *Autumn of Glory*, p. 236.
9. Ibid., p. 241; OR 52-2-538.
10. OR 30-2-67,68; Connelly, *Autumn of Glory*, pp. 238–240.
11. OR 30-4-705,706.
12. Connelly, *Autumn of Glory*, p. 241.
13. Ibid., pp. 241–242.
14. Ibid.
15. Ibid., p. 249; Judith Lee Hallock, *Braxton Bragg and Confederate Defeat*, p. 97; Irving Buck, *Cleburne and His Command*, pp. 158–159.
16. OR 30-4-735; Buck, *Cleburne and His Command*, pp. 158,159; William C. Davis, *Jefferson Davis, The Man and His Hour*, p. 519.
17. Davis, *Jefferson Davis*, p. 519; Connelly, *Autumn of Glory*, pp. 243–245.
18. Connelly, *Autumn of Glory*, pp. 238,243,246; Hallock, *Braxton Bragg and Confederate Defeat*, pp. 99,107,121; Davis, *Jefferson Davis*, p. 516; OR 52-2-549,550.
19. OR 30-4-744; Davis, *Jefferson Davis*, p. 521.
20. Davis, *Jefferson Davis*, p. 522.
21. Connelly, *Autumn of Glory*, pp. 242,243.
22. Patricia L. Faust, *Historical Times Illustrated Encyclopedia of the Civil War*, p. 569.
23. Ibid., p. 208.
24. Wiley Sword, *Embrace an Angry Wind*, pp. 20,21; Davis, *Jefferson Davis*, pp. 523,526.
25. Davis, *Jefferson Davis*, pp. 689–706.
26. OR 30-4-404,744.

CHAPTER 5: "Everything Will Come Out Right"
1. OR 30-1-146.
2. OR 30-1-146–148.
3. OR 30-1-147.
4. OR 30-1-147,194; OR 30-3-760.
5. OR 30-1-150–154,194.
6. OR 30-1-149,152; OR 30-3-762.
7. OR 30-1-151,153,154,160,195.
8. OR 30-1-155,156,195,196.
9. OR 30-1-155,158.
10. OR 30-1-160.
11. OR 30-1-169-179; OR 30-2-25; OR 30-4-721,765.
12. OR 30-1-148.
13. Carl Sandburg, *Abraham Lincoln, The War Years*, vol. 2, p. 426.

14. OR 30-1-161,197; OR 30-3-946; Theodore Clarke Smith, *The Life and Letters of James Abram Garfield,* vol. 1, p. 240.
15. OR 30-1-168; OR 30-3-792.
16. Sandburg, *Abraham Lincoln,* vol. 2, p. 426.
17. Ibid., pp. 426–427.
18. Ibid.
19. Ibid.
20. Ibid.
21. OR 30-1-200,215,478,885.
22. OR 30-1-200.
23. OR 30-1-196,197,198.
24. OR 30-3-816,892.
25. OR 30-3-836.
26. OR 30-1-205; OR 30-2-723; OR 30-3-951,952,956; OR 30-4-9,37–45,58–68,99.
27. OR 30-3-951,956; OR 30-4-9,43.
28. OR 30-4-279,307,361,385.
29. OR 30-1-218; OR 30-3-846,890,891; OR 30-4-9,307,413.
30. OR 30-3-948; OR 30-4-36,63,64,102.
31. OR 30-1-214,215.
32. OR 30-1-214,215.
33. OR 30-1-215.
34. Ibid.
35. OR 30-4-404,450,479.

CHAPTER 6: A "Dazed and Mazy Commander"

1. OR 30-1-202; William Lamers, *The Edge of Glory: A Biography of General William S. Rosecrans, U.S.A.,* p. 383.
2. Charles A. Dana, *Recollections of the Civil War,* p. 10ff.; OR 30-1-204ff.; OR 30-3-946.
3. Lamers, *The Edge of Glory,* p. 383.
4. Carl Sandburg, *Abraham Lincoln, The War Years,* vol. 2, p. 426.
5. OR 30-4-57,79; Lamers, *The Edge of Glory,* p. 380.
6. OR 30-1-216,219; OR 30-4-322,414,415.
7. OR 30-1-217; OR 30-4-244.
8. OR 30-4-414,428.
9. OR 30-1-210,215,218,219.
10. OR 30-1-198–201,1051; Lamers, *The Edge of Glory,* p. 384; Sandburg, *Abraham Lincoln,* vol. 2, p. 433.
11. OR 30-1-217,218; Lamers, *The Edge of Glory,* p. 410; Theodore Clarke

Smith, *The Life and Letters of James Abram Garfield,* vol. 2, p. 868ff.
12. Lamers, *The Edge of Glory,* pp. 407,408,413; T.C. Smith, *Garfield* vol. 2, p. 872; Sandburg, *Abraham Lincoln,* vol. 2, p. 434.
13. OR 30-1-146,149; OR 30-3-755,770,808; OR 30-4-306.
14. Lamers, *The Edge of Glory,* p. 396.
15. OR 30-1-202.
16. OR 30-4-55,236,355.
17. OR 30-4-274,354.
18. Lamers, *The Edge of Glory,* p. 380.
19. OR 30-1-215.
20. OR 30-1-218,219.
21. Lamers, *The Edge of Glory,* pp. 407,413.
22. OR 30-4-404; Lamers, *The Edge of Glory,* p. 407.
23. OR 30-1-684.
24. OR 30-4-404,429.
25. OR 30-4-404; John Y. Simon, ed., *The Papers of Ulysses S. Grant,* vol. 9, p. 281; Ulysses S. Grant, *Personal Memoirs of U. S. Grant,* p. 281.
26. Grant, *Personal Memoirs,* p. 308; Lamers, *The Edge of Glory,* p. 397; James H. Wilson, *Under the Old Flag,* vol. 1, pp. 259–260.
27. Simon, ed., *The Papers,* vol. 9, pp. 256, 298n.; Lamers, *The Edge of Glory,* p. 407; OR 30-31-945.
28. Grant, *Personal Memoirs,* pp. 309,312; Simon, ed., *The Papers,* vol. 9, p. 298; OR 30-1-221.
29. Grant, *Personal Memoirs,* p. 312; OR 30-4-479.
30. Grant, *Personal Memoirs,* p. 312; Simon, ed., *The Papers,* vol. 9, p. 301; OR 30-4-479.

CHAPTER 7: "What Does It Mean?"

1. OR 30-1-220; OR 30-41-389,415,435,436,467,479; William Lamers, *The Edge of Glory: A Biography of General William S. Rosecrans, U.S.A.,* p. 391; Theodore Clarke Smith, *The Life and Letters of James Abram Garfield,* vol. 2, p. 353.
2. Lamers, *The Edge of Glory,* p. 391ff.; Isaac Roseberry, diary 9-26-1863, Emory University; James E. Withrow, diary 10-19-1863, CHICK-CHATT; OR 30-4-404,478; OR 31-1-77; Herbert M. Schiller, ed., *Autobiography of Major*

General William F. Smith, 1861–1864, pp. 75–76; William F. Smith, "An Historical Sketch of the Military Operations around Chattanooga, Tennessee, Sept. 22 to Nov. 27, 1863," *Papers of the Military Historical Society of Massachusetts,* vol. 8, pp. 168–172.

3. Lamers, *The Edge of Glory,* pp. 392,393; OR 30-4-478.

4. Lamers, *The Edge of Glory,* pp. 392,393.

5. Ibid., pp. 392–396; OR 30-4-478.

6. John Y. Simon, ed., *The Papers of Ulysses S. Grant,* vol. 9, p. 304n.; OR 30-1-670; Ulysses S. Grant, *Personal Memoirs of U. S. Grant,* pp. 312, 313.

7. OR 30-1-219,221; OR 30-4-446,467,477,478; Lamers, *The Edge of Glory,* p. 398; Edward G. Longacre, *From Union Stars to Top Hat, A Biography of the Extraordinary General James Harrison Wilson,* p. 88.

8. Grant, *Personal Memoirs,* p. 313; OR 30-4-446.

9. OR 30-1-218; OR 30-3-890; OR 30-4-415,421,426; OR 31-1-69,693,706; Simon, ed., *The Papers,* vol. 9, p. 222n., 317; Grant, *Personal Memoirs,* p. 313.

10. OR 31-1-70; Simon, ed., *The Papers,* vol. 9, pp. 317,318n.

11. Longacre, *From Union Stars,* p. 90; Horace Porter, *Campaigning with Grant,* pp. 1–2; James H. Wilson, *Under the Old Flag,* vol. 1, pp. 269–274.

12. Wilson, *Under the Old Flag,* vol. 1, pp. 273–276.

13. Ibid.

14. OR 31-1-43,69,684,700.

15. Porter, *Campaigning with Grant,* pp. 4–6.

16. Schiller, ed., *Autobiography of William F. Smith,* pp. 75–76; William F. Smith, "Sketch of Military Operations," pp. 168–172; OR 31-1-77.

17. Porter, *Campaigning with Grant,* pp. 5–6; B&L 3–714.

18. B&L 3-714.

19. OR 31-1-70,712.

20. OR 31-1-712,713,716,738.

21. OR 31-1-717,729; Simon, ed., *The Papers,* vol. 9, pp. 334,335; Porter, *Campaigning with Grant,* p. 5.

22. OR 31-1-45,77; Simon, ed., *The Papers,* vol. 9, p. 334.

23. OR 31-1-706.

24. OR 31-1-738.

25. OR 31-1-72,739.

26. OR 31-3-15.

27. OR 31-1-15.

CHAPTER 8: Whom Should the Soldiers Trust?

1. Edwin H. Rennolds, diary 10-13-1863, CHICK-CHATT.

2. OR 30-4-744.

3. Ibid.

4. Edwin H. Rennolds, diary 10-17-1863.

5. Thomas Lawrence Connelly, *Autumn of Glory: The Army of Tennessee, 1862–1865,* p. 247.

6. Ibid., pp. 239, 247, 249.

7. Ibid., pp. 246,252,253.

8. Ibid., pp. 240,241; John Allan Wyeth, *Life of Nathan Bedford Forrest,* pp. 264–266.

9. Wyeth, *Life of Nathan Bedford Forrest,* pp. 264–266.

10. OR 31-3-603,604.

11. Connelly, *Autumn of Glory,* pp. 250,251.

12. Ibid., p. 253ff.

13. Ibid., pp. 75,239,318; Howell and Elizabeth Purdue, *Pat Cleburne Confederate General,* pp. 182,183, 238.

14. Perdue, *Pat Cleburne,* p. 29.

15. Ibid., pp. 9,31,63,89,118,219, 220.

16. Ibid., pp. 82,90,97; Wiley Sword, *Embrace an Angry Wind,* pp. 17,18; OR 20-1-682–684.

17. Purdue, *Pat Cleburne,* p. 52.

18. OR 30-4-696,713.

19. OR 30-4-684,696,698,710,711.

20. OR 30-4-698.

21. OR 30-4-711–713.

22. OR 30-4-726,735.

23. OR 30-2-666,723ff.

24. OR 30-4-708,741.

25. OR 30-4-743,747,762.

26. OR 30-4-762.

27. OR 30-4-763; OR 31-1-25,30; OR 31-3-586,587,676,763.

28. OR 30-2-729; OR 30-4-748.

29. OR 30-4-726.

30. OR 30-4-745,746,761.

CHAPTER 9: Bragg's "Least Favorable Option"
1. OR 30-4-701.
2. OR 30-4-705,706.
3. OR 30-4-706; OR 52-2-549,550.
4. OR 30-4-705,706.
5. OR 30-4-709,710.
6. James Longstreet, *From Manassas to Appomattox, Memoirs of the Civil War in America,* pp. 466–468.
7. OR 30-4-742.
8. OR 31-1-220; Judith Lee Hallock, *Braxton Bragg and Confederate Defeat,* vol. 2, p. 122ff.
9. Longstreet, *From Manassas to Appomattox,* pp. 466–468; OR 52-2-548,554.
10. OR 31-1-220,221; OR 31-3-589–595.
11. OR 30-2-543,545,603,604,614; OR 30-4-749; OR 31-4-616,644.
12. OR 30-2-547,606; OR 30-4-649,707; OR 52-2-526.
13. OR 30-4-716,725.
14. OR 30-2-547,551; OR 30-4-739.
15. OR 30-2-547.
16. OR 30-4-749,753.
17. OR 30-4-749,756,760,761.
18. OR 30-2-606; OR 30-4-761,762; OR 31-3-576,593,594.
19. OR 31-1-6,7; OR 31-3-576,586; OR 52-2-534,548,554,555,561.
20. OR 31-3-601,607.
21. OR 31-3-593,594; OR 52-2-554; Dunbar Rowland, ed., *Jefferson Davis Constitutionalist, His Letters, Papers and Speeches,* vol. 6, pp. 70,71.
22. OR 52-1-478,481.
23. OR 31-1-712,756.
24. OR 31-3-607.
25. OR 52-2-554,555; Rowland, *Jefferson Davis Constitutionalist,* vol. 6, pp. 69–73; Thomas Lawrence Connelly, *Autumn of Glory: The Army of Tennessee, 1862–1865,* p. 262.
26. Longstreet, *From Manassas to Appomattox,* pp. 468,469; Rowland, *Jefferson David Constitutionalist,* vol. 6, p. 73.
27. OR 31-1-218; OR 52-2-555; St. John R. Liddell, journal, Govan Papers, SHC.
28. OR 31-1-455; OR 52-2-557,560; Longstreet, *From Manassas to Appomattox,* p. 480.
29. OR 52-2-557–558.
30. OR 31-1-455; OR 31-3-626,634; OR

52-2-555,560; Longstreet, *From Manassas to Appomattox,* p. 481.
31. OR 52-2-560; Ulysses S. Grant, *Personal Memoirs of U. S. Grant,* p. 344.
32. OR 31-3-634.
33. OR 52-2-559,560.
34. OR 52-2-560.
35. OR 31-3-634,635.
36. OR 31-3-635–637.
37. OR 31-3-670,671,672,680.
38. OR 31-3-680,681.
39. OR 31-3-680,681; OR 52-2-563.
40. Braxton Bragg, letter to wife, November 14, 1863, Bragg Papers, Missouri Historical Society, St. Louis, Missouri.
41. OR 31-3-681,687,696.
42. Braxton Bragg, letter to wife, November 14, 1863, Bragg Papers, Missouri Historical Society, St. Louis, Missouri.

CHAPTER 10: "One of the Wildest Places You Ever Saw"
1. James Withrow, diary, October 24, 1863, CHICK-CHATT; Josiah H. Bender, letter, September 28, 1863, USMHI; Axel Reed, diary, October 31, 1863, Chick-Chatt; 104th Illinois Infantry file, CHICK-CHATT; Zella Armstrong, *The History of Hamilton County and Chattanooga, Tennessee,* vol. 2, p. 33.
2. Armstrong, *The History of Hamilton County,* vol. 1, p. 152; John Y. Simon, ed., *The Papers of Ulysses S. Grant,* vol. 9, pp. 334,335.
3. Arnold Gates, ed., *The Rough Side of War, The Civil War Journal of Chesley A. Mosman, 1st Lieutenant, Company D, 59th Illinois Volunteer Infantry Regiment,* pp. 90,91.
4. Armstrong, *The History of Hamilton County,* vol. 1, p. 118ff.
5. Ibid., p. 151.
6. Ibid., vol. 2, p. 59.
7. Gates, ed., *The Rough Side of War,* p. 87.
8. Armstrong, *The History of Hamilton County,* vol. 2, p. 31ff.
9. Ibid., pp. 33,34.
10. Ibid., p. 59.
11. Loren J. Morse, ed., *Civil War Diaries & Letters of Bliss Morse,* p. 88.

12. Armstrong, *The History of Hamilton County,* vol. 1, p. 152.
13. Ibid., p. 137; Gates, ed., *The Rough Side of War,* p. 93.
14. Armstrong, *The History of Hamilton County,* vol. 2, p. 34; John W. Sparkman, diary, September 22, 1863, CHICK-CHATT.
15. Lyman S. Widney, letter, November 10, 1863, CHICK-CHATT; Isaac Roseberry, diary, September 16, 1863, Emory University Library; Cecil Fogg, letter, August 23, 1863, collection of Wiley Sword.
16. R. Lockwood Tower, ed., *A Carolinian Goes to War, The Civil War Narrative of Arthur Middleton Manigault, Brigadier General, C.S.A.,* pp. 129–130; Arthur B. Carpenter, letter, October 4, 1863, Yale University Library.
17. Morse, ed., *Civil War Diaries,* p. 84; Withrow, diary, September 25, 1863.
18. Gates, ed., *The Rough Side of War,* pp. 85,86; Withrow, diary, October 2, 1863.
19. Gates, ed., *The Rough Side of War,* pp. 85–87.
20. Ibid., Edward F. Betts, Map of the Battlefield of Chattanooga and Wauhatchie, Chickamauga-Chattanooga National Park Commission, 1896; OR 31-1-217.
21. Gates, ed., *The Rough Side of War,* pp. 86–87; Josiah Bender, letter, September 28, 1863, USAMHI.
22. Morse, ed., *Civil War Diaries,* pp. 84–85.
23. Ibid.; Carpenter, letter, October 10, 1863; William W. Calkins, *The History of the One Hundred and Fourth Regiment of Illinois Volunteer Infantry, War of the Great Rebellion, 1862–1865,* pp. 164–165; Bender, letter, September 28, 1863.

CHAPTER 11: "Ain't That a Queer Kind of War?"
1. Ralsa C. Rice, *Yankee Tigers, Through the Civil War with the 125th Ohio,* p. 72.
2. Ibid.; OR 52-2-534.
3. Arnold Gates, ed., *The Rough Side of War, The Civil War Journal of Chesley A. Mosman, 1st Lieutenant, Company D, 59th Illinois Volunteer Infantry Regi-* ment, p. 89; John Obrieter, *The Seventy-seventh Pennsylvania at Shiloh, History of the Regiment,* p. 203; OR 30-1-514; OR 30-3-876.
4. OR 30-1-566; Gates, ed., *The Rough Side of War,* pp. 89,90.
5. OR 30-3-872,893; Loren J. Morse, ed., *Civil War Diaries & Letters of Bliss Morse,* p. 84; Gates, ed., *The Rough Side of War,* p. 93.
6. Gates, ed., *The Rough Side of War,* p. 92.
7. Morse, ed., *Civil War Diaries,* p. 83; Gates, ed., *The Rough Side of War,* p. 93; Arthur B. Carpenter, letter, October 4, 1863, Yale University Library.
8. OR 30-1-205; Gates, ed., *The Rough Side of War,* pp. 93,94.
9. Thomas Green, letter, September 30, 1863, USAMHI; Glenn Sunderland, *Wilder's Lightning Brigade—And Its Spencer Repeaters,* p. 95.
10. Isaac Miller, letter, October 15, 1863, catalog of Olde Soldier Books, Gaithersburg, Maryland, catalog # 69, item 191.
11. Lyman S. Widney, letter, November 18, 1863, CHICK-CHATT; Richard Watson, letter, October 31, 1863, USAMHI.
12. OR 30-1-208; J. A. Reep, *Guttmachrala, or Four Years at the Front as a Private,* p. 12; Morse, ed., *Civil War Diaries,* pp. 90–91. Gates, ed., *The Rough Side of War,* pp. 90–91.
13. John S. H. Doty, letter, November 18, 1863, collection of Wiley Sword; Carpenter, letter, October 10, 1863.
14. Carpenter, letter, October 10, 1863.
15. Axel Reed, diary, October 5, 1863, CHICK-CHATT.; Gates, ed., *The Rough Side of War,* pp. 90,91.
16. Edward G. Whitesides, diary, September 24, 1863, USAMHI.
17. Gates, ed., *The Rough Side of War,* p. 98ff.
18. Widney, letters, November 18 and 20, 1863.
19. Ibid.
20. Gates, ed., *The Rough Side of War,* pp. 102, 120; William R. Glison, diary, November 4,14, and 18, 1863, CHICK-CHATT; Reed, diary, November 13 and 22, 1863; Morse, ed., *Civil War Diaries,* p. 94.

21. Gates, ed., *The Rough Side of War*, pp. 100,103.
22. Ibid., p. 95; James E. Withrow, diary, September 30 and October 1, 1863, CHICK-CHATT.
23. Gates, ed., *The Rough Side of War*, p. 95ff; Withrow, diary, October 1, 1863.
24. Gates, ed., *The Rough Side of War*, p. 104.
25. Morse, ed., *Civil War Diaries*, pp. 93,94.
26. Reed, diary, October 1, 1863.
27. Morse, ed., *Civil War Diaries*, p. 95; Gates, ed., *The Rough Side of War*, p. 99.
28. Reep, *Guttmachrala*, pp. 14,15.
29. Gates, ed., *The Rough Side of War*, p. 101.
30. Withrow, diary, October 17 to 23, 1863.

CHAPTER 12: "This Is Starvation Camp"
1. Arnold Gates, ed., *The Rough Side of War, The Civil War Journal of Chesley A. Mosman, 1st Lieutenant, Company D, 59th Illinois Volunteer Regiment*, p. 89.
2. Ibid., pp. 90,92; James E. Withrow, diary, September 27 and 28, 1863, CHICK-CHATT.
3. OR 30-3-803,806ff.
4. OR 30-3-846,877,922.
5. OR 30-1-212,214.
6. Loren J. Morse, ed., *Civil War Diaries & Letters of Bliss Morse*, pp. 85,86; Gates, ed., *The Rough Side of War*, p. 95.
7. Withrow, diary, October 1,8,10,16,20 and 21, 1863.
8. Morse, ed., *Civil War Diaries*, pp. 90,91; J. A. Reep, *Guttmachrala, or Four Years at the Front as a Private*, p. 15; Gates, ed., *The Rough Side of War*, p. 105.
9. Morse, ed., *Civil War Diaries*, p. 91; William W. Calkins, *The History of the One Hundred and Fourth Regiment of Illinois Volunteer Infantry, War of the Great Rebellion, 1862–1865*, pp. 183,184.
10. Isaac C. Doan, *Reminiscences of the Chattanooga Campaign*, pp. 8,9; John

McClenahan, memoirs, CHICK-CHATT.; Almon Browner, letter, October 20, 1863, USAMHI.
11. OR 30-4-206.
12. OR 30-4-57,58.
13. Gates, ed., *The Rough Side of War*, p. 89.
14. OR 30-4-9,36,38.
15. OR 30-4-306,307.
16. OR 30-4-307,323,414,456.
17. OR 30-4-206; Morse, ed., *Civil War Diaries*, pp. 90,91.
18. Reep, *Guttmachrala*, p. 14; OR 30-4-413.
19. Withrow, diary, October 19, 1863; OR 30-4-478.
20. OR 30-4-479.
21. Gates, ed., *The Rough Side of War*, p. 106.
22. Emerson Opdycke to wife, October 25, 1863, the Ohio Historical Society, Columbus, Ohio.
23. OR 30-4-479.

CHAPTER 13: "Oh, What Suffering This War Entails"
1. Elizabeth Whitley Roberson, *Weep Not for Me Dear Mother*, p. 117; Joab Goodson, letter, September 28, 1863, CHICK-CHATT; Ray Mathis, *In the Land of the Living, Wartime Letters by Confederates from the Chattahoochie Valley of Alabama and Georgia*, pp. 76,77.
2. Goodson, letter, September 28, 1863.
3. Thomas W. Davis, diary, September 20,21,23 and 24, 1863, CHICK-CHATT; Hezekiah Rabb, letter, September 23, 1863, CHICK-CHATT.
4. Edwin H. Rennolds, diary, September 21,23, and 24, 1863, CHICK-CHATT.
5. Andrew Jackson Neal, letter, October 1863, CHICK-CHATT.
6. John Snow, letter, September 30, 1863, CHICK-CHATT; Thomas W. Davis, diary, September 21 and 30, 1863, CHICK-CHATT; John W. Sparkman, diary, September 20 and 22, 1863, CHICK-CHATT.
7. Mathis, *In the Land of the Living*, p. 77.
8. Robert Watson, journal, September 27, 1863, CHICK-CHATT.

9. Ibid., September 28 to October 19, 1863.
10. W. R. Montgomery, letter, October 24, 1863, CHICK-CHATT; Ambrose Deas, letter, October 25, 1863, CHICK-CHATT.
11. Sparkman, diary, September 26, 1863; Deas, letter, October 25, 1863; Neal, letter, October 1863.
12. OR 30-4-547–553,713; Larry J. Daniel, *Soldiering in the Army of Tennessee,* p. 55ff.
13. OR 30-4-549,550,553,713,714.
14. OR 30-4-699,700,757,761; Sparkman, diary, September 26, October 3 to 10, 1863.
15. Montgomery, letter, October 24, 1863; Rennolds, diary, October 24, 1863; Robert Bullock, letter, October 5, 1863, Georgia Department of Archives.
16. G. E. Goudelock, letter, October 5, 1863, CHICK-CHATT; Montgomery, letter, October 18, 1863; Watson, journal, October 1,5, and 6, 1863; Bullock, letter, November 1, 1863.
17. Bullock, letter, October 11, 1863; Washington Ives, letters, October 5,11 and 14, 1863, CHICK-CHATT.
18. Ives, letters, November 5 and 12, 1863; Rabb, letter, October 9, 1863.
19. Bullock, letter, October 5, 1863.

CHAPTER 14: Brown's Ferry and Smith's Pontoons
1. Alfred L. Hough, *Soldier in the West; The Civil War Letters of Alfred Lacy Hough,* p. 153.
2. Ibid., p. 159.
3. OR 31-1-740; Horace Porter, *Campaigning with Grant,* p. 5.
4. Porter, *Campaigning with Grant,* p. 8.
5. OR 31-1-70,77,739,780; B&L 3-714,715; Schiller, ed., *Autobiography of William F. Smith,* pp. 76–77.
6. Ibid., pp. 676,713; OR 31-1-71.
7. Hough, *Soldier in the West,* p. 162.
8. OR 31-1-77; John Y. Simon, ed., *The Papers of Ulysses S. Grant,* vol. 9, p. 334; B&L 3-713,714.
9. OR 31-1-77; Patricia L. Faust, ed., *Historical Times Illustrated Encyclopedia of the Civil War,* p. 699; Schiller, ed., *Autobiography of William F.*

Smith, pp. x–xv; William F. Smith, "Sketch of Military Operations," pp. 168–172.
10. OR 31-1-79; Steven Dunker, "Rendering Invaluable Service," *Michigan History Magazine,* January/February 1992, p. 42.
11. OR 31-1-77,79,84,89.
12. OR 31-1-84.
13. William R. Glison, diary, October 26, 1863, CHICK-CHATT.
14. Ibid., October 27, 1863; OR 31-1-86.
15. OR 31-1-79,86.
16. OR 30-4-393,726,735; OR 31-1-216,224.
17. OR 31-1-224,225; William C. Oates, *The War Between the Union and the Confederacy and Its Lost Opportunities, with a History of the Fifteenth Alabama and the Forty-eight Battles in Which It Was Engaged,* p. 270.
18. OR 30-4-176,177.
19. OR 30-4-177,183.
20. OR 30-4-177,182; OR 31-1-802.
21. OR 30-4-377,393.
22. OR 30-4-337,393; Spencer Repeating Rifle Company Catalog, 1866, in L. D. Satterlee, *Ten Old Gun Catalogs for the Collector,* p. 14.
23. W. A. McClendon, *Recollections of War Times by an Old Veteran While under Stonewall Jackson and Lieut. Gen. James Longstreet,* pp. 188,189; John Anderson Morrow, *The Confederate Whitworth Sharpshooters,* pp. 7,12,17,20,27, 28,43–45.
24. OR 31-1-830.
25. Satterlee, *Ten Old Gun Catalogs,* p. 19; OR 30-4-441,457.
26. OR 30-4-393.
27. OR 30-4-441,457; OR 31-1-216; McClendon, *Recollections of War Times,* p. 192.
28. OR 31-1-216,224; McClendon, *Recollections of War Times,* pp. 193,194; Oates, *The War Between the Union and Confederacy,* pp. 272,273.
29. Oates, *The War Between the Union and the Confederacy,* p. 275.
30. McClendon, *Recollections of War Times,* p. 194.
31. Ibid.; Robert L. Kimberly, and Ephraim S. Holloway, *The Forty-first Ohio Veteran Volunteer Infantry in the*

War of the Rebellion, 1861–1865, pp. 60–63; OR 31-1-84,86.

32. OR 31-1-78–86.

33. OR 27-2-392; Oates, *The War Between the Union and the Confederacy,* p. 275–277.

34. OR 31-1-86,87.

35. OR 31-1-89; Oates, *The War Between the Union and the Confederacy,* p. 275–277; McClendon, *Recollections of War Times,* p. 194.

36. OR 31-1-225; Oates, *The War Between the Union and Confederacy,* pp. 275–277.

37. OR 31-1-78–87; Dunker, "Rendering Invaluable Service," p. 42.

38. OR 31-1-52,54,56,78; Hough, *Soldier in the West,* pp. 162,163.

39. Hough, *Soldier in the West,* pp. 162,163.

CHAPTER 15: "General Hooker's Balloon"

1. OR 52-2-556; OR 31-1-217,222.

2. OR 31-1-220–222.

3. OR 52-2-548; James Longstreet, *From Manassas to Appomattox, Memoirs of the Civil War in America,* pp. 468,469.

4. OR 52-2-549; OR 31-1-220,221.

5. OR 52-2-547; OR 31-1-221,224.

6. OR 52-2-556; OR 31-1-221,222.

7. OR 31-1-225; William C. Oates, *The War Between the Union and the Confederacy and Its Lost Opportunities, with a History of the Fifteenth Alabama and the Forty-eight Battles in Which It Was Engaged,* pp. 278,279.

8. OR 3-1-34,225.

9. OR 31-1-225.

10. OR 31-1-69 to 72; Charles A. Dana, *Recollections of the Civil War,* p. 134.

11. OR 31-1-43,44,46; Dana, *Recollections of the Civil War,* p. 134.

12. Andrew J. Boies, *Record of the Thirty-third Massachusetts Volunteer Infantry from Aug. 1862 to Aug. 1865,* pp. 45,46.

13. Ibid., p. 46; OR 31-1-58,93,97,99.

14. Puntenney, *History of the Thirty-Seventh Regiment of Indiana Volunteer Infantry,* p. 47; Boies, *Record of the Third-third Massachusetts,* p. 47; OR 31-1-96.

15. OR 31-1-53–55,57,59,60,112,113.

16. OR 31-1-54,46,72,770; Isaac C.

Doan, *Reminiscences of the Chattanooga Campaign,* p. 8; Arnold Gates, ed., *The Rough Side of War, The Civil War Journal of Chesley A. Mosman, 1st Lieutenant, Company D, 59th Illinois Volunteer Infantry Regiment,* p. 108.

17. OR 31-1-58,72.

18. OR 31-1-99; Gates, ed., *The Rough Side of War,* p. 109.

19. OR 31-1-221,222; OR 52-2-550,551,556; OR atlas 50-5; St. John R. Liddell, journal, Govan Papers, SHC.

20. Braxton Bragg, letter to James Longstreet, October 28, 1863, Bragg Reports, WRHS.

21. Braxton Bragg, letter to James Chesnut, Jr., November 9, 1863, WRHS; Liddell, journal, SHC; Longstreet, *From Manassas to Appomattox,* p. 474; OR 31-1-217; OR 52-2-556.

22. OR 31-1-217,219; OR 52-2-552,556; Longstreet, *From Manassas to Appomattox,* pp. 474,475; Liddell, journal, SHC.

23. OR 31-1-217.

24. OR 31-1-217; OR 52-2-553.

25. OR 31-1-217–223.

26. OR 31-1-217,223.

CHAPTER 16: Jenkins's Patrol to Pick Up Wagons and Stragglers

1. Patricia L. Faust, ed., *Historical Times Illustrated Encyclopedia of the Civil War,* p. 394.

2. Ibid., p. 426; William C. Oates, *The War Between the Union and Confederacy and Its Lost Opportunities, with a History of the Fifteenth Alabama and the Forty-eight Battles in Which It Was Engaged,* pp. 338–339.

3. OR 52-2-552.

4. OR 31-1-225; OR 52-2-552,553.

5. OR 31-1-222; OR 31-3-606.

6. OR 31-3-606; OR 52-2-551.

7. OR 31-1-225,226.

8. OR 31-1-226.

9. OR 31-1-217,218,223; OR 52-1-89.

10. OR 31-1-222,223,226.

11. OR 31-1-223.

12. OR 31-1-226,227,231.

13. Faust, ed., *Historical Times Illustrated Encyclopedia,* p. 302.

14. OR 31-1-113,116,117,120,123,131.

15. OR 31-1-113,123,126.

16. OR 31-1-231.
17. OR 31-1-113,114,128,135.
18. OR 31-1-122,133,231.
19. OR 31-1-113,114,125,127,130,133.
20. OR 31-1-114.
21. OR 31-1-124,128,231,232; OR 52-2-553.
22. OR 31-1-115,128; Ulysses S. Grant, *Personal Memoirs of U. S. Grant,* pp. 319–320; Wilson, *Under the Old Flag,* vol. 1, p. 278.
23. OR 31-1-115,135,232.
24. OR 31-1-117,119,124,135,136.
25. OR 31-1-128,133.
26. OR 31-1-232.
27. OR 31-1-124.
28. OR 31-1-232.

CHAPTER 17: "What Were Your Orders, General Schurz?"

1. OR 31-1-72,94; Andrew Boies, *Record of the Thirty-third Massachusetts Volunteer Infantry from Aug. 1862 to Aug. 1865,* p. 47.
2. OR 31-1-72,94,96,97,98,110,149,163, 164,177,182,185,186,193.
3. OR 31-1-73,99,104,106,108,110,150, 151,163,164,166,170,212.
4. OR 31-1-110,150,167,177,186–188.
5. OR 31-1-164,165,172,186,187.
6. OR 31-1-175,184,227; OR 52-1-89,90.
7. OR 31-1-115,116,232,233.
8. OR 31-1-226,227.
9. OR 31-1-61,112,143,171,173,193.
10. OR 31-1-95,177,189–195.
11. OR 31-1-98,101–104.
12. OR 31-1-104; Boies, *Record of the Thirty-third Massachusetts,* pp. 47–49.
13. Ibid.
14. OR 31-1-104,227,230.
15. OR 31-1-104,228,230.
16. OR 31-1-228,233.
17. OR 31-1-63,143,172,190.
18. OR 31-1-64,95,96.
19. OR 31-1-114–117; Mary de Forest Geary, *A Giant in Those Days,* p. 173; Oliver O. Howard, "Chattanooga," *Atlantic Monthly,* no. 38, p. 209.
20. OR 31-1-110,167,218,219; OR 31-3-606,607; OR 52-1-89,90; OR 52-2-556; Thomas Lawrence Connelly, *Autumn of Glory: The Army of Tennessee, 1862–1865,* pp. 261,296.
21. OR 31-1-120,232,233.
22. OR 30-4-765; OR 31-1-218,222,232.

23. Ibid.
24. Arnold Gates, ed., *The Rough Side of War, The Civil War Journal of Chesley A. Mosman, 1st Lieutenant, Company D, 59th Illinois Volunteer Infantry Regiment,* p. 109.

CHAPTER 18: "We Have the River"

1. Arnold Gates, ed., *The Rough Side of War, The Civil War Journal of Chesley A. Mosman, 1st Lieutenant, Company D, 59th Illinois Volunteer Infantry Regiment,* p. 111; James E. Withrow, diary, October 30, 1863, CHICK-CHATT; Allan L. Fahnestock, diary, October 30, 1863, CHICK-CHATT.
2. Gates, ed., *The Rough Side of War,* p. 109; OR 31-1-56,67,74,82; OR 31-4-102.
3. J. A. Reep, *Guttmachrala, or Four Years at the Front as a Private,* p. 20; B&L 3-678.
4. Reep, *Guttmachrala,* p. 20; Gates, ed., *The Rough Side of War,* pp. 111, 112; OR 31-1-74.
5. Isaac C. Doan, *Reminiscences of the Chattanooga Campaign,* p. 9; Withrow, diary, November 10, 1863.
6. Washington Ives, letter, November 10, 1863, CHICK-CHATT.
7. Gates, ed., *The Rough Side of War,* p. 115.
8. Hezekiah Rabb, letter, November 7, 1863, CHICK-CHATT; Ives, letter, November 10, 1863; Charles A. Houghton, letter, November 8, 1863, Charles A. Houghton Papers, USAMHI.
9. OR 31-3-606,607; OR 52-2-556.
10. OR 31-1-218.
11. OR 31-3-607,635; OR 52-2-557; St. John R. Liddell, journal, Govan Papers, SHC.
12. OR 31-1-73; Puntenney, *History of the Thirty-Seventh Regiment of Indiana,* p. 47; William R. Glison, diary, November 29, 1863, CHICK-CHATT.
13. OR 31-2-28,29,52,53; John Y. Simon, ed., *The Papers of Ulysses S. Grant,* vol. 9, p. 557.
14. OR 31-1-784; Simon ed., *The Papers,* vol. 9, p. 406.
15. Horace Porter, *Campaigning with Grant,* pp. 5,10,15; Simon, ed., *The Papers,* vol. 9, p. 352.

16. Porter, *Campaigning with Grant,* pp. 9,10.
17. OR 31-2-57,58.
18. OR 31-2-57,58; OR 31-3-66,73.
19. OR 31-1-57; OR 31-3-73.
20. OR 31-2-57,58; OR 31-3-10,15,84.
21. OR 31-2-58; William F. Smith, "Sketch of Military Operations," pp. 189–195.
22. OR 31-2-58,59; William F. Smith, "Sketch of Military Operations," pp. 189–195.
23. OR 31-2-29,59,92; OR 31-3-84,551,552.
24. OR 31-2-39; OR 31-3-92,93.
25. OR 31-3-93.
26. OR 31-3-216.
27. OR 31-3-93,216.
28. OR 31-2-54,55; OR 31-3-10,26.
29. OR 31-1-73; OR 31-2-53,57; OR 31-3-116.
30. OR 31-3-11,69,74; Simon, ed., *The Papers,* vol. 9, p. 406.
31. Simon, ed., *The Papers,* vol. 9, p. 559.
32. Ibid., pp. 396,397.
33. Porter, *Campaigning with Grant,* p. 5.
34. Simon, ed., *The Papers,* vol. 9, p. 396.

CHAPTER 19: "I Don't Think There Will Be Much Left After My Army Passes"
1. John Y. Simon, ed., *The Papers of Ulysses S. Grant,* vol. 9, p. 396; OR 31-1-706; OR 31-4-476.
2. OR 30-4-236,355.
3. OR 30-1-36,161,162; OR 30-3-592; Simon, ed., *The Papers,* vol. 9, p. 233.
4. OR 30-1-36; OR 30-3-720,721.
5. OR 30-1-37; OR 30-3-732.
6. OR 30-3-840,841.
7. OR 31-2-569.
8. OR 30-3-923; OR 31-2-569,570; William T. Sherman, *Memoirs of General William T. Sherman,* pp. 375ff.
9. Sherman, *Memoirs,* pp. 383,384; Ulysses S. Grant, *Personal Memoirs of U. S. Grant,* pp. 321,322; OR 31-1-713,771; OR 31-21-570,571.
10. Eugene McWayne, letters, October 5 and November 28, 1863, Collection of Wiley Sword.

11. OR 31-1-771,789,797; OR 31-2-571.; OR 31-3-12.
12. OR 31-2-571; OR 31-3-69,70,89.
13. OR 31-3-69,91,97.
14. OR 31-3-54,56,99.
15. OR 31-3-99,118,119.
16. OR 31-3-69,70,119.
17. OR 31-2-571; OR 31-3-139,140.
18. OR 31-2-29,571.
19. OR 31-3-31; B&L 3-715,716; William Wrenshall Smith, "Holocaust Holiday," CWTI 18, no. 6 (October 1979): 31.
20. OR 31-2-67,571; OR 31-3-58; B&L 3-716; William F. Smith, "Sketch of Military Operations," pp. 194–195.
21. OR 31-2-571,572; OR 31-3-168,178; Sherman, *Memoirs,* pp. 388,389.
22. OR 31-3-163,177,181.
23. Alfred L. Hough, *Soldier in the West; The Civil War Letters of Alfred Lacey Hough,* p. 169; Ely S. Parker, letter, November 18, 1863, American Philosophical Society Library, Philadelphia, Pennsylvania; Smith, "Holocaust Holiday," p. 32.
24. Smith, "Holocaust Holiday," p. 32.
25. Simon, ed., *The Papers,* vol. 9, p. 396.

CHAPTER 20: "I Have Never Felt Such Restlessness Before"
1. OR 31-3-178,583; William T. Sherman, *Memoirs of General William T. Sherman,* vol. v, pp. 388,389.
2. OR 31-2-37,572; OR 31-3-178,185,186,189.
3. OR 31-2-584,630.
4. OR 31-2-583–588,630,631.
5. OR 31-3-188.
6. OR 31-2-37,38.
7. OR 31-2-39; John W. Nesbit, letter, November 21, 1863, CHICK-CHATT.
8. OR 31-2-64; OR 31-3-203.
9. OR 31-2-39.
10. OR 31-2-215; OR 31-3-41,216.
11. OR 31-2-64; OR 31-3-179,185.
12. OR 31-2-41,64.
13. OR 31-2-64.
14. OR 31-2-61.
15. OR 31-2-62,216.
16. OR 31-2-38.
17. OR 31-2-30; OR 31-3-145,163,215.
18. OR 31-2-30; OR 31-3-93,145,163, 215,216,225,226,233; Charles A. Dana, *Recollections of the Civil War,* p. 137.

19. OR 31-3-163,181,215.
20. OR 31-2-63.
21. OR 31-2-32,39,40,42.
22. William Wrenshall Smith, "Holocaust Holiday," CWTI 18, no. 6 (October 1979): 31; OR 31-3-402.
23. Smith, CWTI "Holocaust Holiday," p. 31.
24. OR 31-3-402; James Lee McDonough, *Chattanooga—A Death Grip on the Confederacy,* p. 104.
25. OR 31-3-233.

CHAPTER 21: "Can't You Spare Me Another Division?"
1. Lewis L. Poates, letter, November 15, 1863, Collection of Lewis L. Poates.
2. Washington Ives, letters, November 5 and 8, 1863, CHICK-CHATT.
3. Ibid., letters, November 5,8,10, and 12, 1863.
4. Poates, letter, November 15, 1863; Ives, letter, November 12, 1863; Gerald F. Linderman, *Embattled Courage, The Experience of Combat in the American Civil War,* p. 34ff.
5. OR 31-3-685,686; OR 52-2-546.
6. Thomas Lawrence Connelly, *Autumn of Glory: The Army of Tennessee, 1862–1865,* pp. 250,251,252n.; OR 31-3-685,686.
7. Robert Watson, Journal, November 14, 1863, CHICK-CHATT; Ray Mathis, *In the Land of the Living, Wartime Letters by Confederates from the Chattahoochie Valley of Alabama and Georgia,* p. 80.
8. Ambrose Deas, letter, November 13, 1863, CHICK-CHATT; Ives, letter, November 12, 1863.
9. Robert J. Boyd Thigpen, letter, November 15, 1863, CHICK-CHATT; Ives, letter, November 20, 1863.
10. OR 31-3-700,701.
11. OR 31-3-86; Deas, letter, November 13, 1863; J. A. Reep, *Guttmachrala, or Four Years at the Front as a Private,* p. 22; Isaac Miller, letter, November 21, 1863, Collection of Wiley Sword; Charles A. Houghton, letter, November 15, 1863, Charles A. Houghton Papers, USAMHI.
12. OR 31-3-716.
13. Rennolds, diary, October 18, 1863,

CHICK-CHATT; Poates, letter, November 15, 1863.
14. Braxton Bragg, letter to wife, November 14, 1863, Bragg Papers Missouri Historical Society, St. Louis, Missouri.
15. OR 30-4-720; OR 31-3-593,668,680, 681,716.
16. OR 31-3-710.
17. OR 31-3-717.
18. OR 31-2-667.
19. OR 31-2-656,657,667–670.
20. OR 31-3-736.
21. OR 31-3-681.
22. OR 31-3-721.
23. OR 31-3-732.
24. OR 31-3-736.
25. OR 31-3-732.
26. OR 31-2-675; OR 31-3-738.
27. OR 31-3-737,745.
28. OR 31-2-656,673,745,746; *The Eighty-Sixth Regiment Indiana Volunteer Infantry, A Narrative of Its Services in the Civil War of 1861–1865.*
29. OR 31-2-746.
30. Ibid.
31. Ibid.

CHAPTER 22: "Kicking Up Such a Damned Fuss"
1. OR 31-3-233.
2. OR 31-2-42,64,572,591; OR 31-3-231.
3. OR 31-2-32,40,64.
4. OR 31-2-64,100,102,136.
5. OR 31-2-32.
6. OR 31-2-32; Ely S. Parker, letter, November 18, 1863, American Philosophical Library, Philadelphia, Pennsylvania.
7. OR 31-2-32.
8. Ibid.
9. OR 31-2-41.
10. OR 31-2-32.
11. OR 31-2-65,94,128,254.
12. OR 31-2-104.
13. OR 31-2-251,254; Thomas J. Wood, "The Battle of Missionary Ridge," *Sketches of War History 1861–1865,* vol. 4, p. 27.
14. Allan L. Fahnestock, diary, November 23, 1863, CHICK-CHATT; William Wrenshall Smith, "Holocaust Holiday," CWTI 18, no. 6 (October 1979): 33; William R. Glison, diary, November 22, 1863, CHICK-CHATT; J. A. Reep, *Guttmachrala, or Four Years at*

the Front as a Private, chapter 15, p. 2; OR 31-2-288.
15. Reep, *Guttmachrala,* CHICK-CHATT; B&L 3-721.
16. Glison, diary, November 23, 1863; Reep, *Guttmachrala;* B&L 3-721.
17. OR 31-2-254; Smith, "Holocaust Holiday," p. 33.
18. OR 31-2-128,129,254,255.
19. OR 31-2-129,254,347; B&L 3-721; John K. Shellenberger, "With Sheridan's Division at Missionary Ridge," *Sketches of War History 1861–1865,* vol. 4, p. 52.
20. OR 31-2-129,254.
21. Reep, *Guttmachrala,* chapter 15, pp. 2,3,4; OR 31-2-65; Smith, "Holocaust Holiday," p. 33.
22. OR 31-2-65,129,254,263,280,287.
23. *Mobile Daily Register & Advertiser,* December 11, 1863; R. Lockwood Tower, ed., *A Carolinian Goes to War, The Civil War Narrative of Arthur Middleton Manigault, Brigadier General, C.S.A.,* p. 130.
24. R. Lockwood Tower, ed., *A Carolinian Goes to War,* pp. 130,131.
25. Ibid.; John Hoffman, *The Confederate Collapse at the Battle of Missionary Ridge, The Reports of James Patton Anderson and his Brigade Commanders,* pp. 35,58,68.
26. *Mobile Daily Register,* December 11, 1863; OR 31-2-14; Glison, diary, November 23, 1863.
27. Shellenberger, "With Sheridan's Division," p. 50.
28. OR 31-2-287.
29. OR 31-2-65.
30. *Mobile Daily Register,* December 11, 1863.
31. Ibid.; Hoffman, *The Confederate Collapse,* p. 35.
32. Hoffman, *The Confederate Collapse, p. 58.*
33. *Mobile Daily Register,* December 11, 1863; Hoffman, *The Confederate Collapse,* p. 68; OR 31-2-280,295.
34. OR 31-2-280,285,295.
35. OR 31-2-281,295,298.
36. OR 31-2-285,287,295,297.
37. OR 31-2-280,298.
38. OR 31-2-65,251,255,279,281,297; Hoffman, *The Confederate Collapse,* p. 68; Stephen H. Helmer, letter, Novem-ber 26, 1863, Civil War Miscellany Collection, USAMHI.
39. OR 31-2-255,263.
40. OR 31-2-65; Wood, "The Battle of Missionary Ridge," p. 29.
41. Ibid.; OR 31-2-129,137,189,347,348.
42. Smith, "Holocaust Holiday," p. 33.
43. Wood, "The Battle of Missionary Ridge," p. 29; OR 31-2-65.
44. OR 31-2-65,66.
45. OR 31-2-103,130.
46. OR 31-2-42,130,137; OR 31-3-103; Ebenezer Hannaford, *The Story of a Regiment, A History of the Campaigns, and Associations in the Field, of the Sixth Regiment, Ohio Volunteer Infantry,* p. 501; Robert L. Kimberly, and Ephraim S. Holloway, *The Forty-First Ohio Veteran Volunteer Infantry in the War of the Rebellion, 1861–1865,* p. 67.
47. Smith, "Holocaust Holiday," p. 33; OR 31-2-65.
48. Smith, "Holocaust Holiday," p. 33.
49. Shellenberger, "The Battle of Missionary Ridge," p. 53.
50. Tower, ed., *A Carolinian Goes to War,* pp. 132,133.
51. Ibid.

CHAPTER 23: "The Ball Will Soon Open"
1. OR 31-2-745,746.
2. OR 31-2-673,674,746,759.
3. OR 31-2-105,106,347,670,718.
4. Mattie Lou Teague Crow, ed., *The Diary of a Confederate Soldier, John Washington Inzer 1834–1928,* pp. 40,41.
5. R. Lockwood Tower, ed., *A Carolinian Goes to War, The Civil War Narrative of Arthur Middleton Manigault, Brigadier General, C.S.A.,* pp. 133,134.
6. Ibid.
7. OR 31-2-664,666,746; Crow, ed., *The Diary of a Confederate Soldier,* p. 41.
8. OR 31-2-746; John Hoffman, *The Confederate Collapse at the Battle of Missionary Ridge,* p. 36.
9. Hoffman, *The Confederate Collapse at the Battle of Missionary Ridge,* p. 36.
10. Crow, ed., *The Diary of a Confederate Soldier,* pp. 40,41.
11. OR 31-2-31; B&L 3-715,716.
12. OR 31-3-154,155.
13. OR 31-2-31,32,571,589,590.

14. OR 31-2-32.
15. William J. Sherman, *Memoirs of General William T. Sherman*, p. 386.
16. OR 31-2-32,42,572.
17. OR 31-2-13,14,42,43,346,347.
18. OR 31-2-41,65,66.
19. *The Story of the Fifty-fifth Regiment Illinois Volunteer Infantry in the Civil War, 1861–1865*, pp. 280,281; Gilbert R. Stormont and John J. Hight, *History of the Fifty-eighth Regiment of Indiana Volunteer Infantry, Its Organization, Campaigns, and Battles from 1861–1865*, pp. 283,284; J. A. Reep, *Guttmachrala, or Four Years at the Front as a Private*, chapter 15, p. 5.
20. *The Story of the Fifty-fifth Regiment Illinois*, p. 280; Andrew McCornack, letter, November 24, 1863, Collection of Wiley Sword.
21. *The Story of the Fifty-fifth Regiment Illinois*, p. 281; Sherman, *Memoirs*, p. 389.
22. Stormont and Hight, *History of the Fifty-eighth Regiment*, p. 285.
23. Jabez Banbury, diary, November 20, 1863, CHICK-CHATT.
24. Ibid., November 22, 1863; OR 31-2-572,573,589,590.
25. Banbury, diary, November 22, 1863.
26. OR 31-2-590,591; B&L 3-712; Allan L. Fahnestock, diary, November 23, 1863, CHICK-CHATT.
27. OR 31-2-73,503.
28. OR 31-2-503.
29. OR 31-2-73,503.
30. Ibid.
31. OR 31-2-105,106,503.
32. *The Story of the Fifty-fifth Regiment Illinois*, pp. 282,283; OR 31-2-503.
33. OR 31-2-73; *The Story of the Fifty-fifth Regiment Illinois*, p. 283.
34. Ibid.
35. Ibid.; OR 31-2-66.

CHAPTER 24: What is "Wrongly Laid Down"

1. B&L 3-712; Allan L. Fahnestock, diary, November 24, 1863, CHICK-CHATT; *The Story of the Fifty-fifth Regiment Illinois Volunteer Infantry in the Civil War, 1861–1865*, p. 283; OR 31-2-572.
2. *The Story of the Fifty-fifth Regiment Illinois*, p. 283; B&L 3-712; Eightieth Ohio manuscript, no identification, file of Eightieth Ohio Infantry, CHICK-CHATT.
3. OR 31-2-781.
4. OR 31-2-74,75,572; *The Story of the Fifty-fifth Regiment Illinois*, p. 283.
5. B&L 3-712.
6. Ibid., OR 31-2-643; Jabez Banbury, diary, November 24, 1863, CHICK-CHATT; Charles A. Partridge, *History of the Ninety-Sixth Regiment Illinois Volunteer Infantry*, p. 61.
7. OR 31-2-33,66,75.
8. OR 31-2-73,77; B&L 3-722.
9. B&L 3-702; OR 31-2-74,75,108, 348,368,573.
10. OR 31-2-573.
11. OR 31-2-74.
12. OR 31-2-33,75,573.
13. OR 31-2-42,74,573,647.
14. OR 31-2-573,643,645,647.
15. OR 31-2-67,571; OR 31-3-58; B&L 3-716.
16. OR 31-2-58,73,573.
17. OR 31-2-348,401.
18. OR 31-2-348,573; Fahnestock, diary, November 24, 1863; Eli J. Sherlock, *Memoranda of the Marches and Battles in Which the One Hundredth Regiment of Indiana Infantry Volunteers Took an Active Part, War of the Rebellion, 1861–1865*, p. 52.
19. OR 31-2-629,636,646,654; Sherlock, *Memoranda of the Marches*, p. 53; Henry H. Wright, *A History of the Sixth Iowa Infantry*, p. 235.
20. OR 31-2-573,597.
21. OR 31-2-573,629.
22. Ibid.
23. OR 31-2-643,645.
24. OR 31-2-42,108,643,747; Sherlock, *Memoranda of the Marches*, p. 53.
25. OR 31-2-631,640,646,651,654; *The Story of the Fifty-fifth Regiment Illinois*, p. 284.
26. OR 31-2-58,573,597,643; Edward E. Betts, Map of the Battlefields of Chattanooga and Wauhatchie.
27. OR 31-2-24,44,597,631ff.
28. Zella Armstrong, *The History of Hamilton County and Chattanooga, Tennessee*, vol. 2, p. 41; Sherlock, *Memoranda of the Marches*, p. 53; *The Story of the Fifty-fifth Regiment Illinois*, pp. 284,285; William Wrenshall Smith,

"Holocaust Holiday," CWTI 18, no. 6 (October 1979): 35; OR 31-2-67.

CHAPTER 25: "A Sickle of Mars"
1. Mattie Lou Teague Crow, ed., *The Diary of a Confederate Soldier, John Washington Inzer 1834–1928*, p. 24; OR 31-2-664.
2. OR 31-2-747.
3. *Mobile Daily Register & Advertiser*, December 11, 1863; R. Lockwood Tower, ed., *A Carolinian Goes to War, The Civil War Narrative of Arthur Middleton Manigaut, Brigadier General, C.S.A.*, p. 134; Rufus W. Daniel, diary, November 24, 1863, Civil War Miscellany Collection, USAMHI.
4. OR 31-2-708,709.
5. OR 31-2-664,678,706–709.
6. OR 31-2-723.
7. OR 31-2-664,678.
8. OR 31-2-664,674,675,692.
9. OR 31-2-102,103,674n.
10. OR 31-2-41,42,105,106.
11. OR 31-2-106.
12. OR 31-2-107,329,314,329.
13. Charles A. Partridge, *History of the 96th Regiment of Illinois Volunteer Infantry*, p. 263,264; Arnold Gates, ed., p. 125; John N. Beach, *History of the Fortieth Ohio Volunteer Infantry*, p. 56; Gideon S. Stare, letter, December 13, 1863, CHICK-CHATT.
14. Partridge, *History of the 96th Illinois*, p. 264,265; Richard Eddy, *History of the Sixtieth Regiment New York State Volunteers*, pp. 305,306; George K. Collins, *Memoirs of the 149th New York Volunteer Infantry, 3rd Brigade, 2nd Division, 12th and 20th A.C.*, p. 207.
15. OR 31-2-315,390.
16. OR 31-2-315.
17. OR 31-2-107,390,391,424,428; Isaac C. Doan, *Reminiscences of the Chattanooga Campaign*, p. 13; Partridge, *History of the 96th Illinois*, p. 265.
18. Edward E. Betts, Map of the Battlefields of Chattanooga and Wauhatchie; OR 31-2-391,392.
19. OR 31-2-391,392; Collins, *Memoirs of the 149th*, p. 207; Partridge, *History of the 96th Illinois*, p. 266.
20. OR 31-2-718,719.
21. OR 31-2-692,723; Patricia L. Faust, ed., *Historical Times Illustrated Encyclopedia of the Civil War*, p. 800.
22. OR 31-2-315,692,693.
23. OR 31-2-690,693,694.
24. OR 31-2-392; Doan, *Reminiscences of the Chattanooga Campaign*, p. 13; Collins, *Memoirs of the 149th*, pp. 209,210.
25. OR 31-2-392; Partridge, *History of the 96th Illinois*, pp. 267,268; Doan, *Reminiscences of the Chattanooga Campaign*, p. 13.
26. OR 31-2-392,698; Partridge, *History of the 96th Illinois*, p. 268; Eddy, *History of the Sixtieth Regiment New York*, p. 306; Stare, letter, December 13, 1863.
27. Eddy, *History of the Sixtieth Regiment New York*, pp. 306; Partridge, *History of the 96th Illinois*, p. 268; OR 31-2-392,393.
28. OR 31-2-393,690,698,699; Eddy, *History of the Sixtieth Regiment New York*, pp. 306,307.
29. Stare, letter, December 13, 1863; OR 31-2-393.
30. OR 31-2-316,391,393,552,599,698; Partridge, *History of the 96th Illinois*, p. 267.
31. OR 31-2-108,599,600; *Military History and Reminiscences of the Thirteenth Regiment of Illinois Volunteer Infantry in the Civil War in the United States, 1861–1865*, p. 373.
32. OR 31-2-393; Partridge, *History of the 96th Illinois*, p. 266.

CHAPTER 26: The Battle Within the Clouds
1. OR 31-2-692,694.
2. OR 31-2-695.
3. OR 31-2-719.
4. OR 31-2-674,719,720,723.
5. OR 31-2-688; Patricia L. Faust, ed., *Historical Times Illustrated Encyclopedia of the Civil War*, p. 390; E. T. Sykes, *Walthall's Brigade, A Cursory Sketch, with Personal Experiences of Walthall's Brigade, Army of Tennessee, C.S.A., 1862–1865*, pp. 539,600.
6. OR 31-2-704.
7. OR 31-2-704,705,717.
8. OR 31-2-395; Isaac C. Doan, *Reminis-*

cences of the Chattanooga Campaign, pp. 13,14; Partridge, History of the 96th Illinois, pp. 267–269.

9. OR 31-2-395; Partridge, History of the 96th Illinois, p. 269; Lyman S. Widney, letter, November 27, 1863, CHICK-CHATT.

10. Doan, Reminiscences of the Chattanooga Campaign, p. 13.

11. Pennsylvania, Pennsylvania at Chickamauga and Chattanooga, Ceremonies at the Dedication of the Monuments, p. 288; OR 31-2-446,717.

12. OR 31-2-156,165,396,441,446; Doan, Reminiscences of the Chattanooga Campaign, p. 14; Richard Eddy, History of the Sixtieth Regiment New York State Volunteers, p. 307.

13. OR 31-2-396,436,441.

14. OR 31-2-159,165; Partridge, History of the 96th Illinois, p. 270.

15. OR 31-2-705; author's personal notes, Chattanooga field trip, April 7, 1993.

16. OR 31-2-705; Alabama Historical Quarterly, vol. 17, p. 187.

17. Partridge, History of the 96th Illinois, p. 270; OR 31-2-159.

18. Partridge, History of the 96th Illinois, p. 270; Doan, Reminiscences of the Chattanooga Campaign, p. 14; OR 31-2-165.

19. M. S. Schroyer, "Company 'G' History" The Snyder County [Pennsylvania] Historical Society Bulletin 2, no. 2, p. 380; OR 31-2-396,441,449,722.

20. OR 31-2-332,395,396,425,444.

21. OR 31-2-109.

22. OR 31-2-106,316,331.

23. OR 31-2-106,332.

24. OR 31-2-396,397,425,444.

25. OR 31-2-333.

26. OR 31-2-677,694,695,699,705,732.

27. OR 31-2-695,720,719,731,732,436.

28. OR 31-2-55,156,436; Phillip Rutherford, "A Battle Above the Clouds," CWTI 26, no. 5 (September/October 1989): 38.

29. OR 3-2-395,436,720,726,732.

30. OR 31-2-109,705.

31. OR 31-2-732.

32. OR 31-2-690,732.

33. OR 31-2-721.

34. OR 31-2-664,674,675,722.

35. OR 31-2-678,721,723.

CHAPTER 27: Fireflies in the Night

1. OR 31-2-718,728.

2. OR 31-2-110; Mattie Lou Teague Crow, ed., The Diary of a Confederate Soldier, John Washington Inzer 1834–1928, pp. 41,42.

3. Crow, ed., The Diary of a Confederate Soldier, pp. 41,42; OR 31-2-463,701, 720.

4. OR 31-2-721; Christopher Losson, Tennessee's Forgotten Warriors, Frank Cheatham and His Confederate Division, pp. 117,125.

5. OR 31-2-690,721,734.

6. OR 31-2-67,78.

7. Crow, ed., The Diary of a Confederate Soldier, pp. 42,43; Alabama Historical Quarterly, vol. 7, p. 188; Arnold Gates, ed., The Rough Side of War, The Civil War Journal of Chesley A. Mosman, 1st Lieutenant, Company D, 59th Illinois Volunteer Infantry Regiment, p. 127.

8. Frank Wolfe, "Letter to a Friend: From the Foot of Lookout Mountain," CWTI 22, no. 4 (June 1983): 40–42; OR 31-2-78; William Wrenshall Smith, "Holocaust Holiday," CWTI 18, no. 6 (October 1979): 34; Lyman S. Widney, letter, November 27, 1863, CHICK-CHATT.

9. Smith, "Holocaust Holiday," p. 34; Charles A. Dana, Recollections of the Civil War, pp. 147,148; OR 31-2-67, 78.

10. OR 31-2-108,316.

11. OR 31-2-111,316,607,689,720,722.

12. OR 31-2-109,111,333,462,463.

13. OR 31-2-317,334,463.

14. OR 31-2-463.

15. OR 31-2-67; Smith, "Holocaust Holiday," p. 34.

16. OR 31-2-333.

17. OR 31-2-112.

18. OR 31-2-113,114,317,318,463.

19. Walter F. Beyer and Oscar F. Keydel, Deeds of Valor, How America's Heroes Won the Medal of Honor, vol. 1, p. 285; Gates, The Rough Side of War, p. 127.

20. OR 31-2-156; Gideon S. Stare, letter, December 13, 1863, CHICK-CHATT; Isaac C. Doan, Reminiscences of the Chattanooga Campaign, p. 13; Military

History and Reminiscences of the Thirteenth Regiment of Illinois Volunteer Infantry, p. 376.

21. Pennsylvania, *Pennsylvania at Chickamauga and Chattanooga Ceremonies at the Dedication of the Monuments,* pp. 288,289.

22. Crow, ed., *The Diary of a Confederate Soldier,* pp. 42,43.

23. OR 31-2-696,726,732,734.

24. OR 31-2-317; Doan, *Reminiscences of the Chattanooga Campaign,* p. 15, Gates, ed., *The Rough Side of War,* p. 127.

25. *Military History of the 13th Illinois,* p. 377; OR 31-2-156,163.

26. OR 31-2-156,163,399; Doan, *Reminiscences of the Chattanooga Campaign,* p. 15; M. S. Schroyer, "Company 'G' History," *The Snyder County [Pennsylvania] Historical Society Bulletin,* 2, no. 2, p. 381.

27. OR 31-2-156, Doan, *Reminiscences of the Chattanooga Campaign,* pp. 14,15.

28. J. A. Reep, *Guttmachrala, or Four Years at the Front as a Private,* ch. 15, p. 15; William Wirt Calkins, *The History of the One Hundred and Fourth Regiment of Illinois Volunteer Infantry, War of the Great Rebellion, 1862–1865,* p. 187; C. C. Briant, *History of the Sixth Regiment Indiana Volunteer Infantry, 1891,* pp. 273,274.

29. OR 31-2-599; Pennsylvania, *Pennsylvania at Chickamauga,* p. 289; Stare, letter, December 13, 1863.

30. OR 31-2-156,163,336.

31. OR 31-2-113.

32. OR 31-2-690; Doan, *Reminiscences of the Chattanooga Campaign,* p. 14.

33. OR 31-2-318,721.

34. OR 31-2-664.

35. OR 31-2-78; Charles A. Partridge, *History of the Ninety-Sixth Regiment Illinois Volunteer Infantry,* p. 269; Pennsylvania, *Pennsylvania of Chickamauga,* p. 289.

36. Ulysses S. Grant, *Personal Memoirs of U. S. Grant,* p. 336n.; OR 31-2-409.

37. John N. Beach, *History of the Fortieth Ohio Volunteer Infantry,* p. 56; Partridge, *History of the 96th Illinois,* pp. 269,271,272.

CHAPTER 28: "I Mean to Get Even with Them"

1. OR 31-2-67.

2. OR 31-2-43,44,112.

3. OR 31-2-67,68,78.

4. OR 31-2-32,67; B&L 3-723.

5. OR 31-2-115; William Wrenshall Smith, "Holocaust Holiday," CWTI 18, no. 6 (October 1979): 35.

6. OR 31-2-664,707–709.

7. OR 31-2-707,747.

8. OR 31-2-746.

9. Ibid.

10. OR 31-2-746,747.

11. OR 31-2-747.

12. Ibid.

13. OR 31-2-747,748.

14. Ibid.

15. OR 31-2-748; Irving A. Buck, *Cleburne and his Command,* pp. 166,167.

16. Ibid., p. 167.

17. Ibid.; OR 31-2-748,752.

18. Grady McWhiney, *Braxton Bragg and Confederate Defeat,* vol. 1, p. ix.

19. Thomas Lawrence Connelly, *Autumn of Glory, The Army of Tennessee, 1862–1865,* p. 273; OR 31-2-677.

20. Connelly, *Autumn of Glory,* pp. 251,273; Nathaniel Cheairs Hughes, Jr., *General William J. Hardee, Old Reliable,* pp. 171,172; Judith Lee Hallock, *Braxton Bragg and Confederate Defeat,* vol. 2, p. 136.

21. Hallock, *Braxton Bragg and Confederate Defeat,* vol. 2, p. 136.

22. Connelly, *Autumn of Glory,* p. 273; Hughes, *General William J. Hardee,* pp. 171,172; Hallock, *Braxton Bragg,* vol. 2, p. 136; St. John R. Liddell journal, Govan Papers, SHC.

23. St. John R. Liddell journal, Govan Papers, SHC.; OR 31-2-722; R. Lockwood Tower, *A Carolinian Goes to War, The Civil War Narrative of Arthur Middleton Manigault, Brigadier General, C.S.A.,* p. 136.

24. OR 31-2-43,44,574,643; S. H. M. Byers, *With Fire and Sword,* p. 105.

25. OR 31-2-349,573,574,596.

26. OR 31-2-629,633; Allan L. Fahnestock, diary, November 25, 1863, CHICK-CHATT; Eli J. Sherlock, *Memoranda of the Marches and Battles in Which the One Hundredth Regiment of Indiana Infantry Volunteers Took an*

Active Part, War of the Rebellion, 1861–1865, p. 53.
27. OR 31-2-629,633.
28. OR 31-2-13,14,67,78,113,114,349.
29. OR 31-2-643.
30. OR 31-2-67,78,106,113,114; Smith, "Holocaust Holiday," p. 35.
31. OR 30-4-476; OR 31-2-706; OR 31-3-216; John Y. Simon, ed., *The Papers of Ulysses S. Grant,* vol. 9, p. 396.
32. OR 31-2-349,574,633,643.

CHAPTER 29: Hell Turned Loose on Tunnel Hill
1. OR 16-1-934; Howell and Elizabeth Purdue, *Pat Cleburne Confederate General,* pp. 51ff,163.
2. Purdue, *Pat Cleburne Confederate General,* pp. 188,189,296,438.
3. Ibid., p. 438.
4. Ibid., pp. 50–52,137–139,149; Wiley Sword, *Embrace an Angry Wind,* p. 17ff.; Charles Edward Nash, *Biographical Sketches of Gen. Pat Cleburne and Gen. T. C. Hindman,* p. 202.
5. Purdue, *Pat Cleburne Confederate General,* p. 237ff.
6. OR 31-2-13,14,757.
7. OR 31-2-748,749.
8. OR 31-2-748.
9. OR 31-2-748,749.
10. Ibid., 748,749,757.
11. OR 31-2-574,631; Lloyd Lewis, *Sherman, Fighting Prophet,* p. 320.
12. OR 31-2-574.
13. OR 31-2-640; H. W. Hall, January 23, 1908 (Fortieth Illinois Infantry) in Statements of Witnesses, in the file of the Chattanooga National Park Commission investigating the claim of Gen. John B. Turchin as to the capture of the De Long Place during the Battle of Chattanooga, CHICK-CHATT (hereafter referred to as Turchin statements).
14. Norman Brown, ed., *One of Cleburne's Command, The Civil War Reminiscences and Diary of Capt. Samuel T. Foster, Granbury's Texas Brigade, C.S.A.,* pp. 60,61.
15. Ibid.
16. Hall, in Turchin statements.
17. Ibid.
18. OR 31-2-574,636; Henry H. Wright,

A History of the Sixth Iowa Infantry, p. 236.
19. Ibid.; Thomas Taylor, letter, December 20, 1863, Ohio Historical Society, Columbus, Ohio; Brown, *One of Cleburne's Command,* p. 162; OR 31-2-636.
20. OR 31-2-636; Brown, *One of Cleburne's Command,* pp. 162,163; Robert Selph Henry, *As They Saw Forrest, Some Recollections and Comments of Contemporaries,* p. 236; Hall, in Turchin statements.
21. Brown, *One of Cleburne's Command,* pp. 162,163.
22. OR 31-2-636.
23. Brown, *One of Cleburne's Command,* pp. 162,163; OR 31-2-749,750.
24. Ibid.
25. Wright, *A History of the Sixth Iowa,* pp. 236,237; Brown, *One of Cleburne's Command,* p. 163; OR 31-2-750.
26. Brown, *One of Cleburne's Command,* p. 163; OR 31-2-636,750; Wright, *A History of the Sixth Iowa,* pp. 236,237.
27. Ibid.; OR 31-2-636.
28. Brown, *One of Cleburne's Command,* p. 162.
29. OR 31-2-750.
30. Ibid.
31. Ibid.

CHAPTER 30: An Ascent into Hell
1. *The Story of the Fifty-fifth Regiment Illinois Volunteer Infantry in the Civil War, 1861–1865,* p. 286; OR 31-2-750.
2. OR 31-2-349,575,596,634,652.
3. OR 31-2-44,349,633; Ira Bloomfield (Twenty-sixth Illinois Infantry), November 21, 1907, and J. N. King (Twenty-sixth Illinois Infantry), November 21, 1907, in Turchin statements, CHICK-CHATT; Eli J. Sherlock, *Memoranda of the Marches and Battles in Which the One Hundredth Regiment of Indiana Infantry Volunteers Took an Active Part, War of the Rebellion, 1861–1865,* p. 54.
4. OR 31-2-360,633,640; King, in Turchin statements.
5. King, in Turchin statements; OR 31-2-633.
6. OR 31-2-360,364,368,370; Sherlock, *Memoranda of the Marches,* p. 54.

7. OR 31-2-634,652.
8. OR 31-2-643,652.
9. OR 31-2-634.
10. OR 31-2-735,736.
11. Ibid.
12. OR 31-2-368,634; Pennsylvania, *Pennsylvania at Chickamauga and Chattanooga, Ceremonies at the Dedication of the Monuments,* pp. 78,79,160,161.
13. OR 31-2-349,735; Edward E. Betts, Map of the Battlefields of Chattanooga and Wauhatchie; Charles A. Partridge, *History of the Ninety-sixth Regiment Illinois Volunteer Infantry,* p. 66.
14. OR 31-2-68,368,575,634.
15. Partridge, *History of the Ninety-Sixth,* p. 54; Pennsylvania, *Pennsylvania at Chickamauga,* p. 79; OR 31-2-361.
16. OR 31-2-750; Irving A. Buck, *Cleburne and His Command,* p. 169.
17. OR 31-2-750,751.
18. Ibid.
19. OR 31-2-652.
20. Ibid.
21. OR 31-2-653; file of the Ninety-third Illinois Infantry, Company B, pp. 25,26, CHICK-CHATT.
22. Ibid.
23. OR 31-2-652,653.
24. OR 31-2-643,644.
25. OR 31-2-647,648; Pren Methamm, December 10, 1907, in Turchin statements; file of the Ninety-third; Aaron Dunbar, *History of the Ninety-third Regiment Illinois Volunteer Infantry from Organization to Muster Out,* pp. 67,77.
26. OR 31-2-736,751.
27. OR 31-2-727.
28. Wirt Armistead Cate, ed., *Two Soldiers, The Campaign Diaries of Thomas J. Key, C.S.A., and Robert J. Campbell, U.S.A.,* p. 155; OR 31-2-757.
29. Buck, *Cleburne and His Command,* p. 170; OR 31-2-751.
30. OR 31-2-736,737,751.
31. OR 31-2-737,751.
32. OR 31-2-737.
33. OR 31-2-736,737.
34. OR 31-2-737.
35. OR 31-2-737,751.
36. OR 31-2-369,652,653,737.
37. OR 31-2-648,653.
38. OR 31-2-648.
39. OR 31-2-655; Jabez Banbury, diary, November 25, 1863, CHICK-CHATT; S. H. M. Byers, *With Fire and Sword,* pp. 108,109.
40. Byers, *With Fire and Sword,* pp. 108,109; OR 31-2-369,370,655.
41. Thomas Taylor, letter, December 20, 1863, Ohio Historical Society, Columbus, Ohio.
42. OR 31-2-650.
43. OR 31-2-650,751; Buck, *History of the Ninety-third Regiment,* p. 170.
44. OR 31-2-648; Ira Blumfield, November 19, 21, 1907, in Turchin statements.
45. Ibid.; OR 31-2-634.
46. Banbury, diary, November 25, 1863; file of the Ninety-third.
47. B. B. Tarman, letter, December 23, 1863, CHICK-CHATT.

CHAPTER 31: Time for a Demonstration
1. OR 31-2-13,14.
2. OR 31-2-44,115.
3. OR 31-2-43.
4. OR 31-2-575,581.
5. OR 31-2-596,650.
6. OR 31-2-68; William Wrenshall Smith, "Holocaust Holiday," CWTI 18, no. 6 (October 1979): 35,36.
7. OR 31-2-34,96,508; Benjamin P. Thomas, ed., *Three Years with Grant As Recalled by War Correspondent Sylvanus Cadwallader,* pp. 152–153.
8. OR 31-2-45; Smith, "Holocaust Holiday," p. 36; Wilson, *Under the Old Flag,* vol. 1, pp. 297–298.
9. Ibid.
10. Ibid.; OR 31-2-34.
11. OR 31-2-112,113; B&L 3-724.
12. OR 31-2-114.
13. OR 31-2-113,115,146,313,318,336, 600,601.
14. OR 31-2-116; B&L 3-723.
15. Ibid.; OR 31-2-68; Thomas J. Wood, "The Battle of Missionary Ridge," *Sketches of War History, 1861–1865,* vol. 4, p. 24.
16. Wood, "The Battle of Missionary Ridge," p. 34.
17. Ibid.
18. Ibid.
19. Ibid. pp. 34,35.
20. OR 31-2-132; B&L 3-724.

21. Ibid.; OR 31-2-87,209.
22. OR 31-2-596,734,735,749ff.; B&L 3-724.
23. Ibid.

CHAPTER 32: One of the Greatest Blunders
1. Joshua Dewes, diary, November 25, 1863, CHICK-CHATT.
2. *History of the Seventy-ninth Regiment Indiana Volunteer Infantry in the Civil War of 1861 in the United States*, pp. 105,106.
3. J. A. Reep, *Guttmachrala, or Four Years at the Front as a Private*, chapter 15, p. 17.
4. Asbury L. Kerwood, *Annals of the Fifty-seventh Regiment Indiana Volunteers*, pp. 222–224; F. W. Keil, *Thirty-fifth Ohio, A Narrative of Service from August, 1861 to 1864*, p. 168.
5. William H. Newlin, *A History of the Seventy-third Regiment of Illinois Infantry Volunteers*, p. 265; Albert R. Stormont and John J. Hight, *History of the Fifty-eighth Regiment of Indiana Volunteer Infantry, Its Organization, Campaigns, and Battles from 1861–1865*, p. 217.
6. Ibid.; Robert L. Kimberly and Ephraim S. Holloway, *The Forty-first Ohio Veteran Volunteer Infantry in the War of the Rebellion, 1861–1865*, p. 68.
7. Ebenezer Hannaford, *The Story of a Regiment, A History of the Campaigns, and Associations in the Field, of the Sixth Regiment, Ohio Volunteer Infantry*, p. 507.
8. William Wirt Calkins, *The History of the One Hundred and Fourth Regiment of Illinois Volunteer Infantry, War of the Great Rebellion, 1862–1865*, p. 85; *History of the Seventy-ninth Regiment Indiana Volunteer Infantry in the Civil War of 1861 in the United States*, p. 106; John K. Shellenberger, "With Sheridan's Division at Missionary Ridge," *Sketches of War History 1861–1865*, p. 56.
9. Shellenberger, "With Sheridan's Division," p. 57.
10. Ibid.; OR 31-2-264.
11. Thomas J. Wood, "The Battle of Missionary Ridge," *Sketches of War History, 1861–1865*, p. 35; OR 31-2-257.
12. OR 31-2-189,209,213,223,264; Charles T. Clark, *Opdycke Tigers 125th O.V.I., A History of the Regiment and of the Campaigns and Battles of the Army of the Cumberland*, p. 172; Stormont and Hight, *History of the Fifty-eighth Regiment of Indiana*, p. 218.
13. OR 31-2-230,246; Stormont and Hight, *History of the Fifty-eighth Regiment of Indiana*, p. 218; Albion Tourgee, *The Story of A Thousand, Being a History of the Service of the One Hundred Fifth Ohio Volunteer Infantry in the War for the Union from August 21, 1862 to June 6, 1865*, pp. 285,286; Shellenberger, "With Sheridan's Division," p. 57.
14. OR 31-2-508,512; William F. Smith, "Sketch of Military Operations," p. 216.
15. OR 31-2-459.
16. John McClenahan, memoirs, CHICK-CHATT.
17. Clark, *Opdycke Tigers*, p. 172; OR 31-2-190; Ephraim G. Wagley, memoir, Civil War Miscellany Collection, USAMHI.
18. OR 31-2-190.
19. OR 31-2-68,190; James Henry Haynie, *The Nineteenth Illinois; A Memoir of a Regiment of Volunteer Infantry Famous in the Civil War of Fifty Years Ago for Its Drill, Bravery, and Distinguished Services*, p. 280; Benjamin P. Thomas, ed., *Three Years with Grant*, pp. 153–154.
20. OR 31-2-96,132,508; Haynie, *The Nineteenth Illinois*, pp. 279-281.
21. Shellenberger, "With Sheridan's Division," pp. 57,58.
22. Ibid.; Stormont and Hight, *History of the Fifty-eighth Regiment of Indiana*, p. 218; OR 31-2-14.
23. Tourgee, *The Story of a Thousand*, p. 285; Kimberly and Holloway, *The Forty-first Ohio*, p. 68.
24. OR 31-2-13,233,263,531,532; David Bittle Floyd, *History of the Seventy-fifth Regiment of Indiana Volunteers, Its Organization, Campaigns, and Battles (1862–1865)*, p. 232.
25. Asbury L. Kerwood, *Annals of the*

Fifty-seventh Regiment Indiana Volunteers, p. 224.

26. OR 31-2-132; Floyd, *History of the Seventy-fifth Regiment of Indiana,* 233; Shellenberger, "With Sheridan's Division," p. 59.

27. OR 31-2-553; Kimberly and Holloway, *The Forty-first Ohio,* p. 69; Floyd, *History of the Seventy-fifth Regiment of Indiana,* p. 233.

28. Shellenberger, "With Sheridan's Division," pp. 58,59.

29. McClenahan, memoirs; Floyd, *History of the Seventy-fifth Regiment of Indiana,* p. 233; Stormont and Hight, *History of the Fifty-eighth Regiment of Indiana,* p. 219.

30. R. Lockwood Tower, ed., *A Carolinian Goes to War, The Civil War Narrative of Arthur Middleton Manigault, Brigadier General, C.S.A.,* p. 137; Tourgee, *The Story of a Thousand,* p. 280; Shellenberger, "With Sheridan's Division," p. 58.

31. OR 31-2-664,665,739; John Hoffman, *The Confederate Collapse at the Battle of Missionary Ridge, The Reports of James Patton Anderson and His Brigade Commanders,* pp. 38–40,53,54.

32. Hoffman, *The Confederate Collapse,* pp. 36,37; *Mobile Daily Register & Advertiser,* December 11, 1863.

33. Hoffman, *The Confederate Collapse,* pp. 36,37,54,55.

34. Ibid., pp. 53–55; *Mobile Daily Register,* December 11, 1863.

35. Ibid.

36. Tower, ed., *A Carolinian Goes to War,* p. 138; Hoffman, *The Confederate Collapse,* pp. 60,61.

37. Ibid.

38. Ibid., p. 53; Tower, ed., *A Carolinian Goes to War,* p. 138; *Mobile Daily Register,* December 11, 1863.

39. Hoffman, *The Confederate Collapse,* pp. 60,61.

40. *Mobile Daily Register,* December 11, 1863; Tower, ed., *A Carolinian Goes to War,* p. 138.

CHAPTER 33: A Matter of Survival
1. C. C. Briant, *History of the Sixth Regiment Indiana Volunteer Infantry,* p. 274.

2. Robert L. Kimberly and Ephraim S. Holloway, *The Forty-First Ohio Veteran Volunteer Infantry in the War of the Rebellion, 1861–1865,* p. 69.

3. Ibid.

4. OR 31-2-264,267,278; Alexis Cope, *The Fifteenth Ohio Volunteers and Its Campaigns, War of 1861–1865,* pp. 381,382.

5. OR 31-2-264,267,275.

6. OR 31-2-267.

7. Cope, *The Fifteenth Ohio Volunteers,* pp. 179,180,385.

8. Ibid., pp. 179,180; OR 31-2-264,267,282.

9. OR 31-2-264,278.

10. OR 31-2-264.

11. OR 31-2-267.

12. OR 31-2-264,266.

13. J. A. Reep, *Guttmachrala, or Four Years at the Front as a Private,* chapter 15, pp. 17,18.

14. *History of the Seventy-ninth Regiment Indiana Volunteer Infantry in the Civil War of 1861 in the United States,* p. 107; Albion Tourgee, *The Story of a Thousand, Being a History of the Service of the One Hundred Fifth Ohio Volunteer Infantry in the War for the Union from August 21, 1862 to June 6, 1865,* p. 286.

15. OR 31-2-281,282; Kimberly and Holloway, *The Forty-First Ohio,* pp. 69,70.

16. Ibid.; OR 31-2-296.

17. Kimberly and Holloway, *The Forty-First Ohio,* p. 70; OR 31-2-281,282,293.

18. OR 31-2-296; Kimberly and Holloway, *The Forty-First Ohio,* p. 70.

19. OR 31-2-301,304,305.

20. OR 31-2-190,202,203,282.

21. OR 31-2-219,223,233.

22. OR 31-2-199,230,234; John K. Shellenberger, "With Sheridan's Division at Missionary Ridge," *Sketches of War History, 1861–1865,* p. 59.

23. OR 31-2-508,509,513.

24. OR 31-2-68,78; B&L 3-723–725; William Wrenshall Smith, "Holocaust Holiday," CWTI 18, no. 6 (October 1979): 35,36.

25. B&L 3-725.

26. Ibid.; OR 31-2-133,190.

27. OR 31-2-133,190,209,217.

CHAPTER 34: "Who in Hell Is Going to Stop Them?"
1. John K. Shellenberger, "With Sheridan's Division at Missionary Ridge,"

Sketches of War History, 1861–1865, p. 60.

2. Ibid., pp. 60–62.
3. Ibid., p. 63.
4. OR 31-2-217,230.
5. Shellenberger, "With Sheridan's Division," p. 64.
6. Edwin W. High, *History of the Sixty-eighth Regiment Indiana Volunteer Infantry 1862–1865*, p. 150; B&L 3-725.
7. OR 31-2-270; Ebenezer Hannaford, *The Story of a Regiment, A History of the Campaigns, and Associations in the Field, of the Sixth Regiment, Ohio Volunteer Infantry*, p. 508; C. C. Briant, *History of the Sixth Regiment Indiana Volunteer Infantry*, p. 275.
8. OR 31-2-264,267,268,278; Robert L. Kimberly and Ephraim S. Holloway, *The Forty-First Ohio Veteran Volunteer Infantry in the War of the Rebellion, 1861–1865*, pp. 70,71; James G. Watson, letter, November 26, 1863, CHICK-CHATT.
9. Kimberly and Holloway, *The Forty-First Ohio*, p. 70; Alexis Cope, *The Fifteenth Ohio Volunteers and Its Campaigns, War of 1861–1865*, p. 381.
10. OR 31-2-273,274; Kimberly and Holloway, *The Forty-First Ohio*, p. 71.
11. Hannaford, *The Story of a Regiment*, p. 508.
12. John Hoffman, *The Confederate Collapse at the Battle of Missionary Ridge, The Reports of James Patton Anderson and His Brigade Commanders*, pp. 42,69–70; OR 31-2-740; John C. Breckinridge, dispatch to Major Wilson, A.A.G., November 25, 1863, 1:00 P.M., Civil War Miscellany Collection, USAMHI.
13. Hoffman, *The Confederate Collapse*, pp. 73n,74; OR 31-2-741.
14. OR 31-2-740; Breckinridge, dispatch to Wilson, November 25, 1863.
15. OR 31-2-656,657,725,728; Hoffman, *The Confederate Collapse*, pp. 42,68,71; James H. Hallenquist, Report of Guns, Caissons, and Limbers Lost in the Late Battle & Retreat, December 3, 1863, National Archives Service Records, Washington, D.C., copy in CHICK-CHATT, (hereafter referred to as Hallenquist report); Edward E.

Betts, Map of the Battlefields of Chattanooga and Wauhatchie.
16. Hoffman, *The Confederate Collapse*, pp. 42,71,72.
17. Ibid., pp. 42,63.
18. OR 31-2-264,271,275.
19. Hannaford, *The Story of a Regiment*, p. 508; Hoffman, *The Confederate Collapse*, p. 71; R. Lockwood Tower, ed., *A Carolinian Goes to War, The Civil War Narrative of Arthur Middleton Manigault, Brigadier General, C.S.A.*, pp. 142,143.
20. Hannaford, *The Story of a Regiment*, p. 508; OR 31-2-274.
21. Hoffman, *The Confederate Collapse*, p. 71.
22. Hannaford, *The Story of a Regiment*, p. 508.
23. Cope, *The Fifteenth Ohio Volunteers*, p. 381.
24. Tower, ed., *A Carolinian Goes to War*, pp. 139,140; Hoffman, *The Confederate Collapse*, pp. 63,64.
25. Hannaford, *The Story of a Regiment*, pp. 508,509; OR 31-2-296,299.
26. OR 31-2-271; Tower, ed., *A Carolinian Goes to War*, p. 140; Hannaford, *The Story of a Regiment*, p. 509.
27. Hannaford, *The Story of a Regiment*, p. 509; Briant, *History of the Sixth Regiment Indiana*, p. 275.
28. Tower, ed., *A Carolinian Goes to War*, p. 140; Hoffman, *The Confederate Collapse*, p. 64.
29. Tower, ed., *A Carolinian Goes to War*, p. 140; Hoffman, *The Confederate Collapse*, p. 64.
30. OR 31-2-299; Tower, ed., *A Carolinian Goes to War*, p. 140.
31. Ibid.; Hoffman, *The Confederate Collapse*, p. 64.
32. Ibid.; Tower, ed., *A Carolinian Goes to War*, pp. 140,141.
33. Ibid.
34. Hoffman, *The Confederate Collapse*, p. 43; Tower, ed., *A Carolinian Goes to War*, p. 143.

CHAPTER 35: "You Kills Me mit Joy!"
1. *The Eighty-Sixth Regiment Indiana Volunteer Infantry, A Narrative of Its Services in the Civil War of 1861–1865*, p. 150.
2. Ibid., p. 151; Thomas J. Wood, "The

Battle of Missionary Ridge," *Sketches of War History, 1861–1865*, pp. 37,39,40.

3. Ibid.

4. R. Lockwood Tower, ed., *A Carolinian Goes to War, The Civil War Narrative of Arthur Middleton Maginault, Brigadier General, C.S.A.*, pp. 140,141; John Hoffman, *The Confederate Collapse at the Battle of Missionary Ridge, The Reports of James Patton Anderson and His Brigade Commanders*, pp. 64,65; OR 31-2-268.

5. Tower, ed., *A Carolinian Goes to War*, p. 141.

6. *Mobile Daily Register & Advertiser*, December 11, 1863; Hoffman, *The Confederate Collapse*, pp. 64,65.

7. Ibid.; Tower, ed., *A Carolinian Goes to War*, p. 143.

8. Hoffman, *The Confederate Collapse*, pp. 37,42,53,54,63; OR 31-2-301; *Report of the Chickamauga and Chattanooga National Park Commission on the Claim of Gen. John B. Turchin . . .* , p. 10 (hereafter cited as Turchin Report).

9. Hoffman, *The Confederate Collapse*, p. 55; OR 31-2-513,515,519,523.

10. OR 31-2-513,520; Map of A Portion of Missionary Ridge Illustrating the Positions of Baird's and Wood's Divisions, Nov. 23,24, and 25, 1863, CHICK-CHATT (hereafter cited as Baird Map).

11. OR 31-2-513,526.

12. OR 31-2-528,535; affidavit of Axel Reed, p. 23, CHICK-CHATT (see also Fenklyn-Curtiss Wedge, ed., *History of McLeod County, Minnesota*, p. 53).

13. Ibid.; Albion Tourgee, *The Story of a Thousand, Being a History of the Service of the One Hundred Fifth Ohio Volunteer Infantry in the War for the Union from August 21, 1862 to June 6, 1865*, p. 287; OR 31-2-535.

14. Hoffman, *The Confederate Collapse*, p. 43,55; Hallenquist report.

15. Hoffman, *The Confederate Collapse*, pp. 49–51.

16. Ibid., p. 51; OR 31-2-540.

17. Hoffman, *The Confederate Collapse*, p. 51.

18. Joshua H. Horton, *A History of the Eleventh Regiment [Ohio Volunteer Infantry]*, p. 221.

19. OR 31-2-535,538,541,546; Hoffman, *The Confederate Collapse*, p. 51; Hallenquist report; David Bittle Floyd, *History of the Seventy-fifth Regiment of Indiana Volunteers, Its Organization, Campaigns, and Battles (1862–1865)*, p. 240.

20. Hoffman, *The Confederate Collapse*, pp. 74,75; Robert L. Kimberly and Ephraim S. Holloway, *The Forty-First Ohio Veteran Volunteer Infantry in the War of the Rebellion, 1861–1865*, p. 71.

21. Ibid.; OR 31-2-293,296.

22. Hoffman, *The Confederate Collapse*, p. 75.

23. OR 31-2-69; Edward E. Betts, Map of the Battlefields of Chattanooga and Wauhatchie.

24. Alexis Cope, *The Fifteenth Ohio Volunteers and Its Campaigns, War of 1861–1865*, pp. 381–383.

25. Kimberly and Holloway, *The Forty-First Ohio*, p. 72.

CHAPTER 36: "Give 'em Hell, Boys!"

1. H. W. Keddick, *Seventy-seven Years in Dixie, The Boys in Gray of '61–'65*, pp. 16,22.

2. OR 31-2-189,662,740,741; OR 52-1-96–98.

3. OR 31-2-291,293,296; OR 52-1-97; Hallenquist report.

4. OR 31-2-742; OR 52-1-97; James Henry Haynie, *The Nineteenth Illinois; A Memoir of a Regiment of Volunteer Infantry Famous in the Civil War of Fifty Years Ago for Its Drill, Bravery, and Distinguished Services*, p. 281; Hazen, *Narrative*, p. 204.

5. OR 31-2-291,293,296.

6. Ibid.; Robert L. Kimberly and Ephraim S. Holloway, *The Forty-First Ohio Veteran Volunteer Infantry in the War of the Rebellion, 1861–1865*, p. 71.

7. OR 31-2-293; OR 52-1-98.

8. OR 31-2-290,293.

9. OR 31-2-293.

10. Kimberly and Holloway, *The Forty-First Ohio*, p. 71.

11. OR 31-2-740,741; *Florida Times-Union*, June 8, 1888.

12. OR 31-2-740,742.

13. OR 31-2-665,742.

14. I. G. Bennett and William M. Haigh, *History of the Thirty-Sixth Regiment Illinois Volunteers During the War of the Rebellion*, p. 528.

15. OR 31-2-189,190.

16. OR 31-2-230; Bennett and Haigh, *History of the Thirty-Sixth Regiment Illinois*, p. 529; John K. Shellenberger, "With Sheridan's Division at Missionary Ridge," *Sketches of War History, 1861–1865*, p. 64; Albert R. Stormont and John J. Hight, *History of the Fifty-eighth Regiment of Indiana Volunteer Infantry, Its Organization, Campaigns, and Battles from 1861–1865*, p. 222; Asbury L. Kerwood, *Annals of the Fifty-Seventh Regiment Indiana Volunteers*, p. 225.

17. OR 31-2-742.

18. Robert Watson, journal, November 25, 1863, CHICK-CHATT; *Florida Times-Union*, June 8, 1888; Washington Ives, letter, December 4, 1863, CHICK-CHATT; John Hoffman, *The Confederate Collapse at the Battle of Missionary Ridge, The Reports of James Patton Anderson and His Brigade Commanders*, p. 74.

19. Watson, journal, November 25, 1863; Ives, letter, December 4, 1863.

20. Ibid.; E. B. McClean, letter to Mrs. Amanda Bullock, December 8, 1863, Bullock letters, Georgia Department of Archives, Atlanta, Georgia; William Ralston Talley, memoir, p. 33, CHICK-CHATT.

21. OR 31-2-197; William H. Newlin, *A History of the Seventy-Third Regiment of Illinois Infantry Volunteers*, pp. 265,266.

22. OR 31-2-208; *The MacArthurs of Milwaukee*, Milwaukee County Historical Society, Milwaukee, Wisconsin, pp. 6,7.

23. Newlin, *A History of the Seventy-Third Regiment Illinois*, pp. 265,266; OR 31-2-203.

24. OR 31-2-198,199,202; *The MacArthurs of Milwaukee*, p. 6.

25. OR 31-2-202,231.

26. OR 31-2-231,742; OR 52-1-98.

27. OR 31-2-665.

28. OR 31-2-742; Keddick, *Seventy-seven*

Years in Dixie, p. 23; Talley, memoir, p. 33.

29. Watson, journal, November 25, 1863; Private Pasco, *Private Pasco, A Civil War Diary*, p. 82.

30. William R. Hartpence, *History of the Fifty-first Indiana Veteran Volunteer Infantry from 1861 to 1865*, p. 193; Kerwood, *Annals of the Fifty-Seventh Regiment Indiana Volunteers*, p. 220; Shellenberger, "With Sheridan's Division," p. 65.

31. Shellenberger, "With Sheridan's Division," p. 65; Bennett and Haigh, *History of the Thirty-Sixth Regiment Illinois*, p. 529; Joshua Dewes, diary, November 25, 1863, CHICK-CHATT; *The MacArthurs of Milwaukee*, p. 6.

32. Bennett and Haigh, *History of the Thirty-Sixth Regiment Illinois*, p. 529; Shellenberger, "With Sheridan's Division," p. 65.

33. OR 31-2-197; Stormont and Hight, *History of the Fifty-Eighth Regiment of Indiana*, p. 223; Newlin, *History of the Seventy-Third Regiment of Illinois*, pp. 266,267; Philip H. Sheridan, *Personal Memoirs of P. H. Sheridan*, p. 364.

34. Kimberly and Holloway, *The Forty-First Ohio*, p. 74.

CHAPTER 37: "Here's Your Mule!"

1. OR 31-2-318,600,601,610.

2. OR 31-2-147,318,601,610.

3. OR 31-2-147,171,172,318,601; *Military History and Reminiscences of the Thirteenth Regiment of Illinois Volunteer Infantry in the Civil War in the United States, 1861–1865*, p. 379.

4. OR 31-2-147,318.

5. *Military History and Reminiscences of the Thirteenth*, p. 379; OR 31-2-615.

6. OR 31-2-147,184.

7. OR 31-2-171,184.

8. OR 31-2-181,184,185.

9. Mattie Lou Teague Crow, ed., *The Diary of a Confederate Soldier, John Washington Inzer, 1834–1928*, pp. 42–46.

10. Ibid.

11. Charles A. Willison, *Reminiscences of a Boy's Service with the 76th Ohio*, p. 77; OR 31-2-148,602.

12. OR 31-2-171,608; Arnold Gates, ed., *The Rough Side of War, The Civil War Journal of Chesley A. Mosman, 1st Lieutenant, Company D, 59th Illinois Volunteer Infantry Regiment,* p. 129; *Military History and Reminiscences of the Thirteenth,* p. 380.

13. OR 31-2-14,459.

14. OR 31-2-459,463,464.

15. OR 31-2-474,480; James Henry Haynie, *The Nineteenth Illinois; A Memoir of a Regiment of Volunteer Infantry Famous in the Civil War of Fifty Years Ago for Its Drill, Bravery, and Distinguished Services,* p. 271.

16. Joseph E. Riley, "The Military Service of Joseph E. Riley in C.S.A.," transcript, CHICK-CHATT.

17. OR 31-2-483.

18. OR 31-2-474,484.

19. William Wirt Calkins, *The History of the One Hundred and Fourth Regiment of Illinois Volunteer Infantry, War of the Great Rebellion, 1862–1865,* p. 185.

20. Ibid.; Angus L. Waddle, *Three Years with the Armies of the Ohio and Cumberland,* p. 62.

21. OR 31-2-116,172,665; Gates, ed., *The Rough Side of War,* p. 130; Edward E. Betts, Map of the Battlefields of Chattanooga and Wauhatchie; Willison, *Reminiscences of a Boy's Service,* p. 77; Michael H. Fitch, *Echoes of the Civil War As I Hear Them,* pp. 181–182.

22. OR 31-2-665; Norman D. Brown, ed., *One of Cleburne's Command, The Civil War Reminiscences and Diary of Capt. Samuel T. Foster, Granbury's Texas Brigade, C.S.A.,* p. 66; Sam R. Watkins, *"Co Aytch" Maury Grays First Tennessee Regiment, or a Side Show of the Big Show,* pp. 117,118.

23. Judith Lee Hallock, *Braxton Bragg and Confederate Defeat,* vol. 2, pp. 141,142.

24. William Wrenshall Smith, "Holocaust Holiday," CWTI 18, no. 6 (October 1979): 36; OR 31-2-35,69; Haynie, *The Nineteenth Illinois,* p. 281.

25. Smith, "Holocaust Holiday," p. 36ff; Ely S. Parker, letter, December 3, 1863, American Philosophical Society Library, Philadelphia, Pennsylvania.

CHAPTER 38: The Night of the Long Shadows

1. OR 31-2-96,509,510.

2. OR 31-2-697,705,726,727,738; Baird map; Edward E. Betts, Map of the Battlefields of Chattanooga and Wauhatchie.

3. OR 31-2-705,706.

4. OR 31-2-548; Joshua H. Horton, *A History of the Eleventh Regiment [Ohio Volunteer Infantry],* p. 107; Walter F. Beyer, and Oscar F. Keydel, *Deeds of Valor, How America's Heroes Won the Medal of Honor,* vol. 1, p. 290.

5. OR 31-2-705,706.

6. OR 31-2-697,706,727,738; Sykes, *Walthall's Brigade,* p. 542.

7. OR 31-2-510,534,548.

8. OR 31-2-528,535; J. A. Reep, *Guttmachrala, or Four Years at the Front as a Private,* chapter 15, p. 25.

9. OR 31-2-752.

10. OR 31-2-697,752.

11. Robert Watson, journal, November 25, 1863, CHICK-CHATT.

12. Turchin report, p. 33.

13. OR 31-2-191,742; OR 32-1-98; Watson, journal November 25, 1863; Betts, Map of the Battlefields.

14. OR 31-2-191,231.

15. OR 31-2-218,228,229; John K. Shellenberger "With Sheridan's Division at Missionary Ridge," *Sketches of War History, 1861–1865,* pp. 66,67.

16. Shellenberger, "With Sheridan's Division," pp. 66,67; OR 31-2-218,228; I. G. Bennett and William M. Haigh, *History of the Thirty-Sixth Regiment Illinois Volunteers During the War of the Rebellion,* p. 527.

17. OR 31-2-191,210,212,128,228,234.

18. OR 31-2-191; Shellenberger, "With Sheridan's Division," pp. 66,67.

19. OR 31-2-191,192,231,239; Philip Henry Sheridan, *Personal Memoirs of P. H. Sheridan,* vol. 1, p. 170.

20. OR 31-2-679.

21. OR 31-2-665,679; *History of the Seventy-ninth Regiment Indiana Volunteer Infantry in the Civil War of 1861 in the United States,* p. 198.

22. Joshua Dewes, diary, November 25, 1863, CHICK-CHATT.

23. Betts, Map of the Battlefields; Gilbert D. Stormont and John J. Hight,

History of the Fifty-eighth Regiment of Indiana Volunteer Infantry, Its Organization, Campaigns, and Battles from 1861–1865, pp. 223,224.
24. Arnold Gates, ed., *The Rough Side of War, The Civil War Journal of Chesley A. Mosman, 1st Lieutenant, Company D, 59th Illinois Volunteer Infantry Regiment*, p. 130; James Birney Shaw, *History of the Tenth Regiment Indiana Volunteer Infantry*, p. 274.

CHAPTER 39: "The Unaccountable Spirit of the Troops"
1. R. Lockwood Tower, ed., *A Carolinian Goes to War, The Civil War Narrative of Arthur Middleton Manigault, Brigadier General, C.S.A.*, pp. 142,143.
2. OR 31-2-665,666,744; OR 52-1-97,98.
3. Albion Tourgee, *The Story of a Thousand, Being a History of the Service of the One Hundred Fifth Ohio Volunteer Infantry in the War for the Union from August 21, 1862 to June 6, 1865*, p. 277; OR 31-2-35,69,341; Ulysses S. Grant, *Personal Memoirs of U. S. Grant*, p. 343.
4. OR 31-2-656,657.
5. John Hoffman, *The Confederate Collapse at the Battle of Missionary Ridge, The Reports of James Patton Anderson and His Brigade Commanders*, p. 36; OR 31-2-740,742; OR 52-1-97,98.
6. Gilbert R. Stormont and John J. Hight, *History of the Fifty-eighth Regiment of Indiana Volunteer Infantry, Its Organization, Campaigns, and Battles from 1861–1865*, p. 221.
7. OR 31-2-26,27,69,90.
8. OR 31-2-99,682–684; Thomas L. Livermore, *Numbers and Losses in the Civil War in America: 1861–65*, pp. 107,108.
9. OR 31-2-99,100; Hallenquist report.
10. OR 31-2-12,36,88; Livermore, *Numbers and Losses*, p. 106.
11. T. J. Walker and Russell B. Bailey, eds., "Reminiscence of the Civil War," *Confederate Chronicles of Tennessee* 1 (1986): 56,57.
12. Sam B. Watkins, *"Co. Aytch" Maury Grays First Tennessee Regiment, or a Side Show of the Big Show*, p. 120.
13. Ibid., pp. 120,121.
14. Ibid.

15. William T. Alderson, ed., "The Civil War Diary of Capt. James Litton Cooper, Sept. 30, 1863 to Jan. 1865," *Tennessee Historical Quarterly 13 (1954)*: 160; *Mobile Daily Register & Advertiser*, December 11, 1863.
16. Andrew Jackson Neal, letter, November 26, 1863, CHICK-CHATT.
17. Ray Mathis, *In the Land of the Living, Wartime Letters by Confederates from the Chattahoochie Valley of Alabama and Georgia*, p. 182.
18. John W. Sparkman, diary, November 29, 1863, CHICK-CHATT; Frank Wolfe, "Letter to a Friend: From the Foot of Lookout Mountain," CWTI 22, no. 4 (June 1983): 44.
19. Mattie Lou Teague Crow, ed., *The Diary of a Confederate Soldier, John Washington Inzer 1834–1928*, p. 46.
20. Ely S. Parker, letter, November 21, 1863, American Philosophical Society Library, Philadelphia, Pennsylvania.
21. Ibid.; Charles A. Dana, *Recollections of the Civil War*, p. 149.
22. OR 31-2-25,45,191,305; John Y. Simon, ed., *The Papers of Ulysses S. Grant*, vol. 9, pp. 479,480.
23. William Wrenshall Smith, "Holocaust Holiday," CWTI 18, no. 6 (October 1979): 36.

CHAPTER 40: In the Wake of the Stampede
1. Ely S. Parker, letter, December 2, 1863, American Philosophical Society Library, Philadelphia, Pennsylvania; OR 31-2-491.
2. Allan L. Fahnestock, diary, November 26, 1863, CHICK-CHATT.
3. *History of the Seventy-ninth Regiment Indiana Volunteer Infantry in the Civil War of 1861 in the United States*, p. 108; OR 31-2-45,46,491,576.
4. OR 31-2-45,46,69.
5. William Wrenshall Smith, "Holocaust Holiday," CWTI 18, no. 6 (October 1979): 36,37; Ulysses S. Grant, *Personal Memoirs of U. S. Grant*, p. 345.
6. OR 31-2-350,591; Smith, "Holocaust Holiday," p. 37.
7. Ibid.; OR 31-2-26,69,350,351,576; John Y. Simon, ed., *The Papers of Ulysses S. Grant*, vol. 9, p. 453.

8. OR 31-2-491,496,576,711; Fahnestock, diary, November 26, 1863.
9. Fahnestock, diary, November 26, 1863; OR 31-2-492,496.
10. OR 31-2-492,493,500; Sam R. Watkins, *"Co. Aytch" Maury Grays First Tennessee Regiment, or a Side Show of the Big Show,* p. 122; Fahnestock, diary, November 26, 1863.
11. OR 31-2-492,493.
12. OR 31-2-460,477; Gilbert R. Stormont and John T. Hight, *History of the Fifty-eighth Regiment of Indiana Volunteer Infantry, Its Organization, Campaigns and Battles from 1861–1865,* p. 224.
13. OR 31-2-477; *History of the Seventy-ninth Regiment Indiana,* p. 109; Arnold Gates, ed., *The Rough Side of War, The Civil War Journal of Chesley A. Mosman, 1st Lieutenant, Company D, 59th Illinois Volunteer Infantry Regiment,* p. 131.
14. OR 31-2-460,464,469,477,478.
15. OR 31-2-460,464,480.
16. OR 31-2-480,486,487.
17. OR 31-2-119,460,464.
18. Gates, ed., *The Rough Side of War,* p. 131.
19. Ibid., pp. 131,132.
20. OR 31-2-319.
21. OR 31-2-320,341,603.
22. Patricia L. Faust, ed., *Historical Times Illustrated Encyclopedia of the Civil War,* p. 550; OR 31-2-120,344,345,603,616,618,626.
23. OR 31-2-120,320,321,341.
24. OR 31-2-321,341,604,608.
25. OR 31-2-320,616,618,626.
26. OR 31-2-342.

CHAPTER 41: "Have You Any Troops That Won't Run Away?"
1. Irving A. Buck, *Cleburne and His Command,* pp. 175–177.
2. Ibid.; OR 31-2-753,754.
3. Buck, *Cleburne and His Command,* pp. 176,177; OR 31-2-754.
4. OR 31-2-14,599,757.
5. OR 31-2-438,754,755; Howell and Elizabeth Purdue, *Pat Cleburne Confederate General,* p. 265, n. 36.
6. OR 31-2-754,755.
7. OR 31-2-758,759.
8. OR 31-2-755.

9. *Military History and Reminiscences of the Thirteenth Regiment of Illinois Volunteer Infantry in the Civil War in the United States, 1861–1865,* p. 631–633.
10. Ibid.; OR 31-2-604,608,759; Purdue, *Pat Cleburne,* p. 260.
11. Purdue, *Pat Cleburne,* p. 258; OR 31-2-755,756,759.
12. Charles A. Willison, *Reminiscences of a Boy's Service with the 76th Ohio,* p. 79; *Military History and Reminiscences of the 13th,* pp. 384–386.
13. *Military History and Reminiscences of the Thirteenth,* p. 386.
14. Ibid., pp. 386,387.
15. Ibid., p. 632; OR 31-2-608.
16. OR 31-2-604,608.
17. OR 31-2-611–616.
18. George K. Collins, *Memoirs of the 149th New York Volunteer Infantry, 3rd Brigade, 2nd Division, 12th and 20th A.C.,* p. 215.
19. OR 31-2-756,760,774,776.
20. OR 31-2-760,777.
21. OR 31-2-616,760.
22. OR 31-2-403,414; M. S. Schroyer, "Company 'G' History," *The Snyder County Historical Society Bulletin* 2, no. 2, p. 384.
23. Gideon S. Stare, letter, December 13, 1863, CHICK-CHATT; Pennsylvania, *Pennsylvania at Chickamauga and Chattanooga, Ceremonies at the Dedication of the Monuments,* p. 290; OR 31-2-414.
24. OR 31-2-760,761,768,769.
25. OR 31-2-616,623,626.
26. OR 31-2-414,418,623,626,769.
27. OR 31-2-419; Schroyer, "Company 'G' History," p. 389.
28. OR 31-2-617; George L. Wood, *The Seventh Regiment A Record;* p. 167.
29. OR 31-2-404,426.
30. OR 31-2-404,405,438.
31. OR 31-2-438,439; Collins, *Memoirs of the 149th,* pp. 216,217.
32. OR 31-2-322,438,450.
33. OR 31-2-321,322.
34. OR 31-2-345,346,454.
35. Collins, *Memoirs of the 149th,* p. 217.
36. OR 31-2-454; *Military History and Reminiscences of the Thirteenth,* p. 388.
37. Ibid.; OR 31-2-120,405,438; Collins, *Memoirs of the 149th,* p. 217.

38. OR 31-2-120,322; William Wrenshall Smith, "Holocaust Holiday" CWTI 18, no. 6 (October 1979): 39.
39. OR 31-2-403,757.
40. OR 31-2-121,757,774,776.
41. OR 31-2-122,326,757.
42. Smith, "Holocaust Holiday," pp. 39,40.
43. OR 31-2-46,47.
44. OR 31-2-47,323,439,450,452.
45. OR 31-2-47,172,322,323,439; Buck, *Cleburne and His Command*, p. 184.
46. OR 31-2-70,71; OR 31-3-266; John Y. Simon, ed., *The Papers of Ulysses S. Grant*, vol. 9, p. 459.
47. Smith, "Holocaust Holiday," pp. 39,40.
48. *Military History and Reminiscences of the Thirteenth*, p. 389,632.
49. Ibid.
50. Ibid., p. 632.
51. Ibid., p. 633.
52. Ibid., pp. 633,634.

CHAPTER 42: "Such Is Civilized War"
1. OR 31-2-35,71,72; John Y. Simon, ed., *The Papers of Ulysses S. Grant*, vol. 9, p. 496; *The Story of the Fifty-fifth Regiment Illinois Volunteer Infantry in the Civil War, 1861–1865*, p. 289.
2. OR 31-2-26,47,577,592.
3. William Wrenshall Smith, "Holocaust Holiday," CWTI 18, no. 6 (October 1979): p. 40; Arnold Gates, ed., *The Rough Side of War, The Civil War Journal of Chesley A. Mosman, 1st Lieutenant, Company D, 59th Illinois Volunteer Infantry Regiment*, p. 134.
4. Smith, "Holocaust Holiday," p. 40.
5. Ibid.
6. Simon, ed., *The Papers*, vol. 9, p. 496; OR 31-2-35.
7. OR 31-2-35,47,49,139,271,279,280.
8. OR 31-2-35,36,40.
9. Ray Mathis, *In the Land of the Living, Wartime Letters by Confederates from the Chattahoochie Valley of Alabama and Georgia*, p. 81; *Mobile Daily Register & Advertiser*, December 11, 1863.
10. *Mobile Daily Register & Advertiser*, December 11, 1863.
11. Andrew Jackson Neal, letters, November 26 and 29 and December 6, 1863, CHICK-CHATT.

12. *Mobile Daily Register & Advertiser*, December 11, 1863.
13. Robert Watson, journal, November 28 and 29, 1863, CHICK-CHATT; Washington Ives, letter, December 2, 1863, CHICK-CHATT.
14. Neal, letters, November 29, 1863, December 6, 1863.
15. Gates, ed., *The Rough Side of War*, pp. 134,135; Gideon S. Stare, letter, December 13, 1863.
16. Gates, ed., *The Rough Side of War*, p. 135; James Austin Connolly, *Three Years in the Army of the Cumberland, the Letters and Diary of Major James A. Connolly*, p. 62; *Military History and Reminiscences of the Thirteenth Regiment of Illinois Volunteer Infantry in the Civil War in the United States, 1861–1865*, p. 387.
17. George K. Collins, *Memoirs of the 149th New York Volunteer Infantry, 3rd Brigade, 2nd Division, 12th and 20th A.C.*, p. 219; Stare, letter, December 13, 1863.

CHAPTER 43: "Let the Past Take Care of Itself"
1. OR 31-2-681,682; OR 31-3-767.
2. OR 31-2-682; OR 31-3-754,764; St. John R. Liddell journal, Govan papers, SHC.
3. OR 31-2-682,774,775; OR 52-2-567,568.
4. OR 31-2-799.
5. OR 31-2-682; OR 31-3-776; Judith Lee Hallock, *Braxton Bragg and Confederate Defeat*, vol. 2, pp. 25,26.
6. Nathaniel Cheairs Hughes, Jr., *General William J. Hardee, Old Reliable*, pp. 183–186; OR 31-3-860.
7. OR 31-2-873,874.
8. Notes on Bragg presentation sword, Zack C. Waters, Rome, Georgia; Robert Watson, journal, December 1, 1863, CHICK-CHATT; Mathis, p. 81; OR 31-3-776.
9. Andrew Jackson Neal, letter, December 6, 1863, CHICK-CHATT; Wirt Armistead Cate, *Two Soldiers, The Campaign Diaries of Thomas J. Key, C.S.A., and Robert J. Campbell, U.S.A.*, p. 8, Hallock, *Braxton Bragg*, vol. 2, p. 149; Sam R. Watkins, *"Co. Aytch" Maury Grays First Tennessee*

Regiment, or a Side Show of the Big Show, p. 118.

10. Howell and Elizabeth Purdue, *Pat Cleburne Confederate General,* p. 267ff.

11. OR 31-2-758.

12. OR 31-2-25,26,51,52; John Y. Simon, ed., *The Papers of Ulysses S. Grant,* vol. 9, pp. 491,503,504n.

13. Simon, ed., *The Papers,* vol. 9, pp. 522,523n.

14. Wilson, *Under the Old Flag,* vol. 1, pp. 300–301, 325.

15. D. R. Lucas, *New History of the 99th Indiana,* p. 162; James Birney Shaw, *History of the Tenth Regiment Indiana Volunteer Infantry,* p. 274; Michael

Fitch, *Echoes of the Civil War As I Hear Them,* pp. 187,188.

16. E. C. Tillotson, letter, December 17, 1863, CL; Fitch, *Echoes of the Civil War,* pp. 187,188.

17. Ibid.

18. OR 31-2-27,340; Simon, ed., *The Papers,* vol. 9, p. 478,496.

19. Simon, ed., *The Papers,* vol. 9, pp. 480,500; OR 31-2-72.

20. OR 30-1-148; John B. Jones, *A Rebel War Clerk's Diary,* vol. 2, p. 106; C. Vann Woodward, ed., *Mary Chesnut's Civil War,* p. 501.

21. Dunbar Rowland, ed., *Jefferson Davis Constitutionalist, His Letters, Papers, and Speeches,* vol. 6, pp. 95,96.

BIBLIOGRAPHY

ABBREVIATIONS

BHL: Bentley Historical Library, University of Michigan, Ann Arbor, Michigan
CHICK-CHATT: Chickamauga and Chattanooga National Military Park Library, Fort Oglethorpe, Georgia
CL: Clements Library, University of Michigan, Ann Arbor, Michigan
CV: *Confederate Veteran* (published in Nashville, Tennessee)
CWTI: *Civil War Times, Illustrated,* Harrisburg, Pennsylvania
MOLLUS: Military Order of the Loyal Legion of the United States
OR: *War of the Rebellion: Official Records of the Union and Confederate Armies,* Series I, Washington, D.C. Cited with volume, part, and page numbers following (e.g., OR 31-2-235)
SHC: Southern Historical Collection, University of North Carolina Library, Chapel Hill, North Carolina
USAMHI: United States Army Military History Institute, Carlisle Barracks, Pennsylvania
WRHS: Western Reserve Historical Society Library, Cleveland, Ohio

SOURCES

With the exception of background material utilized primarily in the initial chapters, the vast bulk of the information for this book was obtained from primary sources. Much emphasis was placed on obtaining materials contemporary to the events depicted, and, where possible, cross-references were utilized in resolving particularly contradictory or unclear testimony. Due to the nature of the events and the considerable controversy among the principals as to responsibility for certain failures and successes, much care was taken to investigate with objectivity each incident as a separate situation. Since interpretation, logic, and common sense are a part not only of depicting the events but choosing what to include or omit, the author is fully responsible for the degree of accuracy. With regard to key individuals, including Ulysses S. Grant, William Tecumseh Sherman, and Braxton Bragg, every effort was made to assess decisions and motives based upon the actual evidence at hand.

One additional matter requiring explanation is the author's normalizing of spelling and punctuation. In certain quotations from original sources, spelling and punctuation have been corrected. Care has been taken to maintain the veracity of all quotations, and it is simply my opinion that normalization is appropriate for the sake of clarity and to eliminate reader distractions.

MANUSCRIPT MATERIALS

Banbury, Jabez (Fifth Iowa Infantry). Diary, 1863. CHICK-CHATT.
Bender, Josiah H. (Twenty-fourth Wisconsin Infantry). Letter, September 28, 1863. Civil War Miscellaneous Collection, USAMHI.
Benton, Samuel. Letter, October 14, 1863. Schoff Collection, CL.
Bragg, Braxton. Letters, 1862–1871. WRHS.
———, letters, 1862–1864. Bragg Papers, Missouri Historical Society, St. Louis, Missouri.
———. Letter to E. T. Sykes, February 8, 1863. Claiborne Papers, SHC.
———. Letter to Marcus J. Wright. n. d., Wright Papers, SHC.
Breckinridge, John C. Dispatch to Major Wilson, November 25, 1863, 1:00 P.M.; letter captured by Lt. Col. M. H. Fitch, Twenty-first Wisconsin Infantry, November 25, 1863. Civil War Miscellany Collection, USAMHI.
Browner, Almon (Ninety-sixth Illinois Infantry). Letter, October 20, 1863. Civil War Miscellany Collection, USAMHI.
Bullock, Robert. Letters, 1863. Georgia Department of Archives, Atlanta, Georgia.
Carpenter, Arthur B. (Nineteenth U.S. Infantry). Letters, 1863. Yale University Library, New Haven, Connecticut.
Cole, William D. (Thirty-eighth Alabama Infantry). Letters, 1863. Civil War Miscellany Collection, USAMHI.
Daniel, Rufus W. (Sixth Arkansas Infantry). Diary, 1863. Civil War Miscellany Collection, USAMHI.
Davis, Thomas W. (Fifth Tennessee Cavalry). Diary, 1863. CHICK-CHATT.
Deas, Ambrose (Nineteenth Alabama Infantry). Letters, October 25 and November 13, 1863. CHICK-CHATT.
Dewes, Joshua (Ninety-seventh Ohio Infantry). Diary, 1863. CHICK-CHATT.
Doty, John S. H. (104th Illinois Infantry). Letter, November 18, 1863. Collection of Wiley Sword, Bloomfield Hills, Michigan.
Dunbar, Aaron (Ninety-third Illinois Infantry). "Civil War Journals," vol. 2, typescript. Copy in CHICK-CHATT.
Edson, Milan (Sixty-third Illinois Infantry). Letter, November 18, 1863. CHICK-CHATT.

Fahnestock, Allan L. (Eighty-sixth Illinois Infantry). Diary, 1863. CHICK-CHATT.

Finley, J. J. Letter to Governor John Milton, December 16, 1863. Vol. 7, Series 32, Florida State Archives, Tallahassee, Florida.

Fogg, Cecil (Thirty-sixth Ohio Infantry). Letters, 1863. Collection of Wiley Sword, Bloomfield Hills, Michigan.

Fraser, James H. (Fiftieth Alabama Infantry). Letter, September 26, 1863. CHICK-CHATT.

Glison, William R. (Sixth Ohio Infantry). Diary, 1863. CHICK-CHATT.

Goodson, Joab (Forty-fourth Alabama Infantry). Letter, September 28, 1863. CHICK-CHATT.

Goudelock, G. E. (Second Arkansas Infantry). Letter, October 5, 1863. CHICK-CHATT.

Green, Thomas E. (Eighty-fifth Illinois Infantry). Letter, September 30, 1863. Civil War Miscellany Collection, USAMHI.

Hallenquist, James H. (Chief of Artillery, Army of Tennessee). Report of Guns, Caissons, and Limbers Lost in the Late Battle & Retreat, December 3, 1863. From compiled services records, National Archives, Service Records, Washington, D.C., copy in CHICK-CHATT.

Harlan, Isaiah (Texas Infantry). Letter, November 15, 1863. CHICK-CHATT.

Haskett, A. A. (Fifty-seventh Indiana Infantry). Letter, October 12, 1863. Civil War Miscellany Collection, USAMHI.

Helmer, Stephen H. (Ninety-third Ohio Infantry). Letter, November 26, 1863. Civil War Miscellany Collection, USAMHI.

Hemming, Charles C. Reminiscences of, typescript. P. K. Yonge Library of Florida History, University of Florida, Gainesville, Florida.

Hooker, Joseph. Letters to Dr. B. M. Stevens and W. P. Fessenden, December 6, 1863. CL.

Houghton, Charles A. (141st New York Infantry). Letters, 1863. Charles A. Houghton Papers, USAMHI.

Ives, Washington (Fourth Florida Infantry). Letters, 1863. CHICK-CHATT.

Jackson, John S. (Ninth Kentucky Infantry, C.S.A.). Journal, 1863. CHICK-CHATT.

Jenkins, Micah. Letters, 1863. Special Collections, Duke University Library, Durham, North Carolina.

Liddell, St. John R. Journal. Govan Papers, SHC.

Lowrey, Mark. Autobiography. Civil War Miscellany Collection, USAMHI.

McClenahan, John (Fifteenth Ohio Infantry). Memoirs. CHICK-CHATT.

McCook, Daniel. Letter to Major General Reynolds, chief of staff, October 28, 1863, 6:45 P.M. CL.

McCornack, Andrew (127th Illinois Infantry). Letters, 1863. Collection of Wiley Sword, Bloomfield Hills, Michigan.

McWayne, Eugene (127th Illinois Infantry). Letters, 1863. Collection of Wiley Sword, Bloomfield Hills, Michigan.

Miller, Isaac (Ninety-third Ohio Infantry). Letter, November 21, 1863. Collection of Wiley Sword, Bloomfield Hills, Michigan. Letter, October 15, 1863, catalog 69 item 191, Olde Soldier Books, Gaithersburg, Maryland.

Miller, William E. (Forty-sixth Georgia Infantry). Letter, September 29, 1863. Collection of Chris Jordan, Harper's Ferry, West Virginia.

Montgomery, W. R. (Third Georgia Battalion Sharpshooters). Letters, October 18, October 24, 1863. CHICK-CHATT.

Neal, Andrew Jackson (Marion Light Artillery, Florida). Letters, 1863. CHICK-CHATT.

Nesbit, John W. Letter, November 21, 1863. CHICK-CHATT.

Opdycke, Emerson. Letter, October 25, 1863, Opdycke Papers, Ohio Historical Society, Columbus, Ohio, copy provided by courtesy of the General's Books, Columbus, Ohio.

Parker, Ely S. Letters, 1863–1864. American Philosophical Society Library, Philadelphia, Pennsylvania.

Phelps, Frank W. (Tenth Wisconsin Infantry). Letter, December 2, 1863. Civil War Miscellany Collection, USAMHI.

Poates, Lewis L. (Sixty-third Tennessee Infantry). Letter, November 15, 1863. Collection of Lewis L. Poates, Knoxville, Tennessee.

Putney, W. G. (Battery One, Second Illinois Light Artillery). Memoirs. CHICK-CHATT.

Rabb, Hezekiah (Thirty-third Alabama Infantry). Letters, September 23, October 9, and November 7, 1863. CHICK-CHATT.

Reed, Axel H. (Second Minnesota Infantry). Diary, 1863. CHICK-CHATT.

Rennolds, Edwin H., Sr. (Fifth Tennessee Infantry). Diary, 1863. CHICK-CHATT.

Riley, Joseph E. (Thirty-third Tennessee Infantry). "The Military Service of Joseph E. Riley in C.S.A.," transcript. CHICK-CHATT.

Roseberry, Isaac (First Michigan Engineers & Mechanics). Diary, 1863. Special Collections, Emory University Library, Atlanta, Georgia.

Seed, Thomas J. (Sixty-third Illinois Infantry). Journal-diary, 1863. CHICK-CHATT.

Shroyer, Michael Simon (147th Pennsylvania Infantry). Diary, 1863. Collection of Susan Boardman, Sunbury, Pennsylvania.

Simpson, Samuel R. (Thirtieth Tennessee Infantry). Diary, 1863. CHICK-CHATT.

Snow, John (Lumsden's Alabama Battery). Letter, September 30, 1863. CHICK-CHATT.

Sparkman, John W. (Forty-eighth Tennessee Infantry). Diary, 1863. CHICK-CHATT.

Stare, Gideon S. Letters, 1863. CHICK-CHATT.

Statements of witnesses, unpublished, in the file of the Chattanooga National Park Commission investigating the claim of Gen. John B. Turchin as to the capture of De Long Place during the Battle of Chattanooga. CHICK-CHATT.

Talley, William Ralston (Havis's Georgia Artillery). Memoir. CHICK-CHATT.

Tarman, B. B. (Sixty-third Illinois Infantry). Letter, December 23, 1863. CHICK-CHATT.

Taylor, Thomas (Forty-seventh Ohio Infantry). Letters, diary, 1863. Ohio Historical Society, Columbus, Ohio.

Thigpen, Robert J. Boyd (Forty-second Alabama Infantry). Letter, November 15, 1863. CHICK-CHATT.

Tillotson, E. C. Letters, December 8, December 17, 1863. CL.

Wagley, Ephraim G. (Fifteenth Indiana Infantry). Memoir, 1861–1866. Civil War Miscellany Collection, USAMHI.

Watson, James G. (Twenty-fifth Illinois Infantry). Letters, 1863. CHICK-CHATT.

Watson, Richard, H. (Thirty-sixth Illinois Infantry). Letters, 1863. Civil War Miscellany Collection, USAMHI.

Watson, Robert. Journal, September–December 1863. CHICK-CHATT.

Whitesides, Edward G. Diary, 1863. *Civil War Times Illustrated* Collection, USAMHI.

Widney, Lyman S. (Thirty-fourth Illinois Infantry). Letters, 1863. CHICK-CHATT.

Wilcox, Edgar N. (Eighteenth U.S. Infantry). Journal-diary. Collection of Wiley Sword, Bloomfield Hills, Michigan.

Withrow, James E. (First Illinois Artillery–Seventy-eighth Illinois Infantry). Diary, 1863. CHICK-CHATT.

Zeller, Asa (118th Ohio Infantry). Diary, 1863. Civil War Miscellany Collection, USAMHI.

NEWSPAPERS, WAR PAPERS, MAPS, AND PERIODICALS

Alabama Historical Quarterly (published Montgomery, Alabama), 1947,1955.

Alderson, William T., ed., "The Civil War Diary of Capt. James Litton Cooper, Sept. 30, 1861 to Jan. 1865." *Tennessee Historical Quarterly* 13 (1954): 141–173.

Anderson, Harry H. "The Civil War Letters of Lieutenant Samuel B. Chase." *Milwaukee History* 14, no. 2 (Summer 1991): 38–62.

Atlanta [Georgia] Journal, September 22 and 28, 1901.

Atlas of the Battlefield of Chickamauga, Chattanooga and Vicinity (map). Chickamauga-Chattanooga National Park Commission, Washington, D.C., 1901.

Betts, Edward E. Map of the Battlefields of Chattanooga and Wauhatchie. Chickamauga-Chattanooga National Park Commission, Washington, D.C., 1896.

Blackburn, George M. ed. "The Diary of Captain Ralph Ely of the Eighth Michigan Infantry." Central Michigan University Press, Mt. Pleasant, Michigan, 1965.

"Civil War Battlefields, Chickamauga and Chattanooga National Military Park." CWTI 20, no. 1 (April 1981): 40ff.

Confederate Veteran (published Nashville, Tennessee); vols. 1,6,12,14,21,24, 25,26,37.

Detroit Free Press, September–December 1863.

Dunker, Steven. "Rendering Invaluable Service." *Michigan History Magazine,* January/February 1992, pp. 38–45.

Feis, William B. "The Deception of Braxton Bragg, The Tullahoma Campaign, June 23–July 4, 1863." *Blue & Gray Magazine* 10, no. 1 (October 1992): 10ff.

Florida Times-Union (Jacksonville, Florida), June 8, 1888.

Hoffsommer, Robert, ed. "The Rise and Survival of Private Mesnard." CWTI 24, no. 10 (February 1986): 10ff.

Howard, Oliver Otis, "Grant at Chattanooga," *Personal Recollections of the*

Rebellion: Addresses Delivered Before the New York Commandery of the Loyal Legion of the United States, vol. 1, pp. 244–259 (New York, 1891).

Longacre, Edward G. "A General Vanquished in the West." CWTI 24, no. 6 (October 1985): 16ff.

The MacArthurs of Milwaukee. Milwaukee County Historical Society, Milwaukee, Wisconsin, 1979.

Map of a Portion of Missionary Ridge Illustrating the Positions of Baird's and Wood's Divisions, Nov. 23,24, and 25, 1863. CHICK-CHATT.

Mobile [Alabama] Daily Register & Advertiser, December 11, 1863.

Moore, William. "Writing Home to Talladega." CWTI 29, no. 5 (November/December 1990): 56ff.

Rutherford, Phillip. "A Battle Above the Clouds." CWTI 26, no. 5 (September/October 1989): 30ff.

Schroyer, M. S. "Company 'G' History [147th Pennsylvania Infantry]." *The Snyder County [Pennsylvania] Historical Society Bulletin* 2, no. 2.

Shellenberger, John K. "With Sheridan's Division at Missionary Ridge." *Sketches of War History 1861–1865,* MOLLUS, Ohio Commandery, vol. 4, pp. 52–67 (Cincinnati, Ohio, 1896).

Skoch, George. "War Along Southern Lines: A Test of Rebel Rails." CWTI 25, no. 8 (December 1986): 12ff.

Smith, William F., "An Historical Sketch of the Military Operations Around Chattanooga, Tennessee, Sept. 22 to Nov. 27, 1863," *Papers of the Military Historical Society of Massachusetts,* vol. 8, pp. 149–272 (Boston, 1910; reprint edition, Wilmington, North Carolina, 1989).

Smith, William Wrenshall. "Holocaust Holiday." CWTI 18, no. 6 (October 1979): 28ff.

Southern Historical Society Papers, Richmond, Virginia, vols. 8,11, 12,22,39.

Tablet Markers for Battery and Infantry Sites. Chickamauga-Chattanooga National Military Park, Chattanooga, Tennessee.

Walker, T. J., and Russell B. Bailey, eds. "Reminiscence of the Civil War." *Confederate Chronicles of Tennessee* 1, (1986): 37ff.

Waters, Zack C. "Through Good and Evil Fortune: Robert Bullock in the Civil War and Reconstruction." *Proceedings of the 90th Annual Meeting of the Florida Historical Society, at St. Augustine, May 1992,* Tampa, Florida, 1993.

Weber, Daniel B. ed. "The Diary of Ira Gillaspie of the Eleventh Michigan Infantry." Central Michigan University Press, Mt. Pleasant, Michigan, 1965.

Wolfe, Frank. "Letter to a Friend: From the Foot of Lookout Mountain." CWTI 22, no. 4 (June 1983): 38ff.

Wood, Thomas J. "The Battle of Missionary Ridge." *Sketches of War History 1861–1865,* MOLLUS, Ohio Commandery, vol. 4, p. 23ff. (Cincinnati, Ohio, 1896).

BOOKS

Armstrong, Zella. *The History of Hamilton County and Chattanooga, Tennessee,* 2 vols. Chattanooga, Tennessee, 1931.

Aten, Henry. *History of the Eighty-fifth Regiment Illinois Volunteer Infantry.* Hiawatha, Kansas, 1901.

Atlas to Accompany the Official Records of the Union and Confederate Armies. Government Printing Office, Washington, D.C., 1891–1895.

Basler, Roy. *The Collected Works of Abraham Lincoln,* 8 vols. New Brunswick, New Jersey, 1953.

Beach, John N. *History of the Fortieth Ohio Volunteer Infantry.* London, Ohio, 1884.

Beatty, John. *The Citizen Soldier; or Memoirs of a Volunteer.* Cincinnati, 1879.

Bennett, I. G., and William M. Haigh. *History of the Thirty-Sixth Regiment Illinois Volunteers During the War of the Rebellion.* Aurora, Illinois, 1876.

Beyer, Walter F., and Oscar F. Keydel. *Deeds of Valor, How America's Heroes Won the Medal of Honor,* 2 vols. Detroit, 1902.

Bierce, Ambrose. *The Collected Writings of Ambrose Bierce.* New York, 1946.

Bishop, Judson. *The Story of a Regiment, Being a Narrative of the Services of the Second Regiment, Minnesota Veteran Volunteer Infantry in the Civil War of 1861–1865.* St. Paul, Minnesota, 1890.

Boatner, Mark Mayo, III. *The Civil War Dictionary.* New York, 1959.

Boies, Andrew J. *Record of the Thirty-third Massachusetts Volunteer Infantry from Aug. 1862 to Aug. 1865.* Fitchburg, Massachusetts, 1880.

Briant, C. C. *History of the Sixth Regiment Indiana Volunteer Infantry.* Indianapolis, 1891.

Brown, Norman D., ed. *One of Cleburne's Command, The Civil War Reminiscences and Diary of Capt. Samuel T. Foster, Granbury's Texas Brigade, C.S.A.* Austin, Texas, 1980.

Buck, Irving A. *Cleburne and His Command.* Wilmington, North Carolina, 1987 (reprint of 1908 edition).

Byers, S. H. M. *With Fire and Sword.* New York, 1911 (reprint 1992).

Calkins, William Wirt. *The History of the One Hundred and Fourth Regiment of Illinois Volunteer Infantry, War of the Great Rebellion, 1862–1865.* Chicago, 1895.

Canfield, Silas S. *History of the Twenty-first Regiment Ohio Volunteer Infantry.* Toledo, Ohio, 1893.

Carter, W. R. *History of the First Regiment of Tennessee Volunteer Cavalry in the Great War of the Rebellion.* Knoxville, Tennessee, 1902.

Castel, Albert. *Decision in the West, The Atlanta Campaign of 1864.* Lawrence, Kansas, 1992.

Cate, Wirt Armistead, ed. *Two Soldiers, The Campaign Diaries of Thomas J. Key, C.S.A., and Robert J. Campbell, U.S.A.* Chapel Hill, North Carolina, 1938.

Chase, John. *History of the Fourteenth Regiment, O.V.I. from the Beginning of the War in 1861 to Its Close in 1865.* Toledo, Ohio, 1881.

Chesnut, Mary A. *A Diary from Dixie.* New York, 1914.

Cist, Henry. *The Army of the Cumberland.* New York, 1882.

Clark, Charles T. *Opdycke Tigers 125th O.V.I., A History of the Regiment and of the Campaigns and Battles of the Army of the Cumberland.* Columbus, Ohio, 1895.

Cleaves, Freeman. *Rock of Chickamauga, The Life of General George H. Thomas.* Norman, Oklahoma, 1948.

Collins, George K. *Memoirs of the 149th New York Volunteer Infantry, 3rd Brigade, 2nd Division, 12th and 20th A.C.* Syracuse, New York, 1891.

Connelly, Thomas Lawrence. *Autumn of Glory: The Army of Tennessee, 1862–1865.* Baton Rouge, 1971.

Connolly, James Austin. *Three Years in the Army of the Cumberland, the Letters and Diary of Major James A. Connolly.* Bloomington, Indiana, 1959.

Cope, Alexis. *The Fifteenth Ohio Volunteers and Its Campaigns, War of 1861–1865.* Columbus, Ohio, 1916 (reprint).

Cozzens, Peter. *No Better Place to Die: The Battle of Stones River.* Urbana, Illinois, 1990.

——. *This Terrible Sound, The Battle of Chickamauga.* Urbana, Illinois, 1992.

Crist, Lynda Lasswell, ed. *The Papers of Jefferson Davis,* vol. 7. Baton Rouge, 1992.

Crow, Mattie Lou Teague, ed. *The Diary of a Confederate Soldier, John Washington Inzer 1834–1928.* Huntsville, Alabama, 1977.

Curtiss-Wedge, Franklyn, ed. *History of McLeod County, Minnesota,* Chicago, 1917.

Cuttino, George Peddy, ed. *Saddle Bag and Spinning Wheel, Being the Civil War Letters of George W. Peddy, M.D., and His Wife Kate Featherston Peddy.* Macon, Georgia, 1981.

Dana, Charles A. *Recollections of the Civil War.* New York, 1898.

Daniel, Larry J. *Cannoneers in Gray, The Field Artillery of the Army of Tennessee 1861–1865.* University, Alabama, 1984.

——. *Soldiering in the Army of Tennessee, A Portrait of Life in a Confederate Army.* Chapel Hill, North Carolina, 1991.

Davenport, E. A. *History of the Ninth Regiment Illinois Cavalry Volunteers.* Chicago, 1888.

Davis, Jefferson. *The Rise and Fall of the Confederate Government,* 2 vols. New York, 1881.

Davis, William C. *Breckinridge, Statesman, Soldier, Symbol.* Baton Rouge, 1973.

——. *Jefferson Davis, The Man and His Hour.* New York, 1991.

Day, Lewis. *Story of the One Hundred and First Ohio Infantry, a Memorial Volume.* Cleveland, 1894.

Demoret, Alfred. *A Brief History of the Ninety-third Regiment Ohio Volunteer Infantry, Recollections of a Private.* Boss, Ohio, 1898.

DeVelling, C. T. *History of the Seventeenth Regiment [Ohio Volunteer Infantry] First Brigade, Third Division, Fourteenth Corps, Army of the Cumberland.* Zanesville, Ohio, 1899.

Doan, Isaac C. *Reminiscences of the Chattanooga Campaign.* Richmond, Indiana, 1894.

Dodge, William Summer. *A Waif of the War; or, the History of the Seventy-fifth Illinois Infantry, Embracing the Entire Campaigns of the Army of the Cumberland,* Chicago, 1866.

Downey, Fairfax. *Storming of the Gateway, Chattanooga, 1863.* New York, 1960.

Dunbar, Aaron. *History of the Ninety-third Regiment Illinois Volunteer Infantry from Organization to Muster Out.* Chicago, 1898.

Dyer, Gustavius W., and John Trotwood Moore, compilers. *The Tennessee Civil War Veterans Questionnaires,* vols. 1–5. Easley, South Carolina, 1985.

Eaton, Clement. *Jefferson Davis.* New York, 1977.

Eddy, Richard. *History of the Sixtieth Regiment New York State Volunteers*. Philadelphia, 1864.

The Eighty-Sixth Regiment Indiana Volunteer Infantry, A Narrative of Its Services in the Civil War of 1861–1865. Crawfordsville, Indiana, 1895.

Faust, Patricia L., ed. *Historical Times Illustrated Encyclopedia of the Civil War*. New York, 1986.

Field, Henry M. *Bright Skies and Dark Shadows*. Freeport, New York, 1970 (reprint of 1890 edition).

Fitch, Michael H. *Echoes of the Civil War As I Hear Them*. New York, 1905.

Floyd, David Bittle. *History of the Seventy-fifth Regiment of Indiana Volunteers, Its Organization, Campaigns, and Battles (1862–1865)*. Philadelphia, 1893.

Fox, William F. *Regimental Losses in the American Civil War 1861–1865*. Dayton, Ohio, 1985 (reprint of 1898 edition).

Fuller, Claud E. *The Rifled Musket*. Harrisburg, Pennsylvania, 1958.

Gates, Arnold, ed. *The Rough Side of War, The Civil War Journal of Chesley A. Mosman, 1st Lieutenant, Company D, 59th Illinois Volunteer Infantry Regiment*. Garden City, New York, 1987.

Gay, Mary A. H. *Life in Dixie During the War*. Atlanta, 1979 (reprint of 1897 edition).

Geary, Mary de Forest. *A Giant in Those Days*. Brunswick, Georgia, 1980.

Grant, Ulysses S. *Personal Memoirs of U.S. Grant*, 2 volumes. New York, 1885 (1982 reprint in single volume).

Grebner, Constantin. *We Were the Ninth; A History of the Ninth Regiment, Ohio Volunteer Infantry, April 17, 1861 to June 7, 1864*. Kent, Ohio, 1987.

Green, Johnny Williams. *Johnny Green of the Orphan Brigade; The Journal of a Confederate Soldier*. Lexington, Kentucky, 1956.

Grose, William. *The Story of the Marches, Battles and Incidents of the Thirty-sixth Regiment Indiana Volunteer Infantry*. New Castle, Indiana, 1891.

Hallock, Judith Lee. *Braxton Bragg and Confederate Defeat*, vol. 2. Tuscaloosa, Alabama, 1991.

Hannaford, Ebenezer. *The Story of a Regiment, A History of the Campaigns, and Associations in the Field, of the Sixth Regiment, Ohio Volunteer Infantry*. Cincinnati, 1868.

Harden, Henry. *History of the Nineteenth Ohio Volunteer Infantry in the Great Rebellion in the United States, 1861–1865*. Stoutsville, Ohio, 1902.

Hartpence, William R. *History of the Fifty-first Indiana Veteran Volunteer Infantry from 1861 to 1865*. Cincinnati, 1894.

Hattaway, Herman. *General Stephen D. Lee*. Jackson, Mississippi, 1976.

Hay, John. *Letters of John Hay and Extracts from His Diary*. 3 vols. Washington, D.C., 1908.

Hay, Thomas Robson. *Pat Cleburne: Stonewall Jackson of the West*. Wilmington, North Carolina, 1987.

Haynie, James Henry. *The Nineteenth Illinois; A Memoir of a Regiment of Volunteer Infantry Famous in the Civil War of Fifty Years Ago for Its Drill, Bravery, and Distinguished Services*. Chicago, 1912.

Hazen, William. *A Narrative of Military Service*. Boston, 1885.

Head, Thomas A. *Campaigns and Battles of the Sixteenth Regiment Tennessee Volunteers in the War Between the States*. Nashville, 1885.

Henry, Robert Selph. *As They Saw Forrest, Some Recollections and Comments of Contemporaries*. Jackson, Tennessee, 1956.

————. *First with the Most,* Indianapolis, 1944.

High, Edwin W. *History of the Sixty-eighth Regiment Indiana Volunteer Infantry 1862–1865.* Metamora, Indiana, 1902.

History of Tennessee. Nashville, 1886.

History of the Seventy-ninth Regiment Indiana Volunteer Infantry in the Civil War of 1861 in the United States. Indianapolis, 1899.

Hoffman, John. *The Confederate Collapse at the Battle of Missionary Ridge, The Reports of James Patton Anderson and His Brigade Commanders.* Dayton, Ohio, 1985.

Hoobler, James A. *Cities Under the Gun Images of Occupied Nashville and Chattanooga.* Nashville, 1986.

Horn, Stanley F., ed. *Tennessee's War, 1861–1865, Described by Participants.* Nashville, 1965.

————. *The Army of Tennessee.* Norman, Oklahoma, 1952.

Horton, Joshua H. *A History of the Eleventh Regiment [Ohio Volunteer Infantry].* Dayton, Ohio, 1866.

Hough, Alfred L. *Soldier in the West; The Civil War Letters of Alfred Lacey Hough.* Philadelphia, 1957.

Hughes, Nathaniel Cheairs, Jr. *General William J. Hardee, Old Reliable.* Baton Rouge, 1965.

Hunter, Edna J. Shank, *One Flag, One Country, and Thirteen Greenbacks a Month, Letters from a Civil War Private and His Colonel.* San Diego, 1980.

Johnson, Richard W. *A Soldier's Reminiscences in Peace and War.* Philadelphia, 1886.

Johnson, Robert Underwood, and Clarence Clough Buel, eds. *Battles and Leaders of the Civil War,* 4 vols. New York, 1956 (reprint of 1887 edition).

Jones, John B. *A Rebel War Clerk's Diary,* 2 vols. Philadelphia, 1966.

Jordan, Thomas, and J. P. Pryor. *The Campaigns of Lieut. Gen. N. B. Forrest and of Forrest's Cavalry.* Dayton, Ohio, 1988 (reprint of 1868 edition).

Keddick, H. W., *Seventy-seven Years in Dixie, The Boys in Gray of '61–'65,* Santa Rosa, Florida, 1910.

Keil, F. W. *Thirty-fifth Ohio, A Narrative of Service from August, 1861 to 1864.* Fort Wayne, Indiana, 1894.

Kerwood, Asbury L. *Annals of the Fifty-Seventh Regiment Indiana Volunteers.* Dayton, Ohio, 1868.

Kimberly, Robert L., and Ephraim S. Holloway. *The Forty-First Ohio Veteran Volunteer Infantry in the War of the Rebellion, 1861–1865.* Cleveland, 1897.

Kinnear, John. *History of the Eighty-sixth Regiment Illinois Volunteer Infantry During Its Term of Service.* Chicago, 1866.

Lamers, William. *The Edge of Glory: A Biography of General William S. Rosecrans, U.S.A.* New York, 1961.

Leeper, Wesley Thurman. *Rebels Valiant, Second Arkansas Mounted Rifles (Dismounted).* Little Rock, 1964.

Lewis, G. W. *The Campaigns of the One Hundred Twenty-Fourth Regiment Ohio Volunteer Infantry.* Akron, Ohio, 1894.

Lewis, Lloyd. *Sherman, Fighting Prophet.* Lincoln, Nebraska, 1932.

Linderman, Gerald F. *Embattled Courage, The Experience of Combat in the American Civil War.* New York, 1987.

Livermore, Thomas L. *Numbers and Losses in the Civil War in America: 1861–65.* Bloomington, Indiana, 1900 (reprint 1957).

Longacre, Edward G. *From Union Stars to Top Hat, A Biography of the Extraordinary General James Harrison Wilson.* Harrisburg, Pennsylvania, 1972.

Longstreet, James. *From Manassas to Appomattox, Memoirs of the Civil War in America.* Philadelphia, 1896 (reprint 1991).

Losson, Christopher. *Tennessee's Forgotten Warriors, Frank Cheatham and His Confederate Division.* Knoxville, Tennessee, 1989.

Lucas, D. R. *New History of the 99th Indiana.* Rockford, Illinois, 1900.

McCaffrey, James M. *This Band of Heroes, Granbury's Texas Brigade, C.S.A.* Austin, Texas, 1985.

McClendon, W. A. *Recollections of War Times by an Old Veteran While under Stonewall Jackson and Lieut. Gen. James Longstreet.* Montgomery, Alabama, 1908.

McDonough, James Lee. *Chattanooga—A Death Grip on the Confederacy.* Knoxville, Tennessee, 1984.

McGee, B. F. *History of the 72d Indiana Volunteer Infantry of the Mounted Lightning Brigade.* Lafayette, Indiana, 1882 (reprint 1992).

McKinney, Francis. *Education in Violence, The Life of George H. Thomas.* Detroit, 1961.

McMurray, W. J. *History of the Twentieth Tennessee Regiment Volunteer Infantry, C.S.A.* Nashville, 1904.

McMurry, Richard M. *Two Great Rebel Armies.* Chapel Hill, North Carolina, 1989.

McWhiney, Grady. *Braxton Bragg and Confederate Defeat,* vol. 1. New York, 1969.

Manderson, Charles F. *The Twin Seven Shooters.* New York, 1902.

Mathis, Ray. *In the Land of the Living, Wartime Letters by Confederates from the Chattahoochie Valley of Alabama and Georgia.* Troy, Alabama, 1981.

Military History and Reminiscences of the Thirteenth Regiment of Illinois Volunteer Infantry in the Civil War in the United States, 1861–1865. Chicago, 1892.

Miller, J. M. *Recollections of a Pine Knot in the Lost Cause.* Greenwood, Mississippi, 1900.

Morrow, John Anderson. *The Confederate Whitworth Sharpshooters.* Marietta, Georgia: privately published, 1989.

Morse, Loren J., ed. *Civil War Diaries & Letters of Bliss Morse.* Wagoneer, Oklahoma, 1985.

Nash, Charles Edward. *Biographical Sketches of Gen. Pat Cleburne and Gen. T. C. Hindman.* Dayton, Ohio, 1898 (reprint 1977).

Newlin, William H. *A History of the Seventy-Third Regiment of Illinois Infantry Volunteers.* Springfield, Illinois, 1890.

Nisbet, James C. *Four Years on the Firing Line.* Chattanooga, 1914.

Oates, William C. *The War Between the Union and the Confederacy and Its Lost Opportunities, with a History of the Fifteenth Alabama and the Forty-eight Battles in Which It Was Engaged.* New York, 1905 (reprint 1985).

Obrieter, John. *The Seventy-seventh Pennsylvania at Shiloh, History of the Regiment.* Harrisburg, Pennsylvania, 1908.

Partridge, Charles A. *History of the Ninety-Sixth Regiment Illinois Volunteer Infantry.* Chicago, 1887.

Pasco, Private. *Private Pasco, A Civil War Diary.* Privately published, n.d.

Pennsylvania. *Pennsylvania at Chickamauga and Chattanooga, Ceremonies at the Dedication of the Monuments.* Harrisburg, Pennsylvania, 1897.

Perry, Henry. *History of the Thirty-eighth Regiment Indiana Volunteer Infantry.* Chicago, 1906.

Pierce, Lyman B. *History of the Second Iowa Cavalry.* Burlington, Iowa, 1865.

Pinney, N. A. *History of the One Hundred Fourth Regiment Ohio Volunteer Infantry from 1862 to 1865.* Akron, Ohio, 1886.

Porter, Horace. *Campaigning with Grant.* New York, 1897.

Puntenney, George. *History of the Thirty-seventh Regiment of Indiana Volunteer Infantry, Its Organization, Campaigns, and Battles, Sept. '61 to Oct. '64.* Rushville, Indiana, 1896.

Purdue, Howell and Elizabeth. *Pat Cleburne Confederate General.* Hillsboro, Texas, 1973.

Record of the Ninety-fourth Regiment Ohio Volunteer Infantry in the War of the Rebellion. Cincinnati, 1891.

Reep, J. A. *Guttmachrala, or Four Years at the Front as a Private.* Knoxville, Tennessee, 1896.

Report of the Chickamauga and Chattanooga National Park Commission on the Claim of Gen. John B. Turchin and Others That in the Battle of Chattanooga His Brigade Captured the Position on Missionary Ridge Known as DeLong Place, and the Decision of the Secretary of War Thereon. n.d., copy at CHICK-CHATT.

Rice, Ralsa C. *Yankee Tigers, Through the Civil War with the 125th Ohio.* Huntington, West Virginia, 1992.

Ridley, Bromfield L. *Battles and Sketches of the Army of Tennessee.* Dayton, Ohio, 1978 (reprint of 1906 edition).

Roberson, Elizabeth Whitley. *Weep Not for Me Dear Mother.* Washington, North Carolina, 1991.

Rogers, Robert M. *The One Hundred Twenty-fifth Regiment Illinois Volunteer Infantry.* Champaign, Illinois, 1882.

Rowland, Dunbar, ed. *Jefferson Davis Constitutionalist, His Letters, Papers, and Speeches,* 6 vols. Jackson, Mississippi, 1923.

Royse, Isaac. *History of the 115th Regiment Illinois Volunteer Infantry.* Terre Haute, Indiana, 1900.

Rusling, James F. *Men and Things I Saw in Civil War Days.* Cincinnati, 1899.

Sandburg, Carl. *Abraham Lincoln, The War Years,* vol. 2. New York, 1939.

Satterlee, L. D. *Ten Old Gun Catalogs for the Collector.* Chicago, 1962.

Schiller, Herbert M., ed. *Autobiography of Major General William F. Smith, 1861–1864,* Dayton, Ohio, 1990.

Sears, Stephen W. *George B. McClellan, The Young Napoleon.* New York, 1988.

Shaver, Lewellyn A. *A History of the Sixtieth Alabama Regiment, Gracie's Alabama Brigade.* Montgomery, Alabama, 1867.

Shaw, James Birney, *History of the Tenth Regiment Indiana Volunteer Infantry,* Lafayette, Indiana, 1912.

Sheridan, Philip Henry, *Personal Memoirs of P. H. Sheridan.* New York, 1992 reprint of 1888 edition.

Sherlock, Eli J. *Memoranda of the Marches and Battles in Which the One Hundredth Regiment of Indiana Infantry Volunteers Took an Active Part, War of the Rebellion, 1861–1865.* Kansas City, Missouri, 1896.

Sherman, William T. *Memoirs of General William T. Sherman.* New York, 1990 reprint of 1875 edition.

Simmons, Lovis A. *The History of the Eighty-fourth Regiment Illinois Volunteers*. Macomb, Illinois, 1866.

Simon, John Y., ed., *The Papers of Ulysses S. Grant*, vols. 8,9. Carbondale, Illinois, 1992.

Smith, John A. *A History of the Thirty-first Regiment of Indiana Volunteer Infantry in the War of the Rebellion*. Cincinnati, 1900.

Smith, Theodore Clarke. *The Life and Letters of James Abram Garfield*, 2 vols. New Haven, 1925.

Sorrel, G. Moxley. *Recollections of a Staff Officer*. Jackson, Tennessee, 1958.

Stanley, David S. *Personal Memoirs of Major General David Sloane Stanley, U.S.A.* Cambridge, Massachusetts, 1917.

Stormont, Gilbert R., and John J. Hight. *History of the Fifty-eighth Regiment of Indiana Volunteer Infantry, Its Organization, Campaigns, and Battles from 1861–1865*. Princeton, Indiana, 1895.

The Story of the Fifty-fifth Regiment Illinois Volunteer Infantry in the Civil War, 1861–1865. [Clinton, Massachusetts], 1887.

Sunderland, Glenn. *Wilder's Lightning Brigade—And Its Spencer Repeaters*. Washington, Illinois, 1984.

Sword, Wiley. *Embrace an Angry Wind*. New York, 1992.

———. *Firepower from Abroad: The Confederate Enfield and the LeMat Revolver 1861–1863*. Lincoln, Rhode Island, 1986.

———. *Shiloh: Bloody April*. New York, 1974.

Sykes, E. T. *Walthall's Brigade, A Cursory Sketch, With Personal Experiences of Walthall's Brigade, Army of Tennessee, C.S.A., 1862–1865*. Publication of Mississippi Historical Society, 1905.

Thatcher, Marshall P. *A Hundred Battles in the West—St. Louis to Atlanta, 1861–1865—The Second Michigan Cavalry*. Detroit, 1884.

Thoburn, Thomas C. *My Experiences During the Civil War*. Cleveland, 1963.

Thomas, Benjamin P., ed. *Three Years with Grant As Recalled by War Correspondent Sylvanus Cadwallader*. New York, 1955.

Thompson, B. F. *History of the One Hundred Twelfth Regiment of Illinois in the Great War of the Rebellion 1862–1865*. Toulon, Illinois, 1885.

Thurston, W. S. *History One Hundred and Eleventh Regiment O.V.I.* Toledo, Ohio, 1894.

Tourgee, Albion, *The Story of a Thousand, Being a History of the Service of the One Hundred Fifth Ohio Volunteer Infantry in the War for the Union from August 21, 1862 to June 6, 1865*. Buffalo, 1896.

Tower, R. Lockwood, ed. *A Carolinian Goes to War, The Civil War Narrative of Arthur Middleton Manigault, Brigadier General, C.S.A.* Columbia, South Carolina, 1988.

Van Horne, Thomas B. *The Life of Major General George H. Thomas*. New York, 1882.

———. *History of the Army of the Cumberland, Its Organizations, Campaigns, and Battles*, 2 vols. Cincinnati, 1875.

Waddle, Angus L. *Three Years with the Armies of the Ohio and Cumberland*. Chillicothe, Ohio, 1889.

Walton, Clyde C. *Private Smith's Journal, Recollections of the Late War*. Chicago, 1963.

The War of the Rebellion: A Compiliation of the Official Records of the Union and Confederate Armies, series I, 73 vols., Washington, D.C., 1880–1902.

Warner, Ezra J. *Generals in Blue.* Baton Rouge, 1964.

———. *Generals in Gray: Lives of the Confederate Commanders.* Baton Rouge, 1959.

Watkins, Sam R. *"Co. Aytch" Maury Grays First Tennessee Regiment, or a Side Show of the Big Show.* Wilmington, North Carolina, 1987 (reprint 1952).

Willett, E. D. *History of Company B, 40th Alabama Regiment Confederate States Army 1862–1865.* Northport, Alabama, 1963, reprint of 1902 edition.

Willison, Charles A. *Reminiscences of a Boy's Service with the 76th Ohio.* Columbus, Ohio, 1986.

Wills, Brian Steel. *A Battle from the Start, The Life of Nathan Bedford Forrest.* New York, 1992.

Wilson, Ephraim A. *Memoirs of the War of Company 'G' 10th Illinois Veteran Volunteer Infantry.* Cleveland, 1893.

Wilson, James Harrison. *Under the Old Flag,* 2 vols., Westport, Connecticut, 1971 (reprint of 1912 edition).

Wilson, Lawrence. *Itinerary of the Seventh Ohio Volunteer Infantry 1861–1865.* New York, 1907.

Winters, Erastus. *In the 50th Ohio Serving Uncle Sam.* Cincinnati, n.d.

Wood, George L. *The Seventh Regiment [Ohio Volunteer Infantry]; A Record.* New York, 1865.

Woodward, C. Vann, ed., *Mary Chesnut's Civil War.* New Haven, 1981.

———, and Elisabeth Muhlenfeld. *The Private Mary Chesnut.* New York, 1984.

Worsham, W. J. *The Old Nineteenth Tennessee Regiment, C.S.A. June, 1861–April, 1865.* Knoxville, Tennessee, 1902.

Wright, Henry H. *A History of the Sixth Iowa Infantry.* Iowa City, 1923.

Wyeth, John Allan. *Life of Nathan Bedford Forrest.* Dayton, Ohio, 1988 (reprint of 1901 edition).

INDEX

Acton, Thomas, 218
Adams, Daniel W., 165
Alexander, Jessie, 199, 237
Amnesty proposal (Rosecrans's), 48
Anderson, J. Patton, 181, 185, 187, 188,
    272–73, 285–86, 288–89, 290–91, 322
Anderson's Crossroads, 68
Army of Northern Virginia, 26, 70, 75
Army of Tennessee (Confederate), 23,
    240; Bragg's assumption of command,
    21; factionalism, 25, 63–67; morale,
    29, 105–11, 146–47, 164–65, 166–67,
    353–54; personnel changes, 29–35,
    64–67, 165–66, 353–54
Army of the Cumberland, 3, 4, 23, 191,
    259, 357; Grant's opinion, 160–61,
    349; Missionary Ridge, 266–68, 295;
    morale, 44, 100–104, 146–47; North
    Missionary Ridge, 189; rivalry with
    Army of the Tennessee, 103; supply
    shortages, 42–44, 54, 57, 59–61, 99–
    104, 145–46; Thomas's command,
    52–54, 56, 103
Army of the Mississippi, 7
Army of the Potomac, 8, 41, 51, 228
Army of the Tennessee (Federal), 7, 153,
    198; rivalry with Army of the Cum-
    berland, 103; Sherman's assumption
    of command, 61
Artillery: Confederate, 91, 94–95, 129,
    267; Federal, 129, 209, 211, 215–16

Atlanta, Ga., Sherman's campaign, 357
Avery, William L., 281, 300

Baird, Absalom, 178, 260, 268–69, 270,
    280, 292, 313, 314
Banbury, Jabez, 191, 256
Bands, military, 95–96, 157
Barber, Gershom M., 118
Barnes, Bill, 262
Bate, William, 165, 272, 296, 298, 299–
    304, 315–16, 319, 321, 354
Bate's brigade, 286
"Battle Above the Clouds," 229–30. See
    also Lookout Mountain
Battlefield carnage, 345; Chickamauga
    Creek, 3, 105–7, 356; Missionary
    Ridge, 317–18; Tunnel Hill, 246
Beatty, Samuel, 180, 279, 293, 313
Beauregard, Pierre G. T., 21, 33, 72
Benning, Henry L., 133, 139–40, 143
Billy Goat Hill, 199–201, 234–35, 237,
    243
Bird's Mill Bridge, 330
Blanchard, Walter, 336, 337, 345
Bragg, Braxton, 4, 8, 9, 19, 60, 143,
    146–47, 150–51, 153–54, 156–57,
    175–78, 186–88, 238, 272, 296, 301,
    315–17, 334, 354, 359; Army of Ten-
    nessee, 21, 165–66; Brown's Ferry,
    123–24, 128–30; Chattanooga, 67–69,
    87–90, 106; Chickamauga, 26–28;

Bragg, Braxton (*cont.*)
Davis and, 23–25, 31–35, 315; east
Tennessee offensive, 74–80, 169–70;
Longstreet and, 70–73, 76–80, 123–
25, 128–30, 153–54; Lookout Mountain, 168–69, 229, 232–37; Missionary
Ridge, 186–88, 202–5, 208, 221, 311–
12, 319–20; misuse of cavalry, 67–69;
opinions about, 23–26, 30–33, 62,
64–66, 354–55; purges, 29–35, 64–67;
relieved of command, 352–54; rise to
fame, 20–23; Rosecrans's campaign
against, 8–18, 36–45; Sherman's
moves against, 167–70; supply route
strategies, 67–69, 109, 116–17
Brannan, John M., 13, 149
Bratton, John, 133–37, 139–40, 142–44
Breckinridge, J. Cabell, 307
Breckinridge, John C., 25, 65, 147, 223,
235, 286, 296, 299, 343, 358; Lookout
Mountain, 220–21; Missionary Ridge,
235–36; opinion of Bragg, 24
Breckinridge's Division, 166, 168–69
Bridgeport plan, 76–77
Bridges's (Illinois) Battery, 184, 270,
275, 298
Brigade of Tennessee volunteers, 165
Brough, John, 51–52, 53
Brown, John C., 165, 227, 242, 254, 314
Brown's Ferry, 59–60, 61, 113–44, 113
(map), 207–8, 209, 214; Bragg's
counterattack, 123–24, 128–30; Con-
federate damage to, 162, 175; Federal
capture of, 120–21; Smith's plan,
114–16, 118–22, 126–29
Brown's Ferry Road, 132–37
Brown's Ferry-Wauhatchie Road, 138–39
Buck, Irving A., 235–36, 334
Buckner, Simon Bolivar, 30, 32–33, 64,
73, 78
Buckner's Division, 124, 165, 170
Buena Vista, battle of, 20
Bullock, Robert, 109–10, 302
Burnside, Ambrose, 8–11, 16, 18, 38,
43, 50–51, 67, 69, 72–80, 148–50,
156, 161–62, 169–70, 175, 328, 348–
49
Bushbeck, Adolphus, 197, 249–50, 257,
262
Bushbeck's Brigade, 198
Bushnell, Doug, 336, 337
Butler, William L., 182–83
Butterfield, Daniel, 56, 307, 331, 342
Byers, Sam, 256

Cadwallader, Sylvanus, 269
Calvert's Battery, 242, 247
Camplife, Chattanooga, 95–96

Candy, Charles, 218
Carlin, William P., 225–26, 309–10, 330–
31
Carpenter, Arthur B., 94
Casualties: Chickamauga, 3, 27; Crutch-
field Road, 316; Lookout Mountain,
223, 229–30; Missionary Ridge, 321–
22; Orchard Knob, 183; Ringgold,
343; Rossville Gap, 309; Smith's Hill,
142; Stones River, 23; Tunnel Hill,
256; Wauhatchie, 143–44
Catoosa Station, 334
Cavalry, 43–44, 67–69, 75
Chalaron, J. Ad., 298–99, 303
Chalmers's cavalry, 154
Chamberlain, Joshua, 120
Champion, Thomas E., 206, 217–18
Champion's Hill, 358
Chandler, William P., 276, 277
Chase, Salmon P., 40, 41, 50
Chattanooga, Tenn., 9, 16–18, 26, 27–
28, 36–45; artillery bombardment of,
91, 94–95; Bragg's plans, 67–69, 87–
90, 106; camplife in, 95–96; chronology of operations, 370–76; Confederate loss of, 11, 357–59; Davis's views
on, 358; description of town, 83–87;
enemy positionings, 87–90; Federal
holding of, 52–54, 106; geographical
isolation of, 42, 44, 85; Grant's plans,
54, 61–62, 112–14; railroads influence
on, 84; siege of, 37 (map), 47 (map);
Stanton's plan, 39–41, 48–49; supply
routes, 42–44, 54, 57, 59–61, 67–69,
114–18, 121–22, 145–46, 148, 151;
theater of operations, 5 (map);
Thomas's plan, 58–60; truce for evacuation of non-combatants, 176;
weather, 96–98
Chattanooga (supply steamer), 146
Chattanooga Creek, 221
Chattanooga–East Tennessee Operations, 71 (map)
Chattanooga Valley, 86, 106
Cheatham, Benjamin Frank, 25, 33, 65,
149, 166, 223, 237, 313–14, 315, 322
Cherokee (Georgia) Artillery, 222
Chesnut, James C., 31
Chestnut, Mary, 357
Chicago Times, 269
Chickamauga, battle of, 3–4, 11–18, 26–
28, 154; battlefield carnage, 3, 105–7,
356; Confederate and Federal feelings
after, 105–7; hospital truce, 91–94;
political results of, 29–32
Chickamauga Creek, 204
Chickamauga Station, 170, 175–76, 186,
323, 326, 328, 329

Cincinnati Commercial, 7
Citico Creek, 149, 183
Clayton's Brigade, 222–23, 225–26, 306–7, 308, 309–10
Cleburne, Patrick Ronayne, 32, 170–71, 176, 186, 239, 252, 257, 338–43, 358; and Bragg, 24, 354–55; Missionary Ridge, 187–88, 315; North Missionary Ridge, 232–36, 240–42, 294; personality, 66–67; Ringgold, 334–37; Tunnel Hill, 254–55
Cleveland, Tenn., 150
Cobb's Kentucky Battery, 303, 304, 305
Cobham, George A., Jr., 208, 218, 341
Cold Harbor, Va., 359
Colliersville, Miss., 154
Confederate order of battle, 365–69
Coombs, John, 351
Cooper, Samuel, 31, 79, 109
Corinth, Miss., 7, 21, 22, 53
Corse, John M., 243–49, 252, 259, 260
Corse, Montgomery D., 76
Corse's Brigade, 73–74
Cravens house, 204
Cravens house plateau, 208, 209, 211, 213–20, 222, 225
Creighton, William R., 339–41
Crittenden, Thomas L., 7, 10, 11, 12, 39, 49–50
Cruft, Charles R., 307–9, 311, 332, 342–43
Cruft's Division (Twelfth Corps), 189
Crutchfield (farmer), 196
Crutchfield Road, 316–17
Cullen, Theodore, 244
Culp's Hill (Gettysburg), 134, 135
Cumberland Gap, 73, 163, 175
Cumming, Alfred, 223, 250, 254–56
Cummings, J. F., 108
Cummins, J. C., 287

Dana, Charles A., 3, 11, 13, 15–17, 38, 39–40, 42, 54, 61, 100, 125–26, 160, 179, 184, 224, 226, 263, 324, 344–45, 347, 355–56; Granger and, 269–70; Lookout Mountain, 231; Missionary Ridge, 320, 321; Rosecrans and, 44–52
Davis, Jefferson, 20, 21, 63–64, 76, 77, 355; Bragg and, 23, 24–25, 31–35, 353; Longstreet and, 72; personality of, 34–35; views on Chattanooga, 358
Davis, Jefferson C., 16, 91, 123, 176, 189, 197, 198, 329–30
Davis, Newton N., 180–83
Davis, Thomas W., 105–6, 107
Deas, Zachariah C., 188, 272–73, 292–93

Deas's Brigade, 286–87, 289
Dent's Battery, 289, 291, 292
Deserters, 148–49, 162, 167, 175–76, 207
Dick's Ridge, 344
Doss, Ambrose, 167
Doty, John S. H., 94
Douglas, Stephen A., 85
Douglas's Battery, 242, 248
Dowd, William F., 210
Ducat, Arthur C., 43–44
Duck River, Tenn., 9, 25
Dug Gap (Pigeon Mountain), 11
Dunbar (supply steamer), 151, 175, 196

East Tennessee and Georgia Railroad, 232, 249, 329
East Tennessee campaign, 71 (map), 73–80, 109, 147, 161, 169–70
East Tennessee Virginia Railroad, 74
Edwards, Arthur, 146
8th Georgia, Company E, 148
8th Kentucky, 227–28
8th Missouri, 193, 195
18th Alabama, 308, 309
18th U. S. Infantry, 92, 94
18th Wisconsin, 117
80th Ohio, 256
82nd Indiana, 292
85th Illinois, 93
86th Illinois, 326
86th Indiana, 279
88th Illinois, 303
Eleventh Corps, 41, 58, 126–27, 134, 138–39, 140, 154, 189–90, 238, 239, 248, 249, 259, 329, 347
11th Ohio, 292, 293
11th Tennessee, 293–94
Ewell, Richard S., 38
Ewell's Corps, 60, 76
Ewing, Hugh Boyle, 157–59, 162, 169, 198, 237, 243, 248, 250, 253, 257–59

Fahnestock, Allan, 329–30
Farmington, Tenn., 68
Feagin, N. B., 119–20
Federal order of battle, 360–65
Ferguson, T. B., 331
Ferguson's Battery, 334
5th Company, Washington Artillery Battalion of New Orleans, 296–99
5th Iowa, 252, 256, 258
5th Kentucky, 91, 182
5th Tennessee, 106, 109
5th Tennessee Cavalry, 105
15th Alabama, 120, 141–42; Company B, 119; sharpshooters, 116
15th Arkansas, 252
Fifteenth Corps, 155, 159–60, 191

15th Indiana, 268, 316
15th Ohio, 101, 269, 275–76, 287
15th Texas (dismounted) Cavalry, 255
55th Illinois, 193
56th Georgia, 250–51, 255
57th Indiana, 266–67
58th Alabama, 223, 308
58th Indiana, 318
59th Illinois, 95, 318, 331
Finley, Jesse J., 354
Finley's Florida Brigade, 301–2
1st Arkansas, 338–39
1st Battalion Ohio Sharpshooters, 117
1st Florida (dismounted) Cavalry, 301
1st Michigan Engineers and Mechanics, 59, 115, 192
1st Missouri Light Artillery, Battery D, 200, 243, 249
1st Ohio, 278, 294
1st Tennessee, 22, 63, 255
Flags, Confederate, 240
Forrest, Nathan Bedford, 19–20, 27, 38, 39, 42, 65, 67, 358
Forrest's Cavalry, 107
Fort Donelson, 7, 21, 51
Fort Henry, 7, 21, 51
Fort Negley, 88, 90, 271
Fort Wood, 88, 90, 178–79, 180, 271, 330
4th Alabama sharpshooters, 116, 118
Fourth Corps, 50, 178, 263
4th Florida, 110, 165, 302
4th Iowa, 339
4th Ohio, 146
4th Ohio Cavalry, 154
Fourteenth Corps, 189–90, 192, 197, 225, 260
40th Alabama, 217–18
40th Illinois, 243–44
40th Indiana, 316
40th Ohio, 217–18, 228
41st Ohio, 182, 183, 267, 275, 278, 294, 299
42nd Illinois, 268
44th Alabama, 105, 141–42
44th Illinois, 303
46th Ohio, 244
47th Ohio, 199, 256–57
Foster, Samuel T., 243–44, 245–46
Fox, Perrin V., 115
Foy, James C., 119, 120–21
Franklin, battle of, 355
Frazer, John Wesley, 73
Fredericksburg, Va., 8, 51
Fremont, John C., 232
Friendly fire, 244
Fullerton, Joseph S., 232, 264, 281, 284

Gardiner, David, 176
Garfield, James A., 14, 17, 18, 36–38, 40, 41, 50, 55
Garnett, Robert S., 4
Garrity, James, 286
Garrity's Battery, 287–89
Geary, Edward R., 136
Geary, John W., 126, 127, 134–38, 141–44, 206, 213, 220, 222, 228, 307, 331–32, 338, 339, 341, 343; Cravens house plateau, 215–16, 218–20; Lookout Mountain, 207–13
Gettysburg, Pa., 9
Gibson, Randall Lee, 285–86, 309–10
Gist, States Rights, 331
Gist's Brigade, 331
Glass house, 250–51, 252
Glison, William, 116
Goldthwaite, Richard, 335–37, 341, 343
Goodson, Joab, 105
Govan's Brigade, 235, 242, 247, 248
Granbury, Hiram, 246, 247, 335, 337, 343
Granger, Gordon, 12, 17, 41, 50, 56, 178, 179, 184, 268, 300, 311, 324; and Dana, 269–70; Knoxville, 328, 348–49; Missionary Ridge, 263–64, 280–81; Orchard Knob, 180
Grant, Ulysses S., 6, 23, 34, 46, 51, 55, 76, 77, 127–28, 170, 179, 224, 226, 238, 343, 359; accolades from Washington, 355–56; and Bragg's retreat, 175–78, 347–48; Brown's Ferry, 121–22; Chattanooga plans, 54, 61–62, 112–14; command of Chattanooga forces, 56–63, 103–4, 147–55; criticism of Army of the Cumberland, 160–61, 349; favoritism of, 159–60; Lookout Mountain, 205, 229–30, 231–32; Lookout Valley, 161–63; Missionary Ridge, 280–81, 312, 320, 321–22, 324–25; North Missionary Ridge, 155–57, 188–201, 259–65; opinion of Bragg, 62; Orchard Knob, 183–85; personality, 152; post-Chattanooga plans, 326–29, 357; rescue of Burnside, 348–49; Ringgold Gap, 344; and Rosecrans, 7–8, 57; supply route plans, 59–61; and Thomas, 58, 160–61
Graysville, Ga., 330–31, 332, 334, 348
Greeley, Horace, 46
Green, John W., 188, 321
Greene, Charles T., 341
Greene, George S., 135–36
Grigsby, J. Warren, 132, 202–4, 232, 234
Grose, William, 213, 220, 344

Hall, H. W., 243–44, 245
Halleck, Henry, 8, 16, 39, 40, 41, 60, 76, 121, 153–54, 161, 348, 355, 357
Hampton's Legion, 136
Hardee, William J., 25, 26, 64, 147, 250, 272–74, 331, 334, 343, 358; and Bragg, 24, 353; Lookout Mountain, 186–87; Missionary Ridge, 188, 205, 208, 235–37, 313–15, 320; North Missionary Ridge, 234–35, 294
Hardee's Corps, 165, 264
Hardee's Tactics, 272
Harker, Charles G., 279, 300–301, 303, 304, 316–17
Harker's brigade, 267, 284
Harlan, Isaiah, 166
Harris, Samuel A., 335
Havis's Georgia Battery, 304
Hay, John, 16, 39, 40
Hays, William H., 313–14
Hazen, William B., 128, 178–79, 182, 183, 275, 278, 294, 298–300, 301, 303, 313, 317; Brown's Ferry, 115–16, 120, 121; Missionary Ridge, 287–88; Orchard Knob, 180–83
Hazen's brigade, 285
Hecker, Frederick, 140, 141, 142–43
Hill, Daniel Harvey, 30–31, 33, 64
Hindman, Thomas C., 31, 64
Hodges, Henry C., 101
Holston River Valley, 73–74, 76
Holtzclaw, J. T., 222–24, 308
Hood, John Bell, 26, 131, 357
Hood's Division, 117
Hooker, Joseph, 8, 48–49, 57, 60, 76, 77, 102, 132, 138–39, 140–41, 142, 149, 228, 303, 319, 331, 341–44, 348; Lookout Creek, 214; Lookout Mountain, 205–6, 207, 218–19, 224–26, 232; Lookout Valley, 61–62, 114, 125–28, 129, 148, 151; Missionary Ridge, 306–11; North Missionary Ridge, 262–63, 265; Rankin's Ferry, 58–59; and Rosecrans, 41; Ringgold, 331–33, 335, 336, 338–42; Wauhatchie, 148
Hooker's "boys," 190–91
Hornet's Nest assault, 21
Horseshoe Ridge, 16–17, 27
Hough, Alfred L., 18, 112, 121–22
Howard, Oliver O., 126–27, 138, 139, 140, 143, 151, 161, 178, 197, 198
Howard's Corps, 183
Howell's Georgia Battery, 215
Hudson, Peter, 344
Hunger, 99–104, 107–11, 145–47, 164–67

Hunter, David, 156, 157, 162, 179, 232, 262
Huntington, A. C. A., 148–49

Informers, 148–49, 162, 167, 175–76
Inzer, John W., 308–9, 324
Ireland, David, 206, 216–17, 219–20, 341
Iuka, Miss., battle of, 7
Ives, Washington, 110, 165, 302

Jackson, John K., 75, 209, 214–15, 219, 220, 223, 313–14, 358
Jenkins, Micah, 119, 128–30, 131, 132–33, 134–37, 139, 140, 143, 144
Johnson, Andrew, 57
Johnson, Bushrod, 170–71
Johnson, Richard W., 267, 269, 309–11
Johnson's Crook, 128, 132
Johnston, Albert Sidney, 21, 34
Johnston, Joseph E., 24–25, 33, 38, 64, 67, 68, 153, 168; replacement of Bragg, 353–54
Jones, John B., 357
Jones, Samuel, 69, 73–76, 78, 147
Jonesboro, Ga., 16

Kelley's Ferry, 59, 125, 127
Kelley's Ferry road, 224
Kelly's Field, 27
Kennesaw Mountain, 359
Key, Thomas J., 242, 247
Key's Battery, 249, 251–52, 254
Kimberly, Robert L., 278
Kittoe, Edward D., 162
Knapp's Pennsylvania Battery, 135, 137
Knefler, Frederick, 279
Knoxville, Tenn., 11, 73, 161–62, 169–70, 328, 348–49
Koppesser, Peter, 226
Kraemer, G. A., 183
Krzyzanowski, Wladimir, 139, 140–41, 142

Lagow, Clark, 162
Landgraeber, Clemens, 342
Langdon, Bassett, 278, 294
Law, Evander McIvor, 116, 119, 120, 124, 125, 130–37, 139, 140, 142–144
Lee, Robert E., 9, 22, 26, 33, 41, 60, 70, 73, 76, 124, 357
Lee, Stephen D., 67–69, 168
Lee and Gordon's Mill, 11–12, 26
Lender, Robert, 139
Lennard, George W., 279
Lewis, Joseph H., 186
Liddell, St. John R., 128, 129
Lightburn, Joseph A. J., 199, 237
Lightburn's Brigade, 243

Lincoln, Abraham, 7, 9, 10, 15–16, 35, 39, 40–41, 48, 50–52, 348, 355, 357
Little Round Top (Gettysburg), 120
Little Suck Creek, 116–17
Long, Eli, 197
Longstreet, James, 6, 27, 38, 69, 116, 119, 131, 133, 140, 144, 169–70, 176, 229, 328, 349, 358; and Bragg, 30–33, 65–66, 70–73, 76–80, 123–25, 128–30; Brown's Ferry, 123–24, 128–30; Chickamauga, 13, 26; east Tennessee, 76–80, 161; Knoxville, 348; Lookout Mountain, 124–25, 132, 149; Lookout Valley, 147; Missionary Ridge absence, 320; reinforcement of Bragg, 153–54; threat to Burnside, 79–80, 149, 161; Wauhatchie, 143, 148
Longstreet's Corps, 60
Lookout Creek/Brown's Ferry, 125–28, 132–33, 134–37, 140, 207–8, 209, 214
Lookout Mountain, 11–12, 26, 72, 73, 86, 103, 114, 119, 123, 126–27, 149, 150, 203 (map), 204–30; Bragg's plans, 168–69; Breckinridge's reinforcement, 220–21; casualties, 223, 229–30; Confederate artillery on, 91, 94–95, 129; Confederate occupation, 44, 48, 106, 146–47; Confederate retreat, 41, 44, 149, 222–24, 227–29; Federal assault, 206–21, 226–27, 229–31; Federal deception plan, 158–59, 169, 204–6; Geary's moves, 207–8, 209–13; Hardee's stand, 186–87; Hooker's tactics, 205–7, 218–19, 224–26, 232; Jenkins's defense plan, 128–30; Longstreet's plans, 124–25, 132, 149; Stevenson's moves, 213–15, 219–23, 229
Lookout Valley, 11, 48, 59, 61, 76–77, 86, 102, 114, 121, 123, 125, 126, 148, 151, 189, 207; Confederate loss of, 147; Grant's impatience, 160–61; Hooker, 61–62, 114, 125–29, 148, 151
Loomis, John M., 237–38, 249, 260
Loomis's Brigade, 243, 248–50, 257, 264
Lowrey, Mark, 339–41
Lowrey's Brigade, 235, 242, 248
Lumsden's Battery, 106
Lunar eclipse, 241

MacArthur, Arthur, Jr., 302–3, 304
Mahan offensive tactics, 21, 23
Maney, George, 165, 329
Maney's Brigade, 255
Manigault, Arthur M., 87, 180–82, 271, 273–74, 286–89; Missionary Ridge, 291–92, 319; Orchard Knob, 185, 187

Matthies, Charles L., 237, 250, 252, 253–54, 256, 262
Maxwell, Troup, 301–2
McAloon, P. A., 251, 256
McCallie, Thomas H., 84
McClellan, George B., 4
McClenahan, John, 101, 275–76
McCollum, Jimmy, 336, 345–46
McConnell, J. T., 254
McCook, Alexander, 10, 11, 13, 39, 49–50
McCook, Daniel, 192–93
McCowan, John, 25
McLemore's Cove, 11
McMinnville, Tenn., 68
Meade, George, 41
Meigs, Montgomery C., 43–44, 101, 102–3, 224, 229
Memphis and Charleston Railroad, 154, 168
Meteor of 1860, 85
Mexican War, 20
Michigan Engineers and Mechanics, 121
Military Division of the Mississippi, 52
Miller, Isaac, 167
Mills, Roger Q., 246, 255, 257
Milton, W. P., 250–51
Milward, Hubbard K., 117, 118
"Missionary Hills," 198
Missionary Ridge, 27, 67, 86, 149–50, 178, 185, 190, 221, 248, 359; after-action reports, 319–21; base of, diversionary tactic, 263–65, 268, 270–73; battlefield carnage, 317–18; Bragg's fortification, 186–88, 202–5, 208, 221; Breckinridge, 235–37; casualties, 321–22; Cleburne, 187–88, 315; Confederate artillery on, 184, 267; Confederate loss, 271–74, 275–305, 297 (map), 311–12, 322–24, 349–50; Confederate occupation, 106; Federal assault, 271–305; Federal breakthrough on crest, 283 (map), 287–89; Federal plans, 266–71; Federal victory celebration, 324–25; Grant's plans, 231–32; Hardee, 188, 205, 208, 235–37, 313–15, 320; Hooker, 306–11; post-Chickamauga flare ups, 91; spoils, 317, 321–22; Stevenson, 229; Thomas's assault, 259–81, 261 (map), 320–21
Missionary Ridge, North, 188–94, 231–58, 266–67, 313–18; Cleburne plans, 232–36, 240–42, 294; Confederate and Federal maneuverings, 232–39; Grant's plan, 155–57, 188–201; Hardee's ideas, 234–35, 294; Hooker's absence at, 262–63, 265; Sherman,

156–62, 188–201, 233 (map), 234, 237–39, 241–42, 248–49, 259–65; Smith plan, 156–57; Stevenson, 237; Tunnel Hill, 259–65
Missouri horse artillery battery, 342
Mitchell, Robert B., 42
Mobile, Ala., 21
Moccasin Point, 59, 85–86, 95, 114, 123, 187, 208, 209, 211, 215–16
Montgomery, W. R., 108
Moore, Bliss, 100
Moore, John C., 208, 209, 215, 217, 219, 222, 227, 313–14
Morale: Confederate, 29, 105–11, 146–47, 164–65, 166–67, 353–54; Federal, 44, 100–104, 146–47
Morgan, James D., 329
Morse, Bliss, 85
Morton, Oliver, 53
Mosman, Chesley, 88, 92–93, 97–98, 103
Mrs. Shepherd's log farm, 329–30
"mule charge" (Wauhatchie), 148
Murfreesboro, Tenn., 8, 23, 30, 358
Muscle Shoals, Ala., 68

Napoleon smooth bores, 270
Nashville, Tenn., 154
Neal, Andrew Jackson, 106
Needham, Arnold T., 345–46
Negley, James S., 36, 91, 112
Negley's division, 18
New Orleans Daily Delta, 20
New York Tribune, 46
Nickajack, 124, 132, 222
Ninth Corps (Burnside), 74–75
9th Indiana, 307–8, 331
9th Iowa, 307
19th Alabama, 167
19th Illinois, Company G, 270
19th Ohio, 97, 146
92nd Ohio, 292
93rd Illinois, 252–54, 256, 258
93rd Ohio, 167, 182
96th Illinois, 206, 217–18
97th Ohio, 316
No-random-firing agreement, 93
Northrop, Lucius B., 108–9

Oates, William C., 119, 121, 124, 125
Ohio gubernatorial elections, 51–52
Oliver, Paul A., 138, 139
104th Illinois, 94, 267, 311
105th Ohio, 100
110th Illinois, 193
111th Pennsylvania, 135, 136
125th Ohio, 90, 269
137th New York, 136, 216–17

149th New York, 136, 206, 216–17, 226, 342
Opdycke, Emerson, 103, 316, 355
Orchard Knob, 176–94, 202, 271; assault on, 177 (map); Confederate counter-attack, 185, 187; field gun signal from, 268, 269–70
Order of battle: Confederate, 365–69; Federal, 360–65
Osterhaus, Peter J., 189, 192, 211–12, 213, 218–19, 227, 263, 306–7, 309, 311, 331–32, 336–38, 343–44

Paint Rock (supply steamer), 145–46
Palmer, John M., 91, 117, 330, 331
Palmetto Sharpshooters, 136
Parker, Ely S., 157, 324, 326, 344
Parrott rifles, 95
Parry, Augustus C., 199
Pea Vine Creek, 330, 331
Pemberton, John C., 34
Pensacola, Fla., 21
Perryville, battle of, 22–23, 30
Pettus, Edmund W., 165, 219, 220, 222, 223, 227
Phelps, Edward H., 293–94, 313–14
Phelps's brigade, 280
Pickett's Division, 73
Pike, James, 154
Pioneer Brigade, 116–17
Poates, Lewis L., 164, 165
Point Lookout ("Lookout Nose"), 205, 206
Polk, Leonidas, 19, 25, 27, 30–32, 64, 147, 353
Polk, Lucius E., 242, 338–41
Polk's Headquarters, 286
Polk's Spur, 287, 292
Porter, Horace, 112
Preston, William, 64
Price, Sterling, 4
Prisoners, 166–67, 257
Putnam, Holden, 252–53

Raccoon Mountain, 41, 48, 59, 86, 114, 124, 125, 158
Railroads, 22, 41, 43, 67–69, 84, 347–48
Rankin's Ferry, 58–59
Raum, Green B., 253–54, 256, 257, 262
Rawlins, John A., 53, 58, 262
Red Clay, Ga., 329, 347
Reed, Axel, 293
Reep, J. A., 97
Reserve Artillery Battalion, 304
Reynolds, Alexander W., 170, 285–86, 294–95, 299
Reynolds, John A., 135, 137
Reynolds, Joseph J., 12–13, 56

Reynolds's Brigade, 301
Rice, Ralsa C., 90
Richmond, Va., 357
Rickards, William, Jr., 134, 137
Riley, Joseph E., 310
Ringgold Gap, 317, 327 (map), 331–46, 354–55
Robertson, Jerome B., 133, 139, 142
Roddey, Phillip D., 68–69
Rodman guns, 270
Rogersville, Ala., 155
Rogersville, Tenn., 149
Rosecrans, Sylvester, 6, 7
Rosecrans, William Starke, 4–18, 116, 117, 153–54; Chattanooga, 8–18, 36–45, 48–49, 87–90; Chickamauga, 26–28; competence of, 44–52; and Grant, 7–8; life story, 6–8; and Lincoln, 7; Lookout Valley, 126; loss of command, 54–56, 57, 103; personality, 4–6, 29–30; Rossville, 17–18, 36–39; Stones River, 23
Rossville, Ga., 12, 13–15, 17–18, 36–39, 232
Rossville Gap, 19–20, 38, 86, 306–9
Rossville Road bridge, 306
Rousseau, Lovell H., 94
Rowden, Judge, 134
Rowden house, 136

Schurz, Carl, 138–39, 140–41, 142
Scott's Tennessee Battery, 294
2nd Arkansas, 252
2nd Minnesota, 94, 270–71, 292–93, 294
2nd Ohio, 310
2nd South Carolina Rifles, 135
Seddon, James A., 33, 34, 70
Semple's Alabama Battery, 335–37
Sequatchie Valley, 42, 43, 68; supply route raid, 100, 102
7th Florida, 107, 109–10, 166, 301–2, 310
7th Ohio, 339–40
7th Texas, 247, 338–39
Seventeenth Corps, 154
17th Iowa, 256
17th Missouri, 337–38
17th Ohio, 292
73rd Illinois, 302–3
73rd Ohio, 141
73rd Pennsylvania, 249–50, 256; Company B, 251–52
74th Illinois, 91, 93, 279, 303
76th Ohio, 224, 338–39
79th Indiana, 279
79th Pennsylvania band, 157
Seward, William Henry, 41

Shallow Ford bridge, 315
Shannon, H. (Swett's Battery), 242
Sharp, Jacob H., 285
Sharp's Headquarters, 285
Sharp's Spur, 284, 285, 286
Shellenberger, John, 271, 282–84, 301
Sheridan, Philip, 16, 17, 178, 183, 184, 263–64, 266–71, 279–81, 299–300, 303, 304, 305, 316–17
Sherman, Francis T., 279, 284, 300–305
Sherman, William Tecumseh, 38, 41, 51, 60, 68, 168–71, 176, 178, 226, 257, 329, 344; admiration for Grant, 356; Atlanta campaign, 357; Chattanooga, 150, 151, 153–56; command of Army of the Tennessee, 61; Knoxville, 349; Lookout Mountain, 231–32; Lookout Valley plan, 156–62; North Missionary Ridge, 156–62, 188–201, 233 (map), 234, 237–39, 241–42, 248–49, 259–65; post-Missionary Ridge orders, 326–29; railroad track destruction, 347–48; Tunnel Hill, 243–47, 259–65
Sherman's "boys," 190–91
Shiloh, battle of, 7, 21
Signal messages, 205, 262
6th Indiana, 120–21
6th Iowa, 246
6th Kentucky, 182
6th Kentucky Cavalry, 132
6th Ohio, 115, 116, 267, 287–88
6th South Carolina, 92–93, 133, 136
6th Texas, 255
6th Wisconsin Battery, 199
16th South Carolina, 331
60th New York, 206, 210–11, 216–17
60th North Carolina, 285–86, 301, 303
63rd Tennessee, 164
64th Ohio Volunteers, 267, 268, 271, 282–84
Slaves, as enlistees, 355
Slocomb, Cuthbert H., 296–99, 303, 315–16, 319, 321
Slocomb's Battery, 296–99, 301
Smith, Edmund Kirby, 22, 240
Smith, Giles A., 191, 195, 199, 243, 248
Smith, James A., 234–35, 242–43, 244–48
Smith, John E., 154, 191, 196, 198, 199, 237, 248, 250, 253, 259, 260
Smith, Morgan L., 191, 193–94, 196, 198, 199, 243, 248, 259
Smith, Orland, 141–42
Smith, William F. "Baldy," 55–56, 59, 61, 114, 149, 192–93, 196–97, 268, 328, 344–45; Brown's Ferry, 114–16, 118–22, 126–29; Citico Creek, 149;

North Missionary Ridge, 156–57;
    South Chickamauga Creek, 196–97
Smith, William Wrenshall, 185, 343
Smith's Hill, 139, 140–42, 143
Smith's Texas Brigade, 315
Snodgrass farm, 12, 14
Snow, John, 106, 107
South Carolina Battery, 331
South Chickamauga Creek, 189, 191–97,
    232–34, 242, 248, 259
Spears, James G., 41, 44
Spencer Repeating Rifles, 118
Stanton, Edwin, 3, 8–11, 16, 39–41, 45,
    46, 48–50, 51, 52–53, 54
Steinwehr, Adolph von, 138
Stevens Gap, 11–12
Stevenson, Carter L., 69, 74–75, 76, 109,
    149, 168–69, 204–5, 208, 209, 234,
    242, 250, 254–55, 264; Lookout
    Mountain, 213–15, 219–21, 222–23,
    229; North Missionary Ridge, 237
Stevenson's Division, 78
Stewart, A. P., 285, 296, 303–4, 309–10,
    315–16
Stones River, battle of, 8, 23, 30, 358
Stoughton, William L., 309–10, 330–31
Stovall, Marcellus A., 165, 309–10
Strahl, Otho, 309–10
Strategy and tactics: deception and feint-
    ing, 9, 10, 158–59, 169, 204–6; diver-
    sion, 263–65, 268, 270–73;
    entrenchment vs. frontal assault, 90–
    91; offensive dogma, 21, 22, 23; rail-
    road troop transport, 22, 41, 43
Suman, Isaac C. B., 308
Summertown Road, 219–20, 221, 225,
    226, 228, 229
Supply routes: Brown's Ferry plan, 114–
    16, 121–22; Confederate, 107–9; Fed-
    eral, 42–44, 54, 57, 59–61, 67–69,
    100–104, 114–18, 121–22, 145–46,
    148, 151; Forrest's raid, 42; railroad
    routes, 67–69; Sequatchie Valley raid,
    100, 102; Wheeler's raid, 43–44, 67–
    69, 100, 102, 116
Swett's Battery, 242–43, 245–47, 249

Taft, Joseph B., 250, 251
Talley, C. E., 338–39
Tarman, B. B., 258
Taylor, Thomas, 256–57
Taylor's Ridge, 335, 342–43
Telegraphy, 153–54, 157, 162
3rd Battalion Georgia Sharpshooters,
    108
3rd Florida, 296
3rd Missouri, 338
10th Iowa, 252

10th Missouri, 257
10th South Carolina, 291
10th Texas, 255
13th Illinois, 211, 227, 309, 336–37, 345
30th Iowa, 339
31st Missouri, 337–38
31st Ohio, 292, 314
32nd Alabama, 167, 223
32nd Indiana, 276, 287–88
33rd Massachusetts, 138, 141, 142
33rd Ohio, 311, 330
33rd Tennessee, 310
34th Alabama, 286–87, 289
34th Illinois, 216
35th Illinois, 276, 277, 284–85
35th Ohio, 315
36th Alabama, 308
36th Georgia, 255
36th Illinois, 300, 303
36th Ohio, 292
37th Tennessee, 176
38th Alabama, 308, 310
39th Georgia, 250–51, 254
Thomas, George H., 10–18, 27, 40, 45,
    48, 51, 54, 94–95, 114, 127–28, 146,
    148–51, 156, 176, 178–79, 183–84,
    205, 280, 324, 355–57, 359; Chatta-
    nooga plans, 58–60; command of
    Army of the Cumberland, 52–54, 56,
    103; Grant's criticism of, 160–61;
    Lookout Valley, 126; meeting with
    Grant, 58; Missionary Ridge, 259–81,
    261 (map), 320–21; North Missionary
    Ridge, 189, 259–65; personality, 57;
    post-Lookout Mountain orders, 231–
    32; post-Missionary Ridge pursuit
    plan, 328, 330–31; Rossville, 36, 38–
    39
Thomas's "boys," 191
Thompson, Harvey M., 293–94
Thurman house, 296
Treacy, Patrick, 6, 18
Truces: artillerists, 94; Chattanooga
    evacuation, 176; medical, 91–94
Tucker, William F., 285–88, 289, 292
Tullahoma campaign, 9, 10, 25
Tunnel Hill, 234, 237–38, 240–65, 344
Tunnel Hill road, 250, 251
Tupper, Nathan W., 248
Turchin, John B., 115–16, 120, 121, 280,
    292–93, 313–14
Twelfth Corps, 41, 58, 126, 127, 154,
    189–90, 338
12th Missouri, 224, 338
Twentieth Corps, 50
20th Maine, 120
Twenty-first Corps, 10, 50, 91
22nd Indiana, 91

23rd Corps (Federal), 75
23rd Kentucky, 119–20
24th Alabama, 180–82, 183
24th Arkansas, 252
24th Mississippi, 210
24th Texas (Dismounted) Cavalry, 243
24th Wisconsin, 302
25th Iowa, 339, 340
26th Missouri, 252
26th Ohio, 316
27th Missouri, 306
27th Pennsylvania, 250, 251–53, 256
27th Tennessee, 255
28th Alabama, 180, 182, 183, 291
28th Pennsylvania, 340
29th Missouri, 337–38
29th Pennsylvania, 134, 137, 207, 228
Tyler's Brigade, 298, 303
Tyndale, Hector, 138, 139
Tyndale Hill, 138, 139, 140–41, 143
Tyner's Station, 197

Vallandigham, Clement L., 51–52
Van Derveer's Brigade, 280, 292–94, 313–14
Van Dorn, Earl, 4, 6
Van Duzer, John C., 116
Vaughan, Alfred J., Jr., 293–94
Vaught, W. C. D., 298, 303
Vicksburg, Miss., 8, 9, 23, 34, 51
"Vicksburg gophers," 155

Wagner, George D., 14, 268, 279, 281, 284, 300–301, 303, 316–17
Walcutt, Charles C., 244–47
Walden's Ridge, 26, 42, 68, 86, 114, 116, 119
Walker, James C., 314
Walker, William H. T., 165, 166, 187, 202, 234, 235

Walthall, Edward, 204, 208–9, 210–17, 219, 222, 227, 314, 358
Warfield, E., 247, 252, 254–55
Wartrace, Tenn., 68
Waters's Alabama Battery, 292–93
Watkins, Sam, 22
Watson, Robert, 107–8
Wauhatchie, 76, 77, 113 (map), 126–27, 129, 134, 135, 138–44, 148
Wauhatchie Road, 138–39
Weather, 96–98, 103, 109–10, 145
Western and Atlantic Railroad, 249, 334, 348
Wever, Clark R., 256
Wheeler, Joseph, 65, 75, 76, 78, 343; supply route raid, 43–44, 67–69, 100, 102, 116
Whitaker, Walter C., 208, 216–17, 220, 228
Whitaker's Brigade, 206
White Oak Mountain, 335, 337, 338–42
Whitworth sharpshooter rifle, 117–18
Whitworth sharpshooters, 117–18, 125
Wilcox, Orlando B., 163, 175
Wiley, Aquila, 182, 278
Williams Island, 55, 59
Williamson, James A., 306, 339–41
Willich, August, 180–81, 183, 275–78, 284–85, 287–88, 295, 313
Willich's brigade, 269
Wilson, James H., 58, 161, 355
Wilson, John, 228
Withrow, James E., 99
Wolfe, Frank, 224
Wood, Gustavus A., 268
Wood, Thomas J., 12–13, 175, 178, 179, 183–84, 263–64, 267, 268, 270, 275, 279, 281, 284, 290–91, 295, 317
Woods, Charles R., 159–60, 162, 175, 205, 306, 332–33, 341
Wright, Marcus J., 204, 234